The Psychology of Education
2nd edition

Martyn Long, Clare Wood, Karen Littleton, Terri Passenger and Kieron Sheehy

Routledge
Taylor & Francis Group

LONDON AND NEW YORK

First edition published 2000
by RoutledgeFalmer

This edition published 2011
by Routledge
2 Park Square, Milton Park, Abingdon, Oxon OX14 4RN

Simultaneously published in the USA and Canada
by Routledge
270 Madison Avenue, New York, NY 10016

Routledge is an imprint of the Taylor & Francis Group, an informa business

© 2011 Martyn Long, Clare Wood, Karen Littleton, Terri Passenger and Kieron Sheehy

Typeset in Bembo and Helvetica by Wearset Ltd, Boldon, Tyne and Wear
Printed and bound in Great Britain by MPG Books Group, UK

The right of Martin Long, Clare Wood, Karen Littleton, Terri Passenger and Kieron Sheehy to be
identified as authors of this work has been asserted by them in accordance with sections 77 and 78 of the
Copyright, Designs and Patents Act 1988.

British Library Cataloguing in Publication Data
A catalogue record for this book is available from the British Library

Library of Congress Cataloging-in-Publication Data
The psychology of education/Martyn Long ... [et al.]. – 2nd ed.
p. cm.
Prev. ed. cataloged under Long, Martyn.
Includes bibliographical references and index.
1. Educational psychology. 2. Teaching. I. Long, Martyn, 1948– II. Long, Martyn, 1948– Psychology of
education.
LB1051.L774 2011
370.15–dc22
                                        2010020643

ISBN13: 978-0-415-48689-7 (hbk)
ISBN13: 978-0-415-48690-3 (pbk)
ISBN13: 978-0-203-84009-2 (ebk)

Contents

Illustrations

Figures

Tables

Preface

A tremendous amount is known about educational psychology which is useful to people involved in teaching and learning. Condensing and selecting from this vast body of knowledge has therefore meant that we have had to cover some areas rapidly in order to reach key ideas and conclusions. This means, we hope, that you will not have to wade through a lot of information to reach something interesting. If you want to go into more detail, there are plenty of recent references and further reading to follow up.

If you are working or training as a teacher, you should find that this book gives focused and up-to-date coverage of the research findings about many of the areas in which you are involved. If you are simply interested in education, the book describes various findings with implications for what we can expect from schooling and the ways in which it might be organised.

Perhaps the biggest problem with the educational field is that it is a political hot topic and strong opinions about the nature of effective teaching are often held without reference to empirical evidence. There has also been a general trend over the years to see education as being partly responsible for many of society's difficulties with respect to younger people. The question of whether such views are valid is one that can be answered in relation to good-quality educational research.

As far as possible, the information we describe comes from direct applications of psychological knowledge, or from the use of psychological techniques in educational research. However, there are inevitably biases, which come from the evidence selected, and these are the result of attempts to reflect the balance of likely explanations in each area. Despite this, there are certain areas where we feel strongly that the general weight of findings points in a certain direction. If you disagree, then we hope that this book will spur you on to look for opposing evidence and develop your ideas about the area further.

We have also tried to write this book with a theoretical grounding, in order to make knowledge more flexible. This can, however, sometimes obscure any practical implications, so we have put in some additional sections with key implications and a practical scenario as a prompt for some questions.

If you have anything at all to do with education, you should therefore find this book factual, useful and, we hope, interesting.

Acknowledgements

The authors gratefully acknowledge the help of:

- Sue Turner
- Nicky Williams
- Dee Passenger of Oldway Primary School, Torquay
- Professor Neil Mercer (University of Cambridge)
- Amy Clarke
- McVities, for their tireless work producing biscuits that kept us going when times were tough ...

Introduction to psychology and education: some essential background

Chapter overview

- Why do we need psychology?
- What is educational psychology?
- Quantitative and qualitative approaches
- Applying psychology
- Differing perspectives
- The evidence from psychology

Practical scenario

Mrs Smith has been recently appointed as the head teacher of Anytown Junior School. This has a solid middle-class intake and has done well in its Ofsted (Office for Standards in Education) inspections and with recent Standard Assessment Tests and Tasks (SATs) scores. However, she is concerned that the curriculum has become rather narrow, and is keen to foster children's wider educational and social development. Although Mrs Smith has support from most of the staff in this, the governors and many parents have very traditional views of education. They mainly want an emphasis on skill achievements, with a curriculum-centred and didactic approach to teaching.

How could Mrs Smith try to convince them that there are other ways of approaching education?

Why do we need psychology?

Virtually everybody seems to think that they know a lot about psychology, and about how education should be run. After all, most of us have had a lot of experience with other people, and virtually all of us have been to school, or have had some form of experience in which we have learned from others. The majority of our ideas about 'what works' are built up from personal experience, and these beliefs work well in our everyday lives. However, they are not necessarily very effective when they are applied to the particular process of educating children. Here, general rules of thumb and common-sense simplifications can sometimes result in very contradictory perspectives when applied by different people. It can be impossible to 'prove' which of two such opposing views is the more valid.

Activity

Take these sets of opposing statements, for instance. Which do you agree with?

'Formal teaching is too restrictive and puts children off learning.'

versus

'Progressive teaching fails to give children discipline and doesn't teach the harder subjects well.'

'Reducing class sizes would obviously result in improved learning.'

versus

'Class sizes are not important; what matters most is the quality of the teaching.'

'Firm discipline and punishment are important in controlling problem behaviour.'

versus

'Positive behaviour comes from the examples of others; punishment is ineffective and simply brutalises children.'

'Dyslexics are simply middle-class children who can't read.'

versus

'Dyslexia is a genuine, important problem that is due to underlying difficulties with cognitive processes.'

'Children's speech and language develops naturally and should be largely left alone.'

versus

'When children use the wrong speech and language, it is important to correct them so that they don't get into bad habits.'

'Children's teachers are the most important factor in their education.'

versus

'Teachers aren't really important – the key things are a child's own knowledge and motivation.'

Feedback

It is likely that you have some existing ideas about each of these pairs of propositions. However, without getting additional information it is impossible to say which of these opposed views is going to be the most useful to us in understanding the educational process. This can be done by carrying out some form of investigation in a particular area, or by seeing what other people have found out. Each of the areas in these boxes is considered within this book.

What is educational psychology?

Psychological knowledge and the techniques of psychological study can help us understand these problems since psychology involves the logical investigation of what people think and what they do. Psychology includes a wide range of topics and can be applied to many different areas such as education, where human thinking and behaviour are important. Educational psychology therefore refers to an area of applied psychology that uses psychological theories and techniques to consider how we think and learn, and how we can address the learning needs of students.

Ways of investigating

A key feature of psychology as a discipline is its emphasis on developing theories about human behaviour and carrying out investigations to test and modify them. A **theory** is a way of trying to explain as simply as possible what we know (or think we know) about a particular area. For example, a theory that most people have about class size and achievement is that 'smaller classes are better for children and lead to improved achievements'. From this theory we might make the following prediction (**hypothesis**): 'Children taught in classes no bigger than six will have better end of year test results than children who are taught in classes of 30.' This process of identifying a theory, making a prediction that tests it, and then collecting data to see if the prediction is supported, is known as the **hypothetico-deductive method**, and has its roots in science. Other techniques, described later in this chapter, are **inductive** in nature: these approaches actively avoid the initial use of theories, instead allowing theoretical explanations to emerge from more open-ended analysis of the data or evidence obtained.

An **experimental investigation** of class size could look at what happens when we change only the particular thing (or **variable**) that we are interested in, in this case how many children are being taught together. For instance, we could investigate the effects of class size on achievement by setting up different-sized groups and measuring children's progress with their school work. For us to know that class size was the only thing having an effect, we would have to make sure that all other aspects of the classes being compared were as identical as possible, so that we might be confident that if there are differences in achievement, it is because of the difference in class size, rather than other factors, such as who was teaching the class, or the way in which the children were seated in the class. Such unintentional differences between groups in experiments which have the potential to offer an alternative explanation of the results obtained are known as **confounding variables**.

A good experimental investigation would set up different-sized classes with **matched groups** of pupils, to cancel out or 'control for' the effects of student ability. Matching is the process of finding children with similar personal characteristics (such as age, gender or general ability), and allocating them to different groups in an experiment, so that the children in each group are similar to each other. An alternative to matching pupils on the basis of ability would be to randomly allocate students to either a treatment group (in which the children receive some form of educational intervention) or the control or comparison groups. A **control group** is a group used in intervention study designs that have exactly the same experience as the treatment group except for the intervention itself. Often they receive 'normal classroom tuition' but better studies will give the control group a dummy intervention to participate in (i.e. a 'treatment' that we would not expect to have any effect on the performance variable being measured). The reason this is a good idea is that it enables us to control for any **placebo effects**. That is, students receiving something different from the norm may have an expectation that this will benefit them, and this in itself may motivate them to try harder or affect their performance in other ways. By giving both groups something novel to do, it means that both groups have the same level of expectation. Another consideration that researchers have to bear in mind is the potential, indirect, motivational effects that extra attention from a researcher may have on student performance. This is known as the **Hawthorn Effect**. So studies that include a dummy intervention are also a good idea because they enable both sets of children to have similar levels of contact with the research team – having normal classroom tuition as the control experience does not afford this.

There is a lot to be said for directly setting up different educational experiences for children, since the outcomes may then be assumed to be closely related to what was done. However, doing so can be very difficult in practice. Interfering with children's education in this way can also be ethically questionable, since children in some of the groups are likely to learn less well. Many educational investigations therefore avoid these problems by using techniques where the investigator uses only information that is already available, or looks at situations that already exist.

Such **non-experimental investigations** are typically based on observational techniques. These can involve an investigator directly, perhaps watching children in a class, or be based on indirect data such as school records. Such approaches can sometimes be **quasi-experimental** ('quasi' meaning 'as if'), when it is possible to assume that a change in one thing is related to a change in something else. 'Natural experiments' can make this more likely. For instance, if a new form of educational practice (such as the literacy hour) is introduced, we can compare children's educational progress before and after its introduction.

One very common form of observational investigation – perhaps the least experimental – is to evaluate the extent to which one thing naturally varies along with, or **correlates** with, something else. Such investigations are often easy to carry out and can be fertile ground for developing new ideas or hypotheses about the way things work.

The main difficulty with such non-experimental approaches is that any outcomes might not necessarily be the result of any change in some other particular measure. For instance, if we looked only at existing classes of different sizes, we could be fooled by the fact that many schools use small classes for pupils of below-average ability. We might then conclude that small classes have the effect of reducing attainments!

However, since such investigations do not involve interference or control by an investigator, it can be argued that they are more likely to be valid, in the sense that they are more naturalistic, or show what normally goes on. They can also lend themselves to personal involvement, and possibly more meaningful interpretation, by an investigator. This happens in **participant research**, where the investigator might for instance become part of a teaching team. Observational data also fit well with the use of qualitative approaches (see below), with an emphasis on the direct experiences and interpretations of those who are involved.

Quantitative and qualitative approaches

A great deal of educational research involves measuring things. Although such **quantitative** approaches allow us to use powerful statistical techniques, they can often have the effect of simplifying and distorting what is really happening, because things have to be put into categories of some kind. Children, teachers and the processes and outcomes of education are much more than just sets of numbers. A good example is early reading skills, which emphasise decoding using sounds and letters. These are very different from more advanced skills, which involve comprehension and the use of context. It could be very misleading to compare different reading levels along a single scale, as though higher attainments were just more of the same thing.

Qualitative approaches attempt to get closer to reality by looking at information that differs in kind rather than in amount. They may involve using more direct and richer information, such as the recording of complete observations, or descriptions by teachers or pupils about what they are doing or how they feel. This information is close to the way things are, and Glaser and Strauss (1967) argue that it enables researchers to develop a **grounded theory**, one which arises from the information gathered, rather than just depending on modifying existing theories. However, Silverman (2005) notes that modern qualitative research has two main models or perspectives within it which are worth being aware of. The **emotionalist model** is primarily interested in looking at a situation from an individual's point of view, and is interested in perceptions and emotional reactions to situations. The counterpoint to this is the **constructionist model**, which emphasises what people are doing, without necessarily dwelling on the reasoning or emotions behind those actions.

In reality, qualitative and quantitative approaches are closely related. Most quantitative research involves qualitative decisions about which variables to study and about what are appropriate techniques to analyse the data. An initial qualitative approach can also develop into a subsequent quantitative analysis; for example, once individuals' responses have been placed into meaningful groupings, these can then be calculated as percentages or analysed for significant differences.

Describing and analysing findings

With quantitative data, psychological and educational researchers often use statistics to describe and analyse what they have found. It is useful to have a basic idea of some key statistical concepts so that you can understand and be critical of how the information from investigations has been interpreted. The Appendix to this book explains some of the terms and techniques that are referred to throughout the book.

One of the greatest errors, but a typical one, is to assume that because the results of a statistical test are 'statistically significant', this automatically means that the results are psychologically or educationally meaningful. If you understand something about the basic ideas of statistics, you are much less likely to be misled about findings that are marginal or misleading.

Qualitative information typically takes the form of direct recordings of events and their meanings, or of people's own descriptions, often referred to as **narratives**. Interpreting such diverse information can involve selecting key themes and reporting on them by reproducing parts of transcripts. In one example, Walker (1998) carried out an analysis of the functions of secondary school parents' evenings, using parts of her interviews with parents to demonstrate that such meetings were almost invariably perceived as frustrating and distressing.

Qualitative analyses often involve setting up possible categories into which the information can be placed. One advantage of having access to the entire range of original information is that such categories can be modified if alternative groupings subsequently appear to be more meaningful. Although this may make conclusions appear rather fluid and unreliable, they can be confirmed by comparing the views found by different types of investigations or information (**triangulation**), or by repeating the cycle of gathering and analysing information (**replication**). In any case, it can be argued that such approaches are more likely to result in findings that have some real meaning for a particular area. As discussed later in this chapter (see 'Shifting paradigms', pp. 7–10), any categories that we use can be seen as social constructs and are therefore bound to be somewhat arbitrary. However, qualitative researchers value subjective experience and interpretation as valid data which tell us about how individuals experience the world. Whether or not that subjective interpretation is 'right' in absolute terms is not relevant if there are very real consequences to how the individual sees the situation they are in.

Applying psychology

'Pure' psychology tries to arrive at general theories that can help us understand basic areas such as learning, memory, motivation, etc. However, practical education is a complex situation and there are often many factors that interact or combine to give rise to a number of different effects. For example, academic achievement can be the outcome of the interaction between home- and school-based factors, with initial home-based advantages being consolidated by early educational success.

It is therefore always important to evaluate real-life applications of psychological ideas, rather than rely on ideas that are derived purely from the original abstract theories; these are often based on work that was originally far removed from the realities of real-life teaching. Some of the early psychological theories about learning, for instance, were derived largely from studying the responses of rats and pigeons in mazes and cages!

Differing perspectives

Applying psychology to education also often involves viewing areas from a number of different psychological perspectives (see Table 1.1). Applying these perspectives to educational topics can generate alternative ways of approaching problems. Each of the perspectives generates a very different way of understanding the behaviour of children in school. The various approaches are often complementary. For instance, achieving optimum arousal levels by using a dynamic teaching style will facilitate general involvement with learning tasks. When pupils are more alert, they are then also more likely to respond to other strategies that will focus them on their work, such as the use of praise in operant conditioning (associating a voluntary response with a stimulus).

On the other hand, some perspectives can give rise to contradictory approaches. Behaviourism, for instance, can appear rather simplistic and may encourage an approach based on rote learning. Cognitive approaches, however, emphasise the use of meaning and understanding, and seem closer to what we personally experience in learning situations. Despite this, behavioural approaches can still be very useful in analysing and managing problem behaviours. Recent developments consider that behavioural conditioning is the result of developing expectancies about what will happen in certain situations, and that behaviourism can therefore be seen as a particular subset of cognitive processes.

Developmental psychology

Psychology also tries to account for the ways in which children establish basic abilities such as reasoning, problem-solving and language use. General developmental theories that cover these can be applied to education to help us understand learning situations. This can be seen in Chapter 2, which considers the role of Piaget's theory of cognitive development, and Chapter 9, which looks at the way in which language abilities are developed. Other areas, such as the development of social roles and identity, and the establishment of basic academic attainments such as reading, also depend to some extent on progress with other underlying skills and abilities.

The importance of theory

There is a famous remark by Allport (1947) that the aims of science are 'understanding, prediction and control, above the levels achieved by unaided common sense'. This perspective is very useful in

TABLE 1.1 Five key perspectives in psychology

Perspective	Overview
Psychodynamic	This is an approach developed in the early twentieth century from the work of Freud, which is applied in therapeutic approaches for children with problems. It views behaviour as the result of tension between aspects of the subconscious mind (the id, ego and superego), which are also seen to drive human development.
Behavioural	Behaviourism is also referred to as 'learning theory' and characterises human behaviour as conditioned responses to stimuli in our environment. This perspective is associated with the work of Pavlov, Watson and Skinner. Sometimes criticised for being too simplistic to account for all learning, it is still used as the basis for behaviour-modification programmes.
Humanistic	Humanistic psychology emphasises individuality and individuals' potential for self-development. Developed by Maslow to counter the mechanistic perspectives of psychodynamic and behavioural psychology, it underlies child-centred approaches in education.
Psychobiological	Psychobiological approaches seek to understand the role of biological structures and processes in influencing thought and action. It is central to discussions of 'nature vs nurture' (e.g. with respect to intelligence), and arousal and motivation.
Cognitive	Cognitive psychology developed as a reaction to the view, which stemmed from behaviourism, that cognitive processes were not appropriate for study, as they could not be directly observed. This approach seeks to understand behaviour as the product of processes of perception, attention, learning and memory, and the emphasis is therefore on how we process information around us.

guiding psychological investigations, and emphasises that we should be able to use theoretical knowledge to help us with applied areas and to go beyond everyday experience and understanding.

Developments in education often lack this theoretical foundation and are frequently inspired by social processes or ideological beliefs, a fact that can lead to cycles of change as the general social climate alters. For instance, in the 1940s it was commonly believed that the most efficient way of educating children was to select them for different types of schooling using the 'eleven–plus' and also to 'stream' them into different general ability groups. A later ideological emphasis on equality of opportunity subsequently led to the development of comprehensive schools and mixed-ability teaching. However, there are now signs that there is a shift backwards in this perspective, with many schools reverting to increased selection and ability grouping of pupils, even at the primary level.

A psychological perspective could help us to limit such swings of fashion by providing theories and knowledge about the realistic advantages and disadvantages of such developments. For instance, it has been shown that selection of pupils on the basis of the eleven-plus (an intelligence test) is not a very accurate or useful process. Research also indicates that streaming of children into different ability groups within schools leads to only limited improvements with the higher groups. It can also lead to pupils in lower groups receiving inferior education, partly because of teacher expectations, and the negative social groupings that can happen in such classes.

Shifting paradigms

Paradigms are general ways of looking at or understanding an area. Although it can often seem that there is only one way to understand a particular domain of knowledge, paradigms often change radically over time. In the particular fields of psychology and education, earlier paradigms of learning saw the child as relatively passive, simply absorbing information transmitted by a didactic teacher. These perspectives fitted well with the then-current stress on principles of conditioning, which took a very mechanistic approach to the managing of learning. According to this, the emphasis for the teacher was to deliver a standard curriculum and to evaluate stable underlying differences between children.

A popular general paradigm in educational psychology is the cognitive one. This emphasises that the developing child in school is active in constructing new knowledge, skills and ways of understanding. This perspective is largely derived from the original ideas of Piaget, although there have been many substantial revisions of his approach. In particular, writers such as Mercer and Littleton (2007) have emphasised the social nature of this learning process, with knowledge developing as a '"joint construction" of understanding by the child and more expert members of his (or her) culture' (p. 17). The role of the teacher can be seen as that of a facilitator of learning, by generating appropriate experiences and closely monitoring a child's changing attainments and needs.

However, a number of alternative perspectives now question the fundamental underlying premises of psychological and educational knowledge. Based on postmodern ideas, they propose that the classical scientific approach of logical investigation using evidence, often referred to as **positivism**, is deeply flawed and outdated. The rationale for this is based on arguments generated by philosophers such as Foucault (1978) that knowledge and understanding are essentially arbitrary and socially constructed. From this perspective, scientific concepts such as 'intelligence' can be seen as functioning to legitimise the status and power of psychology within society. Language concepts and the ways in which they are used (referred to as 'discourses') also demonstrate the way in which such processes operate. For example, Reay (2007) studied a group of primary school girls to examine the way in which the 'new discourse' that girls are doing better than boys at school is experienced by these children.

The conventional social role of researchers in relation to those being studied can be seen as part of the general domination of classical scientific investigation. It is argued that the balance can be redressed by placing an emphasis on the natural experiences and reports of participants in the educational process. More recently there has been an increased emphasis on trying to find ways of moving away from such models of research, towards ones in which children are given their own voice, and are genuine participants in (rather than subjects of) research (e.g. Fraser et al., 2004; Lewis and Lindsay, 2000). One particularly interesting approach to this issue has been to train children as researchers and to allow them to ask their own research questions, and equip them with the skills to answer them, and to even publish them (Kellett, 2010).

A further perspective is that the study of education has inherent difficulties, since education takes place in a highly complex social system. Such structures may be chaotic, with processes and outcomes that are unpredictable and therefore perhaps unknowable. However, all human development and learning takes place within highly complex social and cultural structures. This is acknowledged in the **ecological model of development** proposed by Bronfenbrenner (1993) in which the individual is seen as situated within a series of interrelated environments, all of which impact on development: the immediate physical, social and cultural setting the person is in at any one moment in time (the **microsystem**); the multiple microsystems that any one individual may inhabit (the **mesosystem**); the way more distant settings might impact upon the microsystems that we inhabit (the **exosystem**) and the patterns of micro-, meso- and exosystems that characterise a culture (the **macrosystem**).

Activity

Think about this idea in relation to your own situation right now. What is the microsystem that you currently inhabit (i.e. where are you now, what are you doing, etc.)? What other microsystems do you also exist within? Think of an example of how the exosystem impacts on you.

Feedback

The answer to this activity will depend on your own personal situation, but we can give you an example of a fictional person to illustrate what we mean here. Consider someone who is reading this book right now. She may be seated in a university library, studying for her course. She has a laptop with her, on which she types her notes, and she has a friend beside her with whom she can discuss her ideas and occasionally talk about other things. She has a pen in her hand as she reads, even though she has no paper to make notes on – she just finds that she thinks better with a pen in her hand. All of these details constitute her immediate environment for learning, or her microsystem. Another microsystem might be her seminar group at university, in which she works with 12 other students and a tutor to discuss and clarify her reading, in a way structured by the ideas and expectations of the tutor. Another might be her family context. All these microsystems that she inhabits together form the mesosystem. The student is married, and her husband works for the local education authority and is about to be made redundant. This more distant influence on the individual (her husband's microsystem) is part of the exosystem.

The idea that research might be, and should be, able to account for the ways in which these aspects of our environments impact on learning and development may sound impossibly ambitious. However, it has been applied to children's experiences in school, in the form of the **Contextual Systems Model** (Pianta and Walsh, 1996). According to this model, we have to understand child development in the context of four systems: the individual child, the family, the classroom and the wider culture. Such a model sees relationships between the child and key adults (e.g. parents, teachers) and other children as central to understanding development. So research in this area can attempt to understand learning through understanding relationships. One example of such research is O'Conner and McCartney (2007) who studied the quality of teacher–child relationships in the US from pre-school to third grade and considered how this impacted on the children's achievement. They found that good-quality relationships were associated with good achievement, that they were mediated by the behaviour of both child and teacher, and that they could protect children from the effects of problematic maternal relationships.

Thus it can be argued that *within* a given system, however ultimately arbitrary it may be, we can still arrive at knowledge and understanding that is useful for us. What postmodernism does in a more positive way, though, is to caution us as to the relatively local and specific nature of knowledge. Part of this is understanding that what might work in one situation may not transfer readily to others. It also guides us towards an emphasis on the direct experiences and interpretations of those most closely involved in the process of education itself.

With their emphasis on cultural determinants of knowledge and identity, these approaches are confirmed by and also have a particular relevance to issues in feminist and ethnic-minority studies, and socio-economic perspectives of class. Given some caveats, a great deal of research can therefore still guide and inform debates and planning in education. As we hope that parts of this book show, it can also often lead us to reconsider the meaning and utility of some concepts and beliefs that are the foundations of educational thought.

The evidence from psychology

When psychology is applied to a number of different areas in education, it has the potential to help us to understand what is happening, and to make more logical, informed decisions about the best way to organise the educational process. Quite often, however, the findings of research or the applications of psychological theories do not give a simple answer, but qualify and extend the original debate. When the findings of educational psychology are applied to the issues that were identified at the start of the chapter, for instance, the findings summarised in this book appear to show the following.

Formal versus progressive teaching

Research indicates that there is no real difference in attainment when we compare children educated by these approaches. Other, underlying features such as classroom organisation or the learning process encouraged seem to be much more important.

Class sizes

Controlled experimental investigations have shown that reducing class sizes *does* improve attainments, but that the effect of doing so is rather limited within the realistic range of possible class sizes. Other factors such as altering the teaching approach used may have a much greater effect.

Punishment

Punishment can be shown to have many negative effects such as failing to teach appropriate behaviours and leading children to regress. It can be effective in temporarily suppressing undesirable behaviour, but there are preconditions that limit its effective use in practice.

Dyslexia

Developmental dyslexia does appear to be a distinctive neurological and cognitive syndrome. However, the nature of effective literacy teaching seems to be the same for all children with reading difficulties, whether or not they have dyslexia, and so the label is useful in research terms and in terms of helping children to understand why they have difficulties, but perhaps is less useful in terms of informing remediation in the classroom.

Language development

Children who have difficulties with language can be helped. Language mainly develops from an intention to communicate; because of this, one of the most effective approaches seems to be for adults to interact with children in an intensive but natural way and to respond mainly to the meaning behind what they say.

Teacher effectiveness

Individual teachers do differ in their effectiveness but the differences are surprisingly small, being greatest for younger children and relatively specific to particular academic subjects. The variations in achievement due to home background appear to be much larger.

It might seem from this that using psychology and educational research is generally a good thing and that all that is needed is to go ahead and apply the approaches described here as much as possible in education. Care should be taken, however, as academic psychology can often lack understanding of the reality of educational practice and classroom practicalities. An important question to reflect on as you read about the research in the book is to think about whether an explanation or intervention approach is likely to be readily integrated into current curricula or teaching approaches. An approach that balances academic research and theory against 'real-world' teaching is likely to result in optimal results. Crucially, however, we argue that *not* using psychology and psychological techniques is likely to lead to greater problems, since people might apply their personal theories, which can only be based on, and limited by, their own experiences and ideas. It is therefore important to ensure that we 'ground' ourselves in a general appreciation of the real issues and processes of education, as we understand them from both practical experience and sound academic research.

Summary

Many commonly held ideas and beliefs about education are the result of limited knowledge or ideological perspectives. These can lead to arguments that can only be resolved by looking for direct evidence or other forms of relevant knowledge. Psychology can help with the search for evidence because it involves the use of logical investigations, and theories about what people think and what they do. These can be based on the use of direct experiments, which look for effects when something is changed, as well as observation and interpretations of naturally occurring processes. Statistics help us to make sense of what we find in such investigations by describing and analysing numerical information. They enable us to look for differences and relationships between sets of data and to see whether they can support our theories. Observational information too can be analysed to look for meaningful relationships and trends. Psychology includes a number of different approaches that can help us to understand what happens in education. These have changed over time, from early behavioural perspectives, to modern beliefs which emphasise that children actively construct their knowledge within a social context. When psychological understanding is applied to areas of real-life educational debate, it can help us to decide between opposing plausible explanations or to change the way in which we view those areas.

Key implications

- We cannot simply trust in common sense when making decisions about education.
- Psychology is useful in this since it is based on logical approaches using evidence.
- It is best to use a range of perspectives when considering particular areas of education.
- These can be guided by contemporary critiques which emphasise the local and constructed nature of knowledge.

Further reading

Breakwell, Hammond, Fife-Shaw and Smith (eds) (2006), *Research Methods in Psychology*: a more detailed text covering both qualitative and quantitative approaches to psychological research. A helpful book if you are already familiar with research methods, but need specific guidance.

Greig, Taylor and MacKay (2007), *Doing Research with Children*: a good basic introduction to designing research projects that involve children as participants.

Martin, Carlson and Buskist (2010), *Psychology*: an introductory text for those who are unfamiliar with psychology as a general discipline.

Discussion of practical scenario

This is a common dilemma, with many teachers being forced into a narrow approach to teaching, but feeling powerless to counter this. One approach could be to look for applications of theories and research evidence about the effectiveness and limitations of purely skills-based approaches. However, practical evidence is more likely to persuade people, particularly if other schools can be shown to be using a more eclectic approach and achieve more rounded pupils who also have good skills. Another way would be to set up an investigation within school, to compare different techniques over time.

If there are differences between schools or classes taught in different ways, then it would be important to control for the effects of a number of variables, particularly varying initial abilities or achievements. The size of any effect is also important to evaluate and, although an approach might work, it is possible that the effort or resources involved would be too great to warrant continuing with it.

A final underlying issue is that the educational agenda may be largely considered as politically driven. From this perspective, initiatives have little basis in reality but originate from politicians pandering to the simple prejudices of the majority of the population. Although the result could be to generate feelings of helplessness, individual schools and teachers can operate creatively within the constraints that they face and achieve intrinsic satisfaction from achieving what they define as real goals.

Learning

Practical scenario

For some time, Mr Jones has become increasingly worried about his teaching abilities. In the past he has considered himself to be a successful teacher, with his pupils achieving well in formal assessments. In his lessons he has usually adopted a brisk pace and aimed to cover the curriculum in some depth. Recently, however, the standard of the school's intake has dropped, owing to local changes in housing policy. Although he has slowed down the rate of teaching, his pupils just don't seem to grasp key concepts and he is wondering if there are more effective ways to develop their knowledge.

How would you describe the possible changes in the underlying abilities of Mr Jones's pupils? Why are such changes likely to affect their learning?

Can you think of any other ways in which Mr Jones could change the way he teaches to become more effective with these pupils?

The importance of learning

Learning has a central role in education. Although curricula tend to be prescribed by governments, school boards or educational authorities, the matter of how to teach that content to students is largely left up to the individual teacher. Psychological research into the nature of learning and the various ways in which it can occur has important practical implications for teaching, and some key psychological theories and research concerned with teaching and learning will be described in this chapter.

What is learning?

Learning can be defined in a number of ways. Some psychologists, such as behaviourists (as you will discover shortly) see learning as a relatively permanent change in an individual's behaviour. Other psychologists see learning as more about changes in the amount or type of knowledge that we have, or the way in which we reason about our world. Learning shows that we have benefitted from experience in some way, and can work or act more effectively as a result. So learning can be evidenced by changes in strategy, or the ability to think differently about a problem. It enables us to anticipate outcomes and therefore act to control our environment.

Categories of learning

A classic and still widely used way of thinking about different kinds of learning is known as **Bloom's taxonomy**. Bloom (1956) categorised learning objectives, covering the three major domains of **cognitive**, **affective** and **psychomotor** development. Cognitive development is concerned with memory, perception, pattern recognition and language use. Affective development relates to the emotions. Psychomotor development relates to movement or muscular activity associated with mental processes. School education has an effect on all three of these domains, but the formal curriculum focuses on the cognitive domain, which Bloom further subdivided into **knowledge**, **comprehension**, **application**, **analysis**, **synthesis** and **evaluation**. Although this has been the most popular way of categorising domains of learning, there have been other schemes such as Gagné et al.'s (1988) approach, which uses the areas of intellectual skills, cognitive strategies, verbal information, attitudes and motor skills.

The idea behind such taxonomies is that the teacher should think about how they are addressing these areas in relation to the specific topic they are planning to teach. However, in practice, it is often too challenging to address the full range of learning domains when teaching or designing a lesson plan. A common approach is to simplify them by using just three headings, usually 'knowledge', and forming two levels from the remaining categories. These often combine Bloom's categories of 'comprehension' and 'application', and use a further heading which includes problem-solving and the ability to use and transfer learning to new situations. For example, we may prefer to use:

- **knowledge** (recall or recognition of specific information);
- **skills** (the ability to carry out meaningful, integrated tasks such as reading); and
- **understanding** (problem-solving and the use and transfer of knowledge).

Again, however, it should be remembered that these distinctions are essentially arbitrary and that there is considerable overlap and difference in the use of many of these terms. Although 'knowledge', for instance, is often thought of as facts which can be memorised, learning of concepts depends to a great extent on understanding their meaning. In practice it is also difficult to separate out 'understanding' and the 'skills' that are involved in this. However, research and theories about the functions of memory discussed later in this chapter give some support for a meaningful distinction between 'knowledge' and 'skills', and also make the links between them more explicit.

Psychologists have attempted to derive general principles of learning which apply to a range of tasks and situations. The sections that follow will consider these areas of learning theory in turn. The ones we have chosen to present you with in this chapter do not form an exhaustive list, however. As you progress through the book, you will see there are other approaches to understanding the nature of learning. However, we do consider the ones we have selected here to be key theories which we will return to throughout the book.

Behaviourism and conditioning

An important form of basic learning is called **conditioning**, and there are two forms that it can take. Both forms involve forming associations between stimuli and responses, and are rooted in a psychological approach known as **behaviourism** (also known increasingly as 'applied behavioural analysis'). These processes were once believed to underlie all types of learning and dominated psychology as a discipline and instructional design, but they are nowadays seen as specific forms which are part of a wider cognitive approach. Conditioning does have a particular relevance to emotional and behavioural difficulties, owing to the structure that it gives to behaviour-management approaches, which you will read about in the final chapters of this book.

Classical conditioning

In **classical conditioning**, an association is formed between an environmental **stimulus** and an involuntary (reflex) **response** – something that one does not have direct control over, such as heart rate. This is based on the original work by Pavlov (1927), who discovered that dogs salivated involuntarily at the presentation of a signal, such as a bell, which the dogs had learned preceded the arrival of food. J.B. Watson (1925) extended these ideas to humans, arguing that psychologists should not speculate about the nature of thought because thoughts and cognition cannot be directly observed, but environments and behaviours can. In a famous experiment on a little boy called Albert, Watson consistently paired a frightening loud noise with the presentation of a white rat (which Albert did not originally fear). Albert eventually became very anxious whenever the rat appeared and had become classically conditioned to show a fear response to the stimulus of the rat.

An example of school-based classical conditioning would be a pupil becoming anxious about going to school, possibly as a result of a stressful experience such as bullying or a bad experience with a teacher. As shown in Figure 2.1, he or she might then come to associate the involuntary reactions involved in anxiety (dry mouth, racing heart, upset stomach, etc.) with the stimulus of school attendance. If the symptoms were severe enough, the case would be one of school phobia.

The original theories of classical conditioning thought of it as merely a strengthening of the association between the stimulus and the response. Recent cognitive theories, however, emphasise that what we are learning is to predict what follows the stimulus; for example, that the experience of school will follow being told to get ready for school in the morning. This expectancy (thinking of attending school and the things that are feared about it) appears to be what triggers off the involuntary response (of anxiety).

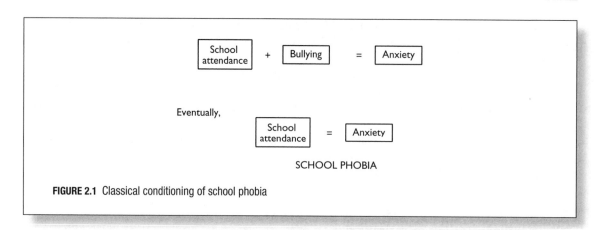

FIGURE 2.1 Classical conditioning of school phobia

Watson confidently argued that classical conditioning could be usefully applied to 'education' in its broader sense too, as indicated by this famous quotation:

> Give me a dozen healthy infants, well-formed, and my own specified world to bring them up in and I'll guarantee to take any one at random and train him to become any type of specialist I might select – doctor, lawyer, artist, merchant-chief and, yes, even beggar-man and thief, regardless of his talents, penchants, tendencies, abilities, vocations, and race of his ancestors.

(Watson, 1930: 82)

Although such a claim indicated the potential of classical conditioning to change behaviour (remember, this was the behaviourist definition of 'learning'), in real life is not so easily controlled or manipulated. Involuntary responses are certainly an important part of the way in which we relate to our environment, but most school learning involves more active participation by the learner, which can be controlled and directed by the teacher. This leads us to consider the second form that conditioning can take.

Operant conditioning

Operant conditioning is a more important form of associative learning and involves voluntary responses rather than reflex reactions. These behaviours are under conscious control, such as a pupil working on a learning task, or calling out in class.

Skinner (1938) said that the concepts and principles involved in such learning apply when an individual acts ('operates') on his or her environment to achieve a desired outcome. In order to control and/or change an individual's behaviour, it is important to analyse the learning situation for the following components:

the antecedents → the behaviour → and the consequences
(what happens before   (what the child   (what the results are
an incident)   actually does)   for the child)

An example of this would be if we were interested in why a child is working well in class:

interesting → pupils get on → praise from
work set   with work   teacher

TABLE 2.1 An illustration of the meaning of 'positive' and 'negative' in the context of reward and punishment

	Reinforcement	Punishment
Positive	Introduction of a reward	Introduction of an aversive stimulus
Negative	Removal of an aversive stimulus	Removal of a 'reward'

This analysis of the learning situation would show that the reason the child is so well-behaved is because the work set was engaging for him or her, and the teacher actively praised the child for being well-behaved. In this analysis, it is important to recognise the antecedent as well as the consequence of a given behaviour. In practice, there may potentially be multiple antecedents, and so observation of the child would need to be conducted over an extended period in order to tease out what combinations of antecedent and consequence are responsible for producing the target behaviour. If the target behaviour is one that we wish to change (e.g. shouting out in class), then we can use such an analysis to change either the antecedent trigger to the behaviour or the reinforcing consequence which is resulting in him/her wanting to repeat the behaviour.

Consequences that strengthen (reinforce) the association between the antecedent situation and a response are called **reinforcers**. An outcome that weakens the association is called a **punisher** and is typically something that is aversive (unpleasant to the individual). An example would be if a pupil was reprimanded for not doing his or her work. A distinction is made between positive and negative reinforcement, and between positive and negative punishment. In this context, 'positive' refers to the introduction of a stimulus into a child's environment, and 'negative' means the removal of that stimulus (it is important to note that 'negative reinforcement' does not mean 'punishment'!). For clarity, we have illustrated this in Table 2.1.

Positive reinforcers strengthen the association and are called **rewards**. For example, receiving praise for doing well in a test might encourage future studying. Negative reinforcers occur when something aversive is stopped, and these also strengthen an association. An example of a negative reinforcer would be allowing the children to stop doing an unpleasant task such as picking up the litter around school if they were well-behaved.

It is important to note that one cannot be sure what a particular child will find motivating (reinforcing) and what they will perceive as aversive (punishing) until you put them into practice. Something that is aversive for one child, such as being shouted at, may prove reinforcing for another child, because they are receiving attention from the teacher that perhaps they do not normally receive.

Punishment

Although the four categories shown in Table 2.1 appear to be equally likely to be effective, there are practical reasons why both types of punishment are generally considered to be less desirable.

- They do not emphasise new, positive behaviours, and children might simply learn to avoid getting caught. Moreover, punishment has also been shown to lead to regression: if a pupil's present behaviour no longer succeeds in getting what the pupil wants, then he or she may return to earlier forms of behaviour. These may previously have been effective for the pupil but could nevertheless be undesirable in class.
- The person who administers the punishment also comes to be seen in a negative way (i.e. the children have **generalised** the aversive experience to include the teacher who administered the

punishment). Although this means that children will be anxious and cautious about that person in the future, it also means that he or she is unlikely to generate any spontaneous cooperative behaviour; the child will just not like the teacher very much. Children who are reprimanded by teachers in front of the class are very unlikely to want to cooperate with them in the future, although they may be careful to avoid a repeat of the punishment. They may do so in a number of negative ways, such as blaming others.

- Punishment also acts as a negative social model for children. The use of punishment by authority figures is likely to set this up as a legitimate process for pupils as well as staff.

Rewards

Positive reinforcements (rewards) can be a very powerful way of managing children's behaviour. They avoid most of the problems with punishments, since their use involves an emphasis on developing new and positive work habits; they establish a pleasant relationship between the teacher and the pupil; and they give positive social roles for pupils. In some situations, however, positive reinforcements may seem inappropriate and can appear to be rather like 'bribing a child to work', with the danger that the child rather than the teacher comes to be in control. This means that pupils can then use the situation to threaten non-cooperation to get what they want.

Also, it often seems wrong to reward a child who is on a programme because of his or her lack of effort. Other children may find it unjust if a difficult child gets extra treats and privileges, whereas they are 'behaving themselves' normally and get nothing. Ways of managing this might involve ensuring that all children are rewarded for positive behaviours, and by the use of negative punishment, where the reward is simply what the other children in the class are already getting for normal behaviour, which can be withdrawn by the teacher.

We revisit the uses and impact of reward and punishment in the classroom in Chapter 5, which discusses student motivation. However, it should be noted that the use of operant conditioning to motivate children's work at school has been strongly criticised as being likely to damage natural, intrinsic motivation. Some researchers argue that children have a natural curiosity and desire to find out about things; however, if they perceive themselves as working only for rewards, their work becomes superficial and geared solely towards the reward, rather than for the sake of learning (e.g. Prabhu et al., 2008). Inappropriate use of praise can also impact negatively on students' attainment, both by lowering a child's academic self-concept (too much praise is seen as patronising) and also be overinflating a child's sense of self-efficacy, resulting in a reduction in the amount of effort put into school tasks.

Learning principles

Skinner established various principles for generating effective learning by the appropriate use of outcomes which are contingent on (dependent upon) some form of behaviour. A key principle is that reinforcements or punishers appear to be most effective when they happen soon after the behaviour. According to this, waiting until the end of the lesson to praise students' work or to reprimand them should not be as effective as praise given just after they have completed a particular section, or verbal comments immediately after the problem behaviour.

Outcomes can also vary in frequency and timing. A very frequent, predictable reward is initially good at training for certain responses. A problem, however, is that such responses are very dependent on the reinforcer: if a pupil is working merely for frequent teacher praise and the praise suddenly stops, then the pupil will probably also stop working. If rewards are less frequent and less predictable, pupils will be more likely to continue their responses when rewards are stopped. Presumably they are less aware when rewards are finally phased out, and, one may hope, they may then develop intrinsic motivation (involvement for its own sake).

Practical implications

When working with a new class or a difficult child, teachers should use a high level of meaningful rewards, along-side firm control. This would be aimed at establishing involvement with class tasks and routines, and at developing positive perceptions of the teacher. After a while, however, the rewards should become more intermittent and attention focused on the performance of tasks and pupils' achievements.

As will be described in Chapter 13, operant conditioning can be applied in the form of 'behaviour modification' to manage problem classroom behaviour and increase work involvement. However, Skinner (1954) considered that it could also be effectively used to directly alter academic progress by a process he called **programmed learning**.

At first, as shown in Figure 2.2, this often involved children initially being given some information. They were then tested on some part of the information they had been given, and a correct response was rewarded in some way (typically with praise); an incorrect response would lead to their being given either a repeat of the original information, or an alternative (simpler) presentation. Programmed learning was often implemented in expensive 'teaching machines' which presented the materials in the appropriate sequence.

The advantages claimed for such early programmed learning systems were that they emphasised success, that the learning was sequential and structured, and that the learning was closely matched to the individual learner's pace. Unfortunately, an approach of this type is difficult to develop properly,

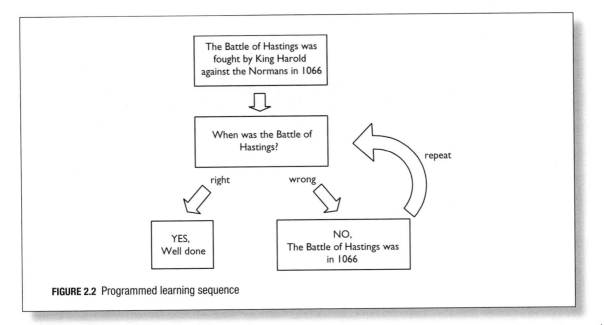

FIGURE 2.2 Programmed learning sequence

owing to the detail involved in the programme design and the emphasis that was placed on developmental testing and the need to demonstrate the effectiveness of the materials before they could be used more widely (Molenda, 2008). Also, students often found the experience of working on such machines socially isolating and somewhat boring. Yet a review by Walberg (1984) of thousands of research studies found that instructional methods based on Skinner's principles yielded the best results in terms of learning relative to other instructional approaches.

This early approach can be seen as the basis of many contemporary computer-based learning systems, although these are becoming increasingly based on sophisticated models of the learner's knowledge base and approach to learning, and there is more of an emphasis on praise as reinforcement, rather than simply being informed that an answer is correct or incorrect.

The principles of operant conditioning have also been implemented in the direct instruction model of teaching developed by Siegfried Engelmann. It was originally developed as a way to help children who were at risk of school failure, and the best-known variant of it is the DISTAR (Direct Instructional Systems for Teaching and Remediation) programme. Applied largely to basic skills work in literacy and numeracy, this approach carefully directs the teaching process by using a script for the teacher, and also specifically incorporates the use of reinforcement – mainly as verbal praise. In the case of reading, it is also a technique that teaches synthetic phonics (see Chapter 10) and, although early evaluations of it showed it to be beneficial (Kameenui *et al.*, 1997), Stahl (1998) notes that when properly controlled comparison studies were conducted, the results observed seemed more likely to be attributable to the phonics emphasis of the programme than the overall instructional approach itself.

Skinner believed that operant conditioning ruled out mentalistic explanations based on thought processes and preferred to limit himself to describing the conditions under which learning occurred. However, it seems that individuals who have been operantly conditioned have in fact learned to predict what will happen in a given situation if they engage in certain behaviour, much as in classical conditioning. This learning process is a cognitive one, and Bandura *et al.* (1963) demonstrated that observational learning (which is the basis of **social learning theory**) depends on predictions and expectations about the consequences of behaviour, rather than direct associations. Whether or not children engaged in a particular behaviour depended on what outcomes (praise or a reprimand) they observed for other people and consequently expected for themselves.

Despite this, conditioning can still be an effective way to describe and understand basic learning situations where there is a direct and predictable link between behaviour and consequences. In many situations, however, behaviour involves more than a simple response, and can comprise a sequence of flexible and skilled activities. Such complex learning can be explained in behaviourism by the linking together of a number of conditioned responses, called 'chaining'. According to this view, pupils might therefore learn to enter a classroom, get out their books and start a particular activity, as a sequence which will gain the approval of their teacher.

Cognitive processes and learning

The cognitive approach in psychology sees the individual as a processor of information, in much the same way that a computer takes in information and follows a program to produce an output. But humans are much more complex and self-directing than computers are, and are able to develop plans and strategies to guide ways of interacting with their environment. To do this, humans also generate and test out internal models of the world, which can act as a guide for future behaviour.

Mental representations

Such cognitive processes involve developing mental representations of events, things or ideas that can act as the basis for thought. Some of these take the form of direct experiences, such as sensations and physical movements, or visual representations which involve imagery. As discussed later in this chapter, these are particularly important at early developmental stages, or with initial learning in a new area of knowledge. 'Higher' levels of thought which develop as children become older are based on symbolic representations such as words, which stand for something else without necessarily having any direct similarity to it. Words can therefore represent concrete and abstract categories and can also express relationships between other symbolic representations.

All these categories and relationships typically take the form of **concepts**, which involve groupings of items that include the same key features or attributes. A conceptual grouping can involve living things, such as 'dogs', which share the attributes of 'four legs, barks, chases cats, can bite', and actions such as 'running', which share the attributes of 'moving fast, all legs off ground at same time'. The use of concepts is a powerful and necessary way of achieving cognitive economy and means that we do not become overloaded by the mass of information we experience. Concepts also enable us to deal with the world rapidly and to infer attributes that we do not directly observe – in Bruner's (1957) phrase, to go 'beyond the information given'. When we meet an animal that we classify as a 'dog', we are then aware that it can bite, and will be able to treat it accordingly.

Propositions involve links or relationships between concepts. They are the smallest unit of information that can be judged either true or false, for example that 'the dog is running' (either it is or it isn't). Such propositions can make up or be assembled into facts, which incorporate information that is generally believed to be valid, for example that 'Hydrogen is a flammable gas', or that 'King Henry VIII had six wives'. This last fact incorporates a number of propositions: that Henry was a king, that he was the eighth king called Henry, as well as that he had six wives.

Knowledge is made up from a body of such propositions and the further relationships between them, which constitute the subject matter of domains of academic study. Propositions can also form the basis for thinking and reasoning, enabling people to make logical inferences by a process of deriving new propositional relationships.

Mental processes can be represented by 'connectionist' models, with 'learning' happening through changes in the strengths of the links between low-level units. Since these models (to be described later in this chapter) are based on the general way in which the brain is believed to function, it seems possible that similar mechanisms may represent the underlying basis of concept formation. It has also been argued that some form of 'spreading activation' links together areas in the brain and that associating concepts and propositions in this way is the basis of thought.

Such concept-based, factual information is often referred to as **declarative knowledge**, and can be contrasted with **procedural knowledge**, which refers to information about how we can do things. Procedural knowledge covers skills such as reading and writing, or fluent calculations in mathematics. Procedural memories appear to be represented as 'condition–action' rules, which are referred to as 'productions'. These specify what to do under certain conditions, and involve the form of 'IF X, THEN Y'. As an example of this, most experienced teachers implicitly use the rule 'IF a student is starting to misbehave, THEN move closer to them'. A large number of such rules linked together must underlie skilled or expert behaviour.

Procedural knowledge often starts off as declarative knowledge but with practice becomes more automated, meaning that we become less conscious of the processes involved in what we are doing. When children first learn to form letters, for instance, they often learn a verbal description and rehearsal of the appropriate movements: writing an 'a' involving the three movement sequences of 'round, up and down'. Fluent writing, however, is a relatively automatic skill, and mature writers are usually aware only of the content of what they are writing. Experienced teachers similarly would probably find it difficult to describe the many skilled elements involved in monitoring and controlling a class, which they normally achieve at the same time as organising and delivering curriculum content. Once established, such procedural knowledge is much less likely to be forgotten than declarative knowledge and, like the ability to ride a bike, skills can often be retained for years with little if any deterioration, even if they are not practised.

Memory

Memory is the storage component of learning such forms of information. A great deal of education is concerned with ways of ensuring that information is input to memory (registered), for it to be subsequently reproduced or used (retrieved). The process can go wrong at any of these stages since information can fail to register or be initially processed, or there can be a failure to retrieve information (which is then available somewhere, but is not accessible). The study of memory is important to education since its models allow us to understand the processes of such losses of information, normally referred to as 'forgetting'. If we understand how forgetting occurs, we may be able to devise techniques to prevent it and to optimise learning and memory.

Short-term memory

The most popular model of memory has been the multi-store model of Atkinson and Shiffrin (1971). In this, short-term memory (STM) is regarded as an initial store which has a short length of time for storage (a few seconds only) and a limited capacity, which is typically about seven 'chunks' or units of information. These are often items that can be verbally encoded, such as words, letters or numbers, and the classic test of STM involves listening to and repeating back sequences of random numbers of increasing length. Information in STM can be 'rehearsed' by a process of repeating items over, as people often do with telephone numbers while they are dialling them. With further processing or encoding, information can be transferred for further storage in long-term memory (LTM; see below, and can also be retrieved from it, as shown in Figure 2.3.

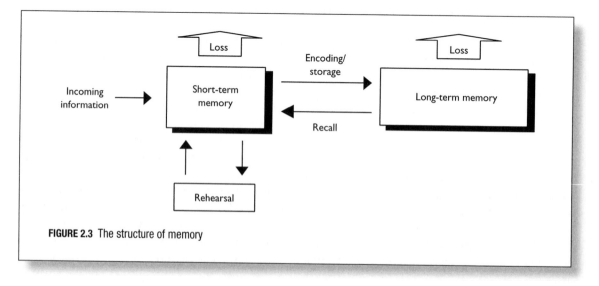

FIGURE 2.3 The structure of memory

Working memory

Because of the active nature of the short-term store, Baddeley (1986) described it as **working memory**. This appears to have a number of modality-specific components that include visual and spatial as well as auditory information (see Figure 2.4). Working memory is best thought of as the conscious part of memory that enables you to generate mental images, think about sounds and concepts and perform mental manipulations upon them. For example, the activity of carrying out the sum '23×6' in your head or reading to yourself (or out loud) is a working-memory task. It is possible to do two things at once in working memory if at least one of the tasks is highly practised and therefore automatised and therefore requires little conscious attention (the central executive is the part of the model that allocates attentional resources to tasks, and it has a finite capacity). It is also possible to do two things at the same time if they are drawing on different components of the model. However, anything that uses the same modality, such as two verbal tasks or two visual tasks, will result in interference and problematic performance.

Long-term memory

Short-term or working memory usually lasts only a few seconds and is in many ways closer to thinking. Long-term memory is the main way in which we store information, and it lasts over hours, weeks and years. It is this that most people usually think about when they refer to memory and forgetting. The main characteristics of LTM are:

- very large capacity (typically more than 40,000 words plus associated facts);
- very long duration (up to a lifetime);
- mainly semantic coding (by meaning);
- loss (forgetting) mainly by interference.

Most theories about the nature of representations in long-term memory see it as a system of associated concepts. Collins and Quillian (1969) originally proposed a hierarchy, with high-level concepts and

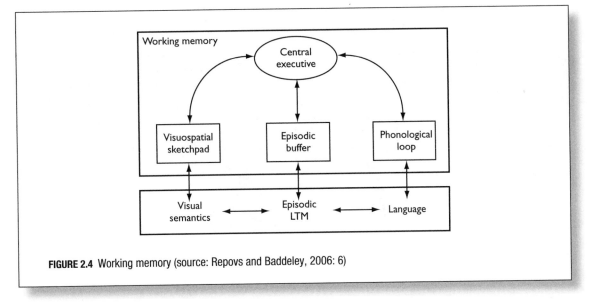

FIGURE 2.4 Working memory (source: Repovs and Baddeley, 2006: 6)

features branching to lower-level subordinate concepts and features. Attributes high up in the structure would generally cover all lower concepts, so 'breathes air' would apply to all animals, and 'has wings' would apply to all birds. Subordinate categories, however, need specific information that can either add to or modify the structure. For example, as Figure 2.5 shows, a robin has a red breast and a penguin cannot fly. Such structures have the advantage of cognitive economy since particular attributes need to be stored only once, with higher attributes covering all lower categories and concepts. A hierarchy such as this is also fairly close to formal scientific classification systems, and developing children's abilities to understand and use hierarchies is one of the aims of teaching.

A difficulty with this theory is that, although people can adopt such structures, they often seem to prefer to use links that are based on similarity of features, rather than logical relationships. Robins and penguins are both types of birds, but the penguin is evidently not very close to what we would normally think of as being 'bird-like'. People are in fact more likely to link it with mammals such as sea lions, which come from a very different branch of classification but also live in cold areas and swim and catch fish.

Such logical hierarchies also depend on concepts that can be well specified. An example of this would be a bicycle, which has the defining or **core attributes** of 'a vehicle, has two wheels, is driven by pedals'. However, the majority of the concepts that people use are generally rather 'fuzzy' and cannot be completely determined in this way. People are therefore more likely to categorise concepts according to how close they are to a typical form, known as a **prototype**. This is usually the norm, or the commonly experienced average of the features of something. The prototype for a bird would usually be something that is small, bird-shaped, has wings, able to fly, eats worms, and chirps. A typical bird would be something like a robin or a sparrow, and people will tend to judge that penguins, ostriches and chickens are not very 'bird-like'.

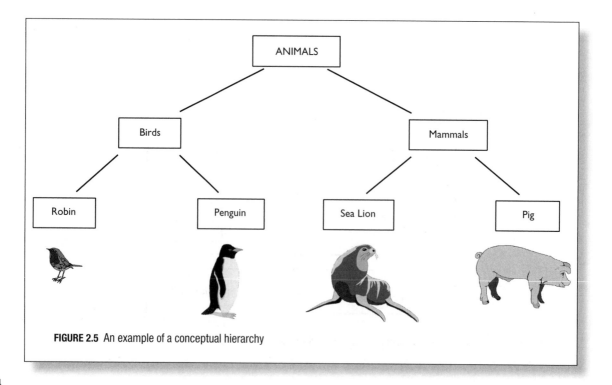

FIGURE 2.5 An example of a conceptual hierarchy

Although such prototypes can be identified and linked in various ways, people tend to prefer to use them at an intermediate level which is referred to as 'basic'. This is the level at which things have the most distinctive features that are of relevance to us. The word 'dog', for instance, is a basic-level verbal concept. It comes under the superordinate category of 'animals' and has subordinate categories which are the various breeds of dogs. Using basic-level concepts means that we are able to communicate effectively without being too general or too specific. In normal conversation, people would tend to say that 'the dog is barking', rather than 'the animal is making a noise' (superordinate concepts), or 'the Chihuahua is yapping' (subordinate concepts).

Concept development

Early conceptual development is often based on establishing prototypes, largely from initial experiences of particular instances known as 'exemplars'. Exemplars become refined over time to 'average out' and represent the typical or key features of a concept. Verbal concepts such as 'doggie' may at first be used by a child to refer only to one particular dog; this is known as the 'underextension' of a concept. After the child has encountered a number of different animals, however, a partial prototype may be established and can lead to 'overextensions', with the child perhaps referring to all four-legged animals as 'doggie'. Eventually an accurate prototype will be formed, based upon the contrasts that can be made between different types of four-legged animals. Even older children or adults will establish new concepts in this way, particularly when encountering a novel area.

It seems that some features of new objects in the environment are more salient to children in terms of categorisation of concepts than others. For example, Quinn *et al.* (2001; see also Quinn and Eimas, 1996) found that infants based their categorisation on the head region of animals that they were shown. Arterberry and Bornstein (2002) also showed that children as young as three and six months could categorise animals and vehicles on the basis of motion cues only (point light displays), but only nine-month-old children could categorise them on the basis of static images, which shows that movement is very important.

Practical implications

Initial teaching of new concepts, particularly with younger children, should focus on exemplars, and lead on to comparisons with other similar categories to establish distinctive features. Concepts are also generally first learned at the basic level, which is the point at which they will have greatest distinctiveness and relevance to children. If basic-level concepts are taught first, they can then lead on to the establishing of subordinate and superordinate concepts.

When teaching about metals, for example, it may be best to start with typical metals such as iron and copper, contrasting these with various non-metals. These features develop the basic-level concept of 'metal', and other exemplar metals can then be identified as subordinate concepts. In this case the superordinate concept of an 'element' is more abstract and would usually be tackled when children reach secondary age.

Schemas

Schemas can be thought of as structured clusters of information which are used to represent events, concepts, actions or processes. Although this explanation may seem rather all-embracing and vague, schemas are very useful ways of understanding how we group together and simplify our general knowledge and understanding. To some extent this is achieved by the use of concepts, but schemas go further, to describe the way in which we generally organise and use conceptual information. Schemas exist because they are ways of achieving cognitive economy; although using them can sometimes lead to inaccuracies through oversimplification, they reduce complexity to a manageable level and speed up the way in which we deal with the world.

A general schema for 'school' might link together the concepts of 'teachers' and 'pupils' with 'school buildings', the fact that 'many children attend schools' and the fact that 'schools are for children to learn reading, writing and arithmetic'. We would also involve our own relationships to school – either as a past pupil or possibly as a parent or teacher. A key feature of such real-world knowledge is that we have associated emotional content and links with our past and future possible actions related to all these constituent parts of the schema.

General schemas have an overall structure that stays the same but with certain aspects that vary with specific instances. When we relate to a particular school, we then adapt the schema to take account of aspects such as its size, location and general reputation, while retaining the key aspects about what generally goes on in schools.

Some schemas cover sequences of possible actions and events, and have been described by Schank and Abelson (1977) as **scripts**. These include the key elements of what is normally carried out in certain situations. For instance, pupils are usually aware of the normal sequence of going into a class, listening to the teacher, getting their books ready and starting work. This general schema has a number of variables, and with particular subjects or teachers the process may vary somewhat. However, in most lessons the key element of the teacher managing the pupil's learning tends to stay the same.

A similar sequencing structure can be seen in written **story grammars**. In the same way that sentences have a structure that conveys meaning, bodies of text also tend to follow certain schematic sequences that enable us to follow their logic. Formal essays, for instance, usually have some form of introduction, a main body that considers evidence and ideas, and a discussion followed by a conclusion. According to Mandler (1987), stories often have the key elements of a setting, and an event structure composed of episodes. Each episode is made up from a beginning, a complex reaction (which sets up a state that the key character wishes to achieve), a goal path (which is the plan and consequences of attempting to achieve the goal) and a final ending. Stories that do not have such structures are hard to understand, and when they are recalled, students tend to distort them to fit them in with the more conventional form.

Schemas are useful ways of understanding general cognitive processes and probably operate at many different levels to organise general life processes, as well as more specific groupings. Schemas have been shown to be useful ways of describing a number of psychological processes, including stereotypical judgements (about what personal attributes we believe are related together), attribution processes (our assumptions of why people do things) and implicit personality theories (about underlying consistencies governing what people think and do).

Prototype concepts can also be seen as low-level schemas, which have average values. The prototype of 'bird' described earlier has the typical size, shape and features of something like a sparrow. According to this perspective, concepts will also tend to have the other attributes of schemas, such as emotional content (sparrows are 'cheeky') and how they relate to ourselves and our actions (we might feed them in the park).

Processes involved in long-term memory

As well as its conceptual structure, long-term storage can involve a number of different systems (see Figure 2.6), according to how information is dealt with. Tulving (1983) considers that declarative memory can be subdivided into the main body of semantic memory, which covers meaningful information such as concepts and propositions, and episodic memory. This involves information about an experienced event or situation, and at one extreme can involve eidetic memory, when the complete experience is recalled. This is relatively rare, however, and usually only the unique or distinctive features of a situation are stored. All learning probably starts off as episodic memory and normally progresses to become semantic memory as it is processed and assimilated. A few days after a particular Christmas, the specific events are still fresh in our memory, but a few years later, all Christmases can seem much the same.

Squire (1992) also considers that memory can be subdivided into two major categories relating to whether recall is conscious, referred to as **explicit memory**, or unconscious, referred to as **implicit memory**. Many forms of knowledge may initially involve conscious processes; for instance, early reading may at least partly be based on the explicit recall and use of letter sounds, which eventually becomes part of the unconscious process of skilled reading. Explicit and implicit memory also appear to involve very different brain processes. When involved in conscious recall, the brain becomes generally more active, and consumes more energy. Surprisingly, with the implicit recall involved in skilled performance, the activity of the brain is reduced, as though it were falling into a routine, 'easier' pattern.

The process of learning can also be either explicit, with the use of conscious plans and strategies, or implicit, without any self-awareness that learning is actually taking place. Explicit learning is involved in what we would normally recognise as formal, didactic teaching, where the teacher closely directs

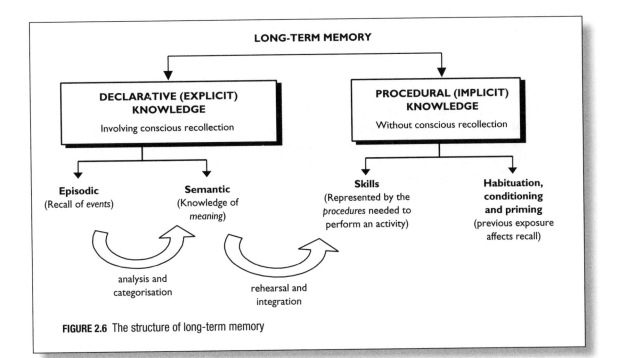

FIGURE 2.6 The structure of long-term memory

pupils on what they are learning and (often) how they should go about it. Pupils are very aware that they are in a learning situation and of what it is that they are learning. As noted above, however, once something is learned, recall may become less conscious over time, particularly if there has been over-learning or close integration with other abilities, as in skilled performance of some kind.

Implicit learning happens when pupils are not aware that they are acquiring information. Although it may at first seem rather unlikely that such learning could occur, implicit learning does nevertheless underpin many 'natural' learning processes such as children's learning of their first language. As you will see in Chapter 9, most vocabulary and grammar development occurs with little effort or aware-ness, and there is evidence that direct teaching may actually inhibit progress, by interfering with the child's own implicit hypotheses. It may seem somewhat strange to talk of high-level cognitive proc-esses such as hypothesis formation as being non-conscious. However, there is evidence (reviewed by Baddeley *et al.*, 2009) that people are able to develop rules (for example, when learning the grammar of a new language) and to control complex systems without being able to describe how they are doing this.

One possible explanation of this comes from connectionist theories, which will be discussed later in this chapter. According to this perspective, it is entirely possible for a complex system with modifi-able connections to generate rules without necessarily having any high-level (conscious) controlling functions. However, if people develop such implicit knowledge to a high level, the knowledge does appear to become more accessible to conscious awareness. It seems that people are eventually able to work out what they are doing, particularly if they are helped to do so. This is shown in the way that pupils are eventually able to learn to analyse and to reflect on their use of grammar in language with formal teaching.

It can be argued that implicit learning is an effective and more natural approach to learning in many situations. As regards the learning of a second language, for instance, it is believed that 'immer-sion learning' is an effective approach, whereby pupils are involved in hearing and using the new lan-guage in practical situations, in much the same way as they learned their first language.

In general, however, the evidence tends to support the value of directed and explicit experiences in most fields of learning. Scott (1990), for instance, studied the development of French in conversa-tional classes with students who were either given certain language rules or experienced them in sto-ries. Even though students in the 'implicit' group were given ten times the amount of experience that those in the 'explicit' group received, their eventual learning was still inferior. Similarly, Ellis (1993, 1994) compared the effectiveness of teaching Welsh grammar either by providing examples of certain rules, by teaching the rules, or by teaching the rules but then requiring students to practise applying them to examples. Only the latter group showed that they could generalise from their learning to new examples. Such results suggest that a combination of explicit teaching and experiential learning, in which students can apply what is being learned in a meaningful way, is perhaps the best approach to take.

Problems with learning

Failure to register information initially or to process it subsequently for LTM storage is what we nor-mally call 'failing to learn'. Subsequent loss or distortion of information, or the inability to retrieve it, is normally called **forgetting**.

Initial encoding depends on the active direction and involvement of working memory, and with-out this, learning will not progress any further. This is effectively the process of paying attention, and most theories about attention, from that of Broadbent (1958) onwards, stress that further processing depends upon information having some form of relevance to the individual. Eysenck (1979) has also emphasised that whether information is processed into LTM depends on its 'distinctiveness' – on whether it has a special, meaningful relationship for us.

When we first transfer information into long-term storage, we do so largely in terms of its meaning. The process usually involves some form of interpretation in terms of our existing schemas (knowledge and ideas). Although interpretation can help students to contextualise new learning and to link it in with existing knowledge, it can also produce **interference** and **distortions**. Distortion can also have an effect on information that has already been learned, to produce forgetting. This can happen when memories become progressively reconstructed over time to fit in with our pre-existing concepts and ideas. In a famous study, Bartlett (1932) studied subjects' recall of a Native American folk-tale called *The War of the Ghosts* which comprised an unusual story narrative. Over a number of successive recalls, the subjects progressively shortened and distorted the content, largely to fit in with their own schemas. Our expectations of commonly experienced social events can also distort our recall of specific events by 'filling in gaps' with what we might expect to have happened, rather than what actually did occur.

School learning should therefore monitor recall and compare this with the original material when necessary. Teachers need to be aware of this potential for distortion of learned information; when carrying out revision programmes, they should encourage pupils to check back on key points in the original material. Butler and Winne (1995), for instance, review findings that feedback is most effective when it emphasises and corrects items that students get wrong, rather than just giving grades or reinforcing their correct responses.

Early theories about forgetting focused on the idea that memories simply faded over time – the **trace decay** theory (e.g. Broadbent, 1958, but see also Gold *et al.*, 2005). However, this idea is not as straightforward, as one might assume from this that a period of inactivity after learning, such as sleep, would result in reduced recall. This has not been found to be the case. Backhaus *et al.* (2008) have found that children's declarative knowledge improves after a period of sleep, but not after a period of wakefulness, and suggest that sleep is essential for the consolidation of factual knowledge during childhood. This implies that children need to ensure that they sleep well after a day of studying at school for best results.

When we are awake, we are exposed to an enormous amount of new information, and it may be the case that this information may influence our ability to learn or recall new knowledge. For example, **interference theory** has been very popular in explaining forgetting and has a number of important implications for effective teaching and learning. This essentially proposes that when similar material is learned, it becomes difficult to distinguish one part from another. This will lead to a retrieval failure, when the information may be learned and in memory but cannot be successfully separated (Anderson and Neely, 1996).

As shown in Figure 2.7, interference can happen when the retrieval of new information is affected by its similarity to previously learned material (**proactive interference**) and when new information affects the recall of older material (**retroactive interference**).

All learning is embedded in previous and subsequent learning and is liable to both forms of interference. This appears to be a likely explanation for the general progressive loss of information (forgetting) over time, since the longer information is in memory, the more likely it is that both types of interference will build up. However, older memories are more robust to the effects of interference than more recent memories are (known as 'Jost's Law').

Interestingly, there are data that suggest that children may outperform adults with respect to susceptibility to interference, at least with respect to procedural memory. Dorfberger *et al.* (2007) found that 9- and 12-year-old children outperformed a group of 17-year-olds on such a motor sequence

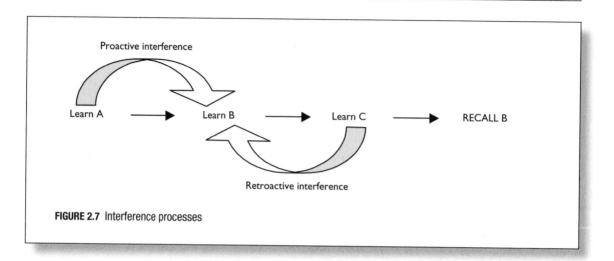

FIGURE 2.7 Interference processes

learning task after exposure to an interference task. In fact, the children showed evidence of continued improvement in performance of the original sequence, even after exposure to the interference task. The results suggested that younger children are best able to resist interference in procedural memory, and that this ability declines after puberty.

Managing learning and improving memory

The implications of the interference explanation of forgetting are, first, that teaching and learning techniques should as far as possible attempt to encode factual information in distinctive ways. Information which is similar to existing knowledge is hard to encode separately and will be difficult to retrieve. Second, the effective retrieval of information will depend on some form of strategy which emphasises the links it has with existing (available) knowledge. Perhaps the most general technique which has been shown to improve memory in this way is the use of organisation. A classic investigation of this by Bower *et al.* (1969) gave subjects the task of learning 112 words organised into conceptual hierarchies (they were all types of minerals). The subjects learned much more effectively than subjects who simply learned the list in its unorganised form. Even pre-school children are observed to benefit from structure when learning new information, and it seems that this may be a strategy that we learn from our parents: Larkina and Güler (2008) found that 40-month-old children's recall of pictorial stimuli was associated with the use of category-based strategies to organise the stimuli by their mothers (mothers were able to assist their children in whatever way they wished).

Such meaningful content and organisation can be enhanced by the technique of constructing **knowledge maps**. These involve students in generating a spatial–semantic display covering a particular area of knowledge, in which the physical layout embodies meaningful relationships. The process of construction appears to activate and also to develop a schema covering that area and can form the basis for initial learning, revision or essay writing. The example in Figure 2.8 shows some concepts and connections for the role of trees in the environment. The activity of constructing this (not simply learning it from a book) would enable a student to appreciate the impact of clearing the rainforests for farming.

Such approaches often involve **visual encoding**, based on the ideas of Paivio (1969), who demonstrated that concrete imagery (visualising things) forms a much stronger basis for long-term memory than do verbal processes (when students work from written or spoken information). One important

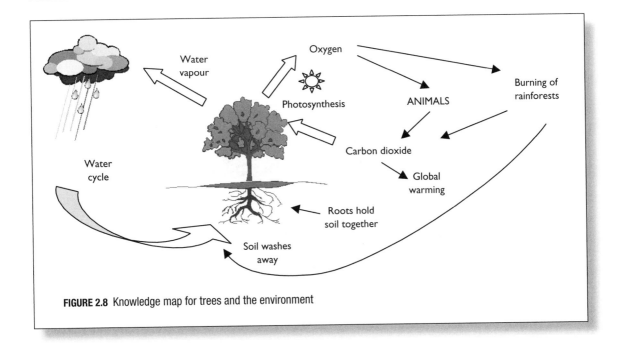

FIGURE 2.8 Knowledge map for trees and the environment

feature of visually encoding information is that it produces material that is much less likely to be similar to other items and as a result is much less liable to interference. Chmielewski and Dansereau (1998) found that the use of such approaches not only improved students' recall of subject areas for which they had prepared knowledge maps, but also transferred to their learning in other areas. This indicates that using such maps trains students to adopt a deeper approach to learning, one which emphasises relationships and organisation.

Coding techniques can reduce the memory load, allow for specific retrieval cues and prevent the effects of both reconstruction and interference. One particular approach utilises both reduction and elaboration of information. Typically it first reduces the original information to key elements such as initial letters. These can then be elaborated into a larger structured system, such as a meaningful sentence, that can be used to reconstruct the original material when needed. In the sentence 'Richard Of York Gave Battle In Vain', the first letters of the words act as the cues for the colours in the spectrum: as red, orange, yellow, green, blue, indigo, violet. This technique is particularly popular with medical students, who have large amounts of anatomical and clinical information to learn.

The keyword mnemonic is another effective approach for learning associations. This works by forming a linked image between one concept and a concrete word (the keyword) representing the other concept. As shown in Figure 2.9, when a student is trying to learn that the French word for 'bald' is 'chauve', he or she could achieve this by forming an image linking a bald head with the keyword 'shaver', which is phonologically similar to the word 'chauve'.

Although such techniques can be very effective, they do require a lot of initial preparation, and the learning tends to be rather superficial. Wang and Thomas (1995) found that, after only two days, keyword learning loses its initial superiority over normal learning procedures. This finding indicates that such approaches are best limited to specific areas such as the learning of foreign vocabulary, where there is limited semantic information. Even here it may be important to move rapidly into more implicit learning situations and to start to use the new vocabulary.

FIGURE 2.9 Keyword mnemonic learning

Cramming versus spacing: the importance of distributed practice

A strong finding in learning and memory research has been that if a certain amount of study time is spread out or distributed between a number of sessions, the result usually is improved learning (Cepeda *et al.*, 2006; Kornell and Bjork, 2007a, b). When learning is combined or 'massed' together (as is often the case when students are revising for examinations), it is likely that students will become overloaded and reduce their attention and active involvement. For example Kornell and Bjork (2007a) asked participants to learn the styles of 12 artists by studying six different paintings by each artist. For half of the artists, their paintings were grouped together and therefore studied intensively; for the others, their paintings were interleaved and therefore spaced out. After the learning phase, new paintings were presented and the students had to correctly identify the artist. A total of 78 per cent of the participants did better in the spaced condition than in the condition where the content was grouped together, but interestingly only 22 per cent of participants felt that they had done better in that condition. This suggests that students need to be told to pace their study rather than cram, particularly as cramming is a style of studying that appears to make students feel that they have learned more effectively.

A variation on the idea of spacing material to be learned is the idea of 'expanding rehearsal', which originated with the work of Landauer and Bjork (1978). This is a technique in which material to be learned is initially re-tested after a short delay, and is re-tested regularly, but with increasing intervals between test sessions over time. The effectiveness of this technique has been demonstrated across a wide range of curriculum areas (Pashler *et al.*, 2007). The spacing of the tests is important and it is recommended that it should be between 10–20 per cent of the period between first test and final assessment (Baddeley *et al.*, 2009). So, for example, if you were going to take an examination in ten days' time, you might initially test every day (10 per cent), increasing to once every two days (20 per cent) over time.

Practical implications

It seems likely that basic skill work might benefit particularly from regular and short sessions since children are more likely to become bored with such low-level activities. These skills might include early literacy attainments such as phonic skills (letters in words) and phonological abilities (sensitivity to spoken sounds), as well as numeracy development such as number bonds and multiplication tables. However, with general curriculum content it is probably more important to teach for periods which have meaningful content and to avoid too many changes during a day, which might become disruptive. More complex and integrated subject work such as investigations can be achieved only with lessons of a certain length, but again it would seem to be best if they could be spaced out during the week rather than combined into 'double periods', as often happens in the secondary school.

Cognitive development and learning

Piagetian theory

The major theory in the area of cognitive development and learning was proposed by Piaget (1966, 1972) and is largely based around the development of the mental structures called 'schemas' described earlier in this chapter. For a young child, a schema could involve the actions involved in 'reaching out and grasping an object', or for an older person it might involve the mature and complex sequence of expectations and actions involved in 'going to a restaurant'.

From an adult perspective, children's schemas appear relatively uncomplicated, and early on these involve ways of representing direct interactions with the physical world. As children mature, Piaget believed that schemas become progressively more complex and can ultimately be capable of representing abstract features, enabling older students to carry out high-level thought processes. Piaget was interested in how this development happens, in terms of children's experiences and the influence of new information on their knowledge structures.

Assimilation and accommodation

Piaget believed that much of the time, new information is only **assimilated**, or 'fitted in' with existing schemas, in a way similar to the process of accretion mentioned earlier. So, for instance, a child may have a general conceptual schema of 'fish', based largely upon early experiences of his or her own pet goldfish. This could be in the form of a prototype concept, and involve features such as 'lives in water' and 'has fins'. New experiences of different types of fishes might fit in neatly with this, and at such times schemas and incoming information are in a state of balance, known as **equilibrium**, as shown in Figure 2.10.

When subsequent information does not have quite the same attributes, there is a tendency at first to continue with assimilation. At this point, however, things do not fit together too well and there is a state of imbalance or **disequilibrium**, as shown in Figure 2.11. When young children first encounter dolphins, perhaps by seeing them on the television, they may tend to see them as being a kind of

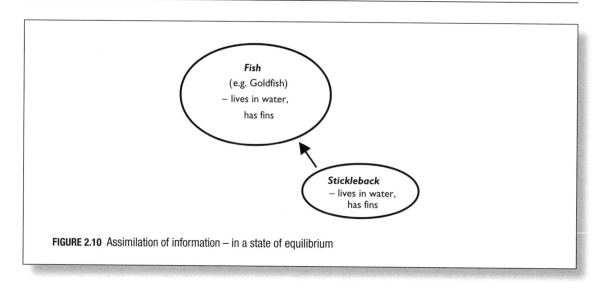

FIGURE 2.10 Assimilation of information – in a state of equilibrium

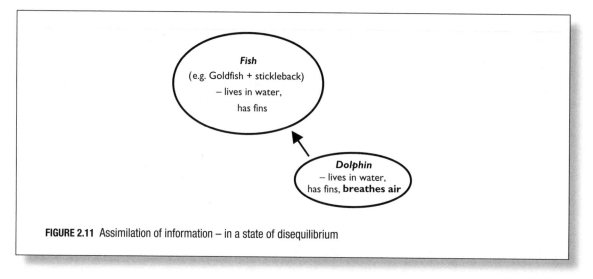

FIGURE 2.11 Assimilation of information – in a state of disequilibrium

fish. The dolphins will be assigned to that concept on the basis of their most evident features, even though they may be seen to come to the surface and breathe air.

If further information does not fit too well with the existing schema, then the disequilibrium that this produces eventually becomes too great and forces a process of restructuring or adjustment to the information, known as **accommodation**, as shown in Figure 2.12. This could happen if the child then has experiences about whales, which not only breathe air but are also very large and are harder to fit in with the original goldfish schema. A possible resolution for this would then be to create a new category of 'whale-type' creatures.

Following this process, there is a new state of equilibrium. New information can again fit in; for instance, 'killer whales' could now be assimilated without difficulty. It will of course probably be much later before features such as 'bear live young' are incorporated and the label of 'cetacean' is used. Some people may never assimilate these latter characteristics of whales and dolphins.

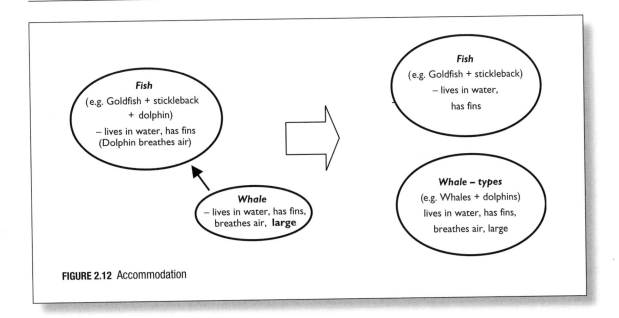

FIGURE 2.12 Accommodation

Piaget developed these ideas largely from close studies of the intellectual development of his own children, including how they misapplied concepts and developed them with further experiences. His basic idea that young children have simplified schemas, which become more complex and differentiated with increasing experiences, is accepted by most people as quite plausible. It fits in with a number of psychological findings such as the overgeneralisation of early language (calling any four-legged animal a 'doggie'), and the increase in complexity of ethnic stereotype judgements when people are exposed to different cultures.

Stage theory

A less commonly accepted belief held by Piaget is that children's mental abilities go through a series of developmental stages. He proposed that these stages affect the ways in which children are able to represent the world and how they are able to use their representations of the world as the basis for thought. Piaget also believed that the various stages are due to changes in fundamental logical processes of thought and therefore affect all mental abilities at about the same time.

The earliest, **sensori-motor stage** covers from zero to two years of age. Schemas are primarily based on direct (sensory) experiences and early physical (motor) reactions and responses. At this stage, thinking is very much doing; it is only towards the end of this period that the infant is able completely to retain the identity of things when they are not present.

The **pre-operational stage** lasts from two to seven years of age. At this stage, children are able to think about things in terms of consistent physical features. Their understanding depends very much on their own perspective, however; children seem to have difficulties understanding that a change in the way that something looks does not necessarily mean a change in other attributes, such as number or quantity. The ability to do this is called 'conservation' and relies on children's ability to represent things to themselves and to carry out logical mental changes, referred to as 'operations'. In the examples in Figure 2.13, children will say that there is more liquid in the tall beaker and that there are

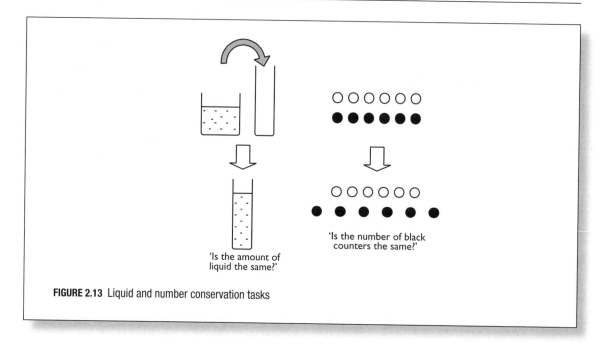

FIGURE 2.13 Liquid and number conservation tasks

more black counters. They appear to be able to take account only of the height of the liquid, and the length of the line of counters.

The **concrete operational stage** lasts broadly from 7 to 12 years of age. By this time, children are able to think about a number of different features of things, but are still largely restricted to doing this with physical objects. Thought is now becoming more logical and shows properties such as 'reversibility', which means that things can be transformed, then returned back into their original form. Children are also able to take on different perspectives, Piaget thought, and are no longer dominated by their own experiences and needs – or no more so than adults are.

The **formal operational stage** from 12 years of age onwards involves abstract thought processes. Children no longer need to use physical objects but can use the features and properties of things as a basis on which to reason. Scientific thought now becomes possible, with the ability to make hypotheses, to think deductively and to carry out experimental investigations by isolating variables. Piaget acknowledged, however, that many people never develop these abilities. Rogoff (2003) also observes that successful performance on classic assessments of formal operations is associated with education in UK-/US-style classroom contexts, and so appears to be culturally influenced.

Modifications of Piaget's ideas

Piaget's ideas have generally been subject to a great deal of criticism and modification. First, there is considerable evidence that children are often able to carry out tasks at an earlier age than his theory says they should be capable of (Siegler and Alibali, 2005). Whether they can do so seems to depend on whether the tasks have meaning or relevance to the children, as illustrated by the following classic study.

Classic study

Children's abilities with conservation appear to depend on what the child believes is expected of them. In a classic investigation of number conservation by McGarrigle and Donaldson (1974), a 'naughty teddy' accidentally disrupted the second row of counters and spread them out. Under these conditions, 72 per cent of four-to-six-year-old children were able to say correctly that the number remained the same, whereas only 34 per cent of those who saw the spreading as carried out by the experimenter did so. A likely explanation for such findings is that when the experimenter asks a child in a classic conservation task if anything has changed, this is taken by the child to imply that something *must* have changed (otherwise, why ask the question?). The child therefore looks for an answer that might fit in with this, for example that there is a change in the height of the liquid or the spread of the counters. According to this, children become able to conserve when they understand that they can describe things without worrying about what other people want. This therefore represents a development in social understanding rather than logical awareness.

Children are certainly capable of carrying out many tasks earlier than Piaget would have predicted. Despite this, there are still some limits to their attainments, and one would not, for example, expect very young children to be capable of certain types of abstract thought, no matter what experiences they had had, or how particular tasks were presented to them.

Biological correlates

Piaget believed that, although children's abilities are developed by interacting with their environment, the basis of this progress is ultimately due to the biological maturation of the nervous system. He considered that this acts as the foundation for the development of intelligence and enables the qualitative changes in logical abilities that are characteristic of each stage. There has been some support for this belief, with Hudspeth and Pribram (1990) finding that measurements of direct brain activity showed regional developmental changes that were broadly consistent with Piagetian stages. Those areas of the brain most associated with perceptual input and physical control, for instance, showed their greatest development during the first few years, whereas those most associated with higher-level processes showed a major increase in late adolescence. Similarly, Kuhn (2006) notes that processing speed and inhibitory control develop during childhood and adolescence, as do self-regulation and management of information processing. Adolescents are argued to show evidence of second-order cognition of the kind implied by Inhelder and Piaget's (1958) conception of formal operations.

Capacity limitations

Although the brain does show progressive physical maturation, it is still possible that this just results in a gradual change in the amount of processing capacity, rather than the discontinuous stages suggested by Piaget. This is supported by findings that the short-term or working memory shows progressive improvements with age. In one study by Dempster (1981), performance on the digit span task improved steadily from just over 2 at two years of age to just below 7 at 12 years of age. One explanation for this is that children develop more expertise as they grow older. Numbers evidently have more meaning for a 12-year-old than for a two-year-old, and differences in processing may be due merely to the fact that the information is less of a load for older children. This is shown in the work of Cowan *et al.* (1998) and others who have found that short-term memory capacity is related to the speed at which individuals are able to talk. These findings are consistent with the idea that short-term memory as measured by digit span is largely due to a form of internal verbal rehearsal. Differences in our apparent capacity with such tasks are therefore probably the result of how much we are able to rehearse in a given time. However, attempts to improve short-term memory by training children to speak more quickly have been unsuccessful (Cowan *et al.*, 2006).

Consistency

Piaget's theory predicts that children's progress in different areas should generally be the same, owing to their dependence on the same underlying logical abilities. However, much evidence indicates that children's progress in different domains of knowledge or expertise often shows only a limited connection between stages. Conservation studies by Tomlinson-Keasey *et al.* (1979), for instance, found that about 60 per cent of children at age seven were able to conserve for mass, but that conservation for volume occurred about two years later. These differences appear to be the result of the conceptual difficulty of each area. Although children's abilities to carry out conservation tasks do show overall progress from age six years to about nine years, this is quite different from the single discrete stage that Piaget originally believed existed.

Children have also been shown to make great progress with specific abilities if they have additional intensive support. Gardner (1993) argues that developments in areas such as linguistic and mathematical abilities can be relatively independent, with some unusual individuals showing high levels of attainment in one area alone. This suggests that there does not have to be a single underlying process determining development. It could therefore be the case that children's apparent consistency of progress with attainments is due in part to the consistency of what happens to them. If all children have roughly the same general experiences in life, then different areas will move forward at a similar rate and it will appear that they are connected.

Within a particular domain, however, such as linguistic abilities, there can be a high level of interconnection of skills, with some attainments acting as a general basis for further progress. Focusing on specific attainments may then easily show 'stage-like' progressions. As an example of this, word-reading abilities show a relatively rapid increase in most children from about seven years of age. This is not, however, due to the sudden onset of operational thought, but is related to the development of generalised phonic attack skills. Different areas may also interact in specific ways, as with reading and language abilities, where verbal knowledge and understanding can support reading comprehension but are also themselves developed by the process of reading.

Although there have been many criticisms of Piaget, there is still general support for his belief that cognitive progress in children can be seen as their active construction of mental structures, utilising new information from their environment. It also seems plausible that children's thought has qualitative differences from that of adults and shows progressive development. The early years show an emphasis on direct experiences. Subsequently the child attains greater ability to represent and manipulate experiences mentally, eventually acquiring more abstract conceptual abilities. However, this progress does not appear to be dependent on underlying general logical structures and is relatively domain-specific. Different areas and abilities can, however, be connected when there are necessary, dependent relationships between them.

Social constructivism

Piaget was mainly concerned with the cognitive and logical nature of children's development. Although he believed that children's abilities develop through their interactions with their environment, he tended to focus on the mental adaptations involved, rather than the role of the environment. However, other theorists, such as Vygotsky, a contemporary of Piaget, have emphasised the way in which children's experiences underlie their cognitive development. Those experiences are determined by the particular individuals (usually parents) who interact closely with children from an early age.

Vygotsky saw the progression of children's cognitive abilities as developing in a generally similar qualitative way to that proposed by Piaget, with initial abilities dependent on direct experiences and actions, leading eventually to more complex and abstract thought. He also believed that children build up or construct their own meaning and understanding of their environment. Unlike Piaget, however, he believed that they do so mainly through their ability to internalise experiences. The experiences themselves he saw as being largely provided by parents interacting with their own children. For example, Vygotsky (1978) described young children learning to point when they see their parents doing so in response to something that they want.

As will be discussed in Chapter 9, Vygotsky considered language to be a key feature of children's development. At first they use it mainly to interact with others, but from the age of two years onwards, they use it increasingly as a basis for 'thinking out loud'. Eventually a form of simplified language becomes internalised at about seven years of age and acts to regulate and organise thought when necessary. Vygotsky saw language as the result of early socialisation, but believed that, by its use in social contexts, it is also the main vehicle for developing later knowledge and understanding.

Anticipating modern perspectives, Vygotsky also believed that children's development can be best understood in terms of the acquisition of their culture. This is embodied in language, art, and ways of seeing and understanding the world, including elements such as metaphors and other models, songs and play. This emphasis implies that there will be significant differences in the thinking of children from different cultural backgrounds, and is supported by findings that basic features such as values and attributional styles can vary widely. Kivilu and Rogers (1998), for instance, found that children from Kenya considered that their academic success depended largely on how they were taught. By contrast, children from Western and Asian countries generally consider ability and effort to be much more important.

Vygotsky particularly believed that children's early understanding came from the support that they were given by interacting with knowledgeable adults. Such support enables children to function in an

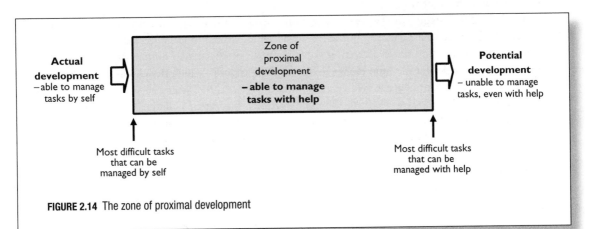

FIGURE 2.14 The zone of proximal development

area he named the **zone of proximal development** (see Figure 2.14), which is beyond children's normal independent abilities. When children are given such support, they are then able to internalise the actions of adults and to make further progress.

This approach implies that teaching should focus on activities within this zone, since it is here that learning progress is occurring. In Piagetian terms, this is the area of greatest disequilibrium and accommodation, and these processes underlie children's interest, curiosity and intrinsic motivation. A further important aspect is that children with the same level of ostensible development may actually have different proximal development zones. As an example of this, two children could have the same basic word-reading vocabulary but one of them may be more likely to make progress if he or she has better abilities with speech and letter sounds. As we will describe in Chapter 3, an assessment of children's ability to make progress could therefore involve teaching them within this zone – a procedure known as **dynamic assessment**.

Scaffolding

The process by which children can be taught within the proximal development zone has been described by Wood *et al.* (1976) as similar to the process of **scaffolding** in building. This apt metaphor implies that the adult supplies initial support to enable children to construct their understanding, and that this support is then withdrawn when they have independent abilities. Wood *et al.* studied parents teaching three-to-five-year-old children simple physical construction tasks. In this situation, effective teaching appeared to be based on two main 'rules':

■ when a child was struggling, the tutor immediately offered more help;
■ conversely, when the child was successful, the tutor gradually reduced the support he or she provided and gave less help until the child was managing the task alone.

This is known as **contingent tutoring** (i.e. the tutor's behaviour is contingent upon the behaviour of the learner).

Another key element of scaffolding appeared to entail involving a child – 'luring' him or her into the activity. This was often done by demonstrating interesting parts of the task that the child could do straight away, such as fitting easy parts together. Also the task was often made easier, so as to fit with the child's actual abilities at that time. This could involve taking away parts, or helping the child to see things in a different way.

Unsuccessful strategies that were used by some parents involved demonstrating the whole task, which just overloaded the children. Either the children attempted to leave the situation, or the parents forced them to become more actively involved. Other parents relied almost exclusively on verbal instructions, such as 'Put the little blocks on top of the big ones', which the children were not able to understand without first being shown.

When scaffolding does work well, then, as Vygotsky suggested, children seem to internalise the actions they have observed. A key role for the adult is to demonstrate or 'model' correct behaviours, as well as maintain children within their 'zone of proximal development'. Adults can also function to remind children of their overall goal or objective, since otherwise children might lose their motivation when they have completed part of the task.

Learning from adults does not always involve the tight structure and interactivity of scaffolding, and children can often learn by simply observing or being told what to do. Tharp and Gallimore (1998) refer to the processes of support (including scaffolding) as 'assisting'. These are more applicable to class teaching and involve the techniques of instructing, questioning and cognitive structuring. These are recognisably what most teachers do, but Tharp and Gallimore emphasise that they should enable students to develop their own understanding, rather than merely assimilate information. For example, teachers can use questioning that leads children to think about topics, rather than just having right or wrong answers. Teachers are also an important source of information that can enable pupils to organise their own knowledge and understanding, by the use of explanations or strategies and rules.

Reciprocal teaching

Children in the same teaching group will often be at about the same level of development within a particular area. In Vygotskyan terms, they are therefore operating within the same zone of proximal development and might learn from being exposed to each other's thinking. The idea is used in a technique known as **reciprocal teaching**, whereby groups of children work together and discuss their ideas and ways of solving problems. The teacher's role in this is mainly to set up and manage the group, rather than providing a direct teaching input, since this could interfere with what the children learn from other pupils.

Socio-cultural theory

Research into the processes of learning and cognitive development has been transformed in the last 20 years through the significant influence of sociocultural theory. Also described as 'socio-historical' and 'cultural–historical' theory, its origins are to be found predominantly in the work of the Russian psychologist Lev Vygotsky (see above, pp. 39–41). As Mercer and Littleton (2007) explain, sociocultural research is not a unified field, but those working within it treat communication, thinking and learning as processes shaped by culture, whereby knowledge is shared and understandings are jointly negotiated and constructed. As communicative events are shaped by cultural and historical factors, thinking, learning and development cannot be understood without taking account of the intrinsically social and communicative nature of human life.

From a sociocultural perspective, humans are seen as having a unique and distinctive capacity for communication – their lives are normally led within groups, communities and societies based on shared ways of using language, ways of thinking, social practices and tools for getting things done. Education is thus seen as a dialogic process, with students and teachers working within settings that reflect the values and social practices of schools as cultural institutions. A sociocultural perspective raises the possibility that educational success and failure may be explained by the quality of educational dialogue, rather than simply by considering the capability of individual students or the skill of their teachers. It encourages the investigation of the relationship between language and thinking and also of the relationship between what Vygotsky called the 'intermental' and the 'intramental' – the social and the psychological – in the processes of learning, development and intellectual endeavour (Mercer and Littleton, 2007). Partly through the influence of these ideas, social interaction has increasingly come to be seen as significant in shaping children's cognitive development. We give special attention to this topic in Chapter 8.

Implications of developmental theories for teaching

Educational limitations of cognitive development

 Piaget appears to have overemphasised the possible limits to children's attainments, and it would certainly be misleading to use his stages as guides to what can or cannot be taught at specific ages. However, within domain areas there are still general qualitative differences in thought, which over the age range of pupils in school progress from the more concrete and direct, to abstract understanding. Although teachers should take account of the level of children's understanding, this will often be due to the children's underlying expertise, which can be developed to enable further progress. An example of this in mathematics is 'subtraction with decomposition', as with the sum '43 minus 17'. Children often have particular difficulties with this procedure (which is normally achieved at about eight years of age), probably because in order to take away the unit value of 7, you need to break down (decompose or partition) the 40 into 30 and 10 and then transfer the 10 across to the units. This is much more complex than just taking away in columns, and would probably be difficult for children to achieve unless teaching had first enabled them to develop sufficient expertise with place value.

Developing new knowledge

Most developmental sequences imply that learning experiences for younger children should be based on more practical, physical (concrete) experiences, eventually leading, with older children, to more indirect knowledge and ideas, and should finally involve more complex and abstract information. Bruner (1966a) extended this idea, considering that the earliest type of thought involving direct physical experience (which he has termed the 'enactive mode') is present at every age and that this can be the basis for all initial learning, even in adults. The principle has been applied in a number of different curriculum developments, an early example of which was the *Nuffield Science Teaching Project* (1967), which based the initial learning of scientific principles on direct experiences by the pupil and only then goes on to develop generalisations and more complex reasoning. A more recent example comes from Kammi (1994) who observed that adult-based methods for computation in mathematics can be problematic for children and that better understanding is often achieved if the children invent mathematical rules and procedures for themselves. Mathematical activity is also embedded in daily classroom activities and routines, so that it has meaning and relevance, and children's board games are adapted to teach children about number concepts and allow them to rehearse their understanding of them during 'play'. Kammi's (1994, 2004) evaluations of her methods for teaching maths reveal that students taught by her method have the same attainment as children taught by more traditional techniques, but her children show greater understanding of what they have been taught and have displayed greater autonomy in their learning.

Importance of active, guided involvement

The active involvement of the child is central to most recent theories about cognitive development. Piaget's original ideas on this were sometimes interpreted as implying that learning should take the form of pure discovery learning. However, this is not necessarily the case, and Piaget did state that a child's environment can involve a teacher facilitating this involvement. The ideas of Vygotsky also emphasise that learning mainly happens in the zone of proximal development and that this can happen through the guided, social interaction of a knowledgeable adult.

Play and learning 🐦

Piaget (1951) described play as essentially early, self-directed cognitive development. This is part of the process of intrinsic (self-directed) motivation, and these ideas have been successfully implemented in a number of learning programmes, and is well illustrated by the approach described by Kammi (1994) earlier. Play therefore is learning, Piaget believed, and many intrinsically motivated learning activities can be described as play, even when carried out by older children or adults. Early educational experiences that are based on play have often been shown to have better long-term developmental and motivational outcomes than do more formal approaches (see Chapter 5 for a discussion of this).

Language and learning

The ideas of Vygotsky and Bruner emphasise that language is the primary medium for socially interactive learning, and that it is also the main basis of knowledge and understanding. These ideas are supported by findings such as the research of Hart and Risley (1995), which demonstrates the massive and cumulative effects of language experiences on children's long-term cognitive development.

The role of disequilibrium

Piaget believed that development is prompted to occur when information does not fit with existing mental structures, and new equilibrium have to be formed. According to this, it should also be possible for an external agent (a teacher) to stimulate a child with new information and produce disequilibrium and cognitive change (learning). A teacher can identify a child's current level of functioning, then bring in new experiences to push along the process of assimilation (relating the new experiences to the child's existing ideas or knowledge), which should eventually lead to accommodation. However, the most effective way of initiating disequilibrium is through **socio-cognitive conflict** between peers, rather than through a teacher and pupil. That is, Piaget argued that because of the difference in status between children and adults, children are less likely to question assertions made by adults, but that this process is important for learning to occur. However, if a peer presents a child with a differing perspective or explanation of something compared to their own, they are likely to engage in discussion and some internal reflection on the ideas exchanged. A good illustration of this process comes from the work of Doise and Mugny (1984). In this study 100 five-to-seven-year-old children were pre-tested on their ability to take a perspective other than their own in a task where they had to reconstruct a model village. Based on their responses, the children were labelled as Level 1 (the least able), Level 2 or Level 3, and were assigned to mixed-ability pairs (Level 1 and Level 2 or Level 1 and Level 3) and were instructed to work on the task together. Following this, all the children were re-tested on their own. The Level 1 children who were assigned to Level 2 partners were observed to make the most progress, as there was more discussion in these pairs, compared to the Level 1–Level 3 pairs, in which the Level 3 imposed their solution on their partner.

The meaning of errors

Most developmental perspectives see children as actively constructing their understanding of the world. This implies that teachers, when analysing pupils' work, should treat a 'wrong' answer as a child's attempt to make sense of a difficult task, using his or her existing logical abilities and knowledge. The approach to the assessment of reading known as 'miscue analysis' uses a child's errors to direct subsequent teaching targets. Effective feedback should therefore be based on the nature of children's errors and give information on how they could develop their abilities.

Use in assessment

Developmental theories have also formed the basis for a number of approaches to assessing children's underlying abilities, and we will discuss assessment in more detail in the next chapter. However, the work of Piaget, for example, has recently been used to problematise current approaches to the assessment of children's intelligence (Shayer, 2008).

Optimising learning

The various findings about learning and cognitive development have a number of general implications for how teaching and learning situations should be organised.

Match

Perhaps the most important and pervasive concept is that the tasks given to an individual child should be appropriate to his or her learning needs. The simplest interpretation of match is that it involves ensuring that the work given to pupils is neither too hard nor too easy, and that the content is related to their existing knowledge, skills and understanding. In practice, it can be achieved with a specific sequential curriculum, and continuous formative assessments. These provide feedback for teachers, to enable them to place pupils on the curriculum and to modify subsequent learning experiences. Dockerell (1995) has described the implementation of such a system in a secondary school, which resulted in changes in teaching and significant improvements in students' learning. Specific feedback is important for students, not only to develop their sense of self-efficacy and motivation but also to guide their own learning towards work that is most appropriate for their attainments.

The mastery learning technique is an individualised learning approach that depends upon a close match between pupils' initial attainments and their work. Most reviews, such as that by Kulik *et al.* (1990), have concluded that mastery learning can be more effective than conventional teaching, where class or group work means that individuals often have to study in areas where they have a weak skills foundation.

In the normal classroom it is difficult to match work closely to each child, owing to the range of abilities and attainments. Teachers usually compromise by pitching work at the average range, and then setting up different learning experiences for children whose needs differ significantly from this range – termed **differentiation**.

Withers and Eke (1995), however, criticise this view of 'curriculum match' as being mechanistic and over-simplistic, arguing for a more active cognitive developmental perspective. They emphasise the Vygotskyan perspective of learning as a social activity, with the teacher working within the 'zone of proximal development' for students, and with learning being constructed rather than transmitted. According to this, 'match' becomes a more dynamic concept, with the role of the teacher being to foster learning through appropriate and responsive scaffolding, rather than just running through a curriculum sequence at what is presumed to be the right level.

High levels of success seem to be important for natural, intrinsic motivation (see Chapter 5), and curiosity and interest are generated by ensuring that the task involves some novel or challenging information. In Piagetian terms, the teacher's job is to generate disequilibrium, which Withers and

Eke imaginatively describe as 'putting the bit of grit into the equilibrated structure of the oyster which forces it to accommodate and produce a pearl'. Unfortunately, of course, disequilibrium does not always lead to the immediate generation of new schemas. When pupils are challenged, this may sometimes be too much for them and they may need further support and direction.

Connectionism

One of the problems for most of the above theories of learning is that they tend to involve the development of rather abstract features such as concepts and schemas without any links to what this could all be actually based on. **Connectionism** is a way of looking at thought and learning that is based upon highly complex parallel logical systems that have similarities to the structure and possible working of the human brain. The new approach can account for a range of complex functions, including concept formation and identification. It represents a radical departure from classical cognitive descriptions, which are usually couched in terms of a clear sequence of logical processes.

The human brain is made up from a huge number of cells, probably more than a trillion of the main ones, known as neurons. Each of these links with thousands of others, and together they form a dense and highly complex web of interconnections. Basic brain processes such as perceptions happen relatively quickly – typically in less time than it takes for information to pass between ten neurons. This, combined with findings from neurophysiological research, makes it seem likely that much of the brain's processing takes place in parallel, with many neurons becoming activated at the same time, and hence many processing operations occurring simultaneously. This perspective sees learning as the process by which different connections between the neurons become strengthened or weakened, producing specific patterns of pathways which are the basis for new concepts and ways of thinking.

The key elements of this process can be represented in a system called a 'neural network', which can be either a computer program or an integrated circuit. The system is made up from layers of artificial 'cells' or units, which are connected with each other. One layer acts as the 'input', rather like the initial sensory processes of the brain. Another layer usually acts as a 'hidden' or interconnecting level, where the main biasing and routing of information happens. A final layer acts as the 'output' and is the result of the combinations of the various biases in the connections. Like neurons, each unit in the network will become activated and pass on information only if the information it receives goes above a certain critical threshold.

Neural networks have to be 'trained' using feedback to give the desired output for specific inputs. This is done by repeatedly giving the network a range of possible input experiences, then using the accuracy of the output to modify the biases of the connections between the units. When a particular output is incorrect, the biases are given a slight nudge in their values towards what would give a correct answer, in a technique known as 'back propagation'.

As an example, Figure 2.15 shows a basic neural network set up to receive input as five letters of the alphabet and analyse these to 'recognise' five simple words. At first, a naive network will just give random outputs. After a number of training sessions, however, the appropriate connections shown for the word 'sit' might be strengthened, as shown in Figure 2.16. If units are activated only when they receive two inputs, then the specific combination of letters in 'sit' will trigger the appropriate output unit.

Connectionism has been applied in a broadly similar way to this by Sejnowski and Rosenberg (1987) to train a neural network called NETtalk to 'read' text. This was set up to accept text input and to output phonetic codes that could be turned into sounds. The training input involved a large amount of normal English text, coupled with its corresponding phonetic output. At first, the network

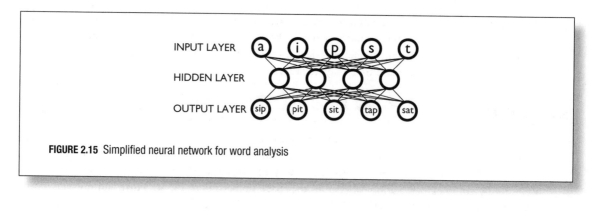

FIGURE 2.15 Simplified neural network for word analysis

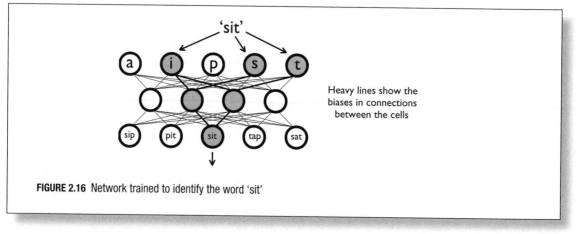

Heavy lines show the biases in connections between the cells

FIGURE 2.16 Network trained to identify the word 'sit'

emitted only random sounds, then went through a stage of 'babbling', which then became closer to normal speech, eventually developing a fairly accurate spoken representation of what was written. The trained network was able to 'read' new text that it had never encountered before.

Neural networks have also been used to develop language capabilities that were once thought to involve sophisticated high-level cognitive processes. Rumelhart and McClelland (1986), for instance, developed a system that learned to identify the past tense of regular and irregular verbs, and Elman (1991) was able to train a network to make grammatical predictions for missing words.

The reason for carrying out such investigations is that they could be telling us something about how the brain may be working. One key feature is that the above networks did not need any special predisposition to learn certain types of structures. This appears to throw some doubt on the idea that humans must possess some specific inherited abilities in order to learn apparently complex behaviour. Nor do networks need any form of 'rule processing', even though the final set of connections does reflect whatever regularities and patterns there were in the original information. In NETtalk, for instance, the hidden layer units showed distinct separate patterns of activation for vowels and consonants. Combined with the fact that it is difficult to argue that such networks are 'conscious' in any meaningful way, this throws some doubt on the need for classical, 'rule-seeking' cognitive processes in basic learning.

For example, a child developing language may make what appears to be an overgeneralisation of a rule, as when saying 'mouses' instead of 'mice'. This can be taken to indicate that he or she is consciously generating and testing hypotheses about the underlying structure of adult language. However, at one stage of training, Rumelhart and McClelland's (1986) network made the very same type of error, indicating that such learning could in fact be largely automatic and unconscious, with the properties of implicit learning described earlier in this chapter.

There are large numbers of units in any practical neural network, and their connections represent a highly complex system. For this reason, it is not possible to know exactly how the various weightings in a trained system are operating. In a similar way, it may be that we cannot actually know the exact nature of human learning and can only describe possible associations between input experiences and output responses – representing a rather unexpected return to some of the original ideas of behaviourism.

It is fair to say, however, that the relevance of connectionism is still hotly debated, and there are still many uncertainties about how the brain really works. There are also difficulties in getting neural networks to reproduce general relationships between symbolic representations; they tend to be relatively specific to what they have been trained up on. Despite this, neural networks have many strengths that come from their distributed nature. This means, for instance, that they are able to represent complex, probabilistic concepts such as the use of prototypes or schemas (discussed earlier in this chapter). It seems likely, therefore, that connectionist approaches will continue to be a useful way of describing general learning processes, and may have a basis in the underlying biological functioning of the brain.

Educational neuropsychology

One area of psychology enjoying a period of growth and influence is that of educational neuropsychology. This is a field of psychology that seeks to understand the nature of learning and learning difficulties by analysing neurological structures and processes, and in so doing aspires to offer teachers new ways of thinking about teaching and learning. However, as Goswami (2006) notes, although there is a good deal of useful research ongoing in this field, telling us about the neurological basis of areas of educational and behavioural difficulties in the classroom, there are also several commercially marketed classroom interventions that claim to boost children's academic performance and present themselves as based on neuropsychological principles, but in fact have limited or no scientific basis for their claims.

A study by Weisberg et al. (2008) perhaps holds the solution to why so many schools adopt these schemes so enthusiastically. In their study Weisberg et al. presented lay people, students and neuroscience experts with explanations of psychological phenomena that were either plausible or bogus, and those explanations either had or did not have neuroscience included in them. They were then asked to rate how satisfactory the explanations were. The lay people and students showed that the explanations that included neuroscience were rated as more satisfactory than the answers that did not include neuroscience, even when the explanation itself was inappropriate. The inclusion of (irrelevant) neuroscience in the explanations was also found to influence the judgement of the neuroscience experts. This study demonstrates why neuroscience has been used as a marketing tool in the past, and so care and judgement needs to be used when evaluating interventions that are sold in this way. As with any educational intervention, it is important to look at the empirical evidence for any claims made, and satisfy yourself that they are persuasive studies.

The promise of Information and Communications Technology

Information and Communication Technology (ICT) involves the use of technology such as computers as the basis for teaching systems that use complex software programs. It also increasingly acts as the basis for communication through systems such as email and enables pupils to access a range of information via the Internet. Such resources have a great deal of potential but to date there is limited evidence of their effectiveness at raising attainment (e.g. Andrews *et al.*, 2007; Torgerson and Zhu, 2003), although research in this area is increasing.

Ultimately, ICT-based systems appear to have the general potential to provide optimal individualised and interactive learning experiences up to and beyond the level of individual instruction. For example, recent research into the use of a specially designed set of resources to support reading development, known as 'ABRACADABRA', has shown that it can be effective in raising young children's attainment in literacy (e.g. Comaskey *et al.*, 2009), and can counter the effects that attentional difficulties can have on reading attainment (Deault *et al.*, 2009). It seems that even children's informal use of technology may impact positively on children's development. For example, there is evidence that children's use of text-message abbreviations when texting on mobile phones may contribute to progress in literacy skills, because it affords children the opportunity to rehearse key skills that underpin both the ability to make text abbreviations and progress in reading and spelling (Plester *et al.*, 2009).

Summary

Learning is a central and pervasive concept in education, and involves changes in pupils' knowledge, skills and understanding. Memory is the storage and retrieval of information by the brain. It initially involves short-term or working memory, which has capacity limitations and depends on our encoding abilities. Long-term memory has a very large capacity, and information is mainly stored in terms of its meaning, with different forms of conceptual organisation. We can fail to learn or subsequently forget material, particularly as a result of interference, which is the result of difficulties in separating information. Learning and memory can be improved by techniques that improve the way in which we structure what we learn. The most effective and useful forms involve an emphasis on organisation and understanding. Learning is also most effective when it is spread out over time.

Learning can be seen as the active construction of mental representations (schemas) by pupils. Piagetian theory describes the key developmental processes involved in this as assimilation of new information, and accommodation, as schemas are adapted. Modifications of this perspective emphasise that pupils construct their knowledge and understanding in social contexts and that expertise can be developed in specific domains, often without any necessary logical connections between them. Applying these ideas to education emphasises that the role of the teacher is to facilitate learning. Key aspects of the facilitation of learning are to match experiences with pupils' abilities, and to encourage appropriate levels of challenge or dissonance to generate change. Some theories see the underlying basis of such learning structures as the formation of complex connectionist patterns, in the same way as the basic units of the brain operate. These simple systems can be very effective in producing apparently sophisticated learning, which implies that it is not necessary to consider innate predispositions for development.

The use of Information and Communication Technology (ICT) appears to be potentially capable of optimising learning by individualising pupils' experiences. Teaching systems that develop from an understanding of the ways in which children learn are just starting to realise this potential.

Key implications

- Effective learning involves the use and application of knowledge, which takes the form of complex, interrelated internal representations.
- Such learning is best described as an active construction by pupils within a social context.
- The role of teachers is primarily to facilitate this by organising and directing experiences that are matched with pupils' abilities and attainments.
- Pupils can also construct meaning from simplified experiences involving actions and consequences (behaviourism).
- Optimal learning comes from individually matched, responsive teaching systems.

Further reading

Bodrova and Leong (2007), *Tools of the Mind*: a thoughtful book that shows how Vygotskyan theory can be usefully applied to support the development and education of preschool and primary-school-aged children. A nice book to read if you want some sense of how these ideas might be used in practice.

Wood (1998), *How Children Think and Learn*: a popular classic on cognitive development and learning that has been updated. It might be best to have some existing knowledge of educational psychology before you read it, but the book would make an ideal follow-on from this chapter.

Discussion of practical scenario

It seems likely that the children Mr Jones now teaches have lower levels of personal resources, in terms of their existing knowledge base, orientation to learning and home support. They will probably have difficulty with learning experiences if these are not matched with their level of knowledge and understanding, and if topics have limited relevance to their own lives.

Using parts of the earlier curriculum might be a partial answer, but there is a danger this will also reduce the coverage of key areas. It might be better to search for ways in which to cover the age-appropriate curriculum but using approaches that are more accessible and relevant to his pupils.

One approach might involve an emphasis on more experimental work, using pupils' own background and interests where possible. Some work might involve broadening out pupils' general knowledge in order to make specific information more relevant. He could also look at the possibility of peer-group tutoring, cooperative learning and programmes to develop children's thinking skills.

Given the constraints of learning time and the wide variations in pupils' initial abilities, it seems unrealistic to expect all children to achieve at the same level. Goals should be realistic, and should be relative to where children start from.

Assessment

Chapter overview

- Why assess?
- What can we assess?
- Functions of assessment
- Types of tests
- Test content and structure
- Intelligence testing
- Other forms of assessment
- National Curriculum assessments

Practical scenario

Mrs Smith trained as a primary school teacher in the 1970s and has spent most of her career in one primary school on the outskirts of a former mining town in Yorkshire. The town has always hosted a residential park for Traveller families and has now also been chosen as the site for a large Japanese motor-manufacturing factory. Mrs Smith openly admits to feeling 'nervous about coping' with the children joining her class of Year 1 (six-year-old) children in September.

What range of educational needs might Mrs Smith expect to encounter?

How would Mrs Smith go about assessing the needs of the children?

What other support could be offered to Mrs Smith?

Why assess?

If pupils' attainments were not assessed in some way, teachers would not be able to 'move children on' by addressing their needs and planning appropriate learning experiences to enhance their existing skills. It would be impossible to tell whether children had made any progress and whether adjustments needed to be made to either the content or the presentation of their learning experiences. It is now

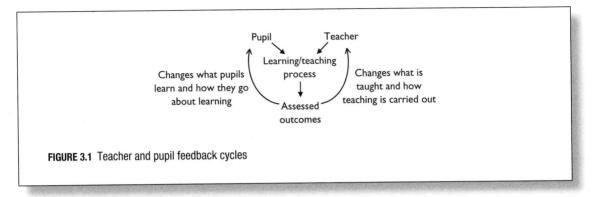

FIGURE 3.1 Teacher and pupil feedback cycles

also increasingly clear that learning effectiveness is increased by appropriate and informative feedback to pupils and to teachers, and that, as shown in Figure 3.1, some form of assessment must be part of an effective learning–teaching cycle.

Assessment is endemic in education, and for the most part is ongoing, informal, hourly and daily and involves a dialogue between pupil and teacher (Boyle and Charles, 2009). Whilst this type of assessment is still relatively informal, teachers still turn to a range of formalised, published test materials in order to find out more information about individual ability (be it skills or knowledge) so that they can make judgements about children's achievements, both as individuals and as compared with their peers.

With the introduction of the National Curriculum in parts of the UK, the call for assessment has become more explicit with regular, government-directed assessment. Results of these assessments at 'Key Stages' in children's education are used for assessing not only individual pupil performance but also for evaluating teacher effectiveness and the overall standards of schools and education authorities. The Key Stages of assessment and how they fit into children's overall school experience are shown in Table 3.1.

Clearly, without any assessment, teaching would become a rather unfocused activity as teachers would be unable to determine what their pupils had learned and what they needed to learn. However, as discussed later in this chapter, there has been growing concern that in some classrooms, lesson content may all too often be determined by the requirements of externally imposed tests such as the National Curriculum SATs (Standard Assessment Tests and Tasks) – and, if this is so, then the tail may be wagging the dog. Thus, it is important to know about what we can assess, how to choose the most appropriate means of assessment and the ways in which results should be interpreted and used to greatest effect.

What can we assess?

Attainment

The most common type of assessment looks at **attainment**, which is a pupil's present level of functioning or ability in a particular area. Most formal tests assess a specific attainment. For example, the NFER Single Word Reading Test (Foster, 2007) described later in this chapter measures word-reading ability – how well a child can read a list of separate words. Educational publishers' catalogues are full of tests that set out to assess abilities such as reading, comprehension, spelling, mathematics, as well as underlying skills such as working memory and phonological processing.

Psychologists and teachers have sought constantly to identify (and then promote) the skills that children need to succeed in education and ultimately in the workplace. For decades, it has been assumed that abilities tend to be generally related to each other, and if people score well on one test

TABLE 3.1 The National Curriculum Key Stages

Age	Year	Key Stage (KS)	Assessment	Expected level
3–4		EYFS*		
4–5	Reception	EYFS*		
5–6	Year 1	KS1		
6–7	Year 2	KS1	Teacher-marked tasks: English, Mathematics Teacher assessments: English, Maths, Science	Most children will be at Level 2
7–8	Year 3	KS2		
8–9	Year 4	KS2		
9–10	Year 5	KS2		
10–11	Year 6	KS2	Externally-marked National Tests: English, Maths Teacher assessments: English, Maths, Science	Most children will be at Level 4
11–12	Year 7	KS3	Ongoing teacher assessments	
12–13	Year 8	KS3	Ongoing teacher assessments	
13–14	Year 9	KS3	Teacher assessments: English, Maths, Science and other foundation subjects	Most children will be at Level 5
14–15	Year 10	KS4	Some children take GCSEs	
15–16	Year 11	KS4	Most children take GCSEs or other national qualification	

Source: www.directgov.uk.

then it is likely they will score well on others. The quality that enables them to do so is known as 'general ability' or intelligence, and, as discussed towards the end of this chapter, it is assessed by using specialised intelligence tests.

However, the main abilities that teachers are interested in are related to the curriculum. Educational targets can be subdivided into a number of different categories, with the simplest and most commonly used approach covering **knowledge** (of factual information), skills (how to do things), **understanding** (the ability to use information) and, more recently, **affective areas** (confidence, motivation and attitude). Although there is general agreement about the need for such broad aims, it has been argued that National Curriculum assessments or SATs with their emphasis on knowledge and skills form a major part of teacher assessment.

Knowledge

A concept is a basic element of thought that links with other concepts to form a web of knowledge or information. Explicit knowledge is generally thought of as what a person knows in terms of facts and information. This **factual knowledge**, for example, about a flower, can be readily assessed by means of questions such as, 'What do we call the part of the flower that receives pollen?'

More general, **schematic knowledge** refers to making associations within a system of related schemas. Assessment can therefore focus on the development of generalised schemas within a subject domain, as well as the knowledge of specific features that vary from example to example. Older science students, for example, might be introduced to the concept of 'catalysts' with generalised information about molecules, change and effect. The general concept could then be related to specific examples of body catalysts, and tests carried out to investigate the function of enzymes such as trypsin (in the body) and lipases and proteases (in the washing machine).

Skill

The term **skill** describes the procedural aspects of how to do things and is often used in a relatively loose way to describe any activity that is done 'well'. It normally refers to an ability that is relatively complex and comprises a number of other linked or coordinated abilities. 'Having a skill' also implies that an individual is able to carry out a task both competently and at a specific level. For instance, division is a mathematical skill that depends on the knowledge and use of number, place value and tables. The Assessment Focus (AF<HS>) at each of the levels of the National Curriculum are examples of stages of functional skill. For instance, the reading assessment guidelines issued to teachers (see Figure 3.2) show, that at level 2 for Reading, pupils need to demonstrate they can 'use a range of strategies, including accurate decoding of text, to read for meaning' by reading 'with some fluency and expression' (QCA, 2009a).

Reading assessment guidelines: levels 1 and 2

Pupil name _____ Class/Group _____ Date _____

	AF1 – use a range of strategies, including accurate decoding of text, to read for meaning	AF2 – understand, describe, select or retrieve information, events or ideas from texts and use quotation and reference to text	AF3 – deduce, infer or interpret information events or ideas from texts	AF4 – identify and comment on the structure and organisation of text, including grammatical and presentational features at text level	AF5 – explain and comment on writers' use of language, including grammatical and literary features at word and sentence level	AF6 – identify and comment on writers' purposes and viewpoints, and the overall effect of the text on the reader	AF7 – relate texts to their social, cultural and historical traditions
Level 2	**In some reading:** • range of key words read on sight • unfamiliar words decoded using appropriate strategies e.g. blending sounds • some fluency and expression, e.g. taking account of punctuation, speech marks	**In some reading:** • some specific, straightforward information recalled, e.g. names of characters, main ingredients • generally clear idea of where to look for information, e.g. about characters, topics	**In some reading:** • simple, plausible inference about events and information, using evidence from text, e.g. how a character is feeling, what makes a plant grow • comments based on textual cues, sometimes misunderstood	**In some reading:** • some awareness of use of features of organisation, e.g. beginning and ending of story, types of punctuation	**In some reading:** • some effective language choices noted, e.g. '"slimy" is a good word there' • some familiar patterns of language identified, e.g. once upon a time; first, next, last	**In some reading:** • some awareness that writers have viewpoints and purposes, e.g. 'it tells you how to do something', 'she thinks it's not fair' • simple statements about likes and dislikes in reading, sometimes with reasons	**In some reading:** • general features of a few text types identified, e.g. information books, stories, print media • some awareness that books are set in different times and places
Level 1	**In some reading, usually with support:** • some high frequency and familiar words read fluently and automatically • decode familiar and some unfamiliar words using blending as the prime approach • some awareness of punctuation marks, e.g. pausing at full stops	**In some reading, usually with support:** • some simple points from familiar texts recalled • some pages/sections of interest located, e.g. favourite characters/events/ information/pictures	**In some reading, usually with support:** • reasonable inference at a basic level, e.g. identifying who is speaking in a story • comments/questions about meaning of parts of text, e.g. details of illustrations diagrams, changes in font style	**In some reading, usually with support:** • some awareness of meaning of simple text features, e.g. font style, labels, titles	**In some reading, usually with support:** • comments on obvious features of language, e.g. rhymes and refrains, significant words and phrases	**In some reading, usually with support:** • some simple comments about preferences, mostly linked to own experience	**In some reading, usually with support:** • a few basic features of well-known story and information texts distinguished, e.g. what typically happens to good and bad characters, differences between type of text in which photos or drawings used
BL IE							

Overall assessment (tick one box only)   Low 1 ☐   Secure 1 ☐   High 1 ☐   Low 2 ☐   Secure 2 ☐   High 2 ☐

FIGURE 3.2 NC reading guidelines (source: http://nationalstrategies.standards.dcsf.gov.uk/node/153537)

Skills are generally assessed by actually carrying them out, although they can also be part of more complex activities. For example, a reading comprehension exercise would involve a range of basic skills including accurately reading the text, understanding the meaning of the text and, possibly, recording the answers in writing. Although these involve complex, integrated abilities and may be well-rehearsed, they also entail conscious, planned processes and would probably be better described as abilities that involve understanding and use of knowledge.

Understanding

At a basic level, **understanding** can involve the retrieval and use of knowledge in new situations. This can be seen when applying a series of simple mathematical calculations $(2 \times 2 \times 15)$ to questions such as, 'If Laura and Fred both need two pencils and each pencil costs 15p, how much money will they need altogether?' Other, more complex tasks place a greater emphasis on the need to recognise what knowledge is appropriate. For example, in the question, 'What could you use to separate iron cans from aluminium cans?', pupils would need to be aware of the relevance of magnetic properties of different metals and how to separate them. Real-life problem-solving tasks require more holistic understanding together with the ability to select and transfer appropriate knowledge. In English, for instance, creative writing will benefit from the generating of ideas but will also depend on existing knowledge and ideas. An example in mathematics that involves some understanding and application of knowledge at Key Stage 2 is shown by the question in Figure 3.3.

Aptitude

Aptitude assessments look at the potential for future attainment. Research has consistently shown that phonological abilities underpin and are the greatest predictors of progress with early literacy, and there are a number of tests that now assess these pre-reading skills. The Phonological Assessment Battery (Frederickson et al., 1997) for instance, sets small tasks that assess a child's early phonological skills (awareness of rhyme, awareness of individual sounds within words) to identify whether there are any specific phonological deficits that will need to be addressed in order for the pupil to successfully learn to read and spell. Many such tests are only weak predictors, however, unless the ability assessed is a necessary precursor of the target ability. The most accurate predictor at later ages is simply children's progress within a particular area, such as their present reading ability, because early reading skills are not only the basis for future progress but also, probably, an indication of other ongoing positive factors such as the support given at home. Intelligence tests are often taken to imply general learning

---

50 children need one pen each. Pens are sold in packs of 4.
How many packs of pens need to be bought?

$$\frac{50}{4} = 12 \text{ r } 2 = 13 \text{ boxes}$$

FIGURE 3.3 Mathematics question involving use of knowledge

potential, but other factors, such as motivation, confidence and even life opportunity, can influence subsequent achievement.

One London education authority is currently proposing to introduce aptitude tests for all children prior to entry to secondary school in an attempt to ensure that all comprehensive schools take children of all abilities. In order to qualify for a place, primary school children will sit a test (likened to an intelligence test) that will be marked 'independently of the schools' and from the results, the children will be placed in bands according to ability. Each secondary school will then be required to offer places to children across the ability range (Camden Girls School, 2009).

Functions of assessment

Assessment, particularly educational assessment, for the most part can be divided into two major types: **summative assessment** (which gives a level of achievement) and **formative assessment** (which guides future learning). In practice, a particular assessment often has both these functions. For example, a mainly summative assessment such as a GCSE grade shows a level of achievement but can also be used to guide future studies, possibly by indicating a suitable direction for further education studies. However, as Newton (2007) suggests, the assessment takes a quite similar form in both cases, but the distinction hinges on how the results are interpreted and used.

Summative assessment

The classic and best-recognised forms of assessment involve summarising levels of achievement. As well as formal tests and examinations such as GCSEs and A levels, these include commonly used informal measures such as review tests. Such evaluations (often carried out at the end of a block of teaching) typically involve assessment of a pupil's general level of functioning in a particular curriculum area. Formal assessments such as exams often have great importance to the pupils involved since they may provide access to employment or higher levels of education. They are also important to schools since they are increasingly being used to evaluate the performance of schools and teachers. They are therefore often referred to as 'high-stakes assessment' and bring with them pressures to achieve well.

This can result in effects such as **curriculum backwash**, whereby the content of tests comes to dominate what is taught. Although this need not necessarily be a bad thing, one cannot expect a limited test to give a realistic assessment of performance across the whole curriculum. Black (1998) reviewed evidence that, to provide adequate coverage, a science assessment would need to take about 35 hours, and that 13 different assignments would be needed to obtain a satisfactory measure of writing achievement. Most formal tests therefore have to be selective and tend to focus on what can most easily be assessed in an examination situation. Teachers are of course aware of this and it is easy to see how they might be inclined to deliver a narrow curriculum, focusing their coverage on the curriculum content and forms of questions that are most likely to be assessed.

General-ability tests are also mainly summative, and their primary function in the past (with the 'eleven-plus' exams) was to allocate children to different 'streams', different types of secondary school or, within the field of special needs, to different forms of education. However, as discussed later, judgements that determine schooling and discriminate between pupils based on the results of such formal, summative tests are now less likely, as in the current climate of educational 'inclusion' most children will attend their local, catchment area school.

Doig (2006) argues that, while it is possible for teachers to use data from such summative assessments to evaluate the effects of their classroom practice, this rarely happens. Ironically, however, pupils often use the results of such formal assessments to make judgements about their own competence and relative standing. Such comparisons form an early basis for establishing academic self-concept, and as pupils go through school this seems to become increasingly important in determining their involvement. When pupils perceive themselves to be successful with meaningful tasks, they are more likely to establish independent motivation and to make subsequent academic progress. When teachers emphasise the evaluative (summative) function of testing in the classroom, the tests may have short-term, positive effects on achievements but appear to have a negative effect on children's long-term attributions and their subsequent independent involvement with school work.

From a large review of research into assessment and learning, Harlen and Crick (2003) reported the negative effect on motivation for learning caused by the 'drill and practice' activities taking place in some classrooms and, perhaps as a result, children being faced with tests in which they were unlikely to succeed. The association of testing and poor motivation contrasts sharply with the widely held view of politicians that testing pupils raises standards. Furthermore, the use of test scores and examination results for 'high-stakes' purposes, which can affect the status or future status of pupils, teachers or schools, often results in teachers focusing their teaching on the test content and training their pupils in how to pass tests. When this happens, teachers make very little use of formative assessment to help the learning process (Broadfoot and Pollard, 2000).

Formative assessment

Formative assessments, in contrast to summative assessments, are those used to help direct or 'inform' the educational process for students. Most formative assessments are 'diagnostic' in that they highlight pupils' strengths (where learning has been successfully accomplished) and also pupils' weaknesses (where further teaching and learning is required). NVQs (National Vocational Qualifications) are national assessments based on specific criteria and, since they are competence-based, can direct subsequent learning experiences.

According to the body responsible for National Curriculum assessments, assessment is formative only when comparison of actual and targeted levels gives information which is then used to narrow the gap between the two (QCDA, 2009). To conform to this definition, the National Curriculum involves teacher assessments that demonstrate how pupils are progressing based on a set of individual targets (known as the 'Assessment Focus', mentioned earlier). Although knowing which targets are still to be met by some pupils can undoubtedly inform a teacher's planning, there is considerable academic and media criticism that these assessments have come to take on a purely evaluative function, to assess the performance of schools and teachers.

A now seminal study by Black (1998) reviewed 600 research studies from around the world, and concluded that formative assessment in classrooms appeared to be the most effective way of improving standards of achievement in schools, even when such achievement was measured by traditional tests and examinations. Black and his colleagues followed this review with their own study (Black et al., 2003) and found that improving formative assessment in the classroom raised GCSE scores by more than half a grade per student per subject. However, their results demonstrated that, although the most common feedback in classrooms was when teachers graded a piece of work, this was of no value in terms of enhancing learning and that giving students marks was no better than giving no feedback at all. On the other hand, giving comments produced substantial improvements in learning. Perhaps the most surprising finding was, however, that giving both marks *and* comments together produced no improvement. When students were given both a mark and a comment, the first thing they looked at was their own mark and the second thing they looked at was their neighbour's mark. The finding was consistent: when awarded a grade and a comment, students rarely looked at the comments. Black and his colleagues reasoned that the students who were given high marks did not need to read the comments, and those who were given low marks did not want to! The study concluded teachers were wasting their time writing 'useful' comments if their students were not acting on them.

Practical implication

Teachers need to consider the needs of their individual students when marking work. For some pupils, it may be better to award a *formative* comment rather than a *summative* grade; for other pupils, it may sometimes be useful to encourage discussion by asking them to evaluate their own work and to suggest the grade they would award themselves.

Although clear in their message (i.e. teaching well is compatible with better results; frequent marking is not), Black and his colleagues did acknowledge that pupils need some feedback in terms of grades or marks but suggest that this should be no more than once every two or three years in primary schools, maybe once a year in lower secondary, and perhaps once a term in the upper secondary years.

Stiggins (2007), following this theme, suggests that feedback should be specific enough that the student knows what to do next, but not so specific that the teacher has done all the work. He suggests the purpose of formative assessment is not to eliminate failure but to ensure that it does not become chronic and inevitable in the eyes of the pupil. He cites an American baseball coach who believes the true key to winning is to avoid losing twice in a row: by using formative assessments, the teacher can ensure that when pupils sense 'failure', they are given feedback that maintains their confidence and their momentum to accept responsibility for their own learning. It is, perhaps, for this reason that teachers now commonly report using assessment checklists which typically include an 'aide-memoire' to help pupils complete the task. In their study of the growing use of checklists, Hamson and Sutton (2000) noted that, for pupils, these checklists helped to increase their awareness of what they were expected to achieve and how they were going to be judged. Teachers meanwhile found that the checklists' clear targets enabled them to record pupils' achievements and award a summative level more readily than the formerly used qualitative comments.

Black and Wiliam (2009) more recently have identified five main types of activity that fall under the 'formative assessment' heading: sharing success criteria with learners; classroom questioning; comment-only marking; peer and self-assessment; and using summative tests formatively (i.e. to help pupils identify for themselves where additional learning is necessary rather than just awarding a 'mark' or 'grade'). They suggest that the dialogue or 'formative interaction' between teacher and pupil is a critical feature in the learning process.

Yet telling children they need to 'try harder' is no better than telling a bad comedian he needs to be funnier and Wiliam (2002) emphasised that teacher feedback must tell students not just what needs to be improved, but also how to go about it and be more involved in their own learning. Although some Government reports and studies of formative assessment in the classroom (for example, QCA, 2004; Watson, 2006) have suggested that, although teachers 'do all the right things', they can tend to focus rather too much on their pupils' awareness of learning *techniques* and too little on the actual *subject* (for example, mathematics).

Some studies have shown that the most 'effective' classrooms are those in which 'formative inter-action' follows an I–R–E (initiation–response–evaluation) format and the teacher, by listening to and formatively assessing pupils' verbal responses, gradually adjusts the questions to guide the pupils towards better understanding and a correct answer (Smith *et al.*, 2004). We will return to the issue of the importance of educational dialogue in Chapter 8.

Practical implication

Teachers who achieve the greatest gains tend to use questions in a general way, to include as many pupils as possible. They usually match the level of difficulty to the children's abilities so that the majority of questions can be answered correctly. When children have problems with answers, teachers will often acknowledge what is correct but then direct the same pupil with additional information until he or she gets the correct answer, as in the following exchange:

TEACHER: What does an adverb do?
PUPIL: Tells you about a noun [*Confusing it with adjective*].
TEACHER: Yes, it tells you more about something, but it's not a noun. Look at the word adverb – the clue's in the word [*Emphasising the 'verb' part of the word*].
PUPIL: It tells you more about a verb.
TEACHER: Yes, that's right.

Range of functions

Assessments can be carried out for a number of different reasons but should always be carried out for a particular purpose, rather than simply testing for its own sake. A teacher might wish to review whether a child (or class) has made significant progress over a year, or a head teacher might wish to check whether a class or their school has a disproportionate number of poor readers.

Formal versus informal assessments

Teachers continually evaluate the progress of the children whom they teach and modify the work that they do with them accordingly. Although most of these judgements are informal, they can be very accurate in terms of comparisons of children. As one might expect, Long (1984) found that when primary teachers were asked to rank their pupils according to their progress with reading, the result for each class was almost identical to the rank order shown by full formal testing.

However, a difficulty is that teachers are also liable to make substantial errors in assessing children's absolute levels of achievement. Budge (1996), for instance, has reported on research with Year 4 pupils which found that, in schools where attainments were generally all at level 4 or higher (above-average), children labelled as having a reading difficulty had an average reading level of 2.28. In schools where overall attainments were at level 2 (below-average), the corresponding average reading level for having a difficulty was 1.65, showing a strong effect of context on judgements.

Unlike primary teachers, subject teachers in secondary education usually teach a large number of children and cannot have the same detailed knowledge of individuals so are more liable to make errors with specific children. Formal tests can address such problems by giving additional information to teachers about absolute levels of achievement and about the comparative abilities of individual pupils. They can also provide more general information, which can be used to compare schools or different types of teaching, and to monitor overall standards.

Types of tests

The two main categories of direct assessment are referred to as **criterion-referenced** and **norm-referenced** tests, and have very different rationales and functions. The purpose of a criterion-referenced test is to measure each individual's specific abilities against a specified set of criteria. The purpose of a norm-referenced test, by contrast, is to discriminate between individuals or to compare them with one another. The content and the use of these two types of test are therefore different, although some tests overlap in their coverage.

Criterion-referenced tests

Criterion-referenced tests assess performance solely on specific features of ability. With reading, this might involve whether a child knows some particular letter sounds, or whether he or she can read certain words from a list. These assessments are closely related to the teaching–learning process and are therefore usually formative, since they identify skills and highlight areas of weakness as a target for subsequent teaching. A criterion-referenced maths test might identify that pupils have weak multiplication skills; this would mean that it would be fruitless to go on to division until they have developed a strong enough understanding of multiplication.

Criterion-referenced achievement testing is a key part of a procedure known as **mastery learning**. This is a technique that was developed from early theories about learning (Carroll, 1963) where, it was suggested, pupils should achieve a level of 90 per cent on the use of specific key skills before further progress or the next level is possible. National Vocational Qualifications (NVQs) are largely criterion-referenced and are mainly based on 'specific elements of competence', which are particular skills carried out in workplace conditions. In order to achieve at a certain level, a student has to be successful with a number of units, and these therefore also give summative information. The National Curriculum targets are still to some extent criterion-referenced but the validity and reliability of these tests have often been questioned.

Norm-referenced tests

A 'norm' is a typical or expected value for something. Norm-referenced tests are designed to measure an individual's abilities against that of a specific population – usually all the other pupils of the same age. They are therefore mainly summative tests, although if they have the capacity to identify specific skills which can be taught, such as particular operations in a mathematical test, then these tests could be said to have a formative component.

Test construction

Norm-referenced tests are developed by first constructing a number of items that assess abilities in a particular domain. With reading, this might involve using a list of words of increasing length and complexity. The test is then checked for reliability (dependability) and validity (meaningfulness), and

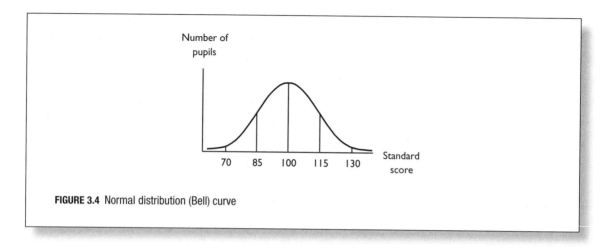

FIGURE 3.4 Normal distribution (Bell) curve

modified until it meets the desired criteria. Reliability and validity are discussed a little later in the chapter.

The test is then standardised by giving it to a sample of children who are broadly representative of the test's target population. This information is then used to construct age-standardised tables that can be used to compare subsequent individual test results. Most normative tests assume that the underlying distribution of abilities is 'normally' distributed (see Appendix), showing the classic bell-shaped curve illustrated in Figure 3.4. Scores can then be standardised, usually with 100 being the mean and 15 being the standard deviation. One standard deviation either side of the mean includes about two-thirds of the population as a whole. About 2 per cent score below 70 and 2 per cent score above 130.

When the test is used, a standard score is calculated from the individual's raw score and this can then be 'translated' using relevant conversion tables to determine how many others in the population would score above or below that level. As an example, the British Picture Vocabulary Scale test (Dunn *et al.*, 2010), described later in this chapter, involves scoring how many times children can correctly identify a picture for a word that is spoken to them. This total can then be compared with age norms to derive a standard score. This can then be used to give a percentile rank score which identifies what percentage of children of the same age would score above or below this level.

A raw score can also usually be referred to tables in the test manual to give a comparison skill-age level. With the increasing pressure on teachers' time, reading tests that have good standardisation yet are easy to administer are in demand. One such test, the Suffolk Reading Scale (Hagley, 2007) can be used with individuals or groups and has recently become part of an online testing system, so that the test can be completed and the results stored digitally for subsequent monitoring purposes.

Problems with normative tests

The standardisation of such tests is obviously very important, and the sample used should be representative of current population attainments. However, many popular tests still used in schools were standardised some time ago and this makes their validity suspect; for instance, particular words (such as 'portmanteau' in the Schonell spelling test) may seem irrelevant and even archaic in today's high-tech, multicultural classrooms.

Other criticisms of normative tests reviewed by the Centre for Language in Primary Education (CLPE, 1989) include:

- the lack of diagnostic information (inevitable with a single normative score);
- the failure of a single measure to represent a complex skill such as 'real reading' which has many different interrelated aspects; and
- problems with interpreting what a single score means.

To some extent, these criticisms can be answered by the development and adequate standardisation of more modern and sophisticated tests. Some of these, such as the Gray Oral Reading Test (Wiederholt and Bryant, 2001) give simple normative information but also cover a range of real reading activities and provide diagnostic (formative) information too.

Individual and group tests

Educational tests can be designed to be administered on an individual basis or to groups of children. The advantage of an individually administered test is that it can be closely monitored and adjusted to a pupil's abilities. With some tests, this means that it is not necessary to do all of the easier items and the assessment can be stopped when it is becoming too hard. Tests can also directly assess an actual skill such as reading, where the assessor may listen to a pupil reading aloud from standard texts. With some tests this can be the basis for diagnostic information when any errors can be recorded and later analysed. The main disadvantage of this approach is the time involved, but this is usually compensated for by the increased accuracy of the test, since close monitoring means that there are fewer errors caused by pupils carrying out the test incorrectly. The Neale Analysis of Reading Ability (Neale, 1997) is a well-known individual test of passage reading that provides normative information and also analyses children's errors. It is meaningful, since it looks directly at the reading process, and it predicts subsequent reading abilities well, with the manual indicating that reading accuracy scores correlate at 0.89 with the same measure a year later.

Group tests are much more common in schools and can be administered to whole classes or year groups at the same time. Such tests are useful for assessing or screening many pupils in a way that is economical of the teacher's time, and all students carry the test out under the same conditions. Unfortunately, with group tests there is less control over what individual children do; such assessments are therefore inherently less accurate and provide less information than individual tests do. Also, group tests are often based on less direct outcome measures of target skills. With the popular Gray Silent Reading Test (Wiederholt and Blalock, 2000), for instance, pupils' reading is assessed by their ability to read some passages of progressively more difficult text and to answer five multiple-choice questions.

Test content and structure

Test items

The structure of assessments can vary from relatively open-ended questions (such as essays) to rather restricted questions (such as multiple-choice). Although essays can be a very rich source of information about an individual's knowledge and abilities, they can lack consistency in terms of the marking. For GCSE examinations, the increasing difficulty in recruiting markers from inside the teaching profession has prompted the need to recruit markers from a more general pool (i.e. graduates and student teachers). Results from one study (Royal-Dawson and Baird, 2009) indicated a significant difference between the grades awarded by different markers with no evidence that experience as a teacher had any positive effect on marking skill. From this, it is easy to see that multiple-choice questions have the advantage of providing a highly standardised testing and marking procedure, and can sometimes even be machine marked. Unfortunately, tests using multiple-choice question papers are scarce because they are difficult and time-consuming to design.

Test characteristics

When one is choosing, using or developing a test, the two aspects of **reliability** (dependability) and **validity** (meaningfulness) must be adequate so that the test can be useful in practice. Information on these can usually be found in the test manual; this should give details about how these measures were assessed, and about their interpretation, and should also refer to any other research background. Without such information, any test must be of doubtful value.

Reliability

Reliability in assessment refers to the extent to which the assessment exercise is trustworthy in providing information about pupils' learning. If the assessment is repeated, would the result be the same or would a different set of pupils with a similar range of abilities and backgrounds gain similar scores?

The reliability of a test means the extent to which it is dependable, or how close a particular result is to the 'true' value of what is being measured. It shows itself in the size of the variation in scores, which is the result of various errors. These can be due to factors such as fatigue, guessing or interpreting questions differently, and variations in the administration and scoring. If pupils were given the same test on a number of occasions, then these errors would mean that sometimes they would do well and on other occasions they would not do so well. If the test is a reliable one, their scores would tend to cluster around a 'middle' value which can be thought of as their 'proper' score, the score they would achieve if there were no errors involved. The example in Figure 3.5 shows a typical scatter of scores that you might find if you carried out the same word-reading test 20 times with a ten-year-old child. Clearly, the scores tend to cluster about the middle and usually fit in with the pattern known as the 'normal distribution'. As it is statistically predictable how many values will fall within a certain standard deviation, this means that we can describe the spread or likelihood of errors, renaming this the standard error of measurement (SEM), shown in Figure 3.6.

Proper, standardised tests usually give the standard error in the manual, and you can use this to work out what sort of error there will be associated with a particular score. Plus or minus ($\pm$) one

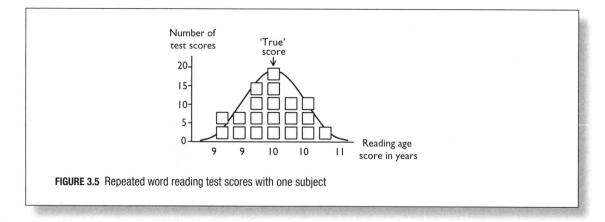

FIGURE 3.5 Repeated word reading test scores with one subject

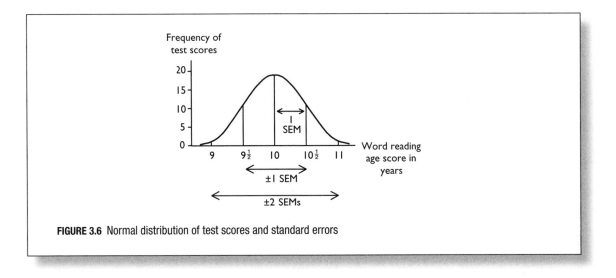

FIGURE 3.6 Normal distribution of test scores and standard errors

standard deviation covers about 68 per cent of all values and plus or minus two standard deviations covers about 95 per cent of all values. In the example above, this means that if a child's actual score was at the ten-year level, about one time out of three that child's true score would be above $10\frac{1}{2}$ years or below $9\frac{1}{2}$ years. It is possible, though even less likely (about one in 20 times), that their true score would be above 11 years, or below 9 years.

It is thus clear that the standard error of measurement is very important, in that it lets us see how much faith can be put in the accuracy of a particular test score. In the example above, it might be rather misleading to compare a child's progress over six months using this test; any real progress might easily be disguised or exaggerated by the normal run of errors. Also, most tests have errors of measurement that are greater than you would normally find with a simple word-reading assessment, particularly if the assessment involves any element of subjectivity or interpretation in the scoring. A good example of this is with reading-comprehension tests, which typically have the much greater standard error of measurement of about one year. If a test does not give a standard error of measurement or some other form of measure of reliability, it would be wise to be cautious about its results. Examples of this are the SATs, which, as discussed later in this chapter, probably have only limited reliability for individual children.

Assessing reliability

In real life, most checks for the reliability of a test cannot be carried out many times with an individual child. Improvements may come with practice, or the child's performance may deteriorate owing to fatigue. Measures of reliability therefore usually depend on correlating only two assessments with each of a number of individuals to cover the range of scores. If the value of the correlation coefficient is high enough, normally above about 0.9, then the reliability is good enough for most practical purposes. Such values can be used as a basis for the underlying correlation between what pupils actually score and an estimate of what their 'true' scores should be, as shown in Figure 3.7.

Test–re-test reliability is what is assessed when a test is given to the same pupils on only two occasions and the results are correlated. This, it is hoped, minimises practice effects that can interfere with the stability of the results. Fatigue or boredom can also have a significant effect on performance, and

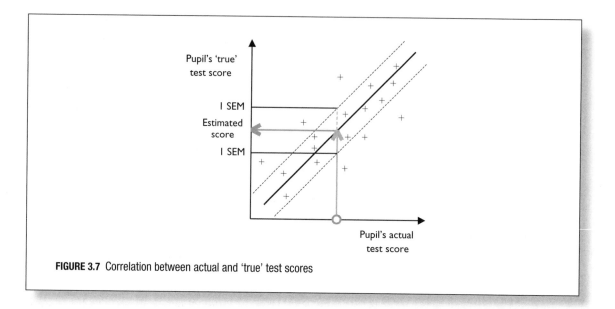

FIGURE 3.7 Correlation between actual and 'true' test scores

to avoid this there has to be a significant delay between the two presentations. This can produce an underestimate in judgements of stability since there will often be some natural variation in scores. With a reading test repeated a week later, some subjects may have improved their true reading ability, while a few might have regressed.

One way around this problem is to carry the test out just once and then to split it into two equivalent halves, often by odd–even items, and then correlate these. The result is called split-half reliability. It depends on test items being fairly homogeneous. Although it is usually justifiable to assume that they are, on some tests certain items may not have an equivalent. In a sense, this approach compares the similarity of two tests (each being half of the overall test) carried out at the same time, and therefore gives some indication of whether pupils answer the questions in a consistent way.

An extension of this approach is to compare all possible splits, and to average these out. One popular example is 'Cronbach's alpha' test, which has been used to assess the reliability of SAT testing. Such indicators are easy to derive since they need only one administration of the test to a number of subjects. However, they will not give any idea of a number of sources of error such as differing assessors and pupil variability on different occasions. Such indices can only really tell us whether the test items are generally of the same level of difficulty and whether the pupils taking the test are consistent in the way in which they perform on such test items. This can, therefore, give an over-optimistic value for the reliabilities of tests and should not be relied on too greatly.

A more complex but more dependable approach is for the test designer to derive two completely parallel forms of the same test. Correlating performance on these should give an estimate of the reliability of a single test. Although it is doubtful whether two forms can ever be completely equivalent, the approach does get around practice effects and is the most stringent of all of the reliability assessments. Well-constructed tests can achieve high correlations: the Gray Oral Reading Test (Wiederholt and Bryant, 2001) with parallel forms A and B has a reliability co-efficient of 0.95 to 0.96 when the two forms are compared. Other advantages of parallel forms are that they can be used to monitor progress more accurately (since practice effects will be reduced), and that, with group testing, the different forms can be alternated in class to prevent copying.

Inherent in any test design must be some consideration of how the test will be marked. The 'startling' finding that the degree of agreement between human markers is quite low (just over 40 per cent agreement) has given rise to considerable research into the possibility of ensuring inter-rater reliability by computerised marking and multiple-choice questions rather than the more usual essay questions (Hutchison, 2006). However, if the purpose of education is in part to develop pupils' coherent writing skills, a skill much valued by employers, then 'adapting' education to suit the mode of testing must be questioned (Ryan, 2009).

Validity

Validity describes the extent to which a test assesses exactly what it is intended to assess. If, for instance, the driving test was based solely on a written exercise, could someone who passed the test be described fairly as a 'good' driver? Validity can be difficult to judge because there may be no consensus of opinion regarding what it means 'to be good at' a subject, or even the level someone might need to achieve to be described as 'good'. The idea of validity is important when devising tests or assessment material to ensure they will enable pupils to demonstrate their knowledge fully. Sometimes 'weak' answers reflect a badly designed paper rather than pupils' lack of knowledge and understanding.

Face validity

A test has face validity if it looks as though it is assessing what it is supposed to. Face validity can be checked by asking people who are knowledgeable in a particular area to give their impressions about the content. To do this with an early-reading test, one might therefore ask for the opinions of some primary teachers, who would presumably look for such features as an early representative sight vocabulary and a progression in the knowledge of letter sounds and their combination. Face validity is typically used in the first stages of developing a test, and is needed to ensure that tests will be accepted by users. In some cases a test may need to have its true purpose disguised and would have a low face validity. For example, in the Rogers' Personal Adjustment Inventory (Jeffrey, 1984) the items are deliberately written to be as neutral as possible so that children taking the test will not give false responses either to please the examiner or to make themselves 'look good'.

Content validity

Content validity refers to whether a test uses items that are part of the general area of skills and abilities that the test is designed to evaluate. Therefore, if a test is supposed to assess reading progress at the secondary level, one would expect the content to be drawn from skills appropriate at that age range; this would probably include the comprehension and interpretation of meaningful text. The WRAT-4 Reading Test (Wilkinson and Robertson, 2006), for instance, is a group 'cloze' test for pupils aged eight years and over, which involves using meaningful paragraphs that have some words missing. In order to fill these in, the person being assessed must understand the rest of the text, which indicates that the test does involve skills that are meaningful at this age.

Content validity can also be assessed numerically, and Hoste (1981) has derived a coefficient measuring the extent to which exam items cover the stated aims and objectives of the syllabus; this has been used to show that the content validity of a test changes significantly when candidates choose between alternative questions (covering different topics), as is common in some exams. Content validity, like face validity, is concerned with what is being examined; it is more precise, however, in that it compares this with a previously defined specification, rather than with some vague notion in the mind of the test user.

Criterion-related validity

Criterion-related validities compare scores on an assessment with values from some external criterion. Concurrent validity is what is measured when the assessment is related to some other assessment that is already available or carried out at the same time. The easiest and most popular way of doing this is to correlate the test with the results from an existing, similar test. However, if these tests are constructed in virtually the same way (for example, both claim to assess vocabulary with a target set of words and corresponding sets of answers to choose from), then a (relatively) high correlation between the two tests is more like a test of reliability and is of limited value in assessing general validity.

Predictive validity relates an assessment to a criterion evaluated at some time in the future. This is perhaps the most stringent of all the validity tests and implies that there is something continuous over time that is affecting both sets of results. Sometimes it can also be taken to imply that the final criterion is in some way a result of the initially assessed skills, although this is not at all logically necessary. Peers and Johnston (1994), for instance, carried out an investigation of the relationship between 'A' level results and the criterion outcome of eventual degree level. 'A' level results are used by university admission tutors for the selection of students, but the predictive validity Peers and Johnston found was quite weak, averaging out at a coefficient of 0.276. They interpreted this as being partly due to the different nature of studies, with 'A' levels being largely factual, whereas degree studies are more interpretative. In some tests that are designed to have a predictive function, this type of validity is much more important. The Infant Rating Scale (Lindsay, 1981) was created to identify children who would have subsequent problems with educational progress. Longitudinal studies carried out by Lindsay to substantiate its validity in this respect found that it did in fact correlate with a range of reading tests two and four years later at around the 0.5 level. Unfortunately, this does not enable one to make very strong judgements for individual children, since the test accounts for only 25 per cent of the variance of later reading scores.

Construct validity

Construct validity is concerned with the match between the assessment and those attributes (or constructs) that are presumed to underlie test performance. To a great extent, looking for construct validity presupposes that the underlying attributes are well-defined, and many tests tend to assume that there is some single global target entity such as 'reading ability' or 'mathematical ability' at which the test can be aimed. However, this may not be the case, and most educational abilities in fact show a qualitative development over time and are based upon a range of different sub-skills. In the area of literacy, young children at first depend mainly upon the component sounds in words (phonemes) and their appearance in written format (graphemes); later abilities depend upon whole-word recognition and the use of meaning, although the earlier skills were still available. A test for younger children that looked mainly for understanding and interpretation would therefore largely miss important early skills.

There is a danger when using tests that they can sometimes be carried out for their own sake, and it is easy to become immersed in the technicalities of validity and reliability. Haylock (2001) distinguishes between the concepts of reliability and validity by giving the example of bathroom scales: bathroom scales, he says, are a *valid* (appropriate) way to measure a person's weight; the scales can be 'reliable' in that they will always respond in the same way to a given weight. However, bathroom scales may not be accurate; that is to say, they may not record the true weight. In educational assessment, accuracy is often 'assumed' within the concept of validity.

Intelligence testing

Origins

The concept of general ability or intelligence has in the past been the most important single way of accounting for individual differences. It is usually assessed by measuring performance on a test of a number of different skills, using tasks that emphasise reasoning and problem-solving in a number of different areas. It can be expressed for an individual as an overall IQ or intelligence quotient. Early assessments of IQ in 1905 were based on work in France by Alfred Binet and were part of an attempt to identify children who needed specialist help to make educational progress. At the same time, general academic interest in the concept of intelligence was developing. Spearman (1904) in particular showed that performances on a number of tests tended to correlate together and believed that this could be explained by the presence of a general ability factor known as '**g**'. This form of testing was continued by Cyril Burt, who became London's first educational psychologist in 1913. Burt set a convenient cut-off criterion of an IQ of 70 for special schooling, and this was subsequently widely applied for many years by psychologists working in education, both in Britain and in the United States.

Developments

There was continued academic interest in intelligence testing, and a general belief by researchers such as Louis Terman in the United States that intelligence was largely inherited and therefore stable over a child's school career. With an increase in the number of children receiving secondary education in Britain, the 1926 *Hadow Report* proposed that, in order to achieve efficient education, there should be different forms of secondary schooling matched to children's abilities and their potential. These ideas were eventually implemented by a wide-scale form of general ability testing, known as the 'eleven-plus', which children sat in their last year of junior schooling. This national test selected out the most 'able' students – those who scored highest in the tests – for grammar schools, where education had a more abstract and academic basis. The eleven-plus was largely discontinued with the advent of comprehensive schooling, although such measures are still used in parts of the country where selective grammar schools remain.

There are tests available that can be used by teachers to assess the abilities of children in school; a good example is the group NFER–Nelson Verbal and Non-Verbal Reasoning Test Series (Hagues and Courtenay, 2009; Smith and Hagues, 2009). The verbal assessments in this series involve a range of language-based tasks and the non-verbal assessments use picture series to assess logical reasoning, and series using abstract shapes to reduce the effects of general knowledge.

Some tests are for use with individual children, and these are often 'closed', meaning that they are for restricted use by qualified workers only, such as educational psychologists. A recent example of this type is the British Ability Scales (Elliott *et al.*, 1997). This test uses a number of different tasks of verbal ability, pictorial (or non-verbal) reasoning ability and spatial ability. The most commonly used form of closed individual intelligence test is the Wechsler Intelligence Scale for Children (the WISC).

This WISC is now in its fourth edition (Wechsler, 2004) and has been fully standardised for use in the UK. The WISC gives four overall scales or Index scores from ten main sub-tests (see Table 3.2).

TABLE 3.2 Scales and sub-tests of the *Wechsler Intelligence Scale for Children* (2004)

Scale	Subtests	Example
Verbal Comprehension	Similarities	In what ways are a chair and a table alike?
	Vocabulary	What is an elephant?
	Comprehension	Why do dogs wear collars?
Perceptual Reasoning	Block Design	Copy a pattern with coloured blocks.
	Picture Concepts	Identify common features from groups of pictures.
	Matrix Reasoning	Select appropriate item to complete the matrix.
Working Memory	Digit Span	Repeat numbers in the same or reverse order.
	Letter–Number Sequencing	Recall numbers in ascending order and letters in alphabetic order.
Processing Speed	Coding	Copy symbols in appropriate box in specified time.
	Symbol Search	Scan line of symbols to identify matching symbol within a specified time.

Note
Adapted from Wechsler (2004).

The number that a child gets correct for each of these sub-tests (the raw score) is referred to age-appropriate tables in the test manual from which scaled scores with a mean of ten are calculated. These standard scores are totalled for the four Indexes (Verbal Comprehension, Perceptual Reasoning, Working Memory and Processing Speed) and for the test as a whole.

By using tables, the total can then be converted to the intelligence quotient, or IQ, which is a relative measure of an individual's score compared with that of the general population. The average **IQ** is 100 and scores have a standard deviation of 15. Intelligence quotients can also be converted to give percentile ranks to give some idea of how many people would achieve at or below this level. If a pupil scores at the seventy-fifth percentile it can be said that he or she has scored at least as well, or better than, 75 per cent of children of a similar age. Percentile scores calculated from intelligence testing suggest only 2 per cent of the population have an IQ of 70 or below. Current intelligence tests, such as the WISC, however, discourage the use of the full-scale score and strongly recommend the use of the more diagnostic individual Index scores to highlight individual strengths and weaknesses.

Standardised, norm-referenced IQ tests are still often used to determine the eligibility of some children to be given additional funding to meet their special educational needs. Defining intelligence has, however, been controversial, and the use and validity of intelligence tests no less so (see Chapter 4). Sternberg considers IQ tests to be only a convenient, partial operationalisation of the construct of intelligence which cannot provide the kind of measurement of intelligence that a tape measure gives of one's height, and suggests there is still 'nothing even vaguely close to a "tape measure" of intelligence' (Sternberg *et al.*, 2005: 47). Yet, as Colmar *et al.* (2006) note, this 'snapshot' type of testing is often chosen to assess children whose very difficulties often reside in their inability to achieve/perform consistently from one day to the next.

Numerous studies have, therefore, sought to identify other abilities or skills that may contribute to how children learn. Rather than the controversial and more heterogeneous intelligence, over the past decade the importance of working memory as an underlying ability has been at the forefront of this research and there are now tests available to assess this ability in young children; one of the most recent takes the form of a teacher-rating scale, where the teacher completes a checklist in order to identify those with a memory deficit (Alloway *et al.*, 2008). In a large study in the West Midlands, Grimley and Banner (2008) found that pupils in the high working memory group achieved a GCSE mean score of 44.4, whereas pupils in the low working memory group achieved a GCSE mean score of 34.3. Growing research evidence has also begun to highlight a complex interplay of three independent variables (working memory, cognitive style and behaviour) in determining achievement in school, and many teachers now see identifying personality styles and learning preferences as important parts of their assessment portfolio.

Jung's theory that differences in behaviour result from people's innate tendency to use their minds in different ways led to the development of the Myers–Brigg Type Indicator or MBTI (Briggs et al., 2000) which focuses on how personality traits can be collated to give an overall indicator of 'personality type'. As a result, tests such as the MBTI and the Cognitive Styles Analysis or CSA (Riding, 1991) are now frequently seen in classrooms. One study of secondary school pupils (Riding et al., 2001) found that educational outcomes (as measured by scores on the Cognitive Abilities Test) were predictable from the interaction between cognitive style (measured on the CSA) and working memory: analytics performed well if they had good working memory but poorly if they had poor working memory, but wholists were found to be generally unaffected by their working memory capacity and performed averagely throughout.

General verbal abilities (verbal intelligence)

Although general ability is assessed by combining scores on a number of different sub-tests, the current trend in intelligence testing discourages the use of the full-scale score and strongly urges the user to use the Index scores to identify specific processing strengths and weaknesses (Kaufmann and Kaufmann, 2004). From the WISC IV sub-tests (Wechsler, 2004), the vocabulary sub-test has the greatest single effect on overall IQ and involves both receptive language (hearing and comprehension) and expressive language (when giving the answer).

A useful test of basic receptive language that can be used by teachers is the British Picture Vocabulary Scale test (Dunn et al., 2010). This is an individual test that can be used across a wide age range from two years, six months to 18 years and is mainly a test of a child's underlying level of verbal concepts. The administration is relatively straightforward, and the person giving the test merely says the target word and asks the child to point to the picture that best illustrates it from a choice of four options. This test can be particularly useful with young children who have only limited spoken language, and with any older children who might have difficulty with the reading that is involved in some written tests of language.

Other tests assess more general verbal abilities. The previously mentioned Verbal Reasoning Test series (Hagues and Courtenay, 2009), for instance, covers the age range from 8 years to 13 years and includes vocabulary, logical verbal reasoning, relationships between words, symbol manipulation using letters and numbers, and the use of words in sentences.

General non-verbal abilities (non-verbal intelligence)

Most tests of general intelligence include some form of assessment of non-verbal ability. The popular Cognitive Abilities Test (Lohman et al., 2009), for instance, covers the age range from seven years, six months to 17 years and is promoted as a means of establishing 'value-added' information. This is done by comparing academic attainments with the abilities assessed by the test which are assumed to underlie such progress. As well as verbal and number skills, the test also incorporates a non-verbal assessment of spatial ability. There are also specific non-verbal tests (e.g. Smith and Hagues, 2009) that cover a similar age range from 8 years to 14 years. The sub-tests here aim to give a reliable indication of how easily a pupil may acquire new concepts in a wide range of subjects including maths, science, and design and technology.

Since non-verbal abilities appear to be less dependent on culture and experience than verbal ones are, it can be argued that they are more representative of general, underlying intelligence. This is often assumed to be innate and is referred to as 'fluid' intelligence (Catell, 1983). Interestingly, abilities on such tests have been reported to peak at an early age, which Long (2000) suggests does imply some role for biological maturation. Fluid intelligence can be contrasted with more verbally based tests which emphasise acquired knowledge, referred to by Cattell as 'crystallised' intelligence. These abilities tend to show progressive improvements during schooling and reach their highest levels from age 30 years onwards, declining significantly only for people over 60.

The *Raven's Matrices* test (Raven, 2008) is one of the most popular ways of assessing non-verbal intelligence. It is open to teachers and can be used either with individuals or as a group test. The various forms cover the entire school age range from 4 years to 18 years, and give a single measure of performance which is standardised for age. As shown in Figure 3.8, the matrices involve analysing logical combinations of geometric shapes in order to select the correct missing pattern.

Although such non-verbal abilities may appear to be more valid assessments of 'true' or underlying intelligence, they are in fact strongly affected by general experience and cultural effects. Evidence that scores on the *Raven's Matrices*, originally published in the 1930s, have shown major improvements over time, may be related to the increasing number of people receiving higher education, as well as greater experience with visual-based technology. This upward shift of standards also incidentally makes the use of any norms difficult, and means that it is particularly important to base any judgements on recent standardisations of such tests.

A further reason for caution concerning the use of non-verbal assessments is that they have only a weak correlation with school achievements. As an example of this, the manual of the WISC (Wechsler, 2004) shows that the correlation between the WISC verbal score and reading comprehension from the Wechsler Individual Achievement Test II or WIATII (Wechsler, 2005) is 0.67 while the correlation between the WISC non-verbal score and reading comprehension is 0.51.

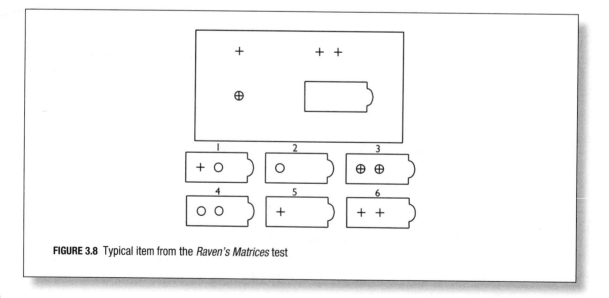

FIGURE 3.8 Typical item from the *Raven's Matrices* test

Reliability and validity of intelligence measures

The reliability of the WISC is well-established and the manual gives a test–re-test coefficient of 0.80, indicating that pupils tend to obtain similar scores on different occasions. The validity of this particular test (and others like it) is, however, more open to question, and raises a number of issues related to the meaning of intelligence and the uses to which intelligence tests results are put.

One might agree that such tests have a certain face validity, since they involve a number of different sub-tests that appear to cover basic mental processes and that relate to each other to some extent. Criterion validities have been the subject of much debate, however, since these depend on how well IQ relates to other attainments.

Construct validity of intelligence measures

As mentioned earlier, the very meaning of the construct of intelligence has been, and remains, the subject of debate. From a statistical perspective, there is certainly a tendency for performances on a broad range of tasks to correlate with one another, supporting the belief in a single general factor. This type of data, however, can be alternatively explained by a number of lower-order factors which will then correlate together weakly. Arguably, these low-order factors could be separate mental skills which, if shared by the separate tasks, would give rise to the general correlations found between those tasks.

Sternberg (1988) argues that broader, naturalistic learning correlates more highly with intelligence. However, one particularly persuasive aspect not refuted by Sternberg is evidence of individuals who are low on measures of general ability, yet have specific areas of high achievement. Some 'autistic savants', for instance, have severely limited interpersonal development, general linguistic abilities and other cognitive skills, yet are able to function at a high level with complex mathematical calculations, on feats of memory or complex visuo-spatial analysis, or they may demonstrate particular strengths in music or art. If certain high-level functions are not at all dependent on a single general ability factor, then this casts severe doubt on the usefulness of the concept of a single overarching factor of intelligence.

Gardner (1999) believes that such evidence indicates that abilities are not restricted to the intellectual domain, but span at least seven other, largely unrelated, areas of intelligence: linguistic, logical–mathematical, musical, bodily-kinaesthetic, spatial, inter-personal and intra-personal. Academic achievements appear to relate most closely to linguistic and logical–mathematical abilities. Despite this, general life success probably also depends on many other factors such as interpersonal skills and specific attainments as well as general motivation. Scores on intelligence tests do correlate to some extent with general success in life, as measured for instance by people's income. However, Ceci (1990) found that this correlation was confounded by the amount of education people had experienced. When education was controlled for, then IQ–income effects disappeared.

In general, there are grounds for strong doubt about the stability of intellectual abilities and questions about the use of intelligence to predict academic progress.

Other forms of assessment

Teachers can gather further information about pupils by using a number of other techniques, such as observational approaches, checklists and interviews.

Observational techniques

Observational techniques are particularly appropriate for gathering information about classroom processes. They are usually carried out by a separate person in the classroom. One early detailed study produced a system of classroom observation still regularly used today (Flanders, 1970). This study used frequent observational judgements throughout the lesson and identified ten types of interaction, such as teacher's use of praise, and children's use of response or initiation. The Flanders schedule was specifically designed to show different types of verbal interactions and highlighted differences between teacher styles, such as whether a teacher encourages pupils' involvement, or whether the teacher tends to dominate classroom interaction. With respect to that point, it is noteworthy that this scheme only includes two codes for pupil talk, and seven codes for teacher talk (and one for silence/confusion).

A more extensive approach was used by Galton and Wilkinson (1992) as the basis of their long-term ORACLE (Observational Research and Classroom Learning Evaluation) where they categorised the behaviour observed every 25 seconds. Merrett and Wheldall (1986) had also looked at the use of positive and negative comments by teachers and how they related to different types of problem behaviours noted in their pupils. The advantage is that observations of this type can directly imply interventions: if teachers are overusing negative comments, this technique may be an effective strategy in monitoring and attempting to reduce this type of comment.

Rating scales and checklists

The introduction of inclusive education now puts a greater demand on teachers in terms of the 'early identification' of any special educational needs. As specific training for this is not generally included in initial teacher training, there are now a number of published rating scales and checklists aimed specifically at identifying children who are most likely to experience difficulty in developing appropriate academic or social skills. There are rating scales and checklists to identify children with attentional (ADHD) problems – for example, the Connors Rating Scale-3 (Connors, 2008) – or difficulties on the autistic spectrum – for example, Childhood Autism Rating Scale-2 (Schopler et al., 2010).

Screening assessments

One of the most important goals of education is learning to read and write. Yet, despite the rigorous structures inherent in the National Literacy Strategy, there are still claims that approximately 20 per cent of children fail to read (or write) at an age-appropriate level by the end of their primary school education (National Literacy Trust, 2009). The early identification of literacy difficulties is therefore important both for the individual child and for the allocation of appropriate resources to address these difficulties. Ever-increasing research into how children learn to read and write has identified a range of requisite skills necessary for successful literacy acquisition, and there are now a number of commercially published 'screening' tests for kindergarten, pre-school and Reception class children. Some claim to identify the specific needs associated with dyslexia such as the Dyslexia Early Screening Test (Nicholson and Fawcett, 2004) or the Dyslexia Screener (Turner and Smith, 2009), while others such as the Phonological Assessment Battery (Frederickson et al., 1997) or the Automated Working Memory Assessment (Alloway, 2007) assess skills that have been found to correlate significantly with proficient literacy.

Interviews

The *Code of Practice* (DfES, 2001) also states clearly that parents have a role to play in supporting their child's education, and regular meetings between parents and teachers are now more commonplace. Parents of children in the primary-school age range will also often participate in a 'Home–School Book' dialogue with their child's teacher where frequent (sometimes daily) written communication will enable the two (parent and teacher) to communicate important information without the necessity for a face-to-face meeting.

Teachers also often meet with parents to report on children's progress or to gather information. These interviews can gather information on which to select or advise on future studies, or, on some occasions, to investigate situations where a pupil has problem behaviour. Walker (1998) described the typical encounter involved in parents' evenings as being a problematic interface between the power bases of home and school, and found that the purpose of the meeting was often unclear to the participants, resulting in some conflict of agendas. Parents were often frustrated by not receiving the information that they wanted, because the time available for discussion was limited and the teachers tended to manage the meeting. A joint home and school approach is, however, now becoming evident in many schools as teachers and parents meet with the intention of agreeing on consistent and positive targets shared between home and school.

It seems likely that today's more 'open door' approach to education, where parents are now actively encouraged to feel welcome in schools and, as a result, feel more relaxed about meeting with teachers, can only serve to enhance children's school experience.

National Curriculum assessments

The introduction of the National Curriculum in England was a major policy change that aimed to enhance standards of pupil achievement and forced teachers to assess pupils summatively against nationally prescribed standards. The Assessment Reform Group (2002) advised, however, that a distinction must be made between assessing *for* learning via classroom assessment and the assessment *of* learning via grading and reporting.

National Curriculum assessments have historically been undertaken in two ways: by teacher assessment and by national standardised testing to 'complement the evidence of attainment collected by teachers through their own assessments'. The balance between these two has, however, changed considerably since the inception of national testing. The results of the tests are then used at an individual level to indicate the achievement of each pupil and, when aggregated, to assess the level of performance of schools and local authorities in England (Ofqual, 2009).

As of 2010, mandatory tests and tasks, developed and administered by the QCA (Qualifications and Curriculum Authority), are undertaken at two points in a child's compulsory education, and are specifically designed to suit the age and predicted attainment of the average child at these ages. These tests are high-stakes tests for teachers, schools and local authorities as the resulting annual performance tables, published on the Internet and in local and national newspapers, are used to evaluate schools' effectiveness. Unlike, say, GCSE examinations, the National Curriculum tests are deemed low-stakes for individual pupils as the results do not generally affect progress to the next year of schooling, although there has recently been considerable concern regarding the validity of Key Stage 2 results in identifying pupils' capabilities as they transfer to their secondary schools. The extent of this concern has resulted in continued, widespread use of the Cognitive Abilities Tests or CAT (Lohman *et al.*, 2009) by primary schools in Year 6, prior to the transfer, or in secondary schools in Year 7 to provide a 'more reliable' assessment of pupils' abilities as they begin their secondary education.

The reluctance of many secondary schools to ability-group based on the results from these National Curriculum Key Stage 2 tests has prompted some research into alternative ways of assessing pupils (Ryan, 2009). As part of this, ten education authorities are currently trialling a scheme where awarding the appropriate level to individual children will be replaced by tests that have a single ability level. This would be much more in line with the way children are tested in music: an able pupil could take a level 4 test in English at the age of nine years (two years earlier than currently) and would then take a level 5 test a year or two later. However, if schools are to be judged by the number of 11-year-olds who achieve the required level (i.e. a level 4), it could be argued there may be no incentive for schools to stretch more-able pupils to enter them for the level 5 test.

Yet, there are reports that national tests together with Ofsted inspections and the publication of school-level results have contributed to real improvements: according to Ryan (2009), a former senior education adviser to the government, the proportion of 11-year-olds reaching the expected standard at Key Stage 2 has risen from 49 per cent in English and 45 per cent in maths in 1995 to 81 and 78 per cent respectively in 2008.

However, criticisms of national testing still abound. The Sunderland Report (2008), which considered the cost, workload and stress involved in national testing, resulted in the abolition of this type of formal testing at Key Stage 3 from 2009. Another recurring concern has been about the lack of independence between the teaching and assessment processes: if SATs are administered in school by the people who have been responsible for teaching the pupils, it seems possible the results could be biased more favourably (Gold, 2002). This concern has been further fuelled by suggestions that schools may have falsified records in order to boost their success rate and place in published league tables (Meadows *et al.*, 2007).

Reliability and validity

Despite the inception of a body accountable to the Secretary of State (DCSF) 'to secure public confidence in the validity, reliability and rigour of the national curriculum assessments' (Ofqual, 2009: 3), the topic of standardised testing is still hotly debated and the tests required seem to be constantly changing.

Doyle and Godfrey (2005) carried out a study where they re-administered past Key Stage 2 tests to several groups of Year 7 pupils. Their study compared the consistency of marking both between markers and between years. They suggested the range of marks within one level was too broad (i.e. a pupil awarded a Level 3 for science could have scored between 23 and 44 points, a range of some 21 points). They similarly noted that these ranges changed from year to year so that in 1997, to attract a Level 3, a pupil must score a minimum of 21 points, whereas in 1998 to achieve a Level 3, a pupil must score a minimum of 24 points. Doyle and Godfrey concluded from their study that the English test results were 'unreliable' for around one-third of the pupils.

The QCA issues annual details for each test, including the total number of marks available for the test, the mean mark for the test as a whole, details of the pre-test sample, and Cronbach's alpha to demonstrate how far the test is measuring a single concept such as spelling, reading or science. In order to address the problem that some questions may not be measuring what they claim to be measuring (for example, if some items in the mathematics tests demanded high level skills in reading in order to understand and answer the question), the QCA is directed to ensure that all National Curriculum tests have coefficients above 0.80.

Assessing Pupils' Progress (APP)

Since 2008, every child's progress is tracked using the APP (Assessing Pupils' Progress) materials, which enable teachers to 'consider the evidence, review the evidence and make a judgment' of children's performance and how this relates to national standards for reading, writing, mathematics, science and ICT (Information and Communication Technology). An example of an APP criterion-referenced guideline was shown at Figure 3.2. As these assessments are criterion-referenced, they can assist in planning and delivering subsequent teaching and can also be used for reporting to parents, and for building up a final summary of pupils' achievements on completing each year or on transition (as they move from primary to secondary school). Perhaps because of the perceived additional workload associated with such monitoring, a number of published programmes are now appearing on the market (for example, *PIE – Progress in English* and *PIM – Progress in Maths*) to identify children's precise position in relation to the national standards.

Value-added measures

Perhaps one of the most important uses of assessments is the way in which they can be used to compare and judge the effectiveness of schools. However, while Key Stage tests offer the possibility of calculating value-added scores for each school based on progress between each Key Stage, crude league tables can be highly misleading, owing to variations between the abilities of pupils going to different schools. As pupils' backgrounds can account for a great deal of the variation in their attainments, the current emphasis on performance data has for some time given rise to concerns that a school could not be judged fairly without some acknowledgement of the initial level (for example, ability or social) of its pupils.

Instead of measuring the performance of one pupil against other pupils (norm referencing), or against specified objectives (criterion referencing), **value-added** pupil performance is measured when current achievement is measured against previous levels of attainment in the same group of children. This is what is meant by **ipsative assessment** when better pupil progress in School A than in schools in the rest of the country might be attributed to the particular effectiveness of School A. The current emphasis on accountability in education has raised the profile of ipsative assessment because of the contribution it makes to value-added assessment. Unlike 'raw' league tables, which do not take into account pupils' prior attainment, ipsative assessment measures gains in personal learning and provides data on the extent to which the pupil, the teacher and the school have been able to improve learning.

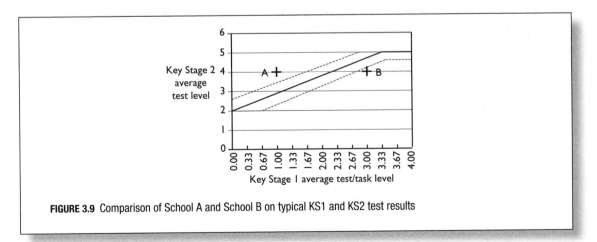

FIGURE 3.9 Comparison of School A and School B on typical KS1 and KS2 test results

In the example in Figure 3.9, School A's pupils achieved an average level 1 at Key Stage 1, but then went on to achieve an average level 4 at Key Stage 2, making better than average progress. School B's pupils, however, achieved an average level 3 at Key Stage 1, but achieved only an average level 4 at Key Stage 2, making less than average progress.

While there is still some concern about the validity and reliability of comparing schools (Hilton, 2005), 'value-added' assessment which now takes into account two measures of 'child deprivation' (the allocation of free school meals and the Income Deprivation Affecting Children Index) would seem to facilitate more informed and useful comparisons between schools.

Summary

Assessment is a key part of the teaching and learning process. Standardised, norm-referenced tests are used in the main to assess achievement (such as literacy or numeracy) or general ability. The assessment of ability includes assessment of knowledge, skills and understanding, while aptitude assessments identify individual characteristics which influence future attainments. Summative assessments indicate the level of pupils' achievements but formative assessments involve regular assessment to inform subsequent teaching and learning experiences. There is still some confusion regarding the distinction between two types of assessment in part because many tests sit along a continuum and have both summative and formative features.

Teachers regularly undertake informal assessments, but the National Curriculum now integrates ongoing formative monitoring with end of Key Stage summative, formal assessments to determine absolute level of achievements. National Curriculum assessments (SATs) involve ongoing criterion-referenced assessment by the teacher supplemented at two points in a child's school life by mandatory tests and tasks. The validity and reliability of these mandatory, sometimes externally marked, tests are still the subject of considerable debate.

Observational techniques are typically used to record patterns of behaviour. This type of assessment often requires an objective observer to collect behavioural data in the classroom if information is to be used to analyse and possibly alter teaching and learning strategies. Interviews and other methods that allow communication between parents and teachers are now considered to play an important part in children's school experiences.

An important function of assessment has come to be in tracking value-added effects, setting targets and evaluating the effectiveness of schools. However, Government efforts to identify the precise 'character' of any individual school are best still seen as a 'work in progress'. As Hallam et al. (2004) suggest, at the current time, only those who have extensive knowledge of the particular circumstances prevailing in a school, i.e. the staff, are in a position to take account of all the information (resource constraints, prior attainment of pupils, numbers of children with SEN, or from disadvantaged backgrounds or with a different home-language) and make informed decisions.

Key implications

- Formative and summative assessment is endemic in education but assessment is only useful when it directs teaching and learning experiences.
- Test reliability and validity must be proven if results are to be valued: understanding of standardisation details for published tests is therefore essential.

■ SATs results can be used to identify strengths and weaknesses but 'teaching to the test' is likely to negate this opportunity.

Further reading

Clarke (2005), *Formative Assessment in the Secondary Classroom*: written by a specialist assessment consultant, this book highlights the key elements of formative assessment – assessment for learning – in the secondary classroom, and how marking and feedback complete the 'learning loop' which starts with learning intentions and success criteria.

Flynn (2007), *What is Intelligence? Beyond the Flynn Effect*: this highly engaging and very readable book holds the reader's attention and demands a rethink of all sorts of issues.

Galton (2008), *Creative Practitioners in Schools and Classrooms: Final Report*: the final report of a study that set out to explore the pedagogy used by successful artists (creative partners) to bring about transformations in pupils' attitudes to (and motivation for) learning, particularly among those disaffected pupils of an anti-school disposition.

Lawrence (2009), *People Types and Tiger Stripes: Using Psychological Type to Help Students Discover Their Unique Potential*: this new edition of the best-selling book about type and how it works in everyday life is especially relevant in the world of teaching. The fourth edition includes two essays by Isabel Myers and provides a detailed explanation of the theory and practice of using type in the education process.

Discussion of practical scenario

Mrs Smith already has a number of children in her class with a range of special educational needs: children with developmental difficulties, with sensory difficulties, with communication difficulties and with motor-skills problems. Working previously with the Traveller families will have already developed Mrs Smith's skill at using criterion-referenced, baseline assessments, particularly with those who may not have had consistent or formal education in the British system. She may need some additional advice/support from the school SENCO (Special Educational Needs Co-ordinator) and her local authority Advisory EAL (English as an Additional Language) and TES (Traveller Education Services) teams. Once she has carried out some initial assessments and has a better view of the children's needs, she may welcome the opportunity for some short-course training sessions. Most importantly, it will be important that her head teacher and the school psychologist 'persuade' her that her teaching experience stands her in good stead and she is more capable than she currently believes!

Individual differences and achievement

Chapter overview

- The importance of differences
- Intelligence
- Home background
- Gifted and talented children
- Creativity
- Thinking skills
- Cognitive style
- Personality

Practical scenario

Christina Agabogo is a newly qualified teacher about to take up her first full-time post at Eastnor School. The school is in a rural area where income levels per head are significantly lower than the national average. The school's catchment area serves a local air force base, a new-build owner–occupier estate and a local council residential home for children. Christina's final University dissertation focused particularly on 'The Importance of Being Different'.

What will be Christina's first tasks before she meets her new class of five-year-olds?

How might her training influence her approach to (1) the children and (2) their parents?

In which areas might Christina need (1) the support of her colleagues or (2) further training?

The importance of differences

Chapters 2 and 3 have looked at general learning principles and ways of assessing attainments. Although these can help teachers to plan what they teach, each child is an individual, with a unique combination of abilities, personalities and learning characteristics. These differences are important since they can determine how teaching and learning experiences may need to be adapted in order to meet children's individual needs.

In the past, one of the most important ways of measuring differences has been to focus on children's 'general ability', and this has often been determined by individual performance on intelligence tests. It is important to know whether or not this might be a good idea since it implies that we could use general ability (or intelligence) to categorise children and to provide appropriate education based simply on the outcome of these tests. The possibility of an inherited, biological basis for intelligence would lend strong support for such an approach since it implies that children have an underlying potential which is relatively stable. This belief has many implications for the way in which education should be organised and its validity continues to be passionately debated.

More recent developments in cognitive psychology – particularly in the study of working memory, human perception, thinking and learning – have provided further insight into how children learn and whether it is possible, by developing these skills, to enhance their academic achievements. There has also been more qualitative research with an emphasis on learning style and personality, and the effect these have on the learning process in different situations.

Intelligence

Activity

When you think about your own general ability, where do you think it 'comes from'? Do you think you take after one or both of your parents? Do you think that it came as a result of your own study and hard work at school or college? Do you think ability is something that is 'fixed' (i.e. does not change substantially over time)? Write down your thoughts and your reasoning behind them now, before reading further.

Historically, it was assumed that intelligence was a fixed, inherited ability, but research in recent years has frequently suggested that intelligence can change. Flynn (1998) found noticeable increases over a period of some 50 years in both verbal and non-verbal scores, and more recently, his further study has revealed an even more marked improvement in non-verbal intelligence. Flynn (2007) attributes this change to the more scientific thinking demanded by today's society with greater emphasis on visual screens, rapid responses and 'bursts' of mental activity. This possibility that intelligence can be enhanced has resulted in a number of accelerated learning programmes (for example, Adey *et al.*, 2002) and these are discussed later in this chapter.

Use of IQ testing

Intelligence tests have often been used in education to predict children's future academic progress, with different levels of measured intelligence being taken to imply the need for different forms of educational experiences (see Chapter 6 for details). More-able children are presumed to respond best to abstract experiences, which result in an accelerated rate of progress, while less-able children, who are presumed to have a slower rate of learning, will respond to more direct, practical experiences.

Intelligence tests have been and still are used to estimate a child's potential for learning. When this 'estimate' matches achievement, then children can be said to be 'fulfilling their potential' at whatever level this might be. Children who are perceived to be of 'lower' ability are described as 'low-achievers', whereas those perceived to be of 'high' ability but who fail to reach the academic levels predicted for or expected of them are often described as 'underachievers'.

Underachievement

There is currently considerable political and media concern about such underachievement and particularly 'underachieving boys'. Recurring evidence suggests that, although boys and girls appear to perform similarly on cognitive test scores at 11 years of age, by the time they reach their GCSEs, the performance of boys is noticeably lower (Deary et al., 2003). As Reyna (2008) notes, boys' poorer performance in examinations may of course arise from attributional stereotyping: teachers who believe they spend too much of their class time managing the behaviour of boys often have low expectations of boys' ability which, in turn, may actually cause the inattentive, arguably reactionary boys' behaviour they are trying to control in the classroom. Conversely, Myhill and Jones (2006) argue that such observable gender-bias (i.e. teachers' over-attentiveness to boys) can suggest that teachers tend to sense greater potential in boys and therefore are focusing 'willing' attention, asking the boys more demanding questions in an attempt to stimulate more problem-solving responses as a result. Classroom studies suggest that teachers often react more positively towards pupils (arguably, girls) who fail for 'uncontrollable' reasons (such as low ability) than they do to pupils who underachieve for 'controllable' reasons (such as low effort): those who are perceived to be 'just not trying' (arguably, boys) will be punished or even 'written-off', whereas those perceived to be working hard will be offered additional support (Jones and Myhill, 2004).

School attainment and intelligence

Focusing on the discrepancy between results from an intelligence test and those from educational tests (such as reading or maths) assumes that intelligence is a good predictor of educational potential, yet there is still much debate regarding the association, if any, between intelligence and performance in school.

In an analysis of earlier studies, Gagné and St Pere (2002) found a correlation of about 0.70 between cognitive ability and academic performance in school, a finding supported by Spinath et al. (2006) in their longitudinal study of over 4,000 twins. Yet, experience tells us, it would clearly be wrong to assume that innate intelligence is the sole factor in academic success. For example, despite some correlation between cognitive ability on starting school and subsequent academic attainment, attentional skills, which contribute significantly to academic attainment, have been shown to be independent of initial cognitive ability (see Feinstein and Duckworth, 2006). Any correspondence, then, that does exist can be open to a number of alternative interpretations: one such possibility is that the academic skill itself might have an effect on IQ, or that both intelligence tests and academic measures may be affected by another general process such as motivation, concentration or self-perceived abilities (Rhode and Thompson, 2007).

Strand et al. (2006) have also suggested that, despite across-gender similarities in *early* cognitive performance, the previously mentioned greater success of girls in GCSE examinations could be attributed to the more specific skills needed for success in GCSEs. These skills, such as verbal fluency, better verbal memory (for information presented orally in class or from reading textbooks) and writing, were more evident in the subsequent academic behaviour of girls, but would not have been assessed by the types of verbal-reasoning tests often used earlier by schools to assess 'intelligence'.

Reading and intelligence

As reading ability is a key basic skill in education, many studies have attempted to investigate whether there is any association between underlying cognitive abilities and subsequent literacy acquisition.

Perhaps the most common and hotly-debated use of IQ testing has been in the assessment of dyslexia (see Chapter 10), where if a child's reading level is significantly below that predicted by his/her score on an IQ test, then he/she is deemed to experience a **specific learning difficulty**, rather than a more generalised learning difficulty. Despite regular reports that children with low scores on intelligence tests can learn to read (Baylis and Snowling, 2007), inherent in the **discrepancy model of identifying dyslexia** is the belief that intensive, specialist teaching will be of greater benefit to those who are 'underachieving' (i.e. those with discrepant scores) than those whose reading level matches that predicted from their IQ score.

However, a British Psychological Society working party report on dyslexia (BPS, 1999) made no mention of any association between intelligence and literacy, proposing only that dyslexia 'is evident when accurate and fluent word reading and/or spelling develops very incompletely or with great difficulty ... the problem is severe and persistent despite appropriate learning opportunities', p. 18). While some studies support this notion that intelligence (as measured by IQ tests) is irrelevant in predicting reading ability (for example, Stuebing et al., 2009), others argue that the cognitive problems (for example, language or working-memory deficits) that impair children's performance on IQ tests may also underpin reading difficulties (Fuchs and Young, 2006).

A further 'reverse' cause–effect argument proposed by Stanovich (1986) was that good reading ability can enhance performance on intelligence tests. Stanovich named this association '**The Matthew Effect**' (after the biblical quotation that 'for whosoever hath, to him shall be given', Matthew 25: 29) and other studies too have suggested that literacy skill may have a causal influence on performance in intelligence tests (Harlaar et al., 2005). As tests of intelligence are largely based on verbal knowledge and understanding, it seems credible that intelligence itself may well be enhanced by the process of reading (see Figure 4.1).

The best way of predicting progress has been to use specific rather than general abilities. When this is done in a particular skill area, correlations can be relatively high. Neale (1989), for instance, quoted research which found that early reading ability correlated at 0.83 with reading age one year later. Correlations are also relatively high if the initial ability measured forms a basis for later progress. Early literacy experiences (nursery rhymes, hearing stories) and pre-literacy skills such as phonological awareness and alphabetic knowledge have often been cited as predictive of literacy in the early school

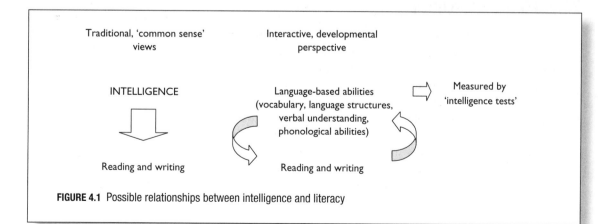

FIGURE 4.1 Possible relationships between intelligence and literacy

years (Nathan *et al.*, 2004). However, there is a growing sense that, while the association between preliteracy skills such as phonological abilities (phonological awareness, rapid naming) and subsequent literacy may be genetically mediated, measures of reading that involve direct instruction (such as letter knowledge) are more likely to show shared environmental effects (Byrne *et al.*, 2002). The results of one longitudinal study (Harlaar *et al.*, 2007) of reading between the ages of seven and ten years concluded that genetic influence is substantial and stable during the elementary school years, which covers the developmental shift from 'learning to read' to 'reading to learn'. Averaging across the ages (seven, nine and ten years), genetic influences accounted for 63 per cent, home background for 13 per cent and school and other influences for 24 per cent.

Public examinations and IQ

Predicting individual differences in educational outcomes was the reason behind Binet's early use of intelligence testing (Binet, 1905). Various studies since that time have set out to determine whether Binet's claim for the association is valid (for example, Sternberg *et al.*, 2001). In Britain there has been a noticeable increase in these studies, not least because of previously mentioned concerns about the markedly poorer performance of boys in national tests and examinations despite no apparent gender differences in cognitive abilities measured during the primary school phase. The Cognitive Abilities Test (CAT2E) (Thorndike *et al.*, 1986) is the most widely used test of reasoning abilities in the UK and is given to approximately one million school pupils each academic year. The test has ten separate sub-tests, grouped into three batteries that give standardised measures of Verbal, Quantitative and Non-Verbal reasoning abilities: a mean score is calculated from the average of the three standardised scores. One large-scale investigation of over 13,000 pupils (Strand *et al.*, 2006) analysed the CAT2E data taken at the age of 11 years and subsequent GCSE results. The results suggested a correlation of 0.81 and reported that a student with average cognitive ability had a 58 per cent chance of obtaining 5 GCSEs at grades between A⋆ and C (an important educational 'goal' in England). Students whose CAT2E scores were one standard deviation higher had a 91 per cent chance of achieving this 'national goal'. However, the authors accede that while 'non-g' factors such as school attendance, pupils' engagement, personality and motivation also have a substantial impact on educational attainment, a weakness of their investigation was that, despite the size of the sample and the rigour of the analysis, no information was collected on family background.

Heritability and abilities

As Chapter 6 will show, some variation in academic progress seems to be accounted for by factors outside of the educational system. One possible explanation for the importance of outside factors could be that general abilities such as intelligence are largely inherited, and that these determine subsequent academic achievements.

Bartels *et al.* (2002b) found a strong genetic correlation between cognitive ability (measured at five, seven and ten years old) and educational achievement at the age of 12 years, while Byrne and his colleagues (Byrne *et al.*, 2007), in their international study of twins, concluded that 'genes are the dominant influence on individual differences in word and non-word reading near the end of the first grade with high heritability also found in reading comprehension scores' (p. 94).

Studies over the years have shown that children show greater similarity of intelligence with increasing genetic similarity, and Bouchard and McGue (1981), summarising 111 studies in this area, found the correlations shown in Table 4.1.

TABLE 4.1 IQ correlations for different family relationships

Relationship	IQ correlations
Identical twins	Reared together 0.86; reared apart 0.72
Siblings	Reared together 0.47; reared apart 0.24
Parent/child	Natural 0.42; adopted 0.19

Source: based on data in Bouchard and McGue (1981).

It is important to realise, however, that most of the above correlations are relatively weak and that comparisons between them are not particularly meaningful. For instance, the parent–natural-child relationship correlation accounts for just above 17 per cent of the variance between the IQs of parents and those of their children, and the parent–adopted-child correlation accounts for just above 4 per cent of the variance. Since many children are adopted after already having been with their biological parent for a few years, the effects of the early home environment, as described below might easily account for this difference.

The strongest evidence supporting heritability comes from twin studies, particularly from the high similarity of the intelligence of identical twins, even when they have been separated and raised in different environments. Identical twins are originally formed from the same fertilised egg cell, or zygote, and their cells have the same genetic information – these twins are known as **monozygotic**. **Dizygotic twins** (non-identical or 'fraternal' twins) are formed from two fertilised eggs and share, on average, half of the segregating genes. So for characteristics that are fully determined by genes, monozygotic twins will be identical and dizygotic twins will be about 50 per cent alike on average. Monozygotic twins have very similar physical structures, including the brain. These findings seem convincing, but they have been subject to a considerable amount of criticism. In particular, the similar appearance of identical twins leads to their experiencing a much more closely similar environment than is usually the case with non-twin siblings. One reason for this is that identical twins who live together are often mistaken for each other and are generally treated in much the same way. Moreover, there is frequently cited evidence (for example, Byrne *et al.*, 2007) that even when siblings are separated, they often continue to have similar environments. For instance, adopted siblings are usually placed with families of similar background. Indeed, they are often placed with members of the extended family (e.g. aunts and uncles), where they can remain in contact with their original siblings and families. When Ceci (1990) had earlier reanalysed some twin study data, separating out the pairs of identical twins reared in dissimilar environments such as rural versus urban, he found that the IQ correlation was massively reduced – to only 0.27, which would only give a negligible role for genetics.

Thus although there are correlations between the general abilities of relatives within families, this does not prove that these are inherited. Greven *et al.* (2009), while reporting that commonalities in IQ and achievement can be primarily attributed to genetic factors, emphasise that 'heritability does not imply immutability' (p. 760), and factors such as personality, attitudes, motivation and early environment that are specific to the individual, also influence ultimate achievement.

Home background

Despite evidence that IQ tends to correlate with school success and attainment, the children of less-educated parents tend to perform more poorly in school and complete fewer years of education compared to children of better-educated parents. A large longitudinal USA study found that parenting quality in early childhood and in early adolescence largely accounted for the continuity in education across generations (Pettit *et al.*, 2009). The authors noted the particular negative effects of less-positive involvement and more harsh discipline in early childhood and less monitoring and academic support in early adolescence.

Family size and birth order

Negative associations between birth order and intelligence level have also been found in numerous studies (see Kristensen and Bjerkedal, 2007, for review). One possible way in which the family context could affect an individual's abilities is by the effects of a child's position within the family. According to Zajonc (2001), 'Birth rank is regarded as a proxy of promise, potential and actual ability' (p. 490). In his earlier (1976) **confluence theory**, he proposed that each successive child is born into a different family context. The first child receives a high level of parental attention, but subsequent children receive a reduced level of general intellectual stimulation since they are also interacting with an older sibling whose intellectual abilities are less than those of an adult. Zajonc estimates the general intellectual climate of the family by assigning a value of 30 to each adult and the actual age for each child (the newborn has a value of zero). Applying this to first- and second-born children in a family would give the outcomes shown in Table 4.2. Thus the theory predicts a reduced intellectual climate for larger families, and also suggests a birth-order effect, with successive children having progressively lower abilities. These predictions have been supported by findings from a study of 2,500 adolescents in Germany (Kirkcaldy *et al.*, 2009). The study demonstrated that family size was significantly correlated with intelligence score categories and that first-borns and only children displayed higher IQs than later-born children.

Zajonc, however, points out the importance of the particular intellectual climate that exists for each child at different ages. For instance, 'only children', who would appear to have the highest possible levels of adult stimulation since this is not shared out with any others, subsequently perform below all other first-born children. Zajonc's explanation for this is that children with younger siblings take on a tutoring role, and that in the process of doing this they further develop their own understanding. Although the picture of a kindly older child patiently helping their younger brother or sister may seem rather 'romantic' to parents reading this, children may nevertheless be able to develop their abilities by being in a more dominant role involving direction and management of their sibling(s). However, Zajonc (2001) insists, results from several studies of birth-order effects on intellectual performance may be discrepant because the effects are both positive and negative dependent on the age of the participants at testing: there should be no influence of birth order on

TABLE 4.2 Family context and intellectual climate

Family composition	Total scores + number in family	Average intellectual climate
Single newborn child	$\dfrac{30+30+0}{3}$	20
Second newborn child with two-year-old sibling	$\dfrac{30+30+2+0}{4}$	15.5

intellectual ability for children younger than 11 years but a positive influence of birth order for children older than 11 years when, arguably, successive children have had opportunities to tutor their younger siblings.

However, other studies have suggested that the relationship between decreasing intelligence and birth order is an artefact: when comparisons between families are made, there is recurring evidence that larger families are associated with lower socio-economic status and that this may cause the reduction in abilities (Rodgers *et al.*, 2000), and that the relation between birth order and IQ is dependent on the social rank of the family, not birth order as such (i.e. the fifth child in a middle-class family is likely to be more intelligent than the fifth child in a poorer family). In direct observations of the effects of family size, Hart and Risley (1995) found that the overall amount of verbal interactions in different-sized families stayed roughly the same but that having more children in a family led to each of them receiving a reduced share of attention. Despite these suggestive findings, family size and birth order are probably rather general effects and are unlikely to be able to account for much of the progress of individual children. To get closer to more powerful determinants, it is likely that one would need to consider those specific experiences that are likely to underlie such outcomes, and most investigations of such experiences have looked at the impact of parents on their children's development.

Direct effects of home background

It has now often been proposed that the cumulative influence of childhood environmental–contextual factors (e.g. parental education, family interactions, school ethos, local community) and individual-ised–personal factors (IQ, personality) shape enduring cognitive styles and outcomes later in life (Dubow *et al.*, 2009).

Parents in different home backgrounds have been found to vary in the extent to which they support their children with early learning tasks and with school work. One study (Elliott and Hewison, 1994) introduced a paired reading project to working-class children and their parents. The results suggested that the project brought the children's academic achievements up to those of children from the other social classes, indicating that parental support can be a direct factor leading to academic progress. Similarly, other studies have shown that middle-class parents typically use and foster the use of an elaborated linguistic code (see Chapter 9). Such a code is supposed to be more capable of embodying abstract ideas and knowledge, and to facilitate formal educational learning more readily. A later study by Locke *et al.* (2002) seemed to confirm that language skills were related to socio-economic factors and that children from good homes experienced a higher quality of verbal interaction with their parents which prepared them well for the verbally presented material in classrooms.

In order to address the effect of any class-based language-bias in intelligence testing, the non-verbal Raven's Matrices test is now often used to measure intelligence (for example, Harris *et al.*, 2009) However, one French study which looked at the performance of a group of six-year-old children on the Raven's Matrices test found that children from lower socio-economic backgrounds performed at a lower level than those from a higher socio-economic background when the test was given in its true, evaluative form. However, no significant difference in the scores between the two groups was noted when the test was subsequently introduced as a game that the children were asked to rate in terms of its suitability for other children of their age (Desert *et al.*, 2009). This would seem to suggest that children from higher socio-economic backgrounds respond more favourably to formal testing situations, a proposal supported by the findings of another longitudinal study (Gottfried *et al.*, 1994) which reported a direct correlation between parenting style and academic attainment. More recent work by Goldstein and Brooks (2009) has reiterated the importance of parents in nurturing 'a resilient mindset' in children. Such a mindset, they suggest, includes feelings, thoughts, perceptions and skills that children possess about themselves that contribute to how successfully they manage and cope with the many challenges that arise in their lives. Perhaps in this instance, such 'challenges' could be the test situations in which children find themselves regularly in school or, it could be wryly added, when they find themselves included in the sample of a research project!

Studies of children who have suffered early deprivation, such as orphans, highlight the important and long-lasting influence of home background. Following a sample of 324 Romanian orphans adopted into UK families, the effects of early institutional deprivation were found to persist up to the age of 11 years (Beckett et al., 2006). Another study of Romanian orphans used PET scans to demonstrate the plasticity of the brain, and the positive impact on intelligence of 'healthy' human interaction, in this study brought about by the children's adoption and dramatic change of home circumstance (O'Connor and Rutter, 2000). Further evidence from brain scans suggests that the home background can affect the way children's brains develop in response to rhyming sounds (frequently found to be a strong predictor of subsequent reading ability). Although only a small-scale study of a group of five-year-olds from mixed SES backgrounds, Raizada et al. (2008) found that in the children whose parents were of higher socio-economic status, language processing appeared to be more localised in the left hemisphere, as seen in most adults.

This perhaps explains the previously mentioned finding (Hart and Risley, 1995) that differences in children's language abilities were related to their different types of home background. Although the children in Hart and Risley's study all started to speak at about the same time, their spoken vocabulary, as measured by the number of different words used, varied significantly. By the age of three years, the observed cumulative vocabulary for children in the professional families was about 1,100; for the working-class families it was about 750; and for the 'welfare' families it was just above 500. There were also major differences in the language the children heard: in professional families, children heard an average of 2,153 words per hour; in working-class families the figure was 1,251 words per hour; and in welfare families only 616 words per hour.

Extrapolating these figures to cover four years of experience would give 11 million words heard by a child in a professional family, six million for a child in working-class family and three million for a child from the most under-privileged background. Hart and Risley's report of a strong relationship (0.78) between home background (gauged by a single parenting index) and children's general linguistic and intellectual development (see Figure 4.2) meant that the parenting measures were able to account for 59 per cent of the cognitive accomplishments of children at this age. Given that Hart and Risley's work was based on only about 26 hours of observations for each child, and that it missed out the first ten-month period, it seems likely that the true relationship between upbringing and ability could be even greater. If this is the case, then although genetics may still have some effect, its role would have to be much less than traditional estimates have indicated.

However, one possible alternative interpretation of the above findings is that children who were inherently more intelligent evoked more verbal interaction with/from their parents, or that intelligent parents (who talk more fluently) simply have more intelligent children. Several studies that have suggested that the effect of home background lessens as the child matures (e.g. Bartels et al., 2002a) raise the possibility that more enduring, genetic effects could have been the underlying basis of the observed differences in performance. The EPPE 3–11 project (a large-scale, national study of pre-school and primary-aged children), while acknowledging that the influence of the home background lessened between the ages of 7 years and 11 years, found that the mother's highest 'qualification level' and the home learning environment (i.e. the level of support offered at home) was still closely linked to children's later academic outcomes (Sylva et al., 2008). For example, mothers with a degree versus

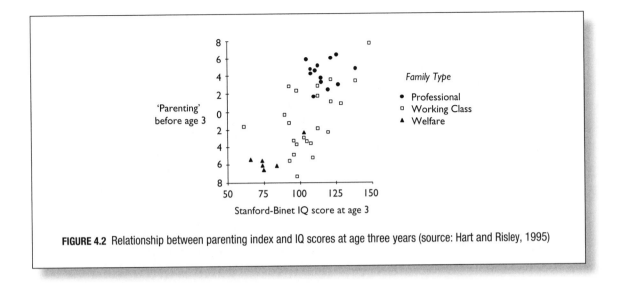

FIGURE 4.2 Relationship between parenting index and IQ scores at age three years (source: Hart and Risley, 1995)

no qualifications had a strong, significantly positive impact on children's English and mathematics attainment by the age of 11 years. Interestingly, the contribution of fathers has seldom been studied, yet Sylva and her colleagues reported the strongest predictor of a child's 'academic self-image' was in fact the father's academic qualification. The importance of the child's 'self-image', which Sylva found to be strongly linked to the child's overall progress in reading and mathematics, was also highlighted more negatively in one longitudinal study that looked at the effect of inter-parental conflict on children's academic attainment. This study found that children's tendency to blame themselves for their parents' arguments, rather than their sense of being rejected by parental hostilities, adversely affected their achievements in school (Harold *et al.*, 2007).

Effects of additional early support

The importance of early home experiences has led to the introduction of a number of programmes of additional early support. Hendriks (2001), in a major Dutch study, criticised the narrow focus on outcomes for *the child* which has been inherent in many early-intervention programmes and insisted that, if governments are to address social inclusion issues, then the involvement of *the whole family* is equally important for the child's development in the longer term. As a result, 'parents as partners' is a key theme underpinning a wide range of government initiatives and programmes to support families and young children (see Chapter 6 for more details).

Heritability and ethnic minorities

Children from certain ethnic minorities regularly underachieve in schools, and writers such as Herrnstein and Murray (1994) have taken this as evidence for an inherited basis for intelligence and achievement. However, other research findings indicate that such differences may be due to cultural factors rather than to any inherited differences in basic abilities. One early study (Scarr and Weinberg, 1976) looked at African-American children who, in view of their backgrounds, would have been expected to achieve at a low level but were adopted at an early age by white, middle-class American families. After being with their new families for some time (an average of about five years), these children came to be above the national average on school achievement tests, and it seems likely that they had taken on their adopted family's cultural experiences and perspectives on education. More recently, Reyna (2008) also attributed the comparatively low achievement of African-American pupils in American schools to the classroom 'culture' where teachers typically give these students less attention than their white counterparts, regardless of academic ability or performance.

So it seems that children's intellectual abilities and academic progress are in part determined by their environments, and that the quality of that environment can contribute to differences in achievements related to social class and ethnic groupings. By the time children come to school, there are already substantial differences in their experiences and achievements, and the continuing effects of children's backgrounds suggest that achieving equality is an impossible target but identifying individual needs and talents and ensuring children achieve their potential may be a more realistic goal.

Gifted and talented children

Gifted and talented children are those whose abilities are well above those of their peers. Historically, the needs of these more-able pupils were reported to have been met by the differentiated school system where grammar schools attracted, and in some areas still continue to attract, additional funding for those deemed 'more able' by an examination at 11 years of age (see Chapter 6).

In 2000, the need for targeted provision for this group (generally referred to as 'the GandTs') was announced by the House of Commons Education and Employment Committee with a specific DfES team dedicated to developing this initiative. This was followed by the inception of the National Academy for Gifted and Talented Youth (NAGTY, University of Warwick and DfES, 2003) to coordinate the development and delivery of specialised education for Gifted and Talented pupils up to the age of 19 years. A set of four grant-funded programmes has been part of the national 'GandT' initiative: these include master classes, summer schools, independent/maintained school partnerships and part of the Excellence in Cities programme.

Aware of criticisms regarding the 'social' advantage of middle-class children, the policy in England has contrasted sharply with other international initiatives in that it was explicitly committed to recognising giftedness and talent across the education system including those schools whose pupils' abilities may previously have been obscured by social or economic disadvantages. *Excellence in Cities* (DfEE, 1999c), an earlier, ambitious initiative, had set out to reverse underachievement in inner-city schools, and proposed 'gifted' pupils were those possessing high ability or potential in academic subjects while 'talented' pupils referred to children with high ability or potential in the expressive or creative arts or sport. By 2005, some 45,000 children had become members of the NAGTY yet, Bonshek (2005) suggests, guidance from Local Education Authorities has tended to focus on identifying skills or attributes, such as advanced language development and a level of knowledge that socially disadvantaged pupils would be unlikely to possess because they lack the 'social capital' to exhibit these. Perhaps in part response to this criticism and in line with the government aim to devolve funding to schools, the Academy is, however, now to be 'scaled back' (Stannard, 2009) with more government emphasis on disadvantaged 14–19-year-olds.

What is meant by 'gifted'?

It can be argued that children with a high level of general ability ('intelligence'), or a specific ability ('talent'), should be considered as a separate group needing identification and specialised forms of education to develop their potential. Rather than the 'compensatory' provision offered to less-able pupils, gifted and talented pupils need a different level, pace and style of teaching, appropriate to their learning abilities.

Ways of defining and identifying such children are, however, still based on inconsistent criteria and, arguably, biased forms of assessment. In the UK, the Qualification and Curriculum Authority acquiesces: 'It is impossible to set one way of identifying gifted and talented pupils ... but 'gifted' generally refers to the top 5% of the school population in academic subjects and 'talented' to the top 5% in other subjects' (Richardson, 2009). Although there is no universally agreed definition of giftedness, ongoing attempts at a definition have expanded to include the importance of non-cognitive factors such as motivation and commitment (Phillips and Lindsay, 2006). One study looking specifically at how to identify gifted pupils stated: 'with regard to standardised tests, it is important to differentiate between giftedness as the result of rapid development, and giftedness as a qualitatively different set of behaviors, attributes and characteristics' (Hartas *et al.*, 2008: 17).

An early checklist from the National Association for Gifted Children (NAGC, 1989) suggested the following attributes of the gifted child:

- learns more quickly than others;
- has a very retentive memory, can concentrate for long periods on subjects that interest him or her;
- has a wide general knowledge and interest in the world;
- enjoys problem-solving, often missing out the intermediate stages in an argument and making original connections;
- has an unusual imagination;
- has an odd sense of humour; and
- sets high standards for him- or herself.

However, using such a checklist might fail to identify pupils who do not show their underlying abilities in school; there may be some children who 'coast' through boredom, while others might hide their abilities so that they can fit in socially. At the same time, there have also been ongoing concerns that pupils from more affluent backgrounds are more likely to be recognised as 'able' by their teachers than their counterparts from more socially deprived backgrounds (Bonshek, 2005). To address this, the World Class Arena, an initiative that identifies and provides specialist support for gifted and talented students across the world and social class, suggests that the group should include those who achieve well above the predicted standard in national tests (SATs) *as well as* other students who may not perform well in traditional tests, but demonstrate keen insight, creative thinking and good problem-solving and mathematical skills (NFER, 2004).

Problems with the use of IQ to identify gifted children

The use of IQ testing to identify the gifted and talented has been criticised in part because of the lack of conceptual clarity as to the level at which 'giftedness' may be determined and in part because of the ever-growing reservations about the validity of such tests which may be culturally and socially biased (Black, 2001). An early study by Terman (1925) used an IQ of 140 or higher (achieved by only about 0.4 per cent of the population) as the identifying feature of gifted children, while others such as Freeman (1991) have used an IQ of 130 (achieved by about 2 per cent of the population). As shown in Figure 4.3, the general distribution of abilities also appears to be continuous, with no 'gap' or 'bump'

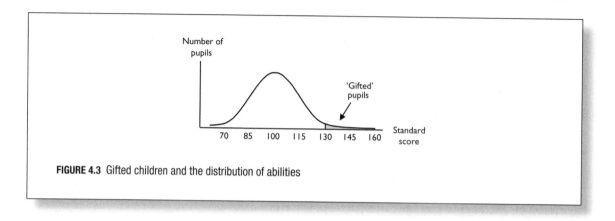

FIGURE 4.3 Gifted children and the distribution of abilities

at the higher end of the range; any cut-off point for higher abilities therefore seems to be as arbitrary as the cut-off for identifying children with lower abilities.

Meanwhile, Sternberg (2003) reports the cultural bias of intelligence assessments that focus on specific, 'narrow' types of measurable mental abilities (vocabulary, comprehension, memory or problem-solving) which, he claims, will identify only those who are 'school smart' or 'book smart'. Sternberg proposed instead the need to assess a broader, triarchic theory of intelligence. This involved measures of analytical intelligence (the ability to complete academic tasks that typically have one correct answer and form the basis of traditional intelligence tests); creative or synthetic intelligence (the ability to deal with new or unusual situations based on existing knowledge or skill) and practical intelligence (the ability to deal with everyday life based on existing knowledge and the context of the situation).

Bar-On (2007) subsequently extended Sternberg's theory to include

exceptionally high cognitive intelligence, potential for superior academic and professional performance, enhanced capability and drive to do one's best and realize one's potential, as well as an advanced ability to apply a variety of different approaches to solve problems in more innovative and creative ways when compared with others.

(p. 125)

However, using this broader view to identify the 'gifted and talented' has, it seems, proven to be a difficult task even for those appointed to teach them. In a review of how students were selected for the National Association of Gifted and Talented Youth summer school, Hartas and her colleagues (2008) noted 'diversity in the selectors' perceptions of what constitutes 'giftedness and talent' resulted in considerable variability in their decisions on which students were deemed 'entitled' to a place on the summer school. One selector described the ideal candidate as 'certainly gifted, enthusiastic, self-disciplining, good at talking (to other students) and really quite mature' which, Hartas warns, highlights the need for a more pluralist approach and acknowledgement of the 'individual characteristics and needs of gifted children' (p. 16).

In line with Gardner's (1993) theory of 'multiple intelligences', high-level achievements are often specific to one particular area such as music or art, and 'general ability' or appropriate social skills are often of little importance to these achievements. Yet, some individuals with an outstanding ability can be severely retarded, have little language and are often dependent on other people for their basic care. One such individual, Stephen Wiltshire, who has autism, is able to make highly detailed architectural drawings from memory, after only a brief inspection. Described as an autistic 'savant', he is not simply reading off from some form of 'photographic memory' since he is able to produce extensions of complex visual themes, and interestingly, his drawings are apparently a 'mirror image' of what he sees. The number of students with Autism Spectrum Disorders has risen sharply in the last few years and Horn (2009) suggests this highlights the importance of discriminating between pupils who excel in abstract thinking and those whose performance may be deemed 'gifted' in retaining factual information. Does an autistic 'savant' who can play every concerto he has ever heard yet scores only 80 on a standardised intelligence test qualify as 'gifted' or 'talented', either or both? If teachers are duty bound to support these pupils to achieve their full potential, it would seem more realistic to look at their particular attainments and special educational needs rather than to use arbitrary criteria and global labelling.

The origin of high abilities

Gifted children often show high attainments from an early age. Along with evidence that supports the possible heritability of IQ, this has been taken to indicate that such abilities are largely inherited. However, in a detailed review of the backgrounds of famous infant prodigies such as Mozart, Howe (1990) found that their abilities were invariably developed following intensive training and involvement, typically involving thousands of hours over many years. Although Mozart was supposedly a brilliant composer and performer by the age of four, his attainments appear to be largely because his father ensured that he spent much of his early life in intensive practice. His father also lied about young Mozart's age when exhibiting him, to exaggerate his uniqueness, and his first real achievements with composing did not come about until the twelfth year of his musical career, after years of rigorous training.

Some children pay a great price for such intensive and unbalanced development. The child prodigy William Sidis, once described as 'the most remarkable boy in the United States' (Wallace, 1986), invented a new table of logarithms at eight years and was able to speak six languages at ten. Unfortunately, this was the outcome of virtually complete domination by his psychologist father, and Sidis subsequently had severe social and emotional difficulties, eventually living an isolated, short and unfulfilling life.

Stimulating environments that are more supportive can nevertheless lead to high-achieving yet balanced individuals. Whether they then go on to make significant contributions, however, probably depends more on personality factors, chance and the opportunities that exist within society at the time (see Gladwell, 2008). Conventional general intellectual abilities may be an important foundation for unusual achievements, but it can be argued that children also need a different type of ability to enable them to generate new ideas or solutions to problems.

Creativity

Most tests used in schools involve homing in on a single correct answer to a problem, a process often referred to as 'analytic' or 'convergent thinking'. Guilford (1950) and subsequently Sternberg (2003), however, argued that it can be important for children to develop 'creative intelligence', or the ability to react to, or cope with, relative novelty. This is similar to de Bono's (1970) ideas about lateral thinking, which emphasise the importance of following different directions, as distinct from conventional or vertical thinking. Most definitions of creativity also emphasise that new ideas or solutions should be useful; generating numerous loose or unconventional associations may be meaningless if done simply for its own sake – although, as Mark Twain once so wryly commented, 'Anyone with a new idea is a crank – until the idea succeeds.'

Measuring creativity

Feldman and Benjamin (2006) found that creativity testing in education has never really 'caught on' (p. 331), in part because of the difficulty in devising appropriate tests. In an attempt to measure creative ability, Guilford *et al.* (1978) devised a series of creativity tests to measure divergent-thinking abilities (which are indicated by the ability to generate multiple, alternative solutions to a problem) rather than the convergent-thinking skills measured by standardised IQ tests (which demand a single correct response). One such test, the Alternative Uses test, for example, seeks alternative uses for a brick, i.e. uses beyond the more usual 'house-building' response. Such ideas might include 'building a wall', 'building a house', 'using as a paperweight' or 'using as a toy for a baby elephant'. These would score 4 for fluency (one for each of the ideas), 3 for flexibility (concepts of 'building', 'weight' and 'toy') and 1 for originality (the 'toy' concept). However, one negative for this approach has been Torrance's finding (1988) that the correlations between creativity (as measured on divergent-thinking tasks) and later creative performance were at best only about 0.3. Runco (2006) suggests this low correlation occurs because 'Divergent thinking is not synonymous with creativity' (p. 250).

Creativity and intelligence

Early studies by Hasan and Butcher (1966) found that children's scores on divergent-thinking tests could show a correlation as high as 0.70 with their intelligence tests results. However, the finding that this relationship seems to hold only when students were told to generate as many ideas as possible would seem to confirm Runco's (2006) claim that intelligent students can be creative when directed, but many of them would not naturally give creative responses automatically. More recent studies have also noted that memory-based strategies often contribute to high performance in divergent-thinking tasks (Gillhooly *et al.*, 2007) yet, as suggested in Chapter 3, scores on working memory tests are found also to correlate highly with overall intelligence (Alloway *et al.*, 2004). So, it seems likely that a certain threshold amount of general knowledge, intelligence and divergent-thinking skills can help in generating a range of different ideas. However, once you have enough of these underlying abilities, then a creative personality style probably becomes important in itself.

Creativity, personality and subject choice

On the basis of their analysis of personality factors, Cattell and his colleagues (1970) found that individuals presumed to be creative, such as university researchers, scored highly on intelligence, but that a number of personality traits were of equal importance. These involved being reserved, thoughtful and self-sufficient (introversion traits), generally imaginative and experimenting, and rather assertive and bold. It seems likely that people with these traits will be interested in and able to generate new ideas, and also will be prepared to persist with them. It is interesting to note, however, that this profile would not necessarily make them the easiest of people to get along with, and Getzels and Jackson (1962) found that creative students were not as well liked by their teachers as the more conformist and conventional ones.

While scores on tests of divergent thinking have also been found to correlate significantly with real-life measures of creative behaviour such as writing novels or plays and entrepreneurial abilities

(Plucker, 1999), earlier research by Hudson (1966) suggests that these divergent-thinking abilities might also be important in determining pupils' choice of academic subjects. In particular, he found that arts students scored higher on divergent-thinking tests and that science students, particularly those doing physics, scored higher on convergent-thinking tests. Later research, however, found that when science students were given some examples of what was expected of them, they were then able to generate more ideas. It seems likely, therefore, that real-life creativity may depend on a number of different intellectual and personality factors coming together in situations that encourage and acknowledge creative ideas. The suggestion from one American study (Phelan and Young, 2003), that creativity is simply the product of high intelligence combined with a low level of inhibition, may prompt the need to consider the importance of confidence in the creative process.

The creative process

Maier (1931) demonstrated the importance of reconceptualising the problem in a classic investigation of creative thinking where he gave subjects the task of joining together two lengths of string that were hanging from the ceiling. The difficulty was that each string was not long enough to allow someone holding one piece to be able to reach the other. When subjects became 'stuck', Maier prompted them towards a solution by brushing against a string to set it swinging. This was usually enough to enable the subjects to restructure the problem to become one of creating a pendulum by using some handy pliers as a weight. This then enabled them to get hold of both strings when the pendulum swing brought them closer together.

According to this approach, a key element of creativity involves breaking a 'set' (a fixed way of seeing or thinking about things that limits the development of new ideas). Known as *functional fixedness*, this was also demonstrated by Duncker (1945) in a task where people were given the task of supporting a candle from a wall using objects that included a box of candles and some tacks. Since people saw the box only as a holder, most of them failed to arrive at the solution, which involved pinning the inside of the box on to the wall to act as a base. This 'set' was overcome by providing the subjects with a different verbal label that enabled them to see the box as having other possible functions.

Sternberg (2006) argues that true creativity requires a confluence (or 'coming together') of six distinct but interrelated resources: intellectual abilities, knowledge, styles of thinking, personality, motivation and environment. This would seem to be eminently demonstrated by Picasso's painting *Guernica* which 'evolved' from earlier, very similar paintings. Arnheim (2006) argues *Guernica* should be regarded as 'research and experiment' not least because of Picasso's own summary: 'I never do a painting as a work of art. I search constantly and there is a logical sequence in all this research' (p. 13). Similarly, the sudden 'discovery' of the structure of DNA in fact took a number of years and depended on a great deal of contemporary work by other researchers.

The *Geneplore model* derived by Smith *et al.* (1995) describes the interplay of generative and exploratory processes in developing new and useful ideas. As shown in Figure 4.4, the 'generative stage' involves a range of normal cognitive processes that can result in 'pre-inventive structures'. These can then be explored to assess their creative possibilities, or the process can be repeated to consider more structures and possibilities. This model also emphasises that the overall process involves considering constraints about the functions of what is needed and the usefulness of what is arrived at.

The implications of this approach are that creativity does not depend on some vague form of 'insight', and that it can be developed by encouraging students to use these types of techniques and processes. There is indeed evidence that creativity and elements of the creative process can be developed in school by the use of appropriate techniques.

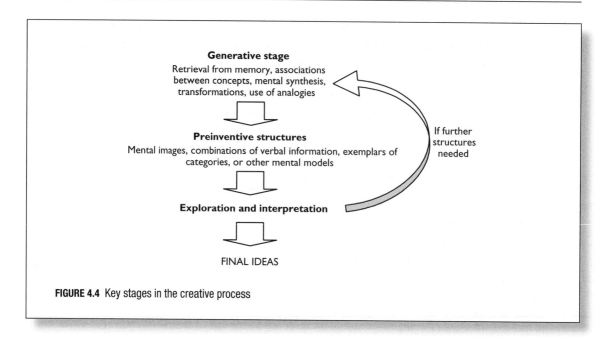

FIGURE 4.4 Key stages in the creative process

Facilitating creativity

Although Torrance (1963) argued previously that teachers tend to discourage creativity (since independence and divergent thinking can interfere with the normal convergent processes of teaching), there is now increased British interest and a co-ordinated, government-sponsored movement to enhance creativity among schoolchildren. Despite the current emphasis on whole-class teaching in British schools, the DfES (2003) and the National Advisory Committee on Creative and Cultural Education Committee have insisted that schools foster the development of greater individuality and creative abilities 'in an atmosphere in which teachers' creative abilities are properly engaged' (NACCCE, 1999: 90). Whilst the implication is that teachers should be aware of the need for creativity in pupils and foster it when possible, Galton (2008) predicts that, without an understanding of the underlying principles of creative practices, teachers are unlikely to sustain the approaches over the longer term. Such understanding could be developed by regular training programmes but it seems unlikely that in-service programmes aimed at encouraging this more 'creative engagement and reflection' would at the moment fit well with the need for schools to cover a prescriptive curriculum in order to meet the exacting targets of, say, the National Literacy Strategy (Cremin, 2006). Following on from this, Pell and colleagues (2007) proposed that the testing regime endemic in National Curriculum classrooms, where achievement rather than effort is rewarded, encourages greater extrinsic motivation which, other studies suggest, undermines creativity (see Prabhu et al., 2008). Interestingly, in an earlier investigation, Lepper et al. (1973) found that children who expected a reward for doing drawings actually produced more of these but they were of lower quality than the drawings of children who did not expect the reward (see Chapter 5).

Covington and Crutchfield's (1965) study demonstrated, however, that students were able to develop their ability to use creative techniques by following a course of programmed instruction.

This involved 16 cartoon text booklets, each featuring mysterious and baffling situations to be explained. As part of their explanation process, pupils were encouraged to generate ideas and then to compare these with a range of illustrative examples of relevant, fruitful and original ideas. Each lesson was designed so that students gradually worked towards the solution and were eventually brought to the stage where they could make the final discovery for themselves. An evaluation of the abilities of children who had completed this course demonstrated more persistence and willingness in their general school work and greater motivation in solving problems that required more diverse 'thinking skills'.

Thinking skills

More recently, investigations into individual differences have attempted to see whether it is possible to develop these thinking skills by appropriate teaching techniques.

A great deal of 'thinking' depends on using existing knowledge or information, and there is now growing evidence that the efficiency of working memory may influence the ability to use thought to learn and to solve problems to a greater extent than intelligence itself (Alloway, 2009). Thinking can act on different types of representations, such as verbal categories or words, when we can literally talk to or reason with ourselves, or imagery, when we visualise a representation of what we are concerned with. Other forms of thought can involve more abstract features, and much of the time we are probably not consciously aware of the processes involved.

Whatever the form that thinking takes, much of it depends upon concepts being activated and linked together in some meaningful way. Eysenck and Keane (1995) considered that the key operations involve **reasoning**, the use of information to make **inferences**, and **decision-making**, by which people evaluate likely outcomes and select between alternatives. These operations can be used to develop further concepts, and to establish additional rules about the ways in which they relate together.

Reasoning can involve logical processes, whereby inferences are made according to certain propositions. The strongest arguments are based on deductive reasoning, where the conclusion must be valid if the original premises are true. For example:

A capital city is a country's seat of government. Lima is the capital of Peru.
Therefore, Lima is the seat of government of Peru.

People appear to be able to follow such logical processes, but also need to use inductive reasoning, which involves reaching a conclusion on the basis of specific instances or information. For example:

Mrs Smith qualified as a teacher. Mrs Smith works in a school.
Therefore, Mrs Smith works as a teacher.

Although this conclusion would probably be correct, it is also possible that Mrs Smith, although a qualified teacher, works in the school as a classroom assistant. In everyday situations, pupils will use their general knowledge and inferential understanding of their world to arrive at likely solutions.

Practical implications

'Wrong' answers to questions asked by a teacher are often due to pupils basing their reasoning on familiar premises and knowledge which are therefore logical and meaningful *to them*. For instance:

TEACHER: What would you usually go into an off-licence for? (*Looking for the answer 'Alcohol'.*)
PUPIL: Some fags, sir.

Rather than criticising or discarding such answers, it would be better for teachers to acknowledge the thinking and knowledge behind them and then to give prompts to extend the reasoning to arrive at the desired outcome, for instance:

TEACHER: Yes, you could, but why do you think they need to be licensed? What do they sell that has to be controlled?
PUPIL: Booze, sir.

Decision-making also appears to be based upon logical, probabilistic judgements. If pupils need to choose between possible solutions for a problem, they will assess the likelihood that each of the outcomes will achieve their goals before making a choice. Much of the time, however, the way in which people think or the decisions they arrive at are simply the result of applying knowledge or behaviour that worked in the past.

People typically generalise from previous situations with similar features, or even use more complex analogies, often with models that incorporate the key elements and functions of a system. In understanding the structure of the atom, for instance, it can be useful to compare it with the solar system, with the sun representing the nucleus and the planets representing the electrons. This can help promote understanding of other features such as electron shells, as being similar to a number of planets in the same orbital sphere. In general, then, although thought can be logical, it is often based on wider knowledge and understanding.

Problem-solving

Many educational tasks involve problem-solving, such as answering higher-level questions and investigative work. Problem-solving corresponds to Gagné's (1965) highest level of learning and involves both reasoning, to combine and apply concepts and rules, and decision-making, to evaluate different outcomes.

Early descriptions of the problem-solving process considered that it covers a number of stages and strategies in progressing towards a final solution. Wallas's (1926) classic description of creative problem-solving included:

preparation: definition of problem, observation and study
incubation: laying the issue aside for a time
illumination: the moment when a new idea finally emerges
verification: checking it out.

In education, many problems are relatively well-defined and discrete. For instance, pupils might be given the task of working out the percentage that corresponds to a particular fraction. One way of

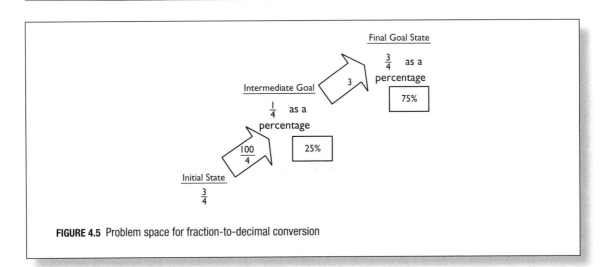

FIGURE 4.5 Problem space for fraction-to-decimal conversion

explaining this involves the use of a 'problem space'. This is a model that demands initial and goal states (Figure 4.5) and indicates how the person tackling a problem can identify intermediate sub-goals and appropriate strategies for achieving them. Whenever possible, pupils should be encouraged to specify where they want to end up – that is to say, what will constitute a solution.

They should also be clear about what they initially know, or need to know, and then should set up intermediate goals that will bring them closer to the final goal. Often, problem-solving can be helped with visual models such as drawings.

Knowledge and rules

Problem-solving that is relatively 'knowledge poor' has to depend on the use of general rules and principles. These can be investigated, and can be developed in children with logical puzzles such as the Towers of Hanoi problem (Figure 4.6). This involves moving three different-sized discs one at a time on to different pegs until they are all stacked in an identical way on the farthest peg, without ever placing a larger disc on top of a smaller one.

A generally important 'rule of thumb' principle (known as a **heuristic**) is to set up an intermediate state that is part-way towards the goal, then to look for ways of solving that simpler problem. This principle is commonly referred to as **the means–end heuristic**. With the Towers of Hanoi, applying it involves the intermediate goal of getting the largest disc on to the farthest peg, as shown in Figure 4.7; this in its turn can be achieved by first moving the two smaller discs on to the middle peg.

As shown in Figure 4.8 the problem can then be completed in three more moves.

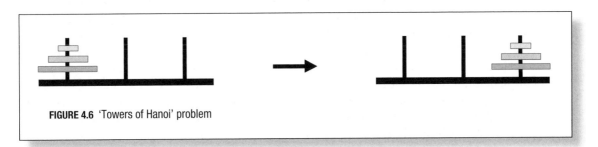

FIGURE 4.6 'Towers of Hanoi' problem

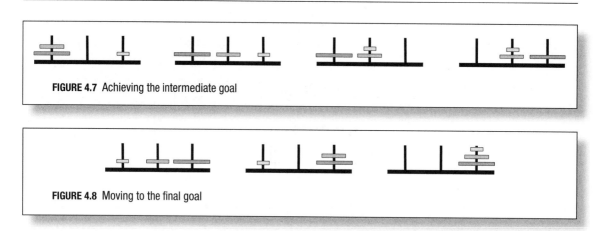

FIGURE 4.7 Achieving the intermediate goal

FIGURE 4.8 Moving to the final goal

The principles involved here can be used across a range of other practical problem areas, and this rule is therefore an example of a 'domain-independent' heuristic. Other heuristics can be more powerful, but these are usually 'domain-specific' and are not so readily transferrable to other areas of knowledge. With the Towers of Hanoi problem, a specific heuristic would be that 'the moves need to take place in a temporally forward direction and often involve separating the upper discs before combining them again', so that problem-solvers typically restrict forward-planning activities to just one or two moves ahead of the current problem state. Davies (2000), however, has suggested that problem-solvers may also engage in retrospective planning processes in order to try to avoid previous states or positions. This could suggest that 'learning from one's mistakes' is also an important problem-solving skill!

Use of thinking skills

A range of thinking skills can be generally useful in school work, including domain-independent strategies such as the 'means–end' heuristic. Other techniques, apart from the one of setting up strategies for achieving goals, involve ways of structuring and linking information, such as Ausubel's (1968) **advance organisers**. Mayer (2003) defines an 'advance organiser' as information that is presented prior to learning and that can be used by the learner to organise and interpret new incoming information. Although, Mayer notes, advance organisers may be used automatically by 'good students', slower learners may benefit from prompts and an initial structure from the teacher. In a classroom setting, this often takes the form of a 'KWL' sheet encouraging the student to identify (before the lesson): 'What I already **K**now', 'What I **W**ant to know' and (after the lesson) 'What I **L**earned'.

Analogies are another common and powerful way to develop pupils' understanding of new ideas and processes. They involve likening something that is already known to whatever is being studied, and effectively involve transfer of knowledge from one domain or context to another. Chenn *et al.* (1995) investigated the way in which analogies can be used by studying eight-year-old children's ability to solve riddles such as: 'A boy walked on a lake for 20 minutes without falling into the water. How did he do this?' One approach to help children with this problem could be to give them an abstract principle which does not include any causal relationship; for example: 'Some liquids can become hard. Heavy things can be held up.' However, when the investigators tried this, the 'abstract' nature of the information actually interfered with the children's ability to solve the problems. Their performance was greatly improved, however, when they were given or encouraged to generate concrete examples alongside the abstract principle; for example, 'Heavy objects can be held up by liquids when the liquids become hard. The truck drove over the hard lava without sinking.'

Practical implications

Analogies therefore seem most effective when they are closely associated with the target problem and where an overarching principle can be applied. One impediment in this process occurs, however, when pupils fail to notice the similarity between the examples and the problem they are being asked to undertake. It may be the case that teachers then initially need to 'guide' their pupils' thinking in line with Bruner's now famous adage, 'Discovery like surprise favours the well prepared mind' (Bruner, 2006).

Learning effective **mnemonic** strategies and other study skills can enable students to develop their knowledge and understanding whilst making it is less likely that forgetting will occur. More recently, understanding of the effectiveness of these strategies has been enhanced by research into how memory affects learning generally and, in particular, by research that indicates how working memory can be improved (Gathercole, 2008).

Activity

Mnemonics are often used as 'spelling' tips, for example:

Big Elephants Can Always Understand Small Elephants ('because')
Only Cats' Eyes Are Narrow ('ocean')
Rhythm Helps Your Two Hips Move ('rhythm')

Can you think of some mnemonics you learned as a child? Can you create a new one?

Metacognitive skills

It is important for students to develop a range of thinking or learning skills, but equally important for them to select and use appropriate strategies when necessary. It may, for instance, be very effective to use a simple rehearsal technique with information that has little intrinsic meaning or that does not need to be retained for very long. Other material, however, which is more fundamental to an area of study, might require deeper learning techniques, based perhaps on links with existing knowledge (by establishing integrating principles), or by establishing an overall schema by using a 'knowledge map' such as the 'KWL' system mentioned previously.

Doing this involves conscious monitoring and planning, and the term 'metacognition' is typically used to describe this conscious reflection by a child on his or her own thinking skills after the problem-solving activity has been completed (Adey *et al.*, 2007). Biggs (1985) found that students who were capable of such metacognitive thought had high general abilities which presumably enabled them to develop and use these skills. These students also had a belief that any progress was due to their own efforts, which appeared to motivate them to utilise their independent abilities. Although a review by Wang *et al.* (1990) indicated that metacognitive ability is one of the most important variables that affect students' progress, Biggs found that many students did not appear to have developed this skill, even at the upper end of secondary school. It has, therefore, become of considerable research interest to know whether metacognitive abilities are just a consequence of high general abilities, or whether it is possible to formally teach this reflective approach to thinking.

Programmes to develop thinking skills

Claxton (2007) suggests that education is not about the amount of knowledge that pupils learn in school, but 'their appetite to know and their capacity to learn' (p. 1), and there have been many attempts to enhance both pupils' appetite and capacity to learn by teaching thinking skills.

Feuerstein *et al.* (1980) developed a programme of assessment and teaching techniques based on instrumental enrichment, as a way of improving general thinking abilities. Following the Second World War, groups of young people flooded into Israel from Europe and North Africa. Many of them had suffered traumatic early experiences and, their results on traditional psychometric tests destined them to be 'ineducable'. Feuerstein worked on discovering what cognitive abilities the young people lacked and then used 'instrumental enrichment' techniques, which helped the students to see problems, make connections, motivate themselves and improve their learning. Early informal evaluations of this by Feuerstein were very positive, but subsequent evaluation of this approach by Blagg (1991) found that, although there did not seem to be any measurable effects on pupils' academic progress, teachers' attitudes towards the approach were generally positive, and pupils appeared to be more active in their learning and more aware of different strategies they could use.

Following on from this, Blagg and his colleagues (Blagg *et al.*, 1993a) therefore developed the Somerset Thinking Skills Course for 10-to-16-year-old children in school, which was subsequently extended into *Thinking Skills at Work* (Blagg *et al.*, 1993b) for people preparing or returning to work. These courses teach a range of general skills including problem-solving techniques, organising and memorising, analysis and synthesis, the use of patterns, and the specific use of analogies and comparisons. They also emphasise the need to analyse and organise responses to the demands of new situations, and use prompts such as 'PLUG' (PLan, Understand, and Go) to trigger the necessary habits of thought. These skills are linked and applied to realistic tasks and settings to ensure transfer and generalisation. A number of evaluations of these courses by Blagg and his team (Blagg *et al.*, 1994) indicate that they appear to result in significant improvements in abilities related to school learning and early vocational development.

However, a number of the successful interventions to enhance cognitive ability (see reviews in Cotton, 2002) have involved high teacher:pupil ratios and as a result were costly. Topping and Trickey (2007), however, undertook a study using a programme that combined the Philosophy for Children (P4C) programme (Lipman *et al.*, 1980) with the Thinking Through Philosophy programme (Cleghorn, 2002). This combination programme was more cost-effective, with minimal teacher input, and relied more on peer interaction incorporating much of the verbal dialogue considered to be a vital factor in providing children with a rich learning environment (Adey, 2001). The multiple-choice Cognitive Abilities Test (CAT3) (Smith *et al.*, 2001) was administered both pre- and post-intervention with a pre–post period of 16 months, and the results suggested significant gains in verbal ability, non-verbal ability and quantitative-reasoning ability that were irrespective of pupil school, class, pre-intervention ability and gender. Interestingly, those in the middle quartile of the pre-test ability range showed the greatest gain, while those in the upper quartile showed the smallest.

Cognitive Acceleration Through Science Education (CASE)

Cognitive acceleration programmes such as this, then, have not only claimed to promote the overall process of cognitive development but also propose that the child will be able to transfer the general intellectual principles (for example, spatial perception) to other tasks without specific instruction from the teacher.

Adey and Shayer (1993) developed a highly effective form of metacognitive training based on developing pupils' general thinking skills in science. Known as Cognitive Acceleration through Science Education (CASE), the programme was designed specifically to promote the type of higher-level or abstract thinking (formal operations) proposed by Piaget. Normally, relatively few children of early secondary age would be capable of such abstract thinking, which involves being able to manipulate the key features of problems, and to ask 'what if?' questions. The programme involved Year 7 and Year 8 pupils, with a session every two weeks. The two-year programme, based on Vygotsky's social construction theory that learning develops best in a social context, encouraged children to reflect on their own thinking and to discuss with each other how they approached problems set by the teacher. The problems were complex, real-life situations such as how to organise food in a larder, or predicting the force needed to raise a heavy load in a wheelbarrow.

These experiences appear to be highly effective in raising the overall long-term level of children's academic achievements, as shown by their GCSE performance three years later. Since the GCSE results for a school are normally closely related to the achievement and ability of its intake, an evaluation by Shayer (1996), shown in Figure 4.9, compared schools in terms of the performance of their intakes. These findings show that the overall effects of running the CASE programme was to increase the number of C grades or above in science by about 18.8 per cent. Achievements were also raised in other subjects, such as mathematics (14.9 per cent) and English (15.6 per cent), indicating that the programme was having a generalised effect on thinking and learning skills across a range of curriculum areas.

Another study (Askew *et al.*, 1997) also found positive effects on mathematics learning when teachers used similar teaching techniques, based on pupils making comparisons between their own problem-solving approaches and those of other students. The CASE approach has also been found to continue to have strong and positive effects when developed by workers other than the original team, indicating that the findings were not just due to early enthusiasm and commitment. The general approach was therefore extended by the original authors to cover mathematics education, and to develop thinking skills at earlier educational stages.

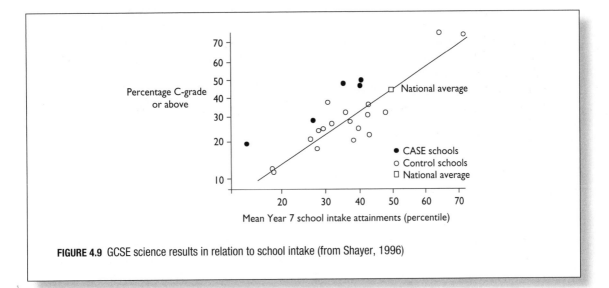

FIGURE 4.9 GCSE science results in relation to school intake (from Shayer, 1996)

In 2007, the CASE model was again used by an inner-London education authority who wished to increase the life chances of its pupils from more disadvantaged areas at the earliest stages of their school life, i.e. at the age of six years (Adey *et al.*, 2007). By targeting the concrete operational stage of cognitive development, the authority hoped not only to enhance academic achievement but also to positively influence subsequent social outcomes such as unemployment, drug abuse and teenage pregnancy. The intervention over one year introduced the children to a range of problem-solving tasks, and when the tasks had been completed, the children were asked to reflect on their thinking by discussing how they had solved the problems. The results suggested that the programme was of particular value 'in a society which had moved rapidly from one needing much thoughtless manual labour to one requiring independent and individual thought-in-action from a far higher proportion of the populace than ever before' (p. 23).

The government's emphasis on raising standards has encouraged many schools to adopt accelerated learning techniques. Many of these programmes are commercially published and, it has been argued, serve to meet the needs of professional teachers who lack confidence in adopting alternative teaching and learning strategies. The comparative absence of reliable evidence as to whether these published programmes lived up to the highly successful reputation claimed by their publishers caused the DfES to commission a review of the programmes. The review concluded that 'accelerated learning is more about rhetoric and rumour than research' (Brain *et al.*, 2006: 419), but acceded that the programmes had encouraged the teachers themselves to experiment and try out new ideas. A further positive note has come from a subsequent study that has reported an improvement in the self-esteem of secondary school pupils, facilitated by some of these programmes (Dewey and Benton, 2009).

Cognitive style

The study of intellectual abilities is usually quantitative; that is to say, it is concerned with the general level of academic attainments. A complementary approach is to look at differences in the way in which individuals deal with information and how these are matched with different types of tasks. 'Cognitive style' is a term used to describe the way individuals think, perceive and remember information, or to describe their preferred approach to using such information to solve problems. It is therefore usually seen as a stable feature that underpins an individual's functioning in a number of different areas. **Cognitive style** is directly contrasted with **cognitive strategies**, which can vary from time to time and can be learned and developed according to the demands of particular tasks (see 'Thinking skills' above, pp. 95–102).

Performance on cognitive style tests has previously led some critics such as Carroll (1993) to argue that analytic thought is really just one aspect of general ability, but more recently Peterson and her colleagues (Peterson *et al.*, 2005) have argued that individual differences on tests of cognitive style are independent of ability and personality.

An early approach by Witkin and his colleagues (Witkin *et al.*, 1977) set out to distinguish between **field-independent** and **field-dependent** cognitive types. Witkin developed a range of tests including the still-popular Embedded Figures Test. In this test (Figure 4.10), the person is shown a shape and asked to find it (embedded) in a large, more complex design.

The judgement of some people (the field-dependent group) is particularly affected by the context (i.e. by the background design), whereas the field-independent group tend to be more autonomous and analytic, and are able to disregard the background complexity. Interestingly, Witkin's original study found that men were significantly faster at identifying the embedded figure than women. The

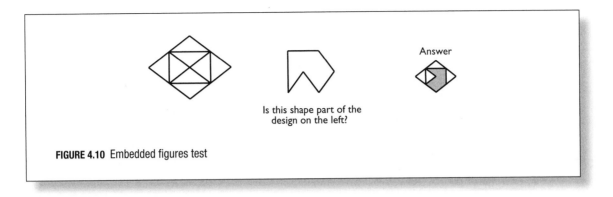

Is this shape part of the
design on the left?

Answer

FIGURE 4.10 Embedded figures test

more recent finding that those with autism, and their first-degree relatives, are also able to complete these tasks significantly faster than the normal population has led to one current theory that autistics might have an extreme form of the normal male brain (Baron-Cohen, 2003).

Other studies have also suggested the **impulsivity–reflectivity** types (Kagan *et al.*, 1964). This cognitive style has often been determined by the speed at which people make decisions under conditions of uncertainty and has typically been evaluated with the Matching of Familiar Figures Test (MFFT). This test assesses how quickly a person is able to match a particular shape with the correct one among a number of alternatives.

Integrating styles

Riding and Cheema (1991) first looked at the way in which individuals are inclined to represent information during thinking and, subsequently, by using a factor analysis of cognitive styles, found that most cognitive styles tend to cluster together into two fundamental groups: the **Verbal–Imager** and the **Wholistic–Analytic** (Riding and Rayner, 1998).

The Verbal–Imagery dimension determines whether an individual, when thinking, represents information verbally or in mental pictures. The two basic dimensions are assessed using the computer-presented Cognitive Styles Analysis or CSA (Riding, 1991). The three sub-tests first assess Verbal–Imagery preferences by presenting verbal statements to be judged 'true' or 'false'; half of the statements contain information about conceptual categories and the other half describe the appearance of items. Visual imagers tend to respond more quickly to the appearance statements.

The second two sub-tests assess the Wholistic–Analytic dimension, which determines whether an individual tends to organise information in wholes or parts by presenting pairs of complex geometrical figures that require a 'same/different' response, and then by presenting a series of one simple and one complex geometrical where the individual has to determine whether the simple shape is contained in the complex shape. As Figure 4.11 shows, Wholists tend to be more successful on the first task and Analysts on the second.

Implications of different cognitive styles

Although controversy exists over the exact meaning of the term 'cognitive style' and whether it is a single or multiple dimension of human personality, it remains a key concept in the area of education.

Witkin and his colleagues (1977) suggested that field-independent (analytic) teachers tended to be generally more formal, focusing on the work content rather than the learner, being more inclined to

Holists ══════════════════════════ **Analytics**

Intermediate

Tend to perceive and organise
information into loosely
clustered wholes and to make
rapid judgements based on
general, impressionistic features

Includes: Field independence,
Impulsivity

Tend to organise information
into clear-cut conceptual
groupings and take more time
over decisions, basing these on
logical and detailed analysis

Includes: Field independence,
Reflectivity

FIGURE 4.11 The wholistic–analytic continuum

criticise learners and explain why they are wrong. Field-dependent (wholist) students preferred group work and responded more to extrinsic motivation; field-independent learners on the other hand were likely to have more self-defined goals and to respond to intrinsic motivation.

Chinn and Ashcroft (2006) have also used the terminology **grasshoppers** and **inchworms** to discriminate between the different learning styles often noted in mathematics. They identified some learners as highly intuitive in the way they learn and do maths (the grasshoppers), who, if asked to find three consecutive numbers that add up to 33 they will divide 33 by 3 and arrive at 11, then quickly complete the trio with 10 and 12. Other children (the inchworms), however, are more analytic and formulaic approaching the task in a step-by-step style, probably adopting a 'trial and error' strategy.

Further research from Newcastle University suggests that additional factors may need to be considered when evaluating the effectiveness of teaching based on learning styles. In order to determine whether this style of teaching has a significant effect on either achievement or motivation, Coffield *et al.* (2004) point to the relationship between cognitive style and working memory. From a study involving a group of 13-year-olds, which included an assessment of working memory, Riding and his colleagues (Riding *et al.*, 2003) found that working-memory skills have a major influence on the performance of Analytics and Verbalisers, possibly because both employ a relatively detailed method of processing information as they learn. By contrast, the Wholists and Imagers were more intuitive, using a more economic method of processing. Recent findings from another study of working memory would seem to suggest that teachers should focus on developing skills innate in the Analytic and Verbaliser cognitive styles (Gathercole and Alloway, 2006).

The importance of working memory could perhaps also explain the earlier finding by Riding and Anstey (1982) that Verbalisers were superior at initially learning to read, which is consistent with the now generally acknowledged contribution of early phonological skills (a combination of phonological awareness and phonological memory) to reading (Passenger, 1997). Further work by Riding and Mathias (1991) also found that reading ability in 11-year-olds was significantly greater for Wholist–Verbalisers, with a mean reading quotient of above 120, compared with the overall mean of about 100. This major difference was presumably due to the superior combination of general abilities and phonological skills.

Riding and Pearson (1994) subsequently reported meaningful differences between school subjects, with students who scored high on the Wholist style being significantly better at school subjects such as French (Figure 4.12). A plausible explanation for this is that such subjects may depend on the ability

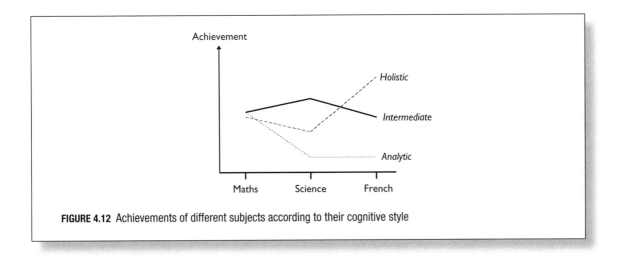

FIGURE 4.12 Achievements of different subjects according to their cognitive style

to retain the overall meaning or to use general patterns in the information studied. The intermediate style appeared to be best for subjects such as science, where analysis is important, but where elements may also need to be combined into general, wholistic theories. The extreme Analytic style appeared to be a disadvantage for learning most subjects, with the exception of mathematics where specific analytic abilities probably compensate for any inability to integrate information.

Riding and Douglas (1993) earlier suggested that mode of presentation can also be crucial in a classroom setting. They used a computer-presented tutorial on the topic of car brakes and found a significant effect in the text-plus-picture condition which appeared to particularly suit the Imager style (Figure 4.13). Although this is perhaps not a surprising finding, the size of the effect suggests presenting verbal information with a pictorial representation may be a sensible teaching strategy.

If a pupil has a similar cognitive style to the teacher, then it seems likely that the pupil will have a more positive learning experience. Similarly, the teacher who acknowledges the importance of cognitive style is more likely to attempt to identify and plan to meet the individual needs of the pupils he or she teaches.

Yet, cognitive style – or, rather, appropriate cognitive style – may, as Greenfield (2007) suggests, be culturally determined: the inattentive, novelty-seeking, risk-taking behaviour typically, and often

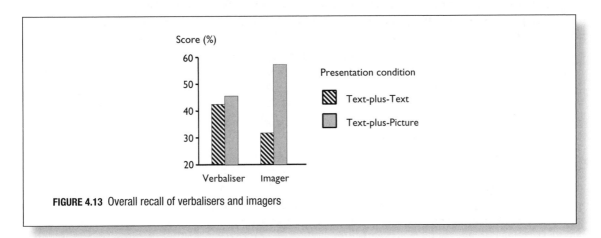

FIGURE 4.13 Overall recall of verbalisers and imagers

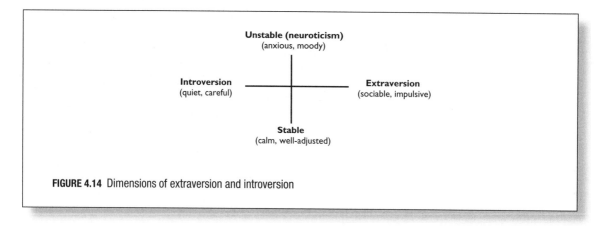

FIGURE 4.14 Dimensions of extraversion and introversion

negatively, associated today with attention-deficit/hyperactivity disorders may have aided the migration, improved the foraging and the early detection of dangers, necessary in early hunting civilisations. These skills, she notes, are not, however, considered 'desirable' characteristics in today's British classroom. However, these skills have evolved from exploration and experience and, as such, should perhaps be considered forms of cognitive diversity. As Greenfield suggests, 'Let's not lose sight of how society might benefit from "the nutters who do the crazy stuff". It must have been a nightmare to teach Mozart' (2007: 21).

Personality

Although results from IQ tests have been consistently associated with academic performance (Deary *et al.*, 2007), intelligence rarely accounts for more than 50 per cent of the variance in academic performance (Rhode and Thompson, 2007), and it has therefore been argued that non-cognitive factors, such as personality or even self-perceived ability (i.e. how good people think they are), may also contribute to academic success or failure.

Mischel (1986) describes personality as 'the distinctive patterns of behaviour (including thoughts and emotions) that characterise each individual's adaptation to the situations of his or her life' (p. 4); Jung (1964) first introduced the idea that these distinctive patterns of behaviour could be 'measured' by assessing individual levels of introversion (a tendency to reflect within oneself) or extraversion (a tendency to focus on the world around). Eysenck (1991) subsequently proposed a personality model based on three factors or traits, measuring high or low extroversion by the tendency to be sociable versus a preference for solitude and routine; high or low neuroticism by the tendency to be anxious versus an ability to cope with stress; and psychoticism demonstrated by the tendency to be aggressive and lack social empathy.

Eysenck's Personality Inventory (Eysenck and Eysenck, 1975), which identified extreme dimensions of personality (Figure 4.14), and subsequent work (Barrett *et al.*, 1998) found that, while stable extraverts tended to perform best in the primary school, this effect starts to reverse in secondary schooling, and by higher education, unstable introverts were found to achieve at a higher level.

One explanation for this could be that primary school learning experiences are more social and therefore favour the outgoing and confident child. Later education probably involves progressively more independent work in isolation, with anxious students being more motivated to work. Petrides *et al.* (2005) made an interesting observation on the contribution of personality to school achievement in their study of secondary-school pupils. They found that verbal ability was a powerful predictor of academic performance at GCSE level, but this was entirely mediated through academic performance at KS3 (two years earlier). Compared to verbal ability, the impact of personality traits on academic performance was weak, but an interesting gender-specific association was found: boys with low verbal ability are likely to perform less well academically if they are extraverted but, by contrast, boys of high verbal ability will perform well academically irrespective of their extraversion or introversion. The authors suggest this is readily explained because extraverts, who are pleasure-seeking and outgoing, and find themselves in a school environment that they perceive as alienating, will direct their interests to activities that are not conducive to educational attainment. Similarly, girls who were tough-minded, non-conformist and emotionally detached (Eysenck's psychotic personality) were less likely to achieve academically in part because their behaviour, perceived by teachers as 'unfeminine', would be likely to attract 'disproportionate penalties', which could result in this group of girls becoming alienated from school with resulting truanting or non-attendance.

Using more factors

One problem with personality research is that using different questionnaires or ways of analysing them is likely to result in the identification of different personality factors. However, developments in personality theory have consistently tended to converge on the importance of a 'five-factor' model, where the main personality traits are thought to be: agreeableness, extraversion, neuroticism, conscientiousness and psychoticism. Wolfe and Johnson (1995) had previously noted the importance of conscientiousness in education, finding that it accounted much of the variance in general grade achievement for college entrants. This effect was revealed by means of a shortened form which only used seven questions based on attributes such as perseverance, carefulness and reliability, so it is perhaps not particularly surprising that students who scored highly on these qualities were also generally good at studying. More recently, one study has proposed a more interesting link between personality and general ability. In a study of 4–6-year-old twins, Harris *et al.* (2007) found that agreeableness and conscientiousness were positively associated to intelligence, while neuroticism and psychoticism correlated negatively with intelligence.

Self-perceived abilities

The past 20 years has seen further evidence that individuals' self-perceived abilities (or SPAs) are also important predictors of academic attainment independent of intelligence (Spinath *et al.*, 2006), and recent studies have found that the association between intelligence, SPAs and academic achievement is relatively stable across the school years. Importantly, one twin study (Greven *et al.*, 2009) has produced evidence that, whilst half the variance in SPAs is due to genetic factors, the rest is due to other environmental factors. Yet to be determined is whether these 'other environmental factors' include the influence of the school, and whether the association between SPAs and academic attainment may be reciprocal.

Different frames of reference

A very different approach to personality is based on the humanistic perspective of Kelly (1955). According to this, an individual's conscious experiences and motivation (or personal 'constructs') help or hinder his or her understanding of the world and subsequent ability to achieve his or her full potential. Salmon (1988) considers that this more dynamic approach, unlike trait theories of personality, which are relatively rigid, enables us to emphasise the possibilities and the processes of change in the ways in which pupils and teachers come to view things. Unfortunately, difficulties can arise if there is a mismatch between the construct systems of pupils and teachers, in particular about what is the purpose of certain types of lessons. In one example quoted by Salmon, pupils regarded their Design and Technology lessons as being about 'making something' while their teachers saw the educational objective to be 'fostering design', a goal which was likely to be frustrated without the pupils' active understanding and involvement in this.

Educational implications

Entwistle (1972) found that certain personality factors correlate with success in certain subjects, and the significant prediction of key personality features such as 'conscientiousness' in general academic success indicates that it may be useful to incorporate measures of this into academic and vocational counselling.

Studies following the humanistic approach, which focus on the importance of the individual's personal construction and understanding of the world, have further identified the significant influence of a sense of 'well-being' on subsequent achievement. In school-aged children, 'well-being' has been seen to involve a positive sense of self or self-perceived ability (SPA), a growing sense of autonomy, a sense of feeling safe and secure and of being supported by an adequate home environment (Fattore et al., 2007).

Recurring evidence that personality, although largely inherited, can be influenced by environmental factors, suggests that effective teachers need the ability to plan activities that not only acknowledge individual attributes but aim to move pupils towards realising their own potential. This will, to a large extent, however, depend on teachers' understanding and determination that 'heritability does not imply immutability' (Greven et al., 2009: 760).

Summary

Differences between children are important because they indicate how learning experiences could be matched with pupils' thinking processes, cognitive style and personality. The growing evidence that intelligence, although biologically based, can be enhanced offers a challenge particularly to those working with pupils from disadvantaged backgrounds. Children with high abilities or who have a specific strength in some area do appear to benefit from interacting with others of similar high ability, but this can sometimes result in negative consequences in terms of their ability to interact with their peers whose ability is not in the 'gifted' range. At the present time, too, attention needs to be given to the financial consequences of providing 'elitist' camps and programmes for a minority group, for whom the exact selection criteria, it would appear, have still not been decided.

Creativity involves generating novel ideas or solutions to problems and appears to depend on a sufficient level of general abilities together with certain personality traits and motivational characteristics. Early ideas about creativity saw it as involving a different way of thinking about a new topic, but more recent theories emphasise the ability to extend and apply existing knowledge and abilities. Creativity in pupils appears to be encouraged by less-formal teaching with an emphasis on intrinsic motivation, as well as specific techniques.

Thinking processes that underlie general ability and creativity can be based on logical reasoning as well as the use of previous experiences and knowledge. With problem-solving, traditional theories have emphasised the role of the unconscious, resulting in a sudden insight into a solution. Recent developments, however, suggest that problem-solving comes from deriving and achieving successive goal states, using heuristic (procedural) rules. In schools there is now a drive to develop general thinking skills with educational programmes, some of which appear to be highly effective.

Pupils can vary according to how they typically organise and process information – their cognitive style. Many of the approaches in this area consider two key dimensions: the Wholistic–Analytic and the Verbaliser-Imager styles. These have important implications in the classroom where learning is likely to be most effective when materials and teaching techniques are matched with pupils' styles.

Personality factors related to effort and involvement contribute greatly to pupils' achievements, but there can also be conflicts due to the different ways in which pupils and teachers view the educational process. Teachers and educationists, then, have a major contribution to make if education is seen as expanding the ways in which children construe the world and develop their sense of self and belief in their own capabilities.

Key implications

- Intelligence is a socially constructed concept in that it relates to the goals and aims of a specific society. In the Western world, the definition of intelligence revolves around academic attainment.
- Children's achievements are no longer assumed to depend solely on some innate unchangeable ability.
- Children's intellectual abilities and academic progress are in part determined by the quality of the environments to which they are exposed (at home and at school).
- Creativity and thinking skills can be fostered by particular teaching approaches.
- Greater emphasis is now being directed towards enhancing a broader learning environment to meet individual needs and encourage individuals to achieve their potential.
- Taking account of the full range of individual differences (ability, social/cultural background, cognitive style and personality) can both inform and enhance the educational experience.

Further reading

Boyle, Matthews and Saklofske (2008), *The SAGE Handbook of Personality Theory and Assessment*: this two-volume series reviews the major contemporary personality models (Volume 1) and associated psychometric measurement instruments (Volume 2) that underpin the scientific study of this important area of psychology.

Gladwell (2008), *The Outliers: the Story of Success*: Gladwell argues that when we try to understand success we normally start with the wrong question. We ask 'What is the person like?' when we should really be asking 'Where are they from?' The real secret of success turns out to be surprisingly simple – it hinges on the culture people grow up in and the way they spend their time.

Shenk (2010), *The Genius in All of Us: the New Science of Genes, Talent and Human Potential*: Shenk dispels the myth that one must be born a genius and convincingly makes the case for the potential genius that lies in us all. By integrating new research from a wide range of disciplines – cognitive science, genetics, biology, child development – he suggests that we are not prisoners of our DNA, and we all have the potential for greatness.

Discussion of practical scenario

Christine will need to read any background notes she is offered about her pupils, particularly those who may be starting school with a history of identified needs and/or the involvement of social workers and medical professionals. She needs to ensure her classroom is physically well-prepared and is a safe, welcoming environment in which she can encourage independence in the children from the start of the term and give herself more time to get to know the children and their parents/carers.

She will initially need to employ a range of informal observational techniques to identify individual abilities, personalities and learning styles. After a few weeks, possibly the first half-term, she may need to follow this up with more formal assessments, perhaps using checklists which she can discuss with her teacher–mentor or the school's Special Educational Needs Co-Ordinator (SENCO). Christine will need to remember that parents have an important part to play in providing background information and, where possible, in supporting the children at home by undertaking regular reading activities.

She may benefit from further training from her local authority Looked After Children Education Service (LACES) and also any advisory staff who can offer her advice in supporting children who are temporarily separated from their family, particularly when family members may be serving in a war zone.

Student engagement and motivation

Chapter overview

- Motivation
- Behavioural approaches to motivating students
- Why is motivation important for education?
- Achievement motivation
- Self-determination theory
- Flow
- Attributional processes
- Academic self-esteem
- Needs
- Student subcultures
- Teacher expectations
- Empowerment
- Task involvement and cognitive development
- Stress in the classroom
- Emotions and their functions

Practical scenario

At King Charles III secondary school, most subject teachers are finding the lowest sets in the final year difficult to motivate. Almost all these pupils have limited academic skills and few will achieve a GCSE. Some subjects do, however, aim for certification when the pupils have completed a relevant course. Although these teaching groups are relatively small (comprising about 14 pupils each), it is hard to involve them in class work and there are often behavioural problems that interfere with attempts to get through any formal work. The various subject heads are wondering if there is anything more that they could do to make this situation easier.

continued

What view do you think the pupils in these classes have of themselves relative to school and how might they have formed these opinions?

What changes might you make to the organisation of classes and curriculum to motivate the children?

This chapter considers how students perceive and react to educational activity in very personal and individualised ways. It focuses on what we know about motivational processes in students, and their emotional reactions to their experiences at school. Part of this will involve examining how students understand the causes of academic success and failure, and how this impacts on their academic self-esteem. As you will see, it has also been suggested that teachers can unintentionally influence these interpretations and influence student progress at school. We will also consider the issue of stress in the classroom, for both students and teachers.

Motivation

What is motivation?

The word 'motivation' has its origins in the Latin word for 'move', and as Boekhaerts *et al.* (2010) observe: 'motivation could best be considered as an inner energy source that pushes people toward desirable outcomes and away from undesirable outcomes ... motivation is concerned with the fulfilment of one's needs, expectations, goals, desires and ambitions' (p. 535).

Some theories about the role and importance of motivation in education tend to portray it as a form of personal quality, which can directly affect learning. Although it is possible to see motivation as a general quality, it can be context-specific. A pupil who puts in very little effort with school work might be said to lack motivation, but might spend a lot of time and energy on a complex and demanding computer game. In the same way, some pupils can also become much more involved and successful in one particular academic subject area than in others. There are many reasons why we do or do not become involved in a specific activity, and this chapter will discuss some of these.

Perhaps the best way of understanding motivation is to see it not as a single quality but rather as a process that comes into play whenever we are involved in an activity. Part of explaining motivation involves reasons for the nature, as well as the level, of involvement. Even if pupils are just chatting with their friends, or staring out of the window and daydreaming, we can still look at explanations for why they are involved in such activity. The problem for teachers is that such behaviours are unlikely to lead to much academic progress. For this reason, educational definitions of motivation tend to focus on academic achievement and involvement with tasks in school.

Intrinsic vs extrinsic motivation

An important distinction that is made in educational psychology with respect to motivation is whether a person is either intrinsically or extrinsically motivated to engage with a given task. **Intrinsic motivation** is where someone is engaged in the activity for its own sake – the task itself is sufficiently engaging and satisfying that the pupil is motivated to complete it. This contrasts with **extrinsic motivation**, which is when someone is motivated to complete an activity because there is some form of external reward or consequence to doing so. The influence of behaviourism on education means that extrinsic rewards are often used to 'shape' children's behaviour in the classroom, but concerns are raised about orientating children towards extrinsic reward as this may replace or reduce the development of intrinsic motivation. The concern is that when no reward is evident, children's willingness to engage in learning activities may be reduced. An example of this is observed when university students choose to attend only those lectures that they know they will be examined on.

Behavioural approaches to motivating students

Operant conditioning, as outlined in Chapter 2, is a powerful way to motivate specific behaviours. It works by linking something that a pupil is already motivated by (**reinforcement**) with an activity that we want the student to engage with. Accordingly, we can try to motivate pupils to work harder in school by using rewards such as praise and merit points, or sanctions such as detentions. For instance, a teacher might encourage pupils to complete some class work by allowing them out to play (the reinforcer being to socialise with their friends) only when they have completed their assignments.

In order for behavioural approaches to work effectively, pupils need to be aware of what is generally expected of them, in the form of 'ground rules'. These should cover classroom routines, with an emphasis on positive, work-directed behaviour. The effective behavioural approach of Assertive Discipline (Canter and Canter, 1992) emphasises a clear and unambiguous set of rules that are agreed on by staff and should be displayed on the classroom wall. These are limited to about six in number, and it can be an effective approach to negotiate these with a new class. Pupils are normally very aware of what is expected of them in school and if anything are rather over-punitive when considering the consequences of disobedience.

Use of punishment

In terms of motivation, pupils need to be aware of the positive and negative outcomes that are associated with such rules. Discipline procedures in schools usually focus on the failure to carry out expectations, and the most common outcome of this is a verbal reprimand. However, punishment is best avoided, as it is only effective at temporarily suppressing unwanted behaviours, but does not eliminate them (Skinner, 1938). Even to achieve suppression, punishment is only effective when it is **immediate**, **severe** and **consistently applied** (Klein, 1996). In reality, punishment is very difficult to implement effectively, as teachers are usually too distracted by other children to apply a severe punishment immediately and consistently, and this is virtually impossible to implement for a class of 30 pupils. It is also difficult to know whether something intended as a severe punishment will be interpreted as such by the child, as some forms of punishment, such as being made to sit at the teacher's desk, can be reinforcing (e.g. the child gains additional attention from the teacher). So a teacher needs to have excellent knowledge of their pupils if they are to know what to use as an effective punishment.

However, one form of intervention that does appear to be effective in improving children's motivation in class is sending letters home to parents. Leach and Tan (1996) found that sending negative letters to parents was highly effective, increasing general on-task behaviour in a class from about 60 per cent to above the 90 per cent level. The letters are likely to be more effective than any punishment that the teacher in the class can administer as the parents are likely to punish the children in a way that they know to be highly effective for that child. The punishment then becomes tailored to the children in an individualised way. However, as noted earlier, consistency of punishment is important here, too, and without the use of appropriate reinforcement when behaviour improves, the effect of such approaches is likely to be short lived.

However, punishment is perhaps best avoided as it can have unwanted effects: there is evidence that it can lead to increased aggression, increased anti-social behaviour and mental health issues (Gershoff, 2002). There is also the risk that its effects may generalise inappropriately: for example, if a particular teacher punishes a child in one context, the child may become fearful and anxious in all lessons with that member of staff.

Praise as reinforcement

A range of rewards are possible in school, the most common form given in classrooms being teacher praise and encouragement. For most teachers, their positive comments are usually outnumbered by negative ones, although these are usually directed towards behaviour rather than achievements. Wheldall *et al.* (1985) found that when teachers were trained to give more positive comments, pupils' on-task behaviour increased significantly. Unfortunately, on-task behaviour is not necessarily the same as actual learning, and a review of the effects of praise by Brophy (1981) found that it does not usually relate very well to students' achievements. One reason for this appears to be that teachers do not normally use praise in a very effective way, tending to use it only with pupils who are already doing well. Although there is a weak positive relationship between praise and achievements for younger pupils and children from deprived socioeconomic backgrounds, this effect disappears with older pupils, and in some studies has even been negative.

Praise is a form of social interaction and its effectiveness therefore depends very much on the relationship between the pupil and the teacher, and whether this is valued by the pupil. In general, pupils up to the age of eight want to please adults, so praise can be effective. After this, the role of the peer group becomes progressively more important, and praise from an adult is likely to have only limited effects – or even negative ones, depending on the peer group's culture.

In order for praise to be at all effective, Brophy (1981) argues that it should emphasise information about achievements and be credible to the pupil. The use of praise should also follow the principles of learning theory, and be reliable and contingent on some specified performance. Pure behaviourists such as Skinner believe that there is no need to consider *why* such motivators work, just *how* they can be used. However, conditioning is effective because it changes individuals' expectations about what will be the outcome of their actions. If pupils are in the class of a teacher who notices good work and regularly gives praise, they should be more likely to work for such recognition.

Praise also seems to be ineffective if it generates a defensive self-concept, with limited approaches to learning. Dweck (1999) describes the way in which a great deal of teacher praise normally emphasises ability ('You're really clever') or achievement ('You've done that work well'). This encourages pupils' efforts and involvement in the short term, but, surprisingly, has long-term negative effects. Such ability- or achievement-oriented praise seems to make students most concerned about maintaining a positive image, which means that they will subsequently tackle only relatively easy tasks, in which success is guaranteed. If pupils experience work that they are less successful with, then this serves to undermine their ability- or achievement-oriented self-concept, leading to a helpless, passive orientation to future work.

Dweck argues that effective praise should emphasise **effort** and **strategy**. This might involve comments such as, 'That's right – you worked really hard on that one' or 'Good – that was a really effective approach'. This type of feedback appears to encourage pupils to see their own abilities and achievements as modifiable. When they encounter difficulties, they are then much more likely to persist and to adopt different strategies. However, too much praise can result in poor performance (Baumeister *et al.*, 2003). Lewis and Sullivan (2005) suggest that this is because the praise leads to an overinflated self-esteem, resulting in less effort being put into the task.

Why is motivation important for education?

Observational studies such as those of Galton *et al.* (1999) have found that pupils work independently most of the time they are in school, showing only limited work-oriented involvement with their teacher or with other children. Whatever learning pupils do achieve is therefore likely to be heavily dependent on their own level of effort and involvement. At all stages in education, progress in a particular subject is mainly determined by students' initial attainments. However, Lange and Adler (1997) found that such predictions for pupils in grades 3, 4 and 5 were significantly improved by taking into account their motivation, as measured by intrinsic goal-orientation (being interested in a subject for its own sake) and academic self-perception (how pupils saw themselves as learners).

Bruner (1966b) pointed out that school experiences differ from other forms of learning because they are **decontextualised**. This means that learning occurs separately from the actual thing or process that is being studied and therefore requires specific and conscious effort to maintain involvement. Children in school who are learning about windmills are likely to receive information from their teacher or books, but only rarely by actually visiting a windmill. Before children come to school, and in societies where formal education does not exist, learning appears to happen with little effort or external pressure. Bruner argued that this is because such learning is contextualised, meaning that children acquire knowledge that has the context of being meaningful and useful for them. All the major early developments, such as walking, talking and social interaction, are not taught in any formal way, but develop because they immediately enable children to interact with and to control their environment.

Before Bruner, the educational theorist John Dewey raised the same point, drawing distinction between:

> the education which everyone gets from living with others ... and the deliberate educating of the young.... Savage groups ... have no special devices, materials, or institutions for teaching save in connection with initiation ceremonies by which the youth are inducted into full social membership.... To savages, it would seem preposterous to seek out a place where nothing but learning was going on in order that one might learn. But as civilization advances, the gap between the capacities of the young and the concerns of adults widens. Learning by direct sharing in the pursuits of grown-ups becomes increasingly difficult.
>
> (1916: 7–9)

The decontextualisation of learning is also partly the product of a prescriptive curriculum and class sizes, which necessarily limit the ability of teachers to respond to individual interests and needs. However, it can also be argued that education must inevitably involve the developing of abstract learning, since it is impossible to experience personally the basis of every new item of knowledge that will be useful to us. Despite this, Bruner argues that it is still possible to develop learning by some form of direct experiences in school and that a process of learning by discovery will maintain children's natural curiosity and motivation. There is some support for these ideas, although the practicalities of covering the curriculum mean that some compromises have to be made.

On the other hand, Pinker has radically argued that school curricula should primarily consist of subjects that will 'provide students with the cognitive tools that are most important for grasping the modern world and that are most unlike the cognitive tools they are born with' (2002: 235). In other words, school should teach children concepts and ideas that they are unlikely or unable to learn about through direct experience and that are necessary for modern society: thus, foreign languages might be dropped from the curriculum in favour of economics. In this way, schooling would be used to teach children about concepts and ideas that they are highly unlikely to be exposed to through experience, and we should rely on direct experience and socialisation to complete the child's education of other subjects that are argued to be less relevant to modern society. And so it would seem that there is a tension between Pinker's argument and Bruner's position that direct experience is necessary to maintain children's motivation to learn and natural curiosity.

One way to judge children's motivation is from the quality and the amount of work that they produce. However, their work also depends on ability, and it is hard to know whether pupils who have not done much work are not trying, or just do not have any knowledge or understanding of what they are supposed to be doing. Teachers try to overcome this difficulty by forming an impression of children's potential abilities, often from how well they cope with other forms of work, or by the consistency of their output. If they find that children can write well on one occasion then it is reasonable to assume that they should be able to do so at other times and that poor work is probably the result of limited effort. However, it can take some time to form these judgements, and some children adopt long-term work-avoidance strategies. Galton *et al.* (1999), for instance, found that a quarter of all children engaged in such 'easy riding', which involved giving the appearance of working while putting in only limited effort, in order to reduce teachers' expectations of them.

Academic motivation may thus be important in determining educational progress, but it is difficult for teachers to monitor directly. There are a number of explanations as to why pupils do or do not become involved with academic tasks in school, and most of these have direct implications for what teachers might be able to do about it. There are so many factors that contribute to motivation, and so many theories that have been proposed to account for it, this chapter is unable to cover them all. In this section, we therefore present you with just a few that offer some useful ways of thinking about sources of motivation.

Achievement motivation

An example of a 'classic' motivation theory that relates well to educational contexts is the achievement motivation theory proposed by John Atkinson (1957, 1964). He proposed that behaviour was the product of motives (the stable tendency of individuals to seek success and avoid failure), probability for success (subjective judgement of how successful you will be) and incentive value (pride in achievement).

This model provides us with some useful ways of thinking about the components of motivation. For example, if we take the idea of motives from this model, we can characterise learners according to whether they have low or high motivation to avoid failure and/or approach success. Covington (1992) suggested that there are four different kinds of learner.

- **Failure acceptors**, who are low on motivation to avoid failure, and low on motivation to achieve success.
- **Failure avoiders**, who are high on motivation to avoid failure, but low on motivation to achieve success.
- **Success-orientated students**, who are low on motivation to avoid failure, but high on motivation to achieve success.
- **Overstrivers**, who are high on motivation to avoid failure, and high on motivation to succeed.

You will see that the emphasis here is on motivation being an internal characteristic of the individual, which is somewhat influenced by outside factors such as task difficulty (which we would expect to affect probability for success).

Atkinson's model attempted to quantify the influences on motivation and the result is a mathematical formula that enables us to generate predictions about what combination of factors will result in the best motivation. For example, one of the predictions from the model is that motivation will be highest when students are presented with tasks of intermediate difficulty. Weiner (1992) found that the experimental literature is supportive of this claim and that most people will select tasks of intermediate difficulty. However, he noted that the motive aspect of Atkinson's model was the most important influence on motivation, with individuals who are high in motivation for success more likely to choose intermediate tasks than individuals who are high in fear of failure. The general tendency to select intermediate-level tasks can be explained both in terms of a **hedonic principle** (minimise negative emotion, maximise positive emotion) and in terms of an **informational principle**. That is, intermediate tasks provide the most information to the individual on their actual abilities than either easy or very difficult tasks do. It should be noted that a contemporary development of Atkinson's theory is the idea that probability for success (**expectancy**) and incentive value (**task value**) are seen as the most important aspects determining academic achievement (e.g. Eccles, 2005).

Activity

Think about what Vygotsky's Zone of Proximal Development tells us about task difficulty. Is it consistent with what Atkinson's model would predict?

Feedback

Both Atkinson's theory and Vygotsky's ideas about the ZPD would suggest that setting student tasks of intermediate difficulty is best. For Atkinson, this is because of the motivational benefits of doing so, but for Vygotsky, the reason is to do with setting a task that is neither too difficult nor too easy, so that the student learns from achieving mastery of the task.

Studies that have looked at the effect of expectancy and self-perceptions of ability have shown that these two factors are able to predict success in mathematics and English better than prior performance on those subjects, and are good at accounting for learners' effort and engagement (persistence) on tasks in these subject areas (Eccles et al., 1989; Wigfield, 1994).

Self-determination theory

Self determination theory (Deci and Ryan, 1991; Ryan and Deci, 2000; Reeve et al., 2004) is perhaps one of the most popular contemporary theories of motivation and how it relates to educational activity. It is based on the ideas of will and self-determination. 'Will' refers to the ability of a person to decide on how to satisfy their needs. According to Deci and colleagues, there are three basic psychological needs: the need for **competence** in one's environment (mastery), **autonomy** (or a sense of control) and **relatedness** (the sense of belonging to a group).

TABLE 5.1 Types of motivation described in Ryan and Deci's self-motivation theory, and how they relate to perceived locus of control

A motivational regulatory style
Low perceived confidence with few links made between behaviour and outcomes, and low perceived task value.

External regulation (extrinsic motivational style) – external locus of control
Motivated by external rewards and punishment. Not a proactive learner.

Introjected regulation (extrinsic motivational style) – slightly external locus of control
Motivated by approval from others. Feel that they 'should' work hard.

Identified regulation (extrinsic motivational style) – slightly internal locus of control
Work is important to them, but because of longer-term outcomes (e.g. getting grades to go to university).

Integrated regulation (extrinsic motivational style) – internal locus of control
Student draws on internal and external sources of information and work because it is important to the student's sense of self.

Intrinsic motivation – internal locus of control
Fully internally motivated by personal enjoyment and satisfaction.

Deci (1980) defines intrinsic motivation as 'the human need to be competent and self-determining in relation to the environment' (p. 27). Self-determination theory values intrinsic motivation, whilst recognising that only some behaviours may be intrinsically motivated. Deci argues that when individuals are unable to exercise some control over their environment by making choices (and thereby being self-determining), intrinsic motivation will decline, and it will also be undermined if an individual thinks that their behaviour is in fact motivated by external rewards (extrinsic motivators). However, the theory also suggests that externally motivated behaviours can become intrinsically motivated through a process of internalisation.

Ryan and Deci (2000) see the different types of motivation as organised along a continuum, as represented in Table 5.1. The lowest level of motivation is 'amotivation', and then there are four different levels of extrinsic motivation that differ in the extent to which they are perceived to be externally or internally controlled, followed by intrinsic motivation as the most satisfying and most internally controlled.

Classic study

Lepper *et al.* (1973) carried out a classic investigation into the effects of extrinsic motivators on natural learning in a study of children's drawing activities. First they observed a group of nursery-school children in a free-play period to see how much time they spent on drawing. They chose a number of children who seemed to like drawing and split them into three groups which subsequently had different expectations and experiences of reinforcement. Only one of the groups was told that they would get a 'good player' award for making drawings, and then all three groups were allowed to 'play' with some drawing materials. After this session, the reward was given to the group that expected it, and a reward was also given to the children in one of the other groups, who did not expect one. There was therefore one group of children remaining who did not expect, and were not given, a reward.

All three groups were then allowed a further free-play session, during which they were observed to see how much time they spontaneously spent on drawing activities. The key finding was that children in the group that had been promised and then received a reward now spent less time than the other two groups on drawing. Lepper *et al.* interpreted these results as indicating that the children who had expected a reward had come to use this as a reason to justify why they were involved in drawing. When the reward stopped, then there was no longer any reason to continue with the drawing; the children's sense of personal control or involvement with the task itself had been removed and drawing was an activity they did only to get something else.

By analogy, in normal school work it would be counter-productive to use any of the normal range of extrinsic rewards such as house points, certificates or various privileges. Although rewards may have short-term positive effects – the group expecting a reward did more work than the other two groups on the second session – they are likely to result in superficial efforts geared solely to getting the reward. The drawings produced by the group expecting the reward were in fact of lower quality than those of the children who were drawing purely for the sake of it.

However, these findings have not always been confirmed when children have had different experiences and expectations. Cameron and Pierce (1994) point out that the group in the original Lepper *et al.* study who did not initially expect a reward, but did receive one, actually performed best of all in the final free-play session. This indicates perhaps that it was not the reward itself, but the expectation of reward that affected subsequent motivation. In a meta-analysis of 96 studies, Cameron and Pierce found that motivation is reduced only in the specific situation when a tangible reward is given merely for doing a task. When a reward is given to children for doing better on a task, a number of studies show that there is generally no damaging effect on subsequent intrinsic motivation.

Practical implications

These findings can be understood in terms of the way in which children interpret and use information. When pupils are rewarded whatever they do, this devalues their efforts and involvement. However, when reward or praise is contingent on what they have done, this gives feedback and is likely to increase feelings of competence and subsequent involvement. The message for teachers is clear. They should attempt to link rewards with specific achievements, and it would also seem safest initially to emphasise performance on the task, rather than the importance of the reward.

Trying to use an intrinsically motivating activity to increase involvement in another activity can also sometimes reduce the desired target activity. Higgins *et al.* (1995) investigated the effects of emphasising different tasks when children were given a book that they could both colour in and read from. When colouring was the main activity in the first session, Higgins *et al.* found that children were subsequently less likely to want to do the reading and seemed to have developed the idea that reading was a subsidiary and less-interesting activity. In general, it seems safest to develop children's interests in activities for their own sake wherever possible. However, some activities are complementary with a natural association, for example following a story in pictures with an explanation underneath that can be read. When this is done, the important aspect is to emphasise the overall task, by saying, 'Let's find out what happens next', rather than, 'If you read this then I'll let you look at the next picture.'

Flow

One concept linked to intrinsic motivation is that of **emergent motivation**, which is seen as the result of engaging with a task or environment and discovering the associated rewards and goals (Csikszentmihalyi, 1978, 1999; Csikszentmihalyi *et al.*, 2005). Crucially, the rewards are such that they cannot be known or anticipated in advance: the reward comes from individuals being able to match their behaviour to their goals within that activity, and so achieving what they wish to achieve. For example, Csikszentmihalyi (1978) observed that when children play with blocks, they do not have an overall sense of what they want to achieve from the activity, but by placing blocks together they start to get a sense of what shape they want to make. This becomes the goal, and it may change as new blocks are placed and suggest different forms, but the motivation for the child comes from matching their actions to what they want to achieve next. The activity becomes worth doing for its own sake: the activity is intrinsically motivating and absorbing or **autotelic**.

When involvement in an activity is so intrinsically motivating that the individual is fully involved and engrossed in the activity, this is known as **flow**. When experiencing flow, you may lose track of time, and even space, and flow is particularly associated with creative activities, but can be experienced in the context of any activity. An important aspect of flow is the positive emotional experience associated with it. Zembylas (2003) has argued that emotional states are not separable from activities and relations with others, and so emotions can be seen as important components of classroom situations that can impact on children's motivation. Csikszentmihalyi (1975) argued that, when individuals experience flow, they also report having clear goals and work towards them, have high levels of effortless concentration, the sense that time passes rapidly, little self-consciousness and a sense that they were able to meet the demands of the activity, even though they were challenging.

Researchers have considered how these different components of flow are present in children's classrooms. For example, Turner *et al.* (1998) found that flow was more common in classrooms that presented children with high levels of involvement and challenge. Moreover, they found that the context of learning can influence the emotional reaction that children will have to it: for example, children who were presented with tasks that were easy for them to complete and were therefore bored, reported high levels of happiness but no pride in their achievements. They argue for the need to consider all aspects of classroom context (interaction type, content, duration, intensity, level of challenge and emotions) in order to understand motivation (Meyer and Turner, 2006).

Attributional processes

There is a strong general tendency for people to want to find out the reasons why things happen. This is probably part of the way in which we model and attempt to make sense of the world. It allows us to think about and plan ways in which we can interact with the various features of our environment. We particularly seek causes or attributions for the behaviour of other people, but we also seem to look for causal links between our own actions and possible effects. When we believe that we can accomplish something, this belief appears to have an important impact on our future involvement or motivation.

Rotter (1966) suggested that one form of attribution is the way in which individuals can have a sense of whether control originates from themselves – an internal locus – or from things separate from them – an external locus. In an educational setting, individuals who have an external locus of control are inclined to believe in 'luck' rather than effort attributions, which tends to result in lower effort and achievements. **Learned helplessness** has been described by Seligman (1975) as an extreme form of an external locus of control and involves a negative, apathetic and withdrawn approach to situations. As described earlier, it is likely to result when students have repeated experiences where their efforts appear to have little or no effect.

Weiner (1985) took this concept further by considering that there are three main dimensions for the perceived causes of success or failure.

- ■ **Stability** – whether the cause changes or not. Ability or intelligence is usually perceived as a stable cause, whereas effort can change.
- ■ **Internal or external** – whether the cause lies within the individual or comes from outside. External causes would be the perceived difficulty or other characteristics of tasks, whereas internal causes include ability and effort.
- ■ **Controllability** – whether the result can or cannot be affected by the individual's expending greater effort. Traits such as 'laziness' are generally seen as being under voluntary control, whereas traits such as mathematical aptitude or physical coordination are not.

Some of the main categories of perceived causes are: **ability**, which is stable, internal and has low controllability; **effort**, which is unstable, internal and has high controllability; luck, which is unstable, external and has low controllability; and **task difficulty**, which is stable, external and has low controllability. If pupils fail on a particular task, they might attribute their failure to any of these categories. If their attribution involves stable and uncontrollable causes such as a belief that they have no ability, or that tasks are always too difficult, they will feel that not much can be done to avoid future failure. The same will happen with attributions for external causes with low controllability, which is the basis for learned helplessness. Even when students are successful, attributing the outcome to 'luck' or 'low task difficulty' means that they are still going to feel that their success was not due to anything that they did, and they are therefore unlikely to be motivated in the future.

On the other hand, students who attribute success at some task to internal causes such as effort or ability are likely to feel positive about their involvement and will be highly motivated in the future. If students fail and attribute the failure to unstable characteristics such as effort or luck, they are still likely to persist in the future, since they are likely to think that they might succeed by trying harder, or by having better luck another time.

Positive attributional styles are most readily developed by successful experiences, where pupils perceive that they are competent and in control, and that it is worthwhile expending effort. Such perceptions can be encouraged and developed by teachers. Mueller and Dweck (1998) found that students who were praised for their effort at solving mathematical problems subsequently showed much greater persistence than students who had been praised for their intelligence. Praising ability led students to worry more about failure and to choose tasks only where they were certain they could be successful. The pupils who had been praised for effort, on the other hand, showed more resilience and persistence, and concentrated on ways to learn different approaches to solving problems.

Attributions and emotions

It is worth noting that an important aspect of student's attributions of the causes of their success or failure is the emotional aspect associated with them. If we consider Weiner's three dimensions of 'locus', 'stability' and 'control' mentioned above, each one is associated with an emotional consequence. Weiner (1994) argued that, in terms of locus of control, an internally attributed success will promote feelings of pride, but a negative outcome internally attributed will result in reduced self-esteem. The dimension of 'stability' is linked to hopefulness or hopelessness, because it is linked to students' expectations for future success. Controllability is linked to feelings of personal responsibility, and therefore feelings of shame or guilt.

Attribution retraining

Once students have established a negative attributional style, however, this will tend to persist, whatever their subsequent experiences of success or failure. Indeed, it is quite possible for it to become more ingrained over time, since they may put in decreased or inappropriate effort and will then experience even fewer successes. Even if the teacher is able to gear the work closely to a student's abilities and thereby ensure a high level of success, students are still likely to devalue this and attribute their achievements to the low level of the tasks. Cooper (1983) has found that this is particularly likely to happen with 'remedial' teaching, if the pupils see the tasks as being closely managed by the teacher, and if comparison with and comments from other children show that they are in fact doing lower-level work.

To break this negative cycle, students can be given tasks they perceive as difficult, but which they are encouraged to persist and to succeed with. When students are unsuccessful, the teacher can emphasise that the lack of success was due merely to lack of effort, or an inappropriate strategy, explaining where they went wrong, then encouraging them to try again. Dweck (1975) found that when treated in this way, students started to attribute success or failure to their own actions and were then able to improve their motivation and achievements. Group work can also increase the effectiveness of such training if pupils see other children making attributions to effort, thereby providing them with models for change.

Classic study

Schunk (1984) designed a study to consider the effect of different combinations of feedback on student performance. Children were allocated to one of four groups: a group that received only feedback on the degree of effort they put into the task, one group received feedback on their ability at the task, one group effort feedback for the first half of the intervention, and then received ability feedback in the second half; and a final group received ability feedback first and effort feedback second. What this study demonstrated was that children who received ability feedback initially showed greater self-efficacy and attributed their success to ability more than those receiving effort feedback. Effort feedback also raised self-efficacy but its effects were weaker than those observed for ability feedback.

Overall Schunk (1984) suggests it is better to offer ability feedback early in children's educational experiences. However, a similar study conducted by Schunk and Rice (1986) with students who had difficulties with reading found that, for these students, it was better to give effort-based feedback first, and then ability feedback afterwards. This is likely to be due to the prior negative educational experiences of these students, which may lead them to dismiss initial ability feedback.

Practical implications

Attributional theories give rise to the rather counter-intuitive prediction that a high level of direction by a teacher might actually reduce motivation and subsequent achievements. If students perceive their own involvement and attainments at school as being mainly under the control of their teacher, then this perception is likely to reduce their own sense of control or involvement. Research summarised by Spaulding (1992) shows that motivation and achievements are decreased by teachers who emphasise their evaluative over their informative role, and who monitor students' behaviour and performance in an intrusive way.

Although high student control and intrinsic motivation may be desirable, schools are organised on the basis of relatively few adults managing large numbers of students. Unfortunately, this type of arrangement tends to require a high degree of external control and direction. To overcome this problem, a number of attempts have been made to allow students to choose their own activities in schools. However, Spaulding's (1992) review indicates that such developments have generally been unsuccessful in achieving conventional curriculum goals and that they were usually rapidly replaced by traditional instruction programmes. One famous surviving British example is Summerhill, a 'free' school operating on the principles of self-direction by pupils, founded in 1921. A study by Bernstein (1968) of the outcomes of this school found significant benefits in terms of social abilities, self-confidence and continuing personal growth. On the other hand, this study also found that parents of children at Summerhill who had themselves attended the school tended to remove their children after the age of 13 because of a lack of confidence in the conventional academic outcomes there. There was also official pressure on the school resulting from its failure to conform to the National Curriculum, but in 2007 it received a positive OFSTED report. The school's policy statement makes interesting reading in the context of our discussions of pupil motivation.

Summerhill General Policy Statement

1   **To provide choices and opportunities that allow children to develop at their own pace and to follow their own interests.**
    Summerhill does not aim to produce specific types of young people, with specific, assessed skills or knowledge, but aims to provide an environment in which children can define who they are and what they want to be.

2   **To allow children to be free from compulsory or imposed assessment, allowing them to develop their own goals and sense of achievement.**
    Children should be free from the pressure to conform to artificial standards of success based on predominant theories of child learning and academic achievement.

3   **To allow children to be completely free to play as much as they like.**
    Creative and imaginative play is an essential part of childhood and development. Spontaneous, natural play should not be undermined or redirected by adults into a 'learning experience' for children. Play belongs to the child.

4   **To allow children to experience the full range of feelings free from the judgement and intervention of an adult.**
    Freedom to make decisions always involves risk and requires the possibility of negative outcomes. Apparently

continued

negative consequences such as boredom, stress, anger, disappointment and failure are a necessary part of individual development.

5 **To allow children to live in a community that supports them and that they are responsible for; in which they have the freedom to be themselves, and have the power to change community life, through the democratic process.**

All individuals create their own set of values based on the community within which they live. Summerhill is a community, which takes responsibility for itself. Problems are discussed. All members of the community, adults and children, irrespective of age, are equal in terms of this process.

(Taken from www.summerhillschool.co.uk/pages/school_policies_statement.html)

Academic self-esteem

Academic self-concept

William James introduced the idea of self-concept in 1890, and saw it as having two distinctive parts: the **I** and the **Me**. According to James, the I is the conscious, mindful aspect of our personality, and the Me is constructed from our experiences and how other people view us. James acknowledged that there were different aspects to the self, with the physical self at its most basic level and the spiritual self at the top. Self-esteem is related to our self-concept, and is best thought of as the difference between our ideal self and our actual self.

Academic self-concept and self-esteem are important topics in motivation because of the way in which they can impact on children's educational attainment. It was noted earlier that sometimes we can be highly motivated in some academic areas but less motivated in others. Accordingly, academic self-concept can differ for different curriculum areas: Marsh et al. (1988) found that academic self-concept appears to have two components, one tied to mathematical ability and the other tied to verbal abilities. Children's academic self-concept appears to change over time, starting relatively high but then declining as they gain more experience and incorporate this into their sense of self until they reach puberty, after which it stabilises and begins to increase during adulthood (Marsh, 1989). It has been suggested by Wigfield and Eccles (2002) that changes in academic self-concept are linked to changes in children's educational environments. From this it would seem that the transition from primary to secondary education it particular is associated with a decline in academic self-esteem.

One of the questions raised by this literature relates to the wisdom of putting children into ability-streamed classrooms. That is, Marsh (1984, 2007) proposed the existence of the **big-fish-little-pond-effect** (BFLPE). According to this idea, one of the sources of information that students draw on when assessing their academic abilities is how well their classmates are performing. So, if a high-ability child is put in a school or a class where their peers are of similar ability or higher than they have, then this may lead them to underestimate their own performance, thereby adversely affecting their academic self-concept. In contrast, placing children who are struggling academically into ability-streamed classes or schools should lead to an increase in academic self-esteem. These ideas have been supported empirically. For example, Marsh et al. (1995) conducted a study of children placed in gifted and talented programmes: their academic self-concepts declined over time and relative to that of a matched comparison group. Ireson et al. (2001) conducted a study of 3,000 UK children who were grouped on ability, and they found a BFLPE on the children's English self-concepts, but not for maths or science. This suggests that perhaps these subject areas may not have as much of a stigma attached to them regarding under-performance (i.e. the pupils were comfortable with the idea of not being the best in their class on these subjects). With regard to less-able students, Tracey *et al.* (2003) found that children with mild learning difficulties (IQ between 56 and 75) who were in special classes had higher academic self-concept in both reading and mathematics than the children who were in regular classrooms.

Self-efficacy

Bandura (1986) argues that our perception of our own ability to perform academic tasks is a form of esteem known as **self-efficacy**. This may be the result of past experiences, and can affect our future academic motivation. Experiences of failure tend to reduce self-esteem, whereas success tends to generate higher expectations and a more positive self-concept, leading to increased motivation, effort and success. Bandura found, for instance, that when students were given negative information about their performance on a mathematics task (irrespective of how they had done), their subsequent success and involvement in similar tasks were often significantly reduced. Bandura (1997) has argued that perceived self-efficacy is a strong influence on actual achievement, and Schunk and Pajares (2005) note that current research suggests a good relationship between self-efficacy and achievement in educational contexts, although the relationship is stronger in older students (secondary school and university level) than in primary-school children.

Bandura considers that children's judgements of their effectiveness come, as well as from task achievement, from comparisons with the achievements of their peers, from their general arousal (see earlier in this chapter) and from advice from key others (such as teachers). Zimmerman *et al.* (1992) have also shown that children will set their goals according to what they perceive they are capable of and will avoid the emotional consequences of failure. Students with good self-esteem set themselves realistic, achievable goals and will expend considerable effort to achieve them. Students with low self-esteem, however, will either set themselves low goals, where they can be certain of success, or unrealistically high ones, where they can blame their failure on the difficulty of the task; in neither of these situations will they need to expend much effort. Self-efficacy therefore seems to impact on the learning strategies that students will adopt. Shunck and Pajares (2005) observe that: 'self-efficacy explains approximately 25% of the variance in the prediction of academic outcomes beyond that of instructional influences. Self-efficacy is responsive to changes in instructional experiences and plays a causal role in students' development and use of academic competencies' (p. 93).

Should teachers try to boost self-esteem?

A key issue is whether self-esteem affects achievements, or whether it is mainly achievements that develop self-esteem. This is important, because if self-esteem determines academic progress, then teachers should make direct efforts to boost it in children. This aspect was investigated by Marsh and Yeung (1997) in a long-term, three-year study of children's academic self-concepts and their achievements in mathematics, science and English. Using a form of path analysis to separate out the different causes, they found that academic self-concept and achievements in each of the subjects had reciprocal effects, but that the impact of achievements was much stronger. The coefficients for the effects of self-concept were of the order of about 0.1, compared with about 0.5 for specific achievements. The effects of self-esteem were related to pupils' marks, as well as teacher assessments, which were presumably fed back to pupils on a regular basis.

Chapman and Tunmer (1997) found that the effects of achievements on self-esteem were only starting to develop in the second year of schooling, as children began to perceive their progress and to make comparisons with the attainments of others around them. Rosenberg *et al.* (1995) found that later in school, the academic self-esteem for grade 10 boys had risen to give a path coefficient of 0.30 for its effects on achievements. It seems likely from this that pupils' academic self-concept develops throughout the process of schooling and may have progressively greater effects on their achievements.

Hay *et al.* (1997) also found that pupils' academic self-concept was affected by the general academic context of the class that they were in. There was a substantial overall correlation of 0.46 between pupils' self-concept and the difference between their achievements and the average of the class they were in, an example of the 'big-fish-little-pond (BFLP) effect' discussed above (p. 124). The outcome of this can be that pupils who are in a group above their achievement level are likely to develop low self-esteem and reduced effort. Conversely, those in a group below their achievement level may develop high self-esteem and improved effort, although there is also the danger that they may reduce their effort to 'fit in' with their social group. These effects would, however, be less likely to happen in a secondary school if pupils were able to make comparisons with other classes.

Part of the process of self-evaluation also appears to be the extent to which pupils are able to achieve the goals to which they aspire. Dweck (1986) has distinguished between **task goals**, where pupils seek to achieve mastery of an area, and **ability goals**, where pupils set what they wish to achieve relative to other children. In general, pupils seem to show more commitment and involvement with task goals, and these seem to involve the same intrinsic motivational processes as those associated with general cognitive development (discussed later in this chapter).

Interestingly, Marsh and Yeung (1997) found that children's sense of academic self-efficacy appears to be relatively specific to their achievements in particular subjects and that it is not very useful to talk about a general academic self-esteem. Although pupils who do well in English are also generally likely to be doing well with mathematics, a surprising finding is that pupils tend to see their achievements in these as relatively separate. Marsh explains this as being due to a combination of external and internal frames of reference. An external comparison with other children's achievements may show pupils that they are doing well in a particular subject such as mathematics. However, any sense of achievement will be cancelled out if they make an internal comparison with another subject such as English where they are doing even better, effectively saying to themselves, 'I can't be that good at maths because I'm not as good as I am at English.'

Taken as a whole, these findings indicate that there are reciprocal effects between achievement and self-esteem, but that self-esteem usually has the minor role. The strongest predictor of progress in an academic area is actually pupils' initial attainments in that area, with Marsh and Yeung (1997) finding path coefficients greater than 0.8 for both mathematics and English test scores. These would give rise to the processes shown in Figure 5.1.

Since self-esteem has only a partial impact on achievement, attempts to boost it may not be the most effective way to improve motivation and achievement. In fact, it is likely that a teacher's attempts to praise pupils' work would be discounted by them if the evidence from marks or what other children were achieving went against this. Since self-efficacy appears to be relatively specific, academic or non-academic self-esteem is also unlikely to transfer over to boost self-esteem and effort in other areas. Pupils who are competent at sports might feel better about themselves, but this would not have much impact on their efforts or achievements with reading.

The most effective ways to affect children's sense of efficacy and effort would probably be to improve pupils' real progress, and also to ensure that they value their achievements. Some approaches are able to alter attributional styles by encouraging pupils to set worthwhile goals and supporting them in attaining these. For children in groups set by ability or achievement, the most motivating situation will be membership of a group where they can see that they are doing as well as or better than the

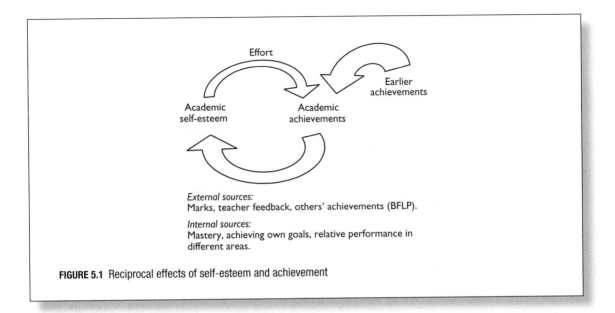

FIGURE 5.1 Reciprocal effects of self-esteem and achievement

other children around them. Although this will be impossible for some children (not everybody can be above average), teachers usually try to avoid any significant mismatches. The negative effects of context can be minimised by avoiding between–class comparisons and by emphasising pupils' individual learning goals.

Needs

A need implies a lack of, or a want for, something. Murray (1938) considered the way in which this can lead to motivated behaviours, originally proposing that there are two main categories of biological and social needs. An example of a biological need would be a lack of food leading to hunger, and a social need would be a lack of contact with other people leading to a desire for this.

Murray also identified a general 'need for achievement', which appears to have some relevance to education. This can be assessed using the Thematic Apperception Test (the TAT), which involves subjects' spontaneous verbal interpretations of a range of ambiguous pictures. For example, when given a picture of a woman sitting in front of a mirror, a pupil might say, 'The woman is daydreaming about doing well at her new job', indicating an interest in achievement-oriented themes. Although this test is not specifically related to education, Wendt (1955) found that students who scored high for need achievement on the TAT did much better on arithmetic tasks than other students, even when they were not directly monitored by a teacher.

The concept of underlying needs was also developed by Maslow (1954) as part of a more general humanistic perspective, with lower levels being a necessary foundation for the higher levels of self-fulfilment. The lowest levels are similar to the basic drives of Hull and are concerned with the physical maintenance and well-being of the individual. As shown in Figure 5.2, the levels rise through social and self-concept needs before cognitive needs can be met; this level involves the need for meaning and predictability, and is similar to Bandura's concept of self-efficacy, to be discussed later in this chapter. The next level involves aesthetic needs, leading to the ultimate stage of self-actualisation where individuals can realise their full potential.

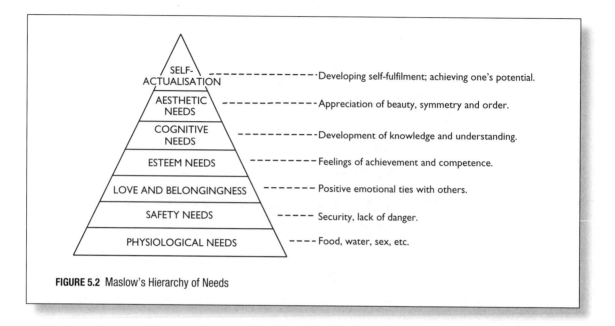

FIGURE 5.2 Maslow's Hierarchy of Needs

According to Maslow, we are unable to proceed to higher levels before our lower needs are secure. Children who are mainly concerned about their physical needs or security are unlikely to be concerned with meeting their higher, cognitive needs at school. This seems quite plausible, and a survey by Kleinman *et al.* (1998) found that children who were regularly hungry in school were about seven times more likely to have social and emotional difficulties, and twice as likely to have special educational needs. Although the specificity of such findings is probably confounded by a number of effects, setting up breakfast clubs has been shown to be associated with significant improvements in some children's attainments.

Maslow's approach appears to bring together a number of different theories of motivation and also anticipated many of the more recent developments, such as intrinsic motivation. A number of different aspects of the theory also appear to have some validity when applied to educational settings. For example, children who have low self-esteem may fail to make progress and meet their cognitive needs, although the effects of such failure are much more specific than Maslow envisaged.

Student subcultures

Not all children conform to school norms or show obedience to their teachers. Some either fail to develop expectations of social roles at an early age, or subsequently adopt certain peer-group roles that are directly in opposition to the work-oriented norms of schooling. Negative roles learned from peer groups can particularly affect boys and children from certain ethnic minorities who need to establish a strong, separate sense of identity. Connell (1989) has described how this can result in a subgroup ethos where academic, cooperative behaviour is seen in a negative way, with pupils who conform to this being labelled as 'swots' and 'wimps'.

The effects of peer conformity increase during secondary schooling, and can be very difficult for schools to counter. One effective approach involves the use of adults from out of school in an individual mentoring role. A study by Miller (1997) of the effects of this in a number of schools found that it improved students' self-reported motivation and significantly increased their grades at GCSE – by an average of just below half a grade for each subject they took.

Teacher expectations

The motivation and the achievements of individual pupils appear to be affected by what teachers believe they are capable of, irrespective of whether this belief is true or not. This is a striking finding and implies that teachers may have a significant effect on their pupils' progress, even though the teachers may not necessarily be aware of what they are doing.

Classic study

The original and classic study in this area is *Pygmalion in the Classroom*, carried out by Rosenthal and Jacobson (1968). In this investigation they first tested all the children in one school with 18 classes, using the 'Test of Inflected Acquisition' from Harvard. This, the investigators claimed, was supposed to identify academic potential and to be particularly sensitive to children who were underfunctioning. Following this assessment, 20 per cent of pupils were identified as being capable of further intellectual progress – the 'late bloomers' – and their teachers were informed of who these children were.

The 'bloomers' were in fact selected on a random basis and the test used was not a test of potential but a new non-verbal test of intelligence. Eight months later, at the end of the school year, the children were again tested for their intelligence. The surprising finding was that the children who had simply been identified to their teachers as having potential had made significantly greater progress than the other children in the same classes. Teachers' expectations that had been formed from one piece of information seemed to be enough by themselves to alter the general intellectual attainments of pupils.

These findings were soon challenged by researchers such as Snow (1969), on the basis of poor experimental design and analysis in the original study. One criticism was that the teachers themselves administered the final intelligence test and may have biased these results by inadvertently helping or encouraging the identified students. Also, the tests used were criticised as having relatively poor reliability, which can give rise to variations in scores and is more likely to produce a 'fluke' effect. These doubts were confirmed when a subsequent replication by Claiborn (1969) failed to produce the same results as the original study.

Despite this setback, further investigations and a review of the key findings by Brophy and Good (1974) supported the basic concept of the effects of teacher expectations. Although some of the criticisms of the original study were valid, students have been shown to make differential progress in real academic skills, such as reading, which were not subject to teacher testing bias or to problems with test reliability. To a great extent, the inability of studies such as Claiborn's to generate effects appears to have been due to the failure of the teachers to acquire the expectancy that the experimenter wanted them to have. When faced with too great a discrepancy, for instance being told that a low-achieving child was supposed to be quite clever, teachers appeared to discount what they were being told and acted according to their own beliefs.

Also, the size of the effect of inducing expectancies is not great and can easily be missed by investigators. An analysis of a number of experimental findings by Rosenthal (1985) indicated that teacher effects account for only about 3 per cent of the overall variance in student achievements. It is possible, however, that the effects in real life could be greater than this, since expectancies are normally formed by the teachers themselves and they are more likely to believe and act on them. Expectancies also probably act over longer periods of time than a short-term experimental investigation and their effects may be cumulative.

How expectations work

Subsequent explorations of the effect of teacher expectations have looked at the effects of naturally occurring expectancies, and have moved on to consider the ways in which these operate in the classroom. Good and Brophy (1978), for instance, have identified that teachers actively construct expectations of students from their earliest contact with them. Much of this initial impression formation may in fact be accurate and appropriate; many teachers are, after all, very experienced and should be able to identify good work styles in pupils.

Teachers can form expectations about children even before they have seen them, perhaps via information from records or comments from other teachers. Baker and Crist (1971) found that teacher expectations for a child (and their subsequent achievements) could be positively or negatively affected by knowing how well an older sibling had done. The effect was confirmed by comparisons which showed that there was no effect on the pupil's progress if the older sibling was not known to the teacher.

Good and Brophy (1978) hypothesised that having formed differential expectations of students, teachers would be led to alter their behaviours. The teachers' behaviour in turn could communicate to each individual student how he or she is expected to behave in the classroom and perform on academic tasks. Good and Brophy also felt it likely that such teacher expectations would have an effect on student self-concept, achievement motivation, level of aspiration, classroom conduct and their interactions with the teacher. Over time, the result could be to reinforce the teachers' original perceptions and eventually lead to differences in student achievements.

A study by Weinstein (2002) appears to support such a hypothesis. School children were interviewed about teacher expectations and found that children monitored teachers' behaviours in order to ascertain the nature of their teacher's beliefs and expectations about their abilities. They noticed differences in the type of work that they were given to do, the kinds of comment that teachers made and the tone of voice that they used. Moreover, Weinstein found that the children reported lower motivation to study subjects that they believed their teacher thought that they were not so good at, and they tended to dislike those subject areas.

When groups are streamed or set by ability, there is also evidence that teachers tend to give greatest attention and preparation to the higher-ability groups. This emphasises the differences between such groupings and reduces the opportunities for lower groups to achieve. Such differential treatment has also been shown to have a direct effect upon students' beliefs about their own abilities and competence. Brattesanti et al. (1984) found, for instance, that teacher expectations predicted 12 per cent of the variance in student expectations about their own performance, over and above the effects of prior student achievement.

Although the general findings on teacher expectancy emphasise the inequalities that can result from this, they also indicate that a generally positive approach to children's abilities and potentials could produce real effects. Research on teacher and school effectiveness by Rutter et al. (1979) indicated that higher expectations for student achievement were part of a pattern of differential attitudes, beliefs and behaviours characterising teachers and schools that maximised their students' learning gains. However, one should perhaps be cautious in assuming that in order to improve attainments, all that teachers need do is expect more from their students.

Empowerment

A humanistic perspective adopted by Lefrancois (1994) emphasises that one of the most important of educational objectives is to empower students. Arnold (2007) agrees, and observes that research on the impact of motivation on achievement demonstrates that students who are empowered (intrinsically motivated and in control of their learning experiences) are engaged in more effective learning strategies and enjoy better outcomes than students who are not. Studies such as Simons *et al.* (2004) have also demonstrated that students who recognise the future impact of their work on their longer-term goals and aspirations do better than students who are more focused on immediate goals and rewards.

Empowerment means that teachers should provide students with the skills and knowledge to do important things they could not do otherwise, and to develop their independent cognitive abilities and intellectual processes. Many of the approaches that develop motivation also involve giving students the power to achieve and to be in control of their own learning. Tasks that are intrinsically motivating and involve a high level of self-efficacy and a positive attributional style enable students to become independently motivated and to extend their learning beyond formal educational experiences. Teachers have a certain moral responsibility to facilitate such development. However, as Arnold (2007) observes, in England at least, there has been a progressive movement away from empowerment of teachers and students, and towards centralised control of the curriculum by the government, amid political discussions re the need to improve academic achievement in schools. Opportunities need to be made and taken to enable some degree of self-determination in the classroom, to maximise student achievement.

Task involvement and cognitive development

Theories based upon self-concept and attributional theory can account for a great deal of behaviour, but they still ultimately depend on some underlying need state such as self-efficacy, or a need for achievement. As discussed earlier, a major problem with this dependence on need is that most activities that people involve themselves in appear to have intrinsic qualities that arise purely from involvement with the task. Understanding this depends on seeing motivation as part of cognitive development, rather than as just a level of activation. Earlier writers such as Hunt (1971) and Rogers (1951) have emphasised that mental activity goes on all the time, and from this perspective, motivation can be seen as involvement directed or redirected towards meaningful activities.

Even when pupils are not directly involved in 'work', they are still actively involved in something, even if it is just 'daydreaming' (a state which is in fact very productive for certain types of goals). Unfortunately, pupils' goals might not be the same as the teacher's, who has a responsibility to cover a specific curriculum. Recruiting children's natural or intrinsic involvement has the potential to develop more meaningful and effective learning experiences. Underlying theories of cognitive development, and practical findings in this area, can offer approaches that are useful for teachers.

Applying Piagetian theories

Eckblad (1981) developed Piaget's concepts of equilibrium/disequilibrium (see Chapter 2) to explain why individuals become involved in some tasks rather than others. According to Piaget's ideas, we are in complete equilibrium with our environment when new information or experiences fit in directly with existing schemas (mental structures). When that is the case, there will be little novelty, challenge or interest in such tasks, and the activation of schemas, as shown by task involvement, will be low. When new information or experiences do not fit completely with existing schemas, then we are in a state of disequilibrium, which, ideally, produces involvement with the environment or task as the schema become modified. This resolution of disequilibrium is called accommodation: changing ourselves to cope with new experiences or information. When disequilibrium is at a high level, however, then everything is new and schemas will be unable to change so as to cope, leading to low levels of involvement. Moderate levels of disequilibrium should therefore lead to higher levels of involvement or motivation, with occasional 'leaps' when schemas undergo general reconfigurations.

Maria Montessori (1936) developed an approach to early (nursery) learning that depends on allowing children to work on simple tasks of their own choice, at their own level, using specially designed physical apparatus. They were designed so that play with and exploration of the objects 'taught' the children key concepts without the need for direct teaching from an adult, who might use unnecessarily complex or inappropriate vocabulary to describe the same concept and therefore impair the children's understanding of it. Montessori described the highly motivating quality of this type of structured play with one particular little girl, who was so engrossed in repeatedly placing wooden cylinders in holes in a block that she did not appear to notice when other children were active around her, or even when her desk was picked up and moved around the room!

Cognitive involvement that is closely matched to an individual's abilities and interests also seems to capture the key features of tasks that are intrinsically motivating, with an emphasis on the process rather than the final outcome. A high level of absorption in self-directed learning tasks is essentially the state of 'flow' described earlier. Bowman (1982) pointed out that such states are also characteristic of children engaged in certain computer games which have the potential to produce higher motivational states combined with more formal educational objectives. For example, Cordova and Lepper (1996) found that students made significantly greater progress with learning when a computer-based mathematics activity was made more intrinsically interesting by the use of individual choices and personalised fantasy elements.

Play and learning

'Play' can also be seen as part of this perspective on cognitive activity. Play is essentially a spontaneous, self-directed activity that involves high levels of success, involvement and progressive development. Play seems to be characteristic of all animals with a certain higher level of development of the nervous system (particularly humans, chimpanzees and dolphins). This appears to indicate that play is something that happens whenever there is the potential for complex cognitive activity.

Play also appears to be important in the development and mastery of skills. Hutt in an early study (1976) described the role of curiosity and exploration in young children's mastery of a novel toy. Children who were more active in this process subsequently showed better long-term development in a number of other areas, indicating that the earlier experiences of play formed a foundation for later, more formal skills. Early theorists such as Herbert Spencer in the mid-nineteenth century saw children's play as merely a peripheral way of using up excess energy. However, recent theories view it as intrinsically motivated learning and an important part of the educational process.

Formal schooling tends to restrict the focus on play to early-years education, largely because of the need to develop certain skills such as reading or number work. Such formal skills cannot be developed by normal play experiences and need a considerable level of direction. However, it is still possible to incorporate some formal goals into less-structured activities, as with number and letter rhymes and games. Such types of experiences were implemented in an American project called High/Scope described by Schweinhart and Weikart (1993), which compared groups of children receiving different early pre-school experiences. Children in the groups whose time was spent on guided play did significantly better than those in groups exposed to narrower, more formal learning experiences. These differences lasted into adult life and affected both educational attainments and social success. Schweinhart and Weikart's work is supported by findings reported on by Judd (1998) that children from countries (such as the United Kingdom) that start formal education at a relatively early age tend to be less successful with later academic achievements. All this implies that play may be a key part of initial learning experiences and that an emphasis on formal objectives can interfere with early development and subsequent progress. Recently the Cambridge Primary Review (Alexander, 2010) recommended that formal tuition should be delayed until children are aged six, but this recommendation was not well-received by politicians at the time because of the emphasis of 'raising standards' and the idea that delaying formal tuition would run counter to such concerns.

Practical implications

From the perspective of the teacher, active, independent learning should come from an initial analysis of a student's abilities, then from learning experiences provided by the teacher which gradually extend these. Ideally, the learning experiences would depend on a pupil's own development, as shown in spontaneous interests and curiosity. Although this closely matched process is difficult to achieve with larger groups of children, it implies that teachers should concentrate mainly on subject matter and individuals' specific progress with ideas and concepts, rather than on gross evaluations, targets and rankings.

Spaulding (1992) in particular recommends that teachers should focus their teaching on skills that pupils can use to guide their own learning, that tasks should be moderately challenging, and that factual information should be acquired through the completion of tasks or projects. Another facet of the instructional role of the teacher should be to support pupils to generate their own subgoals and by demonstrating effective study behaviours. Extrinsic rewards can still be useful when there is no intrinsic motivation to undermine, such as when a student feels incompetent or when a task is inherently uninteresting. Also, marking should emphasise feedback, rather than evaluation, by using specific comments about work, rather than just giving a grade level.

Stress in the classroom

'Arousal' is the general level of physiological and psychological activity, and is an important aspect of the extent to which people are involved in tasks. In the first place, arousal can be a consequence of involvement, since if something is very interesting or important, it will tend to increase the mental and physiological activity of the person carrying it out.

Arousal has also been shown to cause different amounts of involvement and performance, depending upon the level of the arousal and the nature of the task. The effects are relatively generalised, and drinking a cup of coffee and just being more awake at a certain time of day would both facilitate learning. You can have too much of a good thing, however, and Yerkes and Dodson (1908) first demonstrated the classic 'inverted U shape' (Figure 5.3) that is found. Increasing arousal at first increases performance and involvement, up to a certain optimum point. Beyond

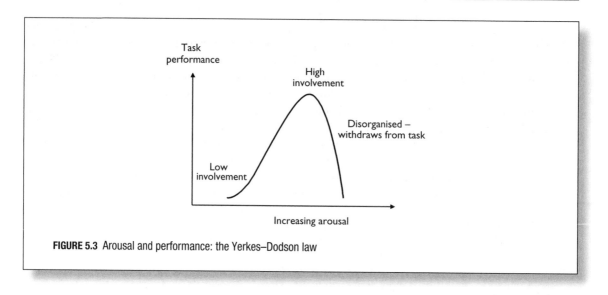

FIGURE 5.3 Arousal and performance: the Yerkes–Dodson law

this, performance deteriorates and individuals will be less likely to be effectively involved in the task.

In school, arousal states can be altered by children's level of alertness and interest in what they are doing. Dynamic and entertaining or 'enthusiastic' teaching has certainly been shown to increase the involvement and achievements of pupils. Arousal states can also be affected by children's anxiety about their performance, particularly in situations such as examinations. Although a certain amount of anxiety can help arousal and performance, high levels of worry can interfere with performance and lead individuals to avoid becoming involved in such situations.

The Yerkes–Dodson law also describes how different tasks can be affected by arousal. Complex tasks, or ones that have only just been learned, are most vulnerable to even moderate arousal states, such as the effects of being watched by an audience. Simple tasks, or ones that are well-learned, are much more resistant to the deleterious effects of arousal, and arousal can promote higher levels of performance. The most vulnerable tasks are cognitive ones, while physical skills, which are normally 'overlearned', are least affected.

Stress

Prolonged and high levels of arousal can have disorganising, negative effects, particularly when an individual is also affected by anxiety. The anxiety can be due to a threat or a lack of perceived control, and is often referred to as a state of stress. Although this term is rather too general for most purposes, a basic physiological process underlies most long-term arousal states. Selye (1956) originally described a 'general adaptation syndrome' in which perceived stressors produce adaptations that initially allow us to function at a higher level. Following interpretation of the meaning of a stimulus, these are at first triggered by the actions of the hypothalamus, a small control centre in the base of the brain.

The 'alarm phase' then involves the sympathetic nervous system, which generally gears up the body into a higher level of activity by stimulating the adrenal glands to release adrenaline and noradrenaline into the bloodstream. These have the effect of increasing heart rate and blood pressure, dilating the pupils, diverting blood flow from the digestive system to the muscles, and generally readying the body to cope with some form of threat. The hypothalamus also activates the pituitary gland, which lies just underneath the brain, to release adrenocorticotrophic hormone into the bloodstream. This stimulates a number of glands, including the outer layer of the adrenal gland, to release a number of other hormones which are involved in the regulation of basic biological processes. These include cortisone and corticosterone, which affect glucose metabolism (to provide energy) and also influence the immune system, reducing reactions such as inflammation.

Continued stressors produce a long-term 'resistance phase', where the body reduces the level of sympathetic activity but continues to involve the stress hormones at a high level. Eventually the body reaches the 'exhaustion phase', when the adrenal glands can no longer function and the immune system and the control of glucose metabolism are no longer effective.

Long-term arousal in this way can lead to an increase in susceptibility to illnesses. Cohen *et al.* (1991) found that individuals who reported the most stressful experiences in their recent past were about twice as likely to become infected with a cold virus. Such infections appear to be particularly likely to happen about four days after emotional disruptions such as a row with someone who is close to you.

Pupils and stress

School-based stresses for children can come from academic pressures, particularly those resulting from the various forms of examinations or other assessments that are now present at all phases of education. For example, Owen-Yeates (2005) conducted a survey of Year 11 Welsh students and asked them about their perceived sources of academic stress. Examinations and deadlines for assessed work were the most frequently reported sources of stress at school, particularly for girls, who also frequently expressed concerns about not being able to do the work as a source of anxiety to them.

Social difficulties such as being bullied or school phobia can also cause long-term problems. These are often associated with high levels of anxiety and can be very debilitating for some children. Long-term stress has also been implicated in a number of physical problems that children may suffer from. Cleare and Wessely (1996), for instance, consider that there is a significant role for stress in the debilitating condition of myalgic encephalomyelitis (ME), also known as 'chronic fatigue syndrome'. This is relatively common and educationally significant, with Dowse and Colby (1997) finding that it accounted for about 42 per cent of all long-term absences from school. However, most stress reactions are not usually so severe, and the most typical signs that teachers should be aware of involve headaches and stomach-aches.

Teachers and stress

The National Union of Teachers in the UK (2008) report figures which show that, between 2003 and 2006, the reported levels of stress for teachers were twice as high as that reported for all professions, and that as many as one in three teachers had taken sick leave as a result of work-related stress. Johnson *et al.* (2005) report that teaching was the sixth most stressful profession out of 26 studied. Research into teacher-stress has shown that pupils' disruptive behaviour is a chief source of work-related stress, amongst both qualified and trainee teachers, and that female teachers experience greater levels of psychological distress than their male counterparts (see Chaplain, 2008). Research also suggests that the head teachers responsible for resolving incidents of challenging behaviour by pupils experience significant stress in relation to these events (Kelly *et al.*, 2007).

Stress and control

Many studies have shown that the key features in producing stress involve the extent to which individuals feel they have control over a situation, particularly one that makes high demands. In a classic experiment, Brady *et al.* (1958) found that many monkeys that had to press a lever every 20 seconds to avoid electric shocks eventually died of stress-induced gastric ulcers. Other monkeys that were given the same level of shocks without the possibility of stopping them were unaffected, so the stress was not simply due to the shocks.

Further investigations indicated that the most important aspect was the lack of feedback to the monkeys about whether they had avoided the punisher. This meant that they could not have any real sense of being able to control the shock and therefore had to be constantly vigilant.

Seligman (1975) also found that individuals' sense of control could be limited by situations where they were repeatedly unable to affect the outcome of events. If animals were given electric shocks that they could not escape from, then they subsequently remained in the situation even when they were allowed the possibility of escaping. This is a state referred to as 'learned helplessness', and individuals who experience it become withdrawn and unreactive, which Seligman considers is similar to the normal development of depression. Hiroto and Seligman (1975) found that humans who were exposed to a loud, stressful noise over which they had no control had subsequent difficulty in learning tasks that would have led to a reduction in the noise. Like the animals, the people involved seemed to have learned that they had no control over this aspect of their environment. These particular types of beliefs about the causes of things (known as 'attributions') are very important in determining motivation.

Rotter (1966) has also shown that such experiences lead people to develop a sense of where control generally comes from. It can be either from within themselves, known as having an 'internal locus of control', or from outside themselves, known as having an 'external locus of control'. When people have the sense of an external locus of control and the feeling that they cannot control events, they are unlikely to take an active approach to dealing with problems and will be more vulnerable to stress. The experience of externally imposed Ofsted inspections appears to be a classic example of this, and Hackett (1998) found that nearly half of all schools reported increased levels of staff sickness in the following two to three months.

In school, children who have made limited progress with basic academic skills are particularly likely to perceive that they are unable to control this aspect of their lives. Although children may attempt to avoid the area where they have problems, the process of normal schooling will repeatedly make demands on them that they cannot manage. Most lessons, for instance, involve some reading and writing, and children who do not have functional literacy skills will repeatedly experience failure. When this pressure is reduced by transferring them to a special school, children usually experience a significant reduction in the academic stress that they experience. This is of course not an option for most pupils, and in any case there is a price to pay in the effects of segregation.

Intervention

If academic pressures and lack of control cause stress, then it should be possible to reduce pupils' anxiety and arousal by increasing their sense of control and effectiveness with school work. One approach that has been successful in improving students' mental health has been a stress-management intervention based on key aspects of **cognitive behavioural therapy**, or CBT (Keogh *et al.*, 2006). Over a ten-week period the students complete one-hour-long sessions that educate students about stress, worry and its effects, as well as teaching relaxation and visualisation techniques. The results showed that, in addition to benefitting the students' metal health, the children in receipt of the intervention achieved significantly better GCSE results than the children in the control group.

The Yerkes–Dodson law shows that overlearning of information should also avoid the disruption caused by high arousal and prevent anxiety and underfunctioning. Children who were very anxious about reading something out loud in an assembly would find it much easier to cope if they had practised the reading so that it was automatic for them. A sense of control in situations such as examinations can similarly be increased by rehearsals with 'mocks', which are made as close to the real experience as possible, but with questions the children can cope with. Students can also be helped to establish greater control by using a structured approach with their revision studies and also when they sit the examination. This can involve working through old papers and identifying key areas for subsequent study, making structured notes covering these, and examination strategies that involve identifying questions and making initial notes as a basis for answers.

Emotions and their functions

It was noted earlier that attributions of success and failure have emotional associations, and that emotion is very much an issue when we discuss student engagement. Emotional states are based on primitive forms of brain–body interactions and involve a range of different types of arousal states and cognitive processes. The initial stages of developing an emotional state usually involve some form of appraisal of the meaning of a situation. Smith and Ellsworth (1987) consider that various features combine to generate a feeling. The examples shown in Table 5.2 show how these can form the foundation for four possible emotions.

Most emotional states involve some form of physiological arousal. This varies according to the emotion: the physical sensations of fear such as 'weak knees' and 'butterflies in the stomach' are very different from the angry sensations of feeling 'tense' and 'heated'. These different states are often triggered by our initial appraisal of a situation. Awareness of our physical state can then feed back to increase our emotional arousal, often setting up a self-maintaining positive feedback. Sometimes, however, the arousal can happen rapidly and without conscious thought, for example if we are startled by something. The generalised physical sensations we experience are then used as cues to develop an emotional state, and this state can then direct our appraisal of what is going on. A teacher might be surprised by an unexpected loud noise caused by a pupil accidentally knocking a chair over. In this case, the teacher is more likely to become angry than if he or she had seen the pupil bump into the chair and was ready for the noise.

Once started, a state of physiological arousal takes some time to dissipate, since the various stress hormones are not broken down immediately. As well as the directly arousing effects of the adrenaline

TABLE 5.2 The cognitive basis of emotions

Did something happen or not?	Was it/would it have been desirable?	Who was responsible for it?	Emotion
Yes	No	Another person	Anger
Yes	No	Me	Guilt
Yes	Yes		Joy
No	No		Relief

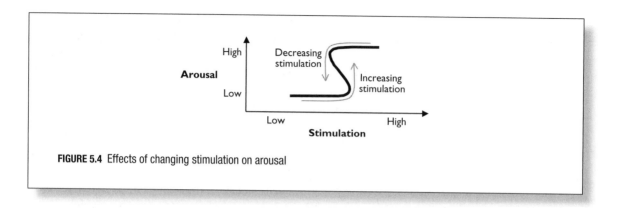

FIGURE 5.4 Effects of changing stimulation on arousal

released into the blood by the adrenal bodies, the noradrenaline too has a generally stimulating indirect effect on the whole of the sympathetic nervous system. There are also psychological feedback processes that operate once a person is physiologically aroused. This means that if your body feels 'hyped up', you will often interpret the feeling as an emotional state and maintain or even increase your general arousal.

Thus emotional or arousal states can escalate suddenly but may take some time to calm down. One way of describing the sudden and discontinuous changes in arousal is with the graph shown in Figure 5.4, which 'jumps' from one level to another, depending on the direction of change of stimulation. This shows that there is an 'overshoot' in both directions before changes happen. Most people will generally avoid getting emotional until they cross a certain threshold, but will maintain their state for some time after any causes have reduced.

Calming down children who are upset or angry may take some time, and at first their heightened emotional state will probably mean that it is not possible to reason with them. In these situations it is often best to have a cooling off period during which the arousal can subdue. For similar reasons, many teachers have a short 'quiet time' when pupils have just come in from an active break or PE session, before starting a class lesson in which high arousal could be disruptive. On the other hand, once pupils are enthusiastic about a subject, their enthusiasm is likely to continue for a while, and it is therefore worth starting off lessons in an upbeat, enthusiastic way in order to generate some ongoing involvement.

'But that's illogical, Captain'

In the original *Star Trek* series, the half-Vulcan Spock was famous for his lack of emotion and his emphasis on the use of pure logic. In education, this sort of cerebral approach can sometimes seem an attractive way to avoid the confounding effects of children's feelings, particularly when there is a need to cover an academic curriculum at speed. Emotions are certainly primitive mental states, and one view of them is that they are merely awkward leftovers from our evolutionary past.

Despite this, there is considerable evidence to support the belief that emotions are vital in energising and maintaining behaviour. One key function seems to be to ensure long-term commitment, which is necessary in maintaining social relationships and effective decision-making. This has been shown by Antonio and Damasio's (1994) description of an individual called 'Elliott' who lost his ability to experience emotions, owing to brain damage caused by a tumour. Although he had a normal IQ and memory, Elliott's life subsequently unravelled in a series of personal and economic disasters.

He was unable to maintain marriages or jobs and appeared to be unable to make effective decisions or to plan ahead for even a few hours. This was apparently related to a break in the connection between Elliott's 'knowing' things and 'feeling' things. Lacking the prompt of emotional commitment, he could weigh up and alter decisions ad infinitum without the 'gut feelings' which normally enable people to maintain consistent behaviour.

Emotional content is also closely involved in our long-term knowledge and understanding, and under the right conditions can facilitate recall. In general, it therefore seems that educational processes should encourage and develop emotional involvement and understanding whenever possible. Interest and enthusiasm for the content of lessons can be readily modelled and encouraged by teachers, which probably accounts for at least part of the large positive effects of 'enthusiastic teaching'.

Summary

Motivation is concerned with how individuals act to achieve their goals and move away from undesirable situations. Intrinsic motivation is where individuals engage in an activity for its own sake, rather than for external reward (extrinsic motivation). Intrinsic motivation is seen as more desirable and educationally less problematic than extrinsic motivation. Praise can be used to motivate children but it should be used with care as it can result in demotivation in some contexts, where it adversely affects a child's self-concept. Effort and task strategy should be the focus of praise. Behaviour can be seen as the product of motives, probability of success and incentive value, and learners can be categorised by the extent to which they avoid failure or seek success. Intermediate-level tasks generate the greatest motivation.

Self-determination theory sees behaviour as motivated by the need to be competent and self-determining. Flow is experienced when an activity is so intrinsically motivating that the individual loses track of time and is fully engrossed in the activity. Success or failure is understood in relation to ability, effort and task difficulty, and can result in internal or external attributions of success and failure. Some degree of self-determination is desirable. There are reciprocal effects between self-esteem and achievement, but self-esteem has limited affects on achievement. Teachers' beliefs about the ability of pupils can influence student achievement. Stress is linked to assessment for pupils, and to managing difficult pupil behaviour for teachers. CBT is an effective way of managing pupil stress and can raise achievement and motivation.

Key implications

- Teaching should focus on pupils' direct active involvement with learning tasks.
- In the short term, this can be achieved with close management and extrinsic (behaviourist) approaches.
- The use of intrinsic involvement (involvement for its own sake) is more effective as a basis for independent and long-term involvement.
- Students' active participation is greater when they have a positive view of themselves as learners.
- Having a positive view also depends on a close match between children's educational experiences and their cognitive development.

Further reading

Elliot and Dweck (eds) (2005), *Handbook of Competence and Motivation*: a comprehensive and detailed book written by leading researchers in the field, covering a wide range of topics relating to competence and motivation. A good book for following up on very specific aspects of the topic.

Schunk, Pintrich and Meece (2010), *Motivation in Education: Theory, Research and Applications – Third Edition*: this gives a broad and technical coverage of the complete range of motivational theories, their developments and how they can be applied by teachers. This book gives in-depth coverage and would be excellent for following up ideas and for reference.

Discussion of practical scenario

It is very likely that the academic self-perception of these pupils is quite negative. By this age, it has been formed over a long period of time involving comparisons between their own achievements and other pupils', as well as the fact of their placement in lower sets.

Modifying and matching the curriculum might go some way to help improve pupil involvement. However, account would need to be taken of the pupils' limited skills, and curriculum matching would probably be difficult to achieve in an academic setting. Although it is possible to be quite creative with the normal curriculum, parts of this can be formally disapplied if necessary, and a broader view of what constitutes education could be adopted.

Using mixed-ability teaching would avoid having 'sink groups', and is likely to give pupils the message that they are worth including. There is, however, the danger that their low achievements might be even more exposed, although some teaching approaches might ameliorate this danger to some extent. These could include using different levels of work and cooperative investigations.

One approach is to consider that, for these pupils, less 'academic' experiences would be more relevant, such as extended work experience and college-based vocational courses. This may seem like getting rid of the problem, but could be much more valuable to the pupils concerned.

The educational context

Practical scenario

Joe Butler has a reputation for being a Head who can 'turn schools around' but on his arrival at Blackbeck Comprehensive has he met his Waterloo? The school has failed an OFSTED inspection, is currently on 'special measures' and the former head teacher is away on long-term sick leave. The school shares a campus with a Sure Start Centre, and a primary school. The buildings are all in a poor state of repair and Joe feels there is currently no sense of community within the school.

What changes might Joe attempt to make in his first week, his first month, his first term?

What should Joe's first moves be in relation (1) to his staff and (2) his pupils?

Which other agencies might Joe invite to assist him to rebuild Blackbeck?

How might Joe integrate the local catchment area community into the work of the school?

The importance of context

Children spend an increasingly large percentage of their lives at school and, historically, the official 'school day' has accounted for nearly one-third of a child's waking life. Ensuring that the years spent at school provide a positive experience both academically and socially is, therefore, an important goal and numerous studies have sought to investigate the principal elements that contribute to this at both school and classroom levels (for example, Siraj-Blatchford *et al.*, 2008).

The organisation of schools is based on a number of variables such as the type of school, the physical environment, the general ethos, the size of the school, the size of the class and different types of pupil grouping, all of which are believed to contribute to differences in educational outcomes. Any discussion of these variables, however, must first acknowledge that schools do not exist in a political vacuum and that these same variables are frequently determined or shaped by governmental legislation.

The legislative context in England

Following the 1944 Education Act, and the introduction of the 'eleven-plus' examination, children's educational placements were determined by age, aptitude and ability. This tiered system introduced secondary-modern schools (for the majority of children), technical schools (for those with scientific aptitude) and grammar schools (for the most-able). In 1965, LEAs (Local Education Authorities) were 'requested' by the then-Labour government to provide 'comprehensive' (i.e. non-selective) education but, despite subsequent government changes, in England there are still some 20 LEAs that are wholly or partially selective (i.e. who assess children based on their academic ability at 11 years of age, with the more-able gaining places at grammar schools).

Pupils assessed as 'educationally subnormal' continued to be educated in special schools until the findings of the Warnock Report (DES, 1978) suggested that, as 'one in five children' would experience learning difficulties at some point in his/her school life, such generalised segregation was no longer appropriate. Thus began a series of legislative moves towards greater inclusion in mainstream schools for children with special educational needs (SEN). No longer were any difficulties in learning to be regarded as 'within the child' but rather as an 'interaction' between the child and the learning environment.

Subsequent Education Acts, the *Code of Practice* (DfES, 2001a) and the Special Educational Needs and Disability Act (DfES, 2001c) reinforced the government commitment to include children with special educational needs in mainstream schools. This in turn promoted a more 'wholistic' approach to children's development with greater multi-disciplinary team-working and the inception of new 'Children's Services' departments within local authorities bringing a range of professionals (social, educational and medical) together more formerly to identify and assess individual needs.

Following this, the Children's Plan (DCSF, 2007) furthered the government aim to put the needs of families, children and young people at the forefront of the political agenda and, as part of this, a growing number of schools are today offering a wider range of childcare services from 8.00 a.m. – 6 p.m. for 48 weeks of the year through the Extended Schools initiative. With the ultimate aim that all schools should offer these extended services by 2010, it seems likely that the widening role of the school is destined to bring even greater influence to bear not only on children's formal academic achievements but also on their social and personal development.

School effectiveness

Do individual schools make a difference?

It may seem obvious that schools do differ, but numerous previous studies have indicated that educational outcomes were mainly linked to influences external to the school: children's basic abilities, their home background and community or cultural influences. In Britain, the *Plowden Report* (CACE, 1967) had found that social class and parental attitudes gave the best explanations for variations in children's performance and there have been and continue to be costly initiatives to address these differences.

One early American project, the 1960s 'Head Start' programme, aimed to enhance the lives of low-income families by offering pre-school placements for children with additional educational advice on child welfare for their parents. Although preliminary conclusions about the effectiveness of the programme were rather negative, long-term follow-ups (for example, Barnett, 1995) found significant educational and social benefits, particularly when the support offered was intensive, long-term and not only involved children but their entire families.

In Britain, similar concern that deprivation was blighting the lives of many children and families, prompted the launch in 1998 of the Sure Start project with the aim of 'giving children the best possible start in life' (DfEE, 1998a) and improving childcare, early education, health and family support by expanding outreach and community development work. One study compared 6,000 three-year-olds who were attending a Sure Start pre-school centre with 2,000 children of similar age and background who were not, and noted improved behaviour in the children involved in the programme, with additionally greater willingness from their parents to encourage learning at home (Melhuish *et al.*, 2008). The conclusion that the gap between less-privileged children and the rest of the population was narrowing assured the continuation of the scheme and, in March 2009, there were over 2,900 Sure Start Children's Centres providing this 'best start in life' to 2.3 million children.

It is easy to see, however, how over-emphasis on the effects of a child's home background *could* conceal weaknesses within a school. For instance, as shown in Figure 6.1, the students from school A (sited in a poor catchment area) may make good progress but still ultimately achieve at a lower level than students in school B (sited in a good catchment area) where less progress is made.

Keen to identify and address any weakness *within* schools, the government insisted that all schools could, and should, be brought up to the level of high-achieving ones with (apparently) comparable intakes and the introduction of the Office for Standards in Education (OFSTED) whose school inspectors form an integral part of this improvement process.

While it has never been feasible to control for variables such as home background by randomly allocating students to different schools, various studies have attempted to make fair comparisons of schools by taking pupils' backgrounds or initial achievements into account. Following on from these studies, in 2003, the government introduced the 'value added' measure to address this perceived range of 'student-body' differences. This measure compares pupil performance in one set of tests (for example, GCSE results) with performance of all pupils nationally who had performed at a similar level in a previous set of tests (in this instance, the Key Stage 2 Standard Assessment Tests – SATs taken at the

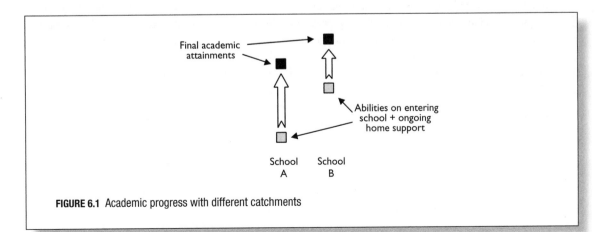

FIGURE 6.1 Academic progress with different catchments

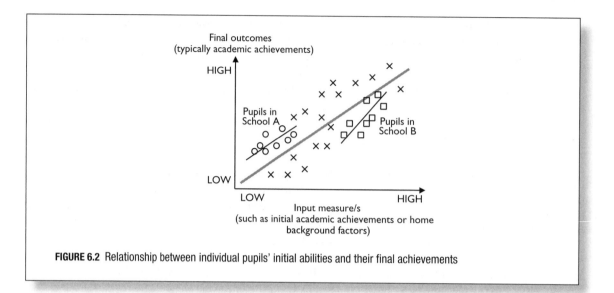

FIGURE 6.2 Relationship between individual pupils' initial abilities and their final achievements

age of 11 years). Thus, a non-selective comprehensive school that offers a broad curriculum for pupils of all abilities can be compared with a more academically focused grammar school that selects children by academic ability. The results of this type of analysis can be shown by a graph (Figure 6.2), where the overall relationship between input variables (such as achievement and/or home background) on starting a phase of schooling can be related to pupils' final achievements.

The data shown in this type of graph can be used to evaluate 'value added' effects by comparing actual progress with predicted progress. Pupils in school A appear to be achieving better results than one would expect from their input measures, while pupils in school B appear to be achieving poorer results than one would expect. Pupils in school B who start off at a lower level also appear to be making relatively worse progress, but it may be the case that this school tends to place an emphasis on the achievements of the more-able pupils.

Using multilevel modelling, which controls for the common effect of each school on the attainment of its pupils, Schagen and Schagen (2003) assessed the variance in national KS3 attainments which could be accounted for by school type (selective or non-selective). They found that the most-able pupils placed in grammar schools in selective LEAs demonstrated no significant benefit over pupils of similar ability educated in comprehensive schools in non-selective authorities. Pupils with an average score at KS2 made only minimally greater progress in a grammar school by KS3 than those of similar KS2 ability in a comprehensive school. The greatest benefit of placement in a grammar school as determined by KS3 results was noted to be in those pupils described as the 'least able' of the grammar school pupils.

Not surprisingly, the selective system remains popular with parents whose children gain access to grammar schools, but other research evidence highlights the inequity of such systems. Recent studies (for example, Levacic and Marsh, 2007) have suggested that these selective LEAs are typically sited in areas of above-average socio-economic status, and as a result, children of average to below average ability from less-advantaged families are concentrated with other less-advantaged and less-able pupils in either comprehensive schools (in non-selective areas) or secondary-modern schools (whose intake consists solely of pupils who fail the grammar school entry test in a selective area). Levacic and Marsh also demonstrated how selective systems disadvantage pupils who 'end up' in secondary-modern schools by undertaking a value-added analysis of GCSE results from a national data set. Using KS2 results as the measure of prior attainment, then awarding points for each GCSE grade (i.e. A★ = 8, A = 7, B = 6, C = 5, D = 4, E = 3, F = 2, G = 1) and adding them together for each pupil, the results indicated that students in grammar schools gained on average five grades more than equivalent students in comprehensive schools and six grades more than pupils in secondary-modern schools.

Primary-school evidence

Historically, the focus in the 1960s and 1970s on the influence of home factors on children's achievements steered research away from the classroom, but more recently there has been renewed interest in investigating these school environments where children spend considerable amounts of their time as they move towards adulthood.

One government-funded longitudinal study, the Effective Pre-School and Primary Education Project (EPPE3–11), followed the progress and development of 2,800 children from pre-school to the end of their primary education (Sylva et al., 2008). The study looked at the relationships between children, their families, their homes and school characteristics, and reported on the effect of these on the children's subsequent attainments in English and mathematics and also on aspects of their social and behavioural development.

Although it has always been assumed that simply attending a pre-school centre or nursery would compensate the more-disadvantaged children, this study set out to measure the importance of *quality* in that provision. As in many previous studies, the final report concluded that two of most significant factors affecting a child's learning during the primary-school years were the academic qualifications of the mother and the home learning environment, but the results highlighted the importance of good quality pre-school provision. The quality of pre-school provision was found to be an important predictor of both cognitive and social behavioural outcomes: while high-quality pre-school provision was found to benefit cognitive attainment across *all* groups, it was found to be especially beneficial to the social development of boys, children with special educational needs and those from disadvantaged backgrounds. Children who experienced poor-quality pre-school provision showed no significant cognitive benefit over those who had not attended pre-school.

Similarly, Melhuish et al. (2006) found significant differences between the educational outcomes of different primary schools after controlling for the influence of child, family and home factors and prior attainment. In general, and perhaps not surprisingly, children made better academic progress in schools described as 'academically-effective' as measured by using the value-added statistics arising from the national measures taken at KS1 and KS2. The key findings of the study are particularly relevant for classroom practice.

Practical implications

It seems that the overall quality of teaching affects children's social behaviour and intellectual development, and the quality of teaching has a more powerful impact on children's academic progress than their gender or whether or not they are entitled to free school meals. Overall quality of teaching tends to be higher in classrooms where teachers use plenary sessions consistently, and attending a primary school that is high in academic effectiveness gives a particular boost to children who have many disadvantages.

Further results from the study found that, while overall teaching quality was associated with progress in reading and mathematics, there was no significant effect on the social or behavioural outcomes for a majority of children. However, the 'academic effectiveness' of the whole school did have a significant effect on the social and behavioural development of those children who had special educational needs, or whose mothers had low educational qualifications. Aspects of the whole school's organisation, such as the emphasis on homework, level of communication with parents and the quality of parental support, was found to play a significant part in promoting better progress. When the powerful influences of child, family and home were controlled, it was the school quality that mattered most: going to a 'better' primary school exerted a positive net influence on children's academic progress and their social/behavioural outcomes.

The final summary (Sylva *et al.*, 2008) concluded that initiatives that promote the overall effectiveness of the school (for example, enhancing the quality of teaching and creating orderly, organised and positive classroom climates) improve educational outcomes for all children, but were particularly important for schools with higher proportions of disadvantaged children. Interestingly, the authors reported another finding that may be particularly relevant in achieving this 'overall effectiveness': in the schools where there were high levels of pupil voice and agency (i.e. where the pupils' views were listened to and they were given greater opportunities to organise activities for themselves) there was a notable increase in hyperactivity and anti-social behaviour.

Practical implications

Moderate amounts of pupil involvement and autonomy may be optimum in the early school years but children in the primary school years may not be developmentally ready to respond well to high levels of autonomy.

Secondary-school evidence

Despite the emphasis on the importance of 'in-classroom' research, Kutnick and colleagues (2005) report that studies in secondary schools are both noticeably fewer and more limited than those undertaken in primary schools.

In their now classic and frequently cited study *Fifteen Thousand Hours*, Rutter and his team (Rutter *et al.*, 1979) sought to challenge the then-contemporary focus on home influences. By investigating the characteristics of effective secondary schools in Inner London they set out to identify those factors that significantly influenced both behaviour and academic attainments. They discovered that the overall ethos of the schools had a marked effect: those schools that had a positive ethos produced both good academic outcomes and good pupil behaviours.

Features that related positively to academic outcomes included: the general level of academic emphasis (shown, for example, by the amount of homework set); involvement of pupils in school life (for example, if there were form representatives); general pupil conditions; and involvement of staff in decision-making. Children in the more successful schools were also more likely to use the library and to have work displayed on the walls. Since these aspects tended to group together, Rutter *et al.* considered that this 'ethos' influenced academic achievement and shaped pupils' behaviour and attitudes long beyond their school experience.

The study was important in refocusing attention on improving the ethos in schools where behavioural and academic outcomes had been less positive (for example, Cassen and Kingdon, 2007a), and the important effect of individual schools on a wide range of subsequent pupil behaviours such as excessive smoking and drinking (West *et al.*, 2004).

Creemers and Reezigt (1996) had previously carried out a review of a number of such studies based on multilevel modelling and found general agreement for the importance of nine main factors. These were:

- an orderly environment/school climate;
- consensus and cooperation between teachers;
- a focus on basic skills/learning time;
- monitoring of student progress/evaluation;
- effective school educational/administrative leadership;
- having a policy on parental involvement;
- high expectations;
- coordination of curriculums and approaches to instruction; and
- quality of the school curriculum.

On the face of it, this list appears to be eminently reasonable. It would be hard to argue that schools should not be organised and run well, or that teachers should not try to manage and deliver learning. Lists such as this are commonly used in inspections to assess schools' effectiveness, and often form the basis for OFSTED recommendations about how schools could be improved.

The full story is more complex, however, and Coe and Fitz-Gibbon (1998) have pointed out that when findings such as these are based only on observational data, any causal direction is not clear as high expectations could *result* from pupils' attainments, rather than cause them. Research by Thrupp (1998) also found that positive organisation and management in schools very much depends on the presence of a 'critical mass' of well-behaved and able pupils. Yet, the majority of primary and secondary schools judged by OFSTED to be 'failing' or which appear to be underachieving on 'value added' measures are largely those schools that have the poorest student intake, a factor over which schools have little control. So, acknowledging that learning, teaching and behaviour are inseparable issues for schools, Steer (2009) proposed an alternative causal link: that poor behaviour may *arise from* an inability to access learning rather than be a *causal* factor in not accessing learning. So, the 'critical mass' of well-behaved and able pupils envisaged by Thrupp may, it seems, *result from*, rather than *contribute to*, the positive organisation and management in schools.

In an attempt to identify other factors that may affect GCSE attainment, Jenkins *et al.* (2006) compared a number of variables. They found that schools with sixth forms performed worse than those without, possibly because teachers in schools with sixth forms may focus greater effort on A-level teaching. Similarly, pupils in single-sex schools and pupils in grammar schools achieved substantially better results. There was also a markedly better performance in denominational schools over non-denominational schools: Roman Catholic schools in particular produced significantly better results. The study focused specifically on resourcing and funding, and concluded that marginal increases in resources, in terms of expenditure per pupil and pupil–teacher ratio, had some positive effect on the least-able pupils and also those entitled to free school meals.

In non-selective authorities, all pupils are educated in comprehensive schools (apart from those in the independent sector); in selective education authorities, approximately 75 per cent of pupils are educated in secondary-modern schools and 25 per cent in grammar schools. The major effect of this selective system of education is that pupils from less-advantaged families (and who are of average to below-average ability) are grouped with other, equally disadvantaged pupils. Using the measure of eligibility for free school meals measure (a standardly used indicator of 'disadvantage'), Levacic and Marsh (2007) found that, on average, in secondary-modern schools some 14 per cent of pupils are entitled to free school meals while in grammar schools only 2 per cent of pupils fall into this category.

Positive effects of schooling

One possible interpretation of the above findings is that most schools are generally doing a similar job, in so far as they are constrained by factors such as their intake, community resources and general funding. It would, therefore, be quite surprising if schools did not have some positive effect on children's progress, and one way of highlighting this is by looking at children when their formal education has been limited for some reason.

One classic finding of this type is the significant decrease in children's general academic attainments that happens during school holidays. Cooper *et al.* (1996) suggested the overall summer loss was equivalent to about one month and that this was greatest for subjects such as mathematics, which pupils are unlikely to work on by themselves. Children from the lower social classes and pupils with special educational needs showed the greatest decline, while middle-class students showed gains on reading tests, presumably due to opportunities and encouragement from their home backgrounds. Similarly, another study of reading loss over the summer holidays (Mraz and Rasinski, 2007) noted this effect particularly in children who have limited access to reading materials at home and whose parents or caregivers may be reluctant or unsure of how to help.

The time of year at which children start school has also been shown to have an effect on their attainments, with Sharp and Hutchinson (1997) finding that if pupils start school two terms later than others, this reduces their end-of-Key Stage 1 attainments by about 10 per cent. A sophisticated analysis by Cahan and Coren (1989) also separated out the effects of age and the amount of schooling for children in grades 5 and 6. This demonstrated that schooling had a significant effect on general intellectual abilities such as non-verbal intelligence, but had the greatest consequences for verbal and academic attainments. The estimated impact of one year's schooling gave an effect size of 0.4 for vocabulary and 0.5 for arithmetic achievements. This could explain Hallam and Ireson's (2007) observation that, by the time they reach secondary school, summer-born children are disproportionately represented in low-ability groups and are more likely to have been identified as having special educational needs.

Schooling does therefore appear to make a big difference to children's academic and cognitive progress. It can also bring about some equity, levelling up the progress of children who come from a less-stimulating home background, although (as noted elsewhere) it is unlikely that it will ever be able to compensate for this completely.

Improving education

The introduction of the Office for Standards in Education (OFSTED) in 1992 aimed to improve education by putting in place regular inspections to identify schools that might be failing (or 'likely to fail') to provide pupils with an acceptable standard of education. Current government directives still attempt to improve 'failing' schools by grafting on features of other schools that seem more successful. However, growing evidence that more-able pupils from disadvantaged backgrounds may be underachieving because they are actually disadvantaged by the 'failing' schools they attend has prompted the government to encourage parental choice so that parents can choose the schools they believe will be 'more effective' for their children.

Currently, schools with an acknowledged poor intake (identified by the number of pupils entitled to free school meals or scoring below the nationally expected levels on Key Stage 2 SATS) have a much more difficult job to do, and it would seem a sensible strategy to allocate increased resources to them, so that key staff could benefit from the resulting opportunities for more non-contact time and further professional development. Macbeath and Galton (2004) comment that 'the English system, for better or worse, is founded on the principle that personal relationships between pupils and teachers are inextricably linked to effective teaching and learning' (p. 249), but several studies (for example, Barmby, 2006) highlight the excessive workload reported by teachers. In many schools, particularly those with an acknowledged poor intake, it seems that teachers have little time to talk to each other, let alone handle any pastoral issues by talking to their pupils outside lesson time.

Internationally, the pastoral curriculum is handed over to other professionals: in the USA, a team of support staff is headed up by a psychologist, while in Sweden, after-school clubs and extra-curricular activities are organised by community youth workers and sited in centres adjacent to the school. This model is in part becoming more evident in the UK with the introduction of school counsellors and the responsibility for after-school clubs being passed to professionals other than teachers (e.g. social services).

The introduction of teaching assistants is also sometimes seen as a means of improving education, enabling teachers to be released from direct teaching duties to follow-up pastoral issues. There is, however, ongoing debate as to the precise role of teaching assistants who, it could be said, provide a more financially feasible solution to the need for extra human resourcing and additional funding in schools.

The physical environment

Although some differences between the performance of schools can be attributed to variations in pupils or pedagogic style, the overall ethos of the school is frequently identified as a factor in studies of pupil attainment. However, a review of some of these studies (Higgins *et al.*, 2005) revealed that evidence, mainly from American studies, suggests not only a significant relationship between physical or structural factors and pupil performance, but also highlights the impact of the physical environment on teachers. These studies can, therefore, offer valuable insight into the ways in which schools should be designed if they are to acknowledge and fulfil the government's aim for enhanced personalised learning with its more subtle view of learning than the traditional 'chalk and talk' environment.

Layout and pleasantness

Alexander (2000) pointed out that school buildings and classrooms vary from country to country because of differing educational philosophies and availability of funding. However, Feilden (2004) notes, the science of designing learning environments 'is currently remarkably under-developed', and Heppell (2004) adds that, whilst school-designers pay great attention to minimising 'heat loss', they give little consideration to minimising 'learning-loss' in their planning.

Rutter's study of British secondary schools indicated that, while the physical layout of schools (split site, age of the buildings) did not account for any variations in academic achievement, variations in the care and decoration of buildings (including the cleanliness and tidiness of rooms and the use of plants, posters and pictures), together with concessions allowing pupils to use the buildings during breaks, with access to a telephone and hot drinks, were related to positive outcomes (Rutter *et al.*,

1979). Buckley *et al.* (2005) found too that a school's ability to comply with health and safety requirements, such as organising fire safety, security and general maintenance, proved to be a reliable predictor of the level of pupil performance on a series of standardised achievement tests.

A problem here is that, since these findings are generally correlational, it is not necessarily the case that these environmental features caused the good outcomes. Some evidence from other studies (for example, Higgins *et al.*, 2005), indeed, suggests a reciprocal effect in that the environmental quality can affect both pupil and staff morale and that the high morale of staff and pupils noted in some schools could lead to greater 'ownership' and better care of the buildings. A direct experimental study by Wollin and Montagne (1981) showed that pupils made better progress when moved from unattractive rooms to ones that were painted in attractive colours and decorated with posters, area rugs, plants and other items. When they were moved back to the less-attractive rooms, their progress also returned to previous levels, indicating that the improvements in progress were due to environmental changes. A similar study by Berry (2002) also noted marked improvement in attitudes in both pupils and staff when the school environment was physically improved.

With the ever-increasing drive to enhance pupil performance, there has been a growth of studies into the impact of the general school environment on classroom practices (see Woolner *et al.*, 2007 for a review). More recently, there has been growing emphasis on the importance of the within-classroom environment, from which Earthman and Lemasters (2009) identify room temperature, heating and air-quality as the most crucial physical influences on pupil achievement.

Seating arrangements

A number of factors that influence teaching and learning in schools have been suggested, and one of these, that children respond directly to the arrangement of the space that they are taught in and their place within it, has focused research attention on the physical organisation of classrooms.

Children in most primary classes tend to be placed around tables in groups of four to six, to work on exercises set by the teacher. In Britain, the *Plowden Report* (CACE, 1967) justified this seating arrangement on the basis that it would enable children to learn from each other through discussion and cooperation. However, several studies (for example, Pollard *et al.*, 2000) finding a lack of correspondence between small group seating and cognitive learning tasks have concluded that seating children around tables does not mean they will interact or work effectively as a small group. Wheldall (1991) had previously noted that groups give greater opportunities for pupils to distract one another. By observing a number of classes for two weeks during which the children first sat around tables, then moved to more traditional rows for two weeks, then eventually returned to the original group pattern, Wheldall found that pupils' on-task behaviour rose by about 15 per cent when they were seated in rows, and fell by the same amount when they returned to sitting around tables. Some pupils' performance rose by over 30 per cent in the row configuration and Marx *et al.* (2000) suggest that learning is further optimised, particularly that of the less-focused and less-successful pupils, when they sit in the 'action zone' across the front and down the middle of the room. In part, this may be because when less-attentive pupils are moved to an 'action zone', they focus more on their school work and lessen the need for persistent 'negative' attention from the teacher. While Marx and her colleagues view this 'action zone' as triangular in shape, Delethes and Jackson (1972) consider it to be 'T' shaped.

Marx and her colleagues also found that in a two-week cycle over an eight-week period when pupils were assigned to sit in a semicircle and then in a row-and-column seating arrangement, they asked more questions in the semi-circle than in the row-and-column arrangement. By way of explanation, the authors proposed that social interaction is encouraged when individuals are able to establish face-to-face contact, so it seems that seating in classrooms should be flexible so that it can be arranged to suit the task, activity or lesson.

Open-plan designs

'Open-space' schools have few interior walls or partitions and are designed to free students from traditional barriers such as conventional seating, allowing them more opportunities to explore the learning environment, with different areas given over to specialist activities. Yet several studies have noted that the physical accommodation in open-plan spaces often failed to encourage or enhance collegiate interaction (Brennan *et al.*, 2002). Studies comparing and evaluating the effectiveness of this design have, however, often been confounded by the way teachers use the space. One early study (Rivlin and Rothenberg, 1976) found that, in many open classrooms, teachers continued to use conventional class teaching and, by staying in one place and 'teaching from the front', they failed to adapt, or encourage their pupils to adapt, to the new opportunities there.

There has also been recurring evidence that students who have educational difficulties find it particularly difficult to cope in open-plan classrooms (for example, Cotterell, 1984). Yet, the current government drive towards inclusive education means that many children with special educational needs are now integrated fully or partially into mainstream classes that are often large and open-plan. Jordan (1999) expresses particular concern for those with Autistic Spectrum Disorders who, acutely sensitive to light, noise and busy environments, are often placed in classrooms populated by colourful wall displays and multiple group activities. Whilst many schools provide 'personalised learning spaces' (often a desk just outside the main classroom), open-plan schools still struggle to adapt the physical environment to meet these specific needs.

Density and crowding

Hall (1966) had previously analysed four zones of personal space that affect the way in which we interact with other people. In most of our lives there appear to be proxemic rules that govern the distances we use in our interactions. Children, however, appear to be less sensitive than adults to these rules, and can sometimes intrude on others' inner zones too readily. A teacher's role would also appear to be somewhat ambiguous, with distances depending on the nature of the task or interaction; directions to the whole class usually involve greater distances, whereas close interactions may be appropriate when working with an individual.

In the average class, many children work together in a single, limited space, and seating and general working arrangements usually position them within each other's casual–personal zone (see Figure 6.3).

Practical activity

Experiment with your zones of personal space. Does it depend on how well you know the other person?
   Which 'space' do you prefer between you and a comparative stranger in these places:

- in a lecture room;
- at the cinema;
- in a bar or pub;
- on a bus.

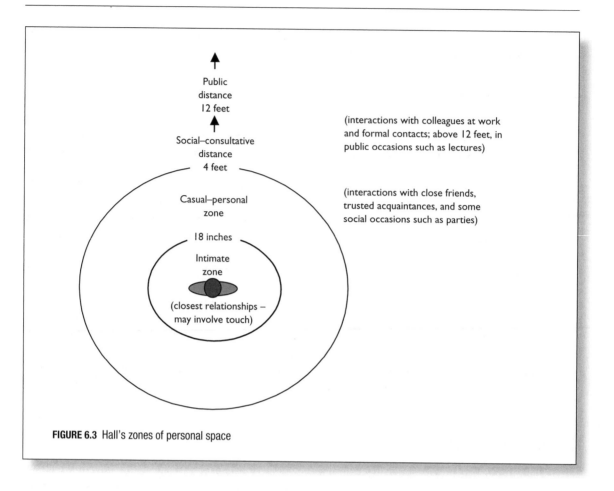

FIGURE 6.3 Hall's zones of personal space

It therefore seems likely that density might have a significant effect on pupils' sense of being intruded upon and their ability to work effectively.

The key feature appears to be whether there is a subjective experience of crowding and whether this affects individuals' feelings of privacy and control over their environment. When tasks are relatively constrained and passive, as in lectures, student performance is not affected by high levels of density. Even when students have contact within their intimate zone, Freedman *et al.* (1971) found that this did not seem to matter so long as the students had their own clearly separated desk space and were able to work independently. However, when tasks are more complex and require higher levels of interaction, then students are more likely to experience crowding. Over a period of time such conditions can also lead students to make attributions that they are not able to control their environments. This can lead to feelings of helplessness and students may then withdraw from active involvement.

The overall density and relationships between pupils and the nature of the task can also affect tolerance of others. Fisher and Byrne (1975) found that students working in libraries (with a low density) were particularly disrupted by strangers sitting close to them, even though they and the strangers were working independently. This appeared to be due to a sense of intrusion, and females especially were affected by a stranger sitting next to them – a position they would normally reserve for interacting with a friend. In school, however, pupils usually know one another well, and it would seem likely they would tolerate close interactions. In designs of seating in public spaces in schools, it may be appropriate to limit the closeness of seating, although conversely, classes may benefit from closer physical groupings, particularly when cooperative group work is being undertaken.

Noise and pupil progress

Teachers often comment that noise in the classroom impedes learning and that open-plan classrooms lead to increased levels of noise and greater distractibility. Some teachers strive to maintain quiet working environments, and their efforts would seem to be supported by research evidence that noise does affect learning (Dockrell and Shield, 2004) – particularly the learning of those with hearing impairments or for whom English is an additional language (Bradlow *et al.*, 2003; Mayo *et al.*, 1997; Nelson and Soli, 2000).

In most classrooms, there are two different types of noise that can affect children's learning: the noise generated by the children themselves and the environmental noise in the classroom caused by heating or lighting systems, computers or external traffic. The noise generated by the pupils themselves can of course be an indication of poor task involvement if pupils are talking off-task or directly calling out to one another. However, pupil-generated noise can also reflect useful inter-pupil discussion and some teachers will aim for more moderate levels, accepting a 'working buzz' as part of active class work. In small-group work, such as a science investigation, a certain amount of noise is to be expected if learning is to occur as pupils discuss their thinking, actions and analysis of their findings.

One investigation (Dockrell and Shield, 2006) compared a group of Year 3 children's performance on a series of non-verbal, reading, spelling and arithmetic tests under three acoustic conditions. The conditions were: a *base* condition – i.e. in a quiet classroom with no-one speaking; a *babble* condition where children were working individually with some interaction; and a *babble plus environmental noise* condition where noise sources that the children found most annoying (sirens and lorries) were recorded and played at random intervals over the typical classroom babble. There was surprising evidence that the children undertaking the reading and spelling tasks in the third condition (babble plus environmental noise) performed better than those exposed to the noise levels in the other conditions. Dockrell and Shield propose that, in the third condition, for the relatively short time-limit of the task, most children were able to actively 'tune out' noise to enhance their focus on their work. Further investigation would be needed to confirm whether children can maintain this high level of attention over lengthier periods. However, the outcome for the children in the study who had special educational needs was poor across all conditions and the babble condition (arguably a typical noise level in an inclusive classroom setting) had a particularly detrimental effect on this group's achievements in the reading and spelling tasks.

Practical activity

Try writing a few paragraphs on 'The House Where I Was Born' in the following three 'noise' conditions:

- in a library;
- in front of the television at home;
- in a café.

An earlier finding that typical class noise levels of 60–65 dB are louder than the normal voice levels of many teachers would seem also to be particularly relevant when including children with special educational needs in class learning which involves verbal interaction between teacher and pupils

(McSporran, 1997). It would seem sensible that, in order for the children to hear teachers' verbal instructions and questions clearly, the teachers' voices should be significantly louder than the background noise (typically, McSporran suggests, by at least 15 dB). As speaking at this volume could cause damage to the teachers' vocal chords, teachers in the study were asked to use a small portable wireless microphone and subsequent results suggested improvements in both learning and behaviour from its use.

Organisation of pupils and teaching

School size

For many years there has been ongoing debate about the optimum size of a school. Budge (1996), reporting on research findings from the United States, suggested the most effective size of a school was between 600 and 900 pupils. More recently, one of the few studies to look at school size in England (Spielhofer *et al.*, 2004) reported that the positive relationship between pupil performance and school size existed in only a certain size of school. The study concluded that the negative effects on performance found in the very smallest and the very largest schools suggested the optimum size of school to be between 180–200 pupils. Yet, according to Kimber (2003), at that time only 22 per cent of secondary schools in England and Wales had fewer than 700 pupils on roll.

One subsequent review reanalysed data from the National Pupil Database and assessed a range of factors affecting pupil attainment in GCSE examinations (Jenkins *et al.*, 2006). The size of the schools they included ranged from 150 pupils to 2,390 pupils on roll, and the results suggested that schools where attainment is higher tend to have low pupil:teacher ratios, but as the number of pupils on roll increases, so the pupil:teacher ratio increases.

This database for over 3,000 schools does, however, include comprehensive schools, secondary-modern schools and a number of grammar schools which, with their selective intake, are usually smaller but would generally achieve at a high level whatever their size.

Primary and secondary school 'culture' clashes

In 2002, a report by the Office for Standards in Education identified the lack of curriculum continuity and progression in pupils' learning between primary and secondary school as 'one of the primary causes of the widening gap in performance, slackening in progress and loss of self esteem for a significant group of learners' (cited in Osborn *et al.*, 2006: 416). Since that time, this 'culture clash' between the primary and secondary stages of schooling has become a cause for concern and a focus of growing research. Osborn and his colleagues catalogued the range of challenges that accompany the primary-to-secondary-school transition as:

- the increased variety and size of the school (both in terms of the location of classrooms and the heterogeneity and size of the pupil population);
- departmentalisation of subjects with individual subject teachers and class streaming;
- increased emphasis on rules with less tolerance for misbehaviour, and a greater emphasis on ability and competition.

Time of day and learning

Most teachers believe that children's learning is more efficient earlier in the day and this has generally led to an emphasis on timetabling the more academic subjects in the morning and, in some schools, the increasing adoption of the 'Continental day' (which involves an earlier start and finish, with a shortened lunch break).

In view of these beliefs, it is surprising to learn that most of the work that has been carried out on arousal and general mental functioning indicates conversely that pupil learning is likely to peak during the late afternoon. Diurnal variations such as body temperature seem to go through a general cycle of a slow rise during the morning, a short dip after lunch, then a progressive rise to higher levels during the afternoon, followed by a fall only much later in the evening. Jones (1992) has summarised the way in which such indices of arousal correspond with changes in real learning ability.

One reason put forward by Jones for the difficulty that most teachers have in believing such findings could be that, in the mornings, less-alert students may be more manageable and therefore appear to be more receptive. Although students may be generally aroused and capable of learning more in the afternoons, they may also be more difficult to control and less likely to be involved in more formal (boring) learning tasks.

When students are older and more likely to be self-motivated, later learning sessions may be even more effective. The findings of a recent Oxford University study of teenagers' responses on a series of memory tests suggested that, from the age of ten years, the human body clock shifts by an average of two hours until it peaks around the age of 20 years (Coughlan, 2009). This means that teenagers are biologically programmed to wake up later and to reach their optimum time for learning later in the day. Some universities are already changing the times of their classes and, in some cases, lectures are being repeated in the evening. This aligns well with Skinner's (1985) findings that teaching courses in the afternoon rather than in the morning resulted in better marks in college examinations.

Learning in groups

Since 1997, the Labour Government has introduced a number of initiatives to improve standards of literacy and numeracy, and these have had an important influence on the grouping procedures adopted particularly by primary schools. One large-scale study of primary schools' organisation (Hallam et al., 2004) reported that, since 1997, 50 per cent of the 2,000 schools in the survey had changed their ways of grouping pupils. Whilst many complied with government guidelines advocating predominantly whole-class, mixed-ability teaching, a number of schools had retained setting and grouping to enhance the personal and social development of the children.

Ability and mixed-ability group work

Most primary schools have historically been organised into mixed-ability, age-determined classes, but there is now a growing tendency for schools to employ more ability-grouping, citing their reasons as to 'raise standards generally' or 'to give [the pupils] the best opportunity in the [National Curriculum] SATs' (Hallam et al., 2004: 126).

Despite evidence from international studies that less differentiation (between schools and within classes) serves to reduce educational inequality (Wiborg and Green, 2006), most secondary schools in the United Kingdom adopt ability grouping (or setting) for at least some curricular subjects, usually using the results of internal tests or National Curriculum SATs (Standard Assessment Tests) to determine placements in sets or groups. In some subjects, such as mathematics, this 'setting' is often done early on, but in other, more practical subjects, such as art, mixed-ability groups are often retained throughout the whole school.

Inaccurate placements in sets, however, can significantly and detrimentally affect pupils' subsequent academic qualifications: for example, in England, top mathematics groups are usually entered for the higher tier of the GCSE and will be taught more in-depth material, often by more experienced and better-qualified teachers, with, perhaps predictably, better progress and examination results (Hallam, 2002).

Although grouping by ability can more readily enable teachers to match work to the pupils' abilities, there is recurring evidence that low-ability groups, in both primary and secondary schools, often include a disproportionate number of children from low socio-economic backgrounds, ethnic minorities, summer-born children (Wilson, 2000) and boys. Kutnick et al. (2002) observed too that these groups of low achievers were often supervised by an adult other than the teacher, while the more-able groups, mainly girls, worked with the teacher.

Despite OFSTED recommendations that pupils should be able to transfer between sets, Kutnick and his colleagues found little evidence of this in reality, possibly because these low-ability pupils, who frequently work alone or in small groups, rarely had sufficient cognitive insights to challenge each other's ideas or elaborate on their own ideas (Kutnick et al., 2002). Further evidence that schools sometimes use 'setting' to separate disruptive pupils seems to overlook Hallam and Ireson's (2007) finding that being placed in a lower set can often cause pupils to become more stigmatised, disaffected and alienated from school and is, therefore, more likely to invoke the very (usually disruptive) behaviour that setting was intended to address.

The outcomes of setting may, then, be real and valuable to schools, but the evidence indicates that there is probably a price to pay in terms of the wider school population's achievements and social adjustment. Hallam and Ireson's (2007) findings that pupils were more satisfied with their class placement if they were taught in mixed-ability classes and, there were no differences in overall attainment between pupils taught in mixed-ability or 'setted' classes, would seem to support the case for mixed-ability teaching in all subjects.

Cooperative group work

Many studies have shown that, with appropriate organisation, cooperative learning (i.e. interacting with other students) can be more effective than independent learning (for example, Chi and Ohlsson, 2005), yet some naturalistic studies (e.g. Pollard et al., 2000) have shown that school grouping is often determined more by the physical constraints of the room rather than by any attempt to promote learning by matching tasks to appropriate group sizes.

In their large-scale study, Kutnick and his colleagues (2002) found that primary-school teachers use small groups more as physical seating arrangements rather than for any pedagogic value, with the most common size of group (4–6 pupils) including pupils of similar ability who worked as individuals rather than collaboratively. Several other studies (for example, Hallam et al., 2004) have suggested that this tendency to group children based on their ability reflects the long tradition of 'selection by ability' endemic in British education and is in sharp contrast to the practices observed in other countries where the emphasis is on effort rather than ability (Broadfoot et al., 2000).

Compared to the government recommendations on the use of grouping in the primary school, secondary-school teachers have been given a relatively free hand regarding classroom organisation, but there is little empirical research to support the notion that pupil groupings at secondary level are organised to actively enhance learning. Indeed, Kutnick *et al.* (2005) suggest that, in the secondary school, seating arrangements are often fixed or constrained either by the location or the availability of apparatus. Groups were also often determined by the physical space available, the furniture and the length of the lesson, and closely linked to a central theme in teachers' planning: controlling pupils. Teachers often associated large (whole-class) grouping with the introduction and assessment of learning material, small grouping for discussion, and individual work for application and practice, but there was inconsistency in the way in which classes were organised from teacher to teacher and from subject to subject. For example, mathematics teachers reported individual learning to be useful for engagement and consolidation of material, whereas English teachers believed they 'lost control' when they allowed pupils to work alone and at their own pace.

Whole-class teaching

Since 1997, the two major initiatives, the National Literacy Strategy (DfEE, 1998b) and the National Numeracy Strategy (DfEE, 1999d), have significantly influenced aspects of primary education, particularly teaching styles and class arrangement. A major feature has been the introduction of interactive whole-class teaching, with a strong emphasis on dialogue and discussion to encourage all pupils to participate. Overall, the groupings in primary classrooms seem to accord with the National Strategies (Literacy and Numeracy), with whole-class teaching occupying 56 per cent of the available teaching time, individual work 36 per cent and group work coming in 'a poor third' (Sammons *et al.*, 2007).

However, the finding that teachers dominated the whole-class section for 74 percent of the time, with the pupils' contribution (24 per cent) consisting of answering mainly closed questions (Smith *et al.*, 2004), suggests there was little evidence that the traditional patterns of whole-class teaching have changed to the 'oral, interactive and lively' exchanges envisaged by the government. Smith and her colleagues found that, while effective teachers displayed a more verbally interactive style than less-effective teachers, the difference proved to be quantitative rather than qualitative, and the teachers' oral contributions in the main consisted of closed, highly structured questions or explanations. Other studies too have concluded that teachers had no clear concept of what was meant by interactive whole-class, shared language teaching (English *et al.*, 2002). If teachers are to succeed with new forms of whole-class teaching, then there must be high-quality in-service professional development that emphasises recent research into class teaching. For example, the results from a recent intervention study by Shapiro and Solity (2008) suggest that breaking whole-class teaching into frequent sessions of short duration (e.g. 12 minutes, three times daily) may provide a more successful format for enhancing children's literacy acquisition in the early years of education.

Practical implication

Research evidence suggests that, in the early years of education, children's literacy acquisition may be enhanced if whole-class sessions are delivered in frequent 'bursts' of short duration.

From 2004, there has been significant funding (£15m) to support the use of ICT and the introduction of interactive whiteboards (IWBs) in whole-class activities. Smith *et al.* (2006), investigating the impact on teacher–pupil interactions in whole-class sessions using interactive whiteboards, reported that, even though the pace of lessons was faster, the traditional patterns of whole-class teaching noted earlier still existed. Again, this reiterated the need for further teacher training to develop the necessary pedagogical skills to benefit from new teaching styles, strategies and techniques.

Overall, Hallam and her colleagues (2004) suggest that there is no one way to group pupils: both whole-class and group teaching can be done well or badly, and either might be more appropriate for certain topics or learning goals. Schools must inevitably make their own decisions based on material resources, human resources (including the expertise of the teachers, additional staffing by teaching assistants and the support of parents), the size of the year group and the numbers of children with special educational needs or for whom English is an additional language.

Class-size effects

It has often been thought that having smaller classes leads to more effective teaching as teachers should then have more time to monitor progress closely and to match the work with the individual needs of the pupils. The STAR ('Student–Teacher Achievement Ratio') project was a major US experimental study that attempted to compare learning progress in different-sized classes (Word et al., 1994). The results indicated that children in small classes performed better in literacy and mathematics, and children from ethnic minorities particularly benefitted from these smaller classes. Its comparative success at a time of growing public concern about education standards in Britain encouraged the Labour government to include limiting the size of primary classes as one of their major aims in their 1997 party political manifesto.

Since that time, a number of studies have continued to monitor both the short- and long-term effects of class size. One of these, a large-scale longitudinal study (Blatchford et al., 2003a), set out to investigate the association between variables such as class size, pupil–adult ratios and classroom procedures and subsequent variations in literacy and numeracy attainment. Overall, the results were similar to those of the STAR project, and a consistent relationship was found between class size and teaching, i.e. the larger the class size, the less teaching. This was perhaps not surprising because of the higher levels of administration or 'non-teaching' (such as taking the register or preparing for an activity) inherent in large classes. In general, children in the larger classes read less frequently to an adult and were twice as likely to be off-task. However, identifying the true relationship between class size and outcome was complicated by the ways in which teachers often compensated for the more negative effects of working in large classes: the results revealed that successful large-class teaching relied heavily on the commitment of individual teachers who regularly gave up their breaktimes (lunchtimes and playtimes) to work with individuals or 'catch up' on administrative tasks and preparation.

Predictably, when a large class of pupils was divided into three groups based on their initial, pre-Reception class abilities, the resulting smaller group sizes had greater beneficial effects on the literacy acquisition of the least-able children. However, Blatchford and his colleagues cautioned, the immediate feedback, so readily available in small class settings, could be seen as 'interruptions' which at times appeared to disrupt the learning of the other pupils or encouraged a level of dependency on the teachers that often resulted in more aggressive peer behaviour. A similarly aggressive behavioural pattern was also noted when small class sizes were introduced later in pupils' school lives with no evidence of any compensatory effect in academic terms. The positive effects then of a small Reception class size, the study concluded, are only sustained if children move forward into similarly small-sized classes.

The longer-term effect of class size has also been investigated using KS2 SAT and GCSE results to produce a 'value-added' model. Jenkins et al. (2006) found that lower pupil–teacher ratios were associated with significantly better GCSE performance overall, but particularly for pupils in the lower quartiles of attainment at KS2. Interestingly, even when controlling for the numbers of pupils with special educational needs, those entitled to free school meals and those for whom English was an additional language, the higher-achieving schools were found to employ more teachers per pupil but fewer non-teaching staff, while in the lower achieving schools, the reverse was found.

Making classes smaller

According to an OECD report (2009), average class sizes in England, currently 26 in primary schools and 24 in secondary schools, are still amongst the highest in the developed world. Moreover, the gulf between class sizes in state-maintained schools and independent schools is widening, with an average of 13 pupils to each class in independent prep schools.

Wasik and Slavin's (1993) idea of one-to-one tutoring for pupils who are most in need has now been adopted by the government with £144 million already allocated to the Every Child a Reader and Every Child Counts programmes, with a further £25 million to be spent on the Every Child a Writer programme to offer intensive one-to-one support for children who are falling behind national standards. While this may go some way to addressing the issue of class sizes, other initiatives have also sought alternative ways of improving pupil:teacher ratios.

Teaching assistants

Changes in educational policy and falling numbers of teachers have prompted significant growth of support staff in schools in England. A report by PricewaterhouseCoopers (2001), commissioned by the government, recommended a substantive increase in non-teaching staff primarily to address the needs of already over-worked teachers, rather than to meet the needs of the pupils they teach.

There is still wide variation in the title given to those 'non-teaching' staff who 'support' children's learning, including classroom assistants (CAs), teaching assistants (TAs), learning support assistants (LSAs) and learning support workers (LSWs). Despite the uncertainty of their title, the number of these 'teaching assistants' increased by 99 per cent between 1997 and 2003 (Blatchford *et al.*, 2007) and now represents more than 25 per cent of staff employed in schools (Bedford *et al.*, 2008). Clearly, government spending on providing these additional, albeit comparatively poorly paid, staff has been considerable, and it could easily be assumed that the provision of additional adults in classrooms was based on evidence that such a strategy would enhance children's learning and overall performance of schools. Recent research findings have, however, questioned the verity of such an assumption.

In an attempt to investigate how the deployment of teaching assistants was perceived, and the effect teaching assistants had on classroom interaction and subsequent pupil attainment, Blatchford *et al.* (2007) carried out a large-scale, three-year study involving some 200 primary schools and over 5,000 pupils. The results suggested that relatively few teaching assistants prepared materials or organised classroom displays, but most were found to undertake more pedagogical, interactive roles with the pupils. Questionnaire responses suggested that teachers regarded 'reiteration, repetition and drilling' by a teaching assistant to be an appropriate way to enhance the children's understanding and, as a result, teaching assistants were mainly 'static' (i.e. they were positioned in one location in the classroom) where teachers had deployed them to support group or individual pupil behaviour or learning. However, whilst primary teachers reported they were largely positive about having these additional adults in the classroom, Blatchford and his colleagues noted that many lacked the experience to manage and oversee other staff who were probably unqualified and lacking in appropriate professional training.

Their results gave little evidence that either the presence or the level of qualification of the teaching assistants had any measurable effect on pupil attainment. However, as only the direct *academic* outcomes for the *whole* class were measured, it could be argued that this may have inadvertently undervalued the *indirect* influence of the teaching assistants. Earlier studies have claimed that, as teaching assistants are more likely to be involved with children who have special educational needs or behavioural problems, the teaching assistants' presence may *indirectly* maximise the opportunity of the remainder of the class to focus on their work, and may also enable teachers to have more interaction with individual pupils (Schlapp *et al.*, 2001). Indeed, OFSTED inspectors have reported a higher quality of teaching in lessons where teaching assistants were present, possibly resulting from this observed increase in pupil engagement and opportunity for more active forms of interaction. However, as Wang and Finn (2000) suggest, one class with 30 children and two adults cannot provide the unique environment of the small class setting of 15 children with one teacher.

Such an observation would not be possible, of course, in the secondary schools, where pupils move from teacher to teacher throughout the day, and this emphasises the very different roles played by teaching assistants in the primary school compared to those in the secondary school. In the primary school, teaching assistants can and do take on a variety of different roles, by offering clerical and technical support, by freeing the teacher to deal with an urgent problem, by reading a story to the whole class or by managing normal occurrences of pupil misbehaviour. In the secondary school, however, the management is more administratively complex, the teaching more specialised and the pupil behaviour more challenging. Unlike their 'Jack and Jill-of-all-trades' counterparts in the primary school, secondary support staff are often recruited and trained in specific tasks such as working in a clerical capacity, working in a Science lab or working with/for the SENCO.

There is still considerable debate as to whether teaching assistants are, or should be, employed to 'support, supplement, extend or replace the teacher' (Lindsay, 2007: 14) and on the inconsistent 'value' attributed to teaching assistants: as Blatchford and his team add, 'There is something paradoxical about the least qualified staff in schools being left to teach the most educationally needy pupils' (p. 20), not least because, as MacBeath and Galton (2004) comment ironically, when there was a shortage of funding, the teaching assistants 'were the first people to go' (p. 49).

Teaching styles and class management

Formal versus progressive styles

Although teachers use a number of ways to organise and manage their work, two styles appear to be based on very different philosophies. The more traditional, **formal** approach is highly structured and based mainly on didactic or teacher-directed processes. The other, more **progressive**, child-centred approach to teaching emphasises freedom, activity and discovery in learning. As with many developments in education, there have been attempts to evaluate the different effectiveness of these styles, but these have often been confounded by weak definitions of the constructs involved and the effects of other variables such as government initiatives.

In a major review of secondary teaching commissioned by the National Union of Teachers, MacBeath and Galton (2004) reported a gradual change from the more formal, whole-class teaching to smaller groupings at different phases of lessons which enabled teachers to build up 'quality relationships' (p. 48) in a less-formal way with their pupils.

Discovery learning versus direct teaching

Further research has tended to isolate more specific aspects of teaching processes and styles to evaluate their effectiveness. One important feature of child-centred approaches has been viewing the pupil as an active and independent learner, with the teacher facilitating that learning. The most common child-centred approach involves discovery learning, where pupils have experiences that lead them to find key concepts for themselves. Bruner (1961a) in particular argued that didactic teaching will result in only a limited ability to apply knowledge to new situations and learners must, therefore, construct their own system of understanding. According to this view, discovery learning will automatically match learning to the appropriate stage in the child's cognitive development and, Bruner argues, children will develop their knowledge further when they revisit curriculum areas, in a spiral fashion.

In line with Bruner's work, Siraj-Blatchford (2009) insists that the acquisition of knowledge and understanding (i.e. the learning activity) must involve language and encourage children to discuss the meanings of their findings. This form of learning would seem similar to 'guided discovery' where, following Vygotsky's (1978) model, pupils' learning is 'scaffolded' (or supported by the teacher) within their individual 'zones of proximal development'. Sammons *et al.* (2007) agree that pupils' eventual knowledge and understanding will be of more use to them if they are involved in 'Sustained Shared Thinking' (SST) which involves the teacher and the pupil in 'questioning', 'demonstrating', 'telling' and 'dialogue'.

This interactive style of teaching contrasts sharply with the more formal and conventional approaches that most teachers employ: mainly direct teaching with the use of whole-class questions to check for understanding. Critics suggest, however, that whilst this type of didactic teaching results in good initial learning, long-term retention tends to be poorer and the learning does not transfer well.

Do teachers matter?

Teachers as a professional body are responsible for applying educational policy inside the classroom and in doing this they mediate between policy and practice. For most people, it probably seems obvious that teachers must have an important effect on pupils' educational progress and there are also many anecdotal examples of individual teachers who people believe made a significant difference to their lives, for good or ill. Growing governmental concern regarding poor recruitment to the profession has prompted a number of surveys that have attempted to identify 'what makes a good teacher' and how life in the classroom can influence or inhibit their teaching.

Teaching is a demanding, stressful job and a large percentage of people who start a teaching career actually leave during the first five years. In a GTC survey (2002) of 70,000 teachers, the factors that de-motivated teachers were reported as: unnecessary paperwork, government-initiative overload, target-driven culture and student misbehaviour. Subsequent research (MacBeath and Galton, 2004) asked 233 teachers in 65 schools to identify and then rank the top five obstacles to their teaching. Across the whole sample, the factors revealed were: poor pupil behaviour; lack of time for discussion and reflection; large class sizes; too many national initiatives; and over-loaded curriculum content in specific subjects. However, when the data set (which included comprehensive, selective and special schools) was reanalysed by school-type, 'pupil behaviour' became a concern only in the comprehensive schools, whilst 'too many national initiatives' became the prime concern in the selective schools, and 'lack of time for discussion and reflection' in the special schools.

In the hurly-burly of classroom life, teachers often seem to do more supervision than teaching, and are often able to have only very limited and often superficial interactions with individual pupils. Yet, teachers' personal traits such as enthusiasm and energy have been found to correlate with pupil achievement (Rosenshine, 1970), and it is easy to see how teachers who have such an approach would be able to motivate children in the classroom, in much the same way as fictional characterisations such as Jean Brody or the inspirational professor John Keating in *Dead Poets Society* have.

Effective teaching

Most people believe that teachers have an important role in pupils' learning, and many assume that teachers alone are responsible for the educational outcomes of the children they teach. While most teachers are effective, much of what they do is constrained by other factors such as pupils' abilities, the curriculum and available resources, and it would, therefore, be wrong to evaluate teachers solely on the basis of their pupils' achievements.

Some studies suggest that schools vary in their effects on pupil progress (for example, Muijs and Reynolds, 2003), while other studies suggest that individual teachers can and do influence children's educational progress (van de Grift and Houtveen, 2007). Some primary-school studies, using a value-added approach, have found a moderately strong correlation between subjects within-school, i.e. teachers who were 'more effective' in one core subject (English, maths or science) were generally 'more effective' in the others. A number of these studies have also consistently identified a range of classroom strategies employed by effective teachers: focusing and refocusing students' attention on the topic (Topping and Ferguson, 2005), taking account of prior learning (Berliner, 2004), providing high levels of verbal instruction and informative feedback (Connor *et al.*, 2004), managing behaviour positively (Hall and Harding, 2002) and encouraging self-direction/regulation (Bohn *et al.*, 2004).

Practical implications

Research evidence suggests effective teachers:

- start at the pupil's own level;
- give positive direction rather than negative criticism;
- use clear instructions;
- refocus the pupil's attention regularly;
- give informative feedback;
- praise only when it is justified.

By comparing the quality of teaching across four European countries (England, Flanders, Lower Saxony and the Netherlands), van de Grift and Houtveen (2007) found the English teachers (i.e. the teachers working in England) to be the most effective with 'effective teaching skills' similar to those cited in previous studies: the ability to give clear instructions; the ability to adapt the lesson to meet the individual needs of the children; and the ability to 'scaffold' children's learning by modelling strategies and giving regular corrective feedback.

Another large primary-school study (Melhuish *et al.*, 2006) reported that teachers' disorganisation (and the resulting behavioural climate of the classroom) were predictors of poorer progress in both reading and maths, and moreover this lack of teacher organisation often led to evidence of increased hyperactivity. It is possible, however, that this lack of pedagogic skill may reflect the classroom practices of inexperienced rather than poor-quality teachers: results from a study by Ross and Hutchings (2003) revealed that schools in disadvantaged areas find it harder to recruit and retain teachers and, as a result, tend to be served by less-experienced or newly qualified staff.

One recent small-scale study undertaken in New Zealand (Rubie-Davies, 2007) also noted significant differences in the student outcomes in classrooms where teachers had high expectations, average expectations or low expectations of their students. Effective teachers also established procedural routines early in the year, so that classroom instructions focused more on new concepts and knowledge to be learned than details relating to administrative routines. They typically had high student expectation and 'scaffolded' their students' learning by taking account of the students' previous experience, linking this to the new concept or topic by giving more instructions and 'bridging' explanations. The teachers with low expectations gave fewer explanations and less regular, topic-related feedback. Although there is recurring evidence that regular praise and formative feedback on tasks can establish a positive socio-emotional climate in the classroom, and that such a climate is important for promoting student motivation and learning (Rubie-Davies, 2006), it has also been argued that praise per se (i.e. praise that is not topic-oriented) is neither useful nor, it can be assumed, valued by pupils (Hattie, 2002).

Sammons and her colleagues noted that teachers' observed practice tended to be better in those schools that had previously been rated more positively in the professional judgement of OFSTED inspectors (Sammons et al., 2006). While a good OFSTED report may give schools a much-needed boost in professional morale, this issue of 'professional competence' is perhaps of even greater importance to the teachers themselves, since a variety of judgements about their effectiveness, made more usually by head teachers and advisers, are increasingly the basis for assessments that determine teachers' pay and career developments.

Professional development

Historically, there were no real prescriptions for efficient teaching, and teachers were seen as autonomous in making sense of and adjusting to their own classroom environments (Schon, 1983). However, it has been argued that the inception of the National Curriculum has lessened the autonomy of the individual teacher, and teacher education has become 'an unproblematic, technical rationalist, procedure' (Furlong, 2005: 132).

In recent years, the routes to becoming a teacher have changed dramatically, and there are now a number of schemes (for example, three-year degree courses, one-year Post-Graduate Certificate courses and, most recently, the Teach First programme, which gives high-achieving graduates six weeks of basic training before 'parachuting' them into schools in deprived areas to teach for a minimum of two years). In response to repeated professional and media reports that many children from ethnic backgrounds are failing to achieve in our schools (for example, Strand and Lindsay, 2009), the Training and Development Agency for Schools (TDA) now requires all trainees to be prepared to teach pupils for whom English is an additional language (EAL). A study by Cajkler and Hall (2009), that investigated the continuing professional development (CPD) of newly qualified teachers in relation to the TDA standards, found that initial teacher-training programmes vary widely in their effectiveness, and the most commonly identified 'gaps' in the training related to practical teaching methods and the development of appropriate resources for EAL pupils, inclusion and differentiation.

Macbeath and Galton (2004) found that teachers were often precluded from attending external training by the pressures of day-to-day teaching, OFSTED inspections, covering for absent colleagues and the unforeseen crises that erupt in schools without warning.

Their data further revealed that the principle and the practice of CPD training did not always converge, as the majority of CPD was taken up by courses relating to national initiatives, delivered in school during the standard number of compulsory training days, with no input on other topics or activities.

Yet, training that is more intensive and based on the use and practice of specific classroom skills has previously been shown to have a significant impact. In one project reported by Waters (1996), teachers in 15 primary schools who were given direct training and support with teaching and management skills recorded gains in their pupils' reading attainments of up to 24 per cent. Similarly, Askew *et al.* (1997) found that the pupils of mathematics teachers who had taken part in longer-term continuing professional development (such as 20-day programmes) achieved significantly higher marks.

Evaluating teachers

Although teachers are increasingly becoming subject to direct inspections and evaluations of their teaching competence, they generally report the opportunity to observe and be observed by colleagues to be a very useful mode of professional development.

However, appraisal procedures when classroom practices are assessed by OFSTED inspectors, head teachers or senior members of staff are sometimes seen in a quite different light. These more 'hierarchical' observations, set on evaluating the competence and effectiveness of individual teachers, are often seen (by the teachers themselves) as more a mechanism of control that can impact on their levels of pay and future careers.

Summary

The school context is an important factor in children's learning. Yet, evaluating the effectiveness of different schools is complex. However, 'value-added' measures or multilevel modelling make it possible to relate input to output measures and compare achievements with average (expected) gains.

Some analyses have found significant differences between schools and have related these to factors involved in organising and delivering education. The size of these differences is rather small and can often seem dwarfed by variations in pupils' abilities and initial attainments, as well as the ongoing effects of home background. Yet schools can and do change children's lives, and it may be possible to improve education by measures that involve reallocating or increasing resources.

There is now growing awareness of the importance of the physical environment of the school, and planners are now being challenged to consider the quality of the air and noise pollution as well as the effect that decoration and types of furniture may have on pupil progress and teacher morale. Open-plan designs are less in evidence as schools seem to be moving towards more formal whole-class lesson delivery in line with curriculum-based initiatives.

Some studies suggest school size influences pupil progress, yet whilst larger schools are sometimes found to be more effective, there would appear to be an optimum size over and above which pupil attainment is lessened. It is commonly believed that small class sizes are better for children's learning, and government manifestos cite reducing the pupil:teacher ratio as a major aim. However, research evidence suggests that reducing class sizes appears to be significantly effective only when this happens in the earliest days of a child's school life.

Formal and progressive teaching styles are difficult to define and evaluate, although aspects of these such as discovery learning and direct teaching can match different learning goals. Secondary schools generally use whole-class teaching for at least some part of each lesson, but the increased government drive for improving standards has changed the way in which many primary-school classrooms are organised, with now greater emphasis on whole-class teaching.

Cooperative group work can improve attainments, but arranging and planning for this type of group working is difficult and, as a result, rarely implemented. It is more common for children to be grouped by their abilities – and, in classes where this is done, the work is often more effectively matched to the pupils' level of attainment. When used to set up different classes, however, separation by ability can lead to a number of negative effects, and appears to benefit only the most-able.

Schools may be constrained by the effects of individual pupils' abilities, their home backgrounds and by general resourcing. Yet, they can and do change many children's lives. Teachers are an important part of the educational process and their effectiveness can only be enhanced by high-quality initial training and regular, focused, continuing professional development.

Key implications

- Pupils spend an ever-increasing part of their daily lives in school.
- High-quality teaching in the early stages of education benefits all children but particularly those from disadvantaged backgrounds or who have special educational needs.
- Inclusive education suggests that most children's needs will be met in the mainstream classroom.
- The performativity culture engendered by the National Curriculum assessments, school league tables and OFSTED may have prompted some improvement in standards, but more emphasis on creativity is needed to encourage further improvement and to re-establish the professional skill and autonomy of many teachers.

Further reading

Alexander (2008), *Essays on Pedagogy*: pedagogy is at last gaining the attention in English-speaking countries that it has long enjoyed elsewhere. To engage properly with pedagogy, we need to apply cultural, historical and international perspectives, as well as evidence on how children most effectively learn and teachers most productively teach. For those who see teachers as thinking professionals, rather than as technicians who merely comply with received views of 'best practice', this book will open minds while maintaining a practical focus.

Bruner (2006), *The Selected Works of Jerome S. Bruner 1957–1978: In Search of Pedagogy Volume 1*: a useful and thought-provoking read that brings together some of Bruner's invaluable ideas on how thinking and learning develops and can be enhanced across the school years.

Day, Sammons and Stobart (2007), *Teachers Matter: Connecting Work, Lives and Effectiveness*: *Teachers Matter* offers a definitive portrait of teachers' lives and work to date. The authors provide powerful evidence of the complexities of teachers' work, lives, identity and commitment.

Discussion of practical scenario

Joe needs to study the OFSTED report and to identify specific short-, medium- and long-term targets (in case the current head teacher does not return from sick leave). With his induction budgetary allocation he may need in his first week to consider enhancing the physical premises of the school, particularly the staffroom, before the start of the new term.

Joe will need to meet with his Senior Management Team and the full staff (including those from the Sure Start Centre), ideally before the children return to school at the start of the term. Within his first month, he will need to review with his Curriculum Co-ordinators the current resources and order new equipment as necessary. He will also need to discuss the Special Needs register and any children who have Statements of Special Educational Need with the school Special Educational Needs Co-Ordinator (SENCO) and discuss any outstanding reviews with the parents.

Joe may need to invite the support of external agencies (local police, health visitors, social workers). He should take advice on creating a suitable activity playground that may in the future become central to the neighbourhood community, and to work with staff, particularly Sure Start staff, to ensure parents, carers, grandparents and friends feel welcome in the school.

7

Society and culture

Practical scenario

Alltown Primary School is concerned about gender issues, particularly the behaviour and achievements of boys. At playtimes there is often a lot of rough play, and football games can sometimes overwhelm the playground. In lessons, some of the boys are rather dominant and noisy, which can disrupt lessons. The school's overall SAT scores are generally representative of the rest of the country, with most of the boys achieving at a level somewhat below the girls. All the teachers are female apart from the head, who teaches two mornings a week.

What could the school do to enhance boys' achievement and performance?

Is there a danger that girls might be sidelined in these initiatives? How could this be prevented?

Society

Psychological perspectives can sometimes bring with them a tendency to neglect the wider social context. Much educational psychology focuses at the level of the individual and is concerned with how people make sense of and react to their environment. In reality, of course, the educational system is part of society and this relationship is implicated in what schooling can achieve. Also, as we have seen, theorists such as Vygotsky believe that the process of education is essentially the development of children's knowledge and understanding of the social culture in which they live.

Culture and schools

According to Hutchins (1995), culture

> is a process and the things that appear on list-like definitions of culture are residua of the process. Culture is an adaptive process that accumulates the partial solutions to frequently encountered problems.... Culture is a human cognitive process that takes place both inside and outside the minds of people. It is the process in which our everyday cultural practices are enacted.
>
> (p. 354)

These practices are learnt, shared and transmitted from generation to generation. The process of developing this in children is often referred to as 'socialisation', and education is an important part of it. The more formal and explicit aims of education are to develop the knowledge, skills and understanding laid down in the curriculum. Quite apart from what is taught in lessons, schools are also important in terms of the informal processes that establish the social identities and behaviours of pupils. These come from the influences of peer contact and values, the general social structure of schools, as well as the processes of management and control within the school.

The process of enculturation does more than just transmit information; it also establishes shared values and beliefs which are necessary for society to function. The relative nature of enculturation is not always apparent, and a particular perspective can seem to be obvious or 'common sense' to people who are raised within a particular culture. Much of what is learned, such as gender roles and our own relationship to them, is also quite subtle. As described later in this chapter, we learn indirectly through observations of the behaviours of others and particular forms of language. The possibility of alternative perspectives and ways of behaving is often apparent only when we look at different cultures, in other countries or at other times. Some of these differences, such as the high level of conformity in the educational systems of some Pacific Rim countries, can seem rather alien to a person who has grown up in Britain, but this is a key part of those countries' general belief in the importance of communal life rather than the individual.

Education is affected to a great extent by general cultural influences since pupils and staff bring their existing beliefs and values to schools. The pre-school years are a critical time for the establishment of basic ideas, and even when children are school age, the majority of their waking hours are still spent out of school, with powerful continuing influences from the family, peer groups and the media. The role of schools is also increasingly open to pressures from the wider society, with recent educational reforms aimed at giving more openness and greater choice to parents.

Sociological perspectives

Sociology complements individually based explanations by emphasising social structures, processes and shared meanings. These can be seen as parts of a complex and interdependent system, whose individual components have certain functions and needs, and which tends to achieve and maintain an overall equilibrium. According to this perspective, known as 'structural functionalism', changes can be difficult to achieve, and what individuals think and do is largely determined by their position within society.

A problem with this sort of approach is that it tends to be rather mechanistic. It does not seem to take account of the ability of individuals actively to think about and to construct and reconstruct their social realities. An alternative perspective, known as **social interactionism**, emphasises the changeable and local nature of social experiences and the importance of processes such as discourses (how we define and talk about things) and specific narratives in defining meanings and self-concepts.

Both these perspectives are important in providing a context for psychological explanations. The earliest functionalist approaches tended to emphasise the determinism of an individual's position within society, with psychology accounting for the ways in which people adjusted to this. However, interactionist perspectives have enabled psychology to describe people as conscious thinkers who are able to define and alter their social environments. It is difficult to argue against the importance of structures in society, but these do not necessarily perform their ostensible functions. They are also made up from individuals who are able, to some extent, to determine their relationships to these structures and with each other.

Social psychology

Social psychology has traditionally attempted to explain social functioning by considering how individuals operate according to their immediate social context. There are a number of areas, however, where it becomes meaningless to distinguish between psychology and sociology, and the most effective approach is to use explanations that inform both societal and individually based perspectives. **Symbolic interactionism** is one important such approach, and is based on the early work of the social psychologist Mead (1934). He believed that our most important psychological feature is the ability to use the symbols involved in language and social meanings, and that our social identity is developed from our interactions with other people, based on the use of these symbols.

Roles and norms

Mead also emphasised the importance of roles in determining such social behaviour. These are expectations about a certain position within a social structure and can be seen as the building blocks of society. Individuals can fill a number of different roles. For example, a pupil in the educational system is also usually a son or daughter, as well as a member of a peer group. Roles carry expected behaviours called **norms** that are associated with them; as far as the school is concerned, basic normative behaviour is that pupils will sit quietly and work in lessons. Behaviour that is in accordance with these norms is called **conformity**, and most of the time roles and norms are powerful ways of understanding and predicting what people will do. Zimbardo (Haney *et al.*, 1973), for instance, carried out a role-play experiment simulating a prison, and showed that student volunteers could very rapidly take on and conform to the roles given to them. The 'guards' in particular soon behaved in a brutal way that was not typical of their normal personality, punishing and isolating the 'prisoners' for minor infractions. Their behaviour was such that, although the simulation had been planned to run for two weeks, it had to be stopped after only six days owing to the severe reactions of the 'prisoners'. These included depression, uncontrollable crying and fits of rage. The students seemed to have no difficulty conforming to roles they had never filled before, and were impelled to continue with these, despite the negative experiences some of them had.

When people fail to conform to a group's norms, they are often rapidly subjected to social pressures to fit in. Early investigations by Asch (1951) placed people in situations where their judgements (about the lengths of lines) were consistently different from those of a group of other people around them. Under this pressure, the subjects regularly changed their stated opinions, even when they were right. The other people in the groups were actually stooges of the investigator and had been instructed before the experiment to make incorrect judgements. They also reacted negatively to any of the subjects' 'incorrect' judgements with non-verbal responses such as looks of surprise, or even brief noises, which the participants appeared to find quite uncomfortable. The knowledge that other people in group apparently had different perceptions and judgements seemed to make the participants embarrassed and anxious. This pressure presumably forced them to agree with the main group and also to alter their beliefs if there was some ambiguity about the stimuli (when the lengths of the lines were in fact quite close).

People generally seem to be anxious about the social effects of disagreeing with normative beliefs and values, and they probably have good cause to do so. Going against a group's norms is a challenge to the identity of the group and its members, and can therefore lead to extreme behaviours to either exclude the individual or to induce conformity. Many norms are, of course, formalised, particularly when they are part of the agreed social structure in some way. In schools these become rules for behaviour and are often written down and displayed for pupils to see. By law (Sections 110 and 111 of the School Standards and Framework Act 1998), schools in England and Wales are directed to set up home–school agreements to ensure that parents also agree about what their children should do.

Many other norms are informal and originate from peer groups, particularly from the age of about eight years, or from wider social influences such as the media. Many of the problems in schools arise when norms are in conflict in some way – if immediate peer-group pressures lead to behaviours that are a challenge to formal school expectations. Girls' developing gender roles may, for example, lead to their adopting behaviours that are hard for schools to tolerate. Measor and Woods (1988) described how some girls refused to wear safety glasses in physical science lessons in order to maintain some distance from a non-feminine subject. As will be described later in this chapter, the norms of many boys' groups can also represent the antithesis of values that schools advocate, and such 'non-conformity' can undermine the possibility of academic progress.

The self

Goffman (1959) extended these ideas and studied the way in which people generally use roles in life, to present a conception of their self to other people. This 'self-presentation' can be seen as a kind of theatre and acts as the basis for a great deal of our social behaviour. Mead has argued that we develop this sense of self from the reactions of other people to us, and through trying out different roles. For example, young children might play at being 'parents' in the house corner of a reception class, or older pupils might adopt a style of dress or behaviour that fits with a particular peer group. In playing roles, children are taking the perspective of the other and this enables children to see themselves as being different from other people and to understand the nature of different roles in society.

Both Goffman and Mead believed that our 'selves' are very much the combination of the roles that we adopt or are socialised into. Tajfel (1981) similarly argues that our sense of identity is largely a product of the social groups that we are part of. Known as **social identity theory**, this view means that we need to emphasise these groups in order to maintain our self-concept. This may involve denigrating an 'outgroup', with some boys' groups condemning others for being 'wimps' and, by doing this, emphasising their own 'toughness' and in-group masculine identity.

Maintaining such differences between groups can entail making inferences about linked characteristics – for instance that doing well with academic work means that you are subservient to figures of authority. This type of association of beliefs is termed a **stereotype** and is the basis for prejudice (usually negative attitudes about others) and discrimination (the behaviour that can result from prejudice). Stereotypes can easily develop from obvious physical differences, such as skin colour or gender. These lead respectively to racial and sexual discrimination, both of which can be important in schools, as well as the wider society.

Social behaviours

Schank and Abelson (1977) believe that our expectations of what is appropriate social behaviour can be understood as a form of **script**. As described in Chapter 2, a script is a type of schema that determines the general sequence of the interactions in a given social situation. It also incidentally emphasises that in some situations we probably have limited choice about our actions. Many of the interactions in school involving teachers and pupils can be seen as fitting such scripts. A typical secondary lesson, for instance, involves pupils entering the room, sitting down at their desks, listening to the teacher, getting out the appropriate books and following the regular sequences of events in that subject.

Roles, norms and scripts are useful because they enable people to predict and understand social behaviour. Roles also usually have role partners with shared expectations (norms) about their interactions. The traditional teacher–pupil relationship, for instance, places the teacher in a position of authority, with the responsibility of organising pupils and passing on information. The pupil's complementary role is to accept this authority and to fulfil expectations about work and behaviour in class. Following the directions of a figure in authority in this way is known as **obedience**, and Milgram (1974) has shown that people will obey authority figures even when unusual or extreme demands are made on them. In a series of investigations, he found that the majority of people would follow instructions to administer what they were told was a dangerous electric shock, so long as they perceived themselves to be in a subordinate role.

Such power relationships are important since they enable hierarchical structures to operate. These are important in the education system since it is based upon a relatively small number of teachers directing and managing large numbers of pupils. When a pupil (or teacher) fails to conform to the more typical behavioural expectations in school, his or her behaviour is often a cause for concern since it interferes with the usual process of transactions. Individuals who do not follow such expectations are therefore often labelled 'abnormal' and literally excluded to enable the normal social processes to continue. The 'free school' movement was an attempt to restructure such relationships in schools, although such schools have often had difficulties meeting the educational expectations of wider society.

Individuals have a range of different roles, and the expectations associated with these can often be in conflict, resulting in role strain for the individual. An individual boy may feel that he ought to work hard to fit in with the role expectations of his parents and teachers. However, such behaviour may not match with the masculinity norms of his peer group, which view working hard as being weak and subservient to authority. The resulting mental conflict (termed 'dissonance') could be resolved by secretly working hard, or by disengaging from one of the roles and emphasising the other. Murphy's (2000) observational research, concerning group-work in science, highlights the complex, difficult dilemmas being negotiated by boys who want to both fit in with the norms of their peer-group and perform well in school work. Earlier work undertaken by Hargreaves (1967) vividly characterises the process by which the failure of some low-band pupils to meet the academic and social expectations of school led to the development of a negative subculture. This rejected the values of school and the wider society, and within these groupings, self-esteem was based on reacting against the norms of the predominant culture. Attempts by the formal school system to control individuals, such as formal punishments, were seen by the group as ways of achieving status. Indeed, there was often competition within the group to see how many punishments each member could get!

As summarised in Figure 7.1, behaviours can be seen as largely determined by individuals' positions within a social structure, and constructed by them to confirm and manage their sense of self-identity.

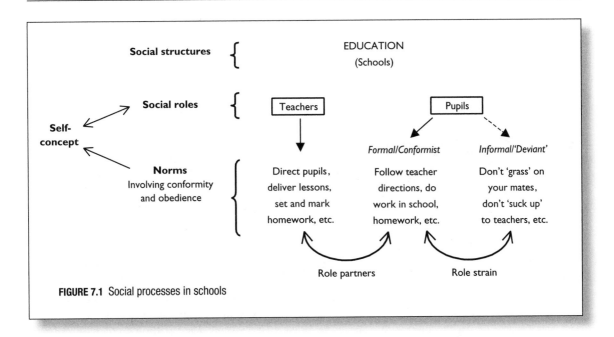

FIGURE 7.1 Social processes in schools

Unfortunately, as mentioned earlier, a functionalist perspective of this kind tends to give a rather rigid and deterministic view of what people are and what they can do. A more interactionist perspective would emphasise that our roles and identities are often more fluid and open to negotiation. Teachers could therefore adopt a relatively egalitarian approach, and discuss with their classes which classroom rules are important. There are limits to such an approach, however, and pupils will usually be aware of what is expected of them and may actually find a lack of adult control and direction uncomfortable.

Developing social knowledge

Bandura *et al.* (1963) argue that children learn social expectations and behaviour largely from observing what others do. This process is called **social learning theory** and involves developing knowledge about what is appropriate or possible in particular situations. In their original investigations, Bandura and colleagues (1963) demonstrated that children were more likely to be aggressive when they had observed others behaving in this way. The studies involved showing children films of an adult either playing aggressively with a 'Bobo' doll (a blow-up toy that can be knocked down and then rebounds) or playing quietly with some other toys. Children were then shown some attractive toys, but were frustrated by being prevented from playing with them. Finally, the children were allowed to play with the 'Bobo' doll and their actions were recorded.

The main findings from these studies were that children who had observed the adult acting in an aggressive way played more aggressively, and that they carried out the same actions that they had seen the adult using. Bandura *et al.* also found that whether children imitated behaviour depended on whether they saw it as relevant to them. This involved whether the model was of the same gender or age and what the children perceived would be the likely outcomes for them. If children believed that a particular behaviour would have negative consequences, they did not have to experience those outcomes personally for the belief to inhibit that behaviour.

Wragg (1984) found that, in schools, critical incidents that happen early on in the relationship between teachers and new classes set expectations for future behaviour. His studies indicated that when minor transgressions by an individual child were promptly dealt with, the teacher's response acted as a signal for other pupils about how to behave with that teacher in the future. Wragg's work therefore gives some support to social-learning theory and to the common belief among teachers that it is best to start off firm and relax later, as in the saying, 'Don't smile until Christmas!'

The functions of education

From a basic structural–functionalist perspective, the educational system exists to teach an agreed body of knowledge to students, in order to enable them to operate within society. This is a largely common-sense approach, and most people would agree that one of the main signs that it is succeeding is for students to pass examinations. Examinations are particularly important since they enable students to access further education and jobs, with Ceci (1990) finding that the most important factor determining people's incomes was not their general ability but the amount and level of their education.

It is often argued that educational attainments are a vital foundation for a society's success, particularly in terms of economic functioning. The logic of such arguments appears to be self-evident since people at work need to be able to manage the intellectual demands that are made on them in order to carry out their job. They require basic skills such as literacy and numeracy, general knowledge and understanding of the world, as well as certain specific technical skills. The need for educational attainments can therefore be used as a justification for the need to improve educational standards, with national and school targets being set to achieve this.

Nevertheless, it has been argued that international comparisons indicate that, above a certain basic level of general competence, educational attainments do not appear to have any significant effect on countries' economic performance (Robinson, 1997). Educational progress may often follow economic development, as a result of a country's increased ability to invest in education. The (apparently mistaken) belief that education is largely responsible for economic development is probably due to people's psychological need to establish simple cause-and-effect relationships. This is not, of course, to say that education cannot, or does not need to, establish useful knowledge in its students, merely that it appears naive to expect education to solve a country's economic problems. Some people argue that the main functions of education are quite separate from economic and even academic goals. Education, they believe, exists largely to inculcate a society's norms and values, and to reproduce its general structure, in terms of economic and class relationships.

Beliefs about the economic importance of education can also lead to concerns that one's own country may be underperforming in certain basic skills when compared with other countries. In fact, it is a difficult and extremely complex undertaking to try to compare like with like. That said, initiatives such as the Programme for International Student Assessment (PISA), which is a triennial survey of the knowledge and skills of 15-year-olds, aim to do just this. For PISA 2006 (conducted under the auspices of the Organisation for Economic Co-Operation and Development – OECD), 400,000 students from 57 countries (making up almost 90 per cent of the world economy) took part. Whilst the focus for PISA 2006 (OECD, 2006) was predominantly on assessing science competencies, the assessment also considered the students' performance in reading and mathematics. In terms of PISA outcomes, the performance of children in the UK is above-average in science, with the UK having an above-average level of top performers and a smaller than average proportion of poor performers. In reading, 15-year-olds in the United Kingdom achieve a mean score of 495 points, on a scale that had an OECD average of 492 score points, and the UK has an average proportion of top-performers. In mathematics, however, the United Kingdom has a below-average proportion of top-performers and students in the UK achieve a mean score of 495 points in mathematics, on a scale that had an OECD average of 498 score points. However, taken overall, the UK ranks internationally among countries with relatively high average educational achievement. That said, perhaps one of the most striking, and alarming, findings to emerge from international comparisons is that the UK has one of the steepest socio-economic 'gradients' in education among similar countries. So, whilst there is relatively high educational achievement, there is also high inequality in achievement (Cassen and Kingdon, 2007c). As Hirsch (2007: 3) explains, children from disadvantaged backgrounds do worse than those from advantaged backgrounds by a greater amount than elsewhere:

> Only about a quarter of students receiving free school meals gain five good GCSEs or equivalent, compared to over half of the overall population.... In Scotland, being in a family poor enough to qualify for free school meals halves a young person's chances of getting to Level 5 in the Scottish Credit and Qualifications Framework.

What matters: culture or poverty?

The underlying processes that determine children's progress appear to be largely related to the quality of their home environments, in particular the nature of adult management and interaction. As we have seen from earlier chapters, this is supported by findings such as those of Hart and Risley (1995), who studied the verbal interactions between parents and their children from ten months to three years of age. As was described in Chapter 4, these measures showed a relatively large correlation of 0.78 with the development of general cognitive abilities. Other aspects of Hart and Risley's study showed that these early interactions also accounted for 61 per cent of the later variance in verbal abilities at ages nine and ten years. This is a very strong effect for long-term prediction at this age and is consistent with the idea that early language-based experiences have a continuing causative impact on general cognitive development. Hart and Risley found that measures of socioeconomic status by themselves were able to account for only 30 per cent of the variance in general verbal abilities at nine and ten years of age.

A large part of this effect was attributable to the fact that the poorest families on welfare almost invariably had the lowest quality of parent–child verbal interaction in the home. It involved an emphasis on negative control, parental rather than child-centred topics and a generally reduced level of talk. From Hart and Risley's observations, this pattern of interaction appeared to be part of a culture that was concerned with established customs and where obedience, politeness and conformity were likely to be the keys for survival. Parents seemed to be preparing their children for lives that were similar to the ones they had experienced themselves, where success would come not from knowledge and skills, but from attitudes and actual performance. More recent work points to the central significance of what has been called the 'home learning environment'. As Cassen and Kingdon (2007c) explain:

> A key factor is the 'home learning environment': the amount parents read to their children, the number of books in the home, the degree to which parents support their children's education in and out of school (Sylva *et al.*, 2004). In the study cited, the home learning environment was only moderately associated with factors such as social class and parental education levels, and what parents did with their children had a more important impact than their own background or

circumstances. Even more strongly: 'In the primary age range the impact caused by different levels of parental involvement is much bigger than differences associated with variations in the quality of schools. The scale of the impact is evident across all social classes and all ethnic groups.

(Desforges and Abouchaar, 2003)

Some investigators have concluded that patterns of interaction within the home are relatively stable and that they tend to be reproduced over successive generations. Adults who are the product of such cultural environments may therefore repeat the cycle with their own children, providing limited stimulation and low expectations. This 'cycle of deprivation' proved resistant to compensatory programmes such as the largely school-based Educational Priority Area initiatives that were set up in the United Kingdom in the late 1960s. Initial analyses of the Head Start programme in the United States similarly indicated that early programmes of support did not improve children's progress.

A key issue, though, is whether such features are characteristic of the culture of a particular class, or whether they are an adjustment to the long-term effects of low social status and poverty. This is important, since if the main problem is that of an impoverished class culture, it should be possible to re-educate children out of this and to break the cycle. If, however, the main driving force behind inequalities comes from the social and economic structure of society, it is less likely that this could be affected by any limited educational intervention. A famous comment by Bernstein (1970) that 'education cannot compensate for society' encapsulates this last perspective, and moreover it can be argued that attempts to drive up standards by setting targets for the educational system are merely a diversion from the real problems of society. Such beliefs are supported by Mortimore and Whitty (1997), whose review of relevant research suggests that educational improvements typically increase stratification since socially advantaged children usually benefit the most, leaving less-advantaged children even further behind. The assertion is that if all schools were brought up to the level of the best, the social-class gap in performance would become even starker unless, that is, positive action were to be taken to provide extra support for disadvantaged pupils (Whitty, 2006). Some DfES research (discussed by Kelly, 2005) appears to lend some credence to this position as it indicated that, while all pupils performed better academically in 2004 than in 1998, those pupils from higher-income families made more progress than those from low-income families, even though schools in deprived areas improved more than those in wealthier neighbourhoods (cited in Whitty, 2006).

Although parent–child interactions may be the most direct cause of inequalities, it seems likely that family experiences of poverty and low status are important underlying factors. When there are limited and variable financial resources, it becomes pointless to plan ahead, encouraging a reactive approach to life. The lack of control over key resources and careers also engenders a form of learned helplessness and a sense of apathy (Mortimore and Whitty, 1997). It is easy to see how parents in this situation would tend to utilise negative control with their children if they feel that there is little that can be achieved in life. The parents' perceived lack of control is also likely to limit their ability to take account of their children's learning needs.

There are also more direct effects on children, in terms of poor-quality housing, heating, clothing and poor nutrition. These lead to an increase in health problems in low-income families which can affect general development, school attendance and learning. For example, Kleinman et al. (1998) found that children from poorer backgrounds who were regularly hungry in school had a range of educational problems and were twice as likely to have special educational needs.

Poverty also restricts children's wider experiences, and Oppenheim (1993) has described how it can affect children socially and emotionally. Without any money, it is difficult to meet friends, and activities such as visits to the cinema or other treats are restricted. Lack of transport means that trips out are limited and many families will rarely go on holidays. Life in this situation can mean often being bored and resorting to low-level entertainment such as watching television or playing video games. Research by Sutton *et al.* (2007) has revealed that, whilst private-school children's free time involved a diverse range of organised sporting and cultural activities, the free time of children from a deprived estate was characterised by unsupervised street play and socialising with friends. This finding resonates with Wikeley *et al.*'s (2007) finding that young people from families in poverty participate in fewer organised out-of-school activities than their more affluent peers. As Hirsch (2007: 6) argues, such activities can be of crucial importance in helping children

> develop confidence in learning, to become active learners and to develop a different kind of relationship with adult instructors or supervisors than in a more formal school setting. In out-of-school settings, they become used to seeing learning as a partnership, rather than as something that is imposed upon them.

Hirsch suggests that through their lack of participation in out-of-school activities, many young people in poverty are denied important informal learning experiences with significant consequences for their engagement in more formal learning in school.

Such findings indicate that poverty is a major driving force underlying cultural deprivation and limiting educational progress. In 1997, Robinson suggested that 'potentially the most powerful "educational" policy might be one which tackles social and economic disadvantage. A serious programme to alleviate child poverty might do far more for boosting attainments in literacy and numeracy than any modest interventions in schooling' (p. 17). There is, however, very little in contemporary educational policy that focuses on explanations based on broader social structures or issues of power (Raffo *et al.*, 2007).

Can education compensate?

There is a danger that such conclusions can lead to a form of paralysis since it seems unlikely that there will be any major changes in British society to prevent or to compensate for structural or economic inequality. However, it is not just poverty but the effects of poverty that are responsible for educational inequalities – this leaves open the possibility of direct action aimed at the processes by which the effects occur.

Unfortunately, this is a rather daunting task and one which is generally beyond the regular remit of the educational system. From the findings of Hart and Risley (1995), the differences between the language backgrounds of children can also be quite massive, with those from the most impoverished homes having only one-third the vocabulary experience of children in professional families. The general findings about the nature of early learning and language development covered in Chapters 2 and 9 also indicate that learning is best when it forms part of children's own environments from the earliest stages, and that it needs to be closely related to their personal experiences.

Given the difficulties that achieving such criteria involves, it is perhaps not surprising that many attempts to overcome inequalities have appeared to be relatively ineffective. It may also be that many of these approaches were simply aimed at the wrong level (schools rather than home background) and were not long-term enough to have an impact. Many of the initial Head Start projects, for instance, lasted only for one summer vacation and were mainly based on providing additional stimulation in a specialist centre. Subsequent analyses, such as that by Barnett (1995), have shown that those parts of the programme that were more lengthy and based on home support did have significant and lasting effects.

But there is room for some optimism, as we know looking historically across a range of studies that even short-term programmes that encourage positive involvement by parents can have a sizeable impact. Whitehurst (1994), for instance, found increases of up to ten points in Verbal IQ scores of three-year-old children when their parents worked with them using a programme of interactive picture-book reading. A more extensive early EPA project in Yorkshire described by Smith (1975) also established significant gains that were equivalent to about four months' mental age. In this case, the intervention involved a one-year home-visiting programme for children aged between one-and-a-half and two-and-a-half years of age. After the programme finished, parents continued with the language interaction and play techniques that they had developed and the group maintained their developmental advantage through to schooling.

It seems likely, then, that although educational disadvantage is closely related to family class and poverty, it is still possible to compensate for this to a significant extent. Intensive school-based programmes can also have a strong effect, and nurture groups, as devised by Bennathan and Boxall (1996), can re-create the management and care in school that would normally be provided by an adequate family. Nurture groups are set up as classes in the ordinary school with about 12 children and two adults, and with an emphasis on developing predictability for the children, together with a generally stimulating environment. An evaluation by Holmes (1982) found that children in a nurture group achieved an average gain of more than ten IQ points over one year and made good long-term adjustments to schooling. A control group of matched children who did not receive this support showed no gains in their IQs, and the majority of these eventually needed some form of special education.

Early intensive programmes such as the High/Scope project described by Schweinhart and Weikart (1993) have shown that such effects can continue through to adult life, with groups that have received this support being more successful economically and having much less involvement with crime. An analysis of these findings also indicated that this programme generated an effective overall saving of more than $7 for every $1 that was initially invested in it.

Gender inequalities

We have already highlighted, earlier in the chapter, that whilst there is relatively high educational achievement in the UK, there is also high *inequality* in achievement. In respect of this, over the last 15 or so years, much academic and public debate has focused attention on the 'gender gap' between the level of boys' and girls' academic performance. Whether it be articulated in terms of the relative paucity of their early literacy skills (see Littleton *et al.*, 2006) or their lower performance in almost all GCSE subjects, concerns have been raised about the relative underachievement of boys. What is striking is that such concerns also appear to be being echoed internationally. In introducing you to the key debates and work in this field, we draw predominantly upon the substantive, DfES-commissioned report, authored by Younger and his colleagues (2005) at the University of Cambridge.

In the United Kingdom, the concern with boys' academic achievement and the allied discussions regarding their experiences of, and engagement with, schooling represented a marked shift of emphasis within the debates in respect of gender and education (Younger *et al.*, 2005). This is because, throughout the 1970s and 1980s, the emphasis had been on characterising and theorising the educational experiences and academic interests and performance of girls. This focus was clearly justified given the compelling research evidence, emerging at the time, suggesting that boys dominated both the linguistic and physical classroom space, monopolising teacher attention such that, whilst girls were willing to participate in classroom dialogue, they were not being enabled to do so (Kelly, 1988). As Younger *et al.* (2005: 16) explain, research was also demonstrating how career expectations and subject choices were being demarcated along traditional gender lines, to the disadvantage of girls (Deem, 1980; Griffin, 1985; Sharpe, 1976), and that facets of the hidden curriculum contributed to the reinforcement of sex roles (Woods, 1990). In the wake of such findings, a raft of initiatives and interventions were introduced specifically designed to reduce gender bias and discrimination, including amongst other things the introduction of new textbooks, language conventions and curricula (see Younger *et al.*, 2005).

Some scholars have articulated reservations and unease with facets of this changed focus. Furthermore, the notion of male disadvantage is one that is hard to sustain if one considers the broader socio-economic context of the Western labour market. For example, The Equality and Human Rights Commission's (2009) *Equal Pay Position Paper* indicates that in Britain women in general earn considerably less than men, even within the same occupational group:

> The gender pay gap – as measured by the median hourly pay excluding overtime of full-time employees – widened between 2007 and 2008. The gap between women's median hourly pay and men's was 12.8 per cent, compared with a gap of 12.5 per cent recorded in April 2007, when it had been at its lowest since records began. When calculated using the mean (the Commission's preferred measure), rather than the median, women's hourly pay, excluding overtime, was 17.1 per cent less than men's pay, showing an increase on the comparable figure of 17.0 per cent for 2007. For women working part-time the gap was 35.6%.
>
> (p. 2)

Women are also underrepresented in the higher levels of many occupations (Institute of Employment Studies, 2009).

There have also been concerns raised regarding the validity of referring to gender differences generally as being about 'girls' or 'boys',

> without recognising that within groups there may be great variation, and between groups considerable overlap. This style of reporting is referred to as an essentialist approach to gender, which assumes that gender difference is attributable to boys or girls as a whole. It is very difficult to avoid this.
>
> (Murphy and Whitelegg, 2006: 1)

Nevertheless, it is the case that there are legitimate grounds for concern regarding the achievement levels of *some* boys.

Activity

There has been intense debate about the reasons for boys' lower levels of achievement than girls'. Can you think of any explanations for why boys are not achieving at the same levels as girls? Take a moment to write these down before going on to read Box 7.1.

Feedback

In Box 7.1 Younger and his colleagues outline the numerous, and diverse, explanations that have been offered by researchers to account for the 'gender gap'. Notice how diverse they are – spanning explanations as wide-ranging as fundamental biological difference, disregard for authority and the gendered nature of classroom interactions. Clearly, each of these explanations brings with it different possibilities, and imperatives, for intervention. Moreover, explaining the gender gap is likely to be complex and multifaceted, with multiple factors in play.

BOX 7.1 Explanations for the gender gap

A variety of different explanations have been offered, and the gender gap is variously construed as resulting from:

- brain differences between girls and boys (Sommers, 2000; Gurian, 2001), with links to boys' testosterone and the 'natural' development of boys (Biddulph, 1998). Similarly, Archer and Lloyd (2002) have argued for a biological construction of masculinity, citing studies that show behavioural sex differences at a very early age, before children are able to form any notions of socially constructed gender (Baron-Cohen, 2003; Connellan *et al.*, 2000);

- boys' disregard for authority, academic work and formal achievement (Harris *et al.*, 1993; Rudduck *et al.*, 1996), and the formation of concepts of masculinity that are in direct conflict with the ethos of the school (Connell, 1989; Mac an Ghaill, 1994);

- differences in students' attitudes to work, and their goals and aspirations (Warrington and Younger, 1999; Younger and Warrington, 1996), linked to the wider social context of changing labour markets, de-industrialisation and male unemployment (Arnot *et al.*, 1998);

- girls' increased maturity and more effective learning strategies (Boaler, 1997; Gipps, 1996), with the emphasis on collaboration, talk and sharing (Askew and Ross, 1988; Fennema, 1996), whilst boys were seen neither as competitive nor as team players, unwilling to collaborate to learn (Barker, 1997), and less inclined to use cooperative talk and discussion to aid and support their own learning (Gipps, 1996);

- differential gender interactions between pupils and teachers in the classroom (Younger *et al.*, 1999).

(Younger *et al.*, 2005: 17)

Boys' general pattern of examination achievements could be seen as lending support to the argument that boys' disregard for authority, academic work and formal achievement (Harris *et al.*, 1993a; Rudduck *et al.*, 1996) is implicated in their relative underachievement, as the distribution of males' achievements at various age levels tends to be more 'spread out' than females'. If males are less affected by educational behavioural norms than females, then this seems a likely explanation for the relatively large 'tail' of underachievers and the overall better performance for females. On the other hand, those males who are actively involved in learning may be studying more from their own personal interest than from any desire to conform. As was discussed in Chapter 5, this 'intrinsic motivation' is more likely to result in effective learning and may produce the small proportion of high achievers who regularly outperform females.

Central to the discussions concerning boys and underachievement has been a consideration of the nature of young masculinities and the associated importance for boys of feeling that they 'belong' within and are accepted by their community of male peers (Frosh *et al.*, 2002). 'Fitting in' with group norms, not marking oneself out as different and acceptance by one's peer-group may entail complex identity negotiations that are constituted, in part, through 'laddishness' and risk-taking behaviour (Jackson, 2002, 2003). Such behaviour often stands in striking opposition to school norms and expectations. But if this helps to establish status and the esteem of peers, protect a strong macho image (avoiding the perceived 'stigma' of homosexuality) and secure acceptance within their peer-group, then this 'cost' is accepted. For many boys, being 'hard', being 'one of the lads' and 'having a laugh' (Mac an Ghaill, 1994) are imperative. There is thus an ethos of misbehaviour, not working hard at school, 'larking about', and of going out in the evenings, rather than staying in to do homework.

The research literature concerning boys' attitudes to work and their learning strategies in addition to emphasising their difficulties in respect of collaborative learning has suggested that, from an early age, boys are less motivated, are overly optimistic about their achievements, and are more likely to have difficulties with concentration and attention. Blatchford *et al.* (1985) have shown that such differences exist on school entry and are present throughout primary education, implying that they could at least partly be the result of early home-based socialisation. Evidence also suggests that boys receive twice as much verbal criticism in class, and they are also many times more likely to be excluded from school or to need special education for behavioural problems. Girls are generally more liked by teachers and are seen as more motivated and helpful (Croll and Moses, 1990).

Activity

At this point, it is appropriate to elaborate on Murphy and Whitelegg's cautions regarding the 'essentialising' of gender and the need for research to acknowledge complexity and diversity.

In Box 7.2 Younger and his colleagues unpack the many complexities inherent in the issue of boys' underachievement. Look particularly carefully at what they say about the need to recognise multiple perspectives on masculinity and femininity. Note too the significance of class and ethnicity.

BOX 7.2 Which boys? Which girls?

As the debate has intensified in the United Kingdom, so it has become obvious that the issue of boys' 'underachievement' is far more complex and multi-faceted than assumed by some commentators.

While it is clear that many boys negotiate a position with respect to the locally dominant masculinity, which preserves their image and status and leads them to take pride in disengagement with school, some boys *also* devise coping strategies which enable them to achieve academically within a legitimised local culture. Not all boys are underachievers, therefore, and the issue of 'underachievement' does not affect all boys. An all-pervasive view of boys as underachieving because of a laddish masculinity ignores the fact that, in many schools, boys are achieving high levels of success in academic, community, sporting and artistic contexts. Indeed, many boys have always done extremely well, and continue to do so (Arnot *et al.*, 1998). Equally, there are those boys who define their sexuality differently from the 'mainstream' macho, football-loving boys: gentle, caring boys who find their comfort zone in the company of girls and women (Mac an Ghaill, 1994; Martino and Pallotta-Chiarolli, 2003). Whilst there are boys who can be aggressive perpetuators of homophobic aggression against other boys, not all boys act in the same way.

Just as it is important to look beneath the stereotype of the 'normal' boy, and acknowledge multiple perspectives on masculinity, so there are different kinds of girls and multiple perspectives on femininity (Frosh *et al.*, 2001; Reay, 2001). Not *all* girls are high achievers and conform to the conscientious, hard-working and well-motivated stereotype, distracted from their endeavours by recalcitrant boys. Indeed, some girls are taking on the 'laddish' attributes of their male peers (Jackson, 2004), and we need to pay greater attention to the monitoring of withdrawn, quiet, 'less visible' girls, whose quietness may hide severe problems (Bell, 2004). Boys do not have a monopoly on such matters: in many schools, there are also disengaged girls who do not reach their potential academically.

[. . .] It is inappropriate, therefore, to generalise uncritically about girls and boys: issues of ethnicity and class, of individuality and sexual inclination, differing images of femininity and masculinity, all affect motivation, attitude and achievement. The emphasis has to be placed upon variety and plurality, more than upon similarity and uniformity. Student interviews themselves reveal that girls and boys often feel uneasy and express disquiet when notions of sameness are attributed to them.

At its simplistic level, then, the 'boys' underachievement' debate ignores the diversity of gender constructions which exist within the schools and societies in which boys and girls operate. Nevertheless, whilst it is nonsensical to accept the simplistic view that the issue is to do with the underachievement of most boys (Arnot et al., 1999), our own research, particularly interviews with hundreds of boys over the last decade, has shown that there are typical patterns of behaviour to which many boys conform. Gillborn and Mirza's research, too, has shown that – when educational performance of boys and girls is compared within social classes, or within ethnic groups – girls as a group invariably do better than boys as a group (Gillborn and Mirza, 2000). There is also evidence to suggest (Warrington and Younger, 1999) that more girls achieve top grades in their school-leaving examinations than do boys.

(Younger et al., 2005: 18–19)

Enhancing boys' attainment

In response to the evidence for, and explanations of, boys' underachievement, a number of different strategic approaches designed to enhance their academic performance have been developed. Younger et al. (2005) summarise these in terms of a four–fold classification outlined below.

Strategies for enhancing boys' attainment

Pedagogic strategies: these strategies are classroom-based and are crucially centred on the processes of teaching and learning, particularly in literacy. It is evident from work undertaken to date that any attempts to improve boys' motivation, interest and achievement in literacy must recognise the complex relationship between product and process and develop a holistic approach across the curriculum.

Individual strategies: essentially a focus on target-setting and mentoring. Research suggests that whilst in some schools, target-setting and mentoring have been transformative in their effects upon motivation, engagement and achievement; in others, they have had minimal impact. This finding underscores just what subtle and complex processes mentoring and target-setting are.

Organisational strategies: are concerned with ways of organising learning at the whole-school level, where the diversity of skills and interests are recognised through the development of an ethos and culture where achievements in different areas are celebrated and accepted as being typical. The essential premise here is that underachieving students are unlikely to engage with learning if schools simply concentrate on adopting narrowly focused and quick-fix solutions in isolation from the ethos of the whole school.

Socio-cultural strategies: these approaches attempt to foster an environment for learning where key boys and girls feel able to work with, rather than against, the aims and aspirations of the school. Research suggests that schools where socio-cultural strategies are most transformative are those where head teachers recognise that there may be conflicts between the cultural contexts, norms and expectations of home and school.

(Younger et al., 2005: 30–31)

This classification is a useful analytic device – enabling the identification of the essence of the different strategies. What is evident is that these strategies are interdependent (rather than self-contained and independent), and that integration is needed in order to maximise impact. That said, the central importance of socio-culturally based strategies in challenging notions of 'laddish' masculinity and 'ladettish' femininity, and engaging peer leaders with their schooling, emerges as a compelling priority for intervention work.

Girls and the physical sciences

In the spirit of recognising complexity and diversity, before leaving our discussion of gender inequalities it is also worth highlighting that, historically, there has been evidence to suggest a different pattern of male–female achievements, with girls in England tending to perform less well in physical sciences, as compared with boys (Murphy and Whitelegg, 2006).

Classic explanations for this pattern have centred on possible differences in underlying cognitive skills, with girls having better verbal abilities and boys having better mechanical and spatial abilities. Whilst early research did find evidence of such differences, longitudinal research by Feingold (1988) established that, over the period from 1947 to 1980, these progressively fell to non-significant levels. Moreover, Brannon (1996) reviews evidence that such assessments of visuo-spatial abilities are strongly influenced by practice. Other explanations for differential achievements have largely been based on sex stereotypes and sex-role socialisation patterns. According to such explanations, there could be generally higher social expectations for girls in verbally based subjects and a belief by girls themselves that it is more appropriate for them to do well in such subjects. Bandura (1986) has proposed that higher self-efficacy will lead to increased motivation, effort and success. One would therefore expect there to be differences between boys and girls, in terms of their academic self-concept and their achievements in different subjects.

More contemporary accounts, reviewed by Murphy and Whitelegg (2006: 48), highlight significant issues in respect of the assessment of competencies. For example, there is evidence to suggest that the content that is more likely to arise in tests and examinations in Physics reflects boys' interests and values more than those of girls. Moreover, performance differences on Physics items in favour of boys are evident within science tests and examinations at Key Stages 3 and 4. As we are aware, from the work of developmental psychologists, the contextualisation of a task and the meanings afforded are crucial determinants of on-task performance (see Light and Littleton, 1999).

Learning in culturally diverse classrooms

An expanding body of educational research is concerned with understanding learning and teaching in culturally diverse classrooms and schools. This research is in part a response to the pressing imperative to understand and meet the needs of the increasing number of migrant students within schools. It is evident that some groups of migrants 'fail' at school (for a detailed account of this body of work, see Elbers, 2010), and researchers have been attempting to understand why this is so. In respect of this, the discrepancy between the expectations and cultural norms associated with the home environment and those associated with the routines and rituals of learning in school has been highlighted.

Activity

Pause for a moment and consider whether there are any criticisms that could be directed towards this idea that it is the cultural discrepancy between home and school that accounts for the underachievement of migrant students. Make a note of your ideas and then go on to read the material in Box 7.3. Here the researcher Ed Elbers summarises some of the problems associated with such an explanation.

BOX 7.3 Critiquing cultural discrepancy accounts

Cultural-discrepancy approaches have been criticised along two lines. Firstly, they bring along the risk of taking cultural differences to be static and fixed. Such a view would lead to teachers ascribing stereotypical characteristics to their students. It would hamper the open-mindedness teachers need in their contacts with students and parents. Rather, individuals and groups are involved in a continuous process of cultural adaptation and innovation. Migrant families see themselves confronted with new challenges. In the process of coping with these challenges, they develop new cultural tools, habits and understandings. Secondly, Ogbu contributed the insight that cultural difference does not necessarily lead to school failure. Some migrant groups are successful, others are not. Migrant and minority groups react variously to the majority culture, and these reactions influence children's motivation to work for school and the assessment of their chances of a successful career after school.

(Elbers, 2010: 306)

It is important to avoid equating discontinuity with deficiency – and teaching in a culturally diverse classroom requires a considered balance between attuning to the students' cultural learning styles and extending the students' repertoire by introducing them to new discursive tools (Elbers, 2010: 207). The *Thinking Together* approach discussed in Chapter 8 affords an example of how teachers might introduce effective discursive tools to students – enabling them to use language to reason in talk in classroom contexts. But the broader experience of schooling also needs to be considered. A significant challenge for teachers in culturally diverse classrooms is the fostering of a positive identification with the school – such that the self-esteem of migrant children is maintained and developed. Many educationalists have therefore advocated building partnerships between the school, parents and the wider community – collectively engaging in collaboration and discussion concerning the nature and purpose of education. A substantive task for educational psychology is thus to study parent–school relationships and ascertain how they are implicated in enhancing learning and teaching (Elbers, 2010).

Summary

The educational system is part of the wider society. It involves enculturation and is influenced by social beliefs and values. Sociology explains this influence by emphasising structural aspects or interactionist perspectives. Explanations in social psychology are based on people's roles, which have associated norms and generate conforming behaviour. Also, people work to present a concept of their self and to maintain the groups of which they are part. In schools, normal scripts and role expectations can lead to obedience to authority, or pupils can be influenced by peer groups to adopt a more informal and deviant role. People develop their knowledge of what is appropriate behaviour from observing and participating in social events.

The functions of education are ostensibly to transmit knowledge and to support society through educational performance. However, it is more likely that its true effect is to reproduce the norms and values and the general structure of society. The UK has a disproportionally large number of underachieving pupils, a problem that is probably related to social inequalities. Children's home backgrounds are a probable cause of these inequalities and can be seen in indirect measures such as entitlement to free school meals, or more direct ones such as early abilities and parent–child interactions. Although differential expectations and values underlie such causes, these are probably generated by economic inequalities. Poverty also has more direct effects on children's experiences and life chances. It is unlikely that education can easily compensate for such differences, although intensive programmes can have a significant impact.

Gender inequalities are present within society as well as the educational system, although, for school, pupils inequality is mainly in the form of differential socialisation and role expectations. Academic achievements of females have progressively outstripped those of males, although there are continuing differences in the types of courses studied and at the higher levels of achievement. There appears to be considerable overlap and flexibility in gender differences, and only limited evidence of a biological basis for them. It seems likely, however, that different social experiences and expectations play an important part in their long-term development, and appear to underlie differences in achievements.

The relative underachievement and behavioural difficulties in boys are also probably due to a general lack of conformity to conventional norms and limited socialisation into roles that would support educational progress. Developing boys' attainments would therefore depend on matching educational experiences and establishing more educationally oriented masculine roles. Challenges associated with meeting the needs of migrant children are also being addressed, and balance between attuning to the students' cultural learning styles and extending the students' repertoire by introducing them to new discursive tools is being considered.

Key implications

- The strategies deployed to enhance boys' attainment are interdependent and that integration is needed to maximise impact.
- The assessment of competencies is complex and the contextualisation of a task (for example, the gendered nature of the task) can be a crucial determinant of on-task performance.
- Teaching in culturally diverse classrooms requires a considered balance between attuning to the students' cultural learning styles and extending the students' repertoire by introducing them to new discursive tools.

Further reading

Arnot and Mac an Ghaill (2006), *The RoutledgeFalmer Reader in Gender and Education*: in this volume, international gender researchers address current debates about gender, power, identity and culture and concerns about boys' and girls' schooling, gender achievement patterns, the boys' education debate, and gender relationships in the curriculum, the classroom and youth cultures.

Elbers (2010), 'Learning and social interaction in culturally diverse classrooms', in Littleton, Wood and Kleine Staarman (eds) *The International Handbook of Psychology in*

Education: framed in relation to the global phenomenon of 'new migration', the chapter explores work that views culturally diverse schools from the perspective of culture and cultural differences.

Raffo, Dyson, Gunter, Hall, Jones and Kalambouka (2010), *Education and Poverty in Affluent Countries*: a comprehensive mapping of research evidence and policy strategies concerning education and poverty in affluent countries.

Discussion of practical scenario

Some schools have set up directed activities (such as organised games) and clubs (such as board-game clubs and computer clubs), particularly at lunchtimes. These can reduce negative peer group effects and encourage some cross-gender socialising.

It would probably be a good idea to try to get more male mentors to come into school, particularly to model academic and cooperative behaviours (not just helping with games). The volunteers could perhaps help with reading or practical activities. Some schemes have used older male pupils from a local secondary school as well as adult volunteers.

It might be worth looking at the books available in school, as well as other curriculum materials, to see whether they incorporate any of the interests of boys – whether, for instance, there are stories that involve boys and activities or topics that might appeal to them (adventures, ghost stories, cars, football, etc.).

Although primary schools are already quite 'girl friendly', it is probably a good idea to incorporate girls in any developments, so as to avoid any overcompensation and encourage cross-gender social interaction. Some activities are relatively gender-neutral, and girls too will benefit from any additional support that is made available in school.

Learning interactions and social worlds

Chapter overview

- Introduction
- How does dialogue with a teacher help children learn?
- The significance of classroom-based interaction between peers
- Types of talk
- Supporting and promoting productive interaction
- The importance of children's playground experiences

Practical scenario

Mr Wright is a primary-school teacher who is keen to foster opportunities for group work in his class. He is, however, concerned about the disputational nature of the group work he frequently observes. He is therefore wondering how he could foster more effective interaction and higher-quality dialogue between his pupils.

What could Mr Wright do to encourage effective group work and educationally productive dialogues between children working together in small groups?

Introduction

Much research within the field of the psychology of education is oriented to understanding educational outcomes, assessment and attainment. It goes without saying that these are important areas of inquiry and many of the chapters you have read thus far have explored these complex issues. In this chapter, however, the central focus is not so much on educational 'outcomes' as on educational 'process'. The aim is to help you understand the nature and significance of the interactions that occur in school contexts. As we explore this topic, we will be focusing predominantly on the research literature concerned with synchronous, face-to-face educational dialogues in classroom contexts. We will, however, also be considering those informal interactions that take place in other school settings – such as those occurring between peers in the playground.

James Paul Gee (2000: 201–202) has argued that any 'efficacious pedagogy should be a judicious mix of immersion in a community of practice and overt focusing and scaffolding from "masters" or "more advanced peers" who focus learners on the most fruitful sorts of patterns in their experience'. Of course what constitutes a 'judicious mix' is contested terrain, but what is being highlighted here are the different kinds of learning relationship children encounter in their classrooms. One way of thinking about these relationships is to recognise how the participants differ in terms of the balance of knowledge and power. In **asymmetrical interactions**, the individuals involved have differing knowledge and social power – a good example being when a child interacts with their teacher. Such interactions are characterised by a complementarity of roles – for example, the child asking for help, and the teacher giving it. While the roles of those involved are inextricably interwoven, the behaviour patterns demonstrated by each one differ markedly. According to Schaffer (2003: 113) the main function of complementary interactions 'is to provide children with security and protection and to enable them to gain knowledge and acquire skills'. By contrast, **symmetrical interactions** between individuals with similar knowledge and social power can be characterised by reciprocal processes rather than complementary ones. A typical example would be a discussion between a group of same-age peers. It has been suggested that one important function of reciprocal interactions is to enable children to 'acquire skills that can only be learned among equals, such as those involving co-operation and competition' (Schaffer, 2003: 113). As we will see later in the chapter, interactions between peers can also constitute important sites for the joint construction of knowledge and understanding. While not absolute, the distinction between interactions in terms of their complementary and reciprocal features is useful because it helps us to understand some important dimensions along which children's classroom-based encounters with others can differ.

Mindful of these features, the first section of this chapter will consider how teachers use talk in whole-class settings to help children learn and develop their ability to reason, whilst the second section will explore the processes through which knowledge and understanding can develop when learners talk and work together in groups relatively autonomously in classroom settings.

From the outset it is important to recognise that (as Littleton and Howe, 2010, explain), there are cultural differences in preferences for each of these modes of organisation. For instance, Alexander (2001) found that, whilst small-group activity is a relatively frequent occurrence in England and the United States, it is rare in France and virtually unknown in India and Russia. It is also clear that, within cultures, there is considerable variation in mode of organisation as a function of teacher preferences: some teachers, so-called 'class enquirers', concentrate activity at the classroom level, whilst others ('group instructors') make significant use of small groups (Galton et al., 1980, 1999). The third section of this chapter extends our consideration of the significance and consequence of school-based interactions into the contexts of break-time and the playground, suggesting that such interactions have a particular role to play in fostering children's social development.

How does dialogue with a teacher help children learn?
Scaffolding and the zone of proximal development

Many psychologists and practitioners seeking to understand the significance of interactions between teachers and their students have turned to the work of the Russian psychologist Lev Vygotsky. This is because Vygotsky's theory directs attention to the developmental significance of asymmetrical interactions, namely, those that occur between individuals who differ in knowledge or ability. Vygotsky sees interaction with adults as a crucial element of successful mental development and offers an account of tutoring that draws attention to the fact that most of what children have to learn, the adults around them already know.

Vygotsky proposed that the interactional processes (discussion, interaction and argumentation) that take place between the child and a more knowledgeable other (intermentally) become internalised as the basis for processes that subsequently occur within the child (intramentally). Language is thus seen as mediating much of our experience of the world and how we come to understand it – holding the key to the processes of internalisation. Originally a social means of communication, in Vygotsky's account language becomes the chief means by which individuals reason and regulate their own behaviour. Meanings constructed through social interaction thus become embedded in individual thought processes.

It was in highlighting the significance of such interactional processes that Vygotsky emphasised the significance of the **Zone of Proximal Development (ZPD)**, which refers to the difference between what a child can do unaided, and what they can achieve with the support of a more knowledgeable other. As we have seen in earlier chapters, 'ability' is typically measured by what children can achieve by their own efforts. Vygotsky, however, argued that what they could achieve with support was a more sensitive measure of children's intellectual potential. The metaphor that has been most widely used to capture the forms of guidance that support learners in their progress through the ZPD is that of '**scaffolding**'. This metaphor, which was first introduced by Wood *et al.* (1976), attempts to characterise the ways in which a learner can be supported by an adult (or more-capable peer) to master a task or achieve understanding through the adult's encouragement, focusing, demonstrations, reminders and suggestions. It thus refers to a special, sensitive kind of help intended to enable a learner to accomplish a task that they would not have been able to do on their own. The scaffolding metaphor was specifically intended to capture the form of 'vicarious consciousness' the adult's intellect provides, as a temporary support for the child's own, until a new level of understanding has been achieved. This image is useful for highlighting the sense in which, for Vygotsky, individual self-supported competence is only possible if successful performance has been established through assisted learning.

Psychologists have attempted to study scaffolding in order to define what constitutes 'effective instruction'. For example, Wood and Middleton (1975) conducted a series of investigations in which they observed mothers' attempts to teach their own four-year-old children how to complete a 3D wooden puzzle of blocks and pegs. Those mothers who were most successful were those who were seen to shift their levels of intervention flexibly according to how well the child was doing – stepping up support when the child was struggling and letting their support 'fade' when the child was making progress. This 'contingent shift' strategy can be seen as a way for the mother to gauge and monitor the child's ZPD as learning proceeds, and to provide scaffolding at the point when the child needs it.

For those interested in conceptualising the educational significance of dialogue with a teacher, concepts such as the ZPD and scaffolding are attractive. This is because they afford appealing metaphors for the active and sensitive involvement of a teacher in students' learning – representing something akin to the essence of a particular kind of good teaching. Given its attractiveness, it is not surprising that the term 'scaffolding' is now very widely used, both in educational research and by teachers discussing their own practice. However, as Mercer and Littleton (2007) argue, there is a need for caution about its casual incorporation into the professional jargon of education. Wood and his colleagues were not using the concept of scaffolding loosely or as a proxy term for 'help' or 'support'.

Rather, they were using the metaphor in a very specific way – to refer to the sensitive, supportive intervention of a more expert other in the progress of a learner who is actively involved in a specific task, but who is not quite able to manage the task alone. Mercer and Littleton also argue that there is a risk that the use of the metaphor to characterise classroom teaching–learning interactions depends on an overly simplistic comparison being made between what parents do when interacting in a dyadic one-to-one situation with their child, and what school teachers have to do in their classrooms. There is a significant disjunction between characterisations of scaffolding and guidance in the ZPD and the kinds of teaching–learning encounters that are feasible in classroom settings (Littleton and Howe, 2010). School teachers and their students are operating under very different circumstances from parents and young children. There is the obvious matter of teacher–learner ratios, and also the more fragmented relationships that are inevitable in school. Teaching–learning interactions in classroom settings are clearly much more diverse and multifaceted:

> Teachers and students interact in classrooms, they construct an ecology of social and cognitive relations in which influence between any and all parties is mutual, simultaneous and continuous. One aspect of this social and cognitive ecology is the multiparty character of the scene – many participants, all of them continually 'on-task' albeit working on different kinds of tasks, some of which may be at cross purposes. Although teachers in group discussion may attempt to enforce a participant framework of successive dyadic teacher–student exchanges, often the conversation is more complicated than that.
>
> (Erickson, 1996: 33)

The implication is that, if concepts like scaffolding and the ZPD are to be of utility in helping us to understand classroom-based interactions, then they have to be separated from the analyses of one-to-one, dyadic interactions and from the imagery of concrete physical tasks. The crucial imperative that emerges is the need for research-based accounts of educational dialogues, and productive interaction, which respect the complex and essentially collective nature of schooling, with its particular aims and goals and inherent diversity and multiplicity (Littleton and Howe, 2010). The work we will discuss in the next section, rooted in classroom realities, exemplifies the variety of forms and functions of language as used in pursuit of teaching and learning in classroom settings.

Teacher-led whole-class interaction

Over the last 30 or so years, much research has sought to understand how teachers use talk to guide learning and construct a shared version of educational knowledge – what Edwards and Mercer (1987) have termed 'common knowledge' – with their students. Drawing on this body of work, Mercer suggests that teachers use talk to do three things:

a   **elicit knowledge from students**, so that they can see what students already know and understand and so that the knowledge is seen to be 'owned' by students as well as teachers;

b   **respond to things that students say**, not only so that students get feedback on their attempts but also that the teacher can incorporate what students say into the flow of discourse and gather students' contributions together to construct more generalised meanings;

c   **describe the classroom experiences that they share with the students**, in such a way that the educational significance of those joint experiences is revealed and emphasised.

(1995: 25–26)

Knowledge elicitation and questioning

When attempting to elicit knowledge from their students, in addition to using direct elicitations, teachers very commonly utilise a technique that Edwards and Mercer (1987) characterise as 'cued-elicitation'. Cued-elicitation is a way of drawing out from students the information that is being sought by providing strong verbal hints and visual cues as to the answer that is required or expected:

TEACHER: So what is the nearest planet to the Sun?
PUPIL 1: Is it Venus, miss?
PUPIL 2: I know, I know, it's Pluto!
TEACHER: Oooh, no, no, not Venus, not Pluto, it is Mer…, Mer…, can you remember?
PUPIL 3: Mercury?
TEACHER: Very good, Mercury.

As in the example given above, teachers often accomplish cued-elicitation through asking questions. And, there has been considerable controversy in educational research more generally concerning the use of questions as a strategy for guiding the construction of knowledge. Specifically, there has been disagreement concerning the functions and value of this characteristic form of classroom interaction (see, for example, Norman, 1992; Wells, 1999). It has been claimed, for instance by Dillon (1988) and Wood (1992), that because most teachers' questions are designed to elicit just one brief 'right answer' (which often amounts to a reiteration of information provided earlier by the teacher), this both limits and suppresses students' contributions to the process of teaching-and-learning. It is, however, evident that all question-and-answer exchanges do not perform the same function and the forms of a language do not have a simple and direct relationship to their functions. In the classroom, teachers' questions can thus have a range of different communicative functions. They can, for example, be used:

to test children's factual knowledge or understanding:
'What is the capital of Finland?'

for managing classroom activity:
'Could we all pay attention and look at the board, please?'

as a way of finding out more about what pupils are thinking:
'Why did you decide to write the character of the magician into your play?'

Even the above account is an oversimplification, because any one question can have multiple functions (for example, the third question above could be used to find out what pupils are thinking and to get them to attend). Moreover, a question takes on a particular, situated meaning in the context of ongoing events. Compare, for example, the function of asking for the name of the capital of Finland before beginning a scheme of work in geography, with asking the same question after it is completed. The key point is that one can only judge the function of questions, and any other forms of language, in dialogic context – there being a need to distinguish between form and function when analysing and evaluating questions in teacher–pupil dialogue.

Similarly, there has also been controversy in respect of the characteristic three-part **I–R–F (initiation–response–feedback)** structure of classroom discourse (sometimes also referred to as 'I–R–E' discourse, with the 'E' standing for 'evaluation'). I–R–E/I–R–F exchanges are those that open with an initiation (I), usually in the form of a question from the teacher, which elicits a response from a student (R), to which the teacher typically provides feedback or an evaluative follow up (F) (see Sinclair and Coulthart, 1975). An example is given below:

TEACHER: So what is the nearest planet to the Sun? (I)
PUPIL: Is it Mercury, miss? (R)
TEACHER: That's right, very good, Mercury, remember we talked about this yesterday? (F)

The pervasiveness of the I–R–F sequence is such that Edwards and Mercer (1987: 9) suggest that 'once seen, [the sequence is] impossible to ignore in any observed classroom talk'. Such sequences appear to be ubiquitous and embedded in classroom practice in diverse cultural settings. Observational studies have, for example, pointed to their prominent use in classrooms across Africa, the United States, England, France, India, Russia and beyond (Alexander, 2001; Cazden, 2001; Pontefract and Hardman, 2005).

Whilst they are frequently used, and are described by some as 'traditional' structures (Cazden, 2001), I–R–F sequences have often been characterised as resulting in dialogue of a rather circumscribed and limited kind. This is largely because of a tendency on the part of teachers to use closed initiatives (e.g. Alexander, 2004, 2008; Galton *et al.*, 1999; Mercer and Littleton, 2007). Closed initiatives are those initiatives, typically questions, which permit a single correct answer, such as: 'What is the Finnish for "cat"?' and 'When did Henry VIII come to the throne?' (incidentally, the answers are 'kissa' and '1509'). Whilst closed initiatives do not necessarily constrain contributions to a single student, they often do not facilitate a range of contributions from students. As a consequence, valuable opportunities for productive dialogue can be lost. Hardman (2008: 133) has therefore suggested that the '"recitation script" of closed teacher questions, brief student answers and minimal feedback … requires students to report someone else's thinking rather than think for themselves, and to be evaluated on their compliance for doing so'. This point is echoed in Skidmore's (2006: 507) comments that the I–R–F sequence results in a 'quiz which requires students to do little more than display their recall of knowledge got by rote', producing 'a pattern of teacher-led recitation which tends to reinforce the teacher's authority as the transmitter of received wisdom and severely restricts the possibilities open to students to contribute thoughtfully to classroom talk.' Given, then, that much of the talk teachers invite from pupils is 'presentational', being proffered for display and teacher evaluation, there is a danger of passivity on the part of students (Barnes, 2008).

Whilst the I–R–F can result in the learners' rote display of recalled knowledge, this is not necessarily and inevitably the case. The I–R–F can also be used creatively by a teacher to 'help students plan ahead for a task they are about to carry out, or to review and generalise lessons learnt from the tasks they have already performed' (Skidmore, 2006: 507). The teacher's follow-up, for instance, can be put to multiple uses – including clarification, exemplification, explanation, expansion or justification of a student's response. It could also invite a student to do any of those things (Wells, 1999). Once again, both the form and the function of the language in use require careful consideration before conclusions concerning its efficacy can be reached.

So, while teachers' questioning certainly can require children to guess what answer is in the teacher's mind, that is merely one possible function. Teachers' questions can also serve other very important functions in the development of children's learning and their own use of language as a tool for reasoning. They can: encourage children to make explicit their thoughts, reasons and knowledge and share them with the class; 'model' useful ways of using language that children can appropriate for use themselves, in peer group discussions and other settings (such as asking for relevant information possessed only by others, or asking 'why?' questions to elicit reasons); and provide opportunities for children to make longer contributions in which they express their current state of understanding, articulate ideas and reveal problems they are encountering (Mercer and Littleton, 2007).

Responding to what students say and describing shared classroom experience

Whilst inappropriate contributions to a classroom discussion may be directly challenged, rejected or ignored, one of the ways in which teachers typically engage with their students is to work with their ideas and contributions, weaving them into the ongoing discussion, thereby making them part of the emergent teaching–learning process. This is often accomplished through the direct confirmation or repetition of things of educational significance (often to underscore their salience to the whole class) and the elaboration of contributions to further explain or highlight their significance, or to make connections with other people's ideas, prior experiences or students' everyday understandings (Edwards and Mercer, 1987; Mercer, 1995; Mercer and Littleton, 2007).

From a student's perspective, school work should ideally have a cohesive, cumulative quality in which specific activities and their goals can be seen to form part of a greater whole – namely, a purposeful educational journey. Given this, research has explored the ways in which teachers attempt to establish and create continuities in the experience of learners – for example, by referring to past events and mobilising them such that they become implicated in the ongoing processes of the guided construction of knowledge. Teachers commonly use recaps to re-introduce, re-state and summarise what they consider to be the most salient features of a past event for the purposes of current activity (Edwards and Mercer, 1987; Mercer, 1995). Recaps can be literal, when a teacher simply sums up what happened ('Last week, we began reading *The Woman in White*') or they can be reconstructive, the latter being where the teacher 'rewrites history', presenting a modified version of events suited to his/her current pedagogic concerns. Elicitations are frequently used to assist students' recall of past events (for example, 'Who can tell me what they found out about the Aztecs in the last lesson?'). It is common too for teachers to mark past shared experiences as significant and relevant by using 'we statements' (as in, 'Remember when we looked at the map of Finland?'). In these diverse and subtly interwoven ways, teachers continually invoke common knowledge, working to highlight the continuities in educational experience, and thereby draw students into a shared, cumulative and progressive understanding of the activities in which they are engaged.

Alexander (2000), Crook (1999) and other educational researchers have argued that coherent knowledge and purposeful understanding do not emerge naturally for students as a consequence of their continuous immersion in classroom life. Thus, if learners are to make sense of their educational experience as part of a progressive 'long conversation', that is cumulative (rather than simply extended in time), then coherence has to be pursued actively as a goal, through the use of appropriate teaching strategies. Talk with a teacher, and with other students, is perhaps the most important means for ensuring that a student's engagement in an extended series of activities contributes to their developing understanding of the subject matter as a whole. In order to understand how classroom education succeeds and fails as a process for developing students' knowledge and understanding, research is now focusing on exploring the temporal relationship between the organisation of teaching-and-learning as a series of lessons and activities, and how it is enacted through talk and joint activity (see for example, Mercer, 2008; Mercer and Littleton, 2007; Rasmussen, 2005; Scott *et al.*, 2006, 2010). The importance of cumulative, rather than simply extended, dialogue is also central to the contemporary notion of 'dialogic teaching' (Alexander, 2004).

Dialogic teaching

Dialogic teaching is a concept that enables us to focus more precisely on the role of the teacher in classroom talk. The concept has emerged from Alexander's (2000) extensive, comparative, cross-cultural research indicating the existence of quite subtle, but nonetheless significant, variations in the interactional 'ground rules' which normally apply in classroom settings. Alexander (2008: 105) has described the essential features of 'dialogic teaching' as being collective (in that teachers and children address learning tasks together), reciprocal (in that teachers and children listen to each other to share ideas and consider alternative viewpoints), supportive (in that children articulate their ideas freely without the fear of embarrassment over 'wrong' answers and support each other to reach common understandings), cumulative (in that teachers and children build on their own and each other's ideas to chain them into coherent lines of thinking and enquiry) and purposeful (in that teachers plan and facilitate dialogic teaching with educational goals in mind). Critically, dialogic teaching can occur in whole-class, group-based and individual interactions between teachers and students (Hardman, 2008). Dialogic teaching is characterised by certain features of classroom interaction: questions are structured so as to provoke thoughtful answers; answers provoke further questions and are seen as the foundations or building blocks of dialogue rather than its terminal point, and individual teacher–pupil and pupil–pupil exchanges are chained into cumulative, coherent lines of enquiry rather than left isolated, stranded or disconnected (Alexander, 2004: 32). Thus dialogic teaching involves both teachers and pupils making substantial and significant contributions. Through these contributions, children's thinking on a given idea, topic or theme is helped to develop and progress.

Dialogic teaching requires a teacher to continually orientate to the state of understanding of their students, engage them in exchanges that will reveal the changing limits and possibilities of their developing interests and understandings, and adjust their communication strategies accordingly as classroom interaction progresses. It involves students taking an active, engaged role in both their own learning and that of their classmates; becoming explicitly part of a collective endeavour. It also requires the creation and maintenance of a kind of dynamic inter-subjectivity that Mercer (1995; Mercer and Littleton, 2007) has called an **Intermental Development Zone** (IDZ).

Unlike the ZPD, which is often construed as an essentially static concept representing the mental state of an individual learner at any one time (rather than the dynamics of development through dialogue), the IDZ is a cumulative, goal-orientated, dynamic contextual-knowledge framework. The notion of the IDZ is intended to help us conceptualise how a teacher and a learner can stay mutually attuned to each other's changing states of knowledge and understanding over the course of an educational activity. For a teacher to teach and a student to learn, they must use talk and joint activity to create and negotiate a shared communicative space – the IDZ – which is built from the contextual foundation of their shared knowledge and aims. This notion of minds being mutually attuned as they pursue a common task is easiest to imagine if there are only two people involved – but one of the characteristics of the effective teacher, as Alexander argues, is that they are able to carry the attention and developing understanding of many, if not all, of a group or even a whole class along with them. The 'dialogic teacher' will use a range of discursive strategies, as appropriate, to establish and maintain a collective IDZ.

As a concept, dialogic teaching is intended to focus attention on the ways in which teachers can encourage students to participate actively in dialogues that enable the students to articulate, reflect upon and modify their own understandings – and, conversely, how they may avoid doing so. The concept highlights the importance of the teacher giving their students frequent opportunities and encouragement to question, state points of view, and comment on ideas and issues that arise in lessons. It also emphasises the significance of the teacher's use of talk to provide a cumulative, continuing, contextual frame, enabling their students' involvement with new knowledge by taking their contributions into account in developing the subject theme of the lesson and in devising activities that enable students to pursue their understanding themselves, through talk and other means. The aim is to enable learners to take the intellectual risks inherent in opening up their ideas and thinking to others, with 'errors' and 'mistakes' being construed as stepping stones to understanding. Alexander also suggests that some key indicators of dialogic teaching concern the ways in which children are seen to talk and work together in collaborative group settings. He emphasises the importance of children listening carefully to each other and respecting minority viewpoints, encouraging each other to participate and share ideas as they build on their own and each others' contributions whilst striving to reach common understanding and agreed conclusions (Alexander, 2004: 3).

As an educational concept, dialogic teaching is both descriptive and prescriptive. It is essentially a specification of good practice, derived from both theory of the nature of dialogue (drawn from the work of Bakhtin, Vygotsky and others) and observations of practice across a range of cultural settings. It represents an approach to classroom teaching which 'aims to be more consistently searching and more genuinely reciprocal and cumulative' (Alexander, 2004: 1) than is usually observed in classrooms.

Our consideration of the significance of teacher-talk in the classroom, and in particular the notion of 'dialogic teaching', indicates that there is huge educational potential inherent in fostering particular forms of classroom dialogue. Recognising this, there is a growing concern amongst educational researchers, teachers and advisers as to how to foster productive educational dialogues in classrooms. This imperative for transformation and change reflects, in part, a recognition that, in schools, the normative environment for talk in most classrooms is incompatible with children's active and extended engagement in using language to construct knowledge and understanding (Alexander, 2005; Mercer and Hodgkinson, 2008; Mercer and Littleton, 2007):

> if we are not careful, classrooms may be places where teachers rather than children do most of the talking; where supposedly open questions are really closed; where instead of thinking through a problem children devote their energies to trying to spot the correct answer, where supposed equality of discussion is subverted by … the 'unequal communicative rights' of a kind of talk which remains stubbornly unlike the kind of talk that takes place anywhere else. Clearly if classroom talk is to make a meaningful contribution to children's learning and understanding it must move beyond the acting out of such cognitively restricting rituals.
>
> (Alexander, 2005: 10)

How, then, are we to move beyond the acting out of 'cognitively restricting rituals' such that the power of classroom talk is harnessed for learning and the joint construction of knowledge and understanding? This is a theme that we will be exploring in some detail in the next section of the chapter, as this question is inextricably linked to the allied issue of how effective group-work can be fostered in classrooms. As we will see, there is now a well-established line of research work focusing on supporting teachers in their endeavours to use dialogue effectively in their classrooms. But for now we want to highlight both the necessity and difficulty of this important educational venture. Supporting and resourcing dialogic teaching–learning encounters is not a matter of engaging teachers in communication skills training. If a teacher is to promote effective educational dialogues in their classroom, the endeavour must be underpinned by a secure understanding of the discipline area being taught and the obstacles to understanding that students face, along with knowledge of appropriate activities around which the dialogues might be staged (Scott et al., 2010).

The significance of classroom-based interaction between peers

In the first section of this chapter, we focused on the educational significance and potential of asymmetrical interactions, where there are differences in respect of knowledge and expertise between the participants. In this section we consider the significance of symmetrical interactions and our discussion begins with a consideration of the work of Piaget, specifically his writing concerning the importance of children's exposure to conflicting ideas through interaction with their peers. This is because it was Piaget's ideas that subsequently gave rise to a long line of work concerned with understanding and promoting children's groupwork.

Piaget and the significance of peer interaction

Piaget was opposed to the transmission of knowledge from adult to child as a model for cognitive development. Interaction with adults was seen at best as irrelevant, or at worst as detrimental, interfering with children's exploration of their physical environment and hence the active construction of their understanding. In contrast to his stance on instruction, and hence on the adult–child relationship, Piaget regarded interaction between children as a particularly powerful source of intellectual progress. Although not central to his main body of work, in his early writings (Piaget, 1932), he offered an argument for the potential productivity of peer interaction in relation to cognitive development, and especially in relation to the achievement of what he called 'concrete operational' modes of thought, when children develop the ability to generate rules based on their own experiences, in the early school years.

Piaget's main argument was that young, preschool-age children are egocentric: they are unable to consider points of view different from their own. A major developmental goal at this stage is to overcome this obstacle, and move towards more advanced forms of cognitive functioning. Although Piaget saw cognitive development as a process of lone discovery, in which encounters with the physical world are crucially implicated, he attributed a central role to peers in learning to decentre and overcome egocentrism. According to Piaget, when confronted with a problem to solve, preschoolers typically fix on the first relevant factor they identify, and respond entirely in terms of that. What the child needs, then, in order to progress, is something that disturbs this centration. Exposure to the ideas of a peer who sees things differently, in a situation that calls for resolution of the conflicting responses, was seen as providing just this kind of disturbance. In contrast, he argued, confrontation with adults' viewpoints would lead to complete disregard or submission as a result of the asymmetry in power relationships. As he put it, 'Criticism is born of discussion and discussion is only possible amongst equals' (Piaget, 1932: 409).

These ideas were taken up during the 1970s and 1980s when a wealth of experimental research was carried out to investigate the facilitative effects of so called '**socio–cognitive conflict**' in collaborative problem-solving tasks, notably, by researchers in the Genevan school (e.g. Doise and Mugny, 1984; Doise *et al.*, 1975, 1976; Perret-Clermont, 1980). The central aim of these studies was to investigate the effects of conflicting perspectives on five-to-seven-year-old children's logical reasoning skills, such as perspective taking, and thus to explore ways in which the socially motivated resolution of conflict impacts children's cognitive development (for more detailed accounts of this work, see Howe, 2010; Light and Littleton, 1999; Mercer and Littleton, 2007). When reviewing this substantial body of research, Perret-Clermont (1980) concluded that the studies provided ample empirical evidence for the positive effects of socio–cognitive conflict on cognitive progress – with socio–cognitive conflict arising most typically when partners who held moderately different perspectives were asked to reach consensus on a problem.

Doise and colleagues' work attracted a good deal of attention, and their work certainly brought the role of interaction in learning into sharper focus. But their work also attracted some criticism. For example, Blaye (1988) raised doubts about the pivotal role of conflict, criticising the concept as vague, ill-defined and hard to operationalise outside experimental research settings. Other researchers pointed to evidence which suggests that, in certain circumstances, peer interaction can result both in regression as well as development (e.g. Tudge, 1989). Crucially, it seemed to some researchers that the observed benefits of collaborative activity could not be explained only in terms of the stimulation of later individual thinking, but had to involve the effects of conflict resolution through dialogue. As, Howe (2010: 35) argues: 'discussing contrasting opinions cannot be sufficient to guarantee growth. Children must also resolve their differences in a progressive direction.'

So, whilst the notion of 'socio-cognitive conflict' remains influential, its most enduring influence on contemporary research has been to foster an interest in the socially constituted and dynamic processes through which learners negotiate and construct knowledge collaboratively together: and it is that interest which we will explore here.

Talking and learning together

Whilst the work of researchers mentioned in the previous sub-section, not to mention the experience of everyday life, would seem to point to the potential value of collaborative learning, educational practice has implicitly argued against it. The history of education suggests that talk amongst students has rarely been incorporated into the mainstream of classroom life (Mercer and Littleton, 2007), and that talk between learners in the classroom has typically been discouraged – often being treated as disruptive and subversive. So in this section we explore what we know about the educational value of students' collaboration and how relevant this is to what can, or should, happen in school.

In everyday contexts, the terms 'collaboration' and 'cooperation' are often used interchangeably, and in very general ways, to refer to the fact that people are working together to accomplish something. In the research literature, however, there has been considerable debate concerning appropriate definitions of terms such as 'collaboration' and 'collaborative learning' (see Dillenbourg, 1999). In this chapter, when we describe children as collaborating or being engaged in collaborative learning, we mean that they are engaged in a coordinated, continuing attempt to solve a problem or in some other way construct shared understanding or common knowledge. Crucially, collaboration is seen as involving a co-ordinated joint commitment to a shared goal, reciprocity, mutuality and the continual (re) negotiation of meaning. Such co-ordinated activity depends upon the collaborators establishing and maintaining what Rogoff (1990) and Wertsch (1991) have termed '**intersubjectivity**'. It will necessarily involve them maintaining a shared conception of the task or problem, and so will require the maintenance of what, in the first section of this chapter, was called an Intermental Development Zone (IDZ). Partners will not only be interacting, as they might in cooperative activity, but inter-thinking.

Whilst the study of children's group-based activity in school has had a relatively brief history, there has been a great deal of contemporary research interest in children's collaborative working, learning and problem-solving. It is evident from the literature that children's joint activity has been researched in diverse ways – for example, through large-scale surveys of life in classrooms; experiments in which pairs or groups of children work on specially designed problem-solving tasks; and detailed analyses of talk between pairs or groups of children working on curriculum-based tasks in school. We will consider each of these in turn.

Perhaps one of the most striking, and worrying, messages to emerge from work surveying classroom activity is that, at least in British primary schools, truly collaborative activity is a relatively rare occurrence. This was the conclusion of the ORACLE project – a large-scale research project conducted during the 1970s (Galton *et al.*, 1980). The ORACLE team of researchers observed everyday practice in a large number of British primary schools. What they established was that, whilst children would frequently be seated together around a table, they would not be collaborating – rather, they would be working, in parallel, on individual tasks. This finding has also been underscored in a number of more recent studies, some of which have shown that even when children are set joint tasks, their interactions are seldom productive (Alexander, 2004, 2005; Blatchford and Kutnick, 2003; Galton *et al.*, 1999). This tells us something important about the nature of everyday educational practice and leads to the conclusion that, if left to their own devices to 'discuss' something or 'talk' together, much classroom-based talk amongst children may be of limited educational value.

Many of the early investigations of collaborative learning were experimental studies of peer interaction designed to establish whether working and solving problems collaboratively was more effective than working alone. Typically children would be given a set task, being allocated to work on it either collaboratively or alone, and their performance on that task would then be assessed. Summarising the findings from such studies, Slavin (1980) concluded that collaborative learning often increased students' academic achievement, self-esteem and motivation. Investigations of this sort subsequently gave rise to a strand of research in which independent variables, notably the size of the group (e.g. Fuchs and Fuchs, 2000), group composition, with respect to, for example, gender and ability (e.g. Barbieri and Light, 1992; Howe, 1997; Webb, 1989; see also Wilkinson and Fung, 2002, for a review of work in this field) and nature of the task (e.g. Cohen, 1994; Light and Littleton, 1999; Underwood and Underwood, 1999) were manipulated, and attempts were made to assess their effects. However, researchers now tend to focus less on establishing the parameters for effective collaboration and more on the ways in which factors such as task design or group composition influence the nature of collaborative interaction (Dillenbourg *et al.*, 1995; Kleine Staarman, 2008; Littleton, 1999). This shift to a more process-oriented kind of investigation has brought with it a resultant interest in the talk and joint activity of learners working together on a task, with attempts being made to identify those interactional features that are important for learning and cognitive change.

Many experimental studies of collaborative interaction have focused on understanding how children talk when they are working together on a task or solving problems collaboratively. The associations between particular features of the learners' talk and on-task success, or subsequent learning gain as indexed by individual performance on a post-test, have been explored using correlational techniques. In this way, Azmitia and Montgomery (1993) established that the quality of children's dialogue is a significant predictor of their successful problem-solving. Barbieri and Light (1992) also found that measures of the amount of talk concerning planning, negotiation and the co-construction of knowledge by partners correlated significantly with successful problem-solving by pairs of children working together on computer-based problem-solving tasks and to successful learning gains in subsequent related tasks by individuals. Similar analytic techniques used by Underwood and Underwood (1999) demonstrated that, for pairs of children working on a computer-based problem-solving activity, those who were most observed to express opinions, analyse the situation in words and express agreement and understanding achieved the best outcomes. Experimental evidence thus supports the view that focused, sustained discussion amongst children not only helps them solve problems but promotes the learning of the individuals involved. This may seem like common sense – after all, we are familiar with the old saying, 'Two heads are better than one' – but if it is so obviously true, then we are led back to the question, raised earlier, of why high-quality peer discussion is not typically seen in many classroom contexts.

Regarding effects on individuals, a series of experimental, and observational, studies by Howe and colleagues (Howe, 2010) have shown that conceptual understanding in science is enhanced by children's discussion of ideas during group work. They found that some features of dialogue are particularly associated with solving complex problems, such as requiring that partners should try to achieve consensus in their discussion (Howe and Tolmie, 2003). Reviewing their own and other (mainly school-based) research, they conclude that the most productive interaction seems to involve pupils proposing ideas and explaining their reasoning to each other (Howe *et al.*, 2007). Moreover, the expression of contrasting opinions during group work was the single most important predictor of learning gain. They also found that the positive effects of group work are often delayed (Howe *et al.*, 1992), and this seems to be because dialogue primes children to make good use of subsequent experiences (Howe *et al.*, 2005). Howe *et al.* (2007) also found that group work seemed most productive when teachers did not intervene, but left pupils to work through problems without intervention – Barnes and Todd (1977) also draw attention to how teachers can inadvertently undermine group collaboration, a point further underscored by Hertz-Lazarowitz (1992).

In the 1970s, Barnes and Todd undertook one of the most important early studies of children's talk while working together in school. It involved secondary-age children (Barnes and Todd, 1977; see also 1995 and Barnes, 2008), but the insights this research afforded have informed much other research since, including that focused on the primary years. Based on their detailed observations, Barnes and Todd suggest that classroom discussion has to meet certain requirements for explicitness which would not normally be expected or required in everyday conversation. One of their key ideas was the concept of **Exploratory Talk**, which they argued was of particular educational significance. Exploratory Talk is talk in which a speaker articulates half-formed thoughts so that they can be tested out in the telling, and so that others can hear them, and comment. In Exploratory Talk, knowledge is made publicly accountable, relevant information is shared effectively, opinions are clearly explained and explanations examined critically. Barnes and Todd also argued that the successful pursuit of educational activity depends on learners sharing the same ideas about what is relevant to the discussion and having a joint conception of what is trying to be achieved by it. These points have been supported by other research based in primary schools (e.g. Bennett and Dunne, 1992; Galton and Williamson, 1992; Kumpulainen and Wray, 2002; Mercer and Hodgkinson, 2008; Mercer and Littleton, 2007).

The educational significance of Exploratory Talk

The educational significance of Exploratory Talk, which was prefigured in Barnes and Todd's work, was highlighted further in the Spoken Language and New Technology (SLANT) project in the early 1990s.

Classic study: the Spoken Language and New Technology project

The researchers working on this project observed the talk of children aged 8–11 years as they worked together in small groups at computers in classroom settings (Wegerif and Scrimshaw, 1997). Detailed analysis of the children's joint sessions of work suggested that most of the interactions recorded were not task-focused. Neither were they productive or equitable. In some pairs or groups, one child completely dominated the discussion, so much so that the other group members often withdrew from the activity, becoming increasingly quiet and subdued. In other groups the children seemed to tolerate, or ignore, each other, taking turns at the computer, each pursuing their own particular ideas when it was 'their turn'. Some groups' talk involved them in unproductive, often highly competitive, disagreements. These disagreements would sometimes escalate, with the children becoming increasingly cross and frustrated with each other and engaging in personal criticism. On the other hand, much group talk was relatively brief, somewhat cursory and bland. Particularly when groups of friends worked together, the discussions involved only superficial consideration of each others' ideas, with the uncritical acceptance of ideas predominating. These observations resonated with those of the other research projects, detailed earlier, that indicated that, although grouping children is a common organisational strategy, talk of any educational value is rarely to be heard. That said, very occasionally there was evidence of a particular, distinctive kind of interaction that was qualitatively different and more educationally productive. Here the children engaged in lively discussions in which they articulated and shared relevant ideas and helped each other to understand problems. Whilst they were mutually supportive, they were also constructively critical of each others' ideas, with challenges and counterchallenges being justified, and alternative ideas and hypotheses being offered. There was more of the kind of interaction that Barnes and Todd called 'Exploratory Talk'.

On the basis of the analysis of the SLANT data, the researchers devised a three-part typology of talk. This typology (described below, was designed specifically to characterise the qualitatively different ways in which children in the project classrooms talked together (Mercer, 1995). In this typology, the concept of Exploratory Talk differs from Barnes and Todd's original usage in the sense that it is less focused on individuals sorting out their thoughts and more on collaborating partners 'thinking together' in talk – a process that Mercer has termed '**interthinking**' (Mercer, 2000; Mercer and Littleton, 2007):

- **Disputational Talk** is characterised by disagreement and individualised decision-making. There are few attempts to pool resources, to offer constructive criticism or make suggestions. Disputational talk also has some characteristic discourse features – short exchanges consisting of assertions and challenges or counter-assertions ('Yes, it is!' 'No it's not!').
- **Cumulative Talk**, in which speakers build positively but uncritically on what the others have said. Partners use talk to construct 'common knowledge' by accumulation. Cumulative discourse is characterised by repetitions, confirmations and elaborations.
- **Exploratory Talk**, in which partners engage critically but constructively with each other's ideas. Statements and suggestions are offered for joint consideration. These may be challenged and counter-challenged, but challenges are justified and alternative hypotheses are offered. Partners all actively participate, and opinions are sought and considered before decisions are jointly made. Compared with the other two types, in Exploratory Talk knowledge is made more publicly accountable and reasoning is more visible in the talk.

(Mercer and Littleton, 2007: 58–59)

The application of the typology is exemplified below in relation to the three short extracts of dialogue presented in the activity box. All the participants are primary-school children who are working at the computer. They are all engaged in the joint task of authoring a conversation between two cartoon characters portrayed on a computer screen. They also have to decide what the characters are thinking as they speak – typing their decisions into the relevant 'speech' and 'thought' bubbles. (Whenever it seemed to the researchers that the children were speaking the voices of the characters, the words have been placed in inverted commas.)

Types of talk

The following three sequences of dialogue are taken from data presented by Mercer and Littleton (2007). Read through the three sequences, making brief notes about the nature of the interactions that are occurring in each of the extracts, then read the commentary by the authors. Did you notice similar things?

Sequence 1: Jo and Carol

CAROL: Just write in the next letter. 'Did you have a nice English lesson.'

Jo: You've got to get it on there. Yes that's you. Let's just have a look at that. 'Hi, Alan did you have a nice English lesson. Yes thank you, Yeah. Yes thank you it was fine.'

CAROL: You've got to let me get some in sometimes.

Jo: You're typing.

CAROL: Well you can do some, go on.

Jo: 'Yes thank you.'

CAROL: [*unintelligible.*]

Jo: You're typing. 'Yes thank you' 'I did, yeah, yes, thank you I did.'

CAROL: You can spell that.

Jo: Why don't *you* do it?

CAROL: No, because *you* should.

Sequence 2: Sally and Emma

SALLY: Yeah. What if she says erm erm, 'All right, yeah.' No, just put, 'Yeah all right.' No, no.

EMMA: No. 'Well I suppose I could.'

SALLY: 'Spare 15p.' Yeah?

EMMA: Yeah.

SALLY: 'I suppose.'

EMMA: 'I suppose I could spare 50p.'

SALLY: '50?'

EMMA: Yeah. 'Spare 50 pence.'

SALLY: '50 pence.'

EMMA: '50 pence.' And Angela says, 'That isn't enough I want to buy something else.'

SALLY: Yeah, no no. 'I want a drink as well you know I want some coke as well.'

EMMA: 'That isn't enough for bubble gum and some coke.'

SALLY: Yeah, yeah.

Sequence 3: Tina, George and Sophie

GEORGE: We've got to decide.

TINA: We've got to decide together.

GEORGE: Shall we right, right, just go round like [take

TINA: [No, go round. You say what you think, and she says.

GEORGE: I think she should be saying, 'Did you steal my money from me?'

TINA: Your go.

Sophie: I think we should put, 'I thought that my money's gone missing and I thought it was you.'

George: 'I think it was you.'

Sophie: Which one?

Tina: Now what was it I was going to say, um, um.

George: No because she's *thinking*, so we need to do a thought. So we could write her saying.

Sophie: 'My money's gone [missing so.'

Tina: [I was going to say if we're doing the one where she's saying, this is *saying* not thinking.

Sophie: 'My money's gone do you know where it is?'

Tina: No, [on the saying one she could say

George: [You should be saying.

Tina: Like she could be thinking to say to Robert, she could be saying, 'Do you know where's my money?' 'Do you know anything about my money going missing?'

George: Yeah, what, yeah that's good. When she's thinking I think she should be thinking, 'Oh my money's gone missing and its definitely Robert.'

Tina: Yeah.

Sophie: No 'cos she's *saying* it to him, isn't she?

Tina: [No she's *thinking* at the moment.

George: [No she's thinking.

Tina: *That's* the speech bubble.

Mercer and Littleton's commentary:

> *The talk in Sequence 1 is an exemplification of Disputational Talk. Whilst both participants take an active part, there is little evidence of joint, collaborative engagement with the task. Much of the interaction comprises commands and assertions. The episode ends with a direct question and answer, but even the exchange has an unproductive, 'tit-for-tat', disputational quality. Sequence 2 has obvious features of Cumulative Talk. Both participants contribute ideas which are accepted and there are no disputes. There is evidence of repetitions, confirmation and elaborations. The interaction is good natured and cooperative, but there is no evaluative appraisal or critical consideration of ideas. Sequence 3 has some characteristics of Exploratory Talk. At the beginning of the sequence Tina and George making explicit reference to their task as requiring joint decision-making, and they make efforts to organize the interaction so that everyone's ideas are heard. The children then pursue a discussion of what is appropriate content for the character's 'thought' and 'speech' bubbles in which differing opinions are offered and visibly supported by some reasoning (For example 'No, because she's thinking, so we need to do a thought.' 'if we're doing the one where she's saying, this is saying not thinking.'). However, their reasoning is focused only on this procedural issue: they do not discuss explicitly or critically the proposed content of the character's thoughts and words.*

What is important to note is that this three-part typology is not simply a means of describing educational dialogues. The typology also has an evaluative dimension allied to a concern with educational effectiveness. This is because the research team found that talk of a mainly 'disputational' type was very rarely associated with processes of joint reasoning and knowledge construction. Whilst there may have been a lot of interaction between the children, the reasoning involved was mainly individualised and tacit. Furthermore, the kind of communicative relationship developed through disputation was defensive and overtly competitive, with information and ideas frequently being flaunted or withheld rather than shared. It was common for this type of talk to consist of tit-for-tat 'Yes it is', 'No it isn't' patterns of assertion and counter-assertion. It was also the case that rather than orienting to the criticism of ideas, the children engaged in disputational talk very often making unconstructive, inappropriate personal criticisms of each another. Disputational argument of this kind has little in common with the kind of reasoned argument that is represented by Exploratory Talk – the children are being 'argumentative' in the negative sense of squabbling and bickering.

In contrast to Disputational Talk, Cumulative Talk characterises dialogue in which ideas and information were shared and joint decisions were made, but there was little in the way of challenge and counter-challenge or the evaluative, constructive conflict of ideas in the process of constructing knowledge. Cumulative Talk represents talk that seemed to operate more on implicit concerns with solidarity and trust, hence the recourse to a constant repetition and confirmation of partners' ideas and proposals.

Exploratory Talk represents a joint, co-ordinated form of co-reasoning in language, in which speakers share knowledge, challenge ideas, evaluate evidence and considered options in a reasoned and equitable way. In the SLANT project it was evident when the children presented their ideas as clearly and as explicitly as necessary for them to become shared and jointly analysed and evaluated. Possible explanations were compared and joint decisions reached. By incorporating both constructive conflict and the open sharing of ideas, Exploratory Talk constitutes the more visible pursuit of rational consensus through conversation. Exploratory Talk thus foregrounds reasoning. Its ground rules require that: the views of all participants are sought and considered by the other group members who listen with respect; proposals are explicitly stated and evaluated, and that explicit agreement precedes decisions and actions. It is aimed at the achievement of consensus. Exploratory Talk, by incorporating both conflicting perspectives and the open sharing of ideas, instantiates the more visible pursuit of rational consensus through conversations. It is a speech situation in which everyone is free to express their views and in which the most reasonable views gain acceptance.

The purpose of this three-part analytic typology is quite circumscribed: to focus attention on the extent that talk partners use language to think together when pursuing joint problem-solving and other learning activities. As Mercer and Littleton (2007) explain, it is not designed to deal with many other important ways that the forms of talk reflect a variety of purposes used, such as the maintenance of social identities, expression of power and solidarity, emotional ties amongst speakers, and so on. Moreover, the three types of talk were not devised to be used as the basis for a coding scheme (of the kind used in systematic observation research). Rather, the typology is intended to offer a way of exploring the functional variation of talk as a means for pursuing collaborative activity. In this respect, it is intended to help an analyst perceive the extent to which participants in a joint activity are at any stage behaving collaboratively or competitively, and whether they are engaging in evaluation/critical reflection or in the mutual acceptance of ideas. The typology has crucially proven to be a valuable tool for helping teachers, advisers and others involved in educational practice gain insights into the functional variety of children's talk.

Interestingly, other educational researchers have independently produced similar characterisations of intellectually stimulating, collaborative and productive classroom talk – though usually with secondary-school students. For example, based on US observations of teacher-led discussions with groups of children, Anderson and colleagues (Anderson *et al.*, 1998; Chinn and Anderson, 1998) have highlighted the educational significance of **Collaborative Reasoning** (CR). During CR discussions, the quality of children's reasoning is high and they actively collaborate on the construction of arguments in complex networks of reasons and supporting evidence (Kim *et al.*, 2007). There are also strong links between the concept of Exploratory Talk (as defined by Mercer and colleagues) and what some educational researchers have called '**accountable talk**' (Michaels and O'Connor, 2002; Resnick, 1999).

From the work considered above, we can conclude that there is evidence to suggest that working and talking together can provide a powerful support for children's learning. However, the evidence also reveals that much of the talk that occurs between children working together in groups in classrooms is educationally unproductive – being 'disputational' or 'cumulative' rather than 'exploratory' in nature. One reason for this may be that many children have relatively little prior experience of or skill in engaging in talk of an 'exploratory' kind. The amount and quality of talk between parents and young children at home varies substantially (see, for example, Hart and Risley, 1995; Wells, 1986), and in some homes rational debates, logical deductions, extended narrative accounts and detailed explanations may seldom be heard. As a consequence, without guidance, instruction and encouragement from a teacher, many children may not gain access to some very useful ways of using language for reasoning and working collaboratively, because those 'ways with words' are simply not a common feature of the language of their out-of-school communities.

It also seems that some teachers may not be aware of children's lack of understanding and skill in using talk for learning; or, at least, they assume that children will know exactly what to do when a teacher asks them to 'discuss' a topic, or 'talk and work together' to solve a problem or carry out a task. The upshot is that children are left to somehow impute what is required and what constitutes a good, effective discussion, but they seldom succeed in doing so. The norms or ground rules for generating particular functional ways of using language in primary school – spoken or written – are rarely made explicit (Edwards and Mercer, 1987). It is often simply assumed that children will just pick these sorts of things up as they go along. But while 'fitting' in a superficial way with the norms of classroom life may be relatively easy, this may conceal children's lack of understanding about what they are expected to do in educational activities and why they should do so. Even when the aim of talk is made explicit – 'Talk together to decide', 'Discuss this in your groups' – there may be no real understanding of how to talk together or for what purpose. Many children may not appreciate the significance and educational importance of their talk with one another. They frequently assume that the implicit ground rules in play in the classroom are such that teachers want 'right answers', rather than discussion. How then are we to support and promote productive small-group interaction between peers?

Supporting and promoting productive interaction

Many opportunities for collaborative learning simply emerge as a consequence of being part of a particular community of learners (Crook, 2000). That said, we still need to understand how best to promote the most effective opportunities for collaborative learning and design strategies for optimising collaboration. This concern is reflected in recent research, in which three factors have been given particular attention: task design, quality of relationships and quality of talk.

Task design

When thinking about the issue of how to support productive group work, many researchers have emphasised the significance of effective task design. It is important that group tasks should be designed such that learners *need* to talk and work together on them. Therefore tasks should not be too simple – for, if each child can easily solve the problem or complete the task alone, then there is no imperative for joint working and talking. Equally, if the task is too difficult and complex for the children, then they will struggle to create understanding and meaning. A good group task is one that requires resources that no single individual possesses, and is one in which students work interdependently and reciprocally – the exchange of ideas and information being vital to success (Cohen, 1994). It is perhaps not surprising, then, that some research indicates that challenging, open-ended, tasks are more effective in facilitating productive interaction than closed tasks focused on finding one right answer (Cohen, 1994; Van Boxtel et al., 2000). This is in part because closed tasks more easily lead to one participant – perhaps, a more knowledgeable person – dominating the discussion (Arvaja, 2005). A clear task structure and provision of feedback is also important, and this might be one of the best ways in which computer technology can resource joint activity (Howe and Tolmie, 1999). That said, it is not simply a case of 'getting the task right'. Of course, good task design helps; but, because the meaning of educational tasks is constituted and created in and through interaction, task design is only part of the story.

Quality of relationships

According to Van Oers and Hännikäinen (2001: 105):

> The main reason why discourses in collaborative learning processes ever lead to improved understandings is that the participants in the process are willing to share their understandings and keep on doing so *despite* their disagreements and conflicts … the fact that they can ever be productive at all relies on the fact that the participants in this process, for the time being, feel obliged to each other, stay with each other and maintain togetherness.

This claim draws attention to the importance of the relationship between interacting partners. Researchers investigating how friendships mediate joint activity (e.g. Azmitia and Montgomery, 1993; Hartup, 1998; Vass, 2003; Youniss, 1999) have found that relational closeness is positively associated with the sharing of ideas, the exchanging of points of view and a collective approach to challenging tasks. It would therefore appear that the development of close relationships, characterised by a sense of trust and mutuality, enhances learning (Howes and Ritchie, 2002; Underwood and Underwood, 1999).

Findings such as these have led some researchers to argue that what is needed is a 'relational' approach to group working, which properly recognises that classroom learning is a social activity (Blatchford et al., 2003b). The suggestion is that training should be given to promote the development of close relationships between classmates through, amongst other things, developing interpersonal trust between the children – something that is often stressed in work investigating collaborative activity in the creative arts (see Miell and Littleton, 2004). To accomplish this, Blatchford and colleagues have developed an educational intervention programme which they characterise as using 'a relational approach' to the development of group working. Influenced by attachment theory and studies of parent–child interactions, the programme engages the participating children in activities designed to foster trust and mutual support, and develop communication skills and joint problem-solving. Evaluations of the programme involving comparisons between experimental and control classes have indicated that this relational approach is not only successful in motivating children to participate in group activity and value it, but that it has a significant impact on their reading and mathematics attainment (Kutnick, 2005). Work by researchers such as Swann (e.g. 1992), which highlights that some peer-based interactions are highly gendered and are characterised by dominance and asymmetry, also add weight to the claim that for group activity to be effective, children need to be taught to relate in positive ways.

Quality of talk

Other researchers, such as Mercer and Littleton (2007), suggest that children have to do more than learn to relate and engage with each other in a positive and supportive way; claiming that they have to be enabled to build constructively and critically on each others' ideas. It is Mercer and Littleton's assertion that it is imperative to teach children how to use Exploratory Talk as a tool for reason together. In collaboration with colleagues, they have developed **Thinking Together**, a classroom-based approach that places a special emphasis on the role of the teacher as a guide and model for language use, who fosters an inclusive climate for discussion while also enabling children to understand better how language can be used as a tool for thinking.

Practical implications

Thinking Together supports children in learning to talk in groups as well as providing them with opportunities for talking to learn. Through the systematic integration of both whole-class teacher-led interaction and group-based discussion, children are helped to understand that aims for group activity and the use of spoken language are as much to do with high-quality educationally effective talk and joint reasoning through Exploratory Talk, in which reasoning is accountable and visible, as with curriculum learning. The processes by which children learn how to learn are thus directly addressed, rather than being left to chance. The approach does more than deliver a particular form of communication skills training. It encourages children to engage in particular ways of talking and working together, and they are explicitly guided in how to use language as a tool for reasoning together. They are encouraged to give reasons, seek clarification, ask questions, listen to each others' ideas and so on. But children learn much more than a model set of talk strategies, and the goal is not that they will simply adhere to the 'ground rules' for Exploratory Talk. The main goal is children's active appropriation of a particular 'educated' way of talking and thinking, one that they understand and appreciate, so that in time they are able to apply, adapt and develop their use of language flexibly and creatively in their discussions.

Evaluations of the approach undertaken with children across a diverse age spectrum shows that teachers' encouragement of children's use of certain ways of using language leads to better learning and conceptual understanding (see Mercer and Littleton, 2007). The most well-established programme of intervention work has focused on enhancing the quality of 8–11-year-olds' group-based educational dialogues – aiming to ensure that children enter collaborative activities with a shared conception of how to talk and think together effectively. The evaluations, focusing on the efficacy of the programme, have revealed that children in target classes (trained in the use of Exploratory Talk) not only come to use significantly more Exploratory Talk than those in control classes, but also demonstrate more successful group-based problem-solving and enhanced individual educational attainment (for further details, see Mercer and Littleton, 2007; Mercer *et al.*, 2004; Wegerif and Dawes, 2004; Wegerif *et al.*, 1999).

Whilst the positive findings arising from this intervention work are compelling, the idea that we should be encouraging children to take up a new set of norms (the 'ground rules') for their classroom discussions has attracted some critical commentary (Lefstein, 2010) and is proving to be controversial in some quarters. Lambirth (2006), for example, has argued that the 'ground rules' associated with Exploratory Talk have no intrinsic value as a basis for collaborative activity, they simply reflect the language habits of the more privileged, educated members of society. Having to make a shift from existing sets of ground rules (those that may operate in the child's out-of-school experience) to those related to Exploratory Talk will, he suggests, undermine the linguistic identities and communicative self-confidence of many children. Whilst the 'subtraction' model of language learning (which proposes that adding any new language genre to a child's language repertoire must involve the deletion of some existing genre) that is implicit in this critique has no scientific foundation, it signals that, for some educators, there are strong ideological reasons why they would not advocate adopting a 'ground rules' approach to the promotion of productive educational dialogues.

There is certainly much more to discover about the ways that language experience in the classroom can contribute to the development of children's abilities to communicate, learn and reason, but what is known now provides a well-informed basis for the creation of a more dialogic, and more effective, educational practice. It is an uncontroversial claim that through social interaction, children learn how language can be used to describe the world, to make sense of life's experience and to get things done. However, what children learn from talk in the classroom, and how significant it is for their psychological development and educational progress, will depend a great deal on the range and quality of the dialogues in which they engage.

The importance of children's playground experiences

Up to this point we have been discussing the nature and significance of children's interactions with others in classroom contexts, largely through considering the nature and significance of teacher-talk and observations of small groups of children working and talking together. However, classrooms are not the only school context in which children engage in meaningful interactions; the playground is also an important site for interactions of significance and consequence. For children of all ages there is a separate, child-governed break-time culture in the playground from which adults are, for the most part, excluded (Blatchford and Baines, 2010). It is evident that this culture is not always a benign one, as there is evidence that racist and sexist teasing, fighting and bullying can occur on occasion (e.g. Kelly, 1994; Short, 1999). But that said, this break-time culture is extremely important to, and for, children. This is because, without adult intervention, children have to learn how to regulate playground games and space, and also how to manage and negotiate teasing and conflictual interactions. In doing so, Blatchford and Baines argue (2010: 237), they begin to develop a sophisticated set of social understandings, acquiring important social skills that are negotiated during the give and take characteristic of the reciprocal interaction between equals: 'The peer group provides arguably the most efficient and highly motivating context for the learning and development of social skills which will ultimately enable children to live effectively as a member of adult society' (Maxwell, 1990: 171).

Whilst there seems to be a reasonably clear consensus that playground experiences help children develop important social skills, other studies indicate that the incidence of bullying and aggression in the playground is sufficiently frequent to occasion some concern (e.g. Whitney and Smith, 1993). Indeed, as Blatchford and Baines (2010: 240) point out: 'One of the most high profile aspects of peer relations in school, and one which has probably done more than any other to suggest the negative consequences of informal peer interaction, is bullying.' This has resulted in a number of initiatives to try to reduce bullying within schools (e.g. in the UK: *Safe to Learn: Embedding Anti-Bullying Work in School*, DCSF, 2007) and improve the quality of playground life. This has been achieved by either changing the physical environment to make it more attractive, or by explicitly teaching children social skills and strategies for dealing with aggression and conflict (see, for example, Blatchford, 1998; Blatchford and Sharp, 1994). As children create their own culture in the playground, an important message for programmes designed to improve the playground climate is that interventions are unlikely to be successful unless they take children's views and knowledge of this culture into account (Cowie, 1999).

Perhaps one of the most challenging issues when considering children's conflicts and disputes concerns the identification of satisfactory criteria to distinguish negative interactions among pupils, especially bullying, from other kinds of dispute. Conflicts and disputes are not of and in themselves a negative experience in children's development (Littleton and Miell, 2004). Children need to learn to understand and recognise the existence of conflicts of interest, furthermore learning how to negotiate those conflicts and how to respect each other's points of view are inevitable and desirable childhood experiences in the context of liberal, democratic societies.

Much 'conflict' takes place in the context of children's play, games and verbal word-play and repartee. As Littleton and Miell (2004: 107) note:

> in these circumstances conflict is understood by those participants in the children's peer culture. This shared meaning system sets the emotional tone of the exchange, the boundaries concerning what is acceptable, and the rules that regulate infringement of what is 'fair'.

Smith and colleagues (1999) suggest that play fighting and play chasing are not only typical among primary-school-age children but are also positively enjoyed among friends as an expression of intimacy within their relationship. That said, Smith *et al.* also recognise that there is not a sharp dividing line between play fighting and real fighting, play teasing and nasty teasing. An important implication for both researchers and teachers alike is that criteria for distinguishing 'positive' from 'negative' conflict cannot be listed and then defined in a detailed observational checklist of unambiguous behaviours that can be used to identify constructive and destructive interactions. The analytic criteria and allied interpretations are highly contextually dependent and fundamentally situated in respect of the customs and beliefs of the peer group in question, the contexts in which the dispute is taking place (e.g. classroom, playground or street) and the standards set by the adults responsible for regulating children's behaviour within a framework of cultural norms. Most crucially, whether a conflict is 'positive' or 'negative' also depends on the subjective experience of those involved. Above, we considered the notions of the subtle 'ground rules' that are implicated in classroom interactions. Ground rules are also significant in framing up participants' expectations in respect of the interactions that occur in less-formal contexts. Friendship pairs and wider peer groups also employ subtle 'ground rules' to distinguish the playful from the non-playful and thus the boundaries of what is seen as acceptable joshing among children who are relative equals (see Littleton and Miell, 2004). This is especially salient in respect of teasing. At worst, just one word, or one subtle action or gesture, can acquire highly provocative symbolic power, to which only one targeted individual may be sensitive. The symbolic power of such words, or gestures, will have their antecedents in the shared history of the interlocutors and are thus not readily visible to observers of (or, indeed, some of the participants in) a given encounter. Thus the perceived playfulness of children's behaviour is only one of the criteria set out by Smith *et al.* in respect of the identification of positive and negative conflict. They argue that, if one is to distinguish bullying behaviour (including 'nasty teasing') from other conflict incidents, to 'count' as bullying, behaviour should be intentional, unprovoked, repeated and dominant.

At this point it is also important to recognise that peer groups are far from homogenous. Competing subcultures are thus likely to adhere to different values, attitudes to authority and expectations for behaviour, including conflict. Pollard's (1987) study of 8-to-12-year-olds' perspectives on school life rendered visible such differences in sub-group values and orientations. Pollard identified three distinct clusters of friendships: the 'goodies', the 'jokers' and 'the gangs'. He also noted that there were clear differences between the children in such groups:

> Children in groups that other children termed 'Good groups' regarded groups which they called 'Gangs' very negatively for their 'roughness' and 'destroying' behaviour. Groups which I termed 'Joker' groups puzzled at the quietness of Good groups, regarded each other as 'good fun' and 'sensible' but were also clear about the 'bigheaded', 'thick' 'roughness' of gangs. Gang groups condemned Good groups as 'soft' and 'goodiegoodies' and Joker groups as 'show-offs' and 'big heads'. Whilst their own gang was regarded as 'great' other gangs were usually labelled as 'soft', 'rubbish' or 'cocky', thus reflecting the extent of inter-gang rivalry.
>
> (Pollard, 1987: 165–166)

Pollard's work highlights the subtlety of interactions between children, and it is through such work that an understanding of the complexity, diversity and multiplicity of children's lived experiences is gained. The complexities of children's social worlds remind us of the dangers inherent in relying on stereotypic assumptions about children's interactions with other children. Also, as the research base we have drawn upon is based largely on research conducted in Western industrialised settings, we are thus unable to address how the nature of peer interactions is influenced by the specific society and cultural contexts within which a child is developing. This is, of course, a significant limitation and it is because of limitations such as these that it is important that psychologists do not over-generalise from interactional patterns observed in a particular society at a particular historical moment in time. Care must be taken not to turn specific, situated research-based descriptions of culturally based patterns of interactions into rigid prescriptions for effective learning and development.

Summary

In this chapter we have described how talk in classrooms, and other contexts, can be understood and analysed in terms of its functions and quality, making clear where there are implications of such analyses for the practice of teaching and learning. What is now known about the psychological functions of interaction and dialogue is not only relevant to the academic study of children's development and learning: it is also of practical value to teachers and parents who are concerned with ensuring that children are offered the best educational opportunities.

Key implications

- Effective teacher talk is dialogic – in that it is collective, reciprocal, supportive, purposeful and cumulative.
- Children need to be explicitly taught how to use talk in educationally effective ways.
- Playground experiences are of developmental significance and consequence.

Further reading

Blatchford and Baines (2010), 'Peer relations in school', in Littleton, Wood and Kleine Staarman (eds), *The International Handbook of Psychology in Education*: a valuable review chapter that focuses on both formal peer relations in classrooms and informal peer relations on school playgrounds. The authors' work not only sheds light on the nature and significance of peer relations but also informs current issues in educational and social policy.

Howe (2010), *Peer Groups and Children's Development*: a book which considers contemporary research regarding the experiences of school-aged children with their peer groups and the implications of these experiences for their social, personal and intellectual development.

Littleton and Howe (eds) (2010), *Educational Dialogues: Understanding and Promoting Productive Interaction*: drawing upon a broad range of theoretical perspectives, this collection examines: theoretical frameworks for understanding teaching and learning dialogues; teacher–student and student–student interaction in the curricular contexts of mathematics, literacy, science, ICT and philosophy; the social contexts supporting productive dialogues; and implications for pedagogic design and classroom practice.

Mercer and Littleton (2007), *Dialogue and the Development of Children's Thinking: a Socio-Cultural Approach*: the authors of this book provide a clear and accessible account of the importance of classroom dialogue for children's intellectual development, considering the relationship between psychological theory and educational practice. Details of the Thinking Together programme of work are provided, together with evaluation data.

Discussion of practical scenario

Mr Wright could think about the nature of the tasks he is setting his pupils – are they such that they ensure that children need to work together, requiring resources that no single person possesses? He may also want to consider introducing activities designed to develop trust between pupils. However, given his concern with the disputational nature of the dialogues he is witnessing, he may want to consider introducing the Thinking Together programme into his class, such that his pupils agree and construct ground rules for talking together in an 'exploratory' way – such that their reasoning is visible in their talk.

Language

Practical scenario

Mrs Peters is a reception-class teacher in a school where children often come in with very poor language abilities, scoring low on their baseline assessments. The children's home backgrounds are often poor and unstimulating, and there are probably limited language models from the parents. Although the children improve during their first year, their inadequate language development still limits their progress with the general curriculum, and particularly with literacy. Mrs Peters is therefore wondering what could be done to accelerate their language abilities, particularly where doing so would also help with their reading and writing.

What could Mrs Peters do to stimulate her pupils' speech and language development?

Should Mrs Peters perhaps concentrate on developing her pupils' language abilities and leave literacy teaching until they have a stronger foundation?

Is there any form of assessment that would help guide support for these children?

The importance of language

There are many interconnected ways in which language can be seen as a central component of the educational process. Perhaps most importantly, language is the major way of forming and developing concepts, and using these to express understanding and to communicate with other people. Language therefore depends on, and is a basis for, learning and memory, as well as general thinking abilities. Because of its central role in education, English is a core subject in the National Curriculum of England and Wales, and children's progress is assessed at the end of the various Key Stages by means of SATs and the GCSE examinations. Traditionally, at school, the emphasis tends to be on developing competency with written forms of language, and less emphasis is put on competency in oral communication. However, there is an increasing recognition of language as the basis for cognitive development and problem-solving, and research has examined the impact that teaching children to 'think together' through spoken language can have on their academic attainment, as you will see.

What is language?

Language can be thought of simply as a system of symbols (vocal noises, marks on a page or hand movements) that we use to communicate with others. According to such a definition, all animals 'speak' a language to other members of their community, but human language is seen as distinct from the communication systems of other species in important ways. In particular, Jean Aitchison (2008) notes that, although there are many similarities between human and non-human languages, human language is distinctive in several key respects.

1 **Semanticity:** the symbols that we use in our language (spoken, written or signed words) carry meaning. It has not yet been demonstrated whether or not units of animal language are 'meaningful' in the same way.

2 **Duality and displacement:** 'duality' refers to the way that the individual components of our language (e.g. letter sounds) do not carry meaning in themselves, but can be combined into larger units that do (e.g. words and sentences). 'Displacement' refers to the ability to use language to talk about things that have happened in the past or will happen in the future, as well as in the here and now. Both these elements have been observed to a lesser extent in some non-human communication systems, but only human language has both these characteristics.

3 **Structure-dependence:** this refers to our ability to recognise that language has patterns within it and a structure that enables us to manipulate and substitute 'chunks' of language (e.g. 'the old lady who lived in a shoe' can also be referred to as 'she', 'her', or 'the old lady' in subsequent sentences).

4 **Creativity:** as the term suggests, this refers to the ability to use symbols to talk about anything the speaker is interested in. Human language may have a finite number of speech sounds or written characters, but these can be combined in a potentially limitless number of combinations.

5 **Intension reading:** sometimes referred to as 'mind reading' or 'theory of mind' in the developmental literature, this is the ability to put oneself in the position of another person, to appreciate what they know or might feel, and to understand that this might be very different to what we know or feel at the same time, or in the same situation. The ease with which humans are able to acquire and use this ability far exceeds what has been observed in non-human animals, although it should be noted that this is not an ability that one either possesses or does not possess – different levels of ability are observed in both humans and other species. This ability is often impaired in individuals with Autistic Spectrum Disorder, for example.

What this list of 'unique' characteristics illustrates is just how complex human language is, and the great potential it offers us as a tool for creative thought, communication and problem-solving. It is easy to take language abilities for granted, and to underuse them in the classroom as a consequence.

As shown in Figure 9.1, spoken and written language can be described at a number of different levels, ranging from the formation and use of sounds to overall structure, use and meaning. **Linguistics** is the scientific study of language. Part of this is the study of grammar, which deals with the form and structure of words (morphology) and the way in which they are combined in sentences (syntax).

Phonetics

There are more than 40 basic phonemes in the English language. Phonemes are the smallest units of sound that we can make with our voice that can change meaning. For example, the difference

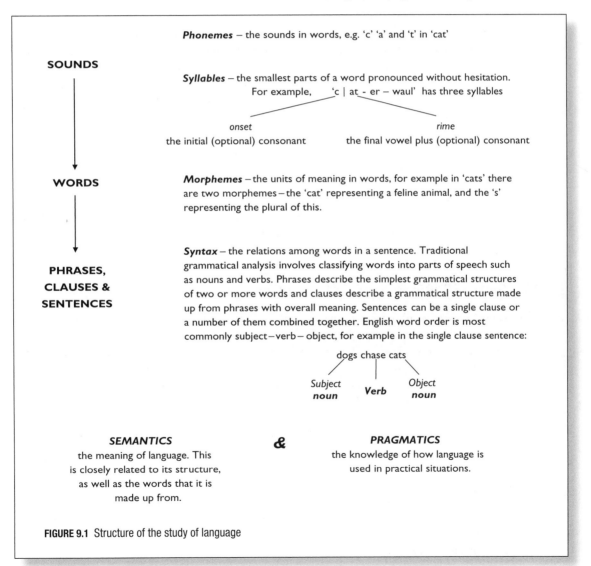

FIGURE 9.1 Structure of the study of language

between the words 'big' and 'pig' is minimal when we consider the movement made in the lips, tongue and throat when we say them, but as words they carry very different meanings. It should be noted that other languages use different numbers of phonemes, and there are 107 different phonemes in the international phonetic alphabet. The majority of these are consonant sounds and are formed by closing or restricting the shape of the vocal tract in some way. For instance, /d/ is formed by taking the tongue away from the alveolar ridge (just behind the teeth) while the vocal cords are active. It is known as a 'voiced' consonant; if the vocal cords were not active, the result would be the 't' sound.

The main vowel sounds are made with a relatively free flow of air and are formed by the shape of the tongue. For instance, the vowel sound in 'bed' is made with the tongue in a mid-position at the front of the mouth. Raising the tongue to a high position would instead produce the different vowel sound in 'bid'. Special types of vowels known as 'diphthongs' are combined with a final glide where the tongue moves to a different position. In 'boy', for instance, the tongue moves all the way from the bottom back to the top front of the mouth.

Accents are distinguished mainly by having modified vowel sounds, as in 'Received Pronunciation' ('posh' English). Dialects also make different use of consonants, as well as having a distinctive vocabulary and syntactic structures. Although a listener unfamiliar with a particular dialect may find it difficult to understand, dialects are used consistently by large groups of people and are normally as effective as other forms of the language in communicating meaning. Standard English is the dominant, high-status dialect in Britain and is required teaching as part of the National Curriculum. Whitehead (1997), however, argues that a child's dialect is a source of personal identity and self-esteem, and believes that, although children should have access to Standard English (for example, through listening to stories), their own dialect should be given equal value.

When sounds are distorted or missing, however, the intelligibility of children's speech can be affected, as is discussed later in the section 'Speech and language problems' at the end of this chapter (pp. 234–235). Moreover, if children have problems hearing or perceiving the sounds in words, this can also affect the development of their ability to read and write, as you will see in Chapter 10.

Syntax and grammar

The general study of word order is known as 'syntax'. Grammar technically refers to any form of rule-based system in language and applies to all levels of analysis, including the regularities in sounds, words, text and meaning. Traditional grammar is a particular form that is derived from classical studies of Greek and Latin. It involves analysing words into the main classes of nouns, verbs, prepositions, articles, pronouns, conjunctions, adjectives and adverbs. Rules then govern the way in which these are modified and form phrases and clauses, how these can be combined to form sentences, and the general organisation of bodies of text.

The main purpose of language is communication: the transfer of meaning from one person to another to achieve practical purposes. Achieving communication must involve some structural system that is able to change thoughts into a form that can be spoken, and a reverse system of altering what has been heard, into its underlying meaning. Chomsky (1965) developed a well-known system of linguistic rules called a 'generative grammar', which governs how this can be done, involving the analysis of sentences into phrases and word classes. According to this approach, the sentence 'The boy kicks the ball' is a single clause with the basic underlying structure of somebody (the boy) carrying out an action, which is to kick the ball. This is analysed as:

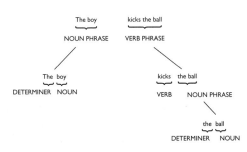

A system of rules applied in this way can account for our ability to produce grammatical sequences, and will rule out a sentence such as 'the boy ball the kicks', which is ungrammatical in English. Chomsky also believed that it is necessary for us to carry out processes called 'transformations', to simplify analyses and to relate together sentences with similar meanings but different structures. For example, the sentence, 'The ball is kicked by the boy' has the same basic meaning as the sentence above but has a very different and more complex phrase-structure analysis. This analysis is simplified by applying a transformational rule, which converts between the active sentence and its passive form. This particular rule is carried out by taking the second noun phrase, adding an auxiliary verb 'is', modifying the form of the verb, then adding 'by', followed by the first noun phrase.

Chomsky argued that spoken language comes from a surface structure, which is the output of the transformational rules and which can then be processed by the phonological system into speech. Underlying this is the deep structure, which is the output of the phrase structure rules and acts as the input to a semantic component. According to this approach, meaning therefore comes from the words in a sentence with information about their grammatical relationships and classes.

Early investigations gave general support to Chomsky's theory, with findings that sentences that have more transformations take longer to process. In the sentence, 'Is Peter not chased by Jack?' there are three transformations, 'passive', 'negative' and 'question', and it is certainly very difficult to understand. However, Slobin (1966) showed that if there are meaningful relationships between actors and the actions they take, then the effect of this knowledge is greater than the effects of transformations. A passive sentence such as, 'The cat was chased by the dog' is as easy to understand as its active form. We already have the general knowledge that dogs chase cats, so we do not have to carry out any additional syntactic work with the passive transformation to know this.

In general, it appears that we are able to use syntax for information, but that linguistic systems that rely on the use of syntax are looking only at our underlying competence – what we are technically capable of when necessary. Real-life performance with communication is likely to also be dependent on meaning, known as semantic information, and what we expect and understand from the general social context, known as 'pragmatics'.

Syntactic complexity does, however, affect ease of comprehension since it can interfere with our ability to use such semantic information. The use of multiple clauses, for instance, can make it particularly difficult to retain the overall meaning, particularly if they are embedded within the overall sentence. An example is:

The dog who chased the cat which was sitting on the wall felt tired.

By the time the receiver gets to the end of the sentence, it might be difficult to remember the initial phrase and work out which animal the 'felt tired' refers to. Since reading or listening has to be mainly sequential, this can place a load on our ability to retain such information. Frazier and Fodor (1978) therefore argued that language input is analysed by a model they named the 'sausage machine', because it divides language input into something like a link of sausages. They propose that, owing to short-term memory constraints, only six words at a time can be initially processed for phrase structure, with a sentence analyser subsequently operating at a higher level.

Research into the 'sausage machine' approach indicate that the first stage involves assigning words to an immediate syntactic category, and that we then make an early initial 'best guess' about what the likely phrase structure will be. The second stage then looks at consistency with other parts of the sentence and will modify the overall analysis if there is other compelling syntactic or semantic information (Harley, 2008). Such a process can account for many natural errors, such as those that occur in 'garden path' sentences. In these, we are 'led up the garden path' by the structure and meaning of the first part of the sentence; for instance:

The cat chased around the house was tired.

The verb 'chased' is ambiguous, and at first the simplest 'garden path' interpretation is that the cat was chasing. The final 'was tired' cannot meaningfully refer to the house and so the overall structure has to be reinterpreted. In reality, of course, people speaking or writing this would want to avoid such ambiguities and would go out of their way to make sure that the receiver understood their meaning. This can involve punctuation, by placing a comma after 'house', or even better by removing the ambiguity early on and adding the additional phrase 'that was' after 'cat'.

Speakers or writers can sometimes become over-involved in their own understanding and lose track of the needs of the listener or reader. Young children, for instance, are very prone to simply rely on the conjunction 'and' when writing. Redrafting is therefore a useful technique, particularly if writers leave their work for a time and are then able to perceive the text from the perspective of a reader. Teachers can also be guilty of communicating in ways that are overly complex or ambiguous, and may need to monitor how they say things, or what they write.

Psycholinguistics

Linguistics by itself can only account for regularities in the structure of language and characteristics of a system which can either produce or analyse this. The complete study of language must also incorporate general psychological processes such as thought, knowledge and meaning, which are closely bound up with the nature of concepts as embodied in words. We can view word meanings as coming from a concept's place within a hierarchical structure, or as sets of linked semantic features, possibly as some form of prototype or schema. Connectionist approaches are able to account for many of the features of schemas, with the advantages of flexibility and swift processing.

When receiving language input, we appear to rapidly identify individual words, and we appear to begin to integrate word information into a semantic context after just 400 ms of input (Van Petten *et al.*, 1999). Word recognition involves a combination of 'top-down' contextual information about what word is likely to occur in a particular place, as well as automatic 'bottom-up' analysis and synthesis of the word's structure. We then seem to have direct access to the features and associations of the concepts represented by words, which is borne out by a classic phenomenon known as the 'Stroop effect' (Stroop, 1935). As shown in Figure 9.2, this involves asking people to read out the colour words are printed in, where the words are either the actual colour or a different one. When people are asked to say the name of the colour that the text is written in, it takes them significantly longer to do this with the top cards. The reason this is so is that we seem to process both the colour and the

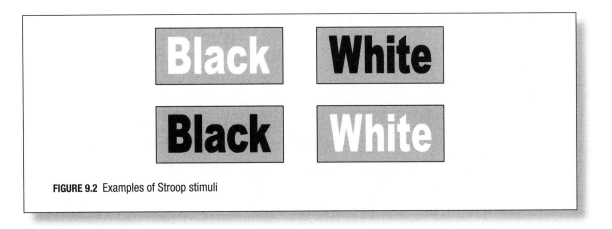

FIGURE 9.2 Examples of Stroop stimuli

word meaning automatically. When there is a difference, this produces a conflict or interference with what we are trying to do. This happens even after practice or with conscious attempts to 'block out' the unwanted information.

Activity

Try the Stroop effect for yourself. Find as many different-coloured pens as you can, and two pieces of paper. On one piece of paper write down the colour of the ink in the pen you are writing with (so you would write 'blue' with a blue pen, 'black' with a black pen, 'red' with a red pen and so on). On the second piece of paper, write down the same colour names but write them in a different-coloured ink (write 'red' with the black pen, 'blue' with the green pen, and so on). Now use a stopwatch or similar to time how long it takes you to name the colour of the ink each word is written in (total time taken for each card). You should find that you are much slower to name the colours on the second card. This is because reading is an automatic process, and you cannot help but process the written words, even though you don't need to read anything to complete the task.

Once the meanings of individual words are activated, these must then be associated in some way to establish some form of thought process or conceptualisation. It seems likely that such conceptualisations can exist in a number of different forms, including direct representations of activities or as a form of imagery. As discussed later in this chapter, it also seems probable that thought can occur as a type of internal language at different levels, either as a conscious form of 'talking to ourselves' or as unconscious symbolic processing.

Constructing overall meaning from spoken or written language in this way involves a significant amount of interpretation and inferential reasoning. As well as understanding individual words, we need to form early hypotheses about the likely structure and meaning of sentences to enable us to make efficient predictions about what follows. One important aspect of sentence structure is the formation of appropriate inferences between sentences. For example:

Tom hit Peter. *He* was angry.

In this case, the word 'he' can refer to either Tom (who hit Peter because he was angry) or Peter (who was angry because Tom hit him). To decide which is meant, we would really need additional information on, say, what was already happening or the different personalities of Tom and Peter.

When we do not have such information, there is a tendency to assume that a pronoun in this position will refer to the person carrying out the action; in this case, that it was Tom who was angry.

Once we have derived meaning from what we have heard or read in a sentence, the specific form of the words is usually lost quite rapidly. Bransford *et al.* (1972), for instance, showed subjects sentences that incorporated certain logical relationships, such as:

> Three turtles rested on a floating log and a fish swam beneath them.

After only a short period, they were unable to distinguish this from the following sentence:

> Three turtles rested on a floating log and a fish swam beneath it.

It seems that when listening to the first sentence, people rapidly construct a mental representation which has the turtles on the log and the fish under the log, which is logically identical to the second sentence.

Schemas

Our ability to understand text can depend to a great extent on general expectations and understanding. One way of describing such expectations is in terms of the activation of schemas. These have already been described in Chapter 2 as general ways of grouping together concepts or features in meaningful ways, for instance to represent particular events, situations or objects. Bransford and Johnson (1972) investigated how a schema could affect understanding of a passage where it was very difficult to work out what was happening from the text alone.

Activity

Below is the passage used in Bransford and Johnson's study (1972). Try reading this yourself and see if you can work out what is being described:

> The procedure is quite simple. First, you arrange items into different groups. Of course one pile may be sufficient depending on how much there is to do. If you have to go somewhere else due to lack of facilities that is the next step; otherwise you are pretty well set. It is important not to overdo things. That is, it is better to do too few things at once than too many. In the short run this may not seem important but complications can easily arise. A mistake can be expensive as well. At first, the whole procedure will seem complicated. Soon, however, it will become just another facet of life. It is difficult to foresee any end to the necessity for this task in the immediate future, but then, one never can tell. After the procedure is completed one arranges the materials into their appropriate places. Eventually they will be used once more and the whole cycle will then have to be repeated. However, that is part of life.

Feedback

When people read this passage by itself, they had great difficulty understanding what it was about and were subsequently able to remember only 2.8 ideas on average. However, when others were given the title 'Washing clothes' before they read the passage, they found it much easier to understand and were able to remember on average 5.8 ideas. The title evidently enabled them to interpret the meaning of the ambiguous information, in much the same way that advance organisers (an integrating preview of what is to be covered at the start of a study unit) have been shown to help with pupils' study and recall. Giving the title after the passage did not help with recall, indicating that the content of the passage had already been lost and could no longer be analysed.

Practical implications

This impact of schemas on comprehension and subsequent recall of information is very clear, and is useful to us when we consider how we introduce material to students in the classroom. It is very easy to 'lose' students by talking about a topic without introducing it adequately or linking it to existing topics that will help them to make sense of it. Making sure that we always invoke schemas by making links between familiar topics and new ones is an easy way to help students integrate new information into memory.

Scripts

Interpretations about the meanings embodied within language can also come from types of schemas known as 'scripts', proposed by Schank and Abelson (1977). These are expectations of what normally happens and is appropriate in certain situations – for example, in the process of 'going to a restaurant'. This would typically involve the social roles of being a customer, related to other roles such as that of waiter, and the sequence of events of entering the restaurant, sitting down, choosing from the menu, ordering and then eating the food, then paying and leaving. Such expectations can have a strong effect on people's analysis and recall of verbal sequences, and when Bower *et al.* (1979) gave people different passages which described going to a restaurant, they found that people tended to distort their recall of the stories. The effect of this distortion was to make the passages fit in with what would normally happen. For example, the subjects would put in any additional features that had been missed out, such as the waiter taking the order. When the stories had additional features, such as the waiter bringing fish instead of steak, then these aspects were remembered well. This indicates that people tend to process and discard language when it fits in with what is already known, but analyse further and store information when it is new and meaningful.

Pragmatics

Pragmatics refers to the intended meaning and functions of what is said, rather than its literal meaning, and depends on our shared knowledge and understanding of social encounters. Children who are on the autistic spectrum often have great difficulty in this respect since they appear to lack the ability to understand the thoughts and intentions of other people. A request by a teacher such as, 'Can you open that window?' would therefore be treated as just a question and the child may merely answer, 'Yes'. Such a reply can appear uncooperative or insolent if the teacher is not aware of the pupil's difficulties.

We evidently have to infer a great deal about what a person really means, and we do this using our knowledge of what is appropriate in certain situations, the intent of the person we are listening to, and social meanings and conventions. There are many situations where the surface meaning is unintentionally different from what is intended, but we can also make deliberate constructions, such as rhetorical questions, irony or sarcasm. The vast majority of simple requests are also indirect and become even less direct when people are trying to be polite. Rather than ask for a window to be closed, a person might therefore ask, 'Don't you find that it's getting a bit cold?' or 'Does anyone feel a draught in here?' Most people appear to understand such utterances immediately, indicating that their general knowledge of social-linguistic conventions and people's needs has primacy over direct linguistic and semantic interpretation.

In conversations, there is usually a strong attempt by each participant to make sure that the other person understands what they are trying to say. This means that new content is often explicitly linked with whatever knowledge the other person already has, as in, 'You know that girl in Miss Penn's class, who's always going on about her new trainers an' that, well, I saw her in town yesterday …' This is also linked with a great deal of verbal information called prosody which involves emphasising different words, using pauses and different tones of voice, as well as general non-verbal behaviour such as eye contact, posture and gesture. Eye contact is particularly used to structure the turn-taking of conversations, with the person who is talking looking away, then looking back at the listener to 'hand over' to them. The listener will also use eye contact as well as nods, gestures and sounds such as 'mm' to show that they are listening and in agreement. A characteristic feature of children who are on the autistic spectrum is that they make little eye contact and are often unaware that facial movements contain a great deal of information.

Characteristics of language development

The acquisition of language appears to most people to be a spontaneous and inborn process. There are in fact strong grounds for believing that humans are naturally prepared to develop some form of language and that children need only a certain level of language experience to develop basic abilities. However, there is also evidence that language development nevertheless very much depends upon experience and that young children need exposure to adequate language models as well as an interactive and supportive environment.

By the time children start school, most of them have already achieved an extensive functional vocabulary and have the basic range of grammatical abilities. Language abilities continue to develop in both these areas, however, and a key role of school can be seen as that of promoting children's general language progress, as well as language's use in studying specific areas of the curriculum. Even a subject such as mathematics, which one would imagine involves relatively independent skills, is in fact dependent on words, concepts and relationships, which often involves reading and talking about problems.

The sound system

Young babies make a wide range of all the possible sounds in their early sound play, or 'babbling', but by about one year of age these are narrowed down to the standard set for the language that the child is being brought up with. Rathus (1988) has shown, however, that at five years of age (i.e. at school entry), many children are still making many errors with the use of sounds, particularly *j*, *v*, *th* and *zh*. As will be described later in this chapter, this can involve the child making substitutions that may need to be reviewed by the teacher. Many children also have difficulty with the use of final consonants, such as saying 'ge' for 'get', and with consonant combinations, such as saying 'bue' for 'blue'. By the age of eight years, children are accurate about 90 per cent of the time, although boys take a year longer than girls to develop a mature phonological system.

Young children are not normally aware of the separate sounds in speech and just 'say words'. As discussed in the following chapter, the ability to perceive and to combine separate phonemes in early reading can be quite difficult for some children and is a strong predictor of subsequent progress with literacy.

Children starting school will also have difficulty with their ability to perceive different intonation and emphases. It can therefore still be difficult for them to resolve an anaphor, which depends upon a stressed word for meaning. In the sentence, 'Peter gave a sweet to Tom and he gave one to Susan', they are likely to fail to notice when there is an emphasis on *he*, to mean that Tom gave the sweet to Susan.

Vocabulary

Children typically say their first word at around nine months, and at about 18 months there is a sudden increase in the rate of word production (Lightfoot *et al.*, 2009), signalling the start of the so-called **vocabulary spurt**. By two years of age, children will be able to use about 200 words (Goldfield and Reznick, 1990). A much more rapid development in general vocabulary then takes place, and by the age of six years the average child knows between 8,000–14,000 words (Anglin, 1993; Biemiller and Slonim, 2001), representing the learning of about seven new words a day up to this time. Although such estimates can vary considerably, children's vocabularies appear to grow by thousands of words each year while they are at school, consistent with the rate shown in Figure 9.3. There is also usually a significant difference between the age at which children start to recognise particular words (their receptive vocabulary), and that at which they start to use them in their own speech (their expressive vocabulary). In the earlier years there is little difference, and indeed sometimes children will use words that they do not yet understand, in phrases which they have learned as a whole. Later on, children will gradually learn features and usage of words for some time before they start to use the words themselves.

The earliest words developed up to the age of two in English-speaking children are mainly nouns, with just one or two verbs. After this age there is an increase in knowledge and use of verbs, with the development of simple structural phrases. Adjectives and adverbs and some interrogative words also start to appear, as well as the simpler prepositions such as 'to', 'in' and 'on'. By the time children start school, they typically have all the main parts of speech, although they continue to develop their understanding and use of words with more difficult logical functions such as linking in complex

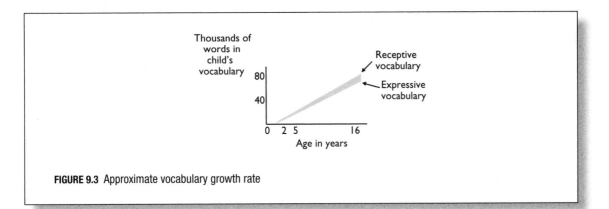

FIGURE 9.3 Approximate vocabulary growth rate

sentences. The main development during children's time in school is now within the classes of nouns, verbs, adjectives and adverbs. These form progressively more abstract, specialised and technical vocabularies according to the subjects that are studied as the children progress through the curriculum.

It should be noted, however, that this pattern of development may be specific to English. For example, very young children learning to speak Korean show greater use of verbs relative to nouns in their early speech (Gopnik and Choi, 1995), and Mandarin-speaking children used similar numbers of verbs and nouns (Tardif, 1996). These differences appear to be rooted in the structure of the various languages that emphasise different word forms.

In general, it seems unlikely that formal teaching can account for more than a small part of this phenomenal rate of vocabulary learning. However, knowledge of new words seems to develop very rapidly when they are experienced in meaningful contexts. Robbins and Ehri (1994) investigated this by reading story books to six-year-old children, which included 11 unfamiliar words such as 'irate' and 'duped' substituted for easier ones. After checking the children's initial general verbal abilities, the stories were then read twice to them over two to four days. There was no direct explanation of the unknown words and the meaning of these could only be gathered from their context. A multiple-choice test then checked whether children had made any progress with the key set of words. The key finding was that just hearing a word a few times in this way accounted for 19 per cent of the variance in their abilities on the final test, indicating that even brief experiences can significantly develop word knowledge, provided that they occur in a meaningful context.

Although watching television is often thought to be a passive activity and to have a negative influence on children's development, there is evidence that educational television programmes can benefit children with some aspects of their spoken-language development: there is evidence that it can help children to acquire new vocabulary, but little evidence that it can impact on grammatical development (Naigles and Mayeux, 2001), which is attributed to the fact that television can only provide one-way language exposure and perhaps aspects like grammar require two-way communication for successful acquisition. Hall *et al.* (1996) found that watching educational and informative educational programmes had a positive effect on children's general knowledge that was on average equal to the effects of their exposure to print. No such effect seemed to occur if children just watched regular television such as game shows or cartoons, and the positive effects appeared only for children who were older than two years. However, Fisch (2004) notes that the programmes need to include careful use of language as there is evidence that where words are used without precision, children's understanding of those terms can be adversely affected. For example, Fisch reports a study by Naigles *et al.* (1995), which found that children exposed to ten episodes of *Barney and Friends* showed decreased understanding of the difference between 'know', 'think' and 'guess', which was traced back to inconsistent use of these terms within the programme.

It seems likely that children learn a great deal of their vocabulary from a range of informal sources such as conversations, or just by listening to the way in which words are used by other people. Markman (1987) considers that, at first, children hearing a new word attempt to map it on to an existing concept that is not yet labelled, using the context in which the word was spoken to guide this process. However, young children might not have developed enough concepts to enable this to happen and may have to develop novel concepts at the same time.

Susan Carey and Elsa Bartlett (1978) looked at whether concept development would happen with limited exposure to the name of a colour that children could not yet identify. She first made sure that a group of three-year-olds did not know the colour 'olive' (the children mostly called it 'green' or 'brown'), then exposed them to a new, non-sense name for the colour. This was done by interrupting their play and pointing to two trays, one coloured blue and the other coloured olive, and casually saying, 'Hand me the chromium tray. Not the blue one but the chromium one.' The child would sometimes pause and perhaps point to the olive tray and say, 'This one?' The experimenter would then reply, 'Yes, that one, thank you.' The children were given no further guidance and a week later they were given some colours to identify. When olive was presented to them, they were still not able to identify it correctly, but they now paused and evidently knew that the colour was not green or brown. It seems that they had started to learn that there was a new property which related to a word but had yet to develop the concept completely. A week later the children were given a colour-naming task, and two-thirds of the children selected an appropriate colour (green or olive) when asked for a chromium-coloured chip.

The ability to make rough guesses at the meanings of unknown words is known as 'fast-mapping', and is observed to occur in children from the age of 15 months. However, the study above indicates that the learning of a new word does not necessarily occur in an all-or-nothing way. A word is normally learned by the progressive development of associated meanings. This is supported by early verbal errors called **overgeneralisations**, which indicate that the first features used tend to be the more general ones. For instance, a child may call all four-legged animals 'doggie' since he or she is using only the concept of 'animals with four legs'. When enough semantic features are acquired (e.g. 'barks', 'chases cats'), then the word can be used accurately and appropriately, and can become part of a child's active vocabulary.

It is likely that word concepts are best seen as **prototypes** – exemplars with classic features – or as schemas with features that are related and are relevant to the individual (Kay and Anglin, 1982). Children will overextend a new concept according to how similar it is to a prototype; cats might be called 'doggie', but a horse is much less likely to be. Parents and teachers appear to utilise this approach intuitively and focus on words that are most accessible and relevant to children, only extending the concept once basic-level terms are established.

Structure

Alongside the development in vocabulary is an early rapid growth in language structure. At about two years of age, children will be putting two words together in a way that involves simple rules. This can involve using **pivot words** such as 'more' to generate utterances such as 'more juice' or 'more tickle'. By the age of about four years, most children have the major elements of normal grammar involving the various parts of speech and rules for combining them.

There is still significant progress to be made during the school years. Work by Berko (1958) with seven-year-olds has shown, for instance, that they still have to develop plurals using -es at the end (rather than the basic –s) and are not yet able to form many irregular past tenses (e.g. sing/sung). It can take even longer for children to acquire the more complex constructions such as passives, which are not fully formed until about age nine. Some sentences, such as those involving double negatives and

led clauses, are logically complex and are often not mastered by even older children
ɔol.

ly language rules are not just parts of the adult system. They often seem to be qualita-
nd, over time, evolve closer towards the mature form. Children appear to develop
t useful language structures (from what they hear and experience) and test these out.
ildren in the early school years appear to establish the rule that putting -ed on a verb
makes it into the past tense, as is shown by their errors, such as overextending the rule and using it
with irregular verbs, such as saying 'runned' instead of 'ran'

Brown *et al.* (1969) found that parents pay more attention to what children say (their meaning)
than to how children say things (the actual structure). When adults correct children's speech, this in
fact slows their progress down (Nelson, 1988), presumably since it inhibits them from developing and
applying their early rule systems. For example, correcting a child for using 'runned' instead of 'ran'
might lead him or her to doubt the general rule about the use of -ed.

Practical implications

In general, the findings from normal language development strongly imply that teachers should not worry too
much about children's language forms but concentrate on involving them in meaningful language work that is
interesting and relevant to each child. The language used by teachers should, however, provide an appropriate
model that is accessible in terms of the content and structures that they use.

A critical period?

You may be aware of the popular belief that it is better to expose children to foreign language when
they are younger, because the older we get, the harder it is for us to learn new languages. Such an
idea is based on a more fundamental principle in language research, the idea that there is a critical
period for language acquisition (both native and non-native languages) (Lenneberg, 1967). During the
critical period, language acquisition is effortless, as long as children are exposed to an appropriate linguistic environment which will stimulate the language-acquisition process. Lenneberg proposed that,
when we are born, both sides (or hemispheres) of the brain have the potential to support language
development, but that between the ages of two and five years there is a process of lateralisation, in
which the left hemisphere becomes adapted to support language processing (neural connections are
typically shorter and greater in number in the left hemisphere compared to the right). This lateralisation is the reason why most people are right-handed – the left side of the brain controls the right side
of the body, so the 'language' side of the brain controls the right side of the body, which results in the
tendency for children to want to write with their right hand.

So, between the ages of two and five years, language acquisition is rapid and effortless, and between
five years of age and 16, language learning requires a little more conscious effort, but is still relatively
easy. After 16, Johnson and Newport (1989) argued, language learning is more difficult, based on
their study of Chinese and Korean immigrants to America. This is because the brain goes from being
relatively plastic to being in a steady state at around this age. However, other researchers have argued
that this change in language ability occurs much earlier, around the age of five years (Birdsong and
Molis, 2001).

Studies of children who have not experienced an appropriate language environment during the proposed critical period show marked impairments in their grammatical development in particular. The most famous of these case studies is that of Genie, a young child who was isolated from the outside world by her abusive father. Her father reportedly barked at her rather than spoke to her and she had no exposure to television or radio. She was 13 years and nine months old when she was discovered. Attempts to teach her to regain language were limited in their success: she was able to acquire vocabulary but was unable to construct grammatical sentences.

The evidence suggests that language abilities do decline steadily with age, but that it is still possible to acquire new languages after the age of 16, and for this reason it is perhaps better to talk about a **sensitive period** for language development (Bialystok and Hakuta, 1994).

Theories of language development

As you can see from the pattern of development just described, children's language does not necessarily develop according to a logical or consistent path, but is characterised by periods of rapid development and relative stability, apparent 'maturity' but then creative but incorrect use of language. Why does language development look like this, and what can it tell us about how children understand language?

The behaviourist account of language acquisition

One early and seemingly plausible explanation of the acquisition of language was the idea that children learn language by imitating the speech that they hear around them. Young children do seem to be capable of such mimicry from an early age, and Skinner (1957) argued that this ability was developed by parents rewarding children with increased attention when they repeat either words or phrases that they have heard. Skinner also believed that early sounds made by a child are selectively reinforced and shaped by parents' responses until they become words. So, for example, the parents of a child who randomly utters 'dada' might respond even more enthusiastically to the times when this sounds more like 'da-dee' ('daddy'), leading the child to gradually improve his or her pronunciation.

However, in 1959 Chomsky heavily criticised this account of language acquisition on a number of counts. Firstly, Chomsky pointed out children are not always reinforced when they produce speech: children often babble to themselves with no feedback from adults. As noted above, it has also been suggested by Brown *et al.* (1969) that if reinforcement really operated on language development in the way suggested by Skinner, children would grow up speaking ungrammatically because adults are more likely to reinforce children's speech when they say something factual (e.g. 'Two bunny!'), even if the utterance is grammatically problematic. They will also be more likely to correct something that a child says that is factually incorrect, whether it is spoken grammatically or not. Another critical point raised by Chomsky was that the language environment that children are exposed to is far from ideal: in speech we often make errors, start sentences over and so on. Children do make mistakes as they learn to speak, but they are not the kind of errors that they hear adults make – as we have seen they are more likely to make creative rule-based errors, such as when they say, 'I goed' instead of 'I went', or 'mouses' instead of 'mice'. Also, Skinner's explanation is unable to account for such examples of children's creative use of language – children are often coining their own versions of words, rather than simply importing the vocabulary that they hear around them. In short, children seem to be forming hypotheses about how language is formed and structured, and then try these ideas out.

Innate theories

So, it seems that children learn the complex rules of language despite having only poor grammatical examples to work from. Normal speech involves much blurring of sounds and words, partial sentences, hesitations and slips of the tongue. Along with the fact that language can appear to develop largely independently of other cognitive abilities, Chomsky (1965) therefore argued that children must have their own separate, inbuilt ability to develop grammatical principles. He refers to this as the 'Language Acquisition Device' (LAD), which he believes is inherited and operates at the level of deep structure. He also argues that its existence is shown by certain universal properties of languages, such as the fact that they all have phonological elements, and syntactic structures such as nouns and verbs. Languages differ in the rules by which they generate the surface structure, although word order still appears to show some universals, such as the fact that all languages tend to avoid placing the object first in the sentence. Pinker (1994) has also argued that humans have a unique, inherited ability to construct grammatical language for themselves. As evidence for this, he uses the progressive evolution of 'pidgins', which are initially formed as simplified hybrids of more than one language with very limited grammatical structures. However, a single generation of children can develop these and establish a complete grammar, creating a language form known as a 'creole'.

Case study

A good example of the process being described here is that of the development of Nicaraguan sign language. That is, prior to the Sandinista revolution in 1979, there was no education for deaf children, and each child developed their own set of 'home signs' that they used to communicate their needs to members of their own family. After the revolution, the new government introduced large-scale education for deaf children, opening two schools for the deaf in Managua. Once in contact with other deaf children, they began to learn and use each other's signs, although the grammar of this newly developing language was not clear. Judy Kegl, an expert in sign language, was given the task of studying this new language. She noted that the teenage children's use of these signs looked similar to a pidgin language, in which words from different languages are combined to allow speakers from different language communities to communicate, albeit in a way that is not grammatical. However, the younger deaf children were much more fluent and rhythmical in their signing, and their signing showed clear signs of a grammatical structure. It seemed that the younger children had been able to learn these signs at a time when their LAD was active and this resulted in their producing a grammatical language from the pidgin that the older children had created.

One implication from this innate perspective is that language acquisition should be a relatively robust process, and Pinker (1994: 29) maintains that 'there is virtually no way to prevent it from happening short of raising a child in a barrel'. If this is the case, then there is little that education can or should do, other than develop the use of language in the various curriculum areas. There is, however, some doubt about this extreme view, based first on the evidence that there are major variations in language development, related to different language experiences. One extreme case affected in this way was 'Jim', reported by Sachs *et al.* (1981), whose only language experience until he was three years of age came from watching television, since his parents were both deaf and non-talkers. Jim did have some spoken language but his grammar was unusual. He would, for example, say, 'Not one house. That two house.' The use of 's' in plurals is normally one of the first morphemes that English-speaking children learn. His failure to establish such rules indicates that they depend on children experiencing language in meaningful contexts as well as some form of innate propensity.

Cognitive ability

Although it may still be that we have some form of general specialisation to enable us to develop language, an additional explanation is that language acquisition depends on the initial development of general cognitive abilities, which tend to search for and to organise information according to patterns or logical principles. If an artificial connectionist system with these properties is set up to process language input, it can learn to generate rules for complex and irregular verbs, or make grammatical predictions for missing words, without any inbuilt initial bias to process for these abilities. This does not of course prove that this is what children are doing, but it does at least show that a complex system can be capable of generating grammatical principles by itself.

Language abilities also tend to develop along with other general cognitive abilities. Piaget (1967) in particular originally argued that we need to develop our schemas, or knowledge and understanding of things and processes, before we are able to represent them symbolically. He believed that the earliest thought is dominated by direct experiences and that it is only at the stage when objects come to have a form of permanence for the child that it is possible for the child to acquire stable concepts and to name them. This happens at around the 12-month level, and it is only after this that dramatic increases in vocabulary occur. Symbolic play, which depends on the development of concepts and their functions, also happens at about this time, and is closely related to the subsequent development of language. Brownell (1988) found that children would use two-word, or more than two-word, sentences in their speech only if they had previously shown sequences in their play, such as pretending to pour the drink from a cup. Such findings indicate that it is necessary to understand the logical meaning of sequences and associations to form a basis for establishing early grammar.

Although it seems very likely that language needs an intellectual basis from which to develop, there is evidence that language can itself act as the basis for the development of thought processes, and that establishing the ability to use language in such a way depends on the presence of a structured and supportive social context.

Social interaction

Children are normally closely involved in a meaningful social environment, and an interactionist perspective proposes that the main way in which language develops is through that social environment. Bruner (1983) considers that a parent provides a 'Language Acquisition Support System' (the LASS) for the child, and that this generates structured information for aspects of the LAD to operate (Bruner's little joke!). Understanding is developed and extended by the process of 'scaffolding'. This involves the parent's providing a directive and supportive framework in which the child can achieve success and develop and extend his or her concepts. By using language that is appropriate to the child's level, the adult first leads the child to use his or her existing language concepts, and later proceeds to extend the child in new situations, so that eventually the child can adopt new language and meanings from the adult's use of language. This process can then be repeated in subsequent experiences for further extension and successive development.

According to this perspective, it is early pragmatics, or the child's and parent's reciprocal knowledge and understanding of one another's intents, that drives the initial development of meaning in language (Tomasello, 2003). From the earliest stages, mothers have been shown to set up 'turn-taking' interactions, starting with feeding sequences where the mother will respond to pauses as a cue for verbal interaction. Any form of action by the child, such as cries, burps or grimaces, is interpreted as though it is meaningful, and is responded to with physical and verbal interaction. As children mature, they seem to establish an early non-verbal basis for sequences of interaction; for instance, a baby may look towards a desired object, then towards a person whom they want to get it for them. Schlesinger (1988) believes that such semantic associations lead directly to early syntactic categories, such as 'agent–action' sequences, without there being the need to consider that such specific abilities are innate.

Nevertheless, it is still likely that humans have some form of general specialisation to develop language, although this is probably less specific or innate than was originally thought. Language must depend to some extent upon aspects of cognitive development, but the relationship is a reciprocal one, with early language abilities acting as a basis for the development of thought. Most recent explanations also emphasise the importance of practical meaning and the social context of the child, implying that education has an important role to play in facilitating children's language abilities.

Language and thought

There are probably many different ways of thinking, depending on the task involved and the individual's abilities. One useful way of categorising these is Bruner's (1966b) description of three main modes: the **iconic mode**, which mainly involves visual representations; an **enactive mode** which involves representation of physical movements or control; and a **symbolic mode** which uses abstractions such as words. In a similar way, Gardner (1993) argued that there are many forms of specific intellectual abilities, although linguistic intelligence is of particular importance to the educational process. A lot of thinking does seem to involve language to some extent, and we are often aware of literally 'talking to ourselves'. Young children in particular will often verbalise when involved with some problem, especially when it is unexpected. At other times, however, learning or the development of ideas or solutions can arise without any awareness, and unconscious processing may be an important aspect of certain types of problem-solving. At such times, creative solutions might be blocked by conventional ways of thinking, including the use of inappropriate verbal labels. If language does have an important role in such ways of thinking, then we should perhaps take account of this in educational processes, by developing verbal skills where they can help children's thought in some way.

Independence of thought and language

At one extreme, linguists such as Chomsky (1965) have argued that language abilities are essentially independent of other cognitive skills. This argument is based upon such evidence as the finding that most individuals above a certain basic intellectual level appear to develop language without any apparent difficulty. One particular example is an unusual genetic disorder known as **Williams syndrome**. Children who have this typically achieve an overall IQ of only 85 but often have well-developed expressive verbal skills, developing complex grammar and a wide vocabulary. However, such abilities are not linked with the same level of general understanding and have only limited usefulness for individuals affected in this way. When making these arguments, linguists are therefore usually focusing only on the limited aspect of linguistic competence rather than general language performance.

Language depending on thought

A virtually opposite argument was made by Piaget (1959), that language abilities are dependent on the development of general cognitive abilities. There is considerable evidence for this perspective, with the findings described above about the development of object permanence and different types of symbolic understanding acting as precursors to early words and grammar. Vygotsky (1962), however, has argued that Piaget's view does not take account of the developmental interrelationship between thought and language, and the importance of the social and cultural context of the child. According to his theories, early language such as crying or calling out to get attention is mainly social and does not involve thought as we normally understand it. When objects are given a verbal label, this mainly functions merely as another property of that object, rather than as a basis for a separate way of representation. Early thought is dominated by direct actions and experiences, and develops before any of the early forms of language.

Vygotsky argued that from the age of about two years onwards, children appear to start to use language to 'think out loud with', particularly when they were trying to do something difficult. He argues that they do so because early thought and language have combined, with language now becoming capable of monitoring and directing internal thought, and of communicating the child's thinking to others. However, these two functions cannot yet be distinguished by the child and a great deal of language is relatively egocentric, resulting in the parallel monologues that are common in younger children.

From about the age of seven onwards, Vygotsky believed, at the time when operational thought develops, children start to internalise such speech as a form of thought, to orient and organise their understanding. Vygotsky found that just before it 'goes underground' in this way, egocentric speech becomes less like normal social language, and is simplified and focused more on the tasks and the child's own needs. In parallel with this process, spoken language now develops separately and becomes more social and communicative, oriented to the needs of others. The two systems continue to relate to each other, with the development of spoken language leading to the assimilation of cultural knowledge, values and beliefs.

Berk (1986) found support for Vygotsky's ideas from observations of six- and eight-year-old pupils working in class on mathematics problems. The younger children generally talked to themselves extensively when they encountered difficulties, but older children did so to a much smaller extent. The use of such 'private speech' correlated positively with intelligence for the 6-year-olds, indicating that private speech was supporting thinking. The correlation was negative for the 8-year-old children, and indicates that speech which had become internalised was now the basis for thought.

Language facilitating thought

Bruner (1966b) extended Vygotsky's ideas and considered that language is even more important in the early stages of the development of thought than Vygotsky had realised. It acts, he believed, to amplify abilities and accelerate cognitive development. Bruner sees language development as dependent on shared social understandings and support from key adults, with the process of progressive 'scaffolding' leading to new verbal abilities and increased knowledge and understanding. Investigations indicate that language used in a meaningful context which is matched with children's conceptual development can develop understanding. In an early study of this, Sonstroem (1966), gave 6- and 7-year-old children training on a conservation task: learning that an amount of plasticine remains the same even when its shape changes. Children who merely observed and talked about the changes did not develop any new abilities. Only children who physically experienced the changes and used language at the same time to describe what was happening made progress. Sonstroem's work is therefore consistent with Bruner's ideas that new language needs a meaningful context in order to affect thinking processes.

Linguistic relativity

Bruner also believes that language acts to free children from direct experiences by providing conceptual categories that can be used as the basis for independent abstract thought. If this is the case, then it is possible that the language concepts which are available to us may have a major role in facilitating or constraining the way in which we can think. This perspective is known as linguistic relativity, and Whorf (1956) argued that the forms of words or grammar in a particular language generate a certain worldview that inevitably affects the type of thinking that we can do about it. Whorf based his ideas on evidence such as the existence of more than 20 words for snow in the Inuit language; this appeared to Whorf to enable Inuit to perceive and attend to the different features of snow in a way that would not be possible for English speakers.

Such strong beliefs do not appear to have much foundation. Harley (2008), for instance, suggests that there are in fact only two root words used by Inuit – *qanik* and *aput* – to describe falling and settled snow respectively, each of which can easily be described by other languages. Even when there are apparent differences, such as Arabic languages having a large number of words related to camels, these are probably more a reflection of the fact that the culture concerned has a general bias in that direction and simply uses more words to accommodate this. All experts in a particular field will have a greater specialist vocabulary and knowledge, which will also correspond with a greater readiness to perceive and think about things to do with that area of expertise.

There has, however, been considerable support for a weaker form of the linguistic relativity argument. This proposes that, rather than determining perception and the ability to establish concepts, language can rather act to direct cognitive processes in a more general way.

Classic study

Carmichael *et al.* (1932) showed that the use of different words to label a specific picture led to correspondingly different reproductions. As shown in Figure 9.4, if an ambiguous shape (of two circles joined by a straight line) was called a pair of glasses, then subsequent drawings by subjects would emphasise the curved nose piece and oval lens shapes; if it was called a dumbbell then reproduction emphasised the connecting bar. The use of the word to label the picture meant that the subject did not need to retain any visual information; recall was therefore mainly from the verbal category, and the subject's drawing emphasised the features of this.

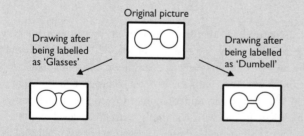

FIGURE 9.4 Differences in the production of a figure after verbal labelling

Language inhibiting thought

Inappropriate use of language concepts can sometimes misdirect our attention or interfere with learning in some situations. Duncker (1945), for instance, originally demonstrated that using conventional labels for an object such as a 'box' prevented subjects from perceiving it as having another possible function; the problem was to support a candle, and people had difficulty understanding that the box the candles came in could also be used as a support. This phenomenon is known as 'functional fixedness', and can be overcome by providing subjects with different verbal labels for objects, which then enables them to be used in other ways. Certain types of learning, called 'implicit learning', may also operate best when there is limited verbal awareness and control. This has been shown to happen with the learning of certain types of physical skills, and it may be that the use of language prevents the appropriate, enactive mode of thought from operating.

In general, however, language abilities have predominantly positive effects on educational progress. Although differences in language forms may not have a great effect, language in general undoubtedly has a key role as the basis for certain types of thought, and spoken language is the principal medium for communicating information between people. Language abilities depend on and also support the development of both knowledge and understanding, which are the main determinants of children's educational progress.

Language and cultural background

Bernstein (1961) proposed that working-class and middle-class children respectively have different forms of language, and that the difference affects the way in which they think and how they react to the educational system. He believes that working-class children have a relatively 'restricted code' which is essentially simplified and limited to the immediate context. A sentence used to communicate the information that a ball had broken a window might therefore be, 'It broke it.' Middle-class children, on the other hand, have an 'elaborated code' which is grammatically complex, more precise and much more capable of embodying abstract ideas and knowledge. In this case, the corresponding sentence might be, 'The ball accidentally broke the window.' Parents appear to provide the models and experiences that develop this style. A working-class parent is therefore likely to say, 'Pack it in', whereas a middle-class parent might say, 'Peter, stop annoying your sister.' Bernstein believed that the language of the educational system is primarily elaborated code and that working-class children are unable to benefit from educational opportunities as much as middle-class children.

Bernstein emphasised that the language capabilities of working-class children are not necessarily inferior and have the same potential to communicate ideas. In one sense this is arguing that restricted code is just a form of dialect, but it is hard to see how the loss of key elements could give the same information, particularly if writing is being used to express ideas when the context is not clear. There are also difficulties with the generalised use of the concept of 'social class', since this can refer to a number of dimensions, such as parental occupation or income, that may relate only indirectly to a child's language culture.

Labov (1979) argued strongly against the idea that minority social groups (mainly African-Americans) with lower social status have inferior language abilities. He pointed out that their language is often more direct and precise, and is certainly capable of expressing sophisticated concepts. Although they typically leave out some parts of speech such as the verb 'to be' in phrases such as 'They mine', this phrase has the same information content and is following the same deletion principle as 'They're mine'. Other languages also commonly contract or leave out unnecessary parts of speech, and Labov saw middle-class language as being unnecessarily complicated and often obscuring the real meaning. Labov believed that the differences between the two forms of language are mainly qualitative and cultural. If there are limits to the educational opportunities of minority groups, he concludes that this is because the control of the educational system is predominantly in white, middle-class hands.

One difficulty in this area is separating out language forms that are just different from language experiences that are deprived. There appears to be a good case for many aspects of working-class and cultural minority languages to be seen as different dialects which are highly functional within their own cultural context. Unfortunately, restricted or socially dependent features do seem to provide a limited match with the requirements of some aspects of formal education. There is also strong evidence that the sheer amount of language experienced by children can vary significantly, and that this variation is related to certain types of social class. As we have seen, an observational study by Hart and Risley (1995) found that, by the age of three, children in professional families had heard more than 30 million words. Children in working-class families, however, had heard only around 20 million, and for the children of the poorest families on welfare, the figure was even lower at around ten million. One study by Heath (1989) also set out to record the interactions between a mother in an isolated poor family with her three children over a two-year period. Over a 500-hour period of tape recording, she initiated talk in only 18 instances, other than to give some brief directions, or to ask about what the children were doing.

Such low levels of verbal stimulation seem bound to limit children's language development. Whitehurst *et al.* (1994) found that a sample of three-year-old children from low-income families had verbal abilities that were generally one standard deviation (15 points) below what would be achieved by the normal population. However, following a six-week programme of interactive picture-book reading which emphasised language involvement and understanding, these children showed gains of up to ten points in their vocabulary scores. This shows that even children from poor backgrounds are able to make significant progress with their language abilities, and also strongly suggests that their initially poor attainments may have been due to a previous lack of such experiences.

Educational implications of language development

If education essentially involves the development of concepts and ideas, and these are primarily taught and encoded using language, then language development must be a central issue in education. Although children starting school have already made much headway with their language abilities, they still have to establish a mature sound system and form the more complex language structures. Children also continue to develop an extensive and integrated vocabulary throughout their school careers, based essentially on meaning and understanding. From the above evidence, however, it appears that the majority of speech and language learning by children is relatively informal and comes primarily from their interest in and involvement with a broad range of experiences, rather than from directed learning. As we have seen in Chapter 8, the nature of discourse around learning activities, both between peers and between children and adults, is an important area of contemporary educational research.

When children start at school, their interactions are often largely based on non-verbal and pragmatic understanding, with relatively egocentric language. As shown in Figure 9.5, it is therefore not uncommon to hear two very 'one-sided' conversations in parallel, where each child seems automatically to assume that others are attending to and aware of what he or she is thinking or wants to say.

FIGURE 9.5 Egocentric conversation

As children become older, they develop awareness of and sensitivity to each other's language needs and undoubtedly learn new language concepts from a range of informal verbal experiences. However, it is unlikely that pupils in school will be able to fulfil the same role as adults. In tutoring situations, children have been shown to be poor at knowing when to intervene, when to withdraw and tend to use simpler, didactic explanations. In a direct comparison, Shute *et al.* (1992) found that adults were better than children on all verbal tutoring measures, and although cooperative group learning may be an effective approach, this is difficult to set up and rarely used.

It seems likely, then, that a primary source of children's language and conceptual development within school must be independent and class-organised activities with curriculum studies. However, this places great stress on children's personal motivation and involvement, and so it is not surprising that these qualities are key determinants of their progress in school.

From the research reviewed earlier, it seems inefficient to spend much time teaching verbal constructs out of context, and it is probably much more effective to concentrate on general subject and content matter. New language concepts and structures should be embedded in a general structure of meaningful features and associations which will enable pupils to refine their own ability to use them. However, the National Curriculum of England and Wales requires that pupils be exposed to Standard English and formally learn parts of speech and grammar. There are dangers that doing so could become an academic exercise, and fail to develop in pupils the ability to acquire new approaches to the use of language.

Should grammar be part of the curriculum?

A specified grammar can be important in ensuring some form of conformity and stability for the language. Unfortunately, languages are constantly changing, and a static grammar will eventually become outdated. The sentence structures in common use, as well as meanings and pronunciations of words, show major changes over time. One has only to look at books written in the eighteenth century which are currently studied for GCSE to realise that phrases such as, 'Lizzy has something more of quickness than her sisters' (from *Pride and Prejudice*, written by Jane Austen in 1797) may be grammatically correct in a technical sense but would not be used nowadays; a more likely expression of the same thing would be, 'Lizzy is more lively than her sisters', and this would have more meaning and relevance to most children.

Formal grammar teaching involves classifying words into the various parts of speech, analysing sentences into the various types of phrases and clauses, and examining ways in which these can be combined to form sentences. The National Curriculum programmes of study for English now incorporate some aspects of this approach, and direct that children should be taught a basic range of technical grammatical terms, the functions of these and their effects. Although this may seem to be an attractive 'back to basics' approach, evidence about how we develop language structures emphasises that they are very much constructed by the child. As discussed earlier, the initial foundation of language comes from shared understandings and needs, and children appear to move through their own stages of progressively more sophisticated grammars. A child does not appear to learn that the past tense of 'to go' is 'went' and not 'goed' from direct instruction; indeed, as noted before, correcting children's language appears to destroy their developing hypotheses about how language works and can lead to slower progress.

In line with evidence of this kind, a number of research studies have shown that the formal teaching of grammar appears to have little if any effect on children's functional abilities with language.

Classic study

Harris (1965) compared the progress of secondary pupils who in addition to their normal English studies either had an extra period of writing, or were taught traditional formal grammar for one period a week from a standard textbook. After two years, the 'grammar' group had certainly improved their performance on a test of their knowledge of grammar, but failed to develop their performance on a writing test – which was marked according to their ability to apply grammatical principles. Furthermore, the pupils who had spent their time writing had made better progress in a number of areas of applied grammar such as the variety and complexity of sentences used. This indicates that learning formal grammar was in effect limiting children's attainments on the very principles that they had been learning about.

A review of such studies by QCA (1998), however, challenges whether there was ever any possibility of transfer from learning traditional grammar in this way to writing and composition skills. Instead, it is proposed that applied skills are more likely to develop by pupils experiencing the demands of different writing tasks, and by drawing explicit attention to the syntactic features of pupils' own writing. In the original study by Harris (1965), this less formal approach was in fact what was happening with the group who practised their writing, with teachers drawing the pupils' attention to the use of sentence structure for stylistic effect, the structure of paragraphs, and techniques for linking them together. When pupils made grammatical errors, these were corrected by example and imitation, and it seems likely that such teaching would indeed lead to improvements in writing technique.

Although the skills of formal grammatical analysis can be taught, it is likely that by itself the teaching of such skills tends to be rather an academic exercise. If the main educational objective is to develop communication skills, then this is most likely to be achieved by the teaching of linguistic features in meaningful contexts. Galton et al.'s (1999) study of children's relative achievements over the period when the National Curriculum of England and Wales was first implemented found that children had improved on specific features such as their use of capitals and appropriate punctuation. However, there was an overall apparent decline in children's language skills, indicating perhaps that there had been too great an emphasis on such surface techniques.

Second-language learning

Learning a first language seems to be achieved best during the early years; bilingual children also appear to achieve the relatively effortless learning of a second language by being exposed to it from an early age. This has been taken as evidence that learning a second language will be more difficult for older students and that, therefore, the teaching of a second language should be started as soon as possible in the primary school (Bialystok, 2001). There is no evidence that children who are exposed to two different languages from an early age are delayed in their language development (Petitto *et al.*, 2001), and they show good awareness of which language they should use when addressing monolingual people. Moreover, there is evidence that children who are bilingual outperform monolingual children on some cognitive tasks: for example, Bialystok and Shapiro (2005) found that when confronted with a classic ambiguous figure image (see Figure 9.6), five-year-old bilingual children are better able to identify both images present, whereas monolingual children of the same age have difficulty seeing more than one image.

Language and behaviour

Since young children appear to use speech to literally instruct themselves and to direct their attention, Meichenbaum (1977) developed an approach to develop these abilities in children who have behavioural difficulties. This is called 'cognitive behaviour modification' and typically uses self-instruction to modify the behaviour of impulsive children. An adult will typically model a simple task for the child, stopping frequently to monitor his or her own behaviour and intentions out loud. The child then imitates the adult's behaviour, and after a few sessions the self-instruction is carried out covertly. When working with a young child on a letter-formation task, this might involve the following when copying a letter 'a':

> *Model:* STOP, What I am doing? I've got to do the rounded bit first. Start at the cross [provided on some lined paper], here I go – round, round. STOP, What do I do now? Make the line down. Down, down, finished.

FIGURE 9.6 An ambiguous figure

A review of findings on the effectiveness of this approach by Robinson *et al.* (1999) indicates that it has a major effect size of 0.74. Such approaches can have a very rapid effect on behaviour, and improvements are often maintained well.

Speech and language problems

By the time they enter school, most children are reasonably intelligible and have developed the majority of their grammatical structures. Unfortunately, usually because of poor home background or medical difficulties, some children have either a general delay with their progress or, less commonly, some form of abnormal development (which is often related to medical problems).

Speaking and listening are part of the English National Curriculum, and if children have moderate difficulties, these can often be managed as part of the normal approach to teaching. In the early years, schools have a strong emphasis on involving children in language work, with listening to stories, talking as part of investigative activities, as well as early literacy activities. After Key Stage 1, problems with grammatical development will be present only in the most severe cases, but more children will have an overall relative delay with their general knowledge and understanding of language concepts. These children would normally be classified as having 'learning difficulties' and their needs would be met with modification and matching of the curriculum, known as 'differentiation'.

When children have more atypical problems, these are less likely to respond to such general educational approaches, and it can be important to obtain expert advice from speech and language therapists (SLTs). Although, in Britain, these are employed by health authorities, they will often visit schools and give advice to whoever is able to work with a child. Formal categories of such difficulties are given in the box below.

Categories of speech and language difficulty

Voice: sounds originating in the larynx (using the vocal cords).

a 'aphonia' – absence of voice;
b 'dysphonia' – impairment of voice.

Articulation: production of speech sounds; using the lips, tongue, jaw, breathing, etc.

a 'alalia' – absence of articulation;
b 'dyslalia' – defects of articulation or slow development of articulatory patterns, including substitutions, omissions and transpositions of the sounds of speech. These problems are common with many young children; for example: 'me do de-a dwin', meaning 'I'm going to get a drink';
c 'anarthria' and 'dysarthria' – absence of and distorted articulation respectively, caused by lack of neuromuscular control;
d 'dyspraxia' – failure to perform the sequence of movements involved in articulation. Also refers to an inability to carry out various other types of sequential processing.

Language: the structure and the content of what is said.

a 'aphasia' – absence of recognition and use of verbal expression;
b 'dysphasia' – incomplete language function. This can affect the structure – whether correct grammatical

---

rules are present. If there is a developmental delay, these may be simple rules characteristic of younger children, for example 'more juice' for 'I would like some more juice';

c   'deviant forms of language' show an uneven and atypical development. Examples include confusions in word order, inappropriate use of pronouns, adverbs, prepositions, phrase and clause patterns, and problems in modifying words as they are used with each other; for example, 'Him is going making very lots of toys';

d   'semantics' – an emphasis on the meaning and knowledge involved in language. Children with a semantic disorder will often limit their conversations to known, safe topics;

e   'pragmatics' – how children communicate in real situations. Children with a pragmatic disorder can therefore have problems initiating and managing conversations, as well as difficulties recognising another person's intent such as what is involved in responding to questions.

(The last two are often combined together into the category of 'semantic–pragmatic disorder', which is often considered to be part of the autistic spectrum of disorders).

Early speech and language difficulties can have long-term negative effects on education. Research shows how children's difficulties with speech and spoken language have a major effect on early literacy development (Catts *et al.*, 2002) and have poorer long-term academic and occupational outcomes (Johnson *et al.*, 2010).

The reported prevalence of speech and language difficulties varies, as do definitions of this and related terms. A recent large-scale Australian study reported that between 12 per cent and 13 per cent of primary- and secondary-school pupils studied experienced communication difficulties, this being the second-highest learning difficulty after specific learning difficulties (which was between 17 per cent and 19 per cent) (McLeod and McKinnon, 2007). Prevalence of specific language impairment has been estimated as being between 2 per cent and 8 per cent (Law *et al.*, 2000).

Special provision

The majority of speech and language support is provided in normal schools, where any additional help in the school can work with programmes provided by SLTs. This can be an effective approach for many children since it continues their social integration and provides a meaningful context in which language can develop.

The most severe language difficulties can be part of a general delay, and educational objectives are then largely related to self-help and independence skills. Such education centres on achieving some form of functional competence in these areas. The focus is often therefore on establishing basic communication such as the expression of needs, and often uses non-verbal techniques such as picture cue cards or early signing such as **Makaton.**

What is Makaton?

Makaton is a sign and (written) symbol-based communication system which is intended to augment (rather than replace) regular spoken and written language to make it more intelligible to children and adults with learning difficulties and language delays. It can also be used by these individuals to enable them to communicate more effectively. The sign language part of Makaton is based on the signs used in British Sign Language, but new signs are developed as they are needed. The written symbolic forms are simple line drawings of the concepts they represent. During speech, a Makaton user would speak at the same time as signing, and so the 'grammar' of Makaton as a sign language follows that of regular speech, and is therefore different to the way that the signs would be combined in British Sign Language.

Recently, Makaton has proved popular amongst parents who want to teach sign language to their children before they can speak, so that they can communicate more effectively with their infant. Some pre-school children's television programmes include Makaton, and so it is increasingly recognised and understood by typically developing children and their parents, as well as families with special educational needs.

Children with more-specific problems are sometimes placed in special schools for children with speech and language problems, or in units, usually with trained teachers and SLTs. Classes are usually small (three-to-six children) and teaching is often intensive, using individual and structured programmes. Units are usually part of a normal school, so that children can integrate with normal-language children for at least part of the day. Many units also try to make sure that children return to their neighbourhood school for part of the week, with the aim of eventual integration. Most children enter such units in their first year of schooling (when problems become apparent) and attend for about two years.

Remediation

Articulation

Improving children's intelligibility by working with their spoken sound system can be a rather technical process and is normally best carried out by SLTs, who are particularly effective in this area. Even when children are very difficult to understand, they normally have a number of correct sounds, and there are usually other sounds that are being established. Some of these could be developed with help, but others may be too abnormal to use as a basis for progress.

It is rare for children to have problems with their vowels; most difficulties are with consonant sounds. These can be missing in particular words and positions, which can be a serious problem requiring expert assessment. Sounds are often changed in some way, and the list in Figure 9.7 gives sets of common substitutions that would be normal immaturities up to the ages shown; for example, saying 'kap' for 'tap' would still be likely up to five-and-a-half years of age. If some remain beyond these ages, they would therefore be a cause for concern.

Initial teaching often involves making sure that children are able to discriminate between different sounds. This can be done by using a number of pictures of words which start with the target and substitution sounds, and then asking them to point to the correct one for a spoken word. If children have difficulties, then they may need more experiences with listening.

The next stage can involve making the sound in isolation, for example by making a hissing noise 'like a snake' for the 's' sound. This may also involve getting children to look in a mirror so that they can see where their lips, teeth and tongue should be. This then leads on to the use of the sound in a whole word. However, if they have been substituting 't' for 's', then they may still leave the 't' sound in and say 'stun' for 'sun' – compounding their problem! A technique to avoid this could involve words where it is possible to make the 's' sound slightly separately, as in 's-poon'.

These techniques are close to the ones involved in phonological sensitivity training and the use of phonics in early reading. It is therefore an area where literacy teaching and speech work should coordinate closely and focus on the same sounds and words. It is very easy to make things worse, and if children are not making easy progress, it is always best to seek expert advice.

5 years		6 years		6 years	
Target sound	Substitution used	Target sound	Substitution used	Target sound	Substitution used
t	k	ch	t	s	th
d	g	j	d	z	th
k	t			l	y
g	d			l	w
f	p			v	w
v	b				
sh	t				
sh	s				
s	t				
z	d				

FIGURE 9.7 Substitution immaturities

Language structures

It seems reasonable to assume that when children have language problems, remedial approaches should utilise goals based on the sequence of normal development. Many programmes therefore involve developing vocabulary and language structures in much the same way as happens with young children. An alternative approach is to use a more logical sequence based on the developing of grammatical rules. In practice, the two approaches are often quite similar, since normal language development involves deriving ways of expressing meaning through increasingly complex language structures.

Speech and language development work is typically done in small groups, where the child with difficulties can hear models from other children and also be part of the overall social context. Much early work to develop vocabulary and understanding is similar to normal early-years practice, with the use of interesting props or pictures to stimulate talk and generate conversations (Whitehead, 2009).

Rees (2001) advocates a psycholinguistic approach to speech and language remediation, which is so-called because it is based on a psycholinguistic model of the different processes and abilities implicated in successful language processing. It begins with identifying which specific aspects of language appear to be problematic for the individual child and then setting short-term and longer-term goals for improving the child's performance, by selecting tasks that focus on developing the child's abilities in those areas whilst activating the child's stronger abilities as a way of supporting development of the weaker areas. Errors are identified and challenged through the tasks, and the child is encouraged to produce new speech patterns. Importantly, explicit links are made between phonology and literacy.

The Derbyshire Language System by Knowles and Masidlover (1982) is popular in schools. It uses the level of information in children's language as an initial index for a sequence of remedial approaches. These involve simple activities that are based largely on play rather than formal teaching. Target language structures are identified, and in teaching them, the emphasis is on the use of language to manage people, to obtain objects and to gain information. Once children have established comprehension, the roles are reversed, and they are then encouraged to use language to control the game themselves.

Evaluating the outcomes of such structured approaches can be difficult, as there are rarely any effective comparison groups. Also, if children have an initially severe delay, it is unlikely that any form of intervention will completely overcome their difficulties. Bruges (1988), for instance, followed up the progress of 62 ex-pupils of language units where structured schemes including Living Language and the Derbyshire Language System had been used. Compared with national norms of outcomes for children with such severe initial difficulties, many but not all of the pupils did appear to have made significant progress, with 68 per cent mixing well with their peers and 60 per cent having literacy attainments in the normal range. Dockrell and Messer (1999) reviewed research which showed that children receiving support made significant progress relative to other children who did not get help (see also Ebbels *et al.*, 2007, for a recent example). There was also evidence that parent-administered interventions were at least as effective as direct clinician-administered treatment (see also Justice *et al.*, 2005, and DesJardin *et al.*, 2008, for examples of parental support for children with language difficulties). However, this was not the case for articulation and phonological disorders, for which direct therapist treatment was more effective.

Summary

Language is both an important goal and a foundation for education. The study of language is mainly based on its structure and meaning, with the sound system acting as an important basis for accent and dialect. Syntax and grammar incorporate rules that determine the structure of language, and these are important in establishing the meaning of what is said. Meaning comes from processing systems that construct and revise plausible interpretations from the sequence of words using their functions and relationships. Interpretation also depends on activating systems of general contextual knowledge and understanding, which can involve the use of known scripts and schemas. In practical situations we also use our knowledge of other people's intentions to interpret what they say.

Language development appears to be natural and autonomous, and the major structures and functions are already in place when children start school. Behaviourist learning theory explains their learning as the result of a process of conditioning, with parents rewarding imitation. This explanation is unlikely, however, as children appear to use rule-based systems from an early age, and some theories argue that this ability is therefore innate. Alternative approaches emphasise the complex, pattern-seeking abilities of the human brain coupled with meaningful experiences in a social context.

The development of the sound system is completed during the early school years. Throughout education, language progress is subsequently most evident in the range and use of verbal concepts. Progress largely depends on experiencing new language in meaningful contexts, and important sources are formal education, conversations, reading and watching television. The majority of the basic structures of language are present by four years of age, although the more complex forms take a long time to develop. Establishing these seems to depend on experiencing language in meaningful situations, and developing and modifying hypotheses about the way in which different forms are constructed and used.

Language and thought appear to be closely related, although competence with language structures is probably an independent ability. Even though it has been argued that the development of language depends upon existing cognitive abilities, it now seems more likely that thought and language combine at an early age and then take separate, more specialised forms when children become older. This seems to happen within a context of shared social meanings and shows that language-based support can facilitate cognitive development.

There is some evidence that language forms can affect thinking processes. Although it was once believed that language had a strong deterministic effect, it now seems more likely that it merely directs attention and ways of thinking. In doing so, it can sometimes limit our ability to consider alternative approaches and solutions to problems. Different forms of language are characteristic of certain social and cultural groupings. The language forms used by some groups can probably result in a certain impoverishment, although some language forms are more like dialects, which are functional within their own cultural context but may be less widely understood than standard forms of the language.

It is rarely possible for education to provide the highly effective, closely monitored and directed language experiences that are possible in the home. Language development in school probably depends on participation in meaningful language-based curriculum experiences, rather than specific instruction. Teaching grammar in isolation is unlikely to be useful unless the emphasis is on its use to communicate meaning. The learning of a second language appears to take place most readily in situations that emphasise its functional usage. Internal language can be a very effective way of developing self-regulation of behaviour.

Many children have difficulties with the development of speech and language: either a delay, or, more seriously, some form of deviance. Speech and language therapists can give expert advice for children, either in the form of support in the normal school, or in special schools or units. There are specific remedial approaches for problems with articulation and language structures. These are generally effective, provided that they emphasise the meaning and practical use of language.

Key implications

- Speech and language develop naturally and informally within meaningful social contexts. Effective learning in school should follow this process.
- New language concepts should be established as part of general curriculum studies.
- Education should acknowledge and utilise children's own forms of speech and language.
- Parts of speech and grammar should be learned as ways of developing effective communication rather than as an isolated academic exercise.
- Speech and language difficulties can benefit from expert assessment, advice and support as part of situations where communication performs useful functions.

Further reading

Harley (2008), *The Psychology of Language: From Data to Theory – Third Edition*: an in-depth consideration of research findings and their interpretation. This book has very wide coverage and would enable its readers to follow up any particular ideas or interests.

Martin and Miller (2002), *Speech and Language Difficulties in the Classroom*: a good practical guide to the kinds of difficulties teachers may experience in the classroom and how to work with them.

Whitehead (2009), *Supporting Language and Literacy Development in the Early Years, 2nd Edition*: a good practical book on the implications of language research for early-years education.

Discussion of practical scenario

Children's speech and language can benefit from a range of activities where communication is necessary and where they are involved with the meaning of what is going on. Examples include turn-taking play activities, role play ('dressing up'), listening to stories, and joining in with rhymes and simple songs. Ideally the activities would have an adult closely involved with small groups of children to prompt and to model good language.

It would certainly be a positive idea to try to encourage parents to be more actively involved with their children. One relatively simple and effective approach is to base this on shared picture books or story book reading by the parent. Ideally, this would be done with pre-school children and would need a supply of appropriate books and periodic meetings with the parents.

It may be tempting to leave literacy until children are 'ready', but this might then produce a double handicap of both academic and language delay. Unless children have a severe problem, they can usually start to work on some words and letter sounds. Moreover, the process of developing early literacy skills is likely to improve children's sensitivity to sounds and their general language abilities.

It would be possible for teachers to check on pupils' underlying vocabulary comprehension by using the British Picture Vocabulary Scales test. This would indicate whether they have basic abilities, which can be built on. The Derbyshire Language System by Knowles and Masidlover uses an assessment procedure, which is directly linked with teaching approaches.

10 Literacy

Practical scenario

James is a Year 5 boy who had problems with his early literacy development despite having normal general knowledge and understanding. Although he has now established basic phonic skills, his reading age is about three years behind and he has problems coping with the level of literacy that is part of normal class work. James receives some help with his reading and writing, but this is limited to two sessions a week in a group with a support assistant and one 20-minute session with a learning support teacher. James's parents are worried about his progress, particularly in view of secondary transfer after next year. They are supportive of school but would like to know if he is dyslexic and if he should get additional help.

What should the school do to help James?

What is literacy?

The term 'literacy' usually refers to the skills of reading and writing. However, these skills are complex and have a number of different components. For example, reading comprises processes of decoding, word recognition, comprehension and articulation. These skills are themselves dependent upon other language-related skills, such as phonological awareness, and cognitive processes, such as working memory. The term 'decoding' highlights the essential nature of reading: we have to crack the code of letter–sound correspondences in order to turn arbitrary marks on a page into the speech and intended meaning of the writer.

Writing, however, involves translating spoken language into its written form – going from the known to the unknown – sometimes referred to as 'recoding'. This is essentially a more difficult process since we have fewer cues from which to 'guess' at the unknown final form. Writing is a specialised form of communication, and because of its formalised nature and permanence, it also acts to focus and direct our thinking.

Although written language skills map on to spoken language skills in various ways, in evolutionary terms literacy has been part of our culture for only a relatively short period, and it is far from universal. Literacy ability is not therefore something that is directly part of our biological and genetic make-up to the same extent that spoken language skills are. However, most of us have the potential to become fully literate because of our spoken language system, our motor and perceptual skills and our flexible learning abilities.

Children need to start to make early links between language, meaning and the written form of words, and in the earliest stages such links appears to relate to children's sensitivity to the sounds in words and their ability to match these to the alphabetic system. Later developments are much more dependent on general language abilities, including vocabulary and structural and semantic abilities. The whole process, then, also becomes more interactive, and as children progress through junior school, literacy increasingly becomes a vehicle for linguistic and general intellectual development.

Home environments and literacy

Children entering school often have some early reading skills, such as the ability to recognise letters and some basic words. Their ability in this respect is very dependent on their home background and varies a great deal between children. Research has therefore considered children's home literacy environment as a source of individual differences in children's early literacy skills. 'Home literacy environment' potentially means everything in children's homes that may impact on literacy outcomes, which may range from the number of books at home, adults' reading and writing activities (such as making shopping lists or looking at the newspaper), to parents' attitudes. By way of an example, a very simple home-literacy environment questionnaire was used by Griffin and Morrison (1997), who asked parents whether they belonged to a library, how often the library was visited, the extent of any newspaper or magazine subscriptions in the home, and how often the parents read to themselves. Subsequent research has shown that responses to the Griffin and Morrison questionnaire were able to explain 6–10 per cent of the total variation in 6–8-year-old children's vocabulary scores (Hart *et al.*, 2009). This is significant as vocabulary is a skill that is linked to later literacy development, both in terms of word reading and comprehension skills.

However, activities such as those assessed by Griffin and Morrison do not necessarily involve the children. To consider the impact of joint literacy activity in the home on children's literacy outcomes, Wood (2002), asked parents of preschool children who showed no signs of reading ability about the activities they did with their children, and how often they engaged in them. This study showed that children who experienced more varied joint activities with their parents had the best literacy outcomes one year later. Moreover, the children's reading attainment, vocabulary and short-term memory increased in line with the frequency of joint story-book reading with parents. In fact, the finding that joint story-book reading is positively associated with literacy outcomes is perhaps the most consistent message from empirical studies in this area.

Not only does the frequency of joint story-book reading impact on young children's literacy outcomes, but the nature of the parents' interactions with their children around the text are also crucial in ensuring the best possible benefits. That is, as adult readers we take for granted the basic conceptual knowledge that one needs to acquire in order to tackle the task of reading appropriately. Simple things like knowing what way up to hold a book (and indeed recognising if a book is upside down!), knowing whether to read from left to right, or right to left, or recognising punctuation marks as different from letters, or even understanding how a word is different from a letter, are essential information for the child starting to learn how to decode text (Clay, 2002). It seems that much of this information is acquired from exposure to books and reading activities in the home. So, the way in which parents direct their children's attention to features of the text and ask questions about what is going on in the story would appear to be important.

This idea is supported by the results of intervention studies in the area. For example, Justice and Ezell (2000) asked the parents of 28 four-year-old children to read two books a week for four weeks, and provided half of the parents with a short video on how to direct their children's attention to important features of the text. The children of the parents who received the instructional video showed significant improvement in their understanding of print concepts, word concepts and a word/syllable counting task. It should be noted that merely reading books to children does *not* teach further-reading skills: Meyer *et al.* (1994) found that there was actually a negative relationship between the amount of time that kindergarten teachers spent reading to children and their subsequent progress with reading. This is apparently due to the 'displacement effect' which such activities had on more direct reading involvement by children. There is evidently a balance to be struck between reading to children, in order to develop their language abilities and interest in reading, and other activities that develop direct reading skills. There is therefore emphasis placed on **dialogic reading techniques**, in which parents or kindergarten teachers engage children with the text that is being read to them through a range of discursive prompts designed to make them think about the narrative of the story and engage in the retelling of it (e.g. Blom-Hoffman *et al.*, 2006; Hargrave and Sénéchal, 2000; Zevenbergen *et al.*, 2003).

The development of reading: reading as 'decoding'

Reading at the very earliest stages can involve learning separate words 'by sight', often from limited physical features. For example, children might remember the word 'look' because the two 'o's in the middle remind them of a pair of eyes. This is referred to as the **logographic stage** of reading (Frith, 1985) or the **pre-alphabetic stage** (Ehri, 2005). However, this approach to reading is not very cognitively efficient, as each new word needs to be memorised, and there is no way in which a child might work out what an unknown word might be, except perhaps by guessing based on the context the word appears in. Consequently, it is important that children progress into the **alphabetic stage** of reading (Frith, 1985), in which children learn about the relationships between letters and sounds. Often children appear to acquire an understanding of the alphabetic principle in their writing before they learn to apply it to their reading, because spelling requires children to learn what sounds go with which letters. The teaching and learning of letter–sound correspondences is referred to by teachers as **phonics** (which we will discuss in more detail later). Phonic tuition focuses on teaching children the letter–sound combinations in a particular sequence that will enable them to tackle the maximum amount of common words as quickly as possible. Phonic approaches also teach the children useful rules about how to cope with more irregular words, such as words with silent letters in them. One example of this is the two-vowel rule: 'the first vowel says its name, the second is usually silent', for example with the words 'tie' and 'eat'. At a reading age of about six years, children are able to work out short, phonically regular words known as 'consonant–vowel–consonant' (CVC) words, such as 'cat'. They are also starting to identify some of the most common irregular words such as 'the', which can be identified only by visual recognition or partial phonic cues.

Subsequent developments involve progressively more complex phonic skills such as consonant blends ('tr' as in 'trip') and consonant and vowel digraphs, where letter combinations result in new sounds such as 'sh', as in 'ship', and 'ou', as in 'out'. Children are eventually able to tackle clusters of letters such as 'ight' and combinations of syllables in complex words such as 'underneath', which has a readability level of just above eight years. The final stage of reading acquisition is the **orthographic stage** (Frith, 1985), or the **consolidated alphabetic stage** (Ehri, 2005). This stage occurs when children are able to rapidly process strings of letters that frequently occur together, such as 'ought' or 'ing' so that laborious letter-by-letter decoding is not necessary, and this frees up cognitive resources for comprehension of what is being read, as well as speeding up the decoding of text itself.

The relationship between reading and spelling

Reading and writing are evidently not the same thing, although they are of course closely related. One reason for this close relationship is that we learn to read and write in parallel. However, the most likely explanation is that both reading and spelling require phonic skills, although to different extents. For example, Ellis and Cataldo (1990) found that children's spelling ability with regular words predicted progress with reading, but not vice versa. This is consistent with the idea that early spellings depend on children's knowledge and use of letter–sound correspondences, whereas reading development can also be based on a visual memory for words, as well as the application alphabetic knowledge (recall Frith, 1985).

In English it is usually more difficult to spell a word than it is to read it. Comparisons of the words used in standard reading and spelling tests indicate that, on average, children can read words about one year before they can spell them. Children may also have specific spelling problems, and in this case the gap can be much greater. Such children may have normal or good reading abilities yet underfunction significantly with spelling. They will often be aware that what they have written is incorrect since it 'reads' wrongly, but they do not know the correct letter sequence. Moseley (1989) has shown that, although all children will tend to avoid words that they are unable to spell, children who have spelling difficulties are much more prone to do so. Their avoidance of problem words can rise to an underestimate of their ability, particularly in secondary schools, where written work is the main way in which attainments are assessed.

Skilled reading: reading as 'word recognition'

The sheer speed at which word identification occurs in skilled readers also implies that it is probably achieved by some form of parallel processing. One such model of skilled reading that has received substantial support is the Dual Route Cascaded Model of reading (DRC; Coltheart *et al.*, 2001), which is based on a computational model of how words are read. Put simply, the idea is that in order to read a word, there are two main routes available. In the first route, the identified letter sequence is matched against a lexicon of all known words. Once a match is found, this then activates both the phonological representation of that word (i.e. how it is pronounced) and its meaning (semantics), and the correct word is spoken aloud. This is known as the **lexical route**. The second route to word reading is available to all words, both known and unknown, and simply involves letter-by-letter decoding of the printed word based on known rules about which sounds go with which letters. This is known as the **nonlexical route**. As the word may be unfamiliar, there is no semantic access on this route. Although these two routes are in one sense separate, they are activated at the same time when a word is encountered, and the number of orthographically similar real words will influence how a non-word or an unfamiliar word will be pronounced via the 'nonlexical' route. For example, the non-word 'zint' may be pronounced so that it rhymes with either 'pint' or 'mint', depending on which pronunciation of '-int' is more common in the person's mental lexicon.

The behaviour of a computer model based on these principles was compared to the behaviour of skilled human readers when presented with the same stimuli, as a way of testing whether this model seems like a plausible way of thinking about how skilled readers process text (Coltheart *et al.*, 2001). The computer model behaves in a very similar way to that of adult readers – for example, in reading highly common words faster than rarer ones, and reading regular words faster than irregular ones. The model can also simulate the behaviour of individuals with acquired dyslexia (i.e. the types of acquired reading difficulty that are observed following head injury). Although the model is still far from perfect, to date it offers a good theoretical model for understanding how the different sources of information about words interact to enable successful reading.

There are three main sources of information that we appear to draw on when engaging in skilled reading: orthography (i.e. printed forms), phonology (i.e. speech sounds) and semantics (i.e. word meanings). These three sources of information can be seen as the three points in a triangle, and connectionist models that draw on the interrelationships between these aspects are therefore referred to as **triangle models of reading**, following a reference to this form in a connectionist study of reading performance by Seidenberg and McClelland (1989). A connectionist model is a computer model that attempts to simulate cognition through the construction of a network of processing units that are similar to neurons in the way that they function and communicate with each other. Although there is considerable overlap between triangle models of reading and dual-route models, in practice the dual route models appear to be able to account for a wider range of reading behaviour than connectionist triangle models can (Coltheart, 2005).

Constructing meaning: reading as 'comprehension'

Reading is of course more than simply the ability to read separate words; it must also involve the ability to assemble grammatical structures and derive meaning from them. In this sense, reading can therefore be seen as successive identification of words and access to their correct meaning. Gough and Tunmer (1986) referred to this as the **simple view of reading**: that reading is about decoding text (as discussed above) plus the ability to comprehend meaning (as assessed by listening comprehension; see Figure 10.1). According to this view, difficulties in comprehension will therefore stem from either difficulties in decoding the words on the page, or difficulties in processing language more generally (or potentially both).

If decoding is difficult for an individual, then it will take up cognitive resources that might otherwise be used to support comprehension of what is being read. You may have experienced this yourself when reading a particularly difficult textbook with a lot of new terminology that you have not come across before; you may finish reading the chapter but have very limited or patchy recall of what it was telling you, and you have to re-read it to access its meaning.

The processing of language required during listening comprehension assessment refers to a great deal of complex cognitive activity. Extracting meaning from a sentence requires the ability to construct from syntax, vocabulary and general knowledge about the world a 'mental model' (Johnson-Laird, 1983) of the situation described in the decoded text. So we will bring all of our script-based knowledge about common events to bear on what we are reading, and this will also lead us to expect certain things to be likely to happen within that context, as well as leading us not to expect others. This is the same when we are trying to make sense of something that someone is telling us about –

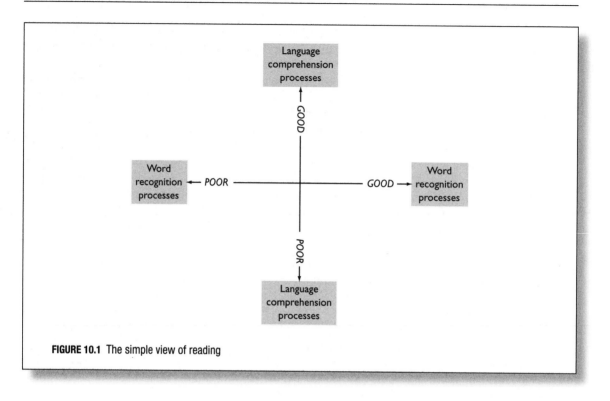

FIGURE 10.1 The simple view of reading

we have to try to represent all the elements of what we are being told in an appropriate way. In fact, the correlation between reading comprehension scores and listening comprehension scores in skilled readers is as high as $r = 0.90$ (Gernsbacher, 1990).

One area of language comprehension that is especially important, and which we can often take for granted, is the ability to make appropriate inferences. For example, if I say, 'Mary heard the ice cream van outside. She rushed to fetch some money from her bedroom', most people will correctly infer that the reason why Mary is rushing to her bedroom is because she wants to buy an ice cream. Such inferences are costly in terms of cognitive effort, but are necessary to maintain a coherent representation of what is going on. Evidence suggests that six-year-old children are able to make inferences that are essential to maintain narrative coherence, but there are age-related differences in the ability to make inferences in general (Barnes *et al.*, 1996). Similarly, studies of individuals with comprehension difficulties show that they are less able to make inferences than more-skilled comprehenders, even when they are able to review the text to help them answer the questions (Oakhill, 1984, 1993). In one classic study, Cain and Oakhill (1999) compared a group of children with reading comprehension difficulties to two groups: a group of children matched on age (called a 'chronological age matched group') and group of typically developing children matched on comprehension ability, who were therefore younger than the children with comprehension problems. This kind of design enables researchers to examine whether difficulties experienced by the poor comprehenders are distinctive to them as a group, or can perhaps be explained by lack of reading-comprehension experience. This study revealed that children with comprehension deficits were worse than both these control groups at making 'gap filling' inferences, for example, such as inferring the likely location of an event from information about what the actors were doing. However, they made inferences at the same level as the younger, typically developing children, when they were asked to make text-connecting inferences, of the kind described earlier, even when they were directed to look at the relevant part of the passage to help them. This study suggests that the difficulties of children with comprehension difficulties may be in part due to relative inexperience with texts or immaturity, but that they do demonstrate specific difficulties processing some aspects of language to build a coherent overall representation.

Teaching reading

Broadly speaking, there have been two major approaches to the teaching of reading, which can be characterised respectively as 'skills leading to reading' and 'reading leading to skills'. These perspectives have often become relatively polarised, and arguments between the respective proponents have sometimes been referred to as the 'reading wars'. However, at the present time, the dominant approach adopted within UK schools is a 'skills leading to reading' approach, and in particular, a phonics-based approach to reading instruction is commonly adopted.

The phonics approach

This approach is based on the theories described earlier, which view early reading development as about 'decoding' text. As noted, children may start with a sight vocabulary for some commonly occurring words and their name, but will not necessarily understand the alphabetic principle. So a phonic approach begins with teaching children the alphabet and how to say the sounds most commonly associated with each letter or letter combination.

This knowledge of letters can then be used to work out simple, regular words that emphasise the use of common, regular patterns such as 'cat', 'rat', 'mat', 'fat', etc. Early reading texts can also be based on such regular words, with the emphasis being on encouraging children to work out unknown words by sounding out all the letters. Children are then taught progressively more complex phonic rules to enable them to tackle a wider range of words.

A more sophisticated approach depends upon learning all the written representations for the 40-plus phonemes (spoken sounds). This means that, as well as single letter sounds, children learn the consonant and vowel digraphs such as 'th' and 'ai' (as in 'rain'). Many of the vowel digraphs have a number of different written forms for the same sound, and the 'ai' sound can also exist as 'rake', 'day', 'great', 'weigh' and 'they'. Learning all these would be quite an initial load for children, and programmes based on this approach such as 'Reading Reflex' (McGuinness and McGuinness, 1998) and 'Jolly Phonics' (Lloyd, 1998) build up their use over time.

Phonics must itself depend on children's phonological abilities (the ability to perceive and process speech sounds). Although phonics teaching has traditionally assumed that children have the necessary ability to perceive and use speech sounds, there is now considerable evidence (discussed later in this chapter) that some children have difficulties in this area. Training for these abilities, particularly when it forms part of the approaches discussed above, provides a stronger foundation for early literacy development and enhances progress.

Classic study

Bradley and Bryant (1983) investigated the phonological awareness skills of 368 four- and five-year-olds, none of whom could yet read. Four years later, they tested the children again for their attainments with reading and writing, and they found that the earlier skills with sound categorisation correlated significantly with subsequent literacy development. These predictive correlations were higher than those for the children's early measures of vocabulary or performance on a memory test, and would appear to indicate that phonological development is an independent cause of early literacy progress. However, it could also be that phonological abilities and literacy are both simply the outcome of early support with literacy: that is, it might be that children who learn to read and write at an early age develop their knowledge of sounds as a result of doing so.

To investigate whether that was the case, Bradley and Bryant carried out an investigation to see whether directly intervening with children's phonological and alphabetic skills would influence their later progress with literacy. To do this, they selected a group of 65 young children with weak sound categorisation skills and divided them up into two experimental groups and two control groups. The first experimental group received training in sound categorisation, with 40 sessions over two years. This involved teaching the children that words could vary by just one sound to make alliterative or rhyming patterns. The second experimental group had the same training as the first, and also learned to identify and match plastic letters that the words had in common, for example 'c' for 'cat' and 'cap'. One control group received training merely in categorising the words into similar conceptual groups, while the other control group was given no training at all. The results shown in Table 10.1 show that the experimental groups made significantly more progress, with the children who had been given both alphabetic and sound training making 12.5 months more progress with reading than the children who had not been given any extra help at all (Comparison 1 in the table). There was an even greater effect with spelling, which at this early stage is very dependent on knowledge of letters and their combinations. These results also show that the sound training by itself had a significant effect, one that was additional to any familiarity with the words involved (Comparison 2 in the table). This gives strong support for the belief that children's initial sensitivities to sounds in words do affect their subsequent progress with literacy.

TABLE 10.1 Final scores in reading and spelling for experimental and control groups given different training

	Sound training	Alphabetic + sound training	Conceptual training	No training
Reading age (months)	92.2	97.0	88.5	84.5
Spelling age (months)	86.0	98.8	81.8	75.2

A great deal of other research has confirmed these findings, and Torgesen *et al.* (1994) found that the strongest predictor of reading in first grade was children's earlier skills with phonological analysis, measured by how well they were able to identify the sounds in words. The effect of phonological analysis was greater than the effect of early measures of language development or even of initial reading progress. Later progress in second grade was, however, more dependent on phonological synthesis, represented by the ability to blend separate sounds into whole words. They also found evidence for a reciprocal relationship, with early pre-school reading abilities independently predicting later phonological awareness, although the effect was smaller than the effect of phonological skills on reading. It seems likely that the processes involved in early reading, such as learning the sounds for written letters, also have some effect on developing children's sensitivities to those sounds in spoken language.

Analytic versus synthetic phonics

A distinction can be made between techniques which initially develop an awareness of sounds within words, known as **analytic phonics**, and those which attempt to teach sounds in isolation first and then showing how to build them up into words, known as **synthetic phonics**. Analytic phonics was incorporated into the original version of England's National Literacy Strategy (NLS) in the 1990s and draws attention to the patterns found between words based on similarities in onsets and rimes. Teaching onsets involves giving children sets of words such as 'bat', 'bin', 'bun' and encouraging them to link the first sound with the first letter(s). Teaching rimes involves showing children how words like fight, light and might sound the same at the end *and* look the same at the end. This approach is based on the idea that one reading strategy available to children who are learning to read is to read unknown words by analogy to known words (Goswami, 1994). For example, if children have learned the words 'pin' and 'tin', they can be taught to use that knowledge to read a new word such as 'bin'. More recent studies of children's reading strategies, in which children are asked to explain how they are tackling unknown words, have shown that children appear to be just as likely to attempt to read words by analogy as they are to use letter–sound conversion rules, even when they have not been taught the technique explicitly (Farrington-Flint and Wood, 2007).

Proponents of synthetic phonics (e.g. Johnston *et al.*, 2009) believe that it is more effective to base learning initially on the 40-plus sounds (phonemes) used in spoken English before moving on to larger structures. Although it may seem that this is a lot for children to learn, it can be argued that the demands are less than those associated with the analytic approach, which requires knowledge of many initial and final consonant clusters as well as a large number of separate rimes. Once the phonemes have been learned, they can then be used in a conventional way to build up initially simple words, progressing on to different forms for the same sounds and more complex and less regular combinations.

In order to discover which phonic approach to teaching reading is most effective, Vousden (2008) conducted a statistical analysis of the characteristics of monosyllabic words in English, with a view to seeing how many words might be successfully read if one adopted a strategy of learning either the most frequent onset–rime or letter–sound correspondences. The results suggest that learning letter–sound correspondences is a more economical strategy for English, in the sense that it will enable you to correctly decode a greater number of words than learning onset–rime units will.

It may be, however, that the differences between the suitability of the two approaches comes down to a question of timing. Although early progress may be accelerated by the limited and more predictable synthetic approach, later progress with less regular patterns of letter combinations will probably benefit from the comparisons and generalisations that come from the analytic approach. It may be unwise to use either technique exclusively, and best to start from an emphasis on the synthetic approach and then incorporate analytic techniques once children are able to manage regular phonics. In a review commissioned by England's Department for Education and Skills, Torgerson *et al.* (2006) recommend that: 'Since there is evidence that systematic phonics teaching benefits children's reading accuracy, it should be part of every literacy teacher's repertoire and a routine part of literacy teaching, in a judicious balance with other elements' (p. 49).

Critics of the phonics approach to teaching reading often attack it on the basis of its artificiality, arguing that reading should be the process of deriving meaning from the written word, and that phonics only produces children who 'bark at print' but who are not able to use what they read. It is also argued that phonics cannot work if taught inappropriately, since letter sounds are very difficult to articulate in isolation. For example, the letters the letters 'b' 'u' and 't' may be incorrectly sounded out as 'buh', 'uh' and 'tuh', which means that blending them together would result in the word 'butter' rather than 'but'. Also as there are around 200 known phonic 'rules' that may be taught to children, for some children this may represent a substantial barrier to learning them.

'Real books'

The alternative approach to phonics is known as the 'real books' approach, based on seeing reading as essentially a psycholinguistic process, and is derived largely from the ideas of Goodman (1968). According to this approach, reading should be acquired (not taught), just as spoken language is. Smith (1973) in particular has argued that children should experience literacy only in meaningful contexts and that learning the finer structure of reading (letters and words) will follow from this. Any early attempt to focus on letter sounds or a limited reading vocabulary is believed to get in the way of the normal process. From the start, it is argued, this should involve immersion in *real reading books* with a complete text, governed mainly by the child's interests and without undue concern for the vocabulary or the difficulty of the words. Goodman (1968) in particular characterises reading as essentially a psycholinguistic guessing game, with readers using whatever cues are available to generate linguistic meaning. These cues can take many forms, including letter sounds and their combinations in words. What Goodman feels is more important, however, is the meaning that is involved in what is read, including the grammatical structure of texts. According to this approach, reading is a process of constructing meaning, using this to make hypotheses about the text and then testing them out. This is evident in a child's errors, which can be seen as attempts to follow a particular hypothesis, rather than just being 'wrong'.

Goodman (1965) originally argued that such strategies were what made good readers, finding that there was a 60–80 per cent improvement in reading accuracy when children read words in context, compared with when they read them in isolation. Good readers also made greater improvements by using context than poorer readers were able to. This suggests that context provides extra-semantic and syntactic cues that good readers are able to use for word identification, and that this ability improves with better reading.

However, Nicholson and Hill (1985) criticised Goodman's original work on the grounds that because his subjects first read the words in isolation, then in the contextual sentences, any improvement might be due just to practice effects. To test this hypothesis, they ran a more stringent counterbalanced study, with eight-year-old readers on two levels of text: easy readability (eight-year level) and hard readability (11-year level). Unlike Goodman, they found that context was *not* a help in reading unknown words. On the easy-readability text, children were able to read all the words and did not need context. On the hard-readability text, the context was simply not powerful enough to reveal the exact words.

Nicholson and Hill concluded that the main characteristic distinguishing good from poor readers (at this age) is not the ability to utilise context, but the ability to decode words independently from context. Similarly, Stuart *et al.* (2000) found that sight vocabulary is better learned out of context on flashcards than in the context of books, or even a mixed approach. This is supported in a study by Harding *et al.* (1985) of the changing reading strategies and abilities used by children from 5–11 years of age. Over this time, whole-word reading strategies progressively increased, with a corresponding decline in the number of syntactic and semantic errors made by children – the opposite of what Goodman would have predicted. Share and Stanovich (1995) also reviewed evidence showing that when poor readers were given text that they could cope with, their comprehension abilities became as good as those of normal readers. When good readers were given text that was beyond their abilities, they too would 'plod' and were unable to use context to aid comprehension. Such findings imply that merely teaching children to guess at unknown words more may not be a very effective strategy for improving early reading.

Integrating approaches

Solity and Vousden (2009) have taken an **instructional psychology** approach to trying to resolve the argument between advocates of real books and phonics. Such an approach analyses the learning environment of children and looks at how this environment influences cognition, rather than starting with an analysis of the cognitive processes associated with reading, and then looking at how they are applied to the task of reading. They discovered, in line with Vousden (2008), that the application of high-frequency letter–sound correspondence rules enable children to read the majority of phonologically regular and irregular words that children are likely to encounter when reading. More surprisingly, they found that such words were *more* likely to occur in 'real books' than in reading schemes. They therefore suggest that real books offer a better basis for the teaching of reading than reading schemes do, but a phonic approach based on the most frequently occurring letter–sound correspondences should be the basis of reading instruction within the context of those texts. They also argue that, just as frequency of words is an important factor that influences children's reading ability, so is the context they are presented in, but in a different way to that originally advocated by Goodman and Smith. That is, Adelman *et al.* (2006) found that it is important for children to see new words presented in a variety of different linguistic contexts, as this seems to enhance retention of those items relative to when they are presented in more restricted contexts (as might be argued is the case in reading schemes). But Solity and Vousden emphasise the need for words to be taught out of context first, alongside a phonic approach which emphasises high-frequency letter–sound correspondences.

The nature of reading difficulties

Various things can go wrong with the process of developing reading and writing skills, and some children, despite many years of tuition in phonics, struggle to acquire literacy. There are a variety of different groups of children who fall into this category. First of all, some children experience difficulties in reading because they have cognitive difficulties that are general and pervasive (i.e. they show generally low performance on all sub-tests of an IQ assessment). These children are generally delayed in their reading development relative to same-age peers, and are referred to in the literature as **poor readers** or even 'garden variety poor readers'.

These children can be contrasted with children who are **underachieving**. Children who underachieve have the cognitive skills and potential to be successful readers, but are falling short of the standards specified by either nationally set targets, or by the levels expected for a child of their age. The reasons for underachievement are not always clear: often this appears to result from disengagement from education and school generally, and sometimes the origins of underachievement can be traced back to factors such as home literacy environment or socio-economic status. As boys are observed to underachieve more than girls at the present time, another possible explanation that has been proposed is the feminisation of education. That is, women are more likely to become teachers, especially in primary school, than men, and this has been seen to be problematic, especially as research has shown that boys do better when educated by male teachers, and girls do better when taught by women (Woolford and McDougall, 1998). It has also been suggested that boys experience contradictory discourses about masculinity inside and outside school, and these can result in confusion about what behaviours are valued in boys (Harris et al., 1993b).

A third group of children with literacy difficulties include those with **specific learning difficulties**. These children have difficulties in reading and have a cognitive profile (as shown on an IQ assessment) characterised by an uneven profile, in which they excel at some cognitive skills, but show marked deficits in others. The specific learning difficulty most commonly associated with literacy difficulties is developmental dyslexia, although it should be noted that other types of specific learning difficulty, such as dyspraxia (difficulties planning and executing motor movements) and specific language impairment, are also likely to result in difficulties with reading and writing.

Dyslexia

The condition that we now know by the term 'dyslexia' ('dys' meaning 'problems with', and 'lexia' meaning 'words') was originally identified by W.P. Morgan as 'congenital word blindness', but the first study of the condition was by James Hinshelwood (a Scottish eye surgeon) in 1917, and was conceived of as primarily a visual difficulty. Samuel Orton also viewed the condition as essentially visual in nature, and used the term 'strephosymbolia' instead. Strephosymbolia literally means 'twisted symbols' and referred to the observation that many of the individuals he studied tended to reverse letters and read or spell words back-to-front (e.g. 'was' might be read as 'saw'). Although this is seen by many as a classic symptom of dyslexia, it should be noted that studies have shown that such reversals are *not* more common among dyslexics and is in fact a characteristic of all poor readers (Rutter and Yule, 1975), and is seen in the reading and writing of young children in early stages of literacy. However, individuals with dyslexia do often report experiencing mild visual disturbances (Lovegrove, 1991).

Specific reading problems that happen as children get older are often termed **developmental dyslexia**, to distinguish the condition from **acquired dyslexia**, which can happen to previously literate people following brain injury. Acquired dyslexia can show a number of different forms, with 'phonological' dyslexia affecting letter–sound conversion, 'surface' dyslexia affecting whole-word recognition and 'deep' dyslexia affecting reading for meaning. It has been suggested that developmental dyslexia might be subdivided in the same way, implying that there may be a similar underlying physical basis. Ellis et al. (1996) found that a dyslexic group of children did show similar differences, with phonological and surface patterns being apparent. However, both normal readers and generally delayed readers showed the same types of differences, which does not support a separate classification of dyslexia based on these.

Dyslexia is best thought of as a neurological syndrome, which results in specific cognitive deficits with respect to working memory (especially phonological memory) and automatisation of learned behaviours. Individuals with dyslexia also appear to have difficulties forming associations between visual and verbal stimuli (Breznitz, 2002), which may explain why learning letter–sound correspondences is so difficult for them. Galaburda (1991) found atypical asymmetry in the planum temporale (in Wernicke's area) in individuals with dyslexia. This area appears to be directly associated with phonological coding deficits which may underlie reading problems. There is some evidence of neuroanatomical abnormalities in the magnocellular visual systems of individuals with dyslexia (Livingstone *et al.*, 1991): this pathway is linked to eye-movement and visual attention, as well as the processing of rapidly changing visual information and motion (Stein, 1994). Best and Demb (1999) found a separate deficit in this for a group of young adults with reading difficulties. The difficulties with learning and automatising new behaviours observed in individuals with dyslexia have been linked to deficits in cerebellar function (Fawcett *et al.*, 2001; Nicolson *et al.*, 1999). There is some physiological evidence to support this idea, as Rae *et al.* (2002) found greater symmetry in the cerebella of adults with dyslexia, and this symmetry was associated with phonological decoding.

Developmental dyslexia is usually identified by comparing reading performance to an individual's IQ performance – if there is a significant discrepancy between the two sets of scores, then the label of dyslexia will be applied. This procedure is known as a discrepancy approach to identifying dyslexia, and is not without controversy because it is not based on a useful definition of what dyslexia actually is. Moreover, it also assumes that IQ is a reliable indicator of reading potential in an individual, and this assumption has been challenged by researchers who have demonstrated only weak but significant correlations between IQ and reading attainment (e.g. Stanovich, 1991). There have been more recent attempts to incorporate the identification of positive behavioural indicators ('symptoms') into the assessment of dyslexia. The British Dyslexia Association definition is helpful in describing a range of difficulties characteristic of the condition:

> Dyslexia is best described as a combination of abilities and difficulties that affect the learning process in one or more of reading, spelling, writing. Accompanying weaknesses may be identified in speed of processing, short-term memory, sequencing and organisation, auditory and/or visual perception, spoken language and motor skills. It is particularly related to mastering and using written language, which may include alphabetic, numeric and musical notation.... Dyslexia can occur despite normal intellectual ability and teaching. It is independent of socio-economic or language background.
>
> (Peer, 2002: 67)

There is also, incidentally, a condition known as **hyperlexia**, when children's reading attainments outstrip their verbal abilities. This can be the outcome of specific problems with language and comprehension disorders such as autism (when reading attainments are sometimes normal but language is retarded), but can also happen when children have very high levels of reading ability. Pennington *et al.* (1987), for instance, describe one boy aged 2 years, 11 months who had a word-reading age of nine years, three months. He was advanced in underlying phonic skills and could also decode both regular and irregular words at the same level. Such cases indicate that word attack skills can develop in a relatively independent way, although reading for comprehension depends on verbal understanding at the appropriate level, and hyperlexic children usually cannot answer questions on the more difficult texts.

The 'dyslexia myth'

One of the areas of controversy surrounding dyslexia relates to whether children with dyslexia have educational needs that are distinctive from those of other children with reading difficulties. As we shall see in a moment, one of the more consistent research findings in reading research shows that the majority of children with reading difficulties have a deficit in processing phonological information (Stanovich, 1994). This is true whether the child is a 'poor reader' or experiences dyslexia. From that point of view, questions have been raised about the usefulness of the dyslexia label in terms of educating children with reading difficulties, as the same programmes of remediation are potentially able to support both groups. There are also doubts about the use of intelligence as a unitary concept, and concerning the extent to which intelligence tests represent an individual's potential for learning. However, as Stanovich (1991) points out, it can be argued that children who have good knowledge and understanding of curriculum subjects but who cannot develop or express this with literacy *do* have particular needs. They are evidently different from those who are behind with literacy but who also have restricted knowledge and understanding of school work, but are they more deserving of extra help? It is a moot point as to where one should draw any line in terms of a definition of special needs and any additional teaching help that might have to come from resources that could be given to other children. Hornsby and Miles (1980), however, argue that children with 'dyslexia' need teaching techniques that integrate auditory, visual and physical work: the **multisensory approach**. Yet, such techniques have the potential to improve learning outcomes for all children, not just children with dyslexia. We will consider different techniques for supporting children with reading difficulties later in the chapter.

The point to take away from discussions of the 'dyslexia myth' is that there *is* evidence that individuals with dyslexia are neurologically and cognitively distinctive from other children with reading difficulties, and that dyslexia can therefore be said to 'exist'. What is disputed is whether such children should be treated differently in terms of programmes of remediation.

Explanations for reading difficulties

Language problems

Early language problems can be a significant factor in early reading progress. In particular, difficulties with a child's spoken sound system can delay his or her progress with phonic analysis and synthesis. Difficulties with language structure, meaning and a limited spoken vocabulary can also limit progress, particularly as reading develops above the eight-year level. Such problems may come from a restricted home environment or be related to underlying medical problems. Webster (1985), for instance, reports that otitis media, or 'glue ear', is present in as many as one-third of all children in early schooling. This has the effect of preventing children from discriminating sounds adequately, and there is a high association of subsequent reading difficulties with such conductive hearing losses.

Phonological deficits

A number of children who start school have not yet developed a mature spoken sound system. Some children also have difficulties with their ability to perceive the separate sounds in words, referred to as 'phonemes', or to recognise patterns of commonality in spoken words, such as which words rhyme with each other. Following a landmark study by Bradley and Bryant (1978) which demonstrated that children with reading difficulties showed pronounced difficulties in tasks that required them to detect the odd word out in sets of words such as 'cat', 'cap', 'hat', 'can' or 'hat', 'fat', 'map', 'rat', there has been much research attention paid to the role of phonological awareness in reading development and reading difficulties. Phonological awareness refers to the ability to detect, isolate and consciously manipulate different sound structures in speech, such as syllables, onset and rime, and individual phonemes. It should be noted that phonological awareness is just about being aware of sound in speech, not how these sounds are represented in print. As a result, it is possible that phonological skills can develop spontaneously, in the absence of formal tuition in reading and writing, although it should be noted that there is no doubt that learning to read and write enhances phonological awareness dramatically. The issue is, however, that if a child has problems achieving phonological awareness, this will impair their ability to learn letter–sound correspondences.

Over the last 30 years there has been a good deal of research that has examined the exact nature of phonological awareness and phonological-processing difficulties observed in children who experience difficulties learning to read. This research has demonstrated that such individuals have impaired phonological working memory (i.e. conscious short-term memory) relative to children of the same age (Johnston et al., 1987). This deficit potentially impacts on their ability to encode information presented to them in a verbal format, or access phonological information from long-term memory effectively. A deficit in phonological short-term memory, as measured by the digit-span task (which requires individuals to recall ever longer strings of numbers) is considered to be a defining characteristic of developmental dyslexia. Most people can recall on average seven items of information in short-term memory, with the typical range being between five and nine (Miller, 1956). However, this capacity is much reduced in individuals with dyslexia, and can be as low as just four items (Snowling, 2000). However, rather than think about short-term memory as being about how many items you can hold in conscious memory, it is perhaps more appropriate to think of phonological short-term memory as a tape-recorder, which can only store four seconds of information (Hulme et al., 1999). There is a strong correlation between speech rate (how quickly you can speak) and phonological short-term memory performance, which suggests that people who can articulate phonological information quickly are able to encode more information in that four-second loop of memory that is available to us. So it appears that speech rate is something that is problematic in individuals with reading problems, too (McDougall et al., 1994).

There is also evidence that individuals with reading difficulties have problems retrieving the names of objects from long-term memory. For example, Snowling et al. (1988) found that even when individuals with dyslexia were matched on vocabulary to typically developing children, they were significantly worse than the controls on a task that required them to name line drawings of objects, even though they were as familiar with the words used as test items as the control children were. This suggests that their representation of word names in memory is somehow impaired, or that access to them is problematic.

The question of whether children with reading problems have difficulties perceiving speech has been raised, and the evidence to date is somewhat mixed, but there is some evidence that they are impaired relative to children of the same age. For example, Metsala (1997) showed that children with reading difficulties require more phonological input before they can recognise a spoken word than typically developing children do. Wood and Terrell (1998) also found that children with poor reading performance were significantly worse than same-age controls at a task which required them to recognise words when they were replayed twice as quickly as normal, but that effect was attributable to individual differences in vocabulary. What was not explained by vocabulary was the finding that the children with reading difficulties had poorer sensitivity to speech rhythm than the controls did. Speech-rhythm sensitivity is an important skill, as we need it to help us to detect word boundaries in speech, and in English it also helps us to identify word meaning (compare 'REcord' with 'reCORD', for example). It also contributes to our awareness of vowels in speech, and onset–rime boundaries. Subsequent research has shown that sensitivity to prosodic information is impaired in both adults and children with dyslexia (see Wood et al., 2009, for a review).

In 1986, Keith Stanovich proposed that the core deficit in dyslexia was a phonological one, and Stanovich and Siegel (1994) showed that all children with reading difficulties (not just children with dyslexia) showed fundamental deficits in tasks that required phonological processing. Snowling (2000) has argued that the evidence is suggestive of a difficulty in representing phonological information in memory.

Automaticity deficits

When we have learned a new skill to the point where it has become automatic, it means that the task typically requires very little conscious attention to perform. For example, when first learning to drive a car, it requires our full attention and lapses of attention can result in errors, such as bumping the kerbside or braking later than we should. However, once we have practised driving for many hours, most of the behaviours become fluent and we are able to divide our attention to talk to passengers without any ill effects. On familiar routes, the attentional demands can require so little attention that we often reach a point in the journey where we have failed to take in how far we have driven or driven past key landmarks without realising!

Like driving, reading and writing are skills that, over time and with consistent practice, should become automatised and fluent, requiring very little conscious effort to perform. However, this is not always achieved by individuals with reading and writing difficulties. This deficit in automatisation of learned behaviours has been of interest in more recent years, and has been examined as a possible cause of the full range of difficulties that are experienced by individuals with dyslexia, which go beyond problems with reading and writing. Nicolson and Fawcett (1990, 1994) observed that even when individuals with dyslexia have overcome their problems with literacy, their reading and writing remains effortful and is not fully automatised. They link this automatisation deficit to problematic cerebellar function.

A task that has been used to assess automatisation deficits in relation to phonological ones is the rapid automatised naming task (RAN for short). A RAN task typically presents participants with a grid of 50 items (usually five items, repeated in a random sequence ten times each). The task is to name each item in the grid in order, as quickly as possible, and the time taken to complete this is noted down. As you may expect by now, we observe slower performance in such tasks in children with reading difficulties, especially when the stimuli to be named are numbers or letters. Wolf and Bowers (1999) have used the results of such studies to propose the **double deficit theory** of reading difficulties. That is, they suggest that reading difficulties may be attributable to either a deficit in phonological processing or a deficit in naming speed. As a result, there are potentially three kinds of children with reading problems: those with a phonological deficit; those with a naming speed deficit; and a third group who have difficulties with both phonological tasks and naming speed tasks (the so-called 'double deficit' group).

Helping children with reading difficulties

One aim of reading research is to try to identify which children are at risk of developing reading difficulties as early as possible, and then putting intervention programmes in place for these children as quickly as possible, so that the impact of experiencing failure is limited as far as possible. Screening children on their phonological awareness early in their school career is one way of identifying these children. Once identified, a phonic training programme may be introduced to support them (recall the Bradley and Bryant (1983) study which showed that, although phonological-awareness training alone can help reading outcomes, the best outcomes are found when phonological-awareness training is combined with alphabetic training, as is commonly found in phonic programmes). Some examples of commonly used, commercially available interventions based on structured phonic teaching include Alpha to Omega (Hornsby et al., 1999), Toe by Toe (Cowling and Cowling, 1993), the Hickey Multisensory Language Course (Augur and Briggs, 1992) and Sound Linkage (Hatcher, 2000).

In England, normal progress with reading is now largely based on class and group activities as part of the National Literacy Strategy. Unfortunately, children with difficulties may find that their achievements are no longer close to the work being done by the rest of the class. Direct involvement by the teacher is often limited, and Plewis and Veltman (1996) found that the average time infant children spent reading to their teachers at the time of their survey was only eight minutes a week. When there are problems, it is therefore important to set up a more intensive and structured approach which can involve general goals for the medium term, and from this, more specific graded targets that can be achieved in the short term. For children with special needs, this can also be part of an Individual Education Plan.

One technique that incorporates this approach is the 'Data Pac' programme (Ackerman *et al.*, 1983), based on the principles of precision teaching. This breaks down overall goals, such as progress through a reading scheme, into manageable targets with key sets of words to be learned each week. The programme sets successive specific targets of accuracy and fluency, aimed at achieving mastery learning before children progress further. A specific daily target could, for instance, be for children to learn a set of six words so that they can identify a random set of 30 of these in one minute, with only two errors.

This technique has been shown to be highly successful, and depends upon the tight structuring and monitoring that are part of the programme. Hui (1991), for instance, looked at the effectiveness of the Data Pac programme with a range of children with early literacy problems. Over a period of 11 weeks, the group more than doubled their reading scores, with children who had specific learning difficulties ('dyslexia') making the greatest progress. However, the programme can be difficult for teachers to apply by themselves and works best when set up and monitored by a separate support teacher.

The importance of the home has been tackled by various paired teaching approaches which give parents a particular role in helping their children. A major review of 155 such projects by Topping and Whiteley (1990) showed that these can be highly effective, with an average gain in reading comprehension of 9.23 months over an average tuition period of just 8.6 weeks. An evaluation of this programme in Britain by Wright (1992) found that it was highly effective, with 96.4 per cent of children reaching average levels of attainments in literacy after a mean of 16.8 weeks of teaching. Long-term follow-up three years later, when the children were nine years old, showed that they maintained these gains and continued to perform as well as their own age group. Unfortunately, the training and intensive teaching are relatively expensive, and most schools are unable to make this sort of investment. Other forms of intensive teaching can be integrated with early academic work and are more realistic in terms of resources. The Early Reading Research project described by Solity *et al.* (1999) can be implemented by teachers as part of the normal teaching day and appears to have a strong preventive role. Fewer than 1 per cent of the children who were given this support were subsequently considered to have literacy difficulties, compared with just over 20 per cent of children in a comparison group.

Children with dyslexia are perhaps best supported by phonic programmes that are multisensory in nature. Programmes like the Hickey Multisensory Language Course and Toe by Toe are structured phonic programmes that also recognise the difficulties experienced by some children in learning letter–sound combinations. In order to overcome this, children are taught to articulate the sounds they are learning, whilst forming the shapes of letters at the same time. In this way, the children receive auditory, visual and kinaesthetic feedback on the information they are learning, and are therefore maximising the input that working memory is receiving at the point of encoding.

Assessing reading

Use of tests

Testing can be a useful way for a teacher to gain additional information about pupils, either to check on overall levels of achievement (summative assessments) or to gain specific information about children's progress to help with future teaching (formative assessments). The most commonly used tests in primary schools are 'normative' ones, mostly used as a rapid test of an individual's overall level. These would have only limited value in the planning of future teaching since they do not give any diagnostic information. At one time, the simplest (and most popular) tests used for reading and spelling were the Schonell Graded Word Reading Test (Schonell, 1955) and the Graded Word Spelling Test (Vernon, 1977). These both involve a list of words of graded difficulty; with the Schonell test, the child reads the words individually to the teacher, and with the Vernon's test the child writes down the words from the teacher's dictation. The spelling test can be done individually or with a group. The Schonell test covers the range from 6 to 12½ years; the Vernon's covers the range from five years, seven months up to 15 years, 10 months. Both of these tests have the virtue of simplicity, which has probably accounted for much of their popularity. As the Schonell test is now somewhat old, the best equivalent with a more modern vocabulary and standardisation might now be the British Ability Scales word reading sub-test (1997).

Such tests can be useful to gain a rapid overall assessment of pupils' reading or spelling, to make sure, for instance, that they can cope with the demands of the normal range of school work. They are typically used on transfer to secondary schooling and the most common are normative group tests such as the NFER-Nelson Group Reading Test II (Cornwall and France, 1997). This takes about 30 minutes and covers the age range from 6 years to nearly 15 years. The sub-tests involve sentence completion and context comprehension tasks, and incorporate skills relevant to general school work at this level.

Individual and group tests

There are many different reading and spelling tests available, and the particular one used will depend on the type of information needed and the circumstances in which it is used. However, individual tests are usually more reliable and often give diagnostic information. For example, on the Neale Analysis of Reading Ability (1997) test, individual children read passages of graded difficulty, and the teacher can note the different types of errors that they make. This assessment also provides questions that enable the user to assess the child's level of reading comprehension, and also provides normative data on reading speed. Group tests for primary-aged children such as the Group Reading Test usually involve selecting the correct word to match with pictures and to complete sentences. Although children are less closely supervised, such tests have reasonable reliability and allow the teacher to test many pupils at the same time. Such tests can therefore be very useful as a means of screening numbers of children for reading difficulties.

Most normative reading tests give relative information about children's levels of ability, such as a reading age, and standard scores that indicate how typical the child's performance is relative to other children of the same age. This may appear to be a simplistic way of summarising children's progress but it can be useful as a general indication of the type of skills that a child has developed. For instance, if children have a reading age above nine years, then they almost certainly have a substantial range of word attack skills. Subsequent teaching should probably emphasise comprehension and the use of reading in general curriculum studies.

Criterion-referenced testing

Criterion-referenced testing is usually less formal and based upon a teacher's own understanding of the learning process. This can involve a sequence of key assessment tasks and criteria for judging whether a pupil has achieved them. For early reading, the tests might cover phonological abilities, letter sound/name knowledge, phonic skills and reading vocabulary from a set of high-frequency words. These can be easily monitored and linked directly with specific phonic teaching approaches, a large number of which have been reviewed and summarised by Hinson and Smith (1993).

Diagnostic testing

Diagnostic testing is a type of formative assessment, and its main purpose is to analyse a child's pattern of abilities to guide future teaching support. Some diagnostic reading tests aim to pinpoint specific key abilities or skills that are weak, implying that subsequent teaching should be aimed at these areas to help to develop reading attainments. The *Observation Survey* (Clay, 2002) is a typical example of this approach and identifies young children's understanding of print concepts, how the children are approaching the task of reading continuous text, their letter identification skills, word reading, writing vocabulary, and hearing and recording sounds in words. The information gathered from these assessments are used to tailor the teaching resources and approach to the child's needs. For children who are failing to make good progress in the context of regular classroom teaching, Clay (1993) recommends the application of a Reading Recovery programme, in which children are taught one-to-one on a daily basis, using texts that challenge the child's current level of ability, but not too much. The focus is on equipping the children with strategies for tackling the text and addressing their areas of weakness. However, it should be noted that Reading Recovery is not characterised by a phonics-based approach to teaching reading and children who fail to make progress in the context of Reading Recovery are further referred for specialist reading support.

A more recent diagnostic assessment is the Phonological Assessment Battery (PhAB, Frederickson *et al.*, 1997), which evaluates children's sensitivity to sounds in words. This covers abilities such as the detection of alliteration and rhyme, speed of naming digits and pictures, the ability to generate spoonerisms, and a test of semantic fluency. The strongest single correlate of reading ability (with a value of 0.85) is the 'spoonerism' test, which involves replacing one sound in a word with another. For instance, a child could be asked to replace the 'l' sound in 'lip' with a 'p' sound, to make a new word. It seems likely that this test involves a number of phonological abilities, such as analysis and synthesis, and encoding in working memory, that are important in early reading. As discussed earlier, this approach has the advantage that it identifies skills that are relatively stable and characteristic of individual children, and which have been shown to improve reading when they are taught.

Choosing the appropriate test

The nature of a test depends to a great extent on what one believes that the reading or writing/spelling process is all about. As this changes at different levels of skill, the abilities looked at should also vary accordingly. As reading progress at the early stages is closely linked with establishing and using letter sounds, an appropriate test would give pupils tasks based upon these abilities. The Word Recognition and Phonic Skills Test, by Carver and Moseley (1994), does so by giving pupils the task of selecting among words according to sounds and their combinations, as read out by the teacher. The test has a relatively early 'floor' of five years and discriminates well between children at the initial stages of reading development.

With intermediate skill development at the top infant and junior level, progress depends on more complex phonic abilities. These include regular and irregular blends and digraphs as well as polysyllabic and low-frequency words with unique spellings. Most tests at this level also incorporate words in meaningful contexts and involve tasks such as selecting between a set of words to complete a sentence. These skills are covered by a wide range of available tests that can be used with groups of children in school.

At higher levels of reading, it may be more appropriate to use tests that are mainly based on comprehension such as the Neale Analysis of Reading Ability, or the York Assessment of Reading for Comprehension (Snowling *et al.*, 2008). Another type of assessment that can cover a broad range of attainments is the Informal Reading Inventory approach defined by Johnson and Kress (1964). This is a way of assessing children's errors using graded passages of real reading material. Based on 'miscue analysis', this looks for children's errors associated with the grammatical, the graphophonic (sound–symbol) and the semantic systems. Children can also be placed at different reading levels in terms of their reading accuracy. The *independent* level means getting 99 per cent or more words correct; the *instructional* level means getting 91–98 per cent correct; and the *frustration* level involves getting 90 per cent or less correct. This type of assessment therefore has direct implications for the level and type of reading material that children should be working on.

Readability assessment

The reading difficulty of texts can vary a great deal. In order for children to read independently, or to need only a low level of support, a text should be closely matched with their abilities – typically so that they can get about 95 per cent of the words correct in order to be at the instructional level. A measure of the level of difficulty of a text can help the teacher to select or to check reading material so that it is in the right range for pupils.

A reader's ability to manage text is affected by a number of measures. As shown in Figure 10.2, these include structural aspects such as sentence structure and the familiarity and complexity of words, as well as the physical properties of the text and how easy it is to understand the concepts involved.

Readability measures are usually based on equations that take into account the complexity of words and of sentence structures. They do so by using parameters such as the average number of syllables, the number of common words in a sentence or the average sentence length.

One of the more reliable of such measures is the Dale–Chall index (1948), which is based on average sentence length and the percentage of words outside a high-frequency list of 3,000 words. This has been shown to correlate at about 0.7 with the average judgements of reading difficulty by groups of teachers and pupils.

However, it can be difficult to calculate such measures without the use of a computer program and the keying in of large amounts of text. The Fry Readability Index (Fry, 1977) shown in Figure 10.3 overcomes this by using word and syllable counts which are then used to read off an approximate reading level. As well as being easy to apply, the Fry Index also covers the range of primary and secondary education and is one of the most popular of all such measures, with a study by Fry (1968) finding a correlation of 0.93 with reading comprehension. It is used as follows.

Randomly select three 100-word passages from a book or an article.

Plot the average number of syllables and the average number of sentences per 100 words on the graph in Figure 10.3 to determine the readability level of the material. Choose more passages per book if great variability is observed and conclude that the book has uneven readability.

Few passages will fall into the grey areas, but when they do, readability scores are invalid. To convert to the reading age in years, add five to the American grade (between the lines).

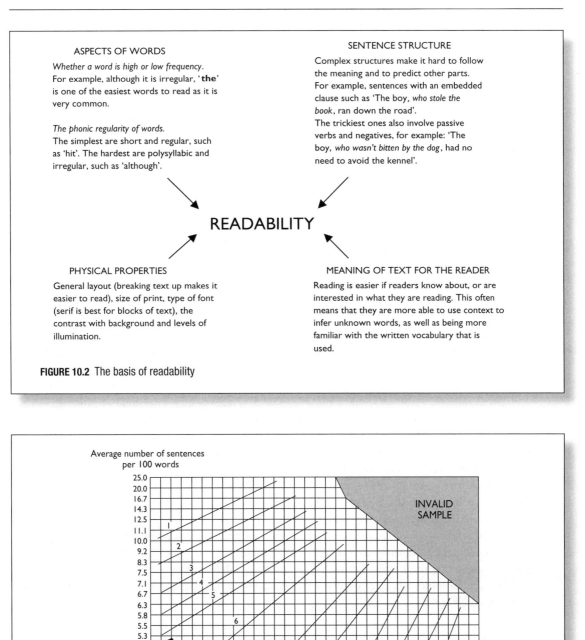

ASPECTS OF WORDS

Whether a word is high or low frequency.
For example, although it is irregular, '**the**' is one of the easiest words to read as it is very common.

The phonic regularity of words.
The simplest are short and regular, such as 'hit'. The hardest are polysyllabic and irregular, such as 'although'.

SENTENCE STRUCTURE

Complex structures make it hard to follow the meaning and to predict other parts. For example, sentences with an embedded clause such as 'The boy, *who stole the book*, ran down the road'.
The trickiest ones also involve passive verbs and negatives, for example: 'The boy, *who wasn't bitten by the dog*, had no need to avoid the kennel'.

READABILITY

PHYSICAL PROPERTIES

General layout (breaking text up makes it easier to read), size of print, type of font (serif is best for blocks of text), the contrast with background and levels of illumination.

MEANING OF TEXT FOR THE READER

Reading is easier if readers know about, or are interested in what they are reading. This often means that they are more able to use context to infer unknown words, as well as being more familiar with the written vocabulary that is used.

FIGURE 10.2 The basis of readability

Average number of sentences per 100 words

Approximate grade level (USA)

INVALID SAMPLE

INVALID SAMPLE

College

Average number of Syllables per 100 words

FIGURE 10.3 Readability chart (source: reproduced from Fry, 1977: 217)

Such measures have been heavily criticised by writers such as Goodman (1986) for their lack of consistency – limited agreement between different indices. It is also argued that they oversimplify the reading process because they fail to take account of the meaning of a text for the reader. Kintsch and Vipond (1979), for instance, found that one of the best predictors of readability was how often readers needed to search their long-term memory to enable them to make sense of what they were reading. It is also argued that readability indices encourage writing that simply involves short words and short sentences, and that such text can be stilted and actually more difficult to read.

An alternative approach, which directly links the difficulty of a text with potential readers, is the cloze procedure. Described by Rye (1982), this involves testing to see how well children can read text that has every fifth word deleted. As shown in Figure 10.4, the percentage of the missing words that the child is able to generate is then used to indicate the ease of reading and comprehension of the complete text.

Unfortunately, this approach is time-consuming and depends upon having access to the students you wish to match the text with. In a study that applied the simpler Fry and the Dale–Chall indices to ten English textbooks, Fusaro (1988) found that they gave similar results to each other and accurate grade levels. Applying the Fry Index to books from current popular schemes such as the Oxford Reading Tree also generally gives readability measures that are very close to the age levels at which they are aimed.

Although they may perhaps be only approximate measures, readabilities can be used to grade books in a library to guide 'free readers'. Without this check it is possible for children to choose books that are a poor match for their reading ability, or even for the overall level of books to be quite inappropriate. Hill (1981), for instance, found that most of the books in one particular primary school library had a readability level above 11 years, although the majority of the school's population had reading ages between 8 and 11 years. A book's readability level can also be used by teachers as a first indicator in placing a child on a reading scheme, provided that they already know the child's reading age.

A further use of readability is to check on the suitability of school textbooks. A study by Chiang-Soong and Yager (1993) used the Fry Readability Index on the 12 science textbooks that were most commonly used in schools. The findings from this study were typical, in that four of the books were found to be too difficult for their intended audience, which indicated that many children would have problems using them.

The difficulty of examination questions can also vary with readability. An investigation by Klare (1975) found that pupils could give a greater number of correct answers for a passage written in an easy style than if the style was more difficult to read (the subject content being kept the same). When preparing worksheets, teachers might therefore want to keep the readability level as low as possible. As previously mentioned, there are dangers in simply writing short sentences and using short words. A good technique is to think about your intended audience while writing.

When you have finished, a readability measure can check whether the level that you have achieved is approximately right.

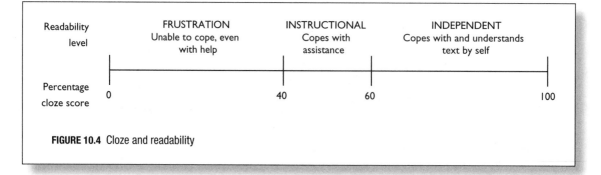

FIGURE 10.4 Cloze and readability

Summary

Literacy is a form of communication based on print and includes reading and writing skills. These are normally closely related, although writing can sometimes fall behind reading level. Home environments in the early years can impact on literacy development. Joint story-book reading is especially important at this stage, as is engaging in a range of joint literacy activities with parents. Reading acquisition is characterised by three phases of development: an initial stage of memorising words holistically, followed by a stage of alphabetic learning, and then a more advanced stage of processing longer strings of letters which commonly co-occur. Skilled reading is perhaps best characterised as a dual-route process, in which words may be processed by reference to a mental lexicon of familiar words and word meanings, or decoded letter by letter. Reading comprehension may be seen as the goal of reading processes but some children show specific difficulties with comprehending what they read. Such children show particular difficulties in making inferences between sentences.

Reading tuition may take one of two forms: phonics or 'real books'. A phonic approach focuses on teaching the sounds in spoken English and showing how these map on to letter combinations. A 'real books' approach takes a psycholinguistic view, and sees reading as a natural process which does not need to be explicitly 'taught'. Recent research suggests that the best approach is to teach phonics in the context of exposure to real books, but emphasises the need for phonic approaches to be incorporated.

Children may have reading difficulties because they have generally poor ability levels, because they are underachieving or because they have a specific learning difficulty such as dyslexia. Dyslexia is a neurological syndrome, and is usually identified by assessing a child's IQ, which is interpreted as indicating the child's potential to learn to read. If there is a significant difference between their IQ and their reading attainment, accompanied by an uneven profile of cognitive ability as indicated on the IQ sub-tests, then an assessment of dyslexia is usually applied. Reading difficulties in general appear to be characterised by a phonological deficit, and there is some evidence of a deficit in the automatisation of learned behaviours in some children. Children with reading difficulties can be helped by structured phonic programmes. Children with developmental dyslexia may require programmes that are multi-sensory in nature in order to learn letter–sound correspondences effectively.

The use of literacy tests can help teachers to match learning experiences with children's needs. Such tests can be carried out with individuals or groups and may involve either normative or criterion-referenced comparisons. The usefulness of tests such as diagnostic assessments depends very much on whether they are based on appropriate models of the reading process. The readability of texts depends on a number of factors but can be estimated using measures such as equations based on word and sentence length. These can be useful to match reading materials with children's abilities.

Key implications

- An important emphasis in early reading should be on developing the rapid identification of words.
- A child starting to read is helped by the ability to analyse and to combine the various sounds that are represented by letters. Children should then be encouraged to read children's literature, rather than reading schemes.
- Literacy difficulties benefit from joint literacy activities in the home and can possibly be prevented by the general use of structured teaching.
- Parents engaged in joint story-book reading should be encouraged to use dialogic prompts to engage their children in the text they are reading together for the best benefits.

- The type of phonics used when teaching is not necessarily important, as long as some form of structured phonic intervention is presented. However, there is some evidence that learning the most frequent letter–sound combinations first will offer the most effective approach initially.
- Recent definitions of dyslexia consider that it has little to do with intelligence, but can be considered as a failure to develop word reading and/or spelling despite appropriate learning opportunities.
- Reading difficulties generally are characterised by phonological deficits, and these can be remediated with appropriate phonic tuition.

Further reading

Cain (2010), *Reading Development and Difficulties*: a good, balanced introduction to research on all aspects of reading development and reading difficulties written by a key researcher in the field.

Hall (2003), *Listening to Stephen Read: Multiple Perspectives on Literacy*: this book centres on a case study of a child who is underachieving in literacy, and presents a range of different perspectives on understanding what may be going on in this case by asking different educationalists to comment on what they think could be done to support him. It presents psycholinguistic perspectives alongside cognitive, social and political ones, and is an interesting exploration of the range of issues impacting on children's literacy development.

Snowling and Hulme (eds) (2005), *The Science of Reading: a Handbook*: a state-of-the-art reference text by leading researchers in the field, that includes review chapters on all aspects of reading, including teaching/intervention.

Wood and Connelly (eds) (2009), *Contemporary Perspectives on Reading and Spelling*: this text attempts to both give an overview of research in the area of literacy, whilst tackling some of the problems and unresolved debates in the area.

Discussion of practical scenario

During his time in school, James has made less than half the normal rate of reading progress. To improve his progress will probably need a significant change. At James's reading level, he is still developing word attack skills. One key alteration would be to ensure that he works on his reading more often to generate greater fluency with these. It is possible that after a year of more-intensive support he could break through to a level where his verbal abilities would help his reading. Reading should be closely matched to his level of attainments (95 per cent-plus accuracy) and linked with a more advanced phonics programme, and with spelling techniques if necessary (the learning support teacher could advise on these).

A particular diagnosis is of use only if it implies a different teaching approach. According to the definition used by the Division of Educational and Child Psychology of the British Psychological Society ('failure to progress despite learning opportunities'), he does have dyslexia, but effective teaching approaches are the same for all children with problems with literacy.

If James had a Statement, this would almost certainly help since it should bring additional support. However, getting one will depend on the criteria applied by the education authority. A reading age of seven years at ten years of age is at the bottom 5 per cent level, and Statements are usually given only to children in the lowest 2 per cent. Some authorities would also take a pupil's general ability into account, although that is not part of the DECP definition.

11

Inclusive education and special educational needs

Practical scenario

A new family has just moved into the catchment of St Marshall's Junior School and the parents have approached the head teacher about their daughter Susan attending there. Susan has Down syndrome and previously attended a special school for children with learning difficulties. Although she has limited educational attainments, she is sociable and has basic language abilities. The school are concerned about whether they can meet Susan's needs or whether she would be better off in a school that has specialist teachers and resources.

- How would Susan benefit from going to St Marshall's?
- What support could Susan expect to help her in school?
- What would be the problems? How might the class teacher feel?
- Do you think that the school might benefit from Susan going there?
- What benefits would Susan gain from attending a special school?

This chapter aims to provide information that would help answer these questions.

Special educational needs and inclusive education

The term 'special educational needs' arose following the Warnock Committee's report on education for 'handicapped' children (DES, 1978) and the subsequent 1981 Education Act. The report rejected the previous categorisation of children in terms of 'handicap', and introduced a notion of individual 'need'. Any child might have special educational needs, at some point, during their school career and they estimated that this flexible and broader approach would be relevant for about 20 per cent of children. The expectation was that, where possible, children should now be educated in mainstream classes and schools. Subsequent guidance for schools has shaped the ways in which they work with children with special educational needs, for example the *Code of Practice on the Assessment and Identification of Special Educational Needs* (DfEE, 1994b). This guidance was updated in 2001 at the same time as, and influenced by, the Special Educational Needs and Disability Act (SENDA) (2001).

> Changes as a result of SENDA have been taken into account and these include: a stronger right for children with special educational needs to be educated at a mainstream school; new duties on LEAs to arrange for parents of children with special educational needs to be provided with services offering advice and information and a means of resolving disputes; a new duty on schools and relevant nursery education providers to tell parents when they are making special educational provision for their child; and a new right for schools and relevant nursery education providers to request a statutory assessment of a child.
>
> (Barron *et al.*, 2007: 6)

This emphasis on rights and a mainstream education for all children can be seen as reflecting an international movement of developing inclusive educational systems.

Inclusive education

The movement towards inclusive schools and inclusive classrooms can be seen as a worldwide phenomenon which has become increasingly significant over the last decade (Mittler, 2004). Inclusive education is underpinned by a belief in children's rights and in equal educational opportunities and access for all learners (UNESCO, 2000). This was encapsulated in the Universal Declaration of Human Rights, which states that there is 'a growing consensus that all children have the right to be educated together, regardless of their physical, intellectual, emotional, social, linguistic or other condition, and that inclusion makes good educational and social sense' (UNESCO, 1999: 9).

The outcome of this stance has been a move towards 'mainstreaming' groups of children who might previously been excluded from mainstream classrooms. This is more than simply integration, in which the child is placed in a mainstream setting and given support to help them 'fit in'. Rather, an inclusive approach is one in which the school and its practices develop in a way to accommodate a diverse range of learners.

This international development has been expressed at national levels in a range of policies. (For example Department for Education and Skills (DfES) (2001); Special Education Needs and Disability Act (2001); Standards in Scotland's Schools Act (2000) and, in the United States of America, The Education for All Handicapped Pupils Act (PL-94–142) and Individuals with Disabilities Education Act (PL99–457) (cited in Lindsay, 2007). There has also been statutory Inclusion Guidance (DfES, 2001a) and the 'Removing Barriers to Achievements' strategy (DfES, 2004c)). Overall, these policies support the view that all children have the right to be educated on equal terms with their peers and contemporaries.

The Special Educational Needs and Disability Act (2001) states that mainstream placement curriculum is the default position unless parents do not wish this or it is incompatible with 'the provision of efficient education for other children' (p. 9). There is also an expectation that psychologists will work in ways that will support inclusive educational practices and that this goes beyond a focus on special needs or difficulties in learning. This wider view of inclusion is illustrated in the British Psychological Society (2005) position paper to inform the practice of psychologists in relation to inclusive education. It states the following principles:

> Rejecting segregation or exclusion of learners for whatever reason – ability, gender, language, care status, family income, disability, sexuality, colour, religion or ethnic origin;
> Maximising the participation of all learners in the community schools of their choice;
> Making learning more meaningful and relevant for all, particularly those learners most vulnerable to exclusionary pressure;
> Rethinking and restructuring policies, curricula, culture and practices in schools and learning environments so that diverse learning needs can be met, whatever the origin or nature of those needs.
>
> (p. 2)

A key contribution of psychologists working in education is in supporting the development of schools and educational institutions as inclusive environments (British Psychological Society, 2005). In doing this, they might be seen as foregrounding an organisational, or systemic, rather than individualised special needs approach. This level of working has parallels with the Index for Inclusion (Booth and Ainscow, 2002) which supports schools in developing their inclusive practice through reflection on pupils' 'presence, participation and achievement' (Hick *et al.*, 2009). This approach sees inclusion as a process of increasing participation, for all students, in the curriculum, and also the cultures and communities of local schools (Ainscow *et al.*, 2006).

Is inclusive education effective?

An important question within this field is whether pupils with special educational needs require specialised teaching approaches and strategies (e.g. Howley and Kime, 2003). Teachers commonly report this belief (Ring and Travers, 2005) and it is a belief that often underpins the provision of segregated teaching (Skrtic, 1991). One way in which this issue has been considered is through research that identifies whether inclusive or separate 'special' education settings produce the best outcomes for children with special educational needs. This type of research occurs because:

> Despite a move toward inclusion being the most significant trend across OECD countries, and widespread belief in the social and emotional advantages of inclusion, the academic consequences of educating students with special needs in inclusive rather than separate settings remain contested.
>
> (Canadian Council on Learning, 2009: 2)

A systematic review of international research looked at the educational outcomes for children placed in special and mainstream settings (Canadian Council on Learning, 2009) and calculated the *effect sizes* found in the studies. The evidence indicated that inclusive settings appeared favourable for pupils across a range of special educational needs and the review concluded:

> All else equal, inclusive settings appear not to academically disadvantage most students with special educational needs (SEN). In many cases they appear to offer an advantage over separate settings. The balance of evidence shows favourable academic outcomes for students with SEN educated in inclusive settings. However, these results are not homogenous and effects are generally small in magnitude. These two caveats suggest that, while inclusive settings are generally preferable, factors other than classroom setting (instructional quality is the most immediately obvious factor) are probably more important determinants of SEN students' academic success.
>
> (p. 7)

Other comparative research, which looks at the outcomes associated with educational placement, has produced similar findings. Some report significant benefits for students in inclusive settings, whilst others have found no specific benefits from segregated special education (President's Commission on Excellence in Special Education, 2002). A longitudinal study compared the development of young people with Down syndrome in mainstream and special education classrooms. It found that the pupils progressed in both settings but that there were large, significant gains in language and communications skills for those pupils in mainstream settings, which did not occur in the special classrooms (Buckley *et al.*, 2007).

Activity

This type of outcomes-based research examines the question of inclusive education from an efficacy perspective (Dyson, 1999), i.e. using empirical evidence to judge its social or educational effect. However, the origins of inclusive education are founded on human rights.

Do you feel that this type of evidence as 'justification' is actually needed to support the idea that children should learn together?

Would you agree that separate can never be equal?

To what extent is inclusive education happening?

The vision of inclusive education that was proposed in the UNESCO Salamanca statement and subsequent policies clearly sees all children learning together. However, the definition of inclusive education within national policies is less clear-cut and is something that has been contested. The ubiquitous nature of these policies means that most people working in education will be familiar with the term 'inclusive education'. However, actual definitions of inclusive education, within the UK, and what this mean in practice have been changing and confusing, and the extent to which education for all pupils in regular mainstream classes is actually supported is likely to remain a focus of political debate. There is a common perception that inclusive education has resulted in the closure of many segregated special education schools in the United Kingdom (BBC, 2005). Indeed in 1987 there were 1,470 special schools and this subsequently fell to 1,148 by 2004 (DfES, 2004). But this fall needs to be considered in the light of falling pupil numbers nationally (Hansard, 2005a, b) and the development of Pupil Referral Units. These Units are designed for children and young people who, due to mainstream exclusion or ill-health, cannot attend their local school or special school. They do not have to deliver the National Curriculum and might be seen as offering a form of segregated special education. Between 2001–2003 the proportion of pupils in Pupil Referral Units rose by 25 per cent (Ofsted, 2004, in Barron *et al.*, 2007). Taking this assumption into account suggests a slight increase (6 per cent in 2005) in special schools at a time of decreasing school numbers elsewhere (Sheehy and Duffy, 2009). Research studies typically reveal an awareness of the potential benefits of inclusion but find little change in the numbers of children with special educational needs in mainstream schools or in the proportion of children in special schools (Barron *et al.*, 2007).

In seeking to explain this lack of change, Hick (2009) notes how the government's strategy of special education needs becomes one whose stated aim is to 'Break down the divide between mainstream and special schools to create a unified system where all school and their pupils are included within the wider community of schools' (DFES, 2004: 38, in Hicks, 2009: 167). This indicates a reconstruction of inclusive education that incorporates and maintains segregated special schools. In this context, inclusive education could mean mixed-ability groups within special schools. Internationally, the terms 'inclusive education' and 'special education' have become used interchangeably. There is also the issue of what is happening within classroom themselves. Ramjhun (2001) noted that, whilst documents and educational officers might use terms associated with inclusive education, within classrooms the language of individuals with specific needs (i.e. problems being located 'within' the child) was more commonly found.

Practical implications

People may use the term 'inclusive education' in different ways.

These different meanings may produce very different ways of thinking about how and where children should learn.

When discussing inclusive education with others, it is therefore necessary to find out what the term means for them.

Concepts of special educational needs: definitions of difference

Whilst the concept of special educational needs, as originally proposed, can be seen as supporting an environmental perspective, there remains a need to consider the degree of progress or attainment of children within this context. This assessment can be carried out in several ways, and how we conceptualise these differences in progress or attainment is a key part of how we respond to children with special educational needs.

Special needs as a continuum

The distributions of the various types of abilities or problems that are relevant to education are almost invariably continuous, without any evident part that can be labelled as special in some way. As examples of this, the plots shown in Figure 11.1 are based on data from the manuals for Behavioural Problems – from the Bristol Social Adjustment Guides (Stott, 1987) – and Reading Ability – from the British Ability Scales (Elliott *et al.*, 1996). If there were parts of these curves that were a separate 'special needs' population, then there would be a discontinuity or a 'bulge' somewhere in the lower range; however, these plots show continuous and smooth curves. The only exception to this general principle happens with the distribution of general intelligence, where there is a small 'bump' somewhere below the IQ 50 level.

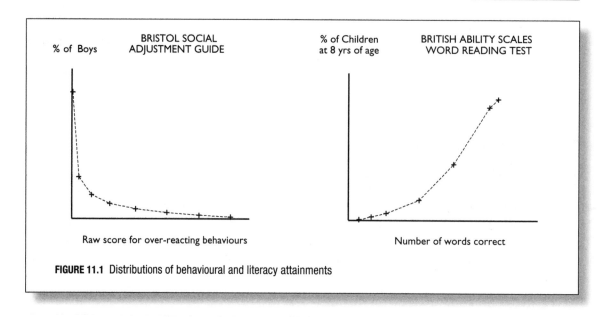

FIGURE 11.1 Distributions of behavioural and literacy attainments

A plausible explanation for this is the presence of specific biological problems such as brain damage or genetic disorders, which would account for only a small proportion of the overall 'special needs population'.

If we were looking to identify a group of pupils who might require additional support or prioritised intervention, one might look along this continuum and select a 'cut-off point'. At one time, schools tended to rely heavily on the use of cut-off points on standardised tests, particularly of reading attainment, in identifying children's SEN. The idea has persisted in the long-standing practice in primary schools that a reading 'age' lag of two years is seen as a 'watershed' for identifying primary-school children with reading difficulties that require additional support (Croll and Moses, 2003). The General Certificate of Secondary Education (GCSE) examination system, used in England, Wales and Northern Ireland, was developed as an 'inclusive' qualification for a wide range of pupils and a candidate's Reading Age of under ten years has been used as a criterion for providing a reader (Woods, 2007).

Special needs as a criterion

Although Warnock's 'cut-off point' at the bottom 20 per cent level appears to be a useful guide for establishing a level of moderate needs, this was based only on studies of teachers' subjective opinions. It is therefore likely that the figure was affected by what teachers considered realistic. This could only have been a relative judgement and might just as easily have been 30 per cent or 10 per cent if more or fewer special-needs resources had been available at the time of the report.

An alternative statistical approach that has been used to define more severe special needs is a criterion of the bottom two standard deviation points of the distribution of a particular ability. If the ability you are looking at has a normal distribution, this identifies a percentage (about 2 per cent) that is not far different from the proportion of children who are in special schools. In fact, Gipps and Stobart (1990) discovered that this figure (which corresponds to an IQ figure of 70) was originally advocated as a criterion by Cyril Burt, the first educational psychologist, who was employed by the former

London County Council. The reason he gave for doing this was as follows: 'For immediate practical purposes the only satisfactory definition of mental deficiency is a percentage definition *based on the amount of existing accommodation*' (Burt, 1921: 167; my italics). It is only from then onwards that quotients of 70 (which correspond to two standard deviations below the norm) were taken to imply some critical level of need. It can be seen, then, that this is essentially an arbitrary level, and again is really dependent only on the level of special-needs provision available.

Special needs as functional abilities

In order to arrive at a more meaningful definition of special needs, some workers, such as Hillerich (1976), have attempted to relate skills to the ability to function in school or within society. Applying this approach to literacy, Hillerich identifies key points along a continuum of skills (Figure 11.2). Using this, one could argue that 'use for basic life functions' should be a minimum level for as many people as possible. This would involve the ability to use key signs for information, such as danger signals or public facilities. In fact, children who would have difficulties eventually achieving this level would normally be recognised as having special educational needs, within the category of 'moderate or severe learning difficulties'. Above this level, the criteria for special needs become more difficult to define, although 'Use for social concerns' should also perhaps be a desirable outcome for the majority of people and could be a reason for identifying special needs. This might involve the ability to read basic newspapers, reading and writing letters, and filling out forms. A study in 1995 of 1,714 adults aged 37 from the long-term National Child Development Study by Bynner and Parsons (1997) found that many people failed to achieve these skills, with 6 per cent scoring below the nine-year level on such basic literacy tasks.

Table 11.1 illustrates the varying levels, as children progress through the educational system, of functional reading problems from the norms of current reading tests. Some people might say that things were better in the past and that these levels are simply evidence for lowered standards. However, a long-term review of the scores after the end of the Second World War found that reading levels had hardly changed (National Commission on Education, 1995). More recently in England and Wales, the National Literacy Strategy has provided focused daily instruction across all classrooms. The effectiveness of this practice has been the source of some debate (Jama and Dugdale, 2010), but it appears that at age 11 approximately 20 per cent of children have not achieved success in reading (and writing), i.e. reading at an age-appropriate level. Unfortunately, even if things are not actually getting worse, the levels of reading problems still mean that a number of children will have difficulties with tasks that are important for them.

The reading age needed for daily tabloid newspapers is from about the 12-year level upwards, with many passages such as descriptions of football skills exceeding this by a wide margin. These levels are evidently beyond the capabilities of a significant number of children at the end of their schooling, and, as mentioned above, many adults fail to make any further progress after leaving school.

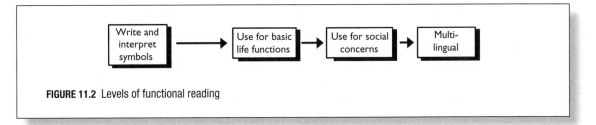

FIGURE 11.2 Levels of functional reading

TABLE 11.1 Level of reading ability at different stages of the education system

Stage	Levels of reading ability
End of infant schooling, age 7½	About one in 25 children will have failed to have made significant progress and will still be reading below the six-year level.
End of junior schooling, age 11½	About one in 20 children will still not be (basic) free readers, with a reading age of eight years or below.
End of secondary schooling, age 16½	About one in 20 children will have a reading age of ten years or below; one in eight children will have a reading age of 12 years or below.

An area in which the assessment of functional abilities is commonly found is for pupils with severe and profound learning difficulties. For example, the EQUALS Key Skills Framework (2009) regards the National Curriculum as being too focused on subject knowledge. This approach seeks to assess and develop key skills, i.e. essential skills for everyday life. These skills are used to define the pupil's educational needs and these areas are addressed across the curriculum areas.

Within-child perspectives

The use of ability measures such as IQ testing, and placing children into special-needs categories, tend to locate the explanation for special needs within the child. A strong 'within-child' belief would be that such difficulties have a biological basis and that little can be done to overcome them. If this is the case, then special education can have only a coping function, educating children at their level and allowing them to achieve only up to their supposedly limited potential.

At the lower end of the ability range, below an IQ of 50, there is strong evidence that many children do have intrinsic biological problems. Simonoff et al. (1996), for instance, review evidence that about one-third of individuals with severe learning difficulties have a known genetic abnormality (such as Down syndrome) and about one-fifth have multiple congenital anomalies, with most of the remainder having some clear evidence of brain damage. However, the majority of children above this level who have moderate learning difficulties do not have any known physical problems, although Simonoff et al. argue that unidentified genetic conditions such as the fragile X syndrome also exist within the moderate learning difficulties population and may lead to a reduction in IQ levels.

In a review of the processes that maintain disadvantage in society, Rutter and Madge (1976) argue that there is a strong heritable basis for general intelligence, and that this has a significant effect on learning at the lower end of the normal range. Research on the similarity of IQ of family members is consistent with this belief, and indicates that the general heritability of intelligence across the range is about 50 per cent. However, as was noted in Chapter 4, the studies on which this finding is based can be criticised for not taking sufficient account of environmental effects, and the level of heritability of intelligence for the majority of children with special needs therefore remains a controversial area.

A within-child measure commonly used in schools is the CAT (Cognitive Abilities Test) test, which is used on over one-million children each year (Deary et al., 2007). It provides schools with standardised measures of pupil's verbal, quantitative and non-verbal reasoning abilities and has a high correlation with IQ scores (Simonoff et al., 2006). Schools typically consider these results to be an accurate predicator of examination performance, when taken at 11, for exams occurring several years later (Galloway, 2009), and teachers often see this as indicating a child's 'potential' for learning: 'Now we do know the child's true ability because we do cognitive ability testing here' (Teacher, in Ireson *et al.*, 2002: 172).

The results of a large (over 70,000 English-school pupils) longitudinal study supports this belief, finding a correlation between CATs and subsequent examination performance (Deary *et al.*, 2007). These test results can be used to 'stream' pupils within schools, to target additional support (Hart *et al.*, 2004) and are also used by some local authorities to allocate funding resources to schools (Florian, 2007). However, once allocated to a stream, pupils tend to remain there (Ireson *et al.*, 2002). Although such tests may have merit in predicting later performance in subject examinations, it may be that this is because the same social processes continue to operate, rather than children being intellectually 'set' by 11 years of age (Hart *et al.*, 2004).

Gender may also affect special educational needs since boys tend to be over-represented in most measures of special provision. A review by Male (1996), for example, found that more than twice as many boys as girls were attending schools for children with moderate learning difficulties. A similar ratio is found in mainstream schools (Dyson and Gallannaugh, 2008). This higher proportion could be interpreted as being due to some underlying biological difference that affects learning, such as the known greater vulnerability of the male foetus to various stresses. However, evidence reviewed in Chapter 7 indicates that there are alternative plausible explanations based on the cultural effects of boys being less actively involved in the educational process. The disproportional representation of particular groups within the special education system has also been noted. For example, Travellers and Black Caribbean children appear to have relatively high levels of being identified as having special educational needs. Dyson and Gallannaugh (2008) explored how minority ethnic groups varied regarding the type of special educational needs that were identified.

The 'normative' disability of visual impairment, identified through relatively objective diagnostic criteria, produces no significant differences between minority groups (except in some specific geographical locations, influenced by an increased rate of consanguineous marriages). These differences are found in the identification of moderate learning difficulties and behavioural, social and emotional difficulties, both of which are less clear-cut and rely more on professional judgement (Dyson and Gallannaugh, 2008).

Less strong 'within-child' views of the basis of general special needs see difficulties as the outcome of stable individual abilities, whatever the cause. Therefore, children with low educational achievements can be seen as having limited general knowledge and understanding, poor general motivation and ineffective learning styles. If these are likely to be long-term characteristics, then they can be taken to imply the need for long-term differences in the type of education that they should receive.

Environmental perspectives

If one excludes those children who have a known physical basis for their difficulties, the majority of children with special needs are consistently found to come from the more deprived sectors of the community. In an analysis of national level data, Strand and Lindsay (2009) examined the Pupil Level Annual School Census for 6.5 million students aged 5–16 in England. Their analysis looked at the factors that were most strongly associated with the identification of special educational needs. They found disproportionate representation of minority ethnic groups, but their further analysis revealed that poverty and gender had 'stronger associations than ethnicity with the overall prevalence of SEN' (p. 2).

This type of evidence is well established. Dunn (1968), for example, argued that moderate learning difficulties were mainly the outcome of social deprivation and that the process of (segregated) special education was not justified as it was effectively discriminatory. However, if special needs are the outcome of a limited home background, it may still be justifiable to attempt to make up for this with whatever form of provision is most effective.

Early compensatory programmes for disadvantaged children, such as the Head Start project in the United States, did not initially appear to be effective, and led Jensen (1973) to conclude that low educational attainments were mainly the result of inherited abilities. There have been mixed results from subsequent evaluations. Barnett (1995) found long-term positive effects and identified that a critical aspect was the involvement of parents. Clark (1983) carried out a comparison analysis of the home processes in socially and economically disadvantaged homes, where children were deemed either successful or unsuccessful in school. This study found that the home lives of all of the unsuccessful children were characterised by much higher levels of social stress, with loose social ties between parents and children, and with limited effective support for education. The Head Start Impact Study (2005), commissioned by the US Congress, suggested small to moderate positive effects, but noted variation among minority groups and how early the intervention began. In the United Kingdom, the Sure Start programme was an initiative by the then Labour Government. It began in 2001 and was focused on children living in the most deprived neighbourhoods in England. It expanded quickly to other areas. By 2004, 400,000 children under four and their families were directly involved in this focused expansion of services and policies.

The National Evaluation of Sure Start (NESS, 2008) noted the complexity of the intervention, as financial support was given to services but the particular intervention methods to follow were not specified. The programme was evaluated through a range of measures, including parental reports, observation, and cognitive, emotional and physical health assessments of children. Whilst the initial outcomes were modest, or non-significant, the longer-term evidence suggests that benefits are developing over time (Melhuish et al., 2008). As we have seen, parental involvement affects language development, general learning style and achievements with basic academic skills. The effects of this appear to be cumulative, and where there might be only minor developmental and cognitive differences between children from different social classes before about 18 months of age, children in deprived social groupings then fall progressively further behind the longer they are in such home environments (Clarke and Clarke, 1974). Regarding Sure Start, Anning and NESS (2007, cited in Siraj-Blatchford and Siraj-Blatchford, 2009) found that certain common characteristics of interventions were associated with better than expected outcomes for children. These included appropriate specialist interventions being delivered as early as possible and the provision of family-based support. This suggests that effective support programmes are those that acknowledge the interaction between within-child and environmental factors.

Interactions and limits to progress

Rutter and Madge (1976) argue that such environmental effects can interact with inherited abilities, generating a 'cycle of disadvantage' as parents with low abilities provide an unstimulating environment for their children, who will in turn raise their own children in similar circumstances. There is also some evidence from Plomin (1995) that the environment of children can itself be modified by their genetic potential. This can happen if an inherited disorder means that children are not very responsive, since their parents will often reduce their level of involvement as a result of the low level of feedback they receive.

When children who face barriers to learning fail to make progress in school, their lack of progress can also lead to different educational experiences. For instance, they may be placed in low sets or even into segregated special education. Although these are normally justified as providing education that is matched to children's attainments and rate of progress, this provision may actually result in a rather restrictive and unstimulating environment. There is evidence, covered in previous chapters, that pupils can make less progress in these situations, owing for instance to the limited verbal abilities of other pupils, reduced expectations from teachers, and the poor self-perceptions and negative social groupings that can arise.

Failure to make progress with basic skills such as reading can also limit a pupil's progress with general knowledge and understanding. Lack of progress can also have negative effects on attribution and motivation – failure leading to apathy and withdrawal from learning situations. Similarly negative interaction effects might occur between learning and behaviour, as limited success leads to disaffection, reactive behaviour and reduced involvement and success in learning. However, there does not appear to be a strong independent effect of learning failure on behaviour, although they probably share similar causes.

The term 'Additional Learning Needs' is commonly used in regard of education funding to support children from significantly disadvantaged backgrounds with special educational and English-language needs.

The law

Various forms of legislation have attempted to make provision for special educational needs and inclusive education. Much of the present philosophy comes from the Warnock Report (Special Educational Needs, 1978), which attempted to set up meaningful descriptions of needs, rather than simple categories, and to identify the proportion of children with such needs. The report found that, at the time, separate special educational provision was catering for 1.8 per cent of the school population, and it also reviewed the existing knowledge about what proportion of children had some form of special needs. In particular, it looked at how many children teachers felt would benefit from additional provision. From this, it identified one-in-five (20 per cent) of all children as needing some form of special educational provision at some time during their school career. The problem with the legal definition of 'special needs' is that it is open to various interpretations since the term 'significant' does not have an exact meaning. In a statistical sense, it means 'unlikely to happen by chance', but here it refers to whether there is a difference that is meaningful in some way. This is because schools have different levels of resources, and 'having special needs' is often just defined as 'needing help that is not normally available'.

The resulting legal guidance has developed differently across the world and even within different parts of the United Kingdom. To illustrate some key concepts, what we provide here is therefore an outline of the law, as it stands, within parts of the United Kingdom. However, it is worth checking on the appropriate government website for the changes in detail and new legislation. The guidance and legislation that supports Government policy is referred to as 'the inclusion framework', and new policies are added to this to develop the framework (for example, *Inclusive Schooling: Children with Special Educational Needs*, DfES, 2001a and *Removing Barriers to Achievement*, DfES, 2004c).

The law in England and Wales

The 1981 Act introduced 'Statements of Special Educational Need'. These legal documents describe both the difficulties experienced by the pupils and the responses that are required to deal with them.

The subsequent Education Act 1993 of England and Wales addressed the same issues and used the same definitions of 'learning difficulty' and 'special educational needs'.

The 1996 Education Act, Section 312(2) identified a child as having special needs if 'he has a significantly greater difficulty in learning than the majority of children of his age'. This could lead to the education authority maintaining a Statement of Special Educational Needs, which is a document that describes a child's needs and how they will be met. As discussed later, getting a 'Statement' is an important way in which children can gain extra educational support, and guidance on the implementation of the law to achieve this is set out in *Special Educational Needs Code of Practice* (DfES, 2001c). This is a graduated approach with three stages.

Within this legal framework, pupils are deemed to have special educational needs if they have 'learning difficulties or disabilities that make it harder for them to learn than most pupils of the same age' (DCSF, 2009). In England, 1.7 million children fall into this category, i.e. about one in five children (DCSF, 2009). Pupils within this large group can fall into three categories, reflecting the level of support that is provided for them within schools.

- *School Action* – where extra or different help is given, from that provided as part of the school's usual curriculum.
- *School Action Plus* – where the class teacher and the SENCO★ receive advice or support from outside specialists (the specialist teacher, an educational psychologist, a speech and language therapist or other health professionals).
- *Statement* – a pupil has a Statement of Special Educational Needs when a formal assessment has been made. A document setting out the child's needs and the extra help they should receive is in place.

(DCSF, 2009)

In 2009, there were over 222,000 with Statements of Special Educational Needs, i.e. 2.7 per cent of all pupils in comparison to 1,434,000 pupils with SEN but without Statements across England. This is approximately 8 per cent of all pupils. There is evidence that the number of pupils at the three levels is increasing, from 18 per cent in 2005 to 21 per cent in 2009 (DCFS, 2009). Whilst the above definitions are based on the level of response, there is also explicit acknowledgement in legislation of different areas of need – these are often described as primary needs and relate to categories of impairment or disability. For example, 'language and communication needs' is the most common type of primary need in Statements for primary-school pupils (24.0 per cent) and 'severe learning difficulties' is the most common type of primary need in Statemented special-school pupils (23.6 per cent).

This definition has been criticised for being open to different interpretations by education authorities (Audit Commission, 1992; Simmons *et al.*, 2006). This has meant that, whilst the 1993 Act gave LEAs responsibility for providing and managing special education provision, how they respond varies in detail across England and Wales (Education Select Committee, 2006; Simmons *et al.*, 2006). The statutory guidance given in *Inclusive Schooling: Children with Special Educational Needs* (DfES, 2001a) had attempted to tighten up the definitions and ensure that inclusive education was supported at local-authority level. However 'the failure of some local authorities to fulfil their legal responsibilities remains a critical issue for parents of pupils with special educational needs and their supporters (House of Commons, 2006)' (Simmons *et al.*, 2006: 9).

The education of children with special needs may therefore involve resources and expertise that would not be part of the range of normal provision. The aims of this support are to allow children with these needs to benefit appropriately from their educational experiences. Educational psychologists have a major role in identifying children's special educational needs, and advising on ways in which they can be helped. Consequently, Educational Psychologists can also be involved in appeals to a Special Educational Needs and Disability Tribunal (SENDIST). This tribunal has the power to change the Statements that are written for children, and psychologists can find themselves acting on behalf of the parents or their employer, usually a local authority. The outcomes of the tribunal are legally binding (Simmons *et al.*, 2006). The tribunals have slightly different remits within England, Wales and Northern Ireland.

The Code of Practice

On 1 January 2002, a new *Special Educational Needs Code of Practice* (DfES, 2001c) came into effect in England. This replaced the 1994 version (DfEE, 1994b) and covered both Special Educational Needs and the Disability Act 2001 (SENDA) (Simmons *et al.*, 2006). The *Special Educational Needs Code of Practice* (DfES, 2001c) does not mention 'inclusion' but emphasises mainstream education for pupils with SEN. The Special Educational Needs and Disability Tribunal (SENDIST) use the *Code of Practice* (DRC, 2002) to inform discussion regarding disability discrimination. Simmons *et al.* (2006) describe several principles underpinning the code:

- a child with special educational needs should have their needs met;
- the special educational needs of children will normally be met in mainstream schools or settings;
- the views of the child should be sought and taken into account;
- parents have a vital role to play in supporting their child's education;
- children with special educational needs should be offered full access to a broad, balanced and relevant education, including an appropriate curriculum for the foundation stage and the National Curriculum.

(p. 17)

The education authority has a duty to identify, assess, issue a Statement where appropriate and arrange appropriate special education provision. The SEN Code of Practice for Wales (2002) is based on broadly similar lines, as is the Code of Practice in Northern Ireland (DENI, 2005). *Removing Barriers to Achievement* (DfES, 2004c) acts to strengthen the polices that comprised the 'inclusion framework' and statutory guidance *Inclusive Schooling: Children with Special Educational Needs* (DfES, 2001a). In particular, it seeks to intervene early and remove barriers to learning that children may experience.

There have also been initiatives to support educational inclusion within a broader social context. Most significantly, *Every Child Matters* (DfES, 2003a, 2004a) seeks to create better 'joined-up' working between the various children's services in order to reduce the incidence of children experiencing educational failure, suffering from ill-health, becoming teenage parents or engaging in anti-social or offending behaviour (DfES, 2003a). It proposes five key outcomes (for children's services to address) in relation to children's well-being: being healthy; staying safe; enjoying and achieving; making a positive contribution; and economic well-being. This is an important initiative given the link between social factors such as poverty and occurrence of special educational needs, and levels of educational attainment (DSCF, 2009). The legislation to support the achievement of these objectives is within The Children's Act 2004.

The law in Scotland

In Scotland the concept of 'Additional Support Needs' is used. This follows from the Education (Additional Support for Learning) (Scotland) Act 2004 and is defined as 'where, for whatever reason, the child or young person is, or is likely to be, unable without the provision of additional support to benefit from school education provided or to be provided for the child or young person' (2:1). The intention is strongly inclusive, seeking to bring a wider group of children within the legal framework and offer them appropriate education within mainstream settings. Pupils' Learning Support Needs might arise from the interaction of factors such as their learning environment, family circumstances, disability or health needs, or social and emotional factors (Section 11, ASL Act, 2004).

In the United States, there has been a drive to improve the educational outcomes for children with learning difficulties through educational reform. Kutash *et al.* (2009) describe how the No Child Left Behind Act (US Department of Education, 2002) uses the term 'evidence-based practice' 110 times, and that the report of the President's Commission on Excellence in Special Education (PCESE, 2002) seeks to develop improved instruction based on research. This suggests that psychological research into classroom practices that support inclusive education are likely to become increasingly important. Therefore, in this chapter, as elsewhere in the book, we draw on research findings to underpin our discussion.

Categories of special needs

Warnock's original conceptualisation of special educational needs was an attempt to move away from identifying children in terms of a single attribute, score, disability or simplistic groupings of children within categories such as 'Educationally Sub-Normal (Moderate)', which merely recorded the fact that they are not coping with normal work, and towards terms such as 'Moderate Learning Difficulties', which puts more of an emphasis on pupils' learning needs. SEN was seen as a continuum. It argued for a more holistic view, taking into account all factors relevant to the child's progress (DES, 1978).

Further special educational needs could be temporary. In doing this it moved the focus away from a medical (within-child) perspective and towards an educational one. This suggests that assessment should have an educational focus that is

> aimed not at allocating a child to a disability category but at producing a rounded analysis of the child's learning characteristics, of the situation in which he or she is expected to learn, and of the modifications, additional support, or alternative provision that might be made.
>
> (Dyson and Gallannaugh, 2008: 37)

Yet the power of a 'medicalised' categorical approach to defining special educational needs persisted. For example, in 2006, Ellen Brantlinger analysed the key texts used in USA teacher training and which shape teachers classroom practices. She found that they were constructed on a category-by-category basis, with associated appropriate 'treatments' and strong expectations from students and colleagues for use of this approach in teaching. Categories of special needs remain common-use, particularly where there are implications for a particular type of educational response. In (English) legislation, 'areas of need' relates to categories of impairment or disability. In practice, these may be ill-defined or overlapping, and with many individual children there is a combination of

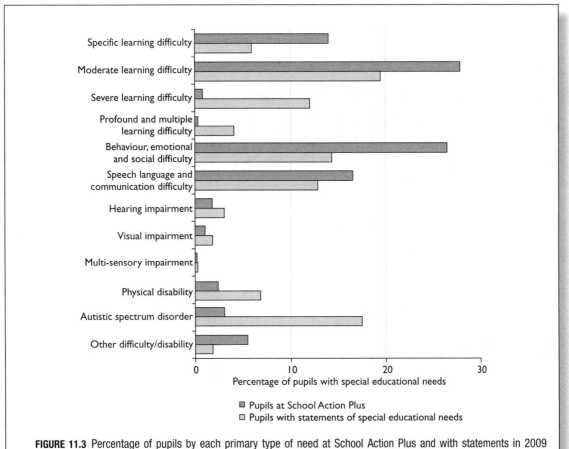

FIGURE 11.3 Percentage of pupils by each primary type of need at School Action Plus and with statements in 2009 (DCSF, 2009)

factors that make it unsafe to generalise from a particular diagnostic classification. For example, a category such as 'moderate learning difficulties' is not necessarily something that some children have and others don't; it might be thought of as a continuum (Keslair and McNally, 2009). However, it suggested that children's 'primary needs' are likely to fall within these areas. The types of 'Primary Need' and their relative frequency, within England in 2009, are illustrated in Figure 11.3.

This show the relative frequencies of the different types of need and also which types of special educational needs are most likely to be associated with Statements.

Activity

Look at Figure 11.3 and consider why some groups are relatively more likely to have Statements than others.

Cognition and learning needs

Over half of pupils with an identified 'type' of special educational need have cognition and learning needs (Keslair and McNally, 2009). This largest single group of children with special educational needs can be subdivided into specific, moderate, severe, and profound and multiple learning difficulties. These subcategories are often determined by levels of key abilities or functional attainments, and there are often different educational approaches associated with each of them.

1 Specific learning difficulties

A large number of children are diagnosed as having specific learning difficulties. They are the second-largest identified group (Keslair and McNally, 2009). Technically, this term refers to a wide group of children and several conditions. This is illustrated in Figure 11.4.

However, the term is most commonly used to indicate dyslexia and dyspraxia. As Figure 11.3 indicates, Autistic Spectrum Disorder is not commonly included as part of this group. The primary feature of dyslexia is a specific difficulty in learning to read and write.

Dyslexia is evident when accurate and fluent reading and or spelling develops very incompletely or with great difficulty. This focuses on literacy learning at the 'word level' and implies that the

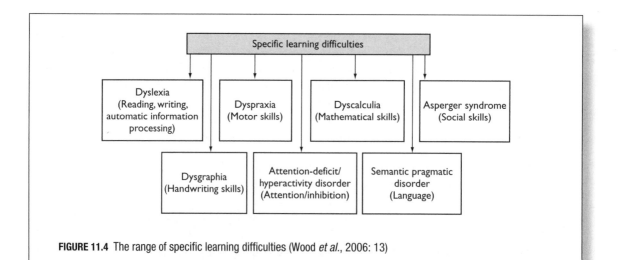

FIGURE 11.4 The range of specific learning difficulties (Wood *et al.*, 2006: 13)

problem is severe and persistent despite appropriate learning opportunities. It provides the basis for a staged process of assessment through teaching.

(British Psychological Society, 1999)

Children with dyslexia may also experience other, associated, problems. The nature of dyslexia and these other issues has been covered previously. Dyspraxia, also known as developmental coordination disorder, is seen in children whose attainment of fine and gross motor skills is substantially below that of their peers, to the extent that it creates a barrier in their daily lives. In the classroom, pupils will struggle with their handwriting but, like dyslexia, may also experience difficulties with planning and coordinating their work. However, there is not a body of research evidence to support 'dyspraxix specific' pedagogy (Portwood, 2005).

2 Moderate learning difficulties

Children with moderate learning difficulties are those who make very limited progress with basic academic skills; for example, failing to achieve functional skills with literacy. Within the classroom they are able to follow a curriculum similar to that of their age-group peers (Fletcher-Campbell, 2005), often with additional help and, for some, this may result from a Statement of Special Educational Needs. This group is the most common primary need of pupils with Statements (DCFS, 2009) and they have the greatest percentage, as a group, on School Action Plus (Daniels and Porter, 2007). Special education for these types of learning problems can take place in either ordinary or special schools, although, as described later in this chapter, there is an increasing emphasis on mainstream support. In England in 2008, pupils with moderate learning difficulties accounted for 27 per cent of pupils in special schools (Keslair and McNally, 2009).

3 Severe learning difficulties

Children with severe learning difficulties are functioning at a low level across a range of basic skills, including self-help and independence. They are likely to be educated in special schools (over 60 per cent – Keslair and McNally, 2009), and the curriculum that they follow can be differentiated versions of the National Curriculum, or include a parallel curriculum such as a personal social and independence skills qualification (ASDAN, 2010). There is a huge variation in academic attainment within this group. However, communication skills and formal academic attainments would normally be relatively less-well-developed. For example, a study of 35 UK special schools for children with severe learning difficulties concluded that relatively few pupils would read and write conventionally (Lacey et al., 2007). Another longitudinal study of five such schools found that, after five years, fewer than 20 per cent of the pupils were able to recognise more than ten familiar words (Chadwick et al., 2005).

The teaching and management of children with severe learning difficulties is often demanding and intensive, and, in special schools, usually takes place in classes with up to six pupils, with one teacher and one teaching assistant. Placements in these special schools are usually made on the basis of early skills, for instance by using developmental checklists. These should not, however, be taken to imply a simple overall developmental level, since children often have an uneven pattern of abilities, which imply different learning needs in each area of attainment. Children with Down syndrome, for instance, typically show higher levels of verbal comprehension than verbal expression, whereas children with autism have particular difficulties understanding social meanings. This raises issues for appropriate and relevant educational targets and curriculum experiences.

DOWN SYNDROME

The largest single group of children who attend schools for children with severe learning difficulties has been those with Down syndrome, although the numbers attending mainstream schools has been increasing (Cuckle and Wilson, 2002), albeit with large variations between education authorities. However, despite inclusive regulations, parents may find that they have to 'battle' for their child to attend a mainstream school (Shepherd, 2009).

Down syndrome affects about one in every 800 children and is the result of additional genetic material, usually in the form of an additional chromosome number 21. Among other things, this affects the central nervous system, and IQs are typically in the range from 40 to 80. Like children with many other types of severe learning difficulties, children with Down syndrome often have associated medical problems such as hearing and visual impairments, breathing disorders and heart defects. For various reasons, children with Down syndrome usually have a relative delay with their expressive language. This can make communication difficult and frustrating for them, and so signed communication systems such as Makaton (a language-development programme using a simplified form of sign language) are often utilised from an early age. This acts to establish concepts and support language development.

Children with Down syndrome seem particularly likely to learn by imitation from other children. Their learning can also tend to plateau in adolescence, although this may be due more to lack of appropriate learning experiences or stereotyped low academic expectations (Wishart, 2005) than to any intrinsic limitation at this age. A survey of research regarding children with Down syndrome educated in either mainstream or segregated schools reported that the children's language and literacy skill developed better within the mainstream settings (Dolva, 2009), particularly where early intervention has occurred. However, difficulties were noted in engaging with some social aspects of school life (Dolva, 2009).

4 Profound and Multiple Learning Difficulty (PMLD)

Children with profound and multiple learning difficulties have pervasive developmental delay, affecting all aspects of everyday lives. This developmental delay occurs regardless of their life experiences or age, and these pupils will remain at an early level in terms of intellectual, social and emotional development and communications skills (Sheehy and Nind, 2005). Consequently these children will need intensive support in all their educational activities. In additional to significant general learning difficulties, they will typically have at least one sensory impairment or medical problem. Hence the responsiveness of, and support provided by, their educational environment is crucially important. Approximately 80 per cent of this group of pupils are likely to be educated in special schools (Keslair and McNally, 2009), where the curriculum may be based upon the range and sequence of skills that children normally develop at a much earlier age. These can be grouped into areas such as communication, mobility, coordination, feeding, toileting, dressing/undressing and social abilities. A sequence of targets can then be identified with each of these areas, according to the child's level of functioning. With feeding this might first involve a child's swallowing liquidised food from a spoon, then holding on to a spoon and feeding himself or herself with guidance, then eventually doing so independently. In practice, such skills normally take many more stages to achieve, and progress can be very variable. It usually depends almost entirely on the specific abilities and experiences of individuals, rather than their age.

These pupils may need work to develop basic responses such as simple eye or limb movements, or generalised responses to sound or light. The curriculum developed for these pupils can draw upon concepts of knowledge and understanding derived from National Curriculum information (QCA, 2009b). However, this is usually balanced with an awareness of the essential key skills the pupils need to develop. These key skills underpin all curriculum areas (EQUALS, 2009).

A particular challenge for teachers is how to include the voice of these pupils, for example as required in annual reviews of Statements Of Educational Need. Whilst simple preferential choices might be used to elicit views on 'here and now' issues, these may become less meaningful for future events (Ware, 2004), and often third-party observation is used to construct the pupils 'voice'.

5 Behaviour, Emotional and Social Difficulty (BESD)

Children with social, emotional and behavioural difficulties make up the second-largest category of those with special educational needs. This group mainly includes children whose behaviours are disruptive, to their own learning or to that of their peers. Disruptive behaviour in class remains a major source of discontent among teachers (Hallam *et al.*, 2003). However, it also encompasses children with problems such as anxiety or depression. Signs of emotional turbulence, social withdrawal or difficulties forming and maintaining relationships therefore might be used as indicators of need (Harden *et al.*, 2003). Not surprisingly, the definition and labelling of children in this way is often contested. Measuring behaviour in school can be difficult, and often rates of exclusion for school have been used as yardsticks in this context (Hallam *et al.*, 2003).

Special provision for children with BESD covers the range from within-school support, pupil referral units to specialist residential provision. The latter is discussed in Chapters 12 and 13, but it is worth emphasising here that problem behaviours are bound up with children's social context at home and at school, and that there is strong evidence for a high 'spontaneous remission rate'. This indicates that any interventions should be the minimum necessary either to ensure the safety and well-being of pupils and staff or to prevent disruption of the educational process. Although it is tempting for teachers to assume that disruptive children should be educated elsewhere, it is usually best to first explore all the possibilities in the school, including parental involvement, additional in-school support and specialist advice.

6 Communication and interaction needs

Boys form the majority of this group, representing 86 per cent of children classified with Autistic Spectrum Disorder and 67 per cent of those classified with speech, language and communication needs (Keslair and McNally, 2009).

7 Speech, Language and Communication Needs (SLCN)

A significant proportion of children have significant speech and language difficulties on starting school, and SLCNs are often identified relatively early. Figure 11.5 indicates the proportion of pupils under seven years of age identified as having special educational needs.

Most children with severe and persistent speech and language impairment attend mainstream schools (McCartney *et al.*, 2009), and these difficulties may continue throughout their education. Speaking and listening are part of the National Curriculum of England and Wales, and Statements consider problems in this area as educational, although severe communication problems can also be classified as a medical need. The *Bercow Review* (2008) looked at improving services for children with communication difficulties, and the resulting initiatives aim to focus on early intervention (e.g. The Every Child a Talker Programme and a National Year of Speech, Language and Communication in

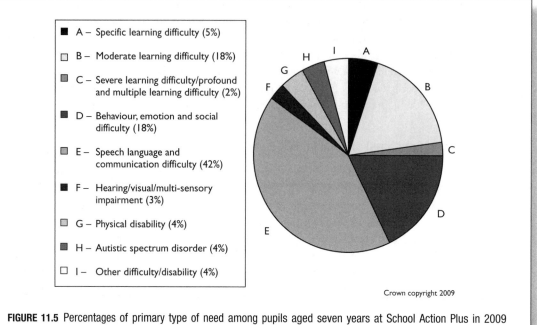

A – Specific learning difficulty (5%)

B – Moderate learning difficulty (18%)

C – Severe learning difficulty/profound and multiple learning difficulty (2%)

D – Behaviour, emotion and social difficulty (18%)

E – Speech language and communication difficulty (42%)

F – Hearing/visual/multi-sensory impairment (3%)

G – Physical disability (4%)

H – Autistic spectrum disorder (4%)

I – Other difficulty/disability (4%)

Crown copyright 2009

FIGURE 11.5 Percentages of primary type of need among pupils aged seven years at School Action Plus in 2009 (DCSF, 2009)

2011). Difficulties with speech and language have a major impact on children's ability to access an appropriate curriculum, to make progress with basic literacy skills, and to interact socially. As was described in Chapter 8, there are a number of different types of approaches and forms of provision, depending on a child's particular difficulties. The key features, however, are an emphasis on developing communication in contexts that are meaningful for children. If possible, therefore, support should be integrated into a child's daily experiences in school, although there is no doubt that the expertise of SLTs to assess and advise on programmes plays a vital part in such support. Teachers are usually able to draw upon curriculum activities, which aim to develop language and communication skills (Learning and Teaching Scotland (LTS), 2008; Qualifications and Curriculum Authority (QCA), 2008), and differentiation of classroom activities has particular importance in supporting the development of this group of pupils (McCartney *et al.*, 2009).

8 Autistic Spectrum Disorder

Autistic Spectrum Disorder (ASD) refers to a group of 'identified disorders of development with life-long effects and that have in common a triad of impairments in: social interaction, communication, imagination, and behaviour (narrow, and repetitive pattern of behaviour)' (Wing, 1997: 253). The most common groups within the ASD category are those with autism and Asperger's syndrome. Children with Asperger's syndrome possess many of the developmental patterns of children with autism, but have no clinically significant delay in their cognitive or language development (DSM, 2004). This is in contrast to children with autism, 80 per cent of whom will have profound or severe learning difficulties (Peeters and Gillberg, 1999).

There has been a significant change in the number of children identified as autistic over the last decade (Volkmar *et al.*, 2004) and, consequently, there has been considerable debate as to the extent to which this is the result of increased public awareness, identification procedures or incidence of the condition. As indicated in Figure 11.3, children with autism are the most likely group to receive a Statement of Educational Need, rather than receive support at School Action Plus level (DCSF, 2009).

Many different theories have been developed to explain the patterns of behaviour found in autism. The most significant have been those that examine the way in which children with autism think in social situations. These 'theory of mind' explanations suggest that a key feature is child's difficulty in understanding and interpreting the mental states of others, such as predicting the beliefs or intentions of other children. Most children with autism fail simple tests in which they need to guess what another child is thinking. However, not all children with autism do so (Colle *et al.*, 2007). This social ability or 'theory of mind' is shown in tasks that involve their understanding of another person who is fooled in some way. In an investigation by Frith (1989), the sequence of events shown in Figure 11.6

FIGURE 11.6 The autistic puppet show (source: Scheffler, 1989)

was enacted for a child by two puppets. Normally, children as young as four years of age are able to realise at the end that Sally will look in the wrong container because she does not know that the marble has been moved. A group of children with Down syndrome who had a mental age of six years were able to correctly answer questions about what Sally would think. However, of a group of 20 autistic children who had a mean mental age of nine years, 16 failed the task. This was despite the fact that they showed that they knew what had happened to the marble and that Sally had not seen the marble move. The key difference seemed to be that they could not grasp the concept that Sally believed something that was not true.

The inability of children with ASD to appreciate another person's understanding and intent has a profound effect on their social functioning. Since language develops from early social interaction, it is also likely that their lack of language abilities comes from this basic difficulty. As this deficit can be relatively specific, however, other, non-language or non-social abilities can develop independently. Other psychological theories of autism focus on explanations for rigidity of thought and a perceptual preferences for detail rather than more holistic processing.

Young people with autism have published accounts of their own experiences, and these often highlight pervasive anxiety and fear as common experiences of being in a social world that they find unpredictable (Grayson, 2005).

Sensory and/or physical needs

9 Physical disability (PD) and medical needs

There are many types of physical difficulties that can affect a child's experience of education. Some of these have direct and obvious effects, such as limits on mobility and access to parts of the school building, or restrictions on working within certain areas of the curriculum. A child in a wheelchair, for instance, may need ramps, special toileting facilities and support in some lessons such as technology, where he or she may not be able to reach certain equipment. Other disabilities, such as epilepsy, may not be so obvious, particularly when well-controlled with drugs. Unfortunately, some forms of medication at high doses have the effect of producing unsteadiness, drowsiness or withdrawn behaviour, which can limit educational progress.

Epilepsy is not a single condition but a group of disorders. Each has differing diagnostic criteria and medical responses (Absoud and McShane, 2009) but most children who develop epilepsy will become seizure-free. Epilepsy is a relatively common neurological disorder in young children, occurring in about 1 in 279 children under the age of 16 years (Deacon and Wigglesworth, 2005), with its incidence tending to reduce as children get older. As many as 5 per cent of all children will have a seizure at one time or another, and the general recurrence risk after a single occurrence childhood is about 30 percent–50 per cent (Absoud and McShane, 2009). There are many different types of epilepsy, but in the more extreme form of 'tonicclonic seizure' there can be a loss of consciousness, difficulty in breathing, convulsions, incontinence and drowsiness on recovery.

Epilepsy is the result of cells in parts or all of the brain firing in synchrony, rather than separately. The cause may be some form of abnormality or brain damage, with a focus that triggers the seizure, or by high temperatures in the brain. In susceptible children, a seizure can be triggered by flashing lights or by general stress. Although children with epilepsy are somewhat more likely to have reading difficulties than other children, these difficulties are often associated with other problems, rather than the epilepsy itself. A review by Bagley (1971) of 118 cases of children with epilepsy, uncomplicated by other handicaps, suggested that epilepsy does not by itself limit intellectual development. Epilepsy is quite common among children with severe and profound learning difficulties, when it is often due to general organic problems in the brain, and 43 per cent of children with epilepsy will receive special education services (Tidman *et al.*, 2003) reflecting this co-morbidity.

Certain types of epilepsy which affect the temporal lobe may be less obvious and involve behavioural problems such as tension, irritability, bad temper, aggressiveness and hyperkinesis (DES, 1962). Although there is an association between epilepsy and cognitive and behavioural difficulties, the exact nature of this association is not clear. 'Absences', brief 'blank' spells in children, are associated with epilepsy and may be difficult to detect since they are transitory and have little outward effect on the child. They often disrupt concentration, however, and may leave the child feeling rather dazed and confused, and liable to react inappropriately. Structured learning programmes can be useful to ensure continuity in such cases, since children can then quickly pick up where they left off. The provision of very clear structure and organisation is useful where the child may have an associated executive function deficit, which affects their planning skills and working memory. In terms of examinations, additional time may be beneficial if tasks are broken down into sub-steps Titus and Thio, 2009). Children with normal cognition do not have a higher risk of injury than their peers; however, close supervision may be needed for potentially dangerous situations, such as swimming and climbing (Absoud and McShane, 2009).

Anti-epilepsy drugs may produce side-effects that can have a profound impact on the children's classroom experiences, such as influencing language processing and memory function (Titus and Thio, 2009). The social stigma of being labelled as 'epileptic' can also be significant for children (Barry *et al.*, 2007), and there is an increased risk for depression and anxiety (Ekinci *et al.*, 2009). Together, these issues can have a significant effect on a child's experience of school and their performance within the classroom (Ekinci *et al.*, 2009).

When poor physical control and coordination are the result of early brain damage, the condition is called 'cerebral palsy'. This affects around two in a thousand children, and is often (but not always) associated with other problems such as difficulties with speech and language or learning problems. Damage to different parts of the brain produces different problems.

- Spasticity is the most common form and is the result of damage to the motor cortex. This produces poor movement control and stiff or weak limbs.
- Athetosis affects far fewer children and is caused by damage to the basal ganglia, which organise the body's motor activity. There are therefore often involuntary movements such as grimacing, dribbling and difficulty with speaking.
- Ataxia is caused by damage to the cerebellum, which controls the body's equilibrium. Children often have problems with walking and negotiating their environment, and can appear rather clumsy and accident-prone.

About half of all children with cerebral palsy have communication problems. These may be due to the effects of the damage on the language areas of the brain, or due to poor control over the speech organs. Children with cerebral palsy also have a higher level of problems with vision (associated with central damage or with control of the eyes), as well as with hearing. In England, approximately 25 per cent of children with cerebral palsy are unable to walk unassisted (Katz, 2009).

If the damage is limited to areas of the brain associated with physical control, then there may be no significant intellectual impairments. However, the damage can often be more widespread, and children with greater physical handicaps were more likely to have cognitive and educational problems. This may be due to difficulties in executive function and working memory which, for example, increase the experiencing difficulties with arithmetic (Jenks *et al.*, 2009). Assessments of children with such physical difficulties must therefore look for evidence of learning or understanding that does not depend on normal physical responses. Many children will therefore benefit from the use of technological aids such as speech synthesisers, communication devices and augmented environments.

Sensory problems

Sensory problems are usually not as evident as other physical difficulties, but they often have the most profound effects on the process of education.

10 Hearing impairment (HI)

Hearing impairment in particular is quite prevalent in young children, and as many as 20 per cent of primary-age children suffer from temporary conductive hearing loss (otitis media with effusion, referred to as 'OME' or 'glue ear', a form of chronic otitis media) (Webster and McConnell, 1987) – when the inner ear is not able to transmit information owing to poor drainage and/or infections. These can affect early speech and language development, and Gottlieb *et al.* (1980) found that 46 per cent of children referred for special help with reading problems had suffered from such middle-ear disorders. However, many children with conductive hearing loss do not have subsequent reading problems. Such difficulties are therefore probably due to a combination of hearing problems along with other factors such as a poor home background. Whilst over 10 per cent of children might experience hearing impairment at some time, potentially influencing their educational classroom attainment, only 0.2 per cent of children will have a permanent loss (Goldstein, 1984). Such long-lasting difficulties can have a major effect on communication skills and educational attainments.

There is an association between degree of hearing impairment and attainment of language skills. Leeson (2009) found the average reading age of school leavers with a profound hearing impairment was only at the nine-year level, and that these abilities depended largely on children's use of visual representations of words. Across the European Union, deaf people remain under-employed, influenced by poor literacy attainment (EUD, 2001, in Leeson, 2009).

Hearing loss is measured on the decibel scale, and this is usually assessed and shown by an audiogram of the type shown in Figure 11.7. This shows the intensity of the sound that can be heard at different frequencies. Normal (modal) hearing ability is at the zero-decibel level, and different levels of hearing loss occur at levels greater than this. The audiogram shows the range of normal speech in the shaded central portion; when hearing loss is greater than parts of this speech curve, then those sounds cannot be heard. A mild hearing loss cuts out the lower and higher frequencies, producing a 'muffled' sound. With a severe hearing loss, one can hear only shouted speech; and, with a profound hearing loss, even this cannot be heard. High frequencies are the most likely ones to be lost, and a specific hearing loss often means that many sounds, such as 's' and 'th', will be lost, reducing overall intelligibility.

As with other abilities, hearing appears to exist as a continuum, as shown by the graph in Figure 11.8. In terms of hearing sensitivity, there are no particular cut-off points that can distinguish separate categories. The trend recently has therefore been away from categorising children as 'deaf' or 'hearing impaired', towards a more functional classification in terms of what can or cannot be perceived. This mainly considers the extent to which children are able to pick up speech, since this has direct relevance to their educational needs.

Conductive hearing losses are normally temporary and improve as children get older and the drainage of the inner-ear improves. However, about one in 200 children suffers from permanent

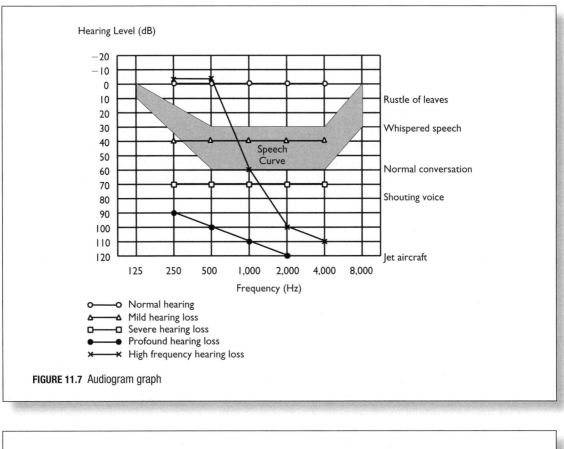

FIGURE 11.7 Audiogram graph

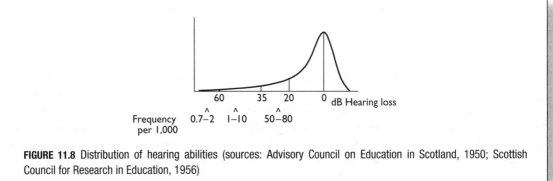

FIGURE 11.8 Distribution of hearing abilities (sources: Advisory Council on Education in Scotland, 1950; Scottish Council for Research in Education, 1956)

conductive losses. Treatment of conductive hearing loss usually involves dealing with any infection, removing fluid from the inner-ear and making a semi-permanent hole in the eardrum with a small plastic 'grommet'; this allows air into the inner ear and improves drainage.

Approximately half of all deaf pupils have a moderate hearing loss, with one-quarter having a profound loss (Fortnum *et al.*, 2002, cited in Gregory, 2005). Permanent loss of hearing is often due to sensori-neural damage, causing the cochlear or the auditory nerves to fail to function, or due to problems with the fine structures of the inner ear. These can be inherited, or due to perinatal (birth) problems or disease. Fortnum *et al.* (2001) estimated that approximately 1.65 per 1,000 children across the UK experienced moderate to profound bilateral deafness.

Many children with long-term hearing problems can benefit from the amplification of sound, using a range of different types of hearing aids. As we have seen, language develops from verbal experience and interactions very early on in a child's life. It is therefore important that hearing aids are used as soon as possible. Unfortunately, detection can sometimes be late, and if the early foundations are missed, long-term problems are likely to result.

In an educational setting, there is often a great deal of background noise such as chatter from other children and scraping of chairs. When amplified, this can all mask a teacher's voice, so a more effective approach can be to use a radio transmitter microphone worn by the teacher. By itself, use of such a microphone can limit a child's exposure to incidental communication with other children, and some aids can therefore be switched between radio and local reception to compensate for this.

With a mild hearing loss, amplification can be very effective and produce good speech perception. Children with this level of loss can therefore usually develop spoken (oral) language and can be taught in the normal way with only limited monitoring and support. With profound hearing loss, amplification is much less effective, and children with this level of difficulty have often been educated in specialist schools or units using manual techniques. These involve the use of a signing system, such as British Sign Language. This is a complete language that is partially separate from spoken English, with some differences in grammatical structure and words/meanings; for example, there is no sign for the word 'the', since it is implied by context. The English Phrase 'I've put in the sugar' is expressed as 'Sugar put in finish' in British Sign Language.

Many children, however, fall between these two extremes, and there has been a historical bias to attempt to develop normal (oral) communication with them so that they can function as independently as possible in the wider (hearing) society. The techniques to achieve this can involve an emphasis on the use of amplification, periods of one-to-one speech training, and tuition with lip-reading. Historically, schools or units adopting this approach have often banned the use of signing since it was felt that it would prevent pupils from developing spoken language.

The proponents of signing argue that when this is developed from an early age, it establishes language concepts that form a basis for later language-based skills. A typical study by Stuckless and Birch (1966) compared two groups of children with a profound hearing loss: those who had been brought up with sign language (because their parents had hearing impairments), and those who used spoken language (because their parents had normal hearing). The main outcomes were that children who had learned sign language at home were half-a-grade ahead with their reading and writing, and that there were no significant differences in speech intelligibility. An issue within this area of education is that of 'Deaf identity'. The Deaf community see themselves as 'a linguistic and cultural minority group' (Gregory, 2005: 18), and sign language is the natural language of this community. This creates a tension with approaches, and pedagogies, designed to 'cure' or remediate.

Conrad (1979) has reviewed a number of studies which indicate that if children with a profound hearing loss use sign language from the earliest ages, their subsequent intellectual abilities are above those of children with a similar loss who do not sign. In his sample, the average age of being fitted with a hearing aid was about 2-and-a-half years. Conrad therefore argued that, if children did not sign, they were likely to suffer from early linguistic deprivation, limiting the development of those cognitive abilities that use language components.

Kumar *et al.* (2009) carried out a systematic research review of children who used speech and signing concurrently. They concluded that, whilst this was associated with learning both spoken and signed languages, there was little empirical evidence to suggest causal effects concerning language development. They recommend that families, wondering which option to choose, consider their own preferences and professional expertise. Although Conrad argues that it would be best to aim to develop sign language with all children who have a significant hearing loss, only about 5 per cent of hearing parents are actually able to use or learn to use signing effectively, and children's sign-language development is delayed in 'hearing homes'. Webster and Wood (1989) therefore argue that, in practice, there is no overall superiority for manual or oral training, and that the key feature is the quality of interaction, whatever the mode used. The method adopted should therefore depend very much on the individual child's abilities and situation. For instance, a child with parents who do sign might well benefit from a combined approach and will certainly not suffer from developing signing. However, a child with limited access to sign language and only a moderate hearing loss is likely to get greatest meaning and information from an emphasis on the development of spoken language.

Recently there has been the development of 'baby signing', the use of manual signs with hearing but pre-verbal infants. Research findings are inconclusive (Johnston et al., 2005), but there is some evidence for positive effects in aspects of child development (see Doherty-Sneddon, 2008, for a discussion of this area).

For some children with hearing impairment, cochlear implants are an option. This is a surgical intervention that can have a significant impact on children's language development, and results for a preliminary study of 86 children reports that implantation in the first year resulted in near-typical language development, in contrast to children receiving later interventions (Ching et al., 2009). It is important that teachers are sensitive to their classroom's acoustic environment (discussed previously) in order to support this approach.

11 Visual impairment (VI)

Visual impairment (VI) can cover a wide range of capabilities, and estimates of its prevalence varies between studies. According to Best (1992) there are about 4.2 visually impaired and 3 blind children per 10,000 of the school-age population, whereas later estimates, looking at VI in Liverpool, reported 1.81 per 1,000 when including multiple impairments across the 0–16 age range (Schwarz et al., 2002).

Far-vision and visual acuity can be assessed by the use of a Snellen test chart (Figure 11.9), and a child's visual abilities will be expressed as the distance that a child needs to be from the chart (usually 6 metres) in order to read print of a certain size. A child at 6 metres who can read only the size 18 therefore has a visual acuity of 6/18.

Near-vision can be assessed by simple reading tasks using print of different sizes, as in the example shown in Figure 11.10. The finding that a child has problems with near-vision has direct implications for the type of text that should be used in a child's normal reading, or for the need to magnify normal reading texts. This can be done using lenses, or with a computer system that can also be used to enhance the contrast.

When children have reading difficulties or a severe visual impairment, which means that they cannot read or identify letters, the ability of the lens to focus light on the retina can be assessed directly using special instruments. Other tests can also assess a child's field of vision, which in school work can be important to pick up peripheral information. An assessment of children's colour vision can indicate whether they will be able to respond to information involving the use of different colours.

The educational implications of these different levels of ability depends to a great extent upon children's understanding of available visual cues, their ability to respond to different types of moving and stationary objects, as well as their field of vision (which is important in reading). When children have some sight, however limited, there has been an increasing emphasis on training residual vision, which

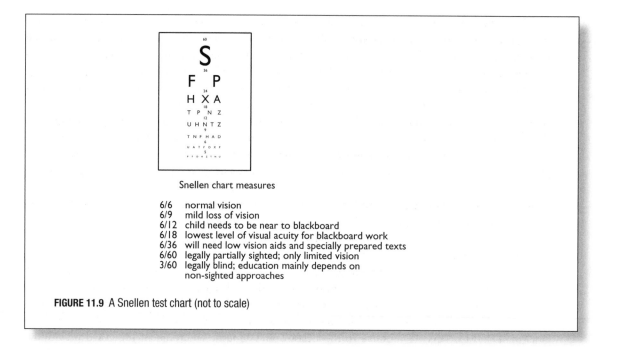

Snellen chart measures

6/6 normal vision
6/9 mild loss of vision
6/12 child needs to be near to blackboard
6/18 lowest level of visual acuity for blackboard work
6/36 will need low vision aids and specially prepared texts
6/60 legally partially sighted; only limited vision
3/60 legally blind; education mainly depends on
non-sighted approaches

FIGURE 11.9 A Snellen test chart (not to scale)

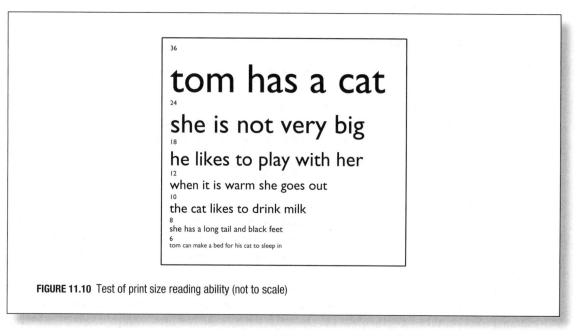

FIGURE 11.10 Test of print size reading ability (not to scale)

means learning to interpret the imperfect or incomplete information that is received. This approach is supported by Gregory's (1970) 'top-down' theory of perceptual processing, according to which normal perception depends on limited visual input, and can be interpreted only according to expectations built up from previous experiences. Gregory thus believes that we construct our perceptions according to higher-level concepts and expectations.

Children with limited visual input may have not learned the relevance of certain types of visual information. They will often have had limited experience of different situations: unplanned incidental experiences and learning through observation and exploring their environment (McCall, 1999, cited in Douglas and McLinden, 2005).

Visual training therefore involves extending children's experiences and encouraging them to independently interpret and use partial visual information in different contexts.

Most children with visual impairment are educated in mainstream schools, or mainstream schools that have been additionally resourced to cater for VI pupils. Fewer than 10 per cent are educated in special schools for visually impaired pupils. They may develop their literacy skills through adapted/enhanced text or the tactile orthographies of Braille and Moon.

12 Multi-sensory impairment (MSI)

Pupils with MSI have a combination of hearing and visual impairments. Some of these children may be deaf and blind, but most will be able to hear or see to some limited extent. Therefore, they experience significant barriers in their everyday lives and learning. Communication intervention is essential for these children, and often uses augmented and alternative communication (AAC) systems. This might include tactile manual signing, tangible objects and texture-enhanced communication boards with associated electronic voice. Sigafoos *et al.* (2008) looked at the outcomes of different approaches for this group of pupils. They found that the majority of children had developmental and or physical disabilities in addition to their sensory impairments. Teachers focused on teaching specific communication skills, utilising AAC approaches, using primarily behavioural approaches. Whilst positive outcomes were reported, the certainty of this evidence was not always evident (Sigafoos *et al.*, 2008).

The process of inclusive and special education

Special education exists to support children who have educational problems and, if possible, to prevent such problems from developing. As we have indicated, the present guidelines for identifying and meeting children's special educational needs differs between countries and principalities, for example in the concept of Additional Support Needs used in Scotland. In England and Wales a Statement Of Special Educational Needs is a document maintained by the education authority for children whose needs cannot be completely met within the normal range of provision. At the time of writing this chapter, parents, carers or a child's school can apply to their Local Education Authority for a Statutory Assessment for a Statement under Section 323 of the 1996 Education Act and, once received, the complete process of assessment and, where appropriate, the issuing of a Statement is required by law to take no more than 26 weeks.

It is based upon assessment information from three main sources: the school, an educational psychologist, the parents and a school medical officer. The child should also contribute their own information to this process. It also includes information from any other agencies that might be involved, such as social services. The Statement itself summarises the child's functioning, his or her educational needs, and how those needs will be met, including facilities and equipment, curriculum modifications and support, and staffing arrangements.

Statements are therefore the way in which children with special needs can gain additional resources within mainstream schools, and how they are placed in special schools. Not surprisingly, therefore, there has been an increasing demand for Statements and such resources. In 2009, DCSF figures suggested that the proportion of pupils with SEN had grown from 14.9 per cent in 2005 to 17.8 per cent in 2009. However, the proportion who received a Statement fell from 2.8 per cent to 2.7 per cent

(221,670). This may reflect targeted funding to schools to support children without a need for a State-ment, and the effects of early identification, with School Action and School Action Plus being extended to early-years settings.

Identification of special needs and levels of provision

There is a graduated approach to the identification and support of special educational needs (DfES, 2001). It begins with an initial identification of a child who is receiving appropriate teaching (e.g. dif-ferentiated work, assumed to be a standard classroom practice) but not making satisfactory progress.

It then moves through School Action to School Action Plus, and then, for relatively few children, a formal assessment by the local authority and the possible issuing of a Statement Of Special Educa-tional Needs. Parents are involved at all parts of this process. Having been initially identified as a child whose progress is unsatisfactory, and following discussion with parents/carers, the school's SENCO and class teacher decide on the nature of any additional support and include this within an Individual Educational Plan. The child's progress is monitored and reviewed three times each year. This process may trigger progression to School Action Plus, when support from specialists from outside the school is most usually sought. This may be in the provision of new equipment or teaching approaches, and such changes are reflected in the child's IEP. As we have seen, the majority of children with SEN will be supported at the level of School Action to School Action Plus.

In cases where this support is not successful, then a formal assessment can be requested. The LEA reviews the school's evidence, parental requests and the child's IEP and decides whether to proceed with the assessment. If they decide to go ahead, then the local authority is required to gather informa-tion from parents, the child themselves, also advice from educational, medical, psychological and social services and any other relevant sources (Simmons *et al.*, 2006). A draft proposed Statement is then produced, a document that sets out the child's needs and the nature of appropriate support that will meet these needs. This may include placement in a particular school or the provision of in-class support. This is circulated and there is a short period of time for comment.

If parents disagree with the outcome of a statutory assessment, they can appeal to a Special Educa-tional Needs and Disability Tribunal (SENDIST). This is chaired by a lawyer and is independent of the education authority. Reviews of tribunals' findings indicate that, although the proceedings can be rather lengthy, they are mainly focused on how the child's needs can be met properly in the future, rather than simply encouraging a legalistic confrontation. Within the SEN system, powerful lobby groups exist for children with dyslexia and autism. Consequently, these groups are over-represented and there is 'clear evidence' that those from more affluent backgrounds are receiving not only more help but more help for less significant levels of difficulty, in comparison to those from poorer back-grounds (Daniels and Porter, 2007).

Under the *Code of Practice* (DfES, 2001c), schools have the responsibility for meeting the needs of the majority of children with special needs without recourse to the provision of a Statement. They are accountable for their actions in this respect, with reports to parents and in their school policy, and are monitored as part of the regular, statutory school-inspection process.

A key element in the meeting of a child's special needs is his or her Individual Education Plan (IEP), which is introduced at School Action level. It needs to include:

- short-term targets set for or by the child;
- the teaching strategies to be used;
- when the plan is to be reviewed;

- success and/or exit criteria;
- outcomes (to be recorded when the IEP is reviewed).

(DfES, 2001c, paras 5:50, 6:58)

IEPs are used in many countries, but their purposes may differ. For example, in the United States of America, an IEP is more akin to a 'Statement' as it is associated with funding. IEPs need to set specific targets that can be evaluated. It is not very effective to use descriptions such as 'to improve reading' since it is impossible to know when the pupil will have done so. It is also important to specify what is going to be done to help the pupil, with details of the strategies and resources to be used, who will help and when. They should also include success criteria and who is responsible for monitoring the pupil's progress.

There is a tension in the use of IEPs, as advice (e.g. DfES, 2004) sees it as focused SMART targets to address within-child needs, rather than being necessarily constructed in terms of the barriers that might exist for the child within the school environment or teaching methods, as referred to in the Code of Practice (Simmons et al., 2006).

Each school must keep a special-needs register of all children who are included on the various stages of the Code of Practice. At a basic level, this will include the names of the children, the nature of their problem and their stage or category of special needs. Ofsted (Office for Standards in Education, Children's Services and Skills in England) inspections of special needs in a school involve selecting children from this register and following up their IEPs or Statements, so as to ensure that the effective provision is being made for them.

Educational psychologists

Chartered educational psychologists in the United Kingdom are employed by education authorities to help children experiencing educational difficulties in some form. They have a degree in psychology, and a Doctorate (England and Wales), or Masters Degree (Scotland), in Educational Psychology, and a teaching qualification (for example, a PGCE – Postgraduate Certificate of Education) or experience of working with young people and their families. They are registered with the Health Professions Council.

Farrell et al. (2006) carried out a review of the functions and contributions of educational psychologists. The review provided evidence that EPs were performing a wide range of tasks, and doing so effectively. (For a review of Scottish EPs, see Review of the Provision of Educational Psychology Services in Scotland, known as the Currie Report (Scottish Executive, 2002).) These tasks include:

- assessing children and young people's learning and emotional needs;
- developing and supporting therapeutic and behaviour-management programmes;
- recommending formal actions to be made about the needs of a child or young person's needs including Statements of special educational needs;
- attending multi-disciplinary case conferences on how social, emotional, behavioural, and learning needs of children and young people might best be met;
- developing and reviewing behaviour, and child development policies.

(AEP, 2008)

In addition, it is common for educational psychologists to advise working/consultation groups on organisation and policy-planning, and to plan and carry out research activities (BPS, 2009). This work occurs across, and between, several areas and levels of organisation.

[T]he core functions of EP work occur in the following domains: (i) early years work, (ii) work with schools (primary, secondary and special), and (iii) multi-agency work, and moreover, that this work is done at the following levels: (a) at the level of the individual child, (b) at the level of groups of children, (c) at the whole school level, and (d) at the LEA level.

(Boyle and Lauchlan, 2007: 76)

The majority of referrals regarding individual children come from primary and secondary schools, and these tend to cover learning problems, usually with a bias towards primary-age children, and behavioural difficulties, mainly involving secondary-age children. Many children are referred before they enter school and these tend to have the more severe learning difficulties that affect general development. Referrals can also come for pupils up to the age of 19, or above for students in further-education colleges.

Whist schools remain the main focus of educational psychologists' work, the development of integrated children's services, following the Children's Act 2004 and Every Child Matters (DfES, 2004a), means that educational psychologists are likely to be working across their community. This may include work in extended provision and children's centres, and as part of multidisciplinary teams within Children's Services, rather than as a completely separate Educational Psychology service. These integrated Children's Services seek to deliver the five outcomes of ECM: Being healthy; Staying safe; Enjoying and achieving; Making a positive contribution; and Economic well-being. EPs contribute to the process of delivering these outcomes.

An increasing number of educational psychologists work as private or independent consultants and, nationally, a shortage of educational psychologists in local authorities has developed (HEPS, 2009). A review by Coopers and Lybrand, in 1996, found that there was, on average, one psychologist for about 4,400 pupils, whereas in Hampshire by 2008 there was one educational psychologist for every 9,000 children between the ages of 0–16 (HEPS, 2008).

Most psychologists carry out assessments of children's educational attainments using individual normative tests. These usually involve tests of reading, spelling and mathematical abilities. Many psychologists also assess various cognitive abilities such as those involved in intelligence tests. The most popular of these continues to be the Wechsler Intelligence Scale for Children (Wechsler, 2003), although many psychologists also use the British Ability Scales. However, some psychologists focus more directly on the nature of a child's learning processes – for example, using teaching–learning tasks, or an analysis of learning subskills. These might, for instance, involve an evaluation of phonological abilities as the basis for the development of literacy skills. It can be argued that this is a more useful approach since it can directly imply appropriate teaching procedures. However, such assessments can as easily be carried out by trained teachers, who are also likely to be the people setting up and delivering subsequent teaching programmes. A more-effective use of psychologists' time and expertise may be to research and develop such teaching approaches and then pass them on to those who are involved in teaching children.

When children have behavioural problems, an assessment may involve observations of their behaviour, or personality assessments. These can lead to the development of a programme involving techniques such as behaviour modification or social-skills training. A review of the work of educational psychologists (Farrell et al., 2006) found that such approaches were often highly effective and that psychologists dealt with a large number of such cases.

There is abundant evidence to suggest that EPs make a contribution to intervention and support for children and young people who present and/or experience behavioural, emotional and/or social difficulties (BESDs).... Work in this area is wide-ranging including direct work with children, parents, teachers, schools and organisations, with a variety of foci including self-esteem, school absenteeism, home–school partnerships and critical incident response development ...

(p. 14)

Educational problems can be found at a preschool age, when an assessment might involve the use of developmental criteria, and consideration of any physical or sensory impairments. Psychologists also deal with complex difficulties such as cases where behaviour and learning problems are present at the same time. In most of these situations, knowledge of psychology can give a particular insight into the nature of a child's problems and avoid over-simplistic labelling.

A psychological assessment can be part of the development of an Individual Educational Plan or part of the statutory procedure for a Statement, when it should outline a child's educational needs and how those could be met. A great amount of educational psychologists' time is therefore taken up carrying out assessments and writing reports, which must be accurate and useful for all those involved. An interesting finding from Farrell et al.'s review was 'There was a universally held view that EPs have been too heavily involved in statutory assessments' (2006: 8) and this commitment is seen as holding them back from important preventative, therapeutic and consultative work.

Nowadays, psychologists' assessments are being increasingly queried in legal or semi-legal situations (such as in a Special Educational Needs And Disability Tribunal). They must therefore be justified in terms of the evidence they are based upon and the logic of their arguments, rather than on 'clinical experience'. A key part of an assessment is often to give advice about the appropriate educational environment for a child, including the nature of provision. This involves a detailed and expert knowledge of what are effective approaches for a range of special-needs issues, as described in this chapter and elsewhere in the book. With a literacy problem, a psychologist might therefore give advice about the teaching techniques to be used, the learning group size and the frequency of teaching. The advice might also cover specific psychological strategies to increase success, such as mastery learning or mediated learning techniques. Some students may also need a particular emphasis on high levels of meaningful success to improve their attributional style and motivation.

Psychological advice can describe key features, such as the nature of the general school curriculum and the social context, which might be characteristic of a certain type of learning environment. Again, however, the psychologist should be aware of the effectiveness of segregated schooling, and its advantages and drawbacks as described later in this chapter.

Psychologists have a relatively ambiguous role since they have the responsibility for identifying needs, but do not normally have the direct power or resources to go along with this. Since psychologists normally have many cases referred to them, they are often limited to making recommendations, and busy, overstretched schools can have difficulties in carrying them out. For many teachers in the United Kingdom, their access to psychological knowledge comes from in-service training on specific concepts and approaches, and there is a danger that their application in the classroom loses touch with the research evidence underpinning them (Hick et al., 2009).

Problem pimps and crocodile hunters

Internationally, there is evidence to suggest that the role of educational psychologists can act to support the maintenance of segregated special schools (Jimerson et al., 2004). Within the UK, there are significant differences between individual EPs regarding the use of segregated provision (Farrell and Venables, 2009). In one large LEA, 'half the EPs were responsible for referring 91 per cent of the children who attend special schools for children with EBD and MLD' (p. 118). However, more-recently trained EPs are less likely to refer children to special schools.

Time constraints and market demands can potentially lead to psychologists carrying out assessments and writing reports that serve only to confirm children's difficulties. Reynolds (1987), for instance, argues that there is a danger that educational psychologists may function as 'problem pimps', living off their ability to provide an apparently legitimate attribution for failure by using general ability testing. The same argument might exist for identifying deficits that elicit funds.

An allegory attempts to illuminate this scenario by describing how a village that was plagued by crocodiles hired an expert crocodile hunter. Every day the hunter would go off into the swamps around the village and devise traps for the crocodiles or shoot them with a special powerful rifle. The crocodiles kept breeding, however, and although the hunter kept their numbers down, it seemed that crocodiles simply had to be accepted by the villagers as being part of their lives.

In this story, the role of the psychologist can of course be likened to the crocodile hunter, using ever-more-specialised techniques and devices to deal with the result, rather than the causes of the problem. Evidently, what the villagers really needed was a civil engineer to drain the swamps and destroy the crocodiles' breeding grounds.

It is, however, not quite so simple to identify or to deal with the causes of educational failure. It seems likely that schools and teachers have fairly similar levels of effectiveness, given the major constraints under which they operate. Overall improvements are therefore normally unlikely to occur, unless there are dramatic changes in key factors – which would generally involve additional funding. If, as seems likely, home background and economic inequality are the main causes of educational problems, then these factors are also unfortunately well beyond the control of any individual, or even of the educational system as a whole.

It is possible, however, that psychologists may be able to influence some parts of the educational system in a developmental or training role. Such a role can involve working with individual schools or across the whole education authority to develop particular techniques or general systems to help children with problems. Burden (1978) in particular has long argued that it is more effective for psychologists to adopt this approach than simply to label and assign children to different forms of schooling. One positive and effective example of this is the 'Sound Linkage' programme developed by Hatcher (1994) to establish phonological abilities as part of general reading development. The 'no blame' approach to bullying by Maines and Robinson (1991) described in Chapter 13 has also been shown to be highly effective, as has 'AcceleRead AcceleWrite', an approach developed by Miles that utilises 'talking computers' for pupils experiencing literacy problems (Brooks, 2007). The latter's recommendation in national strategy documents illustrates the reach that such work can have.

Moving towards multi-agency working and integrated children's service may offer educational psychologists the flexibility to move away from the traditional approach. For example, in the consultancy model (Wagner, 1995), psychologists work in a collaborative way with schools to address individual or more general problems. The idea is that they do not simply give advice but take something akin to a counselling approach, involving a dialogue with schools to seek information and to analyse and reflect back the present situation. This can then act as the basis for a school to develop new ways of solving difficulties or problems. Using this approach seems more likely to generate involvement and commitment to change than the traditional process of 'test and tell'.

Special educational needs support: a range of provision

A range of provision exists for children with special educational needs. In England and Wales this encompasses in-school support, resourced schools, pupil-referral units and special schools.

In-school support

The Special Educational Needs Coordinator (in England, Wales and Northern Ireland), or learning support teacher (in Scotland), is a key professional in creating inclusive educational experiences for children. The SENCO role involves working both at a whole-school level and also with individual children. They advise and collaborate with other teachers in their school and liaise with outside agencies, such as educational psychologists or Behavioural Support Teams. They also bear the brunt of SEN-related paperwork and administration. It is a highly pressured role in which SENCOs may struggle to meet the external accountability demands and providing proactive support with the school (Daniels and Porter, 2007).

There is also learning support within the classroom, perhaps associated with a particular Statemented pupil. There are a variety of terms that are used, including 'learning-support assistant', 'non-teaching assistant', 'learning supporter', 'classroom assistant' and 'non-teaching assistant'. These professionals usually work directly with a child, or small group, to provide targeted support with the curriculum. Their duties may range from: social facilitator, to allow children to work in small groups; sign language translator/interpreter; behaviour programme monitor; amanuensis or providing additional explanations of classroom activity; and task-related support. (In some authorities, a distinction is made between the classroom assistant, who assists the teacher generally, and a learning-support person who works with individual pupils.) For children who have moderate learning difficulties and who have Statements in mainstream schools, the provision and the teaching approaches used are often additional individual or small-group help with specific skills. Such children often need support with the general curriculum. This can be achieved by additional help in class – for example, with an assistant interpreting the normal subject matter or helping with literacy demands. An evaluation of such assistance by the schools inspectorate HMI (Audit Commission, 1992) found that it improved the quality of learning above the level of even withdrawal work (teaching children in small, separate groups). Such support is expensive, however, and is usually possible only for some of a pupil's lessons.

Resourced schools

Some 80 per cent of LEAs have resourced schools (Evans and Lunt, 2002). These are usually designed to support pupils with low-incidence impairments or needs, for example by being resourced with Teachers of the Deaf and sign-language support within the classroom. Cuckle and Wilson (2002) looked at the experiences of pupils with Down syndrome in resourced provision. They highlighted two advantages: access to 'role models' of appropriate social behaviour and 'access to friends with similar needs and whose levels of maturity and interests maybe more evenly matched to their own' (p. 71). Resourced schools allow education authorities to bring together equipment, resources and personnel, which may be scarce. An OFSTED report noted that, whilst there were no differences between special and mainstream school in terms of pupils with SEN making 'outstanding progress', resourced mainstream schools had particular strengths regarding 'ethos, the provision of specialist staff and the provision of focused professional development for staff' (OFSTED, 2006, cited in Daniels and Porter, 2007), i.e. that good or outstanding practice was more likely to be found in resourced mainstream schools. However, these schools are usually not the pupil's local school, potentially undermining the development of inclusive practices within the local school, and there may be issues in maintaining friendships and social activities outside the school day.

Pupil-referral units

In England and Wales, pupils who have been excluded from school following challenging behaviour may attend pupil-referral units. These came into existence following the 1993 Education Act, as an educational provision for pupils not in school. They are discussed in Chapter 13, but it is worth indicating here that pupils with Statements were nine-times more likely, in 2003, to be excluded than pupils without Statements (Wilkins *et al.*, 2003, in Daniels and Porter, 2007).

Special schools

As we have seen, the existence of separate special schools for pupils with special educational needs has continued in parallel to, and increasingly as part of, the development of polices regarding inclusive education. For those who believe that 'separate can never be equal' this is a major issue. The UK Government had committed itself to 'ensure they have a secure long-term future' (DfES, 2003b: 1) and, by 2007, there was an increasing proportion of new Statements of SEN directing children to special schools (Daniels and Porter, 2008).

A key feature of special schools is the low teacher:pupil ratio, at around 6.6 and 4.8 in the maintained and non-maintained special schools respectively. They are also typically small with an average size of approximately 80 pupils (DfES, 2003). Pupils are usually placed in such schools only when they are having significant difficulties, and the majority stay within them for the whole of their education. The curriculum is more closely matched to the achievements and the rate of learning of the children who attend there. However, small class sizes and specialist provision mean that the cost of educating children in such schools is about three-times the level of the cost of normal education (Audit Commission, 1992). Also, Crowther *et al.* (1998) found that special-schooling costs were about 58 per cent higher than the cost of special-needs support for equivalent children in an ordinary school. As we have seen, the need for such segregated provision has been the subject of a great deal of concern and debate. There exists a large body of research that examines the academic efficacy of segregated versus mainstream placements.

Another aspect is the social impact of different types of school placement. Some people argue that children, who may be physically or socially vulnerable, need such support and protection, whereas others argue that segregation can be divisive and limiting. A further important argument against segregated education is that it tends to isolate children socially, separating them from their normal local peer group. A follow-up study by Marra (1982) of children who had attended special schools demonstrated that such isolation does happen, and that over half of the children studied said that they felt a definite inferiority and stigma as a result of having attended a special school. A counter-argument, however, is the general finding by Lewis (1972) that when special-needs children are 'integrated' into the ordinary school, they have lower self-esteem and tend to have poorer social integration than children in segregated special schools. Special schools therefore appear to protect some children to some extent. An important aspect of educational research in this area is the accounts from pupils themselves, and using their insights and understanding to inform policy and practice (Shah and Priestley, 2009). One such study, across 12 secondary schools, suggested that pupils identified as having Autistic Spectrum Disorder experienced less social support and higher levels of bullying than their peers without SEN or those identified as dyslexic (Humphrey and Symes, 2010). They highlighted peer contact and support as ways to address this situation (bullying is discussed in Chapter 13).

General and specific teaching approaches

What does inclusive teaching look like?

There are no simple 'recipes' that might deal effectively with all the life experiences, interests and challenges that are present within a classroom. However, there is some evidence to indicate the features of classrooms that help to successfully include a diverse range of pupils. Many have argued that inclusive educational practice is simply good teaching for all. However, there is a tendency for inclusive recommendations to focus on policy and systems (Nind and Wearmouth, 2004). Whilst this is necessary, there may be a lack of advice and support regarding what actually happens within classrooms. This is of particular concern to mainstream classroom teachers, particularly newly qualified teachers (Nind and Wearmouth, 2004). This is of importance as, in England, the majority of children with special educational needs are in mainstream schools, therefore one should discuss SEN in this context.

Skidmore (2004) analysed how schools responded to providing an inclusive educational experience in their classrooms. His analysis suggested that schools that successfully accommodated a diverse range of learners and pupils with special education needs achieved this by starting from a consideration of the curriculum and subject lessons. From this basis, they develop their inclusive teaching practices, rather than beginning by looking at an individual child's needs. Influenced by this view, Sheehy and Rix (2009) carried out an international systematic review of research looking at the question 'What is the nature of whole-class, subject-based pedagogies with reported outcomes for the academic and social inclusion of pupils with special education needs?' The underpinning assumption in this research was that inclusive education requires a pedagogy which successfully delivers the curriculum within mainstream classes. The outcome of the review was that five characteristics were identified, which appeared to have merit in mainstream classrooms, where learning aims were set for the whole class but not for individual children and learning tasks were subject- (i.e. curriculum-) specific and where the teaching practice was stated or described. These characteristics are: social engagement being intrinsic to the pedagogy; flexible modes of representing activities; progressive scaffolding of classroom activities; the authenticity of classroom activities; and a 'pedagogic community'.

Social engagement being intrinsic to the learning process

This indicates situations where the social interactions within the classroom are prioritised, for example using group-based or cooperative working. A wide range of evidence supported this approach and that it should become part of classroom life (Howe and Mercer, 2007). Clearly, though, pupils will need support in developing the appropriate skills to access and consider the knowledge of other class members, in order to develop their own understanding; and, second, to be given opportunities for developing the skills required to share their own knowledge successfully. Several programmes have now been developed that allow teachers to use this approach in their classrooms. Palincsar et al. (2001) developed a programme known as 'reciprocal teaching', which provides support to allow learners to become active in explicitly sharing their thinking. Pupils gain experience in posing questions, predicting and clarifying. The pupils practice, with their peers, the skills that support effective learning in their classroom lessons. This dialogue also allows the teacher to monitor how the pupils are approaching issues and help develop successful strategies. The approach was originally used successfully to teach reading skills and later extended to science lessons.

Flexible modes of representing activities

Activities can be presented in different ways, by both the teacher and pupils. For example, students might share their thinking more effectively by using graphics and drawings. This allows them to communicate what they want to express, where using text or talk alone could create barriers for some learners (Palincsar *et al.*, 2001). Rules and abstract concepts can be made understandable and memorable through additional language and symbol support. The classroom activities themselves can be presented in different modalities, and how the teacher manipulates the modality of curriculum-related materials appears to allow access to a more diverse group of learners and positive outcomes for all learners in the class. This can be straightforward. Miller *et al.* (1998) used paper plates to represent groups in multiplication problems and plastic discs 'to represent objects in the group' (p. 56). This was an alternative, or augmentation, to providing a verbal account of the relationships between abstract numbers. Not only could the pupils manipulate these objects, but their use allowed the teacher to 'see' how the pupils constructed the relationship between groups of numbers. There were 123 pupils in their study across six classes producing positive learning outcomes for all members of diverse class groups.

The use of new technologies has been cited as having potential in developing this aspect of inclusive pedagogy with options to combine text, picture/symbols and sound in learning activities.

Progressive scaffolding of classroom activities

Scaffolding places an emphasis on the support needed for successful learning to occur. It refers to planned learning activities, which begin at a level appropriate for the learner and allows learners to engage with tasks and concepts that they would not be able to tackle independently, through support (Davis and Miyake, 2004). This can include using mnemonic aids to help pupils guide their own actions. If we are seeking to use a social pedagogy, then some children may need a scaffolded approach to use and develop these interpersonal skills.

The authenticity of classroom activities

Authentic activities are those that learners find meaningful, i.e. it is grounded in the pupils' own experiences or where they can make a clear link to a real-life skill. In addition, this activity is judged by the teacher as having academic merit, being appropriate to the curriculum area. That is to say, they are 'being grounded in the learners "first hand experiences" of phenomena but also seen as authentic practices within the … community' (Sheehy and Rix, 2009: 47). Authentic problems and activities are associated with positive learning outcomes for a diverse group of learners, particularly when a social and collaborative approach to learning is adopted. There is evidence to indicate that contextualising curriculum elements by making what is learned relevant to pupils' experiences can support the academic and social inclusion of a diverse range of pupils (Sheehy and Rix, 2009).

Pedagogic community

This final characteristic describes the relationship between the teacher and the subject they are teaching. At first glance this might seem unusual in discussing inclusion, because typically the focus is on the pupils within the classroom and the support that they might require. Teachers who are delivering a curriculum to a diverse group of pupils are supported when they have a good understanding of the knowledge and skills that are associated with that topic, and the aims of the programme they may be delivering. At one level this may appear obvious – that teachers need to understand the nature and aims of what they are teaching. However, this is the basis for developing educationally inclusive classrooms – rather than beginning from identifying a range of pupil needs. Further, teachers are supported if they have an informed position on how children learn and are able to apply this perspective to facilitate learning across the class. Teachers are supported in developing this if they are part of a collaborative community or teachers and educationalists. This community can develop and support a shared pedagogic model to support educational and social inclusion within their curriculum area.

Activity

Read this account of a small classroom study (Sheehy and Johnston-Wilder, 2005) and consider the extent to which the approach might be deemed 'inclusive'.

A small project investigated the use of Lego robotics with pupils who had been excluded from mainstream school and attended a school for children with emotional and behavioural difficulties. Many of them had been assessed as having other special educational needs (attention-deficit/hyperactivity disorder (ADHD) and dyslexia). A series of lessons were run in which the pupils built, created and programmed their own robots. Initially the pupils were uninterested but became increasingly engaged as the sessions progressed, spending more time working and playing with their robots. Inappropriate behaviour decreased. The pupils voted to extend the lesson time and many positive comments were noted.

Some features that supported the class in their work were subsequently identified. The tasks could be adapted in several ways, some pupils had partially pre-built robots and others built from scratch. Once they decided what they wanted to build, the tutor's support regarding gearing and how to use motors was meaningful for them. The robot's plans were visual step-by-step diagrams, which allowed children who experienced difficulties in literacy to engage fully, and supported their reading and comprehension of the process. The robots were programmed by manipulating icons on a laptop screen. It helped overcome memory and sequencing difficulties. However, the group still required considerable tutor support in their work.

Feedback

You will probably have noted some features.

- This type of topic allows a progressive scaffolding of activities and the task can be represented in different modes (for example, diagrams, icons, construction principles, verbal descriptions). The activity appeared to have authenticity for the pupils and also for the teachers who saw it as a valid academic experience for developing science and maths skills.
- In terms of social engagement, the approach did not begin from the basis of a pupil group and how they would work together to develop knowledge. The children worked on their own projects which they then shared and commented upon.

The sessions were run in a segregated school, so you may have queried the extent to which this example can be seen as inclusive teaching at all. However, this setting meant that the timetable could be adapted to accommodate the topic. The tutors were part of a particular pedagogic community, but existed outside the formal education system. You may also have considered the difference between a short-term 'novelty' project and long-term 'everyday' teaching.

There is an interesting tension in the examples we present here. They suggest that inclusive education is not a static event or something that is put in place by set procedures and policies. Rather, inclusive classrooms are worked towards and negotiated by skilled teachers. Yet, whilst the intended focus in these examples is of inclusive practices rather than individual needs, or deficits or impairments, these concepts are used in our discussion and inform, for example, the degree of scaffolding, the way information is presented and the design of activities.

Differentiation

Children with special needs are likely, by definition, to have problems coping with the normal curriculum in school. It may be that the work is not at their general level of understanding, they may lack specific knowledge in an area or they may not have functional basic educational skills such as literacy. This means that the nature of educational experiences and tasks may need to be altered or differentiated to match such children's abilities.

The most common form of differentiation is simply by outcome. This means that the actual task is the same for all children, but there are different expectations according to children's abilities. Although children's achievements will naturally vary, the key element is that the teacher sets different goals for children and judges their work in terms of their own capabilities.

Work can also be differentiated according to the level at which a child is functioning. In England, the National Curriculum allows material to be selected from earlier Key Stages when necessary, and some reading or mathematics schemes are organised so that each child follows material that is matched closely with his or her abilities.

Children can also be given different teaching delivery, or tasks which cover the same area of knowledge but with a different type of conceptual understanding. Bruner (1961b) argues that it is possible to teach any concept to any child in an intellectually respectable way. In investigating oxidation, a practical lesson might therefore involve direct experiences that depend on describing chemical combinations with oxygen. Other children who have not reached this level of understanding might have differentiated tasks that depend on the concept of 'burning'.

Experiences can also be differentiated in terms of the rate at which children complete tasks set for them, the nature of the organisation of teaching groups, for example with ability sets, and in terms of the different physical resources and teaching support that are available. It is often overlooked, but worth noting, that differentiation by ability can be seen as supporting an inherent-ability approach to teaching. Rather than engaging with the child's learning interactions, it may become part of a hierarchical streaming approach to education (Hart et al., 2004). The use of simplified language and materials is recommended for many groups of pupils with learning difficulties. However, whilst there is a range of evidence that differentiated materials support the comprehension and engagement of pupils – for example, those with Down syndrome – there are also potential drawbacks such as stigmatisation, lack of choice and alienation from the curriculum (Rix, 2004). The development of differentiated approaches has been a key issue within inclusive education. For example, children experiencing difficulties with literacy may also need different forms of reading, such as worksheets written to match their skills, symbol support, group work where other children can read any directions, or adult help to prompt unknown words. Alternative approaches to recording can involve using a digital recorder, an adult to copy a child's dictation, speech-to-text software and the use of summary drawings.

We have previously considered the influence of new technologies on learning. In the area of inclusive education, many such developments are heralded as 'solutions' for difficulties in learning. They are seen as being able to remove the disabling barriers that learners face. They are also able to create new spaces within which learners can interact. For example, children spend an increasing amount of time communicating in virtual spaces through game worlds (such as *World of Warcraft*™) and by 2012 one-hundred-million people may well have a virtual character (an avatar) of some type (Castronova, 2008). These types of spaces are now being created, or utilised, for educational purposes, and within them learners can have an agency that is difficult to achieve within the physical world. These spaces can potentially allow learners to communicate in a variety of ways, from text (via typing, symbol choice or voice recognition), speech, symbols or sign language, and the learner can be represented in different ways, such as an avatar. Similarly the activities within the new educational spaces can be structured and supported in a variety of ways to help pupils access the curriculum.

Specific approaches and programmes: the case of autism

As we have indicated elsewhere in this book, it is common for specialist teaching approaches or specific programmes to be designed for a specific 'type' of need or 'impairment'. This approach is particularly noticeable in relation to children with autism.

A key educational barrier experienced by this group is that they may not respond very well to typical interpersonal interaction. They also tend to have difficulties in generalising learning to different situations, presumably since they may not be aware of the way in which people generally construe them. Queuing for lunch may seem very different from queuing for a bus unless you are aware that this is an agreed social convention. One approach can therefore be to teach children with ASD how to react in specific situations, using basic learning that does not depend on social understanding. In an early study, Lovaas *et al.* (1973), for instance, demonstrated that an appropriate behavioural approach can be effective, reducing unusual behaviours and developing basic independence skills. Lovaas (1996) has described how this can be the basis for a highly intensive approach which takes about 40 hours a week with younger children from two to four years of age, with parents trained to carry out the therapy themselves at home. Early intervention programmes can potentially produce positive changes that reduce the need for later interventions. This approach has remained influential in education since its original development. The Southampton Childhood Autism Programme (SCAmP) is an intensive early-intervention ABA approach, influenced by Lovaas's original model of 40 hours' tuition per week. As a form of early intensive behavioural intervention, it appears successful in producing significant gains in language, daily living and social skills. However these improvements may not necessarily lead to reductions in problem behaviour (Remington *et al.*, 2007).

Within classroom settings, Applied Behavioral Analysis (ABA) has influenced the development of precision teaching approaches. These identify target behaviours, the teaching interaction is analysed and progress in learning recorded. The teacher focuses on improving the pupil's performance in a particular skill or task.

Overall, this type of approach for children with autism has been well evaluated, partly because it is built on measurable learning objectives. This means that data is available and evaluative studies are typically well-controlled, enabling influences such as placebo effects and maturation to be ruled out (Dempsey and Foreman, 2001). There is, however, some concern, as expressed for example by Wood and Shears (1986), that this general approach results in a reduction of children's rights, owing to its emphasis on conformity and simplistic learning approaches. Against this, it can be argued that, within the present framework of educational care, behaviouristic approaches usually bring about positive progress for many children, with increased levels of functioning and independence. An ABA approach presents a model for understanding the effect that our interactions may have on children and vice versa.

The TEACCH programme (Treatment and Education of Autistic and related Communication handicapped CHildren) is largely developed from clinical research findings as to the best ways to structure learning. Parental involvement is an important element, although in the UK, TEACCH is more commonly found within schools. It is based on the relative strengths in the visual processing of children with ASD, for example by using picture prompts, and also has a major emphasis on predictable, explicit routines and contextual cues. A TEACCH approach emphasises the physical structure of the classroom in order to support learning interactions. Teaching activities may be sited in particular school or classroom locations, and visual (pictorial or symbolic) schedules used to indicate transitions between each activity. For example, reading tasks can always be done in a particular place and at a particular time of day. Evaluation of the long-term outcomes of TEACCH has generally been positive. Significant gains have been noted in adaptive behaviour, general cognitive skills and skills of daily living (Panerai *et al.*, 1997; Probst and Leppert, 2008). The long-term impact of such development also appears positive, with Schopler *et al.* (1981) finding that 96 per cent of autistic adolescents and adults who had been educated in this way were able to live in their local community, whereas 39–74 per cent would normally need to be in residential-care programmes. This approach is less easy to evaluate and investigations typically lack control groups or direct comparison with alternative approaches (Dempsey and Foreman, 2001). However, research is emerging that does this. For example, Panerai *et al.* (2009) looked at the effects of TEACCH over three years in either a special residential centre or a home and mainstream school implementation. They compared these settings with a supported mainstream education. Their results suggest that TEACCH can be delivered in both settings, and that this specialist teaching approach is more beneficial than the non-specific comparison approach, particularly for pupils with more severe learning difficulties. This study also highlighted the positive benefits of parents, school and 'programme experts' working collaboratively.

Another approach to teaching children with autism, particularly those with severe and profound learning difficulties, has been through social interactive approaches. One of these, 'Intensive Interaction', adopts a strategy based on early child development to construct a shared experience with the child (Nind and Kellet, 2002). It is based on a style of caregiver–infant interaction, seeking to establish rapport and using this as the basis for social development. The key elements of the approach are:

- responding to the behaviour of the child with autism 'as if' they had an intentional purpose;
- adjusting one's own behaviours to establish social interplay and rapport;
- allowing the person with autism to 'take the lead' in social interactions;
- using rhythm and timing to give the interactions flow;
- allowing the sessions to be enjoyable.

Intensive Interaction sets out to enhance social and communication abilities rather than to reduce stereotyped behaviours. However, findings from two studies of Intensive Interaction (Nind and Kellett, 2002) report the reduction of such behaviours. Intensive Interaction builds on 'natural' processes, as opposed to constructing artificial learning situations. One might see a continuum concerning the child's control over their interactions with Intensive Interaction at one end and ABA at the other.

These examples, although autism-specific, have relevance to other 'types of need' in illustrating different aspects of good practice that have empirical support (Dempsey and Foreman, 2001; Iovannone *et al.*, 2003; Panerai *et al.*, 2009). Successful learning experiences for children with special educational needs are more likely when there is:

1   a pedagogy that is based on an underlying model of learning, applied consistently;
2   a learning environment that is made comprehensible to the children, both socially and physically;
3   a curriculum that is sensitive to the child's cognitive and social requirements;
4   functional treatment for problem behaviour;

5   tailored collaborative support for children and their families;
6   planned and supported inclusion with peers.

Interestingly, these characteristics would not contradict those derived from research into inclusive classrooms. However, specialist teaching approaches are often cited as a reason for *not* including children with special educational needs in mainstream schools. You might reflect upon the degree to which these approaches would work within a mainstream inclusive setting, or where their underpinning view of how learning occurs is complementary or conflicting. The latter is important if one is seeking to develop an eclectic approach.

Summary

Inclusive education is part of a global movement of children's rights. It aims to create a situation of 'learning for all' and to remove barriers that prevent all children from learning together. Inclusive polices have influenced the development of educational provision for children who experience difficulties in learning or have physical impairments, which might prevent educational progress. These children are deemed to have special educational needs, which are formally recognised when they are significantly greater than those of other children. One issue is that special educational needs have become used to refer to 'within-child' difficulties, which can act to downplay the considerable evidence that children's backgrounds affect their progress, and that there are interactions between children's environments and their abilities. Further, the term 'inclusive education' is at risk of being reconstructed.

The major category of 'learning difficulties' includes groups whose problems range from slow progress with the curriculum and academic skills, to limited self-help and independence. Children with 'emotional and behavioural difficulties' form the second largest group; for these children, provision is ideally centred in the normal school.

Medical problems such as physical difficulties, epilepsy and cerebral palsy can affect children's educational progress and require environmental and teaching modifications. Hearing difficulties are quite common and affect language and educational progress. Children with hearing difficulties can benefit from specialist oral and manual communication techniques which match with their needs and preferences. Visual difficulties can create a barrier to curriculum access, but this can be addressed through specialist equipment and in-class support that allows children to develop their use of information.

Special educational needs procedures and terminology differ between countries, but identify children who need additional support. Identifying and providing for needs mainly occurs in schools and involves the class teacher, the special educational needs coordinator and outside agencies. A key element of dealing with a child's special needs is the use of Individual Education Plans.

Educational psychologists have experience and training in education and in psychology, and they assess, advise on and support a broad range of children in schools. They can also have a developmental and training role, and increasingly utilise a more consultative approach.

There are some general teaching approaches associated with inclusive classrooms, for example scaffolding and the differentiation of learning activities. The placement of children within segregated special schools continues to be debated. The educational effectiveness of these is not necessarily greater than that of provision based in mainstream schools, but they may offer a protective environment for some children. Although expectation in policy is of mainstream education, children continue to be educated in special schools, and this situation appears a relatively stable one. Children with severe learning difficulties need an early, developmentally based curriculum to achieve self-help and independence goals. Autistic Spectrum Disorder is related to an inability to appreciate the thoughts and understanding of other people, and can severely limit social abilities, language and cognitive development. Successful teaching approaches for children with severe learning difficulties are often based on direct behavioural approaches.

Key implications

- Special educational needs should be seen as a relative judgement about the level of educational difficulty and the allocation of resources.
- Teachers and parents need to be aware of the formal process of special education so that they can ensure that their pupils'/children's needs are being met.
- The range of children's problems and needs means that teachers may need additional advice and support with specific cases.
- Inclusive classroom practices can allow a diverse range of pupils to learn together successfully.

Further reading

Booth and Ainscow (2002), *Index for Inclusion Bristol: Centre for Studies on Inclusive Education (CSIE)*: this set of materials is designed to support schools in developing inclusive school development. These have been highly influential in helping schools to decide their priorities for change and how they can begin to implement and evaluate them. There is also an *Index for Inclusion for Early Year and Childcare.*

Hart, Dixon, Drummond and McIntyre (2004), *Learning Without Limits*: this is a very readable book that challenges a within-children deficit model of special-needs education. It takes the reader inside classrooms and the reflections underpinning teachers' decision about their work.

Hick, Kershner and Farrell (eds) (2009), *Psychology for Inclusive Education: New Directions in Theory and Practice*: this book brings together psychological theory that might usefully underpin inclusive education and discusses how psychologists might actively support and promote inclusive education.

Lewis and Norwich (eds) (2005), *Special Teaching for Special Children? Pedagogies for Inclusion*: as we have discussed, a key question is whether particular groups of children need specific teaching strategies. This book considers different groups in turn (e.g. dyslexia) and the question of whether a specialist teaching strategy is needed is critically considered for each.

Discussion of practical scenario

In general terms, there is evidence to suggest that Susan would do as well academically and socially in a mainstream school as in a specialist school. Going to her local school would mean that Susan could develop contacts with local children. Susan did not attend mainstream school in her previous authority. This may be because of difficulties in arranging this. As we have seen, some parents still have to battle for their children's inclusion. Alternatively, it may be that Susan has, or had at the time, particular needs that were best supported by a particular special school in her previous authority. As she attended a special school, she will already have a Statement of Special Educational Needs. Susan's needs should now be assessed in the context of her new school. There are a range of possible support options that exist, for example she may need in-class support and activities that develop language and communication skills. It may be that some classroom activities will need to be differentiated for Susan, as well as for other children with the class. If Susan's in-class support is delivered by a learning support assistant, it may be that they work with Susan as part of a group, helping them to learn together. This could benefit the class and help Susan to work collaboratively with friends in her new school.

12

Behaviour problems

Chapter overview
- What are behavioural problems?
- Categories of behavioural problems
- Background and causes of educational and behavioural difficulties
- Psychological theories
- Social roles and expectations
- The social-skills perspective
- The role of gender
- The home
- School factors
- Achievement and behaviour
- 'Giftedness'
- Medical causes of children's behaviour problems
- Anxiety and school attendance
- Categories of emotional and behavioural difficulties
- Assessment of behavioural problems
- Prevalence of behavioural problems
- Reliability of assessments
- Validity of BSAG assessments

Practical scenario

Tom has significant behavioural problems in school which mainly involve calling out and attention-seeking in class. He also regularly gets involved in physical aggression, when he reacts against minor social problems if he does not get his own way.

Tom's teacher is concerned about his behaviour and would like to know the reasons for his difficulties.

Tom was adopted three years ago and his teacher believes that he has seen a child psychiatrist a number of times. His adoptive parents are always supportive of school and appear to have similar difficulties managing Tom at home.

What could be some possible reasons for Tom's difficulties?

To what extent should these guide the way in which his teacher manages him in the future?

Is it likely that it would help his teacher to find out more from Tom's child psychiatrist? What would the psychiatrist's perspective be?

If Tom has had early damaging experiences, does this 'excuse' his disruptive behaviour?

Is it at all likely that Tom will improve? Is mainstream school the best place for him?

What are behavioural problems?

All teachers are bound at some time or another to experience children whose behaviour can be a problem. Surveys have generally indicated that behavioural problems have become a matter of increasing concern to schools. Reviews of teachers' concerns find that disruptive pupils are a major source of personal stress for both experienced and trainee teachers (Chaplain, 2008). This is therefore an important area in education, and one where psychology has developed a number of practical and useful approaches.

One measure that is often seen as an indicator of the extent of behaviour problems in schools is that of school exclusions. In England, the level of permanent exclusions has varied over time. It rose more than four times over the period from 1990–1991 to 1996–1997 (DfEE, 1999b; Parsons and Howlett, 1996). The subsequent reduction that began after this period (see Figure 12.1) may have been due to increased pressures on schools to retain problem pupils rather than to any major improvements in underlying behaviour. This decline subsequently reversed, with an overall 11 per cent rise between 1994 and 2001 as the rules for exclusion 'relaxed' (Evans et al., 2004). More recently, there has been a downward trend. As Figure 12.1 illustrates, in 2008 permanent exclusions in England fell by 6.4 per cent. It also highlights that the majority of exclusions are occurring at secondary-school level.

The number of fixed-period exclusions (i.e. temporary exclusions for a short period of time) fell in 2008, with the average exclusion time being two-to-three days. The most common reason for both permanent and fixed-term exclusions was 'persistent disruptive behaviour'. Exclusions do not affect all groups equally. Children with Statements, in receipt of free school meals, who are boys or who are from particular minority ethnic groups are more likely to be excluded from their school than their peers.

There are, of course, many possible reasons for these changes, other than actual increases or decreases in problem behaviours. One of these could simply be that schools became more or less tolerant over this time, owing to changes in the curriculum and increased pressures on them to achieve academic standards. However, there is also evidence that there has been a real increase in underlying difficulties. Rutter and Smith (1995), for instance, carried out a major review of changes in a range of indices of psycho-social disorders of youth in the post-war period. They found significant increases in crime, alcohol and drug abuse in young people, and a range of psychiatric disorders such as depression, anorexia and suicide. The number of children requiring psychiatric help also rose by one-quarter in the second half of the 1980s, and the number of those under the age of ten with such difficulties doubled over this time. Rutter and Smith concluded from such evidence that there were generally

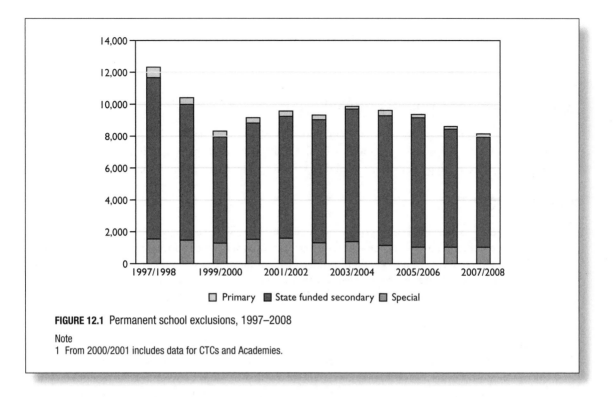

FIGURE 12.1 Permanent school exclusions, 1997–2008

Note
1 From 2000/2001 includes data for CTCs and Academies.

more children with difficult behaviour and that the overall level of pressures and problems experienced by young people in Western society was on the increase owing to factors such as family difficulties and increased expectations. Changes in social poverty creates difficult neighbourhoods and is associated with children experiencing significant difficulties (Watkins and Wagner, 2000). A national survey in 2000 found that approximately one in ten children between 5–15 years of age had a 'mental disorder'. This included 4 per cent with emotional disorders such as anxiety and depression (Meltzer *et al.*, 2000). This group was more likely than their peers to come from low-income backgrounds, with unemployed parents, and live in social-sector housing. This highlights the interplay between social issues and well-being and behaviour. In order to promote the social and emotional well-being of school children, there is therefore a need for a combined comprehensive, universal and targeted approach and a whole-school ethos to promote well-being (Nind and Weare, 2009). In this context it is important that teachers are trained to identify the early signs of emotional distress, anxiety and problem behaviour. This would enable them to assess if specialist help is needed (Nind and Weare, 2009).

Although such findings might suggest that behaviour problems are rampant in schools, it should be emphasised that the vast majority of schools and classes are well-managed and orderly. The Behaviour in Scottish Schools 2009 project found that '97% of teachers and 96% of support staff indicated that all or most of the pupils they encountered around the school were generally well behaved' (Munn *et al.*, 2009, Part 5). When asked specifically about in-class behaviour, this agreement fell slightly, to 93 per cent of teachers and 89 per cent of support staff, but this still indicated a positive change between 2006 and 2009. A review of classroom behaviour in Wales found that, in general, teachers manage behaviour well (Reid, 2009). In the majority of cases, teachers are able to deal rapidly with any problems using techniques such as moving pupils or by gently cautioning them (Galton *et al.*, 1999). Where unsatisfactory behaviour does occur, in the vast majority of cases it involves low-level disruption in lessons. Unfortunately, such low-level disruption is relatively frequent, is wearing for pupils and teachers, impacts upon children's learning and may create situations in which more serious incidents arise (Reid, 2009).

Categories of behavioural problems

The term 'emotional and behavioural difficulties' (EBD) is commonly used, but more recently the term 'behavioural, emotional and social difficulties' (BESD) has become used in legislation. This term positions BESD as a type of primary need (See Chapter 11) and as a possible learning difficulty.

What is BESD?

> The term 'behavioural, emotional and social difficulties' covers a wide range of SEN. It can include children and young people with conduct disorders, hyperkinetic disorders and less obvious disorders such as anxiety, school phobia or depression. There need not be a medical diagnosis for a child or young person to be identified as having BESD, though a diagnosis may provide pointers for the appropriate strategies to manage and minimize the impact of the condition.
>
> (DfES, 2008: 4)

This definition covers the obvious disruptive behaviours but also acknowledges that children can have emotional difficulties such as anxiety or depression, or other mental health problems (DfES, 2001b). Importantly, this view highlights the interactive relationship between mental health and learning. BESD may therefore also draw on disability issues (DRC, 2002). In terms of behaviour, most definitions, such as that by Chazan *et al.* (1994), tend to cover three major aspects. These consider that a child shows emotional and behaviour difficulties when:

- the child's behaviour is a danger to himself or herself, other people or property. This is the most obvious category and can involve physical aggression or less-direct problems such as running out of school.
- the child's behaviour interferes with efficient education of other children or with their own educational progress. Difficult children can deliberately interfere with or distract others, and withdrawn or anxious children may have difficulties concentrating on their work.
- the child has difficulty with social relationships or interferes with the relationships of other children. Again, this might be a deliberate process or it could be simply due to lack of interpersonal skills.

Each of these difficulties can exist by itself or combined together, for instance when children are involved in bullying. This is a common problem and involves prolonged social or physical intimidation, with the added dimension that there is usually the direct intent to have this effect on the victim. In a study of 1,400 secondary-school pupils, 4.9 per cent reported being bullied a lot, and 20.8 per cent a little, in the previous 12 months (Hayden, 2008).

The concept of social, emotional and behavioural difficulties

There are various ways of construing problems in school, and this area overlaps in an interesting way with the field of abnormal psychology. As in abnormal psychology, an unusual behaviour in school is not necessarily a problem. For example, very creative or intelligent children may do their work very differently from the other children around them, but their doing so would usually be seen as desirable rather than a problem.

The 'medical' model

There is a strong tendency for people to see behavioural problems as being primarily located within the child, although such a view is probably less common than it used to be. By implication, any problems should be dealt with by simply considering the child as a difficult individual. (Similarly, the medical model in abnormal psychology sees problems as being due to an 'illness' of the individual or a 'deficit'.) The language used within this way of thinking about issues contains phrases about the identification of symptoms, making an accurate diagnosis of a disease or deficit, and the prescription of an appropriate treatment for the identified syndrome or condition. According to this perspective, problems are the result of an individual child's behaviour, which can be diagnosed and classified and then treated by some expert. From the teacher's perspective, this can mean that the child should be removed from the classroom and educated or 'treated' in some form of specialist provision, away from the school, in the hope that the treatment can 'cure' the behaviour. However, definitions of behaviour, to confirm a condition, occur within a social context. This can make labelling 'emotional disorders' potentially problematic. The example of attention-deficit/hyperactivity disorder (ADHD) illustrates this.

A label often associated with children whose behaviour is problematic in class is that of ADHD. As we will see in Chapter 13, this label occurs following a diagnosis using a defined set of criteria, and there are recommended medical (i.e. pharmacological) and psychological interventions. Children diagnosed with ADHD typically exhibit behaviour that is impulsive, hyperactive and inattentive to a degree that it interferes significantly with their engagement within the classroom. There are a number of diagnostic criteria the children need to meet, over a period of six months, in order to gain such a diagnosis. For example, regarding impulsivity, 'often blurts out answers before questions are completed', 'often has difficulty awaiting turn' or 'often interrupts or intrudes on others (e.g. butts into others' conversations or games)' (DSM-IV-TR, cited in NCCMH, 2008). Following a positive diagnosis, a medical response may be the outcome. This involves prescribing the drug Methylphenidate, commonly known as Ritalin. There is empirical evidence to support the use of this drug, as it is effective in reducing motor activity and improving attention and concentration in some children (NCCMH, 2008). Its use is widespread and growing. In 2001 approximately five-million children were taking Ritalin in the USA (Breggin, 2001). In England there was a 180-fold increase between 1991 and 2005, prescriptions rising from 2,000 to 359,100 in 2005 (Nikah, 2005).

One issue in adopting a medical approach is that it uses social classroom behaviours to identify a 'condition'. There are no clearly discernible biological causes, although there is evidence for association with genetic and maternal risk factors. It has therefore been argued that prescribing drugs in this way is a form of social control rather than the treatment of a medical problem (Baldwin and Cooper, 2000). Prosser (2006) sees this drug treatment as a consequence of thinking about children's behaviour in a particular way:

> if we ask only medical questions about ADHD, we will get only medical answers and more drug treatment. However, if we also ask educational, social and political questions, we will not only gain a better understanding of ADHD, but also possibly identify why drug use for the disorder has skyrocketed in recent years.

> (Prosser, 2006: ix)

As well as producing particular treatment implications giving a child a label of ADHD also has social effects. In a study of the short term effects of Methylphenidate, parents were interviewed before and after treatment. What emerged from this study was that the behaviour of children was interpreted differently with and without medication (Johnston *et al.*, 2000). When children behaved positively, whilst medicated, their mother responded more positively to this behaviour. They also responded less negatively to problem behaviour when the child was medicated. This study suggests that the medication influenced both the children's behaviour and also their parent's perceptions and responses to it. It might be suggested that the same effect could occur for classroom teachers, who are increasing likely to have a child being medically treated for ADHD in their classroom. Of course, a key issue is the effect of such a process on the children themselves. A range of studies indicate that children consistently lack awareness of the educational, situational aspects of their experiences and tend to take on the view that they are defective in some significant way, ignoring their own strengths (Graham, 2006).

The example of ADHD highlights how the 'medicalisation' of a child's behaviour carries with it assumptions about within-child deficits, based on subjective judgements of teachers or parents (Graham, 2006), and also that the label and treatment influences how the child's behaviour is perceived by others and how the child perceives himself or herself.

Activity

What are your own feelings about the use of a drug to treat children's behaviour?

Makes note of the positive outcomes that you would expect to see from a successful intervention for 'impulsive, hyperactive and inattentive' children.

As you read through the chapter, consider to what extent these positive outcomes might be achieved by other means.

A more popular perspective nowadays considers that problems are best seen as an interaction between children and their past and present environments, both at school and at home. This implies that, overall, it may be more effective to manage children and the situation they are in rather than simply medicate or remove them.

Deviation from the norm

Behaviours that are different from what is usually expected (the norm) are often used as the basis for categorisation. For instance, if children fail to obey normal classroom rules, there is certainly a problem, since their behaviour will result in difficulties for teachers in carrying out their job. However, some teachers will have rigid expectations of conformity, whereas others will expect (or tolerate) a certain amount of individuality. This will inevitably lead to inconsistencies between teachers in their judgement of an individual child, and, as discussed later, the reliability of behavioural assessments tends to be quite low between different teachers and different situations.

In fact, the judgements of individual teachers are the most common basis for determining whether a problem exists. When they are asked to give examples of difficulties, teachers will usually talk about behaviours that interfere with class work. A typical survey (Munn *et al.*, 2009) found teachers reported 'low level' disruption such as:

- talking out of turn (e.g. by making remarks, calling out, distracting others by chattering);
- making unnecessary (non-verbal) noise (e.g. by scraping chairs, banging objects);

- hindering other pupils (e.g. by distracting them from work, interfering with materials);
- getting out of their seat without permission;
- persistently infringing class rules (e.g. pupil behaviour, safety).

Similar concerns are found across a range of school contexts (Beaman *et al.*, 2007). Teachers will also include behaviour that is physically dangerous to the child causing the problems, and aggression towards other children or the teacher. However, these are seen as being much less frequent than the above behaviours, which are mainly important because they make it difficult for the teacher to carry on with the process of teaching.

Formal teacher-based assessments of problems typically focus on disruptive and aggressive behaviours, despite their generally low frequency. However, anxiety (phobic states, shyness, etc.) and depression (withdrawn behaviour, unhappiness) can be more important for the individual child. Although they are not necessarily a direct problem for the teacher, these are certainly significant for children in terms of their personal and educational development. It seems advisable to broaden the concept of social and emotional difficulties to cover and emphasise the goal of adaptive behaviour. In school, this would mean being able to use cooperative social behaviours and to adjust to differing situations. The concept has similarities with perspectives in abnormal psychology based on humanistic approaches, which focus on the ability of people to develop and to fulfil their potential.

Background and causes of educational and behavioural difficulties

Psychological theories

Many psychological explanations tend to focus on individuals and try to explain problems from what is going on inside them. However, possibly more powerful approaches take into account the social context and look at the way in which long-term environments develop individuals' strategies and predispositions.

Frustration–aggression

Aggression was originally proposed by Dollard *et al.* (1939) to be mainly an innate response that is always triggered by frustrating situations and events. Although there is some support for this approach, it was subsequently modified by researchers such as Berkowitz (1989) to take account of differing emotional states, environmental cues and cognitive factors such as attributions. According to this, the emotional state of anger towards somebody can result when an individual has an aversive (unpleasant) experience that is perceived to be due to the deliberate intent of another person.

Our existing emotional state can significantly affect the likelihood of aggression. People who are already upset will easily become more aggressive, whereas people who are happy or amused are less likely to become aggressive. Many teachers are of course already well aware of this, and use humour to avoid or defuse tense situations. All emotions are at least partly mediated by arousal, whatever the cause, and an individual who has recently experienced a strong emotion is particularly likely to react in an aggressive way. Zillmann (1988) argues that this happens because physiological arousal takes some time to dissipate; a subsequent minor annoyance can then become intensified by our assuming that it has caused our arousal.

Environmental cues associated with aggression can also increase the likelihood of aggressive behaviours occurring. Berkowitz (1989) originally studied this effect by showing that the presence of a gun would increase the likelihood of subjects giving a confederate of the investigator what they believed to be an electric shock (the apparatus was in fact only a dummy). Although this particular cue is unlikely to occur in British schools, similar effects have also been shown to operate with other associations with violence, for example when people believe that the person they are shocking is more or less belligerent.

Another important feature is whether we attribute an aversive or unpleasant experience to another person, particularly if we believe or perceive that they intended it to have a negative effect. Such attributions are particularly likely when direct physical or verbal provocation, such as insults, is involved. For example, Geen (1968) gave subjects a difficult puzzle that they were sometimes unable to complete. A confederate then proceeded to insult them, attacking both their intelligence and their motivation. Even when they were able to complete the puzzle, the insults led to levels of aggression towards the confederate that were higher than when the subjects had simply been frustrated by being unable to complete the task. Evidently, teachers should be careful in their use of negative feedback and criticism towards pupils. It is also likely that some children have social difficulties due to their use of provocation as an interpersonal style, and such children might be helped to develop more positive ways of getting on with people.

Kelley (1967) has argued that we use logical ways of deciding whether a person's actions are intended to have a certain effect. Attributions of perceived intent are most likely when we believe that another person's actions are different from what other people would do in that situation, when they act consistently in this way (on different occasions), and when they act in the same way with different people. Therefore, if Mrs Smith criticises Peter (but other teachers do not), if she criticises him each lesson, and if she also criticises other students, then Peter is likely to say that Mrs Smith is a generally negative teacher. Similarly, in the case of aggressive behaviours we are likely to be most upset and retaliate when a person repeatedly behaves in an atypical negative way towards us. However, if we are given mitigating information – for example, that the person was upset about something, or that they did not realise the effect that they were having – we are much less likely to be negatively affected.

Although frustration can lead to aggression, Berkowitz (1989) argues that it does so only when it produces negative, unpleasant feelings which result in emotional arousal. Emotional arousal can be strongly reduced by higher thought processes, but these may be undeveloped in some children in schools. It can be difficult to rationalise causes and intents with some pupils, and in these cases it may be appropriate to use a more direct behavioural framework.

Behavioural causes of aggression

Like most other behaviours, aggression (or other problem behaviours) can be seen as the result of operant conditioning. If people act aggressively and receive some reinforcement as a result, they will be more likely to be aggressive on other occasions. Deaux and Wrightsman (1988) have reviewed the evidence that there are a number of effective reinforcers that have been found to increase aggression. These include:

- social approval;
- increased status; and
- evidence of a victim's suffering.

There is considerable evidence of aggressive behaviour being reinforced by processes that take place in the homes of some children. These sometimes involve direct approval for negative acts, for example with attention, laughter or verbal comments. An important type of reinforcement, however, consists of 'escape-conditioning'. This might involve a child learning to use aggressive behaviour to escape from aversive intrusions from other family members (being negatively reinforced). Within such families, aggressive and manipulative behaviours are highly functional since they make it possible for the child to survive in a negative social system.

Activity

Read the following example concerning problem behaviour. Consider why the child might have behaved in the way that was reported and also the teacher's method of helping the child. Are the reasons that you think of similar in nature to the method of helping the child. Do you think that this matters?

Sara, aged five, had been attending a school for two terms. Her mother had insisted on the local authority placing her in this school, refusing to send her to a special school. I attended the annual review for this child before I started my post.

The staff were suggesting that the placement was not suitable for Sara, as she was hitting the children in the playground and this was not appropriate behaviour. They indicated that she would be better off in a special school. I interrupted, having observed Sara in the classroom, and, being an experienced teacher in a special school, I suggested that the special school would not be a 'better place' for her and that once in post I would be able to change her behaviour. I suggested that rather than view her behaviour as disturbed, Sara was trying to communicate with her peers, but did not know how to do this in an acceptable way. Once she was taught this and could learn how to communicate in an appropriate way, she would be able to play with her peers.

Her mother became very emotional and thanked me for my positive view. I was asked by the head teacher how I would implement these changes. I suggested a behaviour modification approach of rewards and clear instructions about how Sara would be expected to communicate with her peers in the playground. I also explained that this would be done in cooperation with the class teacher and the assistant.

After a few weeks, Sara's behaviour had improved. She had learnt how to make friends and how to touch others appropriately. She also had a selection of activities to do at playtime if she became bored. Later, she went on to secondary school with her peers to study for her A-level Art.

(Paige-Smith, 2005: 82)

There are several interpretations that one might make of this example. However, a key focus is that the teacher identified a skill that the child needed to learn and a setting where she needed to be able to use this skill. The teacher then taught the child the skill with positive results. Another aspect is that the teacher thought the child's hitting behaviour served a purpose of some sort. One might have thought that the problem behaviour was caused by a 'within-child' disorder and an alternative response might have been to remove her from the school (she was, after all, hitting other children), or to use some form of punishment to stop her hitting. The behavioural perspective can offer an explanation for the development, or at least increase in frequency, of aggressive behaviour, and it can also be applied to reduce the occurrence of this behaviour – we look at this in Chapter 13. However, the role of punishment is worth considering at this point as a potential cause of aggressive behaviour. To be effective, punishment must be applied consistently, contingent, immediate and severe (Klein, 1996). However, this is almost impossible to do outside of a laboratory and will only, at best, 'suppress a behaviour in a specific context, not eliminate it' (Skinner, 1938). There is also a risk that the 'punisher' will come to evoke an aversive classically conditioned response and, through negative rein-forcement, become more likely to punish the child in future. The results of punishment can be unpre-dictable, stimulating aggressive behaviour in some instances and producing unintended term effects on behaviour – these include poorer mental health, a decrease in the quality of relationships, increased aggression and, longer term, an increase in anti-social behaviour (Huesmann *et al.*, 2003).

Social-learning theory

Social-learning theory proposes that many behaviours develop as a result of our observing what other people do. An investigation by Bandura *et al.* (1963) of behaviour learned from observation showed that children were more likely to be aggressive when they had observed another person behaving aggressively. They were also more likely to be aggressive when they had observed the person being praised for what he or she had done. This indicates that they had learned the social expectations and the likely outcomes for this type of behaviour.

Patterson *et al.* (1967) found that such behavioural processes can be useful in explaining aggression in early-years settings. When aggressive acts by nursery children were followed by rewarding con-sequences, such as passivity or crying by the victim, the aggression was much more likely to be repeated. Children who were non-assertive were often victimised in this way. Eventually, some of them began to copy the aggressive behaviours of other children, and the positive consequences that they then experienced increased the likelihood of these behaviours being used again. Although it seems certain that children are motivated by the consequences of their actions, it also seems to be the case that they develop what they do from the behaviours of others around them.

Such observational learning is a key concept in understanding how children develop their know-ledge of social roles and their sense of identity in school. Wragg (1984) has shown that children do seem to learn from the behaviour of other children in class, particularly about what the consequences would be for themselves if they were to misbehave. These are often critical incidents that set the scene for future expectations and behaviour. The first time a teacher takes a new class, he or she may see a child being naughty but decide to do nothing about it. However, the other children in the class will see the child's bad behaviour being ignored, particularly if the behaviour is a deliberate challenge to the normal rules of the classroom. In these circumstances, children will often recruit attention from those around them and make sure that the teacher is aware of what they are doing. On future occa-sions, the children who observed that naughty behaviour goes unchecked will therefore be more likely to become involved in similar difficult behaviour themselves.

A similar approach can be applied to the influence of the media, where studies have shown the general way in which social learning occurs. Bushman and Huesmann (2006), for example, argue that when children watch media characters dealing with interpersonal problems by using violence, they develop ideas about *scripts* – what events are likely or appropriate in a given situation. When children are confronted with similar situations in their own lives, these scripts may then be activated and increase the probability of overt aggression. An important feature, which increases the likelihood of children believing that such behaviour would be appropriate for them, seems to be the extent to which they identify with the aggressor. This is the perceived similarity of the model, or the ideal role which the model represents, to themselves. They are also more likely to use aggressive behaviour that they have seen as being justified in some way, which has not had upsetting or negative consequences, and, perhaps most importantly, if they see the context and behaviour as being close to reality. Chil-dren learn these new scripts through observational learning more readily than adults do. These scripts influence aggressive behaviour, thoughts and feelings.

Media and aggression

Although the amount of television that children watch varies, it is often a significant part of their daily activities. Even before the onset of multiple digital channels, younger children, two-to-seven years of age, watched around 25 hours per week (Roberts *et al.*, 1999); more recent estimates are that, by the time they enter school, children will have viewed at least 4,000 hours (American Psychology Association, 2005). In Britain, over a decade ago, children's television programmes often contained violence, with around 1,000 programmes featuring 4,000 physical assaults or shootings (Gunter and Harrison, 1997). Some recent analysis puts the occurrence of these incidents as high as 'one violent act every 4 minutes' (Erwin and Morton, 2008). This equates to children typically observing more than 20,000 violent acts during their school career. There is evidence to suggest that children give greater attention to commercials (Alexander and Morrison, 1995), where one-third featuring children also feature violence of some form or other (Larson, 2003). Bandura's early work found that children were more likely to copy behaviours when the actor:

- is seen as attractive;
- is similar to them in age and sex;
- has desirable characteristics.

Bandura's (1986) original view was that children learn through: exposure, acquisition, and acceptance to become less sensitive to violence, and also 'how to do it'. Supporting Bandura's view, the American Psychology Association concluded that the three primary effects of media violence appear to be:

1   reduced sensitivity to the pain and anguish of others;
2   increased fearfulness; and
3   greater aggressive or violent behaviour toward others.

(Cited in Erwin and Morton, 2008)

Long-term studies have shown that children who watch more violence on television tend to be aggressive later in life. However, these findings are correlational, and may just reflect the fact that such children are from backgrounds that encourage this type of viewing and, at the same time, foster the development of aggressive behaviour. One American study looked at the viewing of over 6,500 10–14-year-olds and found half had viewed films featuring 'extreme graphic violence', and explicitly rated as unsuitable for young people (Worth *et al.*, 2008). Their viewing habits correlated with factors such as low socioeconomic status, poor school performance and being a boy from a minority ethnic group. In an attempt to investigate the influence of the child's background, Huesman (1986) carried out a 22-year study that considered the relative importance of a range of different factors. Huesman looked at aggression and the amount of violent television watched at eight years of age, and related these factors to aggression and criminality (including the seriousness of the crimes committed) at 30 years of age. The investigation found that early television watching was a better predictor of later difficulties than early ratings of aggression, indicating that it was the television watching that caused the later difficult behaviour. Others have concluded that the amount of violence children watch is a stronger predictor of later adult violence than economic and early social factors. However, there appear to be a number of other long-term mediating effects, including family background, social integration and academic achievements. It may therefore be that the key feature is the continuity over time of a family background that fostered progressively more aggressive behaviour, as well as poor supervision permitting the viewing of violence. Stronger evidence would need to show a direct effect of watching violence, by comparing the behaviour of groups of children who had either watched or not watched violent television or films, while holding other factors such as home background constant.

Perhaps the ideal way of studying the effects of television would be to carry out a long-term experiment in a real-life situation. This would involve assembling two similar groups of people who had been prevented from seeing television in their lives. One group would then be exposed to television and studied over time to see whether the level of aggression in that population changed, relative to the other control group. Although such an experiment is impossible to arrange, it has been approximated by some 'natural experiments'.

Natural experiments in television watching

In 1973, a small Canadian town (called 'Notel' by the investigators) became able to receive television for the first time when problems with reception were overcome. Joy et al. (1986) investigated the impact of television on this community and used as controls two similar communities that already had television. Using a double-blind research design, 45 first- and second-grade students were observed over a period of two years for rates of different forms of aggression. Although the behaviour in the two control communities stayed the same, the rates of physical aggression among children in Notel dramatically increased by 160 per cent, indicating that television viewing had a strongly negative effect on behaviour.

However, there were very different findings in a similar study by Charlton and O'Bey (1997), who looked at the effects of introducing television to the isolated island of St Helena in the South Atlantic. In this case, the behaviour of children in school, as assessed by direct observation and by teacher ratings, did not worsen over time. There were in fact some improvements among younger children, with a reduction in teasing and fighting behaviour.

As the Notel example illustrates, later work suggests that factors such as the family context of television-watching is vitally important. These effects are mediated in the long term by general real-life cultural and socialising factors (Browne and Hamilton-Giachritsis, 2005), as the family can sometimes be more important than viewing negative models on television. In this context, the St Helena population may have been rather atypical, since it had very close community links, ensuring monitoring and accountability for behaviour. When home and the general community (including schooling) are less cohesive (as in Notel), then it may be that the influences of viewing television can be more negative.

Television and pro-social effects

A further interesting possibility is that some television, particularly programmes specifically made for children, can have pro-social effects, since they often portray positive moral principles and outcomes. A review of research of the effects of educational programmes suggested that they had a positive influence on knowledge and attitudes concerning race, and developed 'imaginativeness' (Thakker et al., 2009). These positive effects have long been noted. Sprafkin and Rubinstein (1979), for instance, found that children who prefer and watch more pro-social programmes tend to behave more positively in school. Young children who watch programmes such as Sesame Street for a couple of hours per week have higher academic attainment scores than peers who did not watch these programmes, or who watched cartoons and non-educational shows (Huston et al., 1981). Thakker et al. (2009)

concluded that, whilst cartoons could have a negative effect on children's attentional abilities, there was insufficient evidence to draw conclusions regarding the effects of these programmes on aggressive or pro-social behaviour.

Computer games, the Internet and violence

Watching television and films is a relatively passive activity, and its importance in children's play and leisure is decreasing as a wider range of interactive media has developed. These media cover computer games and virtual worlds. In 2005, a US survey found that half of the children sampled had a games console in their bedroom and over one-third had a computer (Olson et al., 2009) – and these figures are likely to increase. Whilst it has been debated whether one can make links between new media and the 'television and aggression' data, it is clear that within these new spaces it is possible for young people not only to view violent behaviour but also to enact and instigate it. This raises the question of whether the boundaries between real and virtual behaviours might become blurred, for example if the repeated performance of 'aggressive scripts' in-game develop automatic responses in the real world (Funk, 2005). Within virtual worlds, concerns have been raised regarding a range of significant issues encompassing online harassment and victimisation, and exposure to online stalkers and dangerous adults (Berson et al., 2008; Wishart, 2004). There are also concerns that family interactions are being negatively influenced by immersion in virtual spaces (Byron, 2008), or that this immersion may develop into a form of addiction (Graham, 2009). Research into the effects on children's social and emotional development and their behaviour in 'real life' remains inconclusive. However, what is emerging is an understanding that, as with exposure to extremely violent films, risk factors for virtual spaces are patterned along social lines (Palfrey et al., 2008) and children who are vulnerable online are often also vulnerable in their offline lives (Wolak et al., 2008).

Overall, the implications for parents and schools appears to be that the media can affect children's behaviour, but that the effects can be mediated by children's general social and cultural context. As with television-viewing, there are reports of positive effects from gameplay and evidence of similar mediating factors in the effects of new media on behaviour and well-being.

Social roles and expectations

Chapter 7 described how behaviour in school can be seen as the result of a set of norms and scripts, with pupils and teachers acting to present their concepts of their own selves in social situations. In school there are role expectations for both pupils and teachers, and these determine a great deal of normal behaviour. The role of the teacher is to control, organise and to exercise authority. Pupils will normally show obedience to the teacher's authority, and conformity to the norms of the normal class-room situation. 'Normal' behaviour can be seen as the process of generally following these expectations, with 'scripts' that govern the processes that happen in different situations in school.

In lessons, pupils are expected to enter the class, sit down at their desks, attend to the teacher and get on with their work. Teachers are expected to complement this behaviour by organising and directing the children. Even informal times of the day such as breaks have their own expectations, with limits on where children can go and the type of games they can get involved in. It is not surprising that problems with non-teaching supervisors are particularly likely at these times. They are unlikely to be perceived by the pupils as having the same authority role as teachers, but have the role responsibility of directing and managing behaviour, which leads to role conflict.

Hargreaves (1967) has shown that problem behaviours in school can often be seen as a general social process, with pupils acting against the organisation's norms in order to meet the alternative norms of their own peer group. Meeting the norms of the peer group can lead to challenges and activities that are deliberately in opposition to school rules and expectations of behaviour. For example, they may subvert the school's dress codes or, at the extreme, actively seek punishment to confirm to their peers that they are in opposition to the formal rules.

The implications of such explanations are that behaviour will be more positive when pupils perceive themselves to be part of the social structures of school and identify with groupings such as their own tutor group or 'house'. They are also more likely to feel commitment when they are part of the processes of decision-making and in establishing rules and regulations. These approaches are incorporated in a number of techniques, described in Chapter 13, such as 'Circle Time' and the 'No-Blame approach', which depend on developing pro-social behaviour through social interactions. Cooperative involvement by pupils out of school can be particularly effective in setting up relationships that transfer well to the normal school situation. A review of a number of studies by Hattie et al. (1997) found that the shared experience of going on an 'outward-bound' type of activity resulted, among other things, in significant improvements in pupils' behaviour when they were back in school, with an overall long-term effect size of 0.51.

Deindividuation

Deindividuation happens when individuals lose their sense of personal identity. This is likely to happen when people are part of a crowd, or when they feel anonymous. People can, for instance, lose their sense of individual responsibility if they believe that others will not be able to attribute their actions to them. This loosening of inhibitions may mean that they behave in ways that are not consistent with their usual values. There are links here to children's behaviour in online social networks, where they may be anonymous to, or feel distance from, other users. Dehue et al. (2008), asked over 1,000 primary-school children about their behaviour in these spaces. They found that 16 per cent had bullied others online to some degree. Deindividuation has also been used as a concept to study the effects of class size on pupil behaviour (Engleheart, 2006).

Behaviour in such situations and experiences can be understood from the perspective of people becoming free from the normal roles and scripts that govern what they do. Such situations can sometimes lead to impulsive and aggressive behaviour, if there is even a low level of motivation to behave in this way. In his classic experiment, Zimbardo (1970), for instance, found that participants would follow instructions and deliver greater electric shocks to an innocent victim when they were part of a group or when they were wearing disguises (the 'shocks' and the victim were actually fake).

School classes involve relatively large groups of pupils, and in secondary schools in particular there can be relatively high levels of anonymity. These circumstances are likely to lead to a decreased sense of responsibility by pupils and a tendency to join in with class misbehaviour. A key technique to prevent such deindividuation and its consequences is for a teacher to be able to identify individual pupils as soon as possible, and to make sure that they are aware that the teacher knows them as individuals. Marland (1993) describes practical ways of achieving this, which include insisting on regular seating positions with a key kept by the teacher and regular rehearsal of children's names in the early stages with a new class. Incidentally, a useful technique here is to use the mnemonic strategies mentioned in Chapter 2. For example, a pupil's key visual features can be identified and linked with the pupil's name in some way.

It also seems probable that the use of a standard school uniform could deindividuate pupils and that it might therefore be best to allow individual dress styles. However, such a policy might also encourage the use of clothing as the signals for subgroup membership with a general ethos counter to that of the school. The best option might be to allow some variation but with limits to the more extreme and challenging forms of clothing.

Bystander apathy

Aggression also becomes more likely when children who are not directly involved fail to act to help an evident victim. Bystander apathy is particularly important in the case of bullying, influencing the severity of bullying behaviour, and must be tackled when one is trying to reduce such behaviour problems. Bystander apathy has been extensively studied, since it can seem rather surprising that people will fail to act helpfully in such situations.

Latane and Darley (1970) emphasise that individuals appear to carry out an evaluation of the situation, in terms of whether there is a real problem and whether they could actually do something to help. Piliavin *et al.* (1981) also found that people will weigh up the costs and benefits of helping. On the one hand, helping another pupil who is being bullied might result in social approval from adults and a boost to one's self-esteem. However, becoming involved could also expose a child to social pressures from other children and perhaps some physical danger. At the very least, it would involve some inconvenience, for instance if the child had to be involved in reporting the incident. Owing to such concerns, children in school will often fail to act and may then seek to rationalise their non-action in order to protect their own self-esteem. They may do this by saying that it was the victim's own fault, or that the incident was not really as serious as it seemed.

As already described, being part of a group can also lead to a decrease in individual responsibility and assumptions that somebody else will act. People also tend to conform and take cues for appropriate roles and actions from others around them. Such conformity can have the effect of inhibiting action unless children become aware of their own responsibilities and the need for action. This aspect is part of some approaches to reducing bullying, and it has been shown that when students are aware of the processes of bystander apathy, they are much more likely to help others in need. 'Social loafing theory' states that pupils will exert less effort when in a group, as their individual contributions are likely to go unnoticed; as class sizes increase, there may be less social cohesion and their motivation to join in decreases, particularly with collaborative tasks (Engelheart, 2006).

The social-skills perspective

Some children can have behavioural difficulties that appear to be due to problems with social interaction. These may involve an inability to structure social exchanges, with the normal turn-taking and reciprocity that the structuring of social exchanges entail. Some children appear to misread social cues and situations, causing faulty peer-group entry, misperception of peer-group norms, inappropriate responses to provocation and misinterpretation of pro-social interactions. Inappropriate understanding and responses may lead to aggression, or alternatively to withdrawal and subsequent rejection by the normal peer group. This can in its own turn lead to membership of more deviant peer groups where children with such problems are even less likely to develop positive interaction skills.

Since many behavioural difficulties are present before school and persist when pupils are there, it seems likely that some children fail to develop social skills as a result of their social experiences in the home. Observations by Patterson (1982) in the homes of some families have shown that children's pro-social acts are often ignored or responded to inappropriately. Also, the parental models for positive behaviours can often be limited, with an emphasis on inconsistent, restricted and punitive interactions with children. Sensitive parental responses to young children help to develop secure attachments in middle childhood and support the development of social skills. In contrast, inconsistent rejecting or harsh parental styles are seen as promoting the development of anti-social behaviours (Scott, 2010). Through poor supervision, children can also frequently be intruded upon by others in the family, which can lead them to develop reactive and coercive behaviours such as shouting and hitting as a form of substitute social skill.

The development of effective social skills is one of the most important skills of early childhood, allowing the child to negotiate peer interactions and interpersonal relationships. Failure to do so has serious long-term consequences. Studies of pupils in school by Dodge *et al.* (1986) have found that many children who are ignored, neglected or rejected by their peers are unhappy and lacking in social skills, and Dunn and McGuire (1992) found that such children are particularly at risk of continued maladaptive behaviour such as aggression, disruption and hypersensitivity. It seems likely that an effective way to help some children with such behavioural difficulties would be to focus on the development of specific social-interactions skills, and some of these approaches are described in Chapter 13.

The role of gender

Across a range of schools and countries, boys are consistently perceived as 'more troublesome than girls' (Beaman *et al.*, 2007: 25). This is due to a gender-based style of behaviour in which the externalising nature of boys' behaviours contrast with less-noticeable behaviours of girls. This might explain why boys receive 68 per cent of criticisms directed at classroom behaviour (Croll and Moses, 1990), implying that low-level problems are twice as prevalent in boys as girls. A small-scale study of 18 teachers supports this, finding that boys receive more disapprobation and are less 'on-task' than girls in class (Swinsom and Harrop, 2009). In England, boys at School Action Plus are most likely to have behavioural, emotional and social difficulties as their primary need (DCSF, 2009). Given this, it is not perhaps surprising that boys account for the vast majority of permanent and fixed exclusions, 78 per cent and 75 per cent respectively (DSCF, 2009). There is, however, some evidence suggesting a slight change of pattern in girls' behaviour: an increase in exclusions (Reid, 2009), disruptive gang behaviour (Smith, 2004, in Reid, 2009) and higher rates of truancy than boys in some schools.

Activity

What types of evidence do you think would be needed to understand why boys are consistently found to be 'more troublesome' than girls?

Do you think that the types of evidence that you see as necessary reveal something about your own views on the causes of problem behaviours?

Some explanations for this difference focus on the possibility of biological differences in the aggressiveness of males and females, for instance due to the effect of the male hormone testosterone. Although males with higher levels of testosterone are more likely to commit anti-social acts (Dabbs and Morris, 1990), aggression itself boosts the levels of testosterone, and this is probably unlikely to be a simple cause of difficult behaviour. Cairns *et al.* (1989) found that boys and girls in school did not differ in their experiences of anger or aggression in different situations, but that they did differ in the behavioural expression of anger. Boys tended to use physical confrontation, but girls were much more likely to use 'social aggression' that involved attempts to alienate or ostracise a girl from a social group or to defame her character. These differences appear to be strongly influenced by the development of sex roles and stereotype expectations, described in Chapter 7. This illustrates that psychological development cannot be explained purely with reference to within-child factors, nor by focusing on a single feature of the environment. For example, Scott (2010) highlights the interaction between parenting styles and children's genetic 'vulnerability' and temperament. Therefore children's disturbing behaviour is the result of social and individual factors that interact in a complex and ongoing way.

The home

A large number of studies have shown that children with behavioural problems at school also have stressful home backgrounds (Olweus, 1993). These suggest that children's aggression is related to:

- severity of punishment by the parents;
- disagreement between the parents;
- lack of warmth on the part of the mother;
- lack of supervision; and
- inconsistent management.

Such experiences appear to give children only partial and inconsistent boundaries for their behaviour, with limited internalisation of values. They also give children poor models for interpersonal relationships and behaviour, and prevent them from developing understanding and feeling for the needs of others.

However, since these findings are correlational, it could be that children's behavioural difficulties cause changes in their parents' handling of them and might also generate stresses within the family. To investigate this, a longitudinal study by Farrington (1978) looked at the development of behavioural difficulties in 411 males from age eight until they were 22 years old. Among other factors, this looked at the outcomes for harsh parental attitudes and an emphasis on the use of discipline. The findings shown in Table 12.1 indicate that there was a significant relationship between early behaviour problems and long-term delinquency, but that parents' attitudes and discipline had an even stronger effect. This is consistent with the possibility that the children's home background had a progressively greater impact on them over time. Evidently, many children who were not originally difficult at eight years of age eventually became so, although, also, some must have improved over time.

TABLE 12.1 Prediction of delinquency by early aggression and parental background

Measures at eight-to-ten years	Delinquents at 22 years, identified by earlier measures (%)
Aggression	48.2
Harsh parental attitudes and discipline	61.5

Source: based on data from Farrington (1978).

How might children learn to be aggressive?

The *Dunedin Multidisciplinary Health and Development Study* is a significant ongoing longitudinal investigation, which began tracking 1,000 boys and girls from three years of age in 1973. Interestingly, the data recorded suggest relatively stable patterns of aggressive behaviour between toddlerhood and adolescence (Broidy *et al.*, 2003), with 9 per cent of boys showing consistently high levels of physical aggression. Across this research area, five factors emerge as particularly important.

Activity

Based on what you have read so far, what do you think these five factors might be?
Make a note of your five factors and your reason for choosing them.
Then compare your thoughts with the findings mentioned at the end of this chapter.

Patterson (1986) found that parenting practices and family interactions by themselves account for up to 40 per cent of the variance in general anti-social behaviour. Direct observations and analyses of family-interaction processes indicate that aggressive and non-compliant behaviours are developed from an early age by a process of social learning. At first, the occurrence of relatively trivial behaviours such as whining, teasing and temper tantrums is reinforced either by attention or by positive outcomes if the child gets what he or she wants. As children become older, parents may then continue to use reinforcers and punishments inappropriately and inconsistently. Various intrusions or forms of attack on children are common in some families and may occur hundreds of times each day. These can include simple verbal name-calling, the taking of a toy or other object away from a sibling and direct physical interference. In such families, children rapidly learn that the only way to handle such events is to counterattack, and Patterson (1982) found that about one-third of children's coercive behaviours were a reaction to aversive intrusions by other family members. The child's counterattacks were also functional, in that about 70 per cent of the time they were followed by the attacker's withdrawal, resulting in a positive or a neutral outcome. As children learn to use high rates of negative behaviours, other family members also acquire the same skills and chains of reciprocal behaviour can build up. Analyses have shown that, as the lengths of this increase beyond 18 seconds, family members are at increased risk of hitting each other.

Patterson (1986) argues that such patterns of learned negative and coercive behaviours extend to outside the family and lead to rejection from normal peer groups. Allied to lax parental supervision and academic failure in school, this can then predispose children to join with similar individuals, forming deviant peer groups. The norms that are then established by these groups appear to become the main socialising process for their members and can lead to delinquent activities and substance abuse. Members of such groups can provide considerable positive reinforcement for deviant behaviour and will punish others for socially conforming acts.

A major review of various studies by Campbell (1995) found that difficult home backgrounds were associated with the emergence of problems in early childhood and predicted their persistence to school age. Incorporating such family, peer group and academic factors into a general model enabled Patterson (1986) to account for 54 per cent of the variance in 'delinquency'. This is a strong effect and indicates that there is likely to be a causative process operating. There is also support for this perspective from family-intervention studies. The results of randomised control trials (Scott, 2010) indicates that when more positive family interactions are developed, then the likelihood of children exhibiting aggressive behaviour is greatly reduced, with larger effects reported for children with more severe problems. A range of research studies have investigated the influence of family and child-based characteristics in the development of anti-social behaviour. The significant family characteristics appear to be:

- harsh/authoritative parenting;
- parental psychopathology and criminality;
- interparental and family violence;
- large family size;
- poverty;
- poor educational achievement of parents.

(Bowen *et al.*, 2008)

An important point is that whilst individually these risk factors may only have weak associations with later behaviour, the presence of multiple risk factors significantly increases the likelihood of later negative outcomes (Bowen *et al.*, 2008). Protecting factors include a close relationship with a family member, positive friends network and socially valued personal achievements. This indicates a positive role for schools in this context.

However, even without intervention, a poor start does not guarantee that all such problems will continue. Topping's (1983) review finding of a 'spontaneous remission rate' of about two-thirds over four years has been replicated in most longitudinal research, across all age ranges. Along with this recovery rate, however, new behavioural problems can develop, particularly when there are significant changes in the home environment. In line with the previous Activity, these common events include moving house, loss of employment or separation of parents. Pagani *et al.* (1997), for instance, found that divorce before a child was six years old was associated with long-term increases in anxious, hyperactive and oppositional behaviour during later childhood. Apart from the direct disharmony that precipitates and is the result of such major changes, some children can be subsequently faced with adapting to a new family if their parent remarries. Although children may eventually learn to adjust to such situations, they may take some time to do so, and new behaviour problems might develop.

School factors

Children spend a great deal of their lives in school and it seems almost inevitable that they will be affected by their social experiences there. However, the home is the main early socialising influence for children, and the social environments of different schools are likely to vary less than children's home backgrounds. For example, the positive correlation between a school's percentage of pupils qualifying for free school meals and number of permanent school exclusions (DCSF, 2009) may indicate this. Yet, schools with a roughly similar intake can still show significant differences in the overall level of general behavioural difficulties. Reid (2009) found large variations in policies and practices in that the number of pupils excluded by five secondary schools in Wales accounted for approximately 40 per cent of all fixed-term exclusions in Wales. This suggests that schools do vary to some extent in their effectiveness in dealing with children's behaviour.

Maxwell (1994), for instance, looked at the social intake of 13 secondary schools in Aberdeen and related this to the level of behavioural difficulties in each catchment. The level of free school meals uptake was taken as a measure of social disadvantage since, although free school meals uptake relates only indirectly to the processes in individual families, it does give some indication of the overall levels of social pressures and difficulties. Emotional and behavioural difficulties were assessed based on the number of children who were being educated out of school as a result of such problems.

As shown in Figure 12.2, this correlation is in fact quite high at 0.89, and evidently children from the most disadvantaged areas are much more likely to have emotional and behavioural difficulties. General home background therefore appears to account for the greater part of the variation between schools over this range. Most schools also tend not to be too extreme on either count and it is difficult to separate them. However, schools A and B appear to have roughly similar intakes, yet school A has at least four-times the level of this type of behavioural difficulty as compared with school B. Reid (2009), examining differences in school exclusions, suggested more extreme polarities between 'a zero-tolerance approach to genuine inclusion practice' (p. 166). Previous research (Reynolds and Sullivan, 1981) also found differences in practices. When schools had a perspective they designated 'incorporation', both children and their families were encouraged to take an active and participative role in school. These schools used prefects and monitors, and had good interpersonal relationships between pupils and staff, with minimal use of overt institutional control. Parental involvement was helped by the regular sending home of information, and there was close informal contact with teachers.

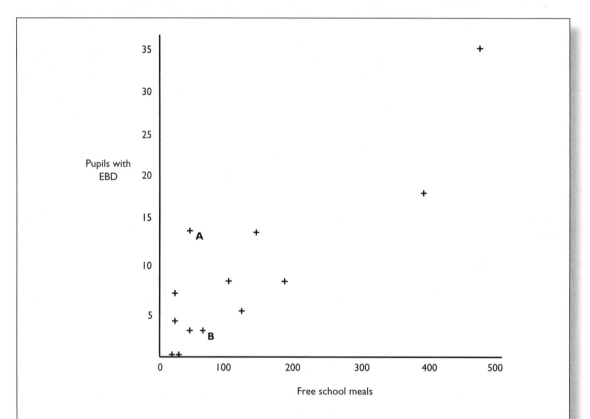

FIGURE 12.2 Levels of emotional and behavioural difficulties (EBD) in relation to social class of intake in 13 Aberdeen schools (source: Maxwell, 1994)

Schools using the alternative perspective of 'coercion' tended to view problems as being mainly due to children's home backgrounds and largely relied upon institutional control, strict rule-enforcement and the use of punishment. Pupils were not involved in the authority structure of the school, since teachers felt that they would abuse that power, and parents were not involved since it was felt that they would not support the school.

However, a caution about such findings is that they are unlikely to account completely for the differences in intakes between schools. Although measures such as entitlement to free school meals may be an indicator of home background, these are likely to be affected by factors such as the local possibilities of employment and cannot accurately account for the general social culture and practices in bringing up children. Also, it is likely that what schools are able to do is strongly affected by their catchment and that factors such as the levels of parental support are mainly affected by a school's social intake. Randall (1997), for instance, describes how interpersonal aggression is very much part of the culture in some school catchments and how some parents encourage their children to continue with aggression in school. The consequences of this aggressive culture may predispose some children to social and emotional difficulties such as depression (Rusby et al., 2005).

Achievement and behaviour

At first glance there appears to be a strong association between learning difficulties and behaviour problems. Older children with behaviour problems of the sort that can lead them into subsequent delinquency (i.e. trouble with the law) often have low levels of basic academic skills. Howe and Mercer (2007) have noted the link between a lack of literacy skills and problem behaviour, and it has been argued that almost the entire secondary-school timetable assumes proficiency. Certainly, good literacy skills and higher abilities are seen as associated with resilience for potentially at-risk children and positive psycho-social outcomes. By contrast, delayed or poor reading skills may be seen as negative influences on children's longer-term development (Stainthorp and Hughes, 2004). Many studies have highlighted positive associations between social skills and academic achievement, in which children with poor social skills performs less well academically (Miles and Stipek, 2006). A typical study by Wilgosh and Paitich (1982) found that more than 60 per cent of a sample of 99 girls and boys who were classed as 'delinquents' at about 14 years of age were underachieving by two or more years in at least one area of academic skills. Similarly, Meltzer et al. (1984) found that as early as second grade, 45 per cent of children who eventually became 'delinquents' were already significantly behind with their reading. Williams and McGee (1994) carried out a long-term investigation with a large sample of boys from the beginning to the end of their schooling. They found that children's early failure with literacy was significantly associated with a subsequent diagnosis of conduct disorder at 15 years of age. A 'life-cycle study' from an ongoing large-scale longitudinal study found a correlation between literacy skills and long-term psycho-social adjustment for males in their teens and at mid-life (Kern and Friedman, 2008). A difficulty in interpreting such findings is knowing whether it was in fact the learning problems that caused the behavioural difficulties. One possibility is that low literacy skills mean that pupils are frequently unable to cope with the work in school and therefore look for other (more deviant) ways in which to boost their self-esteem. However, there is an alternative and plausible explanation which is the complete reverse. This is that early and persistent behavioural difficulties cause learning problems.

There is some support for this explanation in that the literacy attainments of older children with behaviour problems are in fact generally not particularly far behind: in the Wilgosh and Paitich (1982) study, which included children with the most severe behavioural difficulties, the overall delay with literacy was only about one year. Although significant, this would hardly limit their ability to cope with the majority of school work. And such delays are in fact quite common, and the majority of children with such literacy difficulties do not automatically have behavioural problems.

The relationship between the long-term development of literacy and behavioural problems was investigated by McGee *et al.* (1986) with 925 boys from 5–11 years of age. The main finding was that those children who had early behaviour problems at the age of five, particularly poor concentration/attention, subsequently had low levels of learning progress. As they became older, the type of their behavioural difficulties changed and they became more anti-social. This gives support for the idea that early behaviour problems which prevent children from being involved with school work will limit their progress with literacy skills.

In a study of 400 low-income children and families, Miles and Stipek (2006) felt that the patterns of associated behaviours were consistent with aggression being the result of experiencing difficulties in learning. Their argument was that boys were less-attentive and off-task, and that these behaviours, in turn, predicted the development of later aggressive and noncompliant behaviour. However, an alternative explanation is that something else might be causing both the eventual conduct disorder and the long-term reading difficulty. Various types of evidence suggest that this something might be the ongoing effects of negative home environments, coupled with early difficulties with attention and concentration. According to this perspective, children can fail to make initial progress with reading owing to a combination of home-environment factors including limited parental involvement. Early difficulties with concentration and attention would interfere with initial learning and are also strongly associated with conduct disorder, frequently acting as a basis for its later development.

When allowance is made for the effect of social background variables, attainments no longer appear to have a direct effect on behaviour. Fergusson and Lynskey (1997), for instance, followed a birth cohort of 1,265 children in New Zealand from the point of school entry to the age of 16. Children with early reading delays were found to have many negative features in their lives, including high rates of attentional difficulties and conduct problems. They also generally had poor home backgrounds, including a high chance of belonging to a low social class, a high chance of coming from a single-parent family and a high chance of coming from a poorly managed home. When these effects were accounted for, there was no longer any association between the reading skills and behaviour of the children when they were 16 years old.

But, if literacy difficulties did cause conduct disorders, one would expect that academic remediation would lead to a reduction in anti-social behaviour. In fact, a number of studies reviewed by Wilson and Hernstein (1985) have repeatedly demonstrated that this does not happen. Having one's skills boosted and experiencing success in school do not appear to be sufficient in themselves to generate improved behaviour. It could, of course, still be the case that the help was given too late and that it is difficult to overcome established patterns of negative behaviour.

Practical implications

In general, behavioural problems do not seem to be a simple outcome of learning difficulties, although they probably share some causes in terms of poor early adjustment to school and long-term home environmental factors. It still seems likely, however, that the most severe forms of literacy difficulties, such as a reading age below eight years later in the secondary school, will have a direct effect on behaviour. If children are unable to manage any formal work in class (which presupposes that the work they are presented with is inappropriate), they might easily become involved in other activities such as talking to other children, which would be generally disruptive. Even in such extreme cases, it is still not certain that problems would extend beyond academic situations. It is possible, though, that failure would have a negative effect on pupils' self-esteem and that they might seek alternative (deviant) social groups to boost this. This highlights the need for effective literacy teaching early in pupils' school life and also the development of inclusive classroom practices (see Chapter 11) that can support children who experience literacy difficulties.

'Giftedness'

It is often assumed that children with high abilities may have behaviour problems, owing to their becoming bored and disaffected with the normal curriculum (Freeman, 1998). It has been argued that these students may provoke disturbance or switch off if not engaged by lessons (Duckworth *et al.*, 2009). However, this does not appear to generally be the case, and a number of studies show that able children tend if anything to have better adjustment than most children and usually also have high self-esteem. As we have seen, this can act to improve resilience.

Medical causes of children's behaviour problems

Various researchers have proposed a medical basis for children's problems, and various formal psychiatric categories have been proposed. These include the possibility of an inherited or genetic component, brain abnormalities, dietary factors, and also psychodynamic explanations of developmental problems. Although some children can appear to have symptoms characteristic of adult psychiatric states, such as psychotic behaviour, such symptoms are relatively rare, although it is sometimes tempting to look for an underlying cause in this way.

Even so, some major disorders such as autism are characteristically present from an early age and can have important educational implications if they involve difficult social behaviours. As was discussed in Chapter 11, there is now convincing evidence that autism has a genetic basis and that difficulties with social interaction arise from a specific cognitive deficit which influences Theory of Mind.

Genetic basis

Some long-term studies, such as that by Thomas and Chess (1977), have found that newborn babies show stable differences in their general dispositions, such as being 'easy' or 'difficult'. They also found that these characteristics persisted at least until the children were 14 years old, which indicates that there could be an inherited basis for such underlying general behavioural predispositions.

Subsequent investigations have attempted to quantify the extent of the amount of inheritance for different types of specific behavioural difficulties. The investigations are similar to investigations of heritability of intelligence discussed in Chapter 3, and in the same way the heritability of behavioural difficulties has been studied by comparing the behaviour of different types of twins with varying levels of genetic similarity. In one major study of a range of different behavioural disorders, Eaves *et al.* (1997) compared identical twins (who are genetically the same) with non-identical twins, whose genetic similarity is the same as for any other siblings. Table 12.2 summarises part of their findings.

If one assumes that the only difference between identical and non-identical twins is their genetic similarity, then these findings indicate that there is a strong genetic effect on the two behavioural

TABLE 12.2 Average correlation coefficients for parents' assessments of twins' behaviours

	Identical male twins	Non-identical male twins
Attention-deficit/hyperactivity disorder	0.47	−0.045
Conduct disorder	0.69	0.43

Source: based on data from Eaves *et al.* (1997).

categories, particularly for attention-deficit/hyperactivity disorder (ADHD). However, it is likely that twins share very similar environments and that they will be treated the same, especially if their appearance is similar and people confuse them with each other. They are also likely to imitate each other's behaviour, and any conflicts are likely to be with each other. These effects would lead to an increase in the perceived similarity of their behaviour, and the above correlations could therefore be somewhat misleading.

A further difficulty with such findings comes from a study by Levy *et al.* (1996), who found a higher rate for ADHD among twins in general, which would inflate the correlations for this category. They also found that most of the variance in ADHD could be accounted for by language difficulties. These are more common in twins and may be due to the decreased adult involvement with each individual or the tendency of twins to develop their own alternative systems of communication. Language has a close relationship with thought and behaviour, and could underlie any difficulties with attention.

In general, therefore, genetic effects remain controversial and difficult to prove conclusively. Even if they are shown to have a significant effect, it is still likely that they will show interactions with other factors. This might happen, for instance, if traits that involve being more difficult to manage evoke less positive parenting styles. Figure 12.3 illustrates the interactions between child temperament and environmental variables, which are bi-directional and reciprocal.

This simplified model of a complex situation illustrates how the young child's temperament interacts with the family environment and vice versa to produce different outcomes.

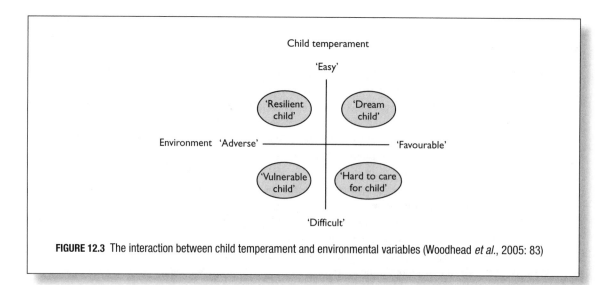

FIGURE 12.3 The interaction between child temperament and environmental variables (Woodhead *et al.*, 2005: 83)

Brain abnormalities

It is possible that problem behaviours may have a physical basis such as abnormal electrical activity in the brain, as in epilepsy (see Chapter 11) (as shown by an electroencephalogram), some form of damage or structural abnormality, or a biochemical imbalance that affects mood. Mood and behaviour can certainly be affected by specific forms of known brain damage. These include tumours, infections and various types of direct physical trauma. Such causes are relatively rare.

Brain function and children's behaviour

As children mature, they develop the skills to inhibit their initial responses to situations and are able to develop more planned responses. (For example, the skill of playing the game 'Simon says' improves as children become older.) The development of this type of inhibition has been extensively studied and the term 'executive function' used to refer to the processes that allow planned, conscious actions to occur rather than initial reactions to events (Hughes et al., 2004). The pre-frontal cortex of the brain is associated with this inhibitory control and planning. It is an extremely important factor in the organisation of children's behaviour. There is some evidence that children labelled as having ADHD may have dysfunction in their prefrontal cortex (Hughes et al., 2004), and consequently struggle which the demands of some school tasks and environments, with consequences for their social and emotional development. Other researchers have made stronger claims between brain and problematic behaviour. For example, activity in the amygdala is associated with fear responses, and abnormal amygdala function has been linked to anti-social behaviour in children. One study looked at how readily 1,795 three-year-olds conditioned to a loud noise. It was found that some children responded significantly less fearfully than others, suggesting a difference in amygdala functioning. Some 23 years later, 8 per cent of the group had criminal records. When matched against two other participants for gender, social adversity and ethnicity, Gao et al. (2009) found that the 'criminal group' were significantly more likely to have been in the less-fearful group of three-year-olds.

The cells of the brain transmit information by passing small amounts of transmitter chemicals, and some of these are specific to certain structures involved in mood and behaviour. Serotonin is involved in mood and emotions and appears to be at a low level in aggressive individuals while being linked to attention-deficit/hyperactivity disorder. There is also some evidence of significantly different levels, from controls, in adolescents with conduct disorder and a correlation between serotonin levels and aggression scores on the Child Behavior Checklist (CBCL) and Overt Aggression Scale (OAS) (Golubchik et al., 2009). Unis et al. (1997), for instance, found these types of serotonin abnormalities in 45 juvenile offenders. There was also a positive correlation between low serotonin levels and the severity of their crimes, as well as how young they were when their difficulties began. On the other hand, negative environmental influences have also been shown to depress serotonin levels, and one would need to carry out long-term controlled studies to prove any causation. If there is a biochemical abnormality, it could perhaps be treated, using drugs such as Prozac, which increase the levels of serotonin, and do have positive effects on mood and behaviour in children. However, there are doubts about the advisability of using such drugs routinely with children, particularly if their problems are mainly the result of difficult environments.

The influence of environmental factors has also been revealed through functional magnetic resonance imaging (fMRI) analysis. Weber et al. (2006) give the following example.

The anterior cingulated cortex (ACC) is a brain structure believed to be involved in the precursors of aggressive behaviour. Individuals likely to exhibit aggressive behaviour show altered activity in this area. Based on functional magnetic resonance imaging (fMRI) analysis, Sterzer *et al.* (2003) found lowered activity in this region in adolescents with conduct and behaviour disorders. This would seem to suggest perhaps a 'brain abnormality' view of the production of such behaviours, or at least their disinhibition. However, Mathews *et al.* (2005) found similar activity patterns in adolescents exposed to higher levels of violent media in the previous year. Teenagers with no 'psychopathological history' demonstrated the same frontal lobe activity as those with behaviour disorders. This led Weber *et al.* (2006) to conclude that the games players were affected by their virtual gaming activities, a consequence of repeatedly eliciting neural activity associated with aggression.

This illustrates how a simple 'brain function' explanation is too simplistic and that we need to consider the transactional relationships between biology and environmental factors in understanding problem behaviour.

Dietary factors

There has been considerable interest in the possibility, initially raised by Feingold (1975), that a number of (mostly artificial) food additives have an effect on hyperactive behaviour. The diet he recommended, which is still in current use, involves exclusion of:

- synthetic colours, particularly tartrazine (yellow – E102) and amaranth (red – E123);
- synthetic flavours, such as vanillin – not usually listed by name;
- antioxidant preservatives, in particular butylated hydroxyanisole (BHA – E320), butylated hydroxytoluene (BHT – E321) and tertiary butylhydroquinone (TBHQ – E319); and
- salicylate and aspirin (salicylic acid).

The Feingold Association provides a list of foods that it believes are safe to eat (Feingold Association, 2009), and it is emphasised that even small amounts of the above substances could trigger a negative reaction.

Early research by Feingold (1976) indicated that 32 per cent–60 per cent of children with behavioural difficulties improved dramatically on this diet, implying that these substances were affecting sensitive children. However, critics have noted that many of the foods on the recommended list do in fact contain salicylates, and that it excluded others that were low in them. More importantly, people's expectations may have influenced how they interpreted or managed subsequent behaviour. There is also the possibility that the apparent effectiveness of the diet may have been mainly due to the different parental management involved in administering the diet; restricting what children eat can involve very firm monitoring and handling, which may improve general behaviour. A number of subsequent studies were therefore based on the strict experimental 'double-blind' design. This means that the diet was set up and run within a clinic and neither the families nor the person administering the diet knew when additives were included in or removed from the diet. Breakey (1997) reviewed 13 studies that used good experimental designs and also used levels of additives and whole foods that would normally be in children's diets. All these found substantial and significant effects on children's behaviour, often with more than half of the children concerned being affected in some way or another. One interesting finding was also that the difficulties were not specific to the hyperactive syndrome (now subsumed under ADHD), but appeared to be affecting mood, particularly irritability.

Most of these studies were based on children who had already been identified as having behaviour problems, but in many of the cases, food problems were already suspected; for instance, there was a family history of allergy or migraines. It is difficult to know to what extent these findings could be applied to the normal population, but it does seem likely that, for some susceptible children, food difficulties could be involved, affecting mood and making a range of behavioural problems more likely. More recently a randomised, double-blinded, placebo-controlled study tested the effects of artificial food colour and additives on 153 three-year-olds and 144 eight-to-nine-year-olds using a computerised test of attention, observed behaviours and teacher and parent ratings (McCann *et al.*, 2007). Both artificial colours and a sodium benzoate preservative (or both) resulted in increased hyperactivity in groups of children representative of the general population. Across a range of studies, the weight of evidence is less universal, but accumulated evidence suggests that for some children with attention-deficit/hyperactivity disorder (ADHD), food colours exacerbate their condition (Stevenson, 2009).

It remains the case that, for the majority of children with behavioural problems, there is normally no known physical basis. Also, the fact (mentioned earlier) that most behavioural difficulties are relatively temporary, with a high rate of spontaneous remission, makes such biological explanations unlikely in the majority of cases and might distract parents and teachers from other explanations.

Anxiety and school attendance

Anxiety in school can happen when a child is fearful of things that have happened or might happen. These could include social difficulties such as bullying, or problems with work such as a feeling of inability to cope with examinations. In terms of clinical diagnosis, there are over a dozen anxiety disorders and phobias that might be diagnosed in children, a key feature of each being disruption of social and academic situations (Davis *et al.*, 2009).

'School phobia' is an example of a seemingly irrational anxiety regarding a specific feature of school life (Kearney, 2008). Its development and continuation can be explained by Gray's (1975) two-process theory. An initial precipitating event, such as being bullied at school, may produce a negative involuntary emotional state, which becomes classically conditioned to thoughts about or attendance at school. If the pupil then avoids attending, this can result in operant conditioning of this behaviour in the future since the non-attendance is effectively being rewarded with reductions in anxiety. School phobia is relatively rare, for example in comparison to school refusal and truancy (Kearney, 2008). Although these terms are often used interchangeably, typically school refusers experience anxiety regarding leaving home and attending school, and may be supported in this behaviour by their parents, whereas truants experience no anxiety and are likely to experience academic difficulties and be at risk of anti-social behaviour outside of school. Although school phobia can be triggered by an unpleasant school-based experience such as bullying, a range of other factors can be a part of its development and help to keep it going. Many of these are home based and involve anxieties about separation (from the home or from the mother) rather than a fear of something to do with school. Such anxieties are typically increased by parental management, which gives more attention to anxious behaviour from the child. Various family stresses can trigger this off, such as the loss of a relative. A very common starting point is when a grandparent dies, particularly if the child knew them well. This death also has a major effect on parents, who are then themselves less able to cope. For various reasons, children may also become anxious about the possible loss of a parent and fear that being away from home may make this more likely.

Non-attendance is also much more likely after periods of absence due to illness or holidays. At these times, the child will often become progressively more anxious as the prospect of school comes closer. Since each non-attendance effectively reinforces the phobia, approaches to dealing with this should therefore attempt to get the child back to school as soon as possible.

Practical implications

Functions of school refusal and possible treatment

When looking at children who avoid school, Kearny (2008) argues that one should look at the functions that their behaviour has, and suggests four areas to consider:

1   Avoidance of specific stimuli in the school setting.
2   Escape from aversive social situation.
3   Engaging in behaviour that will result in attention from parents or teachers.
4   Engaging in more rewarding experiences outside school.

Think of some examples that might fit with each of Kearney's functions, and then consider how each situation might be addressed. Make a note of your thoughts and then compare them with Kearney's suggestion, given below.

Interestingly Kearney (2002) has developed an assessment tool (The School Refusal Assessment Scale–Child) which asks children about their reasons for staying away from school. The children's responses can then be linked to the 'four functions'.

You are likely to have thought of a variety of responses and the following ideas are not exclusive or all-encompassing. Clearly each situation needs to be considered individually – for example, some children may have a medical condition interfering with their school attendance.

Responses to function 1

The first function may suggest anxiety problems, so these could be addressed through relaxation training or medication. The child could be gradually exposed to the school and the anxiety-provoking situation (systematic desensitisation).

Responses to function 2

You may have considered checking that the child is not being bullied at school and, if so, addressing this issue. If social anxiety is an issue, then this might be addressed through a cognitive behavioural approach, social skills programmes or gradual exposure to a range of social situations, beginning with low-anxiety situations, to develop their ability to cope in these situations.

Responses to function 3

A variety of responses are possible here, for example working with parents to change the way they are dealing with non-attendance (in the UK, parents can be subject to an educational supervision order or prosecuted for failing to send their children to school), setting up a contract regarding attendance that incorporates some form of reward, looking to change the child's engagement with teachers in other aspects of their school life.

Responses to function 4

Again, a wide range of responses exist. These may range from the formal escorting and supervision of children's attendance to a formal contract with defined contingencies. Kearney (2008) also indicates the option of 'peer refusal skills training' for situations where there is a peer group culture of non-attendance.

Depression

The term 'depression' refers to a condition that influences three aspects of children's lives: their affect (mood), behaviour and cognition (their thinking). Typically, children will become sad or irritable, their thoughts self-critical and their levels of activity lowered, sometimes accompanied by a loss of interest in activities they previously enjoyed. Their lowered self-esteem may be accompanied by an internalised explanation for their perceived failures or lack of motivation. The way in which children's symptoms present is not clear-cut but they indicate a significant impairment in their social functioning (NCCMH, 2005). Depression is more common in adolescents than younger children, with incidences of 3 per cent and less than 1 per cent respectively (Angold and Costello, 2001). Adolescents are more likely to report 'cognitive' issues (poor attention, self-criticism) and younger children describe aches and pains (NCCMH, 2005). For most children who experience a period of depression, it will not be a precursor to recurrent adult depression (NCCMH, 2005). For children, a significant complication is the effect that depression has on their ability to maintain friendships and manage the demands of school successfully.

There are a number of social factors that are associated with depression in children. In a review of research evidence, NCCMH (2005) concluded that 95 per cent of major depressive illness in children can be associated with longstanding psycho-social difficulties such as 'family or marital disharmony, divorce and separation, domestic violence, physical and sexual abuse, school difficulties, including bullying, exam failure, social isolation' (p. 33). In these circumstances, an acute event may act to trigger depression.

One explanation of depression is that it can be the result of a loss of self-esteem or self-effectiveness, which may be related to school processes. If children experience long-term failure, they may come to feel that they have no control over events, a condition known as 'learned helplessness'. Seligman (1975) has found that individuals who develop this remain passive and have a low sense of self-worth. This can continue even if they subsequently experience success, since even their success is attributed to external processes such as luck. Although self-esteem appears to be relatively specific, children spend a lot of their lives in school and it is likely that long-term academic failure will have a significant impact in this way.

Some medical explanations are based on the belief that such disorders, such as anxiety and depression, are due to biological malfunctioning of the brain. Anxiety might be the result of an overactive autonomic nervous system (the system that manages general physiological arousal), for instance by releasing adrenaline into the bloodstream. Depression, on the other hand, is believed to be due to a lack of certain chemical transmitters in the brain which relate to mood, in particular a substance called 'noradrenalin' which is mainly found in the brain stem.

However, the common view of such conditions is that they occur through an interaction between biological and social factors. Biological malfunctions could be a result of psychological factors, since repeated stresses or a perceived lack of control may themselves bring about specific physiological changes. Nevertheless, medication can still be useful and bring about rapid and positive changes for some individuals, particularly when other techniques have not been effective.

An issue for teachers is the difficulty of discriminating between children's mental health needs and the features associated with labels of particular special educational needs, for example ADHD, autism or PMLD (NASS, 2007). For some children, their SEN label can act to 'mask' underlying mental health problems. This is clearly seen in children with PMLD or ASD, where changes in behaviour might easily be misinterpreted, attributing their behaviour to their 'SEN label' rather than indicating a mental health issue. Yet, pupils with complex needs are more likely to develop mental health problems than other children. Rose *et al.* (2009) found that few teachers in residential specialist schools had received training in mental health issues, and that they perceived this as a significant source for concern. Their perception was that children's mental health problems are increasing in frequency and yet support for children, within education, remains relatively lacking.

Categories of emotional and behavioural difficulties

In a review of the various perspectives, Chazan *et al.* (1994) consider that there is a general tendency to put problem school behaviours into two major groups. The first of these is the category of anti-social/over-reacting behaviour, often termed 'acting out', which includes aggression and hyperactivity, or behaviours that are generally disruptive. The second category involves withdrawn/under-reacting behaviour and includes anxiety, such as school phobia, and depression, which can involve unhappiness, passivity and social isolation. Like the classification systems used in abnormal psychology, however, this approach is largely based on what can be observed of the behaviour. It is not necessarily linked with a knowledge of specific causes or with particular techniques to help with the behaviour.

Psychiatric classifications of childhood disorders are also based on the use of symptoms and use similar categories. These come from two main schedules, the *American Diagnostic and Statistical Manual of Mental Disorders*, fourth edition (DSM-IV, 1994), and the *International Classification of Diseases*, tenth revision (ICD-10, 1993), which is mainly used in Europe. Diagnosis is based on a clinical interview with a child's parents and this is used to assess whether a child has a certain number of problem behaviours, as set out in a standard list, and for a significant length of time – usually six months. Both schedules separate out emotional difficulties from disruptive behaviours, and the major categories that cover behavioural problems of children are shown in Table 12.3.

There is evidently some overlap between these two systems, for example with the common use of the category 'conduct disorder'. Also, hyperactivity disorder in the DSM is similar to hyperkinetic disorder in the ICD. However, there are also major contrasts between the two approaches, which highlights the fact that these systems probably reflect different medical customs and practices, and there must be a certain arbitrariness about the use of categories.

There are also many shared features and associations between categories within the classification systems. For example, most children who have ADHD have other disruptive behaviours as well.

TABLE 12.3 Psychiatric classification of childhood disorders

DSM-IV	ICD-10
Attention-deficit and disruptive behaviour disorders	Hyperkinetic disorder
Attention-deficit/hyperactivity disorder	Conduct disorders
Conduct disorder	Mixed disorders of conduct and emotions
Oppositional defiant disorder	Emotional disorders with onset specific to childhood
Oppositional defiant disorder	Disorders of social functioning with onset specific to childhood and adolescence
Anxiety disorders are now included with adult categories as they are not considered to be specific to childhood, apart from separation anxiety disorder	Other behavioural and emotional disorders with onset usually occurring in childhood and adolescence

Because of this imprecision, specific diagnoses should perhaps be viewed with some caution and interpreted in terms of their usefulness for helping children with such problems.

Assessment of behavioural problems

Teacher questionnaires

A common way of identifying and categorising behaviour problems in schools has been by the use of a behavioural checklist administered by a teacher who knows the child well. Two rating scales commonly used in clinical practice are the Strengths and Difficulties Questionnaire (SDQ) (Goodman, 1997), a short behavioural screening questionnaire, and the Child Behaviour Checklist (CBCL) (Achenbach, 1991), which was developed in America. The CBCL is a 113-item standardised rating scale for both parents and teachers.

One of the most popular of the behavioural checklists has been the BSAG (Bristol Social Adjustment Guides, Stott, 1971), which covers the age range from 5–16 years. Each guide is made up from 33 categories of behaviour, such as 'paying attention in class' and 'ways with other children'. All these categories have a number of possible descriptors such as 'attends to anything but his work' or 'on the whole attends well'. A teacher goes through the questionnaire, circling the Statements that he or she judges are most appropriate for each of the categories. The questionnaire is then scored by using an overlay that puts these responses into two general groupings, as shown in Table 12.4. The assessment therefore results in two scores that can be referred to normative tables to see how often they are likely to occur. These tables are adjusted to take account of the higher levels of behaviour problems for boys. So, for example, an 'Over-reaction' score of 21 would be achieved by only 4 per cent of all boys and by 1 per cent of all girls.

Although still featured in research literature, the BSAG is rather old now and a more modern variation on this approach which covers the same age range is the Devereux Test (Naglieri et al., 1992), which uses 40 statements with five rating categories. The statements use specific problem behaviours, similar to 'During the last four weeks, how often did the child …' 'act aggressively to others?' or 'seem anxious or distressed?' Each of the behaviours is rated for frequency, with the categories 'never', 'rarely', 'occasionally', 'frequently' and 'very frequently'. Scoring is similar to that for the BSAG, with answers placed into the subscales of Interpersonal Problems, Inappropriate Behaviours/Feelings, Depression, Physical Symptoms/Fears, as well as an overall total problem score.

A range of assessment tools have been developed to look at emotional and social competence. These range from pre-school measures, such as the Penn Interactive Peer Play scale (Fantuzzo et al., 1995) and those that span the entire school age, such as the Behaviour and Emotional Rating Scale (Epstein et al., 2002). Two other popular and longstanding behaviour-rating scales that can be used with primary-aged children are the Rutter (1967) Child Behaviour Scale and the Conners et al. (1998) Teacher Rating Scale. Both these involve a number of items describing problems behaviours, which are rated by the teacher for a particular child. The Rutter scale is primarily

TABLE 12.4 Major dimensions of British social-adjustment guides

Under-reaction	Over-reaction
Includes the core syndromes of unforthcomingness, withdrawal and depression.	Includes the core syndromes of inconsequence and hostility, as well as the associated grouping of peer-maladaptiveness

designed to be used as an initial screening instrument, but the Conners scale enables scores to be grouped into four subscales of Conduct Problems, Inattentive–Passive, Tension–Anxiety and Hyperactivity.

Pupil questionnaires

Other approaches also include questionnaires, which are filled out by the pupil instead of a teacher, such as the Behaviour in School Inventory (Youngman, 1979). This involves 34 questions about school such as, 'Are you usually quiet in class?' and 'Do you answer back if a teacher tells you off?' The answers are grouped into the three categories of Studiousness, Compliance and Teacher Contact, and are added together to give a single overall score. Scores can again be compared with norms to see how likely it would be for a particular pattern of responses to occur.

Whole-school approaches

In contrast to these individualised diagnostic approaches are whole-school approaches that look at the context of the school. The Child Development Project (CDP) (Solomon *et al.*, 2000) was developed from a large sample of 8–12-year-olds and examines supportive and collaborative relationships with the classroom. Its aim is to help teachers create a caring school community and supportive positive schools experiences, and therefore gains pupils' perspectives as part of this process. At a similar level, the Index for Inclusion (Booth and Ainscow, 2002) allows a school community to explore and develop its practices in terms of creating an inclusive school community. These latter two approaches are not focused on potentially negative aspects of individuals on whom to target interventions, but rather they have a proactive approach to creating supportive educational environments for all learners.

Classroom observation

A further type of approach avoids all concepts of classification and, instead, just records observations of problem behaviours. Identification in this way is often part of an overall approach to dealing with behaviour problems. An example is the Behavioural Approach to Teaching Package (Wheldall *et al.*, 1983), in which standard schedules are used to record observations of both pupil and teacher behaviours. Observation categories are specified beforehand and involve positive and negative teacher behaviours and on- or off-task pupil behaviours.

Sociometry

Sociometric techniques can also be used to establish the social links and organisation in classes. Such techniques involve first asking all the children in a class to nominate those other children whom they like, or some other index of the same thing, such as naming two other children they would want to work with (Rodkin and Hodges, 2003). As shown in Figure 12.4, the results are typically analysed by drawing a visual representation of the groupings and the popularity of each individual.

The technique can then be used to establish groupings, key individuals and individuals' social situations. For instance, if the individual pupil C is disruptive, his or her behaviour might have a disproportionate effect because of C's influence on a number of other children. The general behaviour of the whole group might be improved if that child's role could be modified to become more positive.

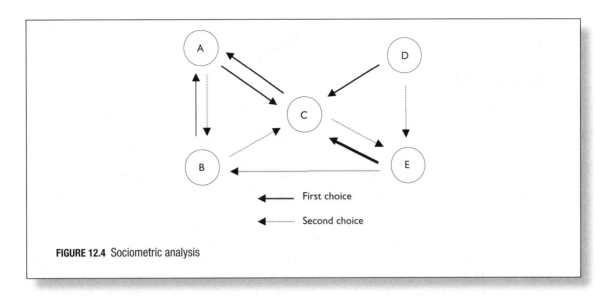

FIGURE 12.4 Sociometric analysis

The approach can also show up children who are relatively isolated (such as D) and not chosen by any others. This could give the opportunity to set up some limited social engineering or social-skills work (see Chapter 13) to encourage the formation of relationships.

Sociometry has been used in classrooms to collect information in relation to bullying and victimisation (see Chapter 13). Typically, children would be asked to indicate three children they like the most (LM) and the least (LL). Indicators of children's social status can be derived from this data (Rodkin and Hodges, 2003): their social preference (LM minus LL) and their social impact (LL plus LM) within the class. This can also be used to understand the types of bullying that may be taking place, such as bullying that is supported by peers (Rodkin and Hodges, 2003). Although sociometry can be a very useful approach, it can cause problems if the results are not kept confidential since there is the possibility that it could expose isolated children.

Prevalence of behavioural problems

In all the various assessment techniques referred to above, there is no single obvious cut-off criterion beyond which a behaviour suddenly becomes a problem (see Chapter 11). This means that there cannot be a definitive value for the frequency of problems. A high criterion score on a questionnaire such as the BSAG will result in relatively few children being identified as having problems; a low criterion score will identify many more.

In one study reported by Sue et al. (1990), when all possible types of problem were identified, a surprisingly high level of about 56 per cent of 101 pre-adolescents (6–12-year-olds) received a medical diagnosis of one type or another, on the basis of the DSM-III-R. The diagnoses were based on interviews with the parents and children, none of whom had a prior history of psychological or psychiatric disturbance. Most of these problems would be relatively minor or a reaction to some temporary circumstances. What is more important, perhaps, is the number of children who teachers find are a significant problem for them in school. A teaching union survey reported that teachers felt there had been a significant increase in incidents of serious verbal abuse and physical assault in their schools. Half of primary-school staff and 20 per cent of secondary-school teachers felt that physical assaults (on pupils and teachers) were more common. In addition, many felt at risk from being cyber-bullied by pupils (ATL, 2010).

Reliability of assessments

In order for any form of assessment to be of use, it must reach a certain level of consistency or reliability, as measured by whether different parts of an assessment agree with each other, whether running the assessment again will give a similar result, and whether different forms of the assessment agree with each other. Most research findings show that when scores on two halves of a behavioural checklist are compared with each other, they typically show a high level of agreement. The BSAG, for instance, has an internal reliability of the order of 0.82 for the grouping of 'Under-reaction', and 0.91 for the grouping of 'Over-reaction'. Re-testing of children tends to show lower reliabilities, although they are still fairly substantial. Again, a typical result in the case of the BSAG for reassessment one year later gives coefficients of 0.74 for 'Under-reaction' and 0.77 for 'Over-reaction'.

Such consistency between such assessments could indicate that a test is accurately evaluating some stability in behaviour problems. An alternative interpretation, however, would be that instead of assessing the fixed attributes of the child, it is demonstrating the fixed attitudes of the teacher. Teacher attitudes and judgements have been shown to be stable over time, and there is evidence that a negative set towards a child can actually generate and perpetuate success or failure.

Another explanation of consistency might be that the test is assessing merely the specificity of the situations that children find themselves in. This means that consistencies in a teacher's assessments might be due to a child's responding to that particular teacher and class in a specific way. Tattum (1982), for instance, found that problem pupils chose certain teachers and lessons to misbehave with. This would produce a high level of consistency for individual teachers' ratings, even though the children's behaviours were actually quite variable between different teachers and lessons.

The reliabilities for assessments between different raters and different situations tends to be relatively low. The more different either of these factors are, the lower the coefficients become. For example, in a study by St James-Roberts (1994), there was only 38 per cent agreement between different staff about which children posed definite problems. This was despite the fact that the test–retest reliability coefficient of the test itself was 0.88 over two weeks.

When very different situations such as home and school are compared, there is usually only limited agreement. With the Devereux test, the correlation between assessments by teachers and by counsellors who saw children in a residential setting was only 0.40 (Naglieri et al., 1992: 45). In the Isle of Wight study by Rutter (1989), 2,193 children were screened by means of both a parent questionnaire and a teacher questionnaire, each of which had been previously piloted extensively. Of these, 157 were selected as being 'maladjusted' on the basis of the teacher questionnaire, and 133 were selected as being 'maladjusted' on the basis of the parent questionnaire. Only 19 children (less than 1 per cent) were selected on the basis of both teacher and parent questionnaires. It seems likely that this minimal overlap could be due to the different role expectations for children in the two situations. At home, children have relatively few constraints, and self-centred behaviour can often be tolerated. At school, on the other hand, firm role expectations and management can limit behaviours that would cause difficulties if they happened at home.

When behaviour assessments are carried out by pupils themselves, these can achieve much greater reliability coefficients. This is not surprising if we consider that this type of test is probably assessing an individual's self-concept, which is more likely to be stable than the judgements of different people. The difficulty with such assessments is of course that teachers are often more concerned about a pupil's behaviour as they see it. Also, there are likely to be significant differences between teachers' behavioural assessments and pupils' own self-ratings. The differences are at least partly due to a tendency for pupils to see their own behaviour as a reasonable response to the particular situation they are in, avoiding responsibility when things go wrong. This is an example of 'self-serving' bias, and is one of the different types of attribution that people use to preserve their self-esteem.

Reliabilities are also affected by the level of specificity of the behaviour described. For example, many descriptions in the BSAG such as 'a good mixer' are vague and open to different interpretations. Reliabilities are greatest when an assessment technique identifies specific observable behaviours, uses agreed categories, and has trained and experienced assessors. In one such investigation, for instance, Wheldall *et al.* (1985) carried out a study in which inter-rater agreements for specific pupil behaviours achieved an average of 94 per cent.

Validity of BSAG assessments

In order for such assessments to be of any use, it is also essential that they have validity, and evaluate something to do with behavioural problems.

Content validity

'Content validity' refers to whether a test focuses on the appropriate problem behaviour. One would expect that a questionnaire that is supposed to be evaluating problem behaviour at school would consider things like 'attitudes to school and school work' and 'relationships with teachers'. If some items involve more general problems with adjustment, such as sleep problems, it is less likely that they will have much to do with school behaviour. Most tests initially generate many of their items from teacher reports, and the BSAG is based almost exclusively on this approach. They can also be based on previous educational research findings which have themselves been validated. Both of these approaches can reasonably claim to have validity of this sort.

Concurrent validity

Concurrent validity involves relating scores on a test to other features that are already present and that most people would agree show problem behaviour. Sometimes this is done simply by correlating the test scores with other assessments of behaviour or personality. Most tests correlate fairly well, particularly if they are of the same type, and St James-Roberts (1994) found a correlation of 0.83 between the Child Behaviour Checklist (the most commonly used US teacher checklist) and the Preschool Behaviour Checklist (a similar device for young children). However, a more persuasive assessment of the concurrent validity of a behavioural test would relate it to a range of current problem behaviours such as absenteeism or disruptive behaviour. Unfortunately, these relationships tend to be low, and in a study by Youngman and Szaday (1985), the Youngman's Self-Report Inventory correlated at only around the 0.5 level with the number of times that a pupil was sent out of the room in a particular year.

Predictive validity

A more stringent test is predictive validity – the extent to which an assessment relates to problem behaviours that happen later in time. The BSAG, for instance, has been shown to relate significantly to subsequent delinquency and criminality. Kamphaus *et al.* (2007) developed a short screening test, derived from the Teacher Rating Scale–Child (TRS–C) of the Behaviour Assessment System for Children. Having found their short 'screener' to be reliable and valid, they then tested its predictive validity over a two-year period. They brought together a variety of measures that included: days absent from school, days suspended/expelled, teacher rating on a number of aspects of metal health, and behaviour and academic results. The 'screener' appeared to correlate reasonably well with teachers' ratings of behaviour and behaviour problems (a level of 0.5), but not very well with attendance records. This led Kamphaus *et al.* (2007) to see their 'screener' as a useful tool in targeting early intervention.

The best predictors are usually measures that are closest to the eventual target behaviour. If one wished to predict disruptive behaviour in a child when he or she gets older, the best measure will probably be an assessment of the child's present behaviour. An exception to this, however, is when other factors such as home background can be shown to act as a basis for behaviour development. As already described, detailed models that incorporate home management, peer-group influences and school attainments predict later delinquency better than do measures of early behaviour.

Construct validity

'Construct validity' refers to how meaningful are the basic constructs identified in the assessment. The criterion of meaningfulness could apply to the very concept of measuring a 'behavioural problem', or to particular dimensions from a behavioural assessment. Since much of behaviour is situation-specific and measures of it have the poor reliability mentioned above, it can be argued that 'behaviour problems' do not have much construct validity.

As many of the assessment devices depend upon factor analysis, they are also subject to some basic criticism that the factors derived depend largely on what items are included and the technique of analysis that is utilised. One might finally consider whether an assessment is of any value in allowing one to deal with problem behaviour. Although assessments may be useful in general research, such as in determining how stable behaviour problems are over time, the ultimate pragmatic evaluation is how far they will allow a school or teacher to directly help or deal with a child with problem behaviours. In order for the child to be helped, perhaps any assessment needs to be derived from a particular treatment or management approach.

Approaches such as direct behavioural evaluations or social analyses would appear to be most valid in this respect since, as Chapter 13 will show, there are immediate implications for setting up a programme of behavioural management or some form of social manipulation.

Summary

There are signs that schools have become increasingly concerned over pupils' behaviour and that modern life puts children under greater pressure. Severe problems are still relatively infrequent, however, although low-level difficulties can significantly limit children's educational progress.

The most common term nowadays is 'behavioural emotional and social difficulties', which covers aggressive and disruptive as well as disturbed behaviours. These can be seen as related to individual differences or to a failure to conform, although teacher concerns tend to focus on direct difficulties with adapting to the educational situation.

Most psychological theories emphasise individual experiences and reactions, such as frustration and attributions of responsibility for unpleasant experiences. Children also seem to be more likely to use problem behaviour when it has positive outcomes for them. However, it is likely that they learn more from observing others and judging what is appropriate and likely to succeed for themselves. Children's engagement with violent behaviours through passive viewing or online simulations can have similar effects, particularly if children see events as being realistic and relevant, although appropriate experiences can also have pro-social effects.

Social causes may involve pupils conforming to deviant peer-group norms, and teachers can combat these by strengthening positive school norms. Group effects can lead to deindividuation and bystander apathy, when pupils may have a weakened sense of responsibility and fail to conform to normal behaviours or to help others in trouble. Owing to their home background, some children seem to lack positive social-interaction skills. Boys are much more likely to have behavioural difficulties than girls and, although there may be a biological reason, their greater incidence of problems appears to be largely due to the development of gender roles.

A poor home background appears to be strongly linked with the development of behavioural problems such as aggression. These appear to be learned as a coping strategy within the home and can later be perpetuated in negative peer-group membership. Such difficulties start early and are affected by different types of home situations.

Schools appear to have differential effects on behaviour, although their effect is much less than the impact of their intake's social background. Although it is widely believed that low achievement can cause poor behaviour, it is likely that early and long-term behavioural difficulties cause both the low achievement and later behaviour problems. 'Gifted' pupils do not seem to have any higher level of behavioural or emotional difficulties.

There are some suggestive findings which indicate that there is a biological basis for certain types of behavioural problems such as attention-deficit/hyperactivity disorder (ADHD) and mood disorders. Dietary factors may be important in affecting ADHD, although the way in which it works and the number of children affected is not yet clear. For most behavioural difficulties there is no known medical cause. Anxiety and depression can result from past learning experiences and a perception of lack of control. They can also be associated with certain biological factors, although these could be a result as well as a cause.

Problem behaviours can be grouped as 'acting out' or as anxiety and depressive states. Psychiatric classifications break these down into further groupings which have some overlap. Whole-school approaches can help schools to assess and develop a proactive response to context that might create problem behaviours.

Problem behaviours can be assessed using techniques such as teacher and pupil questionnaires, direct observation and sociometry. Such assessments usually have low reliabilities, owing to the varying effects of different contexts and relationships with whoever carries out the assessment. Most assessments have reasonable content and concurrent validities but are relatively poor at predicting future behaviour, and their meaningfulness depends on how they are going to be used.

Key implications

- Home background and peer-group influences appear to be the significant factors in the causes of behavioural difficulties.
- Behaviour difficulties are the result of an interaction between personal, social and environment factors.
- Education can probably have only a limited impact on these.
- The possibility of medical or biological causes remains uncertain.

- We should not place too much reliance on classifying individual children as having behavioural problems.
- The most useful approaches are those that are directly linked with management strategies.

Further reading

Howarth and Fisher (2005), *Emotional and Behavioural Difficulties*: this is written for teachers, and an interesting feature of this book is the discussion of 'you as a teacher', which considers teachers' skills and attributes. The role of learning support assistants and communicating with parents about SEBD issues are also discussed.

Hunter-Carsch, Tiknaz, Cooper and Sage (eds) (2006), *The Handbook of Social, Emotional and Behavioural Difficulties: Educational Engagement and Communication*: this book looks at how to approach the issue of SEBD through a range of interesting and relevant international contributions. It introduces some helpful practical classroom strategies and foregrounds the importance of educational practices in relation to SEBD.

Wearmouth, Richmond, Glynn and Berryman (2004), *Understanding Student Behaviour in Schools*: the explanation and understanding of pupil behaviour is approached through sections looking at cultural, psychological and medical perspectives. A particular strength of this book is exploring how we can gain insights into understanding problem behaviours in the context of school and national cultures, and this area is well-illustrated and discussed.

The 'five factors' activity

The five factors that emerged as having particular importance were: social background/income; parental agreement on discipline; mothers' mental state; fathers' behaviour; marital relationship.

Discussion of practical scenario

Tom is a child who has experienced several of the life events that might be associated with, or precipitate, problem behaviours. He probably focuses mainly on his short-term needs and becomes frustrated when these are not met. Managing Tom in school will therefore involve close monitoring and direction. However, it is important to also consider other aspects of Tom's life, for example the development of his academic skills, communication skills and his peer-group relationships. Counselling and guidance on appropriate ways of relating to others would be useful. This could be part of a class-wide programme. It would be useful to discuss Tom's situation with the school's Behaviour Support Team, who would be able to gain information from the child mental health services and to help develop appropriate responses in the school as part of an assessment of Tom's needs. It seems likely that Tom would meet the criteria for having social, emotional and behavioural difficulties and this could lead to a Statement of Special Educational Needs. Although his behaviour might improve spontaneously without intervention, particularly if his new environment is positive, Tom's current physical aggression could potentially lead to exclusion from school. Providing appropriate support is therefore vital. As we'll see in Chapter 13, there are a range of interventions that are useful in these situations.

Dealing with behaviour problems

Chapter overview

- Behaviour support
- Behavioural approaches to problem behaviour
- Physical control
- Other techniques for managing behaviour
- Specific problems
- School-based behaviour programmes
- Special-needs provision for behaviour problems

Practical scenario

Mr Gray is a newly qualified teacher in his first term who is having difficulties with a new class. Although most of the pupils can be well behaved, some are particularly difficult and regularly disrupt his carefully planned lessons with boisterous and noisy behaviour. The usual approaches, such as keeping them in at breaks, do not seem to be very effective and, if anything, make them more resentful. He is rather reluctant to send pupils out or to ask for support as he would be seen as having poor classroom control. Because of these problems, he is starting to dread taking the class and is wondering whether he should continue with his teaching career.

Is Mr Gray in the wrong job?

Should he try to get help from senior staff or attempt some different stratagems himself?

Could it be that he has just got a difficult class and that things will get better next year?

What techniques could Mr Gray use to achieve more positive control? Is it likely that some form of behavioural approach could be used?

Behaviour support

The general background of behavioural problems has been covered in Chapter 11, along with the various explanations for what might cause them. Many of these explanations directly imply ways of managing and changing what children do, although some of the most important factors, such as home background, are beyond the influence of schools or teachers.

All education authorities have Behaviour Support Plans, which detail the strategies and resources that can be used to tackle inappropriate behaviour and the roles of the various agencies. In some authorities this plan includes the monitoring of, and setting targets regarding, school attendance and academic progress of vulnerable groups (Wilkin *et al.*, 2003).

The range of provision can include behaviour support services, educational psychologists, education welfare, social services and various types of health authority provision. In the United Kingdom, Behaviour Support Units, Educational Guidance Centres or Learning Support Units may become involved with the aim of returning the pupil to mainstream school, or supporting them and the school where exclusion may be an option. The relevant health services are often based in clinics that specialise in child and family problems and have workers such as child psychiatrists, specialist nurses, counsellors and other therapists. Their role is often focused on the home, but some centres are able to link in with schools, their services sometimes being partly funded by the education authority.

Many authorities have a specialist behaviour-support service made up of teachers with particular expertise and experience in this field. They normally work directly with schools, mainly with individual cases, although they can also be involved in projects with groups of pupils such as in social-skills development and whole-school and in-service training activities (Halsey *et al.*, 2005). Behaviour and Education Support Teams (BESTs) are multi-agency teams which may be based within schools or in an education authority location. They focus on identification and early intervention with the aim to promote emotional well-being and positive behaviour across the 5–18-year age range. In assessing their effectiveness, Halsey *et al.* (2005) found a positive impact across the areas of 'attainment, attendance, behaviour and wellbeing' (p. iii). Being multidisciplinary, BEST appeared to improve parental access to services (such as Child and Adolescent Mental Health Services); to help repair home and school relationships; and to be able to address parenting skills (Halsey *et al.*, 2005).

Schools in England are also responsible for implementing 'pastoral support programmes' (PSP) (DfEE, 1999b) for pupils who do not respond to the normal systems of management and are in danger of permanent exclusion. These programmes should be developed with external services and involve appropriate targets, strategies and resources. A PSP will involve drawing up an individual education plan which, where appropriate, also takes account of the pupil's other special educational needs. It is important that the PSP identify achievable behavioural outcomes for the pupil to work towards. The PSPs may involve input from Behaviour Support Teams, for example in providing an anger-management programme. The PSP may also assign a 'key worker' from an outside agency, such as the Behaviour Support team, and consider the options of a managed move to another school, or placement within a unit for children with emotional and behavioural problems, or a temporary placement within a school unit or alternative educational facility.

In-class support

It may be that additional support within the classroom is provided for individual children or at a whole-class level. Teaching assistants working within classes have had an increasingly important, and frequent, role in supporting children with SEBD. Groom and Rose (2005) reviewed the nature and extent of these roles and noted how teaching assistants worked closely with the class teacher and helped to provide 'support for promoting classroom rules, reminding pupils of expectations, dealing with conflict and keeping individual pupils on task' (Groom, 2006: 201). Groom (2006) sees teaching assistants as playing a vital role in maintaining three key relationships that underpin successful learning:

relationship with self, relationship with others and relationship with the curriculum (p. 201). Teaching assistants may also support the effective delivery of a wide range of programmes that have a focus on emotional and social development. For example:

- Circle Time (see p. 539);
- nurture groups;
- anger and conflict management;
- emotional literacy programmes;
- SEAL (Social and Emotional Aspects of Learning) Programme;
- mentoring;
- lunchtime and play support;
- peer-support/befriending programmes;
- self-esteem and social-skills programmes.

(Groom, 2006: 201)

Alternative provision

Even with this type of support, children's behaviour may be such that they are excluded from their school, and authorities' Behaviour Support Plans will include details of available alternative placement options.

Children who are permanently excluded can attend pupil-referral units (PRUs). These have the difficult job of providing a general curriculum for a number of pupils with the most extreme behavioural problems, at the same time as working with their emotional and behavioural difficulties. Each child needs to have an IEP which details their targets for re-admission into mainstream or special schools. Pupils in PRUs can also be registered with a school, with an objective to reintegrate the pupil, although with older pupils it may be more appropriate to prepare them for other life experiences through extended work projects. Other options might include home-tuition services, tutorial centres or residential schools.

However, the majority of the large number of children who have problems are in normal classes and are the day-to-day responsibility of the class teacher. Although there is now a particular emphasis on the academic curriculum with targets to be achieved, achieving targets is possible only if classes are manageable and if the teacher does not have to spend too much time dealing with behavioural problems. It is therefore important for all teachers to be aware of what are appropriate techniques and to develop effective behavioural strategies.

Behavioural approaches to problem behaviour

A behaviourist perspective can be particularly useful for understanding and managing difficult behaviours. Behaviourism, as we have seen, gives a set of rules and principles for describing and manipulating learning. If problem behaviours have been learned in the first place, they can be altered by applying the principles of conditioning. Even if some behaviours are due to inherited or biological factors, it should still be possible to learn other behaviours that could take their place.

Behavioural techniques can appear somewhat simplistic and mechanistic, largely ignoring children's thoughts and feelings. However, they are in fact part of a broader cognitive perspective since they work by altering children's expectations about what will happen in certain circumstances. Their simplicity can also be a major advantage when one is designing and running a behavioural programme, as they avoid the distractions and interference of supposed causes and processes. Children are often not consciously aware of why they do things and just repeat actions that have been effective in the past. Asking children to explain the reasons for something they have done can lead to their making up a plausible cause, or rationalisation. This could be very misleading if it was used as the basis for any further action.

Although operant conditioning is generally the most important approach that is used in behavioural programmes, classical conditioning also underlies many learning experiences.

Classical conditioning

Both anxiety and phobias in school involve involuntary behaviours and can be the result of classical conditioning.

An initially classically conditioned response (e.g. anxiety) is created. This anxiety is not reduced through exposure to anxiety provoking situations, because the child avoids these situations. This avoidance behaviour reduces the child's level of anxiety and is therefore negatively reinforced. This makes the avoidance behaviour more likely to occur again in this context.

When one is trying to manage such problems, it might therefore be appropriate to attempt to break down the learned association. With school phobia (described later in Chapter 12), this could involve exposing the child to situations that become progressively closer to the reality of school, while reducing their anxiety, a technique called 'systematic desensitisation'. This might involve the use of relaxation techniques, combined with trips that gradually get closer to school, home visits from teachers, other pupils, and any other links with school. If a child was anxious about going into the school hall for assemblies (a common problem with young children), the desensitisation could involve experiences such as brief play sessions in the hall or attendance for only part of class assemblies. It is important that if the child becomes anxious at any stage, the process is halted until he or she is able to cope. This can be a very time-consuming therapy and it may take weeks until a child is able to tolerate the difficult situation.

An alternative approach called 'flooding' is much more rapid and involves forcibly exposing the child to the feared experience and keeping him or her exposed to it until the anxiety decreases naturally. In some situations this approach has proved effective, since it normally works quickly, typically after a few days. When carried out for school phobia with a pupil's parents, it can also give them encouragement in positive techniques for handling their child. Unfortunately, it does place great strains on parents, who may be very anxious about their child. As described later in this chapter, they may have inadvertently generated the problem in the first place by excessive concern and by allowing the child to stay away from school for minor problems.

Activity

Imagine a pupil who is anxious and refuses to attend or avoids school. Can you see problems with implementing a flooding approach?

Feedback

With school phobia, parents would need to physically take children in and keep them there, no matter how extreme their behaviour became. Allowing children to escape the situation on even one occasion will undermine the process, since their behaviour will have been reinforced by the reduction in anxiety. They will then have an expectation on future occasions that their anxiety/escape behaviour might be reinforced again. There are issues with how to physically keep a pupil in a school. You may also have thought of situations where flooding would not be addressing the issue that is causing the problem. Flooding is not used for children with chronic problems, or who do not attend school due to social anxieties, for younger children or where their anxiety levels are high. There are also issues around establishing pre-school routines that contribute to the likelihood of a child attending school and the extent to which the child is aware of the process they are engaged in. Because of these issues, you might conclude that flooding could be inappropriate in many cases.

Operant conditioning

Operant (or instrumental) conditioning involves learned voluntary behaviours. When it is applied to children's problem behaviours, it should be possible to reduce negative behaviours and increase the positive ones by altering the outcomes and antecedents for these.

Figure 13.1 shows the three key elements in the process of behaviour modification. Consequences can affect the likelihood of a child engaging in a behaviour. They are termed 'reinforcers' if they increase the behaviour and involve experiences that are positive, such as getting house points, stickers on a chart or attention from a teacher. 'Punishers' are aversive events that act as punishment and decrease the frequency of a behaviour, and include experiences such as detentions or cleaning the board.

If a child's behaviour can be explained through an ABC model, as illustrated in Figure 13.1, where the consequence appears to be the attention that they receive, then it might appear sensible to adopt an 'ignore it' strategy to the child's behaviour. In practice, this is difficult. First, behaviours for whom reinforcement has stopped are likely to increase a little in the short term (known as 'extinction burst'). An increase of the behaviour, for example a temper tantrum, can be problematic in a classroom. Second, ignoring behaviours is often very difficult, for the teachers and other pupils, and so a positive planned approach that addresses the development of an appropriate behaviour is often the best strategy for the classroom teacher.

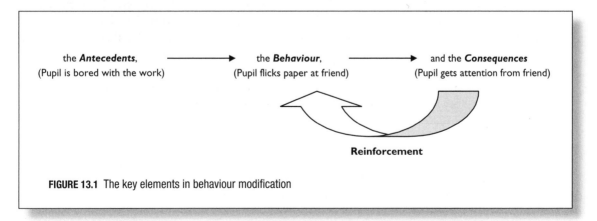

the **Antecedents**,
(Pupil is bored with the work)

the **Behaviour**,
(Pupil flicks paper at friend)

and the **Consequences**
(Pupil gets attention from friend)

Reinforcement

FIGURE 13.1 The key elements in behaviour modification

The use of rewards/reinforcers and punishments

Reinforcers can take many different forms and their use is often purely empirical. That is to say, you use whatever seems to work with a particular child in a particular situation. This can often be completely different for different children. Some young children really like to hold a teacher's hand during break, but doing so could be highly aversive to another child, particularly an older one. This is an important point: a reinforcer is something that increases the frequency of the behaviour that it follows. If it doesn't do this, it is not a reinforcer and it is easy for adults to assume what will act as a reinforcer for a child, rather than testing it. A study, looking at reinforcers for toddlers, found that a mixture of teacher-identified possibilities and direct assessment proved the most useful way of identifying effective reinforcers (Cote *et al.*, 2007).

A useful strategy to influence the frequency of a behaviour is the Premack Principle (Klatt and Morris, 2001). This indicates that following a low-frequency behaviour with a high-frequency behaviour is likely to increase the likelihood of the low-frequency behaviour occurring. Children might finish a low-probability task, such as completing a handwriting task, and then engage in a preferred activity.

As a general rule, effective reinforcers with younger children tend to be more direct and physical, and can involve adult attention, whereas older children tend to prefer reinforcers that give them more freedom, control and contact with their peer group. Studies of the effectiveness of different reinforcers in school by Harrop and Williams (1992) indicate that the most powerful ones involve sending information to parents.

As described in Chapter 2, the use of punishment is generally frowned on in most behavioural approaches. Nevertheless, there are arguments for their use in some situations.

Should we ever use punishment?

Most teachers (and parents) mainly use punishments such as reprimanding children, keeping them in at break and so on. Although training as used in 'Assertive Discipline' (covered towards the end of this chapter, pp. 377–378) can reduce the use of such negative controls, there seems to be a natural tendency to regress, and the effect of Assertive Discipline will normally fall off after a couple of years unless there is some maintenance support.

Punishment has traditionally been seen as ineffective by psychologists, and it seems strange that people naturally tend to prefer to use something that is not supposed to work very well. One reason why punishment is favoured could be that it is a 'quick fix', and that it is easier to be negative than positive. With negative control, you respond only to the misbehaviour, whereas with positive control, you have to go out of your way to look for and reward the good behaviour. Another reason is that a 'quick fix' negatively reinforces the person who punishes, making them more likely to punish in future.

Another reason may be that, in many situations, negative approaches can work quite well in the short term. O'Leary *et al.* (1970), for instance, found that private individual reprimands were an effective way of reducing disruptive behaviour with specific disruptive children when the following criteria were met:

- there is an alternative behaviour known to the child;
- the feedback is consistent and specific; and
- the teacher has a positive relationship with the child.

Most children are probably aware of what they should be doing, and it should also be possible for teachers to ensure that they respond in the same way to problem behaviours. It is also possible for teachers to establish positive relationships with children, and it has been consistently found that teachers who have the personal quality of 'warmth' are generally more effective and are less likely to have behavioural problems in their classes.

The longer-term consequences of punishment are unclear; however, research suggests that its use is associated with poorer relationships with carers and decreased mental health (Gershoff, 2002; Klein, 1996).

Time-out

A particular procedure known as 'time-out from positive reinforcement' is often used in behavioural programmes to prevent such problem behaviour being reinforced. Rather than just ignoring problem behaviour (which might sometimes be dangerous), the child is removed from the room to somewhere less reinforcing for a short period of time, about five-to-ten minutes. The approach is intended to prevent the child from getting the immediate reinforcement of attention or control that the behaviour usually generates.

It needs to be carefully planned and thought through. The length of time-out that is appropriate for the child, the contingencies if, for example, the child repeats the behaviour entering or exiting the time-out room and the precise circumstances that result in time-out.

Time-out techniques have been shown to be effective as part of a strategy to reduce aggressive behaviour in young children (UNESCO, 2004). For children with severe behaviour problems, time-out has been a successful feature of early-intervention programmes (Roberts et al., 2003) and, in classrooms, in reducing inappropriate impulsive behaviour that gains attention from peers (NICE, 2008).

The removal of difficult children from a classroom for a short period can be very (negatively) reinforcing for the teacher and so it is important that a clear programme is adhered to avoid overuse or over-extension of the length of time-out. Also, it is vital that the reinforcement that is happening during 'time-in' is considered, as time-out will not teach the child to develop new skills or ways of behaving. It therefore needs to be part of a broader strategy:

> While a school needs to pursue appropriate counselling and welfare provisions for such students, they will often need to learn how to behave appropriately. While most students respond to the normal socialisation into rights-respecting behaviour, some will need to be specifically taught:
>
> how to put their hand up without calling out;
> how to move through the room – without disturbing and annoying others;
> how to get teacher assistance and support appropriately (instead of yelling out, 'Miss!! Eh, Miss!' or tugging at the skirt, or butting in when the teacher is assisting other students ...);
> how to use positive language, instead of easy swearing and put-downs; how to stay on task; how to sit 'four on the floor'.
>
> These learning targets can be developed as specific behaviour plans that involve teacher modelling, student-rehearsal and feedback and encouragement in the natural setting of the classroom.
>
> (Rogers, 1994: 166–167)

Many schools have designated 'time-out rooms' (Hallam et al., 2003). However, these are not necessarily used as described above. Children may attend these rooms during entire breaks and lunch periods. In this way they are functioning as a means of separating children from places where they are likely to experience or create problem behaviour, rather than being used as part of a planned time-out programme that incorporates the learning of new behaviours. Some schools may also use the term 'time-out' to indicate periods of withdrawal from mainstream lessons for alternative teaching.

Implementing a behavioural programme

Most teachers naturally use a number of rewards and punishments in their classes without much thought about how this is done. However, when something is going wrong, they may need to analyse the situation and to use a more specific approach. Such an approach is often referred to as a 'behaviour modification programme' and involves the following sequence.

- The first stage involves identifying the specific problem behaviour(s). These must be directly observable and capable of being assessed. For example, the category 'Stands up and shouts in class' is better than the rather fuzzy (imprecise) category of 'Being disruptive'.
- The next stage involves identifying alternative behaviours that are appropriate and would displace the problem behaviour – that is to say, ones that cannot be done at the same time. Again, this would have to be specific, such as 'On-task behaviour, involving writing, reading or attending to the teacher'.
- An effective reinforcement now has to be identified. This can involve either observing what individual children will do when they have a free choice of activities, asking other people who know them well, or asking children directly. With younger children it might involve being allowed to play a particular game, and with older children it often involves more freedom or control, such as break sessions (see Premack Principle, p. 352).

  An ideal behavioural programme would involve an initial set of baseline observations so that it is possible to see whether the behaviour does improve. In practice, it is often important to get a rapid improvement, for instance to prevent an exclusion from school, so this stage is often left out.
- Running the programme now involves setting targets, monitoring the positive behaviour(s) and applying the reinforcer(s) consistently. So, for example, a positive behaviour could involve 'being on task' and the reinforcer might be 'being allowed to play with a favourite toy'. A realistic target should first be set for the child, such as 70 per cent of the time on task. The child's behaviour is then monitored, which could involve the teacher checking the child on regular occasions. If the target is reached by playtime, then the child would be allowed to play with the toy. Although negative behaviours sometimes have to be dealt with, as far as possible they should be ignored, to avoid inadvertently reinforcing them with attention.

It is important that children are aware of the target that they are aiming for and exactly how they are doing. For the latter, they need some form of regular feedback. With younger children this can take the form of a chart system, for instance with stickers for good behaviour. Some form of tokens can be used such as plastic counters or coloured table-tennis balls placed in a large container in front of the child. These would be given for positive behaviours and can then be counted up at the end of a lesson and exchanged for desired rewards. Older children will be able to operate with less immediate reinforcers and their behaviour can be reviewed at the end of each lesson. The normal reports that are commonly used in secondary schools can be modified for daily monitoring and linked in with outcomes such as being given weekly pocket money or being allowed out to a youth club.

Approaches that work well in developing appropriate behaviour with primary-school pupils have some factors in common (Evans *et al.*, 2003). As might be predicted, choosing 'rewarding' reinforcers is vital, for example minutes of free play or listening to music following periods of on-task behaviour. Further, children were able to see how their behaviour was progressing through visual feedback provided by the teacher – this might be a graphic representation or 'smiley faces' which signal how close the child was getting to, for example, a period of free play (Evans *et al.*, 2004). However, although these behavioural token systems are effective in the short term, their effectiveness can be limited to the period when the intervention was running, and therefore a strategy is needed to incorporate a longer-term socialisation element into the programme. This type of approach can be used effectively with individual pupils and also with whole classes. There is a consensus across research reviews (Evans *et al.*, 2003; Reddy and Newman, 2009; Roberts *et al.*, 2003) to indicate that this is an effective approach for dealing with a range of school-based problems, and that it results in generally more positive classroom environments, cooperative behaviours and improved learning.

Following the principle of operant conditioning, initial reinforcement schedules should involve a high, constant ratio; that is to say, the child's behaviour should be reinforced frequently and predictably. As one does not usually wish to continue a behavioural programme indefinitely, as soon as possible the schedule should be switched to a low-frequency variable ratio; this means reinforcing less often and less predictably. The reason for the change is that, although there will be a fall in the positive behaviour, this is then much more likely to become stable and to be maintained in the long term without the reinforcers.

Strict behavioural theory states that the key feature of a conditioning programme is the close matching of reinforcers with particular behaviours. More recent developments in learning theory, however, emphasise the cognitive nature of this process, with the individual developing expectancies about what will happen in certain situations. This implies that it would be useful to involve individuals as much as possible in the process, possibly by monitoring their own behaviour and deciding on desirable behaviours, targets and rewards. This can be particularly effective with older pupils, and McNamara (1979), for instance, has shown how such self-rating systems can be used with secondary-school pupils. Self-rating systems involve the use of reports where pupils make assessments of their own behaviours during lessons. Their assessments are usually surprisingly close to teacher assessments and encourage pupils to acknowledge their difficulties and to enter into a discussion about what they are doing.

Antecedents

A number of studies have emphasised the role of the context in determining problem behaviour. Context acts as the antecedent stage in behaviour modification and provides cues and information for the pupil. These might simply alert children that a certain type of behaviour from them is likely to have a desirable outcome. For instance, when a particular teacher enters the room, pupils might anticipate that shouting out will confuse him or her and delay the start of the lesson.

There are other effects that are more than a signal for the opportunity for misbehaviour. These include the pupil's active involvement, or lack of involvement, in more positive activities, such as concentrating on the lesson. Teachers vary, for instance, in the amount of time they spend setting up and changing activities. Teachers who are alert to the processes going on in the classroom and who minimise the opportunity for problems certainly appear to experience fewer behavioural difficulties in their lessons. The study by Rutter *et al.* (1979) compared different schools and showed that behaviour problems were less likely when work was well-organised and at the right level for pupils, when staff were themselves prompt in starting lessons, and when the student–staff relationships were positive. Certain peripheral school features also appeared to have a positive effect on general behaviour, including the use of carpets and the presence of plants in classrooms.

Activity

You have read about the effectiveness of behaviour approaches to problem behaviour. However, the approach has been criticised.

Consider how you feel about using behavioural approaches in the classroom and make a note of possible criticisms.

Although the behavioural approach has been shown to be very powerful in changing behaviour, it is often said that its superficiality may miss the true underlying difficulty in a child. For example, children who have behaviour problems in school may be acting in a particular way because they are the victim of abuse or bullying. Failing to take account of such difficulties can, of course, be a real problem, and any possible causes should first be investigated. However, it should also be borne in mind that behaviour can be relatively specific to particular situations.

A further criticism of behavioural approaches is the effect that they may have upon children's motivation. Lepper and Greene (1978), for instance, showed that the use of extrinsic rewards was effective in changing behaviour but that the behaviour became dependent on it. However, provided that rewards are not over-emphasised, appropriate behavioural techniques should probably bring the child back to normal motivators. Bornstein and Quevillon (1976), for example, showed good long-term maintenance following a behavioural programme, which they interpreted as being due to the 'behavioural trap' of the normal classroom. This means that when children's behaviour becomes more positive, they gain from increased task involvement and naturally positive teacher responses.

At a more practical level, a classroom teacher, already charged with developing lesson plans, monitoring learning objectives, collating class performance data and perhaps managing several IEPs, can find additional record keeping and the dispensing of reinforcers challenging (Theodore *et al.*, 2003). Where additional in-class support is lacking, a significant barrier to implementing an individual programme can arise.

One way in which this issue can be ameliorated is the use of group contingencies. This can reduce input time by having an entire class follow a contingency programme. It has the advantage of allowing children 'not on a programme' to have their good behaviour rewarded, and also reduces the possible stigmatisation that might result from targeting an individual child (Theodore *et al.*, 2003). This can be set up in many ways, for example with individual pupil targets, small group targets or an average performance on the tasks across the class. Teachers need to consider the relative advantages and disadvantages of each, in particular how children with learning difficulties might be treated by the approach or how 'fair' the approach may be to those who reach a criteria themselves but are not rewarded, or vice versa. This type of approach has, however, proved effective in reducing a variety of inappropriate classroom behaviours in a wide range of contexts and with children of different ages. Theodore *et al.* (2003) makes the point that, because the reinforcement is delivered to the whole class, a 'caste system' is avoided and an opportunity for whole-class success is offered.

Physical control

It is no longer legal for British teachers to use physical punishment with children, and such approaches have, in any case, been shown to be largely ineffective. School records of children who were caned demonstrated that the same children continued to be punished regularly, with no evident deterrent effect on their misbehaviour.

Unfortunately, some children may need to be physically restricted in some way, to prevent them from physically harming themselves, other people or property, or from disruption of the educational process. Yet, Piper and Smith (2003, in Hayden and Pike, 2005) argue that childcare and educational settings in the UK have become '"no touch" zones, because of fear, confusion and moral panic' (p. 879). The issue of the misperception of physical contact has been clearly indicated in educational guidance and legislation. For example, 'Physical contact may be misconstrued by a pupil, parent or observer. Touching pupils, including well intentioned gestures such as putting a hand on a shoulder, can, if repeated regularly, lead to serious questions being raised' (DfES, 2004b). However, government guidance has sought to make it explicit that teachers, within the UK have a legal right to 'use reasonable force to prevent pupils committing a criminal offence, injuring themselves or others or damaging property, and to maintain good order and discipline' (DCSF, 2010: 4). Further, it is also explicitly stated that teachers who use such reasonable force will have a robust defence against accusations of unlawful action and that the guidance is 'intended to help staff feel more confident about using force when they think it is right and necessary' (p. 4).

The power to restrain evidently has a very broad coverage and would appear to enable a teacher to (safely) restrain a child who was causing significant problems in school. Such restraint is of course likely to be aversive to the child and perceived by them as a punishment. If at all possible, the use of such physical approaches should therefore be carefully thought out and used as part of a behavioural programme that is aimed at developing positive behaviours, rather than just controlling negative ones. With a young child who enjoys playing on the computer, this might mean preventing his or her access to it, so that being allowed to use it once more can be used as a reinforcer for cooperative behaviour. Limiting children in this way could of course lead to disruptive attempts by them to get their own way. It might then be appropriate to consider using physical restraint (in line with the guidance mentioned above) to prevent their behaviour interfering with the educational process. In the United Kingdom, schools are expected to draw up their own policies that relate to their specific context. However this needs to accommodate a wide range of relevant policies and guidance, therefore frameworks may be supplied by local authorities for schools to adapt. Reviewing the extent to which positive handling procedures are used suggests that this is a 'very small part of an overall behaviour management programme in schools, notably special schools' and 'was always a last resort' (Fletcher-Campbell et al., 2003: viii, cited in Hayden and Pike, 2005: 12).

It can also be difficult to know quite what forms of restraint are safe for the child and for the person applying them. Merely holding a child by one arm could be damaging if he or she then struggles against the restraint. Therefore, if it looks as though this procedure might be necessary with a child, it is important for teachers to inform senior staff and to involve parents so that they are aware that what is being done is in their child's best interests. If schools are concerned, it may be appropriate to involve an educational psychologist or specialist support teacher, who would usually be able to advise on the best approaches to be used, how to monitor and record progress, help establish appropriate parental reporting procedures and ensure that incident logs are monitored by appropriate personnel.

Research on the use of physical interventions indicates that intervening staff must be specifically trained (Ryan and Peterson, 2004) and at least one member of school staff should have accredited training in this area. It is important that staff training is able to 'live up' to the policies and acknowledges the complexities of the situations in which teachers and pupils find themselves (Cornwall, 2000). For some pupils with SEN, an individual risk-assessment will be necessary, for example where children have:

1   communication impairments that make them less responsive to verbal communication;
2   physical disabilities and/or sensory impairments;
3   conditions that make them fragile, such as haemophilia, brittle-bone syndrome or epilepsy; or
4   dependence on equipment such as wheelchairs, breathing or feeding tubes.

(DCSF, 2010: 15)

'Team-Teach' is a training approach that combines knowledge of the legal context with a whole-school approach and developing awareness of a range of classroom strategies such as de-escalation and positive handling techniques (restraint) (Hayden and Pike, 2005). In practice, this approach appears to be mostly used in special-school settings.

Within secure settings, such as secure children's homes and young offenders institutions, a variety of intervention approaches that incorporate restraint are practiced. A review of how these methods were used, for behaviours which would be much more extreme than found in mainstream settings, recommended the importance of situating such techniques within a proactive positive behaviour management approach, having suitably graded responses and the removal (or review) of the use of 'pain compliant' methods (Smallridge and Williamson, 2008).

Other techniques for managing behaviour
Social skills training and social manipulation

If children's behavioural problems appear to be related to social difficulties, it seems reasonable to train up specific abilities or to modify children's social situation in some way. In an approach devised by Spence (1995), children's abilities can first be analysed and then programmes run to work on areas of deficit. These areas of deficit can include non-verbal abilities such as making appropriate eye contact and having good posture and good listening skills. Role-play situations can also be used to structure and deal with problem situations such as teasing, bullying or confrontation by an adult (to model some pupil–teacher interactions).

A review evaluation of a wide range of research in this area by Ogilvy (1994) found that children can make progress with these specific abilities but that they are unlikely to transfer these skills to other situations. Most research on the outcomes of social-skills training has failed to demonstrate any changes in children's normal social functioning, which may be partly due to the rigidity of peer expectations and stereotypes. When social development is carried out in a meaningful social context, it is much more likely to have a generalised impact. In one programme by Bierman and Furman (1984), children with social difficulties were trained in conversational skills, either individually or as part of a task with peers that required coordination to achieve a superordinate goal. Children who were trained individually showed no transfer of conversational skills, whereas those who had developed them in a group situation continued to use them in other situations. It is, however, rare for social training to be carried out in this way, and the evidence generally indicates that there will be little transfer of skills unless considerable effort is put into developing their use in a child's normal social context. Consequently, school-based teacher social-skills programmes tend to produce significant positive effects but changes in behaviour are less likely to be maintained longer term (Evans *et al.*, 2004). Social Effectiveness Therapy for Children and Adolescents (SET-C) is a programme designed for children with social anxiety and social phobia, which has proved effective in a range of studies, including randomised control trials (Silverman *et al.*, 2008). It combines several strategies: social-skills training for individual and groups, 'peer generalisation' and in-vivo exposure activities. This allows the development and transfer of skills missing from purely individual approaches and incorporates a parental education element.

Difficulties with social organisation in the classroom can be elicited by the sociometric technique outlined in Chapter 12. The technique might make it possible to reduce the impact of key disruptive individuals who have a disproportionate effect on the class through their range of contacts, perhaps by moving their seating position or changing their teaching group for some lessons. The converse is also true: socially isolated children might benefit from setting up greater contact for them with other children who are likely to be open to social involvement. This could be achieved by setting up small adult-directed games groups during break times or by seating children together. However, in a five-year longitudinal study, Coie and Dodge (1983) found the social dynamics of classrooms was a complex process, with many problem situations resolving naturally. Social status also tended to change over time without any intervention, which indicates that such social engineering may be difficult to achieve.

An alternative approach is one that begins from a basis of looking at developing socially and educationally fruitful interactions. This relational approach focuses on developing the supportive relationships that underpin the children's learning and utilises activities designed to develop respect and communication. The rationale is that '[e]nhanced learning in groups of children is apparent when there are close relationships ... characterised by a sense of "trust" and interdependence' (Kutnick *et al.*, 2008: 85). Kutnick *et al.* (2008) implemented and evaluated a relational approach with 5–7-year-olds over one year. Their results, measured against a control group, indicated that the approach had a significant effect in several areas. These young pupils were able to engage in productive group work and outperformed the control group in curriculum-related tests (English, maths and vocabulary). A time-sampling analysis indicated that children's talk was more constructive and that they spent more time on-task than the control group. This type of approach would not be a suitable response to behaviour problems per se but does indicate potential as being a proactive way of developing social skills and positive affect at the start of children's school careers. The Social Pedagogic Research into Group-Work (SPRinG) programme used a relational approach in the context of teaching science and also found that pupils experienced more positive social interactions and outperformed a control group in terms of academic attainment (Baines *et al.*, 2007). A strength of the relational approach is that it is part of authentic curriculum tasks, combined with practical support for teachers, within 'real-life' classrooms.

Systemic models of behaviour change look at the broader organisational context in which problem behaviour occurs and intervene by altering the context itself, such as pupils' grouping and classroom layout, Significant short-term improvements in time on-task and reduction in inappropriate behaviours have been achieved through arranging where children sit and how they are grouped (Evans *et al.*, 2004). One example of a systematic approach that looks at social relationships is 'Circle Time'.

Circle Time

Circle Time is a specific technique described by Bliss *et al.* (1995) that aims to promote pro-social behaviour and positive climates in schools by means of regular class work with groups of children.

TABLE 13.1 Sample Circle Time plan (Canney and Byrne, 2006: 20)

Introductory phase	(Group gelling and to mark the beginning of the session) Opening game, e.g. *Pass the Action* – any action passed around the circle as fast and as smoothly as possible. Opening round – each child takes a turn in completing a scripted sentence, e.g. 'I feel happy when …'
Middle phase	(Open forum) (Open discussion for problem-solving and target-setting) The facilitator might ask, 'Is there anyone here who needs help with their behaviour?' pupil can respond by raising their hand and saying, 'I need help because I …' Other group members offer supportive suggestions for change beginning, 'Would it help if …?'
Closing phase	(Celebrating success and a calming game to end) Group members offer thanks to others for kind acts noted in the week before, e.g. 'I'd like to say thank you to John for …' Closing game, e.g. 'Chinese Whispers' (sic).

The actual session involves an interactive process that has firm ground rules whereby children (and staff) are required to listen to each other with respect and to take turns in speaking. It is a whole-class approach for class issues, including problem behaviour. Children can, for instance, each identify positive aspects about other group members, or commit themselves to specific ways in which they could help a child who is having difficulties. The sessions may run weekly, are usually in the children's own classroom and have a basic structure (see Table 13.1).

A complete circle of turns can lead on to children working in small groups on key social areas that they can then bring back to the main group. As with general counselling approaches, the emphasis is on commitment to and resolution of problems, but this time in the form of the overall social group. Controlled evaluations of Circle Time approaches are lacking; however, several research studies of teachers' and pupils' attitudes suggests that it raises the self-esteem of participants (Miller and Moran, 2007).

Circle of Friends

Circle of Friends (CoF) is based on peer support and aims to facilitate the inclusion of children experiencing difficulties in learning. It has also been adapted to support children experiencing social, emotional and behaviour difficulties in schools and aims to establish a supportive social network for a 'focus child through a buddy system'. Qualitative and case-study evaluations of CoF suggests that it can achieve this support and inclusion. This benefits the 'buddy' in terms of self-confidence and awareness of difference, and the focus child in terms of self-esteem and community access (Holtz and Tessman, 2006). This interaction potentially helps change the behaviour and attitudes of both children. The class will discuss the child's strengths and aspects that need development. A small group of pupils form the 'circle of friends' and consider how they will support them. Comparative outcomes-based quantitative research is lacking on CoF; however, a long-term study by Fredrickson *et al.* (2005) found that the whole-class meeting was a significant influence on improving social acceptance. They also found that teachers were skilful in choosing 'socially inclusive, supportive children' who were likely to be responsive to the programme. As with other approaches that we have considered, the maintenance and generalisation of positive changes is likely to be limited without specifically targeted intervention.

Restorative Justice in schools

Whilst social approaches can be seen as proactive, there are obviously occasions where schools need a system that is capable of being appropriately reactive. In this context, Restorative Justice is an approach that offers an alternative to punitive sanctions. Its key feature is a negotiated reparation for damage or hurt caused by inappropriate actions, with the offender taking responsibility for the consequence of their actions. This is quite a challenging approach to dealing with problem behaviour as it goes against an ingrained desire to blame and punish (Hopkins, 2005), and successful mediation requires sensitivity and skill. It is underpinned by five key principles:

1   full participation and consensus of all the affected parties;
2   to repair what has been damaged for all those involved, including the offender;
3   the offender confronts those they have hurt or offended, and accepts responsibility;
4   there is a reintegration of both offender and victim into the community;
5   pro-active measures are developed to prevent further harm.

(Sharpe, 1998: 7)

The approach developed in the context of criminal justice and, subsequently, youth offending. It was then trialled in schools in New Zealand and Australia. It appears to be successful in reducing criminal violence and school bullying. Reports indicate that

> Applied to the school context, restorative justice shifts the emphasis from seeing anti-social behaviour as challenging the authority of the school to seeing it as damaging to relationships within the school. The effect is then that it allows a way forward for the individuals concerned because, rather than their having to bow to authority, they are required to take responsibility for repairing the damage to those they have hurt and to the school community as a whole.

(Varham, 2005: 95)

A pilot of the approach in 32 schools across England and Wales was implemented by Youth Offending Teams. Conferencing and mediation was able to resolve 95 per cent of disputes and conflicts. The schools became perceived as being safer, and there were significant reductions in victimisation and bullying (Varham, 2005). Whilst positive findings are emerging regarding the impact of restorative justice, take-up and application remains inconsistent (Varham, 2005). This may be because the time needed for training in conflict and relational-management strategies or awareness of the risks of poorly implemented strategies in sensitive and difficult areas (Hopkins, 2005).

Cognitive approaches

Some approaches such as counselling and cognitive behaviour modification involve individual work with children. These attempt to modify ways in which children with problems think about and deal with their difficulties.

Counselling

Originally based largely on the work of Rogers (1951), school-based counselling is a helping process that depends on the development of a relationship between a counsellor and a child. This should be sufficiently supportive to enable children to explore aspects of their life more freely. A final goal should be the possibility of arriving at more adequate ways of coping with whatever children perceive as a problem in their lives.

Counselling is normally based on uncritical acceptance of what children have to say, and matching in with their 'frame of reference' – the way in which they construe the world. The frame of reference incorporates views about the roles and motivations of others, and children with problems will often have a very different perspective compared with other people in the school. However, this can be a difficult stance for teachers to take, as they have to uphold the rules and regulations of school. As far as possible, counselling is therefore carried out by a neutral person, and some schools employ professional counsellors or counselling services.

As shown in Figure 13.2, counselling starts with listening and reflecting back what the child has said. This is followed by a number of questions, mostly open-ended to allow the child to expand on his or her perceptions. During this time, the counsellor is trying to build up an understanding of the child's situation using non-verbal as well as verbal information. He or she will often then try to interpret the problem, via a remark such as, 'So perhaps a lot of your problems start with your friends?' The final stages involve the counsellor prompting for solutions. Although it is very tempting for counsellors to impose their own ideas at this stage, it is important for them to be non-directive. The key element here is for children to generate their own realistic options, since they are then more likely to be committed to them.

Some schools using this approach allow pupils to refer themselves. Counselling can be an effective way to help pupils with anxiety and/or depression, and Lawrence (1971) used volunteers to visit schools and talk regularly with underachieving children. This counselling was shown to help them with adjustment difficulties and resulted in improved self-esteem and improvements in academic skills such as reading.

Referrals can also be made by senior staff, whose concerns are often prompted by challenging or worrying behaviours. In these situations, children may be less motivated, and it can be difficult for the counsellor to get pupils involved in considering the need to change. Bergan and Tombari (1976) found, however, that once pupils had committed themselves to implementing a plan, there was then a very high correlation (of 0.977) with eventual resolution of the original problem. In this study, the effect of the counsellors was greatest at the stage of problem identification, and counsellors who did not have very good interviewing skills were the least effective.

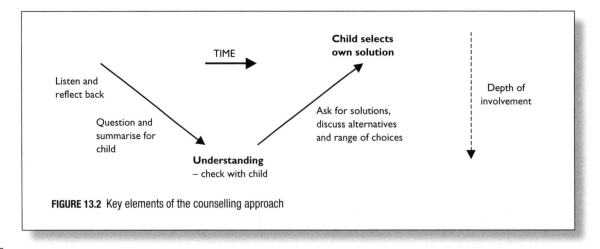

FIGURE 13.2 Key elements of the counselling approach

A development allied to traditional counselling is solution-focused brief therapy. Rhodes and Ajmal (1995) describe this approach, which can be used with individuals or groups in schools. It involves only about four sessions, and from the start it emphasises solutions, rather than what the problem is, or what caused it.

The solution-focused approach is largely congruent with research on the nature of effective problem-solving techniques. The key elements of this are to first identify or construct the goal end-state, then an intermediate achievable goal that can be linked with the final one. In solution-focused therapy, the therapist starts off by asking the child about what the child's life would be like if there were not a problem. Ways of working towards this desired state are then identified by looking for 'exceptions' – times when the problem is not present. A child might, for instance, find that there are no problems in school on days when the child did not first have a row with his or her parents. Small changes in a child's life may then lead to many other positive changes through a 'ripple effect'. This happens as children realise that there are different ways of seeing and doing things, ways that are under their control.

As with conventional counselling, there is an emphasis on adopting the frame of reference of the client. Some children who have been forced to see the therapist are described as 'visitors' (and will probably have little commitment to change), and others, such as teachers, who perceive problems with a child, are described as 'information givers'. A third category who believe that their actions can bring about change are described as 'customers', and following a session they can be given tasks to carry out. For example, parents might be asked to make a positive comment to their child each morning.

Rhodes (1993) has reviewed findings that indicate the effectiveness of this approach is similar to that of other forms of therapy. In view of the short-term nature of the approach, combined with its simplicity and respect for the client, he argues that solution-focused brief therapy should therefore be a first choice for most interventions. There is growing evidence to support its use in this way. For example, a study of 67 children found that a solution-focused brief therapy was effective in reducing classroom-related behaviour problems in comparison to control groups (Franklin *et al.*, 2008).

Cognitive behaviour modification

Cognitive behaviour modification has been developed on the premise that various problems can be modified by altering the way a pupil thinks. This moves away from a purely behavioural approach and acknowledges the child's ability to represent actions and reflect on them through language. Self-monitoring and reflection might therefore be built into behaviour-modification programmes (Evans *et al.*, 2004).

Cognitive behaviour modification usually involves attempts to use verbally mediated self-control to direct attention and to modify behaviour. Therapists will first model a task, which involves 'talking out loud' to themselves about what they are doing and what is going to be done next. The child then imitates the therapist's actions and progressively internalises the verbal instructions.

Such approaches have often been shown to be highly effective with impulsive behaviour. A meta-analysis of 23 such studies by Robinson *et al.* (1999) also found an overall effect size of 0.74 on reducing hyperactive-impulsive and aggressive behaviours in school settings, indicating that this could be a useful routine approach for children with such behavioural difficulties. A systematic research review (Evans *et al.*, 2004) found some evidence that a cognitive behavioural approach was useful in tackling disruptive or off-task behaviour in an example where children were taught outside the classroom to self-monitor their behaviour, and were given adult and peer modelling of self-talk, in addition to opportunities to practise their new skills. There was more evidence for its usefulness in reducing aggression and developing social skills, albeit in the short term. This included counselling sessions to help young boys deal with frustration and feelings of anger and teacher-awareness training. Cognitive behaviour therapy can be delivered to individuals or groups, such as parents and their children. Interestingly, a meta-analysis of research evidence suggests that there are no significant differences between individual and group treatments in the treatment of anxiety and social phobias (Silverman *et al.*, 2008). Overall, cognitive behavioural approaches seem to work well with a broad range of problem behaviours.

Non-verbal behaviour and authority

Non-verbal information comes from a range of aspects such as posture, gesture, general body positioning and eye contact. Paralanguage also involves the volume, tone and rhythm of speech. All these have a great influence on communication processes. Teachers who say that they are going to carry out some discipline behaviour, and yet at the same time physically act in an indecisive way, are unlikely to be believed and will have less impact. A teacher who threatens a detention unless a child stops a particular behaviour will not be given much credibility if he or she stands well away, has no eye contact and also 'fidgets'.

The effects of teacher non-verbal communication used to be investigated by showing pupils photographs of teacher postures and asking them to rate these. This method lacks validity, however, and more complex and realistic techniques now utilise videotape analysis of classrooms, which enables researchers to identify common features of teachers with good classroom control. Reviews such as that by Neill and Caswell (1993) find that effective teachers have non-verbal behaviour appropriate to their authority role and matched with the information content of what they say.

Appropriate teacher behaviour covers the general use and control of space, with effective teacher's greeting and directing classes at the door as they come in. According to Hall (1966), every individual pupil has his or her own zone of personal space, which extends to a little over 1 metre around them. If teachers avoid entering this and stay at the front of the class, this can give a message of insecurity to pupils and how they enter this space can indicate respect for the pupil (Rogers, 2000). When there is a minor problem such as inappropriate talking, then if a teacher merely enters the zone of personal space, it can send a message to a pupil that the teacher is aware of what he or she is doing and will usually stop the behaviour progressing. Confident and sensitive use of pupils' territory by the teacher implies high status and also enables the teacher to monitor their work.

Eye contact can also have the same effect, and high-status individuals are able to control interactions by dictating how and when gaze is used. When the encounter has little emotional content, the high-status person is able to give and withdraw eye contact when he or she wishes. With high emotional content, however, the high-status person will concentrate their gaze on the low-status person, who has to either return the gaze or look down.

A high-pitched voice is characteristic of stress or anxiety, and again gives a signal to pupils that the teacher lacks confidence and has limited control. A low-pitched voice has been shown to be characteristic of a relaxed and authoritative style, and is also generally more trusted and believed. Other signs of insecurity and tension that pupils unconsciously detect can involve 'grooming' such as hair or arm stroking, and defensive postures, such as arms, or objects such as a book, held across the body. Even effective teachers appear to have such characteristics, particularly when directing a class to change from one activity to another. However, they are usually able to control these involuntary signs at critical points of the lesson.

Effective teachers were found by Neill and Caswell (1993) to show warmth, enthusiasm for their subject and decisiveness. They used smiles, positive interactions with pupils, and a wide variety of facial expressions, gestures and tones of voice. They used these to illustrate the content of what they were saying and made lessons more vivid and interesting for the class. Effective teachers also showed a keen interest in what pupils had to say, with good eye contact and appropriate head and facial movements such as the 'eyebrow flash' – a strong signal involving raising the eyebrows briefly, which shows interest. When effective teachers watched their performances, they were often surprised at their own exaggerated style, but these ways of interacting with classes had the effect of involving students and prevented them from initiating inappropriate behaviour.

Pupils will often make challenges to the teacher's authority, and effective teachers will monitor for these and act appropriately. 'Closed' challenges are just limited rule-breaking – for instance, two children talking – and can often be safely left. 'Open' challenges on the other hand are a direct test of the teacher's authority and are characterised by 'control checks' by pupils. These involve rapid glances at the teacher just before and after an incident to see if the teacher is monitoring what is going on. A teacher who has 'withitness' will be aware of the first control check by pupils and will respond with a low-level non-verbal control. This can involve eye contact or moving towards them, to let them know that the teacher is aware of what is going on.

Neill and Caswell (1993) found that, when confrontations do occur, the behaviour of effective teachers was both more decisive and more relaxed than that of ineffective teachers. They used more controlling and illustrative gestures and they used animated intonation, showing a lively and often humorous involvement in what they were saying. They also used a loud voice less often, and, although forceful, did not adopt a threatening tone or posture.

In general, the most effective control is achieved by teachers who are relaxed and authoritative, who monitor and are aware of classroom behaviour, who take on the right to control and direct pupils' behaviour, and who show their control by means of matched verbal and non-verbal behaviour.

Medical approaches to problem behaviour

Many treatment approaches based on the medical perspective take place in a clinic setting, often with child psychiatrists in charge. These are doctors who have become qualified in studying and dealing with abnormal behaviour in young people. Referrals are usually made from within the health service, and are usually triggered off when parents go to see their GP and complain about problem behaviours. The focus of these centres is mainly on individual children and their families, and there is normally little contact with the school. Teachers may know that a pupil is attending a clinic of some kind but are often unaware of what approaches are being used. Occasionally centres are set up in conjunction with education, and these can sometimes be particularly effective in drawing together different types of expertise and in setting up joint management approaches.

Psychodynamic techniques

One technique has been to use psychodynamic psychotherapy, based originally on the mental structures and theories proposed by Freud. According to Freud, problems are the result of a child having inappropriate techniques for dealing with unconscious drives. Such maladaptive defence mechanisms may produce behaviours that can appear to be unrelated to what is causing them. The classic example of this described by Freud is the case of a child called 'Little Hans', whose irrational fear (phobia) of horses was analysed as being really due to displaced fear of his father. Simple behavioural approaches are therefore supposed to be unlikely to solve such a problem. Since they tackle the symptom and not the cause, they will only lead to 'symptom substitution', which means that one form of problem behaviour is merely exchanged for another.

Psychodynamic therapy typically involves talking with a patient and analysing his or her unconscious processes. With adults, this can be done by studying a patient's dreams, which are supposed to show unconscious desires. There can also be lapses of control, as in 'Freudian slips', when we make revealing errors, such as calling a disliked teacher 'Mrs Hate', when her name is really 'Mrs Hite'. Using such information, the therapist analyses and reflects back patients' mental processes, enabling them to develop insight. This then enables patients to experience catharsis (an emotional release from tension) and to change themselves – if they want to.

Children are less likely to be able to understand and talk about their mental processes in this way. Play therapy was therefore developed as a way of studying children's unconscious motivations and enabling them to understand and to cope with their underlying difficulties. It involves placing the child in a room with some age-appropriate playthings and encouraging their use. If, say, a boy buries a toy soldier in some sand, this could be interpreted as an unresolved tension concerning his father, and further directed play might encourage him to work through these difficulties.

Freudian theories were derived about a hundred years ago and are nowadays viewed with some scepticism, owing to their unscientific nature. More importantly, many studies of the outcomes of such therapeutic approaches with children have indicated that they are not effective. In a classic early review, Levitt (1957) looked at a range of studies that covered almost 8,000 child patients, and found that those who were treated made only as much progress as those who dropped out and were not treated. Despite this, some elements of psychodynamic approaches are still used, and play or art can be useful ways for children to show their feelings about abuse when they are unable to verbalise them.

Steinberg (1986) has pointed out, however, that much of the work in child psychiatry involves a range of different approaches. These psycho-therapeutic approaches have in common a focus on the complex roots of challenging or problematic behaviour. One might include in this broad approach the use of 'nurture groups' in schools, which developed from attachment theory and an awareness of the long-term effects of early childhood experiences. This began as a response to schools encountering young children with emotional and behavioural problems who struggled to cope with the demands of classroom life. Marjorie Boxall, an Educational Psychologist, believed that this could be the result of impoverished early attachment relations (Bennathan and Boxall, 1996). In essence, nurture groups seek to address the causes of emotional and behaviour problems as early as possible. They provide a small and supportive class within a mainstream school. This setting allows the child to feel secure and to engage in intense one-to-one or small-group work, developing their communication and social interactions.

Due to a relative lack of controlled research, there had been little conclusive empirical support for nurture groups as a psychotherapeutic approach (Evans et al., 2004), although they have remained popular. However, one large-scale and long-term quasi-experimental investigation has provided strong evidence of their influence on children's development. Reynolds et al. (2009) measured changes in children's cognitive and emotional/behavioural factors across groups in 32 schools. They found, in comparison to matched sample groups, significant gains across a wider range of standardised measures, and also in educational attainment.

One important technique described by Sue et al. (1990) is family therapy, when the therapist(s) will attempt to analyse and change the way in which the members of a family interact. Based on systems theory, family therapy argues that the different roles of individuals within the family can contribute to an individual's problem behaviour. For instance, underlying conflicts between a husband and wife might result in their child's misbehaviour. Although parents might bring children to a clinic and say that they want to improve their behaviour, the family system might in fact need to maintain these difficulties. Resolving them might mean that the key relationship of the marriage would be threatened if the parents would no longer be able to blame any problems on the behaviour of their child. Changing the system means encouraging the family members to develop new roles, sometimes by carrying out particular tasks that will force them to realise what is happening. One such technique is the 'paradoxical instruction' whereby the therapist tells the family to try to make things worse. It is hoped that success in doing so will show them how they can also make things better.

It can be difficult to evaluate the effectiveness of such techniques, as target outcomes will vary. With some families, for instance, it may be impossible to resolve any difficulties, and the best resolution would be for the parents to separate and then reconstruct their lives. Some intensive and structured programmes can, however, achieve positive outcomes with standard measures. One example of such a programme is the Functional Family Therapy Program (Alexander *et al.*, 1998), which is based upon improving communication skills and identifying solutions to family problems. Long-term evaluations of this have found that the reoffending rate of older children was reduced by up to 75 per cent and that there was also a preventive influence on younger siblings.

Drug therapies

Since child psychiatrists normally have a medical orientation, children are sometimes prescribed drugs to alter their mood or behaviour. Drugs would typically only be used for the more severe disorders where other approaches are not effective, for instance when the child's behaviour appears to be beyond his or her own control, or when there is some real physical danger to the child (such as a danger of suicide). Children who are highly impulsive and overactive are increasingly often prescribed Ritalin (methylphenidate), whose widespread use was discussed in Chapter 12.

Antidepressant drugs are not recommended for the initial treatment of mild depression in children. When medication is prescribed for moderate to severe depression, following assessment by a child and adolescent psychiatrist, it should only be in conjunction with psychological therapy, supporting family relationships and monitoring potential suicidal thought (Gentile, 2010). Some antidepressant drugs have serious side effects: causing dry mouth, blurred vision, drowsiness and constipation, and can also affect the cardiovascular system. Only one drug, fluoxetine (known as 'Prozac'), at the time of writing, is recommended for children as it is the only case where its benefits outweigh the risks associated with medication (NCCMH, 2005).

Although selective serotonin reuptake inhibitors (SSRIs) such as fluoxetine tend to have fewer medical side-effects, they can still cause agitation, nausea and loss of appetite. Some children taking these, particularly younger children, also become disinhibited, saying and doing things they would not have before. The SSRIs work by preventing the reuptake by cells of the brain chemical serotonin, which again is involved in mood. However, critics of this drug argue that the use of fluoxetine may interfere with the biochemistry of developing brains and could have long-term negative effects.

As well as these largely medical approaches, many clinics also use techniques such as behavioural and social interventions. These could be linked in with schools, but may deal with cases in isolation from other agencies. Within clinics there is often an emphasis on problems as coming from the individual child and, even when the family is included, only infrequent contact outside the home is involved. Even so, there is no doubt that clinics and child psychiatrists tend to be used as a final resort for the more severe cases, where it is difficult to make progress with the techniques and resources available elsewhere.

Educational psychologists and behaviour problems

In Chapter 11 we discussed how educational psychologists work at different levels within educational and community organisations. Their work in relation to social, emotional and behavioural difficulties reflects this diversity, ranging from systemic work in research, training and the implementation of policies and interventions, to direct work with children and their families (Farrell *et al.*, 2006). Examples of this diversity, from a national review practice, included developing anti-bullying policies, consultation and management with staff to deal with challenging behaviour, and therapeutic work (e.g. CBT or solution-focused therapy) and group work on anger management (Farrell *et al.*, 2006).

They might also use a consultation model in which parents or teachers request a meeting, mediated by the psychologist, to discuss and find solutions for a child's emotional and behavioural difficulties. As discussed in Chapter 11, they are increasingly likely to be delivering these services within a multi-professional context. With the possible exception of drug treatments, educational psychologists can be involved at some level in all the interventions and strategies discussed in this current chapter.

Specific problems

Bullying in schools

Bullying is a form of aggression that goes on over a period of time and is focused on a particular individual. It can be defined as 'systematic abuse of power' (Rigby, 2002: 74). The nature of this perceived 'power' may be physical, or derived from a form of social capital such as peer-group popularity. Definitions typically include the following: 'physical abuse (e.g., hitting, kicking or punching), verbal abuse (e.g., threatening, mocking, name-calling, or spreading malicious rumours), and social isolation or exclusion ... in which a person is deliberately ignored' (Monks *et al.*, 2009: 147).

The incidence of bullying appears to rise after children transfer from primary to secondary school (Rigby, 2002). Over a decade ago, the Department for Education and Employment carried out a questionnaire survey of pupils in a range of different British schools (DfEE, 1994a), and found that 27 per cent of children in primary schools and 10 per cent in secondary schools said that they had experienced being bullied. At this time, 66 per cent of children reported that they had been subjected to teasing or to some form of victimisation leading to social exclusion and isolation. Since then, there has been a large increase in public awareness of bullying as a problem in schools, and the nationwide development in schools of anti-bullying policies. Although lower figures (between 9 per cent–12 per cent) are now estimated across the United Kingdom (Bowen and Holtom, 2010), it is easy to find research studies that indicate increased prevalence. The figures reported in such surveys vary depending on how data are collected, the timescale being studied and the definition of bullying that is used. What is clear, however, is that bullying remains a significant issue in the school lives of children.

Bullying can have a major negative impact on a child's academic and social development. In the most severe cases, the result can be removal from school or attempted or actual suicide. Bullies themselves are also likely to experience long-term negative consequences, and a study by Olweus (1993) found that 60 per cent of bullies in grades 6–9 had at least one criminal conviction by the age of 24 years.

Cyberbullying

Online social networks and virtual worlds have created new spaces that are becoming central to children's social lives and their sense of identity. They are also spaces within which bullying can occur. The picture that is emerging is that children who are vulnerable in the classroom are also vulnerable online (Sheehy and Littleton, 2010). The large scale of social networks and the speed at which hurtful information, pictures or shunning practices can be spread is combined with potential anonymity, in some virtual spaces, for bullies. These spaces can act to disinhibit behaviour with negative consequences, For example, university students carrying out academic work in *Second Life* 'engaged in vandalism and bullying on such a scale that the site owners, Linden Lab, banned the whole student body' (Crook, 2008: 36); and online harassment is commonly reported by teenagers (Lenhart, 2007). A developing area of research concerns the moderating effects of families in online game play. Situations in which parents and their children play together online give opportunities to develop online social skills such as collaboration and turn-taking (Ulicsak and Cramer, 2010).

Characteristics of bullies and their victims

Bullies

Bullies are more likely to be boys, and are more likely to engage in, and be the victim of, physical bullying than girls (Monks *et al.*, 2009). Olweus (1993) carried out a series of questionnaire surveys and in-depth investigations of bullying with many thousands of children, staff and parents. He found that in contrast to what is often believed, bullies generally have little anxiety and possess strong self-esteem. They are normally stronger than average and often enjoy physical confrontation. The stereotype of the bully as a coward who will cave in at the first sign of resistance is therefore a dangerous myth to promote among children.

Bullies appear to derive satisfaction from inflicting injury and suffering on others. They seem to have little empathy or feeling for their victims and will often rationalise their actions by saying that their victims provoked them in some way or another. Olweus found that the home background and general environment of such children was typically characterised by:

- limited love and care;
- too much 'freedom' in childhood;
- the use of 'power-assertive' child-rearing methods such as physical punishments and violent emotional outbursts.

When children are brought up in this way, they are likely to fail to establish limits to their own behaviour and will also learn that interacting with others involves the use of control. This type of home background also seems less likely to enable children to develop an understanding of their own mental states and those of others, known as a 'theory of mind'. A failure to develop this ability appears to lead to limited understanding by children about the effects of their actions on others' feelings. Dunn (1984) argues that the normal process of early pro-social development is very dependent on the capacity to feel for others. The developing of this capacity appears to be largely dependent on the quality and quantity of social interactions with parents in particular, as well as the level of development of general thought processes.

Bullies will often claim that they were 'only having a laugh' and play down the importance of their actions. This may be an attempt to divert responsibility, but it might also be that they do in fact have limited appreciation of the affective consequences (empathy) of what they are doing, combined with high impulsivity (Joliffe and Farrington, 2010). There is, however, evidence to suggest that bullies have well-developed theory of mind skills, and consequently are adept in reading social and emotional cues, and in recruiting supporters, suggesting a more complex picture regarding bullies, empathy and theory of mind.

Victims

Victims are characteristically less physically strong than average but it has been shown that they do not usually differ in any extreme way. Although bullies will often focus on one particular characteristic, physical characteristics such as wearing glasses or weight do not appear to be significantly correlated with victimisation per se. However, being disabled or having special educational needs significantly increases the chance of being bullied (Wainscott *et al.*, 2008). Victims are typically more anxious and suffer from low self-esteem, although this might at least in part be because of the experience of being bullied. Victims are also much less likely to have adequate social skills and tend to be socially isolated, lacking the protective effects of a supportive social group. A key feature appears to be that they are much less likely to react in a positive way when bullied, tending to withdraw, and they often fail to communicate their difficulties to either teachers or their parents. Because of this, they become 'easy targets', and attacks can escalate over time. The consequences of this may be reflected in victims of bullying being significantly more likely to experience sleep disturbance and bed wetting and report head and stomach aches (Monks *et al.*, 2006) and depression.

The home background of victims tends to be overprotective, often with particularly strong relationships between the mother and the child. Although it is tempting to assume that an overprotective background is a cause of poor relationships with the child's peers, it could also be at least partly a consequence of the child's isolation.

General environmental factors

Olweus found that school size did not seem to be an important factor, and that there was the same incidence of bullying in small, single-class primary schools. The broader social context does appear to be a key feature, and Randall (1997) has found that in some geographical areas with a generally high level of aggression, bullying is imported into schools and is very resistant to change. Aggressive or conflicting families will often encourage their children to react violently, and parents themselves will sometimes bring disputes into school.

The majority of school-based bullying occurs in the classroom, playground or corridors (Monks *et al.*, 2009) and, although bullying can happen on the way to and from school, Olweus found that two-thirds of incidents occur within the school grounds. Out-of-school bullying was linked to within-school bullying, and it is therefore possible that school events are the main precipitating factor. Bullying incidents happen particularly during breaks and lunch time, and Olweus found that the greater the number of teachers supervising at breaks, the lower the level of bully/victim problems. For children in residential schools, such as children's homes, higher levels of bullying are found than in mainstream settings, and these children are more likely to have been bullied before entering the schools (Monk *et al.*, 2009).

Staff awareness of likely problems also seems to be important, since it can be difficult to distinguish between general processes such as 'play fights' and low-level complaints by children, and more serious difficulties. Bullying is much less likely to go unnoticed where staff (including teachers, assistants and supervisors) are involved in a common policy and provide supervision of free activities.

Techniques to reduce bullying

A major issue when evaluating the success of all anti-bullying programmes is the extent to which they are followed through and implemented as originally intended. However, research evaluations of whole-school interventions typically produce improvements ranging from a 50 per cent reduction in bullying to zero, with some evidence to suggest that increased fidelity to the programme and staff motivation is associated with more positive outcomes. All school have anti-bullying policies and procedures, or have these as part of their school behaviour policy. However, few have procedures for non-teaching staff, (e.g. lunchtime supervisors), non-peer-to-peer bullying or cyberbullying (Smith *et al.*, 2008).

To reduce bullying, Olweus (1993) argues that the key aspect is to promote principles that are the opposite of the child-rearing dimensions that research has shown produce the problem in the first place. He gives details of an approach that involves intervention at the school, class and individual levels. This process involves the following.

- An initial questionnaire is administered to students and adults. This raises awareness of the problem, justifies interventions and serves as a benchmark for subsequent improvements.
- A parental-awareness campaign is launched. This can be done through conference days, newsletters and PTA meetings. The goal is to increase awareness (by using the questionnaire results) and to point out the importance of parental involvement and support.
- Teachers are encouraged to work at the class level to develop rules against bullying. Techniques include formal role-playing and assignments that teach pupils alternative ways of interacting. The aims are also to show other students how they can help victims and create an anti-bullying school climate.
- Interventions with bullies and victims are made at the individual level. Cooperative learning activities to reduce social isolation are implemented. Adult supervision at key times is increased.

Olweus carried out an evaluation of this approach in 42 junior and high schools with approximately 2,500 children. Comparing questionnaire data before and after the intervention, he found that there was a 50 per cent or more reduction in bully/victim problems, with the effects becoming more marked after two years. There were also other positive changes affecting general behaviour, social relationships and school ethos. The Olweus Bullying Prevention Programme has developed this approach further (Merrell *et al.*, 2008). Similar approaches have also been recommended in the DfEE's (2002) publication, Bullying: Don't Suffer in Silence. An Anti-Bullying Pack for Schools.

Many of the approaches already described in this chapter have been used to tackle bullying in schools. Other methods include peer support schemes in which children can practise and develop skills to overcome bystander apathy (see Chapter 12). This can involve the development of supportive networks of friends but also how to directly gain help when in trouble. As with other 'buddy' approaches, there appear to be benefits for the peer helpers, but in the context of bullying there is also the risk of hostility towards the peer helpers (Naylor and Cowie, 1999, cited in Monks *et al.*, 2009). Smith and Watson (2004) evaluated the work of Childline in Partnership with Schools and found a variety of practices including Internet and email support, lunchtime clubs and mentors. Most users felt they had been helped by the service (Monks *et al.*, 2009). In terms of virtual and online spaces, there is a growing consensus that schools should help their pupils to develop safe online behaviours (Crook, 2008), and school guidelines are now being developed regarding cyberbullying and harassment. However, children's access to virtual spaces largely occurs outside school hours and therefore effective online moderation and transparent 'report bullying/abuse' processes will need to be developed externally. Byron (2008) gives an excellent description of recommended national and international practices in this area. She highlights the successful examples of work of the Internet Watch Foundation and The Child Exploitation and Online Protection Centre, which tackle child exploitation issues.

Assertiveness training

Since a key component of bullying is the victim's vulnerability, some approaches aim to strengthen children's ability to cope with social pressures and typical problem situations. Social training can be carried out with individuals or small groups and equip victims with verbal and social skills that they can then use to defuse harassment when it actually takes place. The objective in these approaches is that the situation becomes less rewarding for the bully and that the child will no longer be seen as vulnerable.

Assertiveness is developed by social-skills training and starts by emphasising a child's own needs and rights as being equal to those of others. Using safe role-play practice, techniques are then developed that are neither passive nor aggressive. These include:

- *Broken record* – just repeating an assertive statement, for example:
  'Lend us your football.'
  'I don't lend my football.'
  'We'll pay you for it afterwards.'
  'I don't want the money, I don't lend my football.'

This avoids becoming involved with social pressuring and the logic that others will use to manipulate another child into giving in. In the example above, there was almost certainly no intent to actually pay the child. If this had been challenged, then it could have led on to further pressure, such as, 'Are you accusing me of being a cheat?'

- *Fogging* – this involves responding with a neutral statement that de-escalates the situation. For example, a child might challenge with, 'Are you a swot then?' and the victim could reply, 'It might look that way.' This does not attack the original statement but doesn't agree with it either and prevents the tormentor from making any progress.

As part of these techniques, children may need to rehearse non-verbal behaviour such as appropriate eye contact, body language and tone of voice in these situations. They also need to be aware of the need to get out of the situation and to inform an adult as soon as possible.

Practical implications

Should we punish the bullies?

From a common-sense and behaviourist approach, it would seem logical to focus on bullies as the source of the problem, and to attempt to modify their behaviour. In practice, this often means the use of punishments after incidents have happened, for instance with reprimands and detentions.

However, as pointed out before, the use of punishments is not very effective in developing positive behaviours. In the case of bullying, punishments also run the risk of making the situation worse if the bully then attempts to 'get back' at the victim and to threaten them so that they will not tell again.

Maines and Robinson (1991) argue that the basis of much bullying lies in general social processes, with groups excluding and victimising individuals to enhance their own sense of identity. Techniques to reduce bullying should therefore avoid focusing on an individual as a 'bully', but instead restructure the perceptions and interactions in the whole social system.

Barbara Maines, an educational psychologist, created the 'No Blame' approach, which involves bringing a group of children together, sometimes including the victim, but usually the other children directly involved, and any others around at the time – the 'colluders' and the 'onlookers'. The teacher then explains what the victim has been experiencing and asks the others to comment on this, about their own similar experiences, and in particular about what they think could be done to help the situation. Each group member is then seen alone, one week later, to discover how things are going.

When this technique is applied in schools, the findings have shown it to be highly successful. In a review of 51 cases, Young (1998) reported immediate success for 80 per cent of them, with the victim and other children involved reporting few or no difficulties, and the parents being happy that the bullying had stopped. A further 14 per cent also improved to a similar level over the following three-to-five weeks. Such experiences led the support team to advise schools to always adopt this approach, unless there were compelling reasons why it would not be appropriate. This has some similarities with Restorative Justice described earlier (p. 361). When implemented effectively, bullying has been reduced to low levels (Demko, 2005). It can be seen as having seven 'steps'.

1   Take an account from the victim – who must be really listened to. The circumstances in which the bullying took place are not important, but its effects are. Note the feelings expressed, and allow the victim to elaborate at length, through talking, pictures and writing.

2   Convene a meeting of all those involved in the bullying – to include no more than eight people. Those attending should include the chief instigators and observers, or those who colluded by failing to intervene. The victim should not be present at this meeting.

3   Explain that there is a problem for the victim and clearly describe the distress caused by the bullying.

4   Instead of attributing blame, state that you know that members of the group are responsible and can do something about it.

5   Ask all the group members if they can make suggestions on how they could help. Do not extract a promise of improved behaviour.

6   Arrange to meet the group a week later to check progress.

7   Throughout, convey your belief that the young people are not bad, that they are capable of kind behaviour and that they will help the victim.

(Demko, 2005: 162)

Activity

Reflect on the approaches to problem behaviour that have been discussed in the chapter so far.

To what extent could each be described as 'no blame'?

Having done this, consider your own position in developing a 'No-Blame' approach.

What barriers or problems would you foresee in implementing this type of approach in your school, or a school you know?

Demko critically reviewed her implementation of the 'No Blame' approach in a school. She found that a significant barrier was a lack of staff training and understanding of the approach. This may have been due to competing school priorities, or possibly a lack of motivation regarding 'yet another initiative'. It may have been that staff did not agree with the ethos underpinning the 'No Blame' approach or that it was not seen as an appropriate response for a particular behaviour. Parents of the bullied children may not have agreed or had sufficient explanation of the approach. Demko noted that, 'Parents should not advise their children to tackle the bullies themselves: by definition, the victims do not have the skills or resources to deal with the problem and could end up feeling even more helpless' (2005: 164), suggesting that such advice was given.

Attention-deficit/hyperactivity disorder (ADHD)

Children who have attention and concentration problems often also have a general level of overactivity, particularly when they are young. ADHD is a clinical diagnostic category in the American Psychological Association's *Diagnostic and Statistical Manual* (DSM-IV), and estimates of its prevalence indicate that it is a significant problem. In a review of research on this syndrome, Tannock (1998) found that it occurred in 3 per cent–6 per cent of children from a range of different cultures and

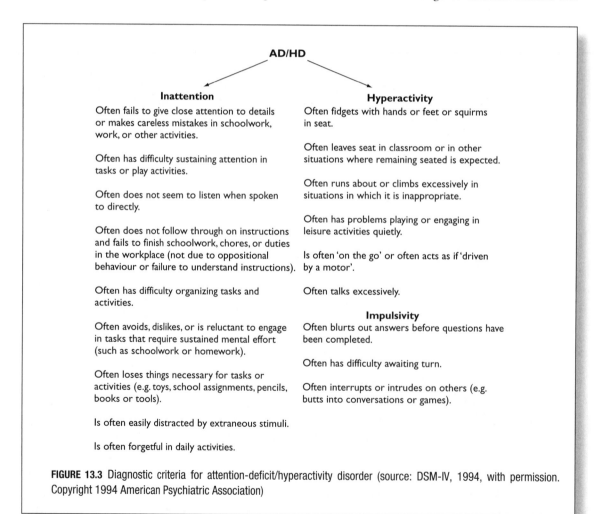

FIGURE 13.3 Diagnostic criteria for attention-deficit/hyperactivity disorder (source: DSM-IV, 1994, with permission. Copyright 1994 American Psychiatric Association)

regions, with boys outnumbering girls by approximately three-to-one. The diagnosis of ADHD appears to be mediated by deprivation, social class and ethnicity, with relative deprivation increasing the risk of diagnosis (NCCMH, 2008). Children with these problems can be particularly demanding and difficult to manage in school.

A long-term study by Fergusson *et al.* (1997) found that if children have difficulties with attention, they often make limited educational progress. About 1,000 children were evaluated for attentional difficulties at eight years of age and their educational progress was subsequently assessed when they were 18 years of age. In total, 35 per cent of those children initially in the top 5 per cent for attention problems eventually scored six years or more behind with their reading, which constitutes a major interference with their educational progress.

DSM-IV lays down specific criteria for diagnosing a child as having ADHD. Figure 13.3 gives the symptoms and criteria that are necessary for such a diagnosis.

Many children with ADHD have a combination of most of these features, but some may have primarily Inattentive type, or primarily Hyperactivity–Impulsivity type. In order to meet the diagnosis, two out of three of the symptoms must be present for at least six months, and they must have been present from an early age (before seven years). Also, symptoms must be at a relatively severe level and present in at least two settings (usually both school and home), and they should not be the outcome of another mental problem.

About 40 per cent–50 per cent of children diagnosed as having ADHD also have associated behavioural difficulties such as conduct disorder, or oppositional defiant disorder. Despite this overlap, factor-analytic studies have found that attentional and behavioural difficulties appear to be distinct domains. Moreover, a longitudinal study by Fergusson *et al.* (1997) found that behaviour problems at the age of 18 years were largely unrelated to earlier specific attentional problems at age eight years.

Drug therapy

In Chapter 12 we introduced ADHD and used it to illustrate issues in treatment by medication and changes in diet. An approach to the treatment of ADHD that is increasingly widely adopted in the United Kingdom involves the use of stimulant drugs, in particular methylphenidate (known as Ritalin) (for a detailed review of ADHD medication and its effects, see NCCMH, 2008).

Such drug therapy does appear to have a positive effect; however, there is a significant placebo effect, with up to 30 per cent of children showing behavioural improvements when they are given an inactive substance that they believe will be effective. Moreover, widespread use of medication is controversial as there are side-effects which, for the stimulant drugs, include insomnia, decreased appetite, weight loss (usually temporary), headaches, irritability and stomach ache. Moreover, the effectiveness of the drugs lasts only as long as they are being taken; they do not 'cure' the behaviour. Ritalin taken in the morning will usually wear off during the day, and this can mean that the child must take another pill at midday while at school.

Using stimulant drugs to treat children who are already overactive seems rather paradoxical.

One possible explanation for their effectiveness is that the brains of children with ADHD lack arousal. According to this, their difficult behaviours are an attempt to seek more stimulation to enable them to function at an optimal arousal level. As shown in Figure 13.4, the stimulant effect of Ritalin is supposed to 'normalise' their brains and allow them to function like everyone else.

Ritalin has the effect of increasing the levels of noradrenaline and dopamine in the brain. These are substances that transmit information between the brain cells and particularly affect arousal and mood. Tannock (1998) has reviewed extensive evidence which indicates that children with ADHD may

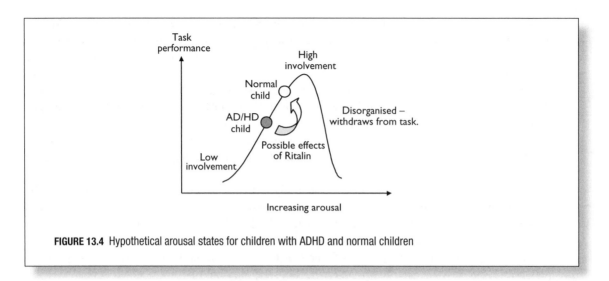

FIGURE 13.4 Hypothetical arousal states for children with ADHD and normal children

inherit a weakness in the dopamine circuits of the brain in the frontal region. This area is believed to be particularly involved with higher thought processes and the inhibition of responses.

For children diagnosed at six years of age, about 70 per cent will still meet the diagnostic criteria of ADHD at adolescence (Langley *et al.*, 2010). However, this also implies that the condition may not necessarily be a long-term one for a significant proportion of children, who may have learned to adjust in some way over time or who have had a complete remission. Whilst medical treatment may be common, its effectiveness in the long term has been questioned or only exists when the person is taking medication. It does not address other aspects of the child's life, such as low self-esteem, poor peer interactions or home factors which might exacerbate ADHD symptoms. Further, a significant number of children do not improve following the prescription of medication or may experience side effects (NCCMH, 2008). Therefore psychological approaches remain central to supporting children with ADHD in school.

Behavioural approaches

The majority of children's difficulties with attention and hyperactivity/impulsivity are short-term and are just a reaction to circumstances in their lives. Lessons that children find boring will lead to attention lapses, and emotional trauma in children's lives may make it difficult for them to focus on a particular activity.

Keown and Woodward (2002) studied the home backgrounds of boys with early-onset ADHD, in particular the quality of their parent–child relationships. In comparison to a control group, the diagnosed children had poor relationships and Keown and Woodward concluded that the way parents interacted with their child made a specific contribution to the child's behavioural difficulties. One possible explanation of this is that poor behavioural management may have generated the hyperactivity, although it is equally likely that this style of parenting was actually a reaction to the frustration and difficulties of having a child with hyperactivity. Whatever the causes, this type of management is unlikely to generate positive behaviours, and there is evidence that parental training based on establishing proactive and authoritative child management can bring about behavioural improvements. A combination of social-skills training and CBT has been shown to be effective (NCCMH, 2008). For the pre-school children, individual parent training has a positive impact on reducing both core ADHD symptoms and behaviour problems. Typically this approach uses behaviourist principles, the provision of information on ADHD and activities such as role play, modelling and recording progress (NCCMH, 2008).

Improvements in behaviour that occur from interventions outside of school do not necessarily transfer to the classroom, although summer holiday programmes (peer-focused behavioural skills approach) appear to have some merit (Pelham and Fabiano, 2008). Therefore, programmes that are carried out within the school are vital. Simple and effective behavioural approaches for both school and home behaviour can be set up by psychologists and teachers. These can involve operant conditioning with targets for self-control and work completion, as well as cognitive behaviour modification as described earlier. As might be expected, a combination of parent behavioural training, together with a teacher-led classroom-based behavioural programme, is particularity effective (Pelham and Fabiano, 2008).

School-based behaviour programmes

In recent years a number of programmes have been designed and evaluated which implement many of the factors that have been shown to help with behaviour problems. Most of these involve whole-class and whole-school approaches and can be delivered by a process of in-service training. We have already covered some of the better-known approaches used in the United Kingdom (e.g. Circle Time and Restorative Justice). The following three examples have been popular whole-school 'packages'.

Assertive Discipline

The *Assertive Discipline* approach (Canter and Canter, 1992) is a commercial (franchised) course developed in the United States that presents teachers with a classroom and school-wide discipline programme. This includes many behavioural objectives, such as the frequent use of positives, clear and stated boundaries to behaviour, clarity of instruction, and the use of non-verbal communication. One particular controversial technique is the process whereby misbehaviour (breaking one of the five classroom rules) results in a child's name being written on either the board or (more recently) a separate clipboard, and sanctions being taken against the child. More misbehaviour results in checks being added to the child's name, and further sanctions are carried out. Other elements are the involvement of parents, and the establishment of a school 'discipline squad' to deal with problem situations.

The firm behavioural rationale behind the programme has resulted in a number of positive evaluations. Teachers' interactions with pupils become more positive having been trained in the approach (Hayden and Pike, 2005). In a typical study, Swinson and Melling (1995) found the statistically

TABLE 13.2 Outcomes for assertive discipline training

	Pre-training	Post-training
Mean pupil time on task (%)	75	89.1
Mean disruptive incidents per lesson	4.8	0.8
Mean teacher praise statements per lesson	7.3	15.4

Source: based on data in Swinson and Mailing (1995).

significant results shown in Table 13.2 after implementing the programme in two schools. Other writers such as Robinson and Maines (1994) have, however, voiced some disquiet about the negative, control-oriented aspects of the overall approach, and the way in which students are seen as the sole cause of misbehaviour. Pupils' reactions to the programme are mixed depending on the extent and perceived justification for the punishment and rewards (Lewis *et al.*, 2008).

Building a Better Behaved School (BABBS)

The authors of the *Building a Better Behaved School (BABBS)* approach (Galvin *et al.*, 1990) have built up a set of extensive resource materials covering nine units dealing with the range of problems in school and effective management techniques. There are three main tiers which cover, respectively, the levels of the whole school, classrooms and individual pupils.

Early units deal with the way in which schools can review behavioural issues and move from this to set up whole-school discipline plans, manage parental involvement and organise the curriculum to minimise behavioural problems. At the level of the classroom, there is an emphasis on the 'lightest possible' approach with organisation and management. With more difficult classes, this can progress on to the use of firmer guidelines and teacher responses. The final level is a highly structured and behavioural approach for use with the most difficult individual pupils.

The BABBS materials can be used by schools as a basis for their own development and in-service training, but they have also formed a basis for the extensive 'Positive Behaviour Project' in Leeds (Galvin and Costa, 1994). This initially included 21 schools covering the primary and secondary age ranges, which were given training and ongoing support over two years.

The approach is strongly based on research findings and has generally been found to be effective. At the end of the Positive Behaviour Project, 69 out of a sample of 100 teachers said that they felt more confident of their ability to control those factors that influence classroom behaviour.

Behaviour Recovery

Behaviour Recovery (Rogers, 2004) is a whole-school approach for primary schools and describes a range of strategies and techniques that can be used by teachers. The emphasis is on practical approaches to a number of common problems such as inattention and disruption in class, as well as aggressive behaviours and problems at break times. The programme is based on researched and valid interpersonal techniques and behavioural principles. The approach has proved to be very popular with teachers, and Rogers' general approaches can also be used with children in secondary schools.

Special-needs provision for behaviour problems

Special schooling

In Britain, when a school's own approaches are not effective, they may exclude a child for a fixed number of days in any one school year. Intractable problems may warrant permanent exclusion, and the child will then have to be educated at another school with available places. If this also fails, then a mainstream school may legally refuse to take the child, and he or she may attend a Pupil Referral Unit. This is usually a small off-site provision, generally with only part-time attendance. Alternatively, as a result of the Statementing procedure that was described in Chapter 11, pupils can be placed in special schools that deal with behavioural problems. The placement can be a residential one if it is felt that there needs to be close coordination between the care of the child and his or her education.

In 2007, over 11,000 Statemented pupils were placed in special schools outside their local authority. Their most common primary type of need was either Autistic Spectrum Disorders or behavioural, emotional and social difficulties. They can be seen as 'potentially the most vulnerable and least visible pupils in the education system' (Audit Commission, 2007: 8).

The ratio of pupils to adults in these specialist schools is usually very low, typically 6:1 or less. As this low pupil-to-staff ratio is often combined with residential provision, this type of education is one of the most expensive of all. The reported costs per child for 'EBD' schooling is more than twice that for children with moderate learning difficulties (which was itself three-times mainstream costs) (Audit Commission, 1992). Between 2001 and 2006, councils' budgets for sending pupils to such schools increased by 28 per cent and the average cost per pupil rose to £57,150 (Audit Commission, 2007). Although this provision takes up a lot of resources, and one would therefore expect it to be effective, this has been questioned by a range of studies which suggest that pupils who had been excluded make poor educational progress and are rarely reintegrated (Audit Commission, 2007).

Alternative approaches

One conclusion from these findings is that it may be best to maintain children in their normal school as far as possible. However, merely waiting for the normal spontaneous improvements to happen can evidently lead to stresses on teachers and interfere with the social and academic development of other pupils.

One behavioural approach which aims to maintain the most difficult children in schools yet avoid these problems has been described by Long (1988). This used a positive daily school report with grades for each lesson, which were totalled and linked with home rewards and management. Of all the cases dealt with in one year, 64 per cent of pupils made virtually immediate progress, with tolerable behaviour and continued attendance. A further 18 per cent made some progress and a similar proportion did not respond at all. The pupils for whom this approach was not effective were usually older ones, for whom 'deschooling' approaches such as further education vocational courses and work experience may be more appropriate.

'Notschool.net' is an alternative personalised approach designed for children who have disengaged or been excluded from formal education. It offers an online learning community, primarily for 14–16-year-olds and has recognition as a form of 'full-time off-site education'. A high proportion of Notschool.net students subsequently go on to further education, employment or training. This form of 'virtual education' is likely to develop in future and it will be interesting to see research evidence regarding its influence in the lives of children who are currently difficult to teach in mainstream settings.

'Non-virtual' options of specially designed educational programmes also exist. For example, for pupils with complex needs and excluded from special schools, Nottinghamshire's Tailor-Made Programmes Team (TMPT) offers long-term support, based at a learning centre. The pupils are offered a personalised curriculum and there is integrated social-care support (Audit Commission, 2007). This approach allows many young people to remain in their local community rather than being placed out of the area.

Schools are ultimately limited in what they can do, and have the task of coping with large numbers of children in sometimes crowded conditions. They are also increasingly judged in rather mechanistic terms, with targets set for the number of children who reach particular academic goals, with little thought for the work that schools do to develop children's social abilities. In view of this, it is perhaps surprising that problems are generally at such a relatively low level. Galton *et al.* (1999) found that most teachers they observed showed highly effective personal and management skills and were able to deal rapidly with the majority of difficult behaviours by the use of low-key but firm strategies. However, later work (Galton *et al.*, 2004) suggested that behaviour problems were becoming of increasing concern for teachers, who, whilst enjoying teaching, found increasing demands on their time in terms of dealing with poor pupil behaviour. Despite the pressures they experienced, the teachers remained committed to their work and those they taught. It is therefore important not only that psychologists research how to create positive learning environments for all, but act to help support the implementation of positive changes in schools and classrooms.

Summary

One of the main ways of dealing with difficult pupils is to use a behavioural approach. For some problems, such as anxiety, this can use classical conditioning, but the main approach is based on operant conditioning to encourage positive behaviours. Programmes need to be carefully implemented. It can also be important to improve the way in which work is organised and monitored. The behavioural approach can be criticised for being superficial and damaging natural motivation, but it is likely that these negative effects can be largely avoided.

Classes can be trained in social skills and ways of interacting directly, through specific social-intervention programmes. Counselling in schools develops children's abilities to solve their own problems, and some approaches work on the links between thought and behaviour. Non-verbal behaviour by teachers and pupils is a powerful source of unconscious information and establishes role relationships.

Medical approaches tend to see problems as related to the individual; there is an increasing use of drug therapies to deal with problems such as ADHD as well as depression and anxiety.

Many of the cases that are referred to educational psychologists involve behavioural difficulties, and these are often dealt with effectively by behavioural or cognitive behavioural programmes.

Bullying is an important problem that affects a large number of pupils in schools. Victims tend to be more socially vulnerable. Most bullying happens within schools, and techniques to reduce it that involve awareness, training and monitoring can be very effective. Individual pupils can learn to be more socially assertive, but the most effective approaches involve managing the social dynamics of groups. Schools also need to develop strategies to give children the skills to be safe in online environments.

ADHD is a medical diagnosis, and the behaviours involved have important negative effects on children's socialisation and their educational progress. An increasingly popular treatment approach is to use drug therapy such as Ritalin, which appears to bring about significant improvements. Dietary changes may help a few children, but home factors appear to be important in maintaining problems, and behavioural and cognitive behaviour modification programmes can be highly effective.

There are a number of whole-school approaches that can improve general ways of dealing with problems. Circle Time, 'No Blame' and Restorative Justice emphasise a social problem-solving approach. Assertive Discipline involves techniques that emphasise rules and positive management, and has been positively evaluated. Building a Better Behaved School is a set of resource materials covering the range of school problems and has been shown to improve teachers' perceived control. Behaviour Recovery is a skill-based set of practical techniques based on research findings.

When children cannot be maintained in their normal school, they can attend special schools or units. The most effective approaches concentrate resources and techniques on the early stages to maintain pupils in ordinary schools.

Key implications

- Behavioural approaches offer a structured and effective way of improving problem behaviour in school.

- Schools should take an active approach to bullying. The most effective approaches increase monitoring and address the social processes involved.

- Children who have significant difficulties with concentration, attention and impulsive behaviour, if diagnosed with ADHD, may benefit from medication. However this is not universally effective and it remains a controversial approach.

- If at all possible, children with behaviour problems should be maintained (with appropriate support) in their normal school.

Further reading

Mosley (2005), *Important Issues Relating to the Promotion of Positive Behaviour and Self-esteem in Secondary Schools*: developing self-esteem through a Circle Time approach is often seen as confined to younger children. Jenny Mosley illustrates here how this important idea can be used with older pupils within secondary schools.

Rogers (2006), *Classroom Behaviour: a Practical Guide to Effective Behaviour Management and Colleague Support*: Bill Rogers is an experienced class teacher and psychologist. A key feature of his approach is that he describes common problems in classroom situations with which teachers will be familiar. He gives insight into practical strategies that have a positive impact on behaviour and illustrates how these work in practice.

Discussion of practical scenario

Mr Gray is not unique in experiencing these problems and finding them stressful. Whilst he plans the content of his lessons thoroughly, it sounds as if he has not considered his classroom-management strategy to the same extent. He should try out some other approaches first, before deciding he is in the wrong career. He might think about developing a positive behaviour programme with the class. This could include changing the seating arrangement, structuring work so that it is accessible to all pupils and ensuring that there are positive results from staying on task. We have discussed some specific approaches in this chapter and it is likely that the school has a behaviour policy that would support one of them. He may find it helpful to observe or team-teach with an experienced colleague. This will help him to develop a repertoire of strategies for 'what do I do when …?' situations and to consider how he will plan for the behavioural aspects of his lessons. If this is not an option, there are video materials that demonstrate these techniques. Bill Rogers produces excellent materials in this area.

He should discuss the situation with an experienced member of staff. Teaching is a demanding job and peer support is essential. It is therefore vital that he is able to discuss the situation with a colleague. All teachers are familiar with 'the hard class', but it may be that some pupils here have social, emotional and behavioural difficulties that require additional support. It would be useful to discuss this with the school special-educational-needs coordinator and decide on the appropriate next steps for supporting these pupils in class. Developing ways of working with this difficult group will stand him in good stead for the future.

Appendix: statistics

Things that we measure can be described and analysed using mathematical techniques. Doing this with a set of numbers is useful because it summarises and simplifies the data and lets us see what it means.

Describing data

Most things that we can measure in education vary quite a bit, and sets of data usually take the form of a bell-shaped curve known as the 'normal distribution'. For instance, children's reading at age ten years covers a wide range of attainments (Figure A.1).

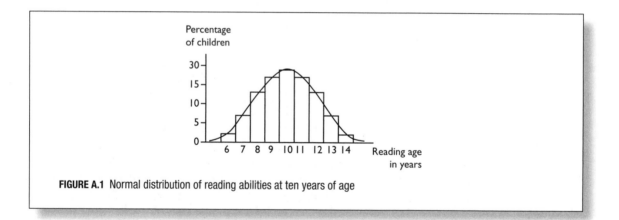

FIGURE A.1 Normal distribution of reading abilities at ten years of age

The extent to which the data is spread out or varies is referred to as the 'variance'; and a measure of this is the 'standard deviation' (Figure A.2), which always includes about one-third of all the values. The middle of the distribution is where most of the scores are and is usually the mean, or average, of all the scores.

This sort of distribution is usually the result of the combination of a large number of factors that have come together in a random way. Children's reading abilities, for instance, can be the result of the interaction between how they have been taught, how much they were helped by their parents, their ability to perceive separate sounds in spoken language, and their motivation and involvement with reading.

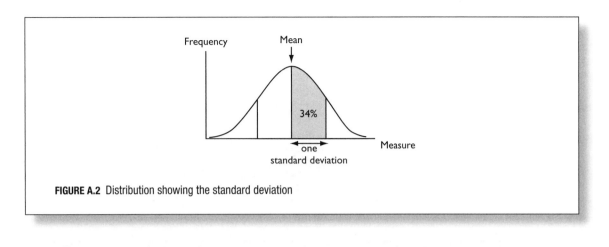

FIGURE A.2 Distribution showing the standard deviation

Analysing data

A statistical analysis can also assess whether what an investigation has found is significant, or whether it is likely to have simply happened by chance. We make a statistical analysis because we have to be careful that any effect we discover is not just part of the variation in scores that normally occurs.

If we found that using a new reading scheme with ten children increased their average reading ability, then we would need to compare their abilities with the range of reading abilities on the normal reading scheme. In the example in Figure A.3, there is a considerable amount of overlap; it could easily have been chance that there were a few more children above the normal average of ten years.

If the effect were greater, or if there were more children on the new reading scheme (as shown in Figure A.4), then it is less likely (or probable) that the improvement only happened by chance. The criterion for significance in statistical testing is usually set at a probability of 0.05 (a probability of 1 means that something is certain to happen). A result is therefore said to be statistically significant when it would have happened by chance only five times or less in a hundred.

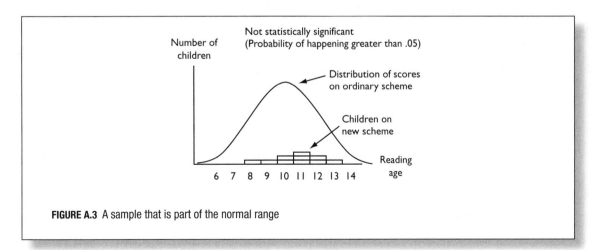

FIGURE A.3 A sample that is part of the normal range

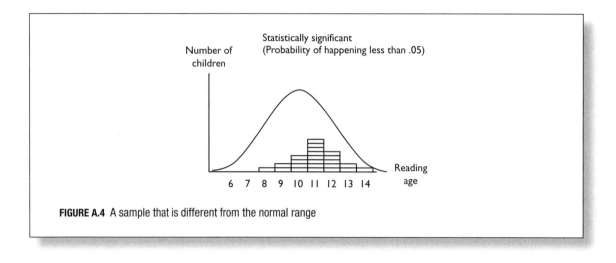

FIGURE A.4 A sample that is different from the normal range

Effect size

There can be problems interpreting the result of this sort of analysis, since a statistically significant effect is not always meaningful in practical educational terms. A good example of this can be seen in the area of school effectiveness. Research since the 1970s began to show that there were significant differences between the effectiveness of different schools. A problem with this research, as discussed in Chapter 6, is that the size of this effect is quite small compared with that of other factors such as home background, and to ignore these can be rather misleading. A lot of educational research therefore looks at effect size. This compares the size of a particular effect with the range of scores that you would normally expect to find, as measured by the standard deviation. For example, as described in Chapter 6, one-to-one teaching has a relatively large effect size of two (see Figure A.5), when compared with the variation of attainments in normal teaching groups.

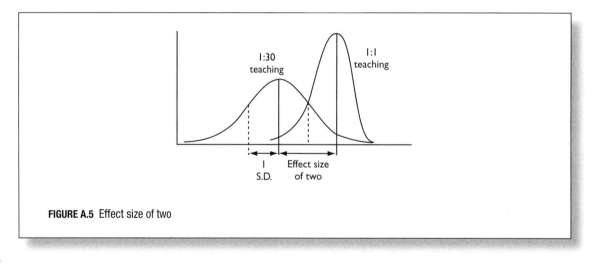

FIGURE A.5 Effect size of two

Effect sizes can also be used to combine and summarise the results of a number of different studies in an area by using a technique called 'meta-analysis'. A meta-analysis gives a more reliable indicator of the general effect size than the result of just one study, which is more likely to have been affected by some form of inaccuracy. An example is a review by Fuchs and Fuchs (1986) of 21 studies into the effectiveness of formative assessment and feedback to children (letting them know how well they had done and how they could make progress). The overall effect size they found was 0.7, which means that teachers can have confidence that the proper use of feedback is likely to have a meaningful effect on children's progress.

Correlation

Another technique that is used a great deal in psychology and education is to look at how two measures relate together. This relationship is known as *correlation* and is shown by a single value that can vary between −1 and +1. A positive correlation means that as one measure increases, the other increases as well. A negative correlation means that as one measure increases, the other decreases. A correlation of zero means that there is no relationship between the two measures. For example, reading attainments tend to improve along with scores on intelligence tests. The correlation between reading attainments and intelligence tests is usually around +0.7, as represented in Figure A.6.

Although correlations are useful and popular ways of showing such relationships, they can be rather misleading and are often assumed to have too great an importance. The correlation of 0.7 at first sounds as though it should explain most of an effect. However, this value will allow one measure to account for only 49 per cent of the variance in the other one (this is calculated by multiplying the correlation by itself, then by 100). If you knew a child's intelligence score at the point shown by the circle in Figure A.6, then as the vertical line on the graph shows, this would cover a relatively wide range of possible reading attainments, albeit with some clustering towards the central part.

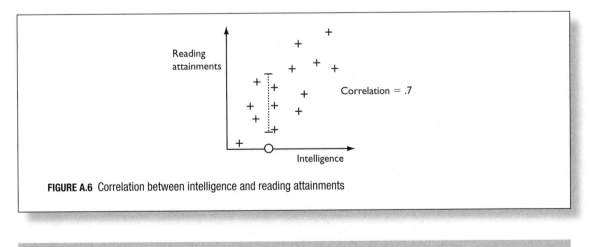

FIGURE A.6 Correlation between intelligence and reading attainments

Causation

In a great deal of behavioural research, it can be difficult to know what it is that *causes* things to happen, and how such processes occur. With correlations in particular, it is often tempting to assume that changes in one measure cause changes in the other measure; for instance, that intelligence directly determines reading attainments. However, this sort of inference is not logically valid, and there is good evidence that reading (and being read to) itself develops verbal abilities and thereby improves children's performance on intelligence tests. It is also possible that another, entirely separate, variable such as motivation is affecting both reading and intelligence test scores at the same time.

Rather than relying on observations and possibly misleading correlations, it is much safer to carry out direct interventions and see what the effect of doing something is. In the STAR investigation of class-size effects, children were randomly allocated to one of two different-sized groups. The better performance of the smaller groups was then much more likely to be due to the group size, rather than pupils in smaller groups somehow having better learning abilities.

Another problem with drawing conclusions is that causation can sometimes go in both directions. Using the example again of literacy and general language abilities, research in this area indicates that speech and language abilities are important as a basis for the development of literacy, and that language abilities in turn are extended by wide reading experiences.

Path analysis

The existence of correlation does not necessarily prove that one thing causes another. However, it can be used to help support or reject a particular theoretical model. In most areas studied in education, there are a number of possible variables and effects, and the theoretical relationships between them can be represented by a structured diagram. This should be derived from existing theoretical ideas and show the direction of effects.

For example, there is good reason to believe that a child's awareness of speech sounds and parental interest in reading both affect the child's motivation towards reading tasks and subsequent reading attainments. This would lead to the path diagram shown in Figure A.7.

A path coefficient is a value that is similar to a correlation coefficient and shows the direct effect that one variable has on another one. It would normally be written next to each straight arrowed line, and an observed correlation is usually the result of a number of path coefficients. In this example, the correlation between motivation and reading ability will be the sum of the direct path coefficient between them and the various indirect effects of parental interest and sound awareness.

A correlation study might support this model, but it is important to remember that it still cannot prove the structure or the causal links. It might be that we would want to consider the mutual influ-

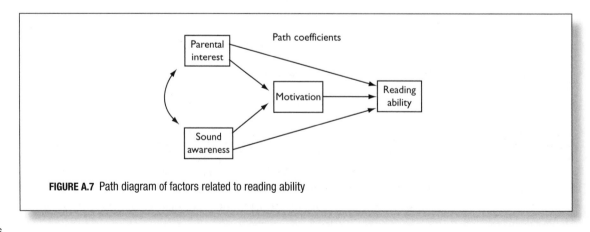

FIGURE A.7 Path diagram of factors related to reading ability

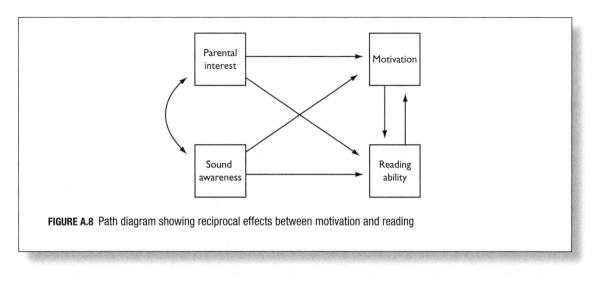

FIGURE A.8 Path diagram showing reciprocal effects between motivation and reading

ences between motivation and attainments, giving the structure the rather different, but possibly more plausible, form shown in Figure A.8.

Factor analysis

Information can sometimes involve a large number of items such as responses to a questionnaire or answers on an intelligence test. Factor analysis is a way of simplifying and summarising the relationships between these, usually in terms of the correlations between the ways in which items are responded to. This technique assumes that if some of the questions tend to be answered in the same way, then they might be measures of the same underlying factor.

If we made up a basic personality questionnaire and gave it to a few people, we might get the answers shown in Figure A.9. Answers to three of these questions seem to be strongly linked: if people in this sample say 'Yes' to liking parties, then they will also dislike reading and have many friends. If people say 'No' to liking parties, then they will like reading and not have many friends. The question about getting bored does not seem to link in with these at all, so it looks as though the

	Susan	Peter	Fred	Jane	Sociability factor loadings
Do you like parties?	Yes	No	Yes	No	+1
Do you get bored easily?	Yes	Yes	No	No	Zero
Do you like reading?	No	Yes	No	Yes	−1
Do you have many friends?	Yes	No	Yes	No	+1

FIGURE A.9 Answers to a simple personality questionnaire

other three items form a factor that we could call 'sociability'. The two questions on liking parties and having many friends are both important positive questions for sociability all the time, so each is given a loading on this factor of +1. The reading question has to be answered negatively to increase this factor, so has a loading of −1.

If we asked a wider range of questions, we would of course probably find more factors. Also, in real life, answers to questions do not go together quite so exactly, and factor loadings are usually fractions rather than whole numbers.

When there is a large amount of information to analyse, specialised computer programs can be used to look for likely factors. They can be set to find either a few factors that are relatively independent of each other, called 'orthogonal factors', or a larger number that have some overlap, called 'oblique factors'. In practice, most investigators tend to go for oblique factors, combining their analysis with techniques to find the simplest or most economical way of describing the data.

Although factor analysis can seem to discover real, underlying processes, it must be remembered that the technique is only a mathematical simplification of whatever data is fed in. The factors that are found will change with different sets of questions or techniques of analysis; with intelligence tests, for instance, factor analysis can show either a single general ability factor or a large number of interrelated mental skills, as described in Chapter 3. As with all statistical techniques, the psychological reality of the concepts involved should still depend on other ideas and knowledge rather than our assuming that the analysis shows us some form of ultimate reality.

References

Absoud, M. and McShane, T. (2009) When should epilepsy be treated? *Paediatrics and Child Health*, 19(5), 216–224.

Achenbach, T.M. (1991) *Manual for the Child Behavior Checklist/4–18 and 1991*, Profile. Burlington: University of Vermont, Department of Psychiatry.

Ackerman, T., Gillett, D., Kenward, P., Leadbetter, P., Mason, I., Matthews, C., Tweddle, D. and Winteringham, D. (1983) Daily teaching and assessment: primary-aged children. *Post Experience Courses for Educational Psychologists*. University of Birmingham: Department of Educational Psychology, 33–52.

Adelman, J.S., Brown, G.D.A. and Quesada, J.F. (2006) Contextual diversity, not word frequency, determines word naming and lexical decision times. *Psychological Science*, 17, 814–823.

Adey, P. (2001) Cognitive acceleration: thinking as intelligence. *Teaching Thinking*, 5, 38–41.

Adey, P. and Shayer, M. (1993) An exploration of long-term far-transfer effects following an extended intervention programme in the high school science curriculum. *Cognition and Instruction*, 11(1), 1–29.

Adey, P., Demetriou, A., Csapo, B., Hautamaki, J. and Shayer, M. (2007) Can we be intelligent about intelligence? Why education needs the concept of plastic general ability. *Educational Research Review*, 2(2), 75–97.

Adey, P., Robertson, A. and Venville, G. (2002) Effects of a cognitive stimulation programme on year 1 pupils. *British Journal of Educational Psychology*, 72, 1–25.

Advisory Council on Education in Scotland (1950) *Pupils Who Are Defective in Hearing*. Edinburgh: HMSO.

AEP (2008) *Occupational Summary Sheet: Educational Psychologist*. Online, available at: www.cwdcouncil.org.uk/assets/0000/.../Educational_Psychologists.pdf (accessed 9 March 2010).

Ainscow, M., Booth, T., Dyson, A., Farrell, P., Frankham, J., Gallanaugh, F., Howes, A. and Smith, R. (2006) *Improving Schools: Developing Inclusion*. London: Routledge.

Aitchison, J. (2008) *The Articulate Mammal: An Introduction to Psycholinguistics* (5th edition). London: Routledge.

Alexander, A. and Morrison, M. (1995) Electronic toyland and the structures of power: an analysis of critical studies on children as consumers. *Critical Studies in Mass Communication*, 12, 344–353.

Alexander, J., Barton, C., Gordon, D., Grotpeter, J., Hansson, K., Harrison, R., Mears, S., Mihalic, S., Parsons, B., Pugh, C., Schulman, S., Waldron, H. and Sexton, T. (1998) *Blueprints for Violence Prevention*, Book Three: *Functional Family Therapy*. Boulder: Center for the Study and Prevention of Violence.

Alexander, R. (2000) *Learning from Comparing: New Direction in Comparative Education Research – Volume 2*. London: Routledge.

Alexander, R. (2001) *Culture and Pedagogy: International Comparisons in Primary Education*. Oxford: Blackwell.

Alexander, R. (2004) *Towards Dialogic Teaching: Rethinking Classroom Talk*. Cambridge: Dialogos.

Alexander, R. (2005) Culture, dialogue and learning: notes on an emerging pedagogy. Paper presented at the International Association for Cognitive Education and Psychology (IACEP), 10th International Conference, University of Durham, UK, July.

Alexander, R. (2008) Culture dialogue and learning, notes on an emerging pedagogy. In N. Mercer and S. Hodgkinson (eds) *Exploring Talk in School*. London: Sage.

Alexander, R. (2010) *Children, their World, their Education. Final Report and Recommendations of the Cambridge Primary Review*. London: Routledge.

Alloway, T.P. (2007) *Automated Working Memory Assessment (AWMA)*. Oxford: Pearson Education.

Alloway, T.P. (2009) Working memory, but not IQ, predicts subsequent learning in children with learning difficulties. *European Journal of Psychological Assessment*, 25, 92–98.

Alloway, T.P., Gathercole, S.E. and Kirkwood, H. (2008) *Working Memory Rating Scale (WMRS)*. London: Pearson/ Psychological Corporation.

Alloway, T.P., Gathercole, S.E., Willis, C. and Adams, A.-M. (2004) A structural analysis of working memory and related cognitive skills in young children. *Journal of Experimental Child Psychology*, 87(2), 85–106.

Allport, G. (1947) *The Use of Personal Documents in Psychological Science*. New York: Science Research Council.

American Psychology Association (2005) Violence in the media: psychologists help protect children from harmful effects. Online, available at: www.apa.org/research/action/protect.aspx (accessed 12 April 2010).

Anderson, M.C. and Neely, J.H. (1996) Interference and inhibition in memory retrieval. In E.L. Bjork and R.A. Bjork (eds) *Memory: Handbook of Perception and Cognition*. San Diego: Academic Press.

Anderson, R.C., Chinn, C., Waggoner, M. and Nguyen, K. (1998) Intellectually-stimulating story discussions. In J. Osborn and F. Lehr (eds) *Literacy for All: Issues in Teaching and Learning*. New York: Guildford Press.

Andrews, R., Freeman, A., Hou, D., McGuinn, N., Robinson, A. and Zhu, J. (2007) The effectiveness of information and communication technology on the learning of written English for 5- to 16-year-olds. *British Journal of Educational Technology*, 38, 325–336.

Anglin, J. (1993) Vocabulary development: a morphological analysis. *Monograph of the Society for Research in Child Development*, 58, 10.

Angold, A. and Costello, E.J. (2001) The epidemiology of depression in children and adolescents. In I. Goodyer (ed.) *The Depressed Child and Adolescent: Developmental and Clinical Perspectives* (2nd edition). New York: Cambridge University Press, pp. 143–178.

Antonio, R. and Damasio, A. (1994) *Descartes' Error: Emotion, Reason, and the Human Brain*. New York: Avon Books.

Archer, J. and Lloyd, B. (2002) *Sex and Gender*. Cambridge: Cambridge University Press.

Arnheim, R. (2006) *Guernica: the Genesis of a Painting*. California: University of California Press.

Arnold, C. (2007) Empowerment, learning and schools: reflections from psychology. *Education Review*, 20(1), 108–113.

Arnot, M., David, M. and Weiner, G. (1999) *Closing the Gender Gap: Postwar Education and Social Change*. Cambridge: Polity Press.

Arnot, M., Gray, J., James, M. and Rudduck, J. (1998) *Recent Research on Gender and Educational Performance*. London: Office for Standards in Education.

Arterberry, M.E. and Bornstein, M.H. (2002) Infant perceptual and conceptual categorization: the roles of static and dynamic attributes. *Cognition*, 86, 1–24.

Arvaja, M. (2005) *Collaborative Knowledge Construction in Authentic School Contexts*. Doctoral Thesis: Institute of Educational Research, University of Jyväskylä, Jyväskylä: University Printing House.

Asch, S. (1951) Effects of group pressure upon the modification and distortion of judgements. In H. Guetzkow (ed.) *Groups, Leadership and Men*. Pittsburgh: Carnegie Press.

ASDAN (2010) *Towards Independence*. Online, available at: www.asdan.org.uk/towards_independence.php (accessed 21 March 2010).

Askew, M., Brown, M., Rhodes, V., Johnson, D. and Wiliam, D. (1997) *Effective Teachers of Numeracy*. London: King's College.

Askew, S. and Ross, C. (1988) *Boys Don't Cry: Boys and Sexism in Education*. Milton Keynes: Open University Press.

Assessment Reform Group (2002) *Assessment for Learning: Ten Principles*. London: Assessment Reform Group.

Atkinson, J.W. (1957) Motivational determinants of risk-taking behaviour. *Psychological Review*, 64, 359–372.

Atkinson, J.W. (1964) *An Introduction to Motivation*. Princeton: Van Nostrand.

Atkinson, R. and Shiffrin, R. (1971) The control of short-term memory. *Scientific American*, 224, 82–90.

ATL (2010) *Over a Quarter of Education Staff Have Dealt With Physical Violence by Pupils*. Online, available at: www.atl. org.uk/media-office/media-archive/ATL-behaviour-survey-2010.asp.

Audit Commission (1992) *Getting In on the Act*. London: HMSO.

Audit Commission (2007) *Out of Authority Placements for Special Educational Needs*. Online, available at: www.audit-commission.gov.uk/nationalstudies/localgov/Pages/placementssen.aspx (accessed 5 February 2010).

Augur, J. and Briggs, S. (1992) *The Hickey Multisensory Language Course* (2nd Edition). London: Whurr.

Ausubel, D. (1968) *Educational Psychology: a Cognitive View*. New York: Holt, Rhinehart and Winston.

Azmitia, M. and Montgomery, R. (1993) Friendship, transactive dialogues and the development of scientific reasoning. *Social Development,* 2(3), 202–221.

Backhaus, J., Hoeckesfeld, R., Born, J., Hohagen, F. and Junghanns, K. (2008) Immediate as well as delayed post learning sleep but not wakefulness enhances declarative memory consolidation in children. *Neurobiology of Learning and Memory*, 89, 76–80.

Baddeley, A. (1986) *Working Memory*. Oxford: Oxford University Press.

Baddeley, A., Eysenck, M.W. and Anderson, M.C. (2009) *Memory*. Hove: Psychology Press.

Bagley, C. (1971) *The Social Psychology of the Child with Epilepsy*. London: Routledge and Kegan Paul.

Baines, E., Blatchford, P. and Chowne, A. (2007) Improving the effectiveness of collaborative group work in primary schools: effects on science attainment. *British Educational Research Journal*, 33(15), 663–680.

Baker, J. and Crist, J. (1971) Teacher expectancies: a review of the literature. In J. Elashoff and E. Snow (eds) *Pygmalion Reconsidered*. Worthington: Jones.

Baldwin, S. and Cooper, P. (2000) How should ADHD be treated? *The Psychologist*, 13, 598–602.

Bandura, A. (1986) *Social Foundations of Thought and Action: a Social Cognitive Theory*. Englewood Cliffs: Prentice-Hall.

Bandura, A. (1997) *Self-Efficacy: the Exercise of Control*. New York: Freeman.

Bandura, A., Ross, D. and Ross, S. (1963) Imitation of film-mediated aggressive models. *Journal of Abnormal and Social Psychology*, 66, 3–11.

Barbieri, M. and Light, P. (1992) Interaction, gender and performance on a computer-based task. *Learning and Instruction*, 2(1), 199–213.

Barker, B. (1997) Girls' world or anxious times: what's really happening at school in the gender war? *Educational Review*, 49, 221–228.

Barmby, P. (2006) Improving teacher recruitment and retention: the importance of workload and pupil behaviour. *Educational Research*, 48(3), 247–265.

Barnes, D. (2008) Exploratory talk for learning. In N. Mercer and S. Hodgkinson (eds) *Exploring Talk in School*. London: Sage.

Barnes, D. and Todd, F. (1977) *Communication and Learning in Small Groups*. London: Routledge and Kegan Paul.

Barnes, D. and Todd, F. (1995) *Communication and Learning Revisited*. Portsmouth: Heinemann.

Barnes, M.A., Dennis, M. and Haefele-Kalvaitis, J. (1996) The effects of knowledge availability and knowledge accessibility on coherences and elaborative inferencing in children from six to fifteen years of age. *Journal of Experimental Child Psychology*, 61, 216–241.

Barnett, W. (1995) Long-term effects of early childhood programs on cognitive and school outcomes. *The Future of Children*, 5, 25–50.

Bar-On, R. (2007) The impact of emotional intelligence on giftedness. *Gifted Education International*, 23, 122–137.

Baron-Cohen, S. (2003) *The Essential Difference: Men, Women and The Extreme Male Brain*. London: Penguin.

Barrett, P.T., Petrides, K.V., Eysenck, S.B.G. and Eysenck, H.J. (1998) The Eysenck Personality Questionnaire: an examination of the factorial similarity of P, E, N and I across 34 countries. *Personality and Individual Differences*, 25, 805–819.

Barron, I., Holmes, R., MacLure, M. and Runswick-Cole, K. (2007) *Primary Schools and Other Agencies. Research Survey 8/2*. Cambridge: The Primary Review.

Barry, J.J., Lembke, A., Gisbert, P.A. and Gilliam, F. (2007) Affective disorders in epilepsy. In A.B. Ettinger and A.M. Kanner (eds) *Psychiatric Issues in Epilepsy: a Practical Guide to Diagnosis and Treatment*. Philadelphia: Lippincott Williams and Wilkins, 203–247.

Bartels, M., Rietveld, M.J.H., Van Baal, G.C.M. and Boomsma, D.I. (2002a) Genetic and environmental influences on the development of intelligence. *Behavior Genetics*, 32, 237–249.

Bartels, M., Rietveld, M.J.H., Van Baal, G.C.M. and Boomsma, D.I. (2002b) Heritability of educational achievement in 12 year olds and the overlap with cognitive ability. *Twin Research*, 5, 544–553.

Bartlett, F. (1932) *Remembering*. Cambridge: Cambridge University Press.

Baumeister, R.F., Campbell, J.D., Krueger, J.I. and Vohs, K.D. (2003) Does high self-esteem cause better performance, interpersonal success, happiness, or healthier lifestyles? *Psychological Science in the Public Interest*, 4(1), 1–44.

Baylis, P.J. and Snowling, M.J. (2007) A longitudinal study of the reading skills of children with Down syndrome attending mainstream schools. Paper presented at BPS Psychology of Education Section Conference, Stoke-on-Trent.

BBC (2005) *Call for Special Schools Review*. Online, available at: http://news.bbc.co.uk/1/hi/uk_politics/4615941.stm (accessed 22 February 2010).

Beaman, R., Wheldall, K. and Kemp, C. (2007) Recent research on troublesome classroom behaviour: a review. *Australasian Journal of Special Education*, 31(1), 45–60.

Beckett, C., Maughan, B., Rutter, M., Castle, J., Colvert, E., Groothues, C., Kreppner, J., Stevens, S., O'Connor, T.G. and Sonuga-Barke, E.J.S. (2006) Do the effects of early severe deprivation on cognition persist into early adolescence? Findings from the English and Romanian adoptees study. *Child Development*, 77(3), 696–711.

Bedford, D., Jackson, C.R. and Wilson, E. (2008) New Partnerships for Learning: teachers' perspectives on their developing professional relationships with teaching assistants in England. *Journal of In-Service Education*, 34(1), 7–25.

Bell, D. (2004) *The Achievement of Girls*. Speech to the Fawcett Society, 8 March.

Bennathan, M. and Boxall, M. (1996) *Effective Intervention in Primary Schools: Nurture Groups*. London: David Fulton Publishing.

Bennett, N. and Dunne, E. (1992) *Managing Classroom Groups*. London: Simon and Schuster.

Bercow, J. (2008) *The Bercow Report: a Review of Services for Children and Young People (0–19) with Speech, Language and Communication Needs*. Nottingham: DCSF.

Bergan, J. and Tombari, M. (1976) Consultant skill and efficiency and the implementation and outcomes of consultation. *Journal of School Psychology*, 14, 3–13.

Berk, L. (1986) Relationship of elementary school children's private speech to behavioural accompaniment to task, attention, and task performance. *Developmental Psychology*, 22, 671–680.

Berko, J. (1958) The child's learning of English morphology. *Word*, 14, 150–177.

Berkowitz, L. (1989) Frustration–aggression hypothesis: examination and reformulation. *Psychological Bulletin*, 106, 59–73.

Berliner, B.A. (2004) Reaching unmotivated students. *Education Digest*, 69(5), 46–47.

Bernstein, B. (1961) Social class and linguistic development. In A. Halsey, J. Flaud and C. Anderson (eds) *Education, Economy and Society*. London: Collier-Macmillan.

Bernstein, B. (1970) Education cannot compensate for society. *New Society*, 387, 344–347.

Bernstein, E. (1968) What does a Summerhill old school tie look like? *Psychology Today*, 2(5), 37–41.

Berry, K. (2002) We drink to think. *Times Educational Supplement* (4510), IV.

Berson, I.R., Berson, M.J., Desai, S., Falls, D. and Fenaughty, J. (2008) An analysis of electronic media to prepare children for safe and ethical practices in digital environments. *Contemporary Issues in Technology and Teacher Education*, 8(3), 222–243.

Best, A. (1992) *Teaching Children with Visual Impairments*. Buckingham: Open University Press.

Best, M. and Demb, J. (1999) Normal planum temporale asymmetry in dyslexics with a magnocellular pathway deficit. *NeuroReport*, 10, 607–612.

Bialystok, E. (2001) *Bilingualism in Development: Language, Literacy and Cognition*. Cambridge: Cambridge University Press.

Bialystok, E. and Hakuta, K. (1994) *In Other Words: the Science and Psychology of Second-Language Acquisition*. New York: Basic Books.

Bialystok, E. and Shapiro, D. (2005) Ambiguous benefits: the effect of bilingualism on reversing ambiguous figures. *Developmental Science*, 8, 595–604.

Biddulph, S. (1998) *Raising Boys: Why Boys are Different – and How to Help Them Become Happy and Well-Balanced Men*. Sydney: Finch.

Biemiller, A. and Slonim, N. (2001) Estimating root word vocabulary growth in normative and advantaged populations: evidence for a common sequence of vocabulary acquisition. *Journal of Educational Psychology*, 93, 498–520.

Bierman, K. and Furman, W. (1984) The effects of social skills training and peer involvement in the social adjustment of preadolescents. *Child Development*, 55, 151–162.

Biggs, J. (1985) The role of metalearning in study processes. *British Journal of Educational Psychology*, 55, 151–162.

Binet, A. (1905) New methods for the diagnosis of the intellectual level of subnormals. *L'Annee Psychologique*, 12, 191–244. (Translated in 1916 by E.S. Kite in *The Development of Intelligence in Children*. Vineland: Publications of the Vineland Training School.)

Birdsong, D. and Molis, M. (2001) On the evidence for maturational constraints in second-language acquisition. *Journal of Memory and Language*, 44, 235–249.

Black, P. (1998) *Testing: Friend or Foe? Theory and Practice of Assessment and Testing*. London: Falmer Press.

Black, P. (2001) Dreams, strategies and systems: Portraits of assessment past, present and future. *Assessment in Education*, 8(1), 30–47.

Black, P. and Wiliam, D. (2009) Developing the theory of formative assessment. *Educational Assessment, Evaluation and Accountability*, 21, 5–31.

Black, P., Harrison, C., Lee, C., Marshall, B. and Wiliam, D. (2003) *Assessment for Learning: Putting it into Practice*. Maidenhead: Open University Press.

Blagg, N. (1991) *Can We Teach Intelligence? A Comprehensive Evaluation of Feuerstein's Instrumental Enrichment Programme*. Hillsdale: Lawrence Erlbaum.

Blagg, N., Ballinger, M. and Gardner, R. (1993a) *Somerset Thinking Skills Course Handbook*. Taunton: Nigel Blagg Associates.

Blagg, N., Ballinger, M. and Lewis, R. (1993b) *Thinking Skills at Work*. Taunton: Nigel Blagg Associates.

Blagg, N., Lewis, R. and Ballinger, M. (1994) *Thinking and Learning at Work – A Report on the Development and Evaluation of the Thinking Skills At Work Modules. Research Series 23*. Preston: University of Central Lancashire Employment Department Group.

Blatchford, P. (1998) *Social Life in Schools: Pupils' Experiences of Breaktime and Recess from 7 to 16 years*. London: Falmer Press.

Blatchford, P. and Baines, E. (2010) Peer relations in school. In K. Littleton, C. Wood and J. Kleine Staarman (eds) *The International Handbook of Psychology in Education*. Bingley: Emerald.

Blatchford, P. and Kutnick, P. (2003) Developing groupwork in everyday classrooms. Special issue of the *International Journal of Educational Research*, 39(1–2).

Blatchford, P. and Sharp, S. (1994) *Breaktime and the School: Understanding and Changing Playground Behaviour*. London: Routledge.

Blatchford, P., Bassett, P., Goldstein, H. and Martin, C. (2003a) Are class size differences related to pupils' educational progress and classroom processes? Findings from the Institute of Education class size study of children aged 5–7 years. *British Educational Research Journal*, 29(5), 709.

Blatchford, P., Burke, J., Farquhar, C., Plewis, I. and Tizard, B. (1985) Educational achievement in the infant school: the influence of ethnic origin, gender and home on entry skills. *Educational Research*, 27(1), 52–60.

Blatchford, P., Kutnick, P., Baines, E. and Galton, M. (2003b) Towards a social pedagogy of classroom groupwork. *International Journal of Educational Research*, 39: 153–172.

Blatchford, P., Russell, A., Bassett, P., Brown, P. and Martin, C. (2007) The role and effects of teaching assistants in English primary schools (Years 4 to 6) 2000–2003. Results from the Class Size and Pupil–Adult Ratios (CSPAR) KS2 Project. *British Educational Research Journal*, 33(1), 5–26.

Blaye, A. (1988) *Confrontation Sociocognitive et Resolution de Probleme*. Unpublished doctoral thesis, University of Provence: Aix-en-Provence.

Bliss, T., Robinson, G. and Maines, B. (1995) *Coming Round to Circle Time*. Bristol: Lame Duck Publishing.

Blom-Hoffman, J., O'Neil-Pirozzi, T.M. and Cutting, J. (2006) Read together, talk together: the acceptability of teaching parents to use dialogic reading strategies via videotaped instruction. *Psychology in the Schools*, 43, 71–78.

Bloom, B. (ed.) (1956) *Taxonomy of Educational Objectives*. Handbook 1: Cognitive Domain. New York: David McKay.

Boaler, J. (1997) Reclaiming school mathematics: the girls fight back. *Gender and Education*, 9: 285–305.

Boekaerts, M., Van Nuland, H. and Martens, R. (2010) Perspectives on motivation: what mechanisms energise students' behaviour in the classroom. In K. Littleton, C. Wood and J. Kleine-Staarman (eds) *International Handbook on Psychology in Education*. Bingley: Emerald.

Bohn, C.M., Roehrig, A.D. and Pressley, M. (2004) The first days of school in the classrooms of two more effective and four less effective primary-grades teachers. *Elementary School Journal*, 104(4), 269–287.

Bonshek, J. (2005) The identification of able socially deprived pupils: LEA advice to primary schools. *Support for Learning*, 20(1), 5–11.

Booth, T. and Ainscow, M. (2000) *The Index for Inclusion: Developing Learning and Participation in Schools*. Bristol: Centre for Studies on Inclusive Education (CSIE).

Booth, T. and Ainscow, M. (2002, new edition) *Index for Inclusion Developing Learning and Participation in Schools*. Bristol: Centre for Studies on Inclusive Education (CSIE).

Bornstein, P. and Quevillon, R. (1976) The effects of a self-instructional package on overactive pre-school boys. *Journal of Applied Behavior Analysis*, 9(2), 179–188.

Bouchard, T. and McGue, M. (1981) Familial studies of intelligence: a review. *Science*, 212, 1055–1059.

Bowen, E., Heron, J. and Steer, C. (2008) *Anti-Social and Other Problems Among Young Children: Findings from the Avon Longitudinal Study of Parents and Children.* Home Office Online Report 02/08.

Bowen, R. and Holtom, D. (2010) *A Survey into the Prevalence and Incidence of School Bullying in Wales Summary Report.* People and Work Unit: Welsh Assembly Government Social Research.

Bower, G., Black, J. and Turner, T. (1979) Scripts in memory for text. *Cognitive Psychology*, 11, 177–220.

Bower, G., Clark, M., Lesgold, A. and Winzenz, D. (1969) Hierarchical retrieval schemes in recall of categorised word lists. *Journal of Verbal Learning and Verbal Behaviour*, 8, 323–343.

Bowman, R. (1982) A 'Pac-Man' theory of motivation: tactical implications for classroom instruction. *Educational Technology*, September, 14–16.

Boyle, B. and Charles, M. (2009) Assessing pupils' progress. *Education Journal*, 117(4), 30.

Boyle, C. and Lauchlan, F. (2007) Applied psychology and the case for individual casework: some reflections on the role of the educational psychologist. *Educational Psychology in Practice*, 25(1), 71–84.

Bradley, L. and Bryant, P.E. (1978) Difficulties in auditory organisation as a possible cause of reading backwardness. *Nature*, 271, 746–747.

Bradley, L. and Bryant, P. (1983) Categorising sounds and learning to read: a causal connection. *Nature*, 301, 419–421.

Bradlow, A.R., Kraus, N. and Hayes, E. (2003) Speaking clearly for learning-impaired children: sentence perception in noise. *Journal of Speech, Language, and Hearing Research*, 46, 80–97.

Brady, J., Porter, R., Conrad, D. and Mason, J. (1958) Avoidance behaviour and the development of gastroduodenal ulcers. *Journal of the Experimental Analysis of Behaviour*, 1, 69–72.

Brain, K.J., Reid, I. and Comerford Boyes, L. (2006) Teachers as mediators between education policy and practice. *Educational Studies*, 32(4), 411–423.

Brannon, L. (1996) *Gender: Psychological Perspectives.* Boston: Allyn & Bacon.

Bransford, J. and Johnson, M. (1972) Consideration of some problems of comprehension. In W. Chase (ed.) *Visual Information Processing.* New York: Academic Press.

Bransford, J., Barclay, J. and Franks, J. (1972) Sentence memory: a constructive versus interpretative approach. *Cognitive Psychology*, 3, 193–209.

Brantlinger, E. (2006) The big glossies: how textbooks structure (special) education. In E. Brantlinger (ed.) *Who Benefits from Special Education? Remediating (Fixing) Other People's Children.* Mahwah: Erlbaum, 45–75.

Brattesanti, K., Weinstein, R. and Marshall, H. (1984) Student perceptions of differential teacher treatment as moderators of teacher expectation effects. *Journal of Educational Psychology*, 76, 236–247.

Breakey, J. (1997) The role of diet and behaviour in childhood. *Journal of Paediatrics and Child Health*, 33, 190–194.

Breggin, P.R. (2001) *Talking Back to Ritalin: What Doctors Aren't Telling You About Stimulants.* US: Common Courage Press.

Brennan, A., Chugh, J.S. and Kline, T. (2002) Traditional versus open office design: a longitudinal field study. *Environment and Behavior*, 34(3), 279.

Breznitz, Z. (2002) Asynchrony of visual–orthographic and auditory–phonological word recognition processes: an underlying factor in dyslexia. *Reading and Writing*, 15, 15–42.

Briggs-Myers, I., Kirby, L. and Myers, D. (2000) *Introduction to Type* (6th Edition). Oxford: Oxford Psychologists Press.

British Psychological Society (1999; reprint 2005) *Dyslexia, Literacy and Psychological Assessment: Report by the Working Party of the Division of Educational and Child Psychology of the British Psychological Society.* Leicester: BPS.

British Psychological Society (2005) *Inclusive Education Position Paper.* Online, available at: www.bps.org.uk/download-file.cfm?file_uuid=CE1DCB9D-1143-DFD0-7EA9-5C1B82EA4596and ext=doc (accessed 21 September 2009).

British Psychological Society (BPS) (2009) *Educational Psychology.* Online, available at: www.bps.org.uk/careers/what-do-psychologists-do/areas/educational.cfm.

Broadbent, D. (1958) *Perception and Communication.* London: Pergamon.

Broadfoot, P. and Pollard, A. (2000) The changing discourse of assessment policy: the case of English primary education. In A. Filer (ed.) *Assessment: Social Practice and Social Product.* London: Falmer Press.

Broadfoot, P., Osborn, M., Planel, C. and Sharpe, K. (2000) *Promoting Quality in Learning: Does England Have the Answer?* London: Cassell.

Broidy, L.M., Tremblay, R.E., Brame, B., Fergusson, D., Horwood, J.L., Laird, R., Moffitt, T.E., Nagin, D.S., Bates, J.E., Dodge, K.A., Loeber, R., Lynam, D.R., Pettit, G.S. and Vitaro, F. (2003) Developmental trajectories of childhood disruptive behaviors and adolescent delinquency: a six-site, cross-national study. *Developmental Psychology*, 39(2), 222–245.

Bronfenbrenner, U. (1993) The ecology of cognitive development. In R.H. Wozniak and K.W. Fischer (eds) *Development in Context: Acting and Thinking in Specific Environments*. Hinsdale: Erlbaum.

Brooks, G. (2007) *What Works for Children with Literacy Difficulties? The Effectiveness of Intervention Schemes*. London: DfES.

Brophy, J. (1981) Teacher praise: a functional analysis. *Review of Educational Research*, 51(1), 5–32.

Brophy, J. and Good, T. (1974) *Teacher–Student Relationships*. New York: Holt, Rinehart and Winston.

Brown, R., Cazden, C. and Bellugi, U. (1969) The child's grammar from 1 to 3. In J. Hill (ed.) *Minnesota Symposium on Child Psychology* (2). Minneapolis: University of Minnesota Press.

Browne, K.D. and Hamilton-Giachritsis, C.E. (2005) The influence of violent media on children and adolescents: a public health approach. *Lancet*, 365, 702–710.

Brownell, C. (1988) Combinatorial skills: converging developments over the second year. *Child Development*, 59, 675–685.

Bruges, A. (1988) The outcome of language unit placement: a survey in Avon (1987). *Educational Psychology in Practice*, July, 86–90.

Bruner, J. (1957) Going beyond the information given. In J.S. Bruner (ed.) *Contemporary Approaches to Cognition: the Colorado Symposium*. Cambridge: Harvard University Press, pp. 41–69.

Bruner, J. (1961a) The act of discovery. *Harvard Educational Review*, 31, 21–32.

Bruner, J. (1961b) *The Process of Education*. Cambridge: Harvard University Press.

Bruner, J. (1966a) On the conservation of liquids. In J. Bruner, R. Olver and P. Greenfield (eds) *Studies in Cognitive Growth*. New York: Wiley.

Bruner, J. (1966b) *Towards a Theory of Instruction*. Cambridge: Harvard University Press.

Bruner, J. (1983) *Child's Talk: Learning to Use Language*. Oxford: Oxford University Press.

Bruner, J.S. (2006) *The Selected Works of Jerome S. Bruner 1957–1978: In Search of Pedagogy Volume 1*. London: Routledge.

Buckley, J., Schneider, M. and Shang, Y. (2005) Fix it and they might stay: school facility quality and teacher retention in Washington, D.C. *Teachers College Record*, 107(5), 1107–1123.

Buckley, S., Bird, G., Sacks, B. and Archer, T. (2007) Mainstream or special education for teenagers with Down syndrome. In J.-A. Rondal and A.R. Quartino (eds) *Therapies and Rehabilitation in Down Syndrome*. London: Wiley and Sons.

Budge, D. (1996) Size does matter: medium is best. *Times Educational Supplement*, 19 April, 19.

Burden, R. (1978) Schools' systems analysis: a project-centred approach. In B. Gillham (ed.) *Reconstructing Educational Psychology*. London: Croom Helm.

Burt, C. (1921) *Mental and Scholastic Tests*. London: King.

Bushman, Brad J. and Huesmann, L.R. (2006) Short-term and long-term effects of violent media on aggression in children and adults. *Archives of Pediatrics and Adolescent Medicine*, 160, 348–352.

Butler, D. and Winne, P. (1995) Feedback and self-regulated learning: a theoretical synthesis. *Review of Educational Research*, 65(3), 245–281.

Bynner, J. and Parsons, S. (1997) *Does Numeracy Matter? Evidence from the National Child Development Study on the Impact of Poor Numeracy on Adult Life*. London: Basic Skills Agency.

Byrne, B., Delaland, C., Fielding-Barnsley, R., Quain, P., Samuelsson, S. and Hoien, T. (2002) Longitudinal twin study of early reading development in three countries: preliminary results. *Annals of Dyslexia*, 52, 49–73.

Byrne, B., Samuelson, S., Wadsworth, S., Hulslander, J., Corley, R., Defries, J.C., Quain, P., Willcutt, E.G. and Olson, R.K. (2007) Longitudinal twin study of early literacy development: Preschool through Grade 1. *Reading and Writing*, 20: 77–102.

Byron, T. (2008) *Safer Children in a Digital World: the Report of the Byron Review*. Online, available at: www.dcsf.gov.uk/byronreview/pdfs/Final%20Report%20Bookmarked.pdf (accessed 4 May 2009).

CACE (Central Advisory Council for Education) (1967) *Children and their Primary Schools: the Plowden Report*. London: HMSO.

Cahan, S. and Coren, N. (1989) Age versus schooling effects on intelligence. *Child Development*, 60, 1239–1249.

Cain, K. and Oakhill, J.V. (1999) Inference ability and its relation to comprehension failure in young children. *Reading and Writing*, 11, 489–503.

Cairns, R., Cairns, B., Neckerman, H., Ferguson, L. and Gariepy, J. (1989) Growth and aggression. 1. Childhood to early adolescence. *Developmental Psychology*, 25, 320–330.

Cajkler, W. and Hall, B. (2009) 'When they first come in what do you do?' Preparation for teaching English as an additional language in primary schools. *Language and Education*, 23(2), 153–170.

Camden School for Girls (2009) *Admissions Policy*. Online, available at: www.camdengirls.camden.sch.uk (accessed 2 March 2010).

Cameron, J. and Pierce, W. (1994) Reinforcement, reward and intrinsic motivation: a meta-analysis. *Review of Educational Research*, 64, 363–423.

Campbell, S. (1995) Behaviour problems in pre-school children: a review of recent research. *Journal of Child Psychology and Psychiatry*, 36(1), 113–149.

Canadian Council on Learning (2009) *Does Placement Matter? Comparing the Academic Performance of Students with Special Needs in Inclusive and Separate Settings*. Online, available at: www.ccl-cca.ca/pdfs/LessonsInLearning/03_18_09E.pdf (accessed 22 February 2010).

Canter, L. and Canter, M. (1992) *Assertive Discipline*. Santa Monica: Lee Canter Associates.

Carey, S. and Bartlett, E. (1978) Acquiring a single new word. *Papers and Reports on Child Language Development*, 15, 17–29.

Carmichael, L., Hogan, P. and Walter, A. (1932) An experimental study of the effect of language on the reproduction of visually perceived forms. *Journal of Experimental Psychology*, 15, 1–22.

Carroll, J. (1963) A model of school learning. *Teachers College Record*, 64, 723–733.

Carroll, J. (1993) *Human Cognitive Abilities: a Survey of Factor-Analytic Studies*. Cambridge: Cambridge University Press.

Carver, C. and Moseley, M. (1994) *Word Recognition and Phonic Skills Test*. London: Hodder and Stoughton.

Cassen, R. and Kingdon, G.G. (2007a) *Tackling Low Educational Achievement*. York: Joseph Rowntree Foundation.

Cassen, R. and Kingdon, G.G. (2007b) *Understanding Low Achievement in English Schools* (June). LSE STICERD Research Paper No. CASE118.

Cassen, R. and Kingdon, G. (2007c) *The Wolverhampton Partnership Development Schools Project*. York: Joseph Rowntree Foundation. Online, available at: www.creativeite.org (accessed 24 July 2010).

Castronova, E. (2008) *Researching Learning in Virtual Environments*. ReLIVE08 Conference, November, Milton Keynes, The Open University.

Cattell, R.B. (1983) *Structured Personality Learning Theory*. New York: Praeger.

Cattell, R., Eber, H. and Tatsouka, M. (1970) *Handbook for the Sixteen Personality Factor Questionnaire (16PF)*. Champaign: IPAT.

Catts, H.W., Fey, M.E., Tomblin, J.B. and Zhang, X. (2002) A longitudinal investigation of reading outcomes in children with language impairments. *Journal of Speech, Language and Hearing Research*, 45, 1142–1157.

Cazden, C. (2001) *Classroom Discourse: the Language of Teaching and Learning*. Portsmouth: Heinemann.

Ceci, S. (1990) *On Intelligence . . . More or Less: a Bioecological Treatise on Intellectual Development*. Englewood Cliffs: Prentice Hall.

Chadwick, O., Cuddy, M., Kusel, Y. and Taylor, E. (2005) Handicaps and the development of skills between childhood and early adolescence in young people with severe intellectual disabilities. *Journal of Intellectual Disability Research*, 49(12), 877–888.

Chaplain, R.P. (2008) Stress and psychological distress among trainee secondary teachers in England. *Educational Psychology*, 28(2), 195–209.

Chapman, J. and Tunmer, W. (1997) A longitudinal study of beginning reading achievement and reading self-concept. *British Journal of Educational Psychology*, 67, 279–291.

Charlton, T. and O'Bey, S. (1997) Links between television and behaviour: students' perceptions of TV's impact in St Helena, South Atlantic. *Support for Learning*, 12, 130–136.

Chazan, M., Laing, F. and Davies, D. (1994) *Emotional and Behavioural Difficulties in Middle Childhood*. London: Falmer Press.

Chenn, Z., Yanowitz, K. and Daehler, M. (1995) Constraints on accessing abstract source information: instantiation of principles facilitates children's analogical transfer. *Journal of Educational Psychology*, 87, 445–454.

Chi, M.T.H. and Ohlsson, S. (2005) Complex declarative learning. In K. Holyoak and R. Morrison (eds) *The Cambridge Handbook of Thinking and Reasoning*. Cambridge: Cambridge University Press.

Chiang-Soong, B. and Yager, R. (1993) Readability levels of the science textbooks most used in secondary schools. *School Science and Mathematics*, 93(1), 24–27.

Children's Act (2004) Online, available at: www.opsi.gov.uk/acts/acts2004/ukpga_20040031_en_1 (accessed 21 March 2010).

Ching, T., Dillon, H., Day, J., Crowe, K., Close, L., Chisholm, K. and Hopkins, T. (2009) Early language outcomes of children with cochlear implants: interim findings of the NAL study on longitudinal outcomes of children. *Cochlear Implants International*, 10(1), 28–32.

Chinn, C.F. and Anderson, R. (1998) The structure of discussions that promote reasoning. *Teachers College Record*, 100, 315–368.

Chinn, S. and Ashcroft, S. (2006) *Mathematics and Dyslexia*. Oxford: Wiley Blackwell.

Chmielewski, T. and Dansereau, D. (1998) Enhancing the recall of text: knowledge mapping training promotes implicit transfer. *Journal of Educational Psychology*, 90, 407–413.

Chomsky, N. (1965) *Aspects of the Theory of Syntax*. Cambridge: MIT Press.

Claiborn, W. (1969) Expectancy effects in the classroom: a failure to replicate. *Journal of Educational Psychology*, 60, 377–383.

Clark, R. (1983) *Family Life and School Achievement: Why Poor Black Children Succeed or Fail*. Chicago: University of Chicago Press.

Clarke, A.M. and Clarke, A.D. (1974) Genetic–environmental interactions in cognitive development. In A.M. Clarke and A.D. Clarke (eds) *Mental Deficiency*. London: Methuen.

Claxton, G. (2007) Expanding young people's capacity to learn. *British Journal of Educational Studies*, 55(2), 115–134.

Clay, M.M. (1993) *Reading Recovery: A Guidebook for Teachers*. Auckland: Heinemann.

Clay, M.M. (2002) *An Observation Survey of Early Literacy Achievement* (2nd edition). Auckland: Heinemann.

Cleare, A. and Wessely, S. (1996) Chronic fatigue syndrome: a stress disorder? *British Journal of Hospital Medicine*, 55, 571–574.

Cleghorn, P. (2002) *Thinking Through Philosophy*. Blackburn: Educational Printing Services.

CLPE (1989) *Testing Reading*. London: Centre for Language in Primary Education.

Coe, R. and Fitz-Gibbon, C. (1998) School effectiveness research: criticisms and recommendations. *Oxford Review of Education*, 24, 421–438.

Coffield, F., Moseley, D., Hall, E. and Ecclestone, K. (2004) *Should We Be Using Learning Styles? What Research has to Say to Practice*. London: Learning and Skills Research Centre.

Cohen, E.G. (1994) Restructuring the classroom: conditions for productive small groups. *Review of Educational Research*, 64(1), 1–35.

Cohen, S., Tyrrell, D. and Smith, A. (1991) Psychological stress and susceptibility to the common cold. *New England Journal of Medicine*, 325, 606–612.

Coie, J. and Dodge, K. (1983) Continuities and changes in children's social status: a five-year longitudinal study. *Merrill-Palmer Quarterly*, 29, 261–282.

Colle, L., Baron-Cohen, S. and Hill, J. (2007) Do children with autism have a theory of mind? A non-verbal test of autism vs. specific language impairment. *Journal of Autism and Developmental Disorders*, 37(4), 716–723.

Collins, A. and Quillian, M. (1969) Retrieval time for semantic memory. *Journal of Verbal Learning and Verbal Behaviour*, 8, 240–247.

Colmar, S., Maxwell, A. and Miller, L. (2006) Assessing intellectual disability in children: are IQ measures sufficient or even necessary? *Australian Journal of Guidance and Counselling*, 16(2), 171–188.

Coltheart, M. (2005) Modelling reading: the dual route approach. In M.J. Snowling and C. Hulme (eds) *The Science of Reading: a Handbook*. Oxford: Blackwell.

Coltheart, M., Rastle, K., Perry, C., Langdon, R. and Ziegler, J. (2001) DRC: a dual-route cascaded model of visual word recognition and reading aloud. *Psychological Review*, 108, 204–256.

Comaskey, E.M., Savage, R.S. and Abrami, P. (2009) A randomised efficacy study of web-based synthetic and analytic programmes among disadvantaged urban Kindergarten children. *Journal of Research in Reading*, 32, 92–108.

Connell, R. (1989) Cool guys, swots and wimps: the interplay of masculinity and education. *Oxford Review of Education*, 15, 291–303.

Connellan, J., Baron-Cohen, S., Wheelwright, S., Batki, A. and Ahluwalia, J. (2000) Sex differences in human neonatal social perception. *Infant Behaviour and Development*, 23, 113–118.

Conners, C.K. (2008) *Conners-3 Rating Scales*. London: Pearson.

Conners, C.K., Sitarenios, G., Parker, J.D.A. and Epstein, J.A. (1998) Revision and restandardization of the *Conners*

Teacher Rating Scale (CTRS-R): factor structure, reliability, and criterion validity. *Journal of Abnormal Child Psychology*, 26(4), 279–291.

Connor, C.M., Morrison, F.J. and Katch, L.E. (2004) Beyond the reading wars: exploring the effect of child–instruction interactions on growth in early reading. *Scientific Studies of Reading*, 8(4), 305–336.

Conrad, R. (1977) The reading ability of deaf school-leavers. *British Journal of Educational Psychology*, 47, 60–65.

Conrad, R. (1979) *The Deaf School Child*. London: Harper & Row.

Cooper, H. (1983) Teacher expectation effects. In L. Bickman (ed.) *Applied Social Psychology Annual*, 4. London: Sage.

Cooper, H., Nye, B., Charlton, K., Lindsay, K. and Greathouse, S. (1996) The effects of summer vacation on achievement test scores: a narrative and meta-analytic review. *Review of Educational Research*, 66(3), 227–268.

Cordova, D. and Lepper, M. (1996) Intrinsic motivation and the process of learning: beneficial effects of contextualisation, personalisation, and choice. *Journal of Educational Psychology*, 88, 715–730.

Cornwall, J. (2000) Might is right? A discussion of the ethics and practicalities of control and restraint in education. *Emotional and Behavioural Difficulties*, 5(4), 19–25.

Cornwall, K. and France, N. (1997) *Macmillan Group Reading Test* (2nd Edition). Slough: NFER-Nelson.

Cote, C.A., Thompson, R.H., Hanley, G.P. and McKerchar, P.M. (2007) Teacher report and direct assessment of preference for identifying reinforcers for young children. *Journal of Applied Behaviour Analysis*, 40, 157–166.

Cotterell, J. (1984) Effects of school architectural design on student and teacher anxiety. *Environment and Behaviour*, 16, 455–479.

Cotton, K. (2002) *Teaching Thinking Skills*. Portland: Northwest Regional Educational Laboratory.

Coughlan, S. (2009) Sleep deprivation is taking a serious toll on children's wellbeing. *TES Magazine*, July, 15.

Covington, M.V. (1992) *Making the Grade: a Self-Worth Perspective on Motivation and School Reform*. New York: Cambridge University Press.

Covington, M. and Crutchfield, R. (1965) Experiments in the use of programmed instruction for the facilitation of creative problem solving. *Programmed Instruction*, 4.

Cowan, N., Elliot, E.M., Saults, J.S., Nugent, L.D., Bomb, P. and Hismjatullina, A. (2006) Rethinking speed theories of cognitive development: increasing the rate of recall without affecting accuracy. *Psychological Science*, 17, 68–73.

Cowan, N., Wood, N.L., Wood, P.K., Keller, T.A., Nugent, L.D. and Keller, C.V. (1998) Two separate verbal processing rates contributing to short-term memory span. *Journal of Experimental Psychology: General*, 127, 141–160.

Cowie, H. (1999) Children in need: the role of peer support. In M. Woodhead, D. Faulkner and K. Littleton (eds) *Making Sense of Social Development*. London: Routledge.

Cowling, K. and Cowling, H. (1993) *Toe by Toe: a Highly Structured Multi-Sensory Reading Manual for Teachers and Parents*. Basildon: K. and H. Cowling.

Creemers, B. and Reezigt, G. (1996) School level conditions affecting the effectiveness of instruction. *School Effectiveness and School Improvement*, 7, 197–228.

Cremin, T. (2006) Creativity, uncertainty and discomfort: teachers as writers. *Cambridge Journal of Education*, 36(3), 415–433.

Croll, P. and Moses, D. (1990) Sex roles in the primary classroom. In C. Rogers and P. Kutnick (eds) *The Social Psychology of the Primary School*. London: Routledge.

Croll, P. and Moses, D. (2003) Special educational needs across two decades: survey evidence from English primary schools. *British Educational Research Journal*, 29(5), 731–748.

Crook, C. (1999) Computers in the community of classrooms. In K. Littleton and P. Light (eds) *Learning with Computers: Analysing Productive Interaction*. London: Routledge.

Crook, C. (2000) Motivation and the ecology of collaborative learning. In R. Joiner, K. Littleton, D. Faulkner and D. Miell (eds) *Rethinking Collaborative Learning*. London: Free Association Press.

Crook, C. (2008) *Web 2.0 Technologies for Learning: the Current Landscape – Opportunities, Challenges and Tensions*. BECTA Research Reports.

Crowther, D., Dyson, A. and Millward, A. (1998) *Costs and Outcomes for Pupils with Moderate Learning Difficulties in Special and Mainstream Schools*. Research Report RR89. Sudbury: DfEE Publications.

Csikszentmihalyi, M. (1975) *Beyond Boredom and Anxiety*. San Francisco: Jossey-Bass.

Csikszentmihalyi, M. (1978) Intrinsic rewards and emergent motivation. In M.R. Lepper and D. Greene (eds) *The Hidden Costs of Reward: New Perspectives on the Psychology of Human Motivation*. Hilsdale: Erlbaum.

Csikszentmihalyi, M. (1999) If we are so rich, why aren't we happy? *American Psychologist*, 54, 821–827.

Csikszentmihalyi, M., Abuhamdeh, S. and Nakamura, J. (2005) Flow. In A.J. Elliot and C.S. Dweck (eds) *Handbook of Competence and Motivation*. New York: The Guildford Press.

Cuckle, P. and Wilson, J. (2002) Social relationships and friendships among young people with Down's syndrome in secondary schools. *British Journal of Special Education*, 29(2), 66–71.

Currie Report (2002) *Review of the Provision of Educational Psychology Services in Scotland*. Online, available at: www.scotland.gov.uk/Publications/2002/02/10701/File-1 (accessed 21 March 2010).

Dabbs, J. and Morris, R. (1990) Testosterone, social class, and antisocial behaviour in a sample of 4,462 men. *Psychological Science*, 1, 209–211.

Dale, E. and Chall, J. (1948) A formula for predicting readability. *Educational Research Bulletin*, 27, 11–20.

Daniels, H. and Porter, J. (2007) *Learning Needs and Difficulties Among Children of Primary School Age: Definition, Identification, Provision and Issues* (Primary Review Research Survey 5/2). Cambridge: University of Cambridge Faculty of Education.

Davies, S.P. (2000) Memory and planning processes in solutions to well-structured problems. *Quarterly Journal of Experimental Psychology: Human Experimental Psychology*, 53A, 896–927.

Davis, E.A. and Miyake, N. (2004) Explorations of scaffolding in complex classroom systems. *Journal of the Learning Sciences*, 13(3), 265–272.

Davis, T.E., Munson, M.S. and Tarcza, E.V. (2009) Anxiety disorders and phobias. In J.L. Matson (ed.) *Social Behaviour and Skills in Children*. New York: Springer.

De Bono, E. (1970) *Lateral Thinking: a Textbook of Creativity*. London: Ward Lock Educational.

Deacon, K. and Wigglesworth, S. (2005) *Epilepsy Prevalence, Incidence and Other Statistics*. Leeds: The Joint Epilepsy Council.

Deary, I., Strand, S., Smith, P. and Fernandes, C. (2007) Intelligence and educational achievement. *Intelligence*, 35, 13–21.

Deary, I., Thorpe, G., Wilson, V., Starr, J.M. and Whalley, L.J. (2003) Survey 1. Population sex differences in IQ at age 11. *Intelligence*, 31, 533–542.

Deault, L., Savage, R. and Abrami, P. (2009) Inattention and response to the ABRACADABRA web-based literacy intervention. *Journal of Research on Educational Effectiveness*, 2, 250–286.

Deaux, K. and Wrightsman, L. (1988) *Social Psychology* (5th edition). Pacific Grove: Brooks/Cole.

Deci, E.L. (1980) *The Psychology of Self-Determination*. Lexington: D.C. Heath.

Deci, E.L. and Ryan, R.M. (1991) A motivational approach to self: integration in personality. In R.A. Dienstbier (ed.) *Nebraska Symposium on Motivation 1990*. Lincoln: University of Nebraska Press.

Deem, R. (1980) *Schooling for Women's Work*, London: Routledge and Kegan Paul.

Dehue, F., Bolman, C. and Vollink, T. (2008) Cyberbullying: youngsters' experiences and parental perception. *CyberPsychology and Behavior*, 11(2), 217–223.

Delethes, P. and Jackson, B. (1972) Teacher–pupil interaction as a function of location in the classroom. *Psychology in the Schools*, 9, 119–123.

Demko, L. (2005) Bullying at school: the no-blame approach. In J. Wearmouth, R.C. Richmond and T. Glynn (eds) *Addressing Pupils' Behaviour: Responses at District, School and Individual Levels*. London: David Fulton.

Dempsey, I. and Foreman, P. (2001) *International Journal of Disability Development and Education*, 48(1), 103–116.

Dempster, F. (1981) Memory span: sources of individual and developmental differences. *Psychological Bulletin*, 89, 63–100.

DENI (2005) *Supplement to the Northern Ireland Code of Practice on the Identification and Assessment of Special Educational Needs*. Online, available at: www.deni.gov.uk/index/7-special_educational_needs_pg/special_needs-codes_of_practice_pg.htm (accessed 22 February 2010).

Department for Children, Schools and Families (DCSF) (2007) *Safe to Learn: Embedding Anti-Bullying Work in School*. London: TSO.

Department for Children, Schools and Families (DCSF) (2009) *DCSF: Special Educational Needs in England: January 2009*. Online, available at: www.dcsf.gov.uk/rsgateway/DB/SFR/s000852/index.shtml (accessed 22 February 2010).

Department for Children, Schools and Families (DCSF) (2010) *Early Intervention: Securing good Outcomes for All Children and Young People*. London: DCSF.

Department for Education and Employment (DfEE) (1994a) *Bullying: Don't Suffer in Silence. An Antibullying Pack for Schools*. London: HMSO.

Department for Education and Employment (DfEE) (1994b) *The Code of Practice on the Identification and Assessment of Special Educational Needs*. London: DfEE.

Department for Education and Employment (DfEE) (1998a) *Meeting the Childcare Challenge (Sure Start)*. London: HMSO.

Department for Education and Employment (DfEE) (1998b) *The National Literacy Strategy*. London: DfEE.

Department for Education and Employment (DfEE) (1999a) *Blunkett Welcomes 3 Per Cent Drop in School Exclusions*. Press release, 272/99.

Department for Education and Employment (DfEE) (1999b) *Circular No. 11/99 Social Inclusion: Pupil Support* (London: DfEE).

Department for Education and Employment (DfEE) (1999c) *Excellence in Cities*. London: HMSO.

Department for Education and Employment (DfEE) (1999d) *The National Numeracy Strategy: Framework for Teaching Mathematics from Reception to Year 6*. London: DfEE.

Department for Education and Employment (DfEE) (2001) *Special Education and Disability Act*. London: HMSO.

Department of Education and Science (DfES) (1978) *Report of the Committee of Enquiry into the Education of Handicapped Children and Young People (The Warnock Report)*. London: HMSO.

Department for Education and Science (DfES) (2001) *Code of Practice on the Identification and Assessment of Special Educational Needs*. London: DfES.

Department for Education and Science (DfES) (2003) *Excellence and Enjoyment: a Strategy for Primary Schools*. Nottingham: DfES.

Department for Education and Skills (DfES) (2001a) *Inclusive Schooling: Children with Special Educational Needs*. London: DfES.

Department for Education and Skills (DfES) (2001b) *Promoting Children's Mental Health Within Early Years and School Settings*. London: DfES.

Department for Education and Skills (DfES) (2001c) *Special Educational Needs Code of Practice*. London: DfES.

Department for Education and Skills (DfES) (2003a) *Every Child Matters*. Green Paper. London: DfES.

Department for Education and Skills (DfES) (2003b) *The Report of the Special Schools Working Group*. Online, available at: www.dfes.gov.uk/consultations/downloadableDocs/214_1.pdf (accessed 21 April 2009).

Department for Education and Skills (DfES) (2004a) *Every Child Matters: Change for Children in Schools*. London: DfES.

Department for Education and Skills (DfES) (2004b) *Physical Contact*. Online, available from: www.teachernet.gov.uk/wholeschool/familyandcommunity/child protection/ (accessed 2 January 2005).

Department for Education and Skills (DfES) (2004c) *Removing Barriers to Achievement: the Government's Strategy for SEN*. Online, available at: www.teachernet.gov.uk/wholeschool/sen/teacherlearningassistant/toolkit/ (accessed 21 September 2009).

Department for Education and Skills (DfES) (2005) *Statistics of Education: Schools in England 2004*. Online, available at: www.dfes.gov.uk/rsgateway/DB/VOL/v000495/schools_04_final.pdf (accessed 22 February 2010).

Department for Education and Skills (DfES) (2008) *The Education of Children and Young People with Behavioural, Emotional and Social Difficulties as a Special Educational Need*. Online, available at: www.teachernet.gov.uk/_doc/12604/ACFD633.doc (accessed 21 March 2010).

DES (1962) *The Report of the Chief Medical Officer, 1960–1*. London: Department of Education and Science.

Desert, M., Preaux, M. and Jund, R. (2009) So young and already victims of stereotype threat: socio-economic status and performance of 6 to 9 years old children on Raven's progressive matrices. *European Journal of Psychology of Education*, XXIV(2), 207–218.

Desforges, C. and Abouchaar, A. (2003) *The Impact of Parental Involvement, Parental Support and Family Education on Pupil Achievements and Adjustments: a Literature Review*. Research Report 443. London: DfES.

DesJardin, J.L., Ambrose, S.E. and Elsenberg, L.S. (2008) Literacy skills in children with cochlear implants: the importance of early oral language and joint storybook reading. *Journal of Deaf Studies and Deaf Education*, 14(1), 22–43.

Dewey, J. (1916) *Education and Democracy: an Introduction to the Philosophy of Education*. New York: Macmillan.

Dewey, J. and Benton, J. (2009) Activating children's thinking skills (ACTS): the effects of an infusion approach to teaching thinking in primary schools. *British Journal of Educational Psychology*, 79, 329–351.

Dillenbourg, P. (1999) *Collaborative Learning: Cognitive and Computational Approaches*. Oxford: Pergamon.

Dillenbourg, P., Baker, M., Blaye, A. and O'Malley, C. (1995) The evolution of research on collaborative learning. In

H. Spada and P. Reiman (eds) *Learning in Humans and Machines: Towards an Interdisciplinary Learning Science*. Oxford: Elsevier.

Dillon, J.J. (ed.) (1988) *Questioning and Discussion: a Multidisciplinary Study*. London: Croom Helm.

Disability Rights Commission (DRC) (2002) *Disability Discrimination Act 1995 Part 4: Code of Practice for Schools*. Online, available at: www.drc-gb.org/uploaded_files/documents/2008_220_schoolscop2.doc (accessed 22 February 2010).

Dockerell, B. (1995) Assessment, teaching and learning. In C. Forges (ed.) *An Introduction to Teaching*. Oxford: Blackwell.

Dockrell, J. and Messer, D. (1999) *Children's Language and Communication Difficulties*. London: Cassell Education.

Dockrell, J.E. and Shield, B. (2004) Children's perceptions of their acoustic environment at school and at home. *Journal of the Acoustical Society of America*, 115(6), 2964–2973.

Dockrell, J.E. and Shield, B.M. (2006) Acoustical barriers in classrooms: the impact of noise on performance in the classroom. *British Educational Research Journal*, 32(3), 509–525.

Dodge, K., Petitt, G., McClaskey, C. and Brown, M. (1986) Social competence in children. *Monographs for the Society for Research in Child Development*, 51(2), 29, 261–282.

Doherty-Sneddon, G. (2008) The great baby signing debate: academia meets public interest. *The Psychologist*, 21(4), 300–303.

Doig, B. (2006) Large-scale mathematics assessment: looking globally to act locally. *Assessment in Education: Principles, Policy and Practice*, 13(3), 265–288.

Doise, W. and Mugny, G. (1984) *The Social Development of the Intellect*. Oxford: Pergamon Press.

Doise, W., Mugny, G. and Perret-Clermont, A.-N. (1975) Social interaction and the development of cognitive operations. *European Journal of Social Psychology*, 5, 367–383.

Dollard, J., Doob, L., Miller, N., Mowrer, O. and Sears, R. (1939) *Frustration and Aggression*. New Haven: Yale University Press.

Dolva, A. (2009) *Children with Down Syndrome in Mainstream Schools: Conditions Influencing Participation*. PhD Thesis. Karolinska Institute, Stockholm, Sweden.

Dorfberger, S., Adi-Japha, E. and Karni, A. (2007) Reduced susceptibility to interference in the consolidation of motor memory before adolescence. *PLoS ONE*, e240(2), 1–6.

Douglas, G. and McLinden, M. (2005) Visual impairment. In A. Lewis and B. Norwich (eds) *Special Teaching for Special Children? Pedagogies for Inclusion*. Maidenhead: Open University Press.

Dowse, E. and Colby, J. (1997) Long-term sickness absence due to ME/CFS in UK schools: an epidemiological study with medical and educational implications. *Journal of Chronic Fatigue Syndrome*, 3, 29–42.

Doyle, L. and Godfrey, R. (2005) Investigating the reliability of the Key Stage 2 test results for assessing individual pupil achievement and progress in England. *London Review of Education*, 3(1), 29–45.

DSM-IV (1994) *American Psychiatric Association: Diagnostic and Statistical Manual of Mental Disorders* (4th edition). Washington, DC: American Psychiatric Association.

Dubow, E.F., Boxer, P. and Huesmann, L.R. (2009) Long-term effects of parents' education on children's educational and occupational success. *Merrill-Palmer Quarterly*, 55(3), 224–249.

Duckworth, K., Akerman, R., Gutman, L.M. and Vorhaus, J. (2009) *Influences and Leverages on Low Levels of Attainment: a Review of Literature and Policy Initiatives*. London: Centre for Research on the Wider Benefits of Learning.

Dunker, K. (1945) On problem-solving. *Psychological Monographs*, 58(5), 270.

Dunn, J. (1984) Changing minds and changing relationships. In C. Lewis and P. Mitchell (eds) *Children's Early Understanding of Mind: Origins and Development*. Hove: Lawrence Erlbaum.

Dunn, J. and McGuire, S. (1992) Sibling and peer relationships in childhood. *Journal of Child Psychology and Psychiatry*, 33(1), 67–105.

Dunn, L. (1968) Special education for the mildly retarded: is much of it justifiable? *Exceptional Children*, 35, 5–22.

Dunn, L.M., Dunn, D.M., Sewell, J. and Styles, B. (2010) *British Picture Vocabulary Scale III*. London: GL Assessment.

Dweck, C. (1975) The role of expectations and attributions in the alleviation of learned helplessness. *Journal of Personality and Social Psychology*, 31, 674–685.

Dweck, C. (1986) Motivational processes affecting learning. *American Psychologist*, 41, 1040–1048.

Dweck, C. (1999) *Self Theories: their Role in Motivation, Personality and Development*. Hove: Psychology Press.

Dyson, A. (1999) Inclusion and inclusion: theories and discourses in inclusive education. In H. Daniels and P. Garner (eds) *Inclusive Education, World Yearbook of Education*. London: Kogan Page.

Dyson, A. and Gallannaugh, F. (2008) Disproportionality in special needs education in England. *The Journal of Special Education*, 42(1), 36–46.

Earthman, G.I. and Lemasters, L.K. (2009) Teacher attitudes about classroom conditions. *Journal of Educational Administration*, 47(3), 323–335.

Eaves, L., Silberg, J., Meyer, J., Maes, H., Simonoff, E., Pickles, A., Rutter, M., Reynolds, C., Heath, A., Truett, K., Neale, M., Erikson, M., Loeber, R. and Hewitt, J. (1997) Genetics and developmental psychopathology. 2. The main effects of genes and environment on behavioral problems in the Virginia twin study of adolescent behavioral development. *Journal of Child Psychology and Psychiatry*, 38(8), 965–980.

Ebbels, S.H., van der Lely, H.K.J. and Dockrell, J.E. (2007) Intervention for verb argument structure in children with persistent SLI: a randomized control trial. *Journal of Speech, Language and Hearing Research*, 50, 1330–1349.

Eccles, J.S. (2005) Subjective task value and the Eccles *et al.* Model of Achievement-Related Choices. In A.J. Elliot and C.S. Dweck (eds) *Handbook of Competence and Motivation*. New York: The Guildford Press.

Eccles, J.S., Wigfield, A., Flanagan, C., Miller, C., Reuman, D. and Yee, D. (1989) Self-concepts, domain values and self-esteem: relations and changes at early adolescence. *Journal of Personality*, 57, 283–310.

Eckblad, G. (1981) *Scheme Theory*. London: Academic Press.

Education (Additional Support for Learning) (Scotland) Act (2004) Online, available at: www.opsi.gov.uk/legislation/scotland/acts2004/asp_20040004_en_1 (accessed 21 March 2010).

Edwards, D. and Mercer, N. (1987) *Common Knowledge: the Development of Understanding in the Classroom*. London: Methuen/Routledge.

Ehri, L. (2005) Development of sight word reading: phases and findings. In M.J. Snowling and C. Hulme (eds) *The Science of Reading: a Handbook*. Oxford: Blackwell.

Ekinci, O., Titus, J., Rodopman, A., Berkem, M. and Trevathan, E. (2009) Depression and anxiety in children and adolescents with epilepsy: prevalence, risk factors, and treatment. *Epilepsy and Behavior*, 14(1), 8–18.

Elbers, E. (2010) Learning and social interaction in culturally diverse classrooms. In K. Littleton, C. Wood and J. Kleine Staarman (eds) *The International Handbook of Psychology in Education*. Bingley: Emerald.

Elliot, C.D., Smith, P. and McCulloch, K. (1997) *British Ability Scales II*. London: GL Assessment.

Elliott, A. and Hewison, J. (1994) Comprehension and interest in home reading. *British Journal of Educational Psychology*, 64, 203–220.

Elliott, C., Smith, P. and McCulloch, K. (1996) *British Ability Scales II*. Windsor: NFER-Nelson.

Ellis, A., McDougall, S. and Monk, A. (1996) Are dyslexics different? Individual differences among dyslexics, reading age controls, poor readers and precocious readers. *Dyslexia*, 2, 59–68.

Ellis, N.C. (1993) Rules and instances in foreign language learning: interactions of implicit and explicit knowledge. *European Journal of Cognitive Psychology*, 5, 289–318.

Ellis, N.C. (1994) Implicit and explicit language processes in language acquisition: an introduction. In N. Ellis (ed.) *Implicit and Explicit Learning of Languages*. London: Academic Press.

Ellis, N. and Cataldo, S. (1990) The role of spelling in learning to read. *Language and Education*, 4, 1–28.

Elman, J. (1991) Distributed representations, simple recurrent networks, and grammatical structure. *Machine Learning*, 7, 195–224.

Englehart, J.M. (2006) Teacher perceptions of student behavior as a function of class size. *Social Psychology of Education*, 9(3), 245–272.

English, E., Hargreaves, L. and Hislam, J. (2002) Pedagogical dilemmas in the National Literacy Strategy: primary teachers' perceptions, reflections and classroom behaviour. *Cambridge Journal of Education*, 32(1), 9–26.

Entwistle, N. (1972) Personality and academic achievement. *British Journal of Educational Psychology*, 42, 137–151.

Epstein, M.H., Ryser, G. and Pearson, N. (2002) Standardization of the Behavioral and Emotional Rating Scale: factor structure, reliability, and criterion validity. *Journal of Behavioral Health Services and Research*, 29(2), 208–216.

Equality and Human Rights Commission (2009) *Equal Pay Position Paper*, March. Online, available at: www.equalityhumanrights.com/legislative-framework/parliamentary-briefings/equal-pay-strategy-and-position-paper-march-2009/ (accessed 13 April 2010).

EQUALS Key Skills Framework (2009) *EYSF and Key Stages 1–3*. Tyne and Wear: EQUALS.

Erickson, F. (1996) Going for the zone: the social and cognitive ecology of teacher–student interaction in classroom conversations. In D. Hicks (ed.) *Discourse, Learning and Schooling*. Cambridge: Cambridge University Press.

Erwin, E.J. and Morton, N. (2008) Exposure to media violence and young children with and without disabilities: powerful opportunities for family–professional partnerships. *Early Childhood Education Journal*, 36, 105–112.

Evan, J. and Lunt, I. (2002) Inclusive education: are there limits? *European Journal of Special Needs Education*, 17(1), 1–14.

Evans, J., Harden, A. and Thomas, J. (2004) What are effective strategies to support pupils with emotional and behavioural difficulties (EBD) in mainstream primary schools? Findings from a systematic review of research. *Journal of Research in Special Educational Needs*, 4(1), 2–16.

Evans, J., Harden, A., Thomas, J. and Benefield, P. (2003) *Support for Pupils with Emotional and Behavioural Difficulties (EBD) in Mainstream Primary School Classrooms: a Systematic Review of the Effectiveness of Interventions.* Slough: NfER.

Eysenck, H.J. (1991) Dimensions of personality: 16, 5 or 3? Criteria for a taxonomic paradigm. *Personality and Individual Differences*, 12, 773–790.

Eysenck, H. and Eysenck, S. (1975) *Manual of the Eysenck Personality Questionnaire (Junior and Adult).* Sevenoaks: Hodder and Stoughton.

Eysenck, M. (1979) Depth, elaboration and distinctiveness. In L. Cermak and F. Craik (eds) *Levels of Processing in Human Memory.* Hillsdale: Lawrence Erlbaum.

Eysenck, M. and Keane, M. (1995) *Cognitive Psychology.* London: Lawrence Erlbaum.

Fantuzzo, J.W., Sutton-Smith, B., Coolahan, K.C., Manz, P., Canning, S. and Debnam, D. (1995) Assessment of preschool play interaction behaviors in young low-income children: Penn Interactive Peer Play Scale. *Early Childhood Research Quarterly*, 10, 105–120.

Farrell, P. and Venables, K. (2009) Can educational psychologists be inclusive? In P. Hick, R. Kershner and P. Farrell (eds) *A Psychology for Inclusion.* London: Routledge.

Farrell, P., Woods, K., Lewis, S., Rooney, S., Squires, G. and O'Connor, M. (2006) *A Review of the Functions and Contribution of Educational Psychologists in England and Wales in Light of 'Every Child Matters: Change for Children'.* Annesley: Department for Education and Skills Publications.

Farrington, D. (1978) The family backgrounds of aggressive youths. In L. Hersov, M. Berger and D. Shaffer (eds) *Aggression and Anti-social Behaviour in Childhood and Adolescence.* Oxford: Pergamon Press.

Farrington-Flint, L. and Wood, C. (2007) The role of lexical analogies in beginning reading: insights from children's self-reports. *Journal of Educational Psychology*, 99, 326–338.

Fattore, T., Mason, J. and Watson, E. (2007) Children's conceptualisation(s) of their well-being. *Social Indicators Research*, 80(1), 5–29.

Fawcett, A.J., Nicolson, R.I. and Maclagan, F. (2001) Cerebellar tests may differentiate between poor readers with and without IQ discrepancy. *Journal of Learning Disabilities*, 24(2), 119–135.

Feilden, R. (2004) Design quality in new schools. In S. Macmillan (ed.) *Designing Better Buildings.* London: Spon Press.

Feingold, A. (1988) Cognitive gender differences are disappearing. *American Psychologist*, 43, 95–103.

Feingold Association (2010) *The Feingold Diet Program for ADHD.* Online, available at: www.feingold.org (accessed 21 March 2010).

Feingold, B. (1975) Hyperkinesis and learning disabilities linked to artificial food flavors and colors. *American Journal of Nursing*, 75, 797–803.

Feingold, B. (1976) *Why Your Child Is Hyperactive.* New York: Random House.

Feinstein, L. and Duckworth, K. (2006) *Development in the early Years: its Importance for School Performance and Adult Outcomes.* London: Centre for Research on the Wider Benefits of Learning.

Feldman, D.H. and Benjamin, A.C. (2006) Creativity and education: an American retrospective. *Cambridge Journal of Education*, 36(3), 319–336.

Fennema, E. (1996) Scholarship, gender and mathematics. In P. Murphy and C. Gipps (eds) *Equity in the Classroom: Towards Effective Pedagogy for Girls and Boys.* London: Falmer Press.

Fergusson, D. and Lynskey, M. (1997) Early reading difficulties and later conduct problems. *Journal of Child Psychology and Psychiatry*, 38(8), 899–990.

Fergusson, D., Lynskey, M. and Horwood, J. (1997) Attentional difficulties in middle childhood and psychosocial outcomes in young adulthood. *Journal of Child Psychology and Psychiatry*, 38, 633–644.

Feuerstein, R. Rand, Y., Hoffman, M.B. and Miller, R. (1980) *Instrumental Enrichment: an Intervention Programme for Cognitive Modifiability.* Baltimore: University Park Press.

Fisch, S.M. (2004) *Children's Learning from Television: Sesame Street and Beyond.* Mahwah: Erlbaum.

Fisher, J. and Byrne, D. (1975) Too close for comfort: sex differences in response to invasions of personal space. *Journal of Personality and Social Psychology*, 32, 15–21.

Flanders, N. (1970) *Analyzing Teacher Behavior*. Reading: Addison Wesley.

Fletcher-Campbell, F. (2005) Moderate learning difficulties. In A. Lewis and B. Norwich (eds) *Special Teaching for Special Children? Pedagogies for Inclusion*. Maidenhead: Open University Press/McGraw Hill, pp. 180–191.

Florian, L. (2007) *Reimagining Special Education: the SAGE Handbook of Special Education*. London: Sage Publications Ltd.

Flynn, J.R. (1998) IQ gains over time: towards finding the causes. In U. Neisser (ed.) *The rising Curve: Long-Term Gains in IQ and Related Measures*. Washington, DC: American Psychological Society, pp. 25–66.

Flynn. J.R. (2007) *What is Intelligence? – Beyond the Flynn effect*. Cambridge: Cambridge University Press.

Fortnum, H.M., Summerfield, A.Q., Marshall, D.H., Davis, A.C. and Bamford, J.M. (2001) Prevalence of permanent childhood hearing impairment in the United Kingdom and implications for universal neonatal hearing screening: questionnaire-based ascertainment study. *British Medical Journal*, 323: 536–539.

Foster, H. (2007*) NFER Single Word Reading Test 6–16*. London: GL Assessment.

Foucault, M. (1978) *Power and Knowledge: Selected Interviews and Other Writings, 1972–1977*, ed. C. Gordon and trans. C. Gordon, L. Marshall, J. Mepham and K. Soper. New York: Panteon Books.

Franklin, C., Moore, K. and Hopson, L. (2008) Effectiveness of solution-focused brief therapy in a school setting. *Children and Schools*, 30(1), 15–26.

Fraser, S., Lewis, V., Ding, S., Kellet, M. and Robinson, C. (eds) (2004) *Doing Research with Children and Young People*. London: Sage/Open University.

Frazier, L. and Fodor, J. (1978) The sausage machine: a new two-stage parsing model. *Cognition*, 6, 291–325.

Frederickson, N., Frith, U. and Reason, R. (1997) *Phonological Assessment Battery (PhAB)*. London: GL Assessment.

Frederickson, N., Warren, L. and Turner, J. (2005) 'Circle of Friends': an exploration of impact over time. *Educational Psychology in Practice*, 21(3), 197–217.

Freedman, J., Klevansky, S. and Ehrlich, P. (1971) The effect of crowding on human task performance. *Journal of Applied Social Psychology*, 1, 7–25.

Freeman, J. (1991) *Gifted Children Growing Up*. London: Cassell.

Freeman, J. (1998) *Educating the Very Able: Current International Research*. London: the Stationery Office.

Frith, U. (1985) Beneath the surface of developmental dyslexia. In K. Petterson, M. Coltheart and J. Marshall (eds) *urface Dyslexia*. London: Lawrence Earlbaum Associates.

Frith, U. (1989) *Autism: Explaining the Enigma*. Oxford: Blackwell.

Frosh, S., Phoenix, A. and Pattman, R. (2002) *Young Masculinities: Understanding Boys in Contemporary Society*. London: Palgrave.

Fry, E. (1968) A readability formula that saves time. *Journal of Reading*, 11, 513–516.

Fry, E. (1977) *Elementary Reading Instruction*. New York: McGraw-Hill.

Fuchs, D. and Young, C.L. (2006) On the irrelevance of intelligence in predicting responsiveness to reading instruction. *Exceptional Children*, 73, 8–30.

Fuchs, L.S. and Fuchs, D. (2000) Effects of workgroup structure and size on student productivity during collaborative work on complex tasks. *Elementary School Journal*, 100(3), 183.

Funk, J.B. (2005) Children's exposure to violent video games and desensitization to violence. *Child and Adolescent Psychiatric Clinics of North America*, 14, 387–404.

Furlong, J. (2005) New Labour and teacher education: the end of an era. *Oxford Review of Education*, 31(1), 119–134.

Fusaro, J. (1988) Applying statistical rigor to a validation of the Fry readability graph. *Reading Research and Instruction*, 28, 44–48.

Gagné, F. and St Pere, F. (2002) When IQ is controlled, does motivation still predict achievement? *Intelligence*, 30, 71–100.

Gagné, R. (1965) *The Conditions of Learning*. New York: Holt, Rhinehart and Winston.

Gagné, R., Brigg, L. and Wagner, W. (1988) *Principles of Instructional Design*. New York: Holt, Rinehart and Winston.

Galaburda, A. (1991) Anatomy of dyslexia: argument against phrenology. In D. Duane and D. Gray (eds) *The Reading Brain: the Biological Basis of Dyslexia*. Parkton: York Press.

Galloway, J. (2009) *Harnessing Technology for Every Child Matters and Personalized Learning*. London: David Fulton Publishers.

Galton, M. and Wilkinson, J. (1992) *Group Work In the Primary Classroom*. London: Routledge.

Galton, M., Hargreaves, L., Comber, C., Wall, D. and Pell, A. (1999) *Inside the Primary Classroom: 20 Years On*. London: Routledge.

Galton, M., MacBeath, J., Steward, S., Page, C. and Edwards, J. (2004) *A Life in Secondary Teaching: Finding Time for Learning*. Cambridge: Cambridge Printing (Report for National Union of Teachers).

Galton, M., Simon, B. and Croll, P. (1980) *Inside the Primary Classroom (the ORACLE Project)*. London: Routledge and Kegan Paul.

Galton, R. (2008) *Creative Practitioners in Schools and Classrooms. Final Report of the Project: the Pedagogy of Creative Practitioners in Schools*. Cambridge: University of Cambridge.

Galvin, P. and Costa, P. (1994) Building better behaved schools: effective support at the whole-school level. In P. Gray, A. Miller and J. Noakes (eds) *Challenging Behaviour in Schools*. London: Routledge.

Galvin, P., Mercer, S. and Costa, P. (1990) *Building a Better Behaved School*. Harlow: Longman.

Gao, Y., Raine, A., Venables, P.H., Dawson, M.E. and Mednick, S.A. (2009) Association of poor childhood fear conditioning and adult crime. *American Journal of Psychiatry*, 167, 56–60.

Gardner, H. (1993) *Frames of Mind: the Theory of Multiple Intelligences* (10th Anniversary Edition). New York: Basic Books.

Gardner, H. (1999) *Intelligence Reframed: Multiple Intelligences for the 21st Century*. New York: Basic Books.

Gathercole, S.E. (2008) Working Memory in the classroom. *The Psychologist*, 21(5), 382–385.

Gathercole, S.E. and Alloway, T.P. (2006) Practitioner review: short-term and working memory impairments in neurodevelopmental disorders: diagnosis and remedial support. *Journal of Child Psychology and Psychiatry*, 47(1), 4–15.

Gee, J. (2000) Discourse and socio-cultural studies in reading. In M. Kamil, B. Mosenthal, P. Pearson and R. Barr (eds) *Handbook of Reading Research*, Volume III,. London: Lawrence Erlbaum Associates.

Geen, R. (1968) Effects of frustration, attack and prior training in aggressiveness upon aggressive behaviour. *Journal of Personality and Social Psychology*, 9, 316–321.

Gentile, S. (2010) Antidepressant use in children and adolescents diagnosed with major depressive disorder: what can we learn from published data? *Reviews on Recent Clinical Trials*, 5(1), 63–75.

Gernsbacher, M.A. (1990) *Language Comprehension as Structure Building*. Hillsdale: Erlbaum.

Gershoff, E.T. (2002) Parental corporal punishment and associated child behaviors and experiences: a meta-analytic and theoretical review. *Psychological Bulletin*, 128, 539–579.

Getzels, J. and Jackson, P. (1962) *Creativity and Intelligence*. New York: Wiley.

Gillborn, D. and Mirza, H. (2000) *Educational Inequality: Mapping Class, Race and Gender, a Synthesis of Research Evidence*. London: Office for Standards in Education.

Gillhooly, K.J., Fioratou, E., Anthony, S.H. and Wynn, V. (2007) Divergent thinking: strategies and executive involvement in generating novel uses for familiar objects. *British Journal of Educational Psychology*, 98, 611–625.

Gipps, C. (1996) Review and conclusions: a pedagogy or a range of pedagogic strategies? In P. Murphy and C. Gipps (eds) *Equity in the Classroom: Towards Effective Pedagogy for Girls and Boys*. London: Falmer Press.

Gipps, C. and Stobart, G. (1990) *Assessment: a Teacher's Guide to the Issues*. London: Hodder and Stoughton.

Gladwell, M. (2008) *The Outliers: the Story of Success*. London: Allen Lane.

Glaser, B. and Strauss, A. (1967) *The Discovery of Grounded Theory*. Chicago: Aldine.

Goffman, E. (1959) *The Presentation of Self in Everyday Life*. Harmondsworth: Penguin.

Gold, J.M., Murray, R.F., Sekuler, A.B., Bennett, P.J. and Sekuler, R. (2005) Visual memory decay is deterministic. *Psychological Science*, 16, 769–774.

Gold, K. (2002) Great results fudge true picture. *Times Educational Supplement*, 10 May.

Goldfield, B. and Reznick, J. (1990) Early lexical acquisition: rate, content, and the vocabulary spurt. *Journal of Child Language*, 17, 171–183.

Goldstein, D. (1984) Hearing impairment, hearing aids and audiology. *Asha*, 26(38), 24–35.

Goldstein, S. and Brooks, R. (2009) Does it matter how we raise our children? *Communique*, 38(1), 19.

Golubchik, P., Mozes, T., Maayan, R. and Weizman, A. (2009) Neurosteroid blood levels in delinquent adolescent boys with conduct disorder. *European Journal of Neuropsychopharmacology*, 19, 49–52.

Good, T. and Brophy, J. (1978) Teachers' expectations as self-fulfilling prophecies. In H. Clarizio, R. Craig and W. Mehrens (eds) *Contemporary Issues in Educational Psychology*. Boston: Allyn and Bacon.

Goodman, K. (1965) A linguistic study of cues and miscues in reading. *Elementary English*, 42, 639–643.

Goodman, K. (1968) *The Psycholinguistic Nature of the Reading Process*. Detroit: Wayne State University Press.

Goodman, K. (1986) Basal readers: a call for action. *Language Arts*, 63, 4.

Goodman, R. (1997) The Strengths and Difficulties Questionnaire: a research note. *Journal of Child Psychology and Psychiatry*, 38, 581–586.

Gopnik, A. and Choi, S. (1995) Names, relational words and cognitive development in English and Korean speakers: nouns are not always learned before verbs. In M. Tomasello and W.E. Merriman (eds) *Beyond Names for Things: Young Children's Acquisition of Verbs*. London: Routledge.

Goswami, U. (1994) The role of analogies in reading development. *Support for Learning*, 9, 22–26.

Goswami, U. (2006) Neuroscience and education: from research to practice? *National Review of Neuroscience*, 7(5), 406–411.

Gottfried, A., Fleming, J. and Gottfried, A. (1994) Role of parental motivational practices in children's academic, intrinsic motivation and achievement. *Journal of Educational Psychology*, 86(1), 104–113.

Gottlieb, M., Zinkus, P. and Thompson, A. (1980) Chronic middle ear disease and auditory perceptual deficits. *Clinical Paediatrics*, 18, 725–732.

Gough, P.B. and Tunmer, W.E. (1986) Decoding, reading and reading disability. *Remedial and Special Education*, 7, 6–10.

Graham, L.J. (2006) Caught in the net: a Foucaultian interrogation of the incidental effects of limited notions of inclusion. *International Journal of Inclusive Education*, 10(1), 3–25.

Graham, R. (2009) *Some Clinical Observations on Computer Games*. Video of talk at Game Based Learning 2009. Online, available at: www.gamebasedlearning2009.com/proceedings/video/905-video/209-dr-richard-graham-tavistock-clinic (accessed 9 May 2009).

Gray, J. (1975) *Elements of a Two-Process Theory of Learning*. London: Academic Press.

Grayson, A. (2005) Autism and developmental psychology. In C. Wood, K. Littleton and K. Sheehy (eds) *Developmental Psychology in Action*. Oxford: Wiley-Blackwell.

Greenfield, S. (2007) Someone needs to do crazy stuff. *Times Educational Supplement Magazine*, April, 20–21.

Gregory, R. (1970) *The Intelligent Eye*. London: Weidenfeld and Nicolson.

Gregory, S. (2005) Deafness. In A. Lewis and B. Norwich (eds) *Special Teaching for Special Children? Pedagogies for Inclusion*. Maidenhead: Open University Press, pp. 15–24.

Greven, C.E., Harlaar, N., Kovas, Y., Chamorro-Premuzic, T. and Plomin, R. (2009) More than just IQ: school achievement is predicted by self-perceived abilities – but for genetic rather than environmental reasons. *Psychological Science*, 20(6).

Griffin, C. (1985) *Typical Girls? Young Women from School to the Job Market*. London: Routledge and Kegan Paul.

Griffin, E.A. and Morrison, F.J. (1997) The unique contribution of home literacy environment to differences in early literacy skills. *Early Child Development and Care*, 127, 233–243.

Grimley, M. and Banner, G. (2008) Working memory, cognitive style and behavioural predictors of GCSE exam success. *Educational Psychology*, 28(3), 341–351.

Groom, B. (2006) *Supporting Pupils with Social, Emotional and Behavioural Difficulties: Effective Provision and Practice*. London: Paul Chapman.

Groom, B. and Rose, R. (2005) Supporting the inclusion of pupils with social, emotional and behavioural difficulties in the primary school: the role of teaching assistants. *Journal of Research in Special Educational Needs*, 5(1), 20–30.

GTC (General Teaching Council for England) (2002) *Better Support for Schools to Implement the Race Relations (Amendment) Act 2000 in Schools*. London: GTCE.

Guilford, J. (1950) Creativity. *American Psychologist*, 5, 444–454.

Guilford, J.P., Christensen, P.R., Merrifield, P.R. and Wilson, R.C. (1978) *Alternative Uses: Manual of Instructions and Interpretations*. Orange: Sheridan Psychological Services.

Gunter, B. and Harrison, J. (1997) Violence in children's programmes on British television. *Child Society*, 11, 143–156.

Gurian, M. (2001) *Boys and Girls Learn Differently!* San Francisco: Jossey-Bass.

Hackett, G. (1998) An ordeal that still upsets teachers. *Times Educational Supplement*, 20 November, 9.

Hagley, F. (2007) *Suffolk Reading Scale*. London: GL Assessment.

Hagues, N. and Courtenay, D. (2009) *Verbal Reasoning 8–13*. London: GL Assessment.

Hall, E. (1966) *The Ridden Dimension*. New York: Doubleday.

Hall, K. and Harding, A. (2002) Level descriptions and teacher assessment in England: towards a community of assessment practice. *Educational Research*, 44(1), 1–16.

Hall, V., Chiarello, K. and Edmondson, B. (1996) Deciding where knowledge comes from depends on where you look. *Journal of Educational Psychology*, 88(2), 305–313.

Hallam, S. (2002) Mixed up? The pros and cons of ability grouping. *Education Journal* 64, 24–26.

Hallam, S. and Ireson, J. (2007) Secondary school pupils' satisfaction with their ability grouping placements. *British Educational Research Journal*, 33(1), 27–45.

Hallam, S., Ireson, J. and Davies, J. (2004) Grouping practices in primary school: what influences change? *British Educational Research Journal*, 30(1), 117–141.

Hallam, S. and Rogers, L. with Rhamie, J., Shaw, J., Rees, E., Haskins, H., Blackmore, J. and Hallam, J. (2003) *Evaluation of Skill Force London*. London: Institute of Education, University of London.

Halsey, K., Gulliver, C., Johnson, A., Martin, K. and Kinder, K. (2005) *Evaluation of Behaviour and Education Support Teams*. Slough: National Foundation for Educational Research. Research Report RR706.

Hamson, R. and Sutton, A. (2000) Target setting at Key Stage 3. *Teaching Geography*, 25(1), 8–11.

Haney, C., Banks, C. and Zimbardo, P. (1973) Interpersonal dynamics in a simulated prison. *International Journal of Criminology and Penology*, 1, 69–97.

Hansard (2005a) Lords Hansard text for 18 January 2005 (250118–19). Online, available at: www.publications.parliament.uk/pa/ld199900/ldhansrd/pdvn/lds05/text/50118–19.htm (accessed 22 February 2010).

Hansard (2005b) School Closures, 6 June 2005: Column 340W. Online, available at: www.publications.parliament.uk/pa/cm200506/cmhansrd/cm050606/text/50606w32.htm (accessed 22 February 2010).

Harden, A., Thomas, J., Evans, J., Scanlon, M. and Sinclair, J. (2003) *Supporting Pupils with Emotional and Behavioural Difficulties (EBD) in Mainstream Primary Schools: a Systematic Review of Recent Research on Strategy Effectiveness*. London: Institute of Education.

Harding, L., Beech, J. and Sneddon, W. (1985) The changing pattern of reading errors and reading style from 5 to 11 years of age. *British Journal of Educational Psychology*, 55, 45–52.

Hardman, F. (2008) Teachers' use of feedback in whole class and group-based talk. In N. Mercer and S. Hodgkinson (eds) *Exploring Talk in School*. London: Sage.

Hargrave, A.C. and Sénéchal, M. (2000) A book reading intervention with pre-school children who have limited vocabularies: the benefits of regular reading and dialogic reading. *Early Childhood Research Quarterly*, 15, 75–90.

Hargreaves, D. (1967) *Social Relations in a Secondary School*. London: Routledge and Kegan Paul.

Harlaar, N., Dale, P.S. and Plomin, R. (2007) From learning to read to reading to learn: substantial and stable genetic influence. *Child Development*, 78(1), 116–131.

Harlaar, N., Hayiou-Thomas, M.E. and Plomin, R. (2005) Reading and general cognitive ability: a multivariate analysis of 7-year-old twins. *Scientific Studies of Reading*, 9(3), 197–218.

Harlen, W. and Crick, R.D. (2003) Testing and motivation for learning. *Assessment in Education*, 10(2), 169–207.

Harley, T.A. (2008) *The Psychology of Language: From Data to Theory* (3rd edition). Hove: Psychology Press.

Harold, G.T., Aitken, J.J. and Shelton, K.H. (2007) Inter-parental conflict and children's academic attainment: a longitudinal analysis. *Journal of Child Psychology and Psychiatry*, 48(12), 1223–1232.

Harris, B., Plucker, J.A., Rapp, K.E. and Martinez, R.S. (2009) Identifying gifted and talented English language learners: a case study. *Journal for the Education of the Gifted*, 32(3), 368–393.

Harris, J.A., Vernon, P.A. and Jang, K.L. (2007) Rated personality and measured intelligence in young twin children. *Personality and Individual Differences*, 42(1), 75–86.

Harris, R. (1965) The only disturbing feature ... *Use of English*, 16, 197–202.

Harris, S., Nixon, J. and Ruddock, J. (1993a) Schoolwork, homework and gender. *Gender and Education*, 5, 3–14.

Harris, S., Wallace, G. and Rudduck, J. (1993b) 'It's not just that I haven't learnt much. It's just that I don't understand what I'm doing': metacognition and secondary school students. *Research Papers in Education: Policy and Practice*, 10, 254–271.

Harrop, A. and Williams, T. (1992) Rewards and punishments in the primary school: pupils' perceptions and teachers' usage. *Educational Psychology in Practice*, 7(4), 211–215.

Hart, B. and Risley, T.R. (1995) *Meaningful Differences in the Everyday Experience Of Young American Children*. New York: Brookes.

Hart, S., Dixon, A., Drummond, M.J. and McIntyre, D. (2004) *Learning Without Limits*. Maidenhead: Open University Press.

Hart, S.A., Petrill, S.A., DeThorne, L.S., Deater-Deckard, K., Thompson, L.A., Schatschneider, C. and Cutting, L.E. (2009) *Journal of Child Psychology and Psychiatry*, 50(8), 911–919.

Hartas, D., Lindsay, G. and Muijs, D. (2008) Identifying and selecting able students for the NAGTY summer school: emerging issues and future considerations. *High Ability Studies*, 19(1), 5–18.

Hartup, W.W. (1998) The company they keep: friendships and their developmental significance. In A. Campbell and S. Muncer (eds) *The Social Child*. Hove: The Psychology Press.

Hasan, P. and Butcher, H. (1966) Creativity and intelligence: a partial replication with Scottish children of Getzels and Jackson's study. *British Journal of Educational Psychology*, 57, 129–135.

Hatcher, P. (1994) *Sound Linkage: an Integrated Programme for Overcoming Reading Difficulties*. London: Whurr.

Hattie, J.A.C. (2002) Classroom composition and peer effects. *International Journal of Educational Research*, 37(5), 449.

Hattie, J., Marsh, H., Neill, J. and Richards, G. (1997) Adventure education and outward bound: out-of-class experiences that make a lasting difference. *Journal of Educational Research*, 67(1), 43–87.

Hay, I., Ashman, A. and van Kraayenoord, C. (1997) Investigating the influence of achievement on self-concept using an intra-class design and a comparison of the PASS and SDQ-1 self-concept tests. *British Journal of Educational Psychology*, 67, 311–321.

Hayden, C. (2008) *Staying Safe and Keeping Out of Trouble: a Survey of Young People's Perceptions and Experiences*. Portsmouth: ICJS, University of Portsmouth.

Hayden, C. and Pike, S. (2005) Including 'positive handling strategies' within training in behaviour management – the 'Team-Tech' approach. *Emotional and Behavioural Difficulties*, 10(3), 173–188.

Haylock, D. (2001) *Teaching Children 3–11: a Students' Guide*. London: Paul Chapman.

Head Start Impact Study (2005) First year findings. Available at www.acf.hhs.gov/programs/opre/hs/impact_study (accessed 22 February 2010).

Heath, S. (1989) Oral and literate traditions among black Americans living in poverty. *American Psychologist*, 44, 367–373.

Hendriks, L. (2001) *Therapeutic Toddler Classes in Dutch Rehabilitation Centres*. Nijmwegen: Nijmwegen University Press.

Heppell, S. (2004) Trump card in our pockets. *Times Educational Supplement*, 3–3.

HEPS (2009) *Hampshire Educational Psychology Service. Service Statement. Educational Psychology as a Resource for Communities*. Online, available at: www3.hants.gov.uk/heps-service-statement.pdf (accessed 22 February 2010).

Herrnstein, R. and Murray, C. (1994) *The Bell Curve: Intelligence and Class Structure in American life*. New York: Free Press.

Hertz-Lazarowitz, R. (1992) Understanding interactive behaviours: looking at six mirrors of the classroom. In R. Hertz-Lazarowitz and N. Miller (eds) *Interaction in Cooperative Groups: the Theoretical Anatomy of Group Learning*. Cambridge: Cambridge University Press.

Hick, P. (2009) Reframing psychology for inclusive learning within social justice agendas. In P. Hick, R. Kershner and P. Farrell (eds) *Psychology for Inclusive Education: New Directions in Theory and Practice*. Abingdon: Routledge, pp. 165–176.

Hick, P., Kershner, R. and Farrell, P. (eds) (2009) *Psychology for Inclusive Education: New Directions in Theory and Practice*. Abingdon: Routledge.

Higgins, E., Lee, J., Kwon, J. and Trope, Y. (1995) When combining intrinsic motivations undermines interest: a test of activity engagement theory. *Journal of Personality and Social Psychology*, 68, 749–767.

Higgins, S., Hall, E., Wall, K., Woolner, P. and McCaughey, C. (2005) *The Impact of School Environments: a Literature Review*. London: Sage.

Hill, L. (1981) A readability study of junior school library provision related to children's interests and reading abilities. *British Journal of Educational Psychology*, 51, 102–104.

Hillerich, L. (1976) Towards an assessable definition of literacy. *English Journal*, 65, 50–55.

Hilton, M. (2005) Damaging confusions in England's KS2 reading tests: a response to Anne Kispal. *Literacy*, 40(1).

Hinson, N. and Smith, P. (1993) *Phonics and Phonic Resources*. Stafford: NASEN.

Hiroto, D. and Seligman, M. (1975) Generality of learnt helplessness in man. *Journal of Personality and Social Psychology*, 31, 311–327.

Hirsch, D. (2007) *Experiences of Poverty and Educational Disadvantage: Round Up Reviewing the Evidence*. York: Joseph Rowntree Foundation.

Holmes, E. (1982) The effectiveness of educational intervention for pre-school children in day or residential care. *New Growth*, 2(1), 17–30.

Holtz, K. and Tessman, G. (2006) Evaluation of a peer-focused intervention to increase knowledge and foster positive attitudes toward children with Tourette Syndrome. *Journal of Developmental and Physical Disabilities*, 19(6), 531–542.

Hopkins, B. (2005) *Just Schools: a Whole School Approach to Restorative Justice*. London: Jessica Kingsley Publishing.

Horn, B. (2009) Gifted students with Asperger syndrome. *Gifted Education International*, 25, 165–171.

Hornsby, B. and Miles, T. (1980) The effects of a dyslexia centred teaching programme. *British Journal of Educational Psychology*, 50, 236–242.

Hornsby, B., Shear, F. and Pool, J. (1999) *Alpha to Omega: the A–Z of Teaching Reading, Writing and Spelling* (5th edition). Oxford: Heinemann.

Hoste, R. (1981) How valid are school examinations? An exploration into content validity. *British Journal of Educational Psychology*, 51, 10–22.

Howe, C. (1997) *Gender and Classroom Interaction: a Research Review*. Edinburgh: The Scottish Council for Research in Education.

Howe, C. (2010) Peer dialogue and cognitive development: a two-way relationship. In K. Littleton and C. Howe (eds) *Educational Dialogues: Understanding and Promoting Productive Interaction*. London: Routledge.

Howe, C. and Mercer, N. (2007) *The Primary Review: Research Survey 2/1b, Children's Social Development, Peer Interaction and Classroom Learning*. Cambridge: Cambridge University.

Howe, C. and Tolmie, A. (1999) Productive interaction in the context of computer supported collaborative learning in science. In K. Littleton and P. Light (eds) *Learning with Computers: Analysing Productive Interaction*. London: Routledge.

Howe, C. and Tolmie, A. (2003) Group work in primary school science: discussion, consensus and guidance from experts. *International Journal of Educational Research*, 39, 51–72.

Howe, C., Tolmie, A. and Rodgers, C. (1992) The acquisition of conceptual knowledge in science by primary school children: group interaction and the understanding of motion down an incline. *British Journal of Developmental Psychology*, 10, 113–130.

Howe, C., Tolmie, A., Thurston, A., Topping, K., Christie, D., Livingston, K., Jessiman, E. and Donaldson, C. (2007) Group work in elementary science: towards organizational principles for supporting pupil learning. *Learning and Instruction*, 17, 549–563.

Howe, C.J., McWilliam, D. and Cross, G. (2005) Chance favours only the prepared mind: incubation and the delayed effects of peer collaboration. *British Journal of Psychology*, 96, 67–93.

Howe, M. (1990) *The Origins of Exceptional Abilities*. Oxford: Blackwell.

Howes, C. and Ritchie, S. (2002) *A Matter of Trust: Connecting Teachers and Learners in the Early Childhood Classroom*. New York: Teachers College Press.

Howley, M. and Kime, S. (2003) Policies and practice for the management of individual learning needs. In C. Tilstone and R. Rose (eds) *Strategies to Promote Inclusive Practice*. London: Routledge.

Hudson, L. (1966) *Contrary imaginations: a Psychological Study of the English Schoolboy*. London: Methuen.

Hudspeth, W. and Pribram, K. (1990) Stages of brain and cognitive maturation. *Journal of Educational Psychology*, 82, 881–884.

Huesmann, L.R. (1986) Psychological processes promoting the relation between exposure to media violence and aggressive behaviour by the viewer. *Journal of Social Issues*, 42(3), 125–139.

Huesmann, L.R., Moise-Titus, J., Podolski, C.L. and Eron, L. (2003) Longitudinal relations between children's exposure to TV violence and their aggressive and violent behavior in young adulthood: 1977–1992. *Developmental Psychology*, 39, 201–221.

Hughes, C., Graham, A. and Grayson, A. (2004) Executive function in childhood: development and disorder. In J. Oates and A. Grayson (eds) *Cognitive and Language Development in Children*. Oxford: Blackwell, pp. 207–230.

Hui, E. (1991) Using Data Pac for Hong Kong Chinese children with reading difficulties. *Educational Psychology in Practice*, 7(3), 180–186.

Hulme, C., Newton, P., Cowan, N., Stuart, G. and Brown, G. (1999) Think before you speak: pauses, memory search and trace redintegration processes in verbal memory span. *Journal of Experimental Psychology: Learning, Memory, and Cognition*, 25, 447–463.

Humphrey, N. and Symes, W. (2010) Perceptions of social support and experience of bullying among pupils with autistic spectrum disorders in mainstream secondary schools. *European Journal of Special Needs Education*, 25(1), 77–91.

Hunt, J. McV. (1971) Intrinsic motivation and psychological development. In H. Schroder and P. Suedfeld (eds) *Personality Theory and Information Processing*. New York: Ronald Press.

Huston, A.C., Wright, J.C., Wartella, E., Rice, M.L., Watkins, B.A., Campbell, T. and Potts, R. (1981) Communicating more than content: formal features of children's television programs. *Journal of Communication*, 31(3), 32–48.

Hutchins, E. (1995) *Cognition in the Wild*. Cambridge: MIT Press.

Hutchison, D. (2006) An evaluation of computerised essay marking for National Curriculum assessment in the UK for 11-year-olds. *British Journal of Educational Technology*, 38(6), 977–989.

Hutt, C. (1976) Exploration and play in children. In J. Bruner, A. Jolly and K. Sylva (eds) *Play: its Role in Development and Evolution*. London: Penguin.

ICD-10 (1993) *International Classification of Diseases and Related Health Problems*. Geneva: World Health Organisation.

Inhelder, B. and Piaget, J. (1958) *The Growth of Logical Thinking from Childhood to Adolescence*. New York: Basic Books.

Institute of Employment Studies (IES) (2009) *Encouraging Women into Senior Management Positions: How Coaching Can Help*. Sussex: IES.

Iovannone, R., Dunlap, G., Huber, H. and Kinkaid, D. (2003) Effective educational practices for students with autism spectrum disorders. *Focus on Autism and Other Developmental Disabilities*, 18, 150–165.

Ireson, J., Clark, H. and Hallam, S. (2002) Constructing ability groups in the secondary school: issues in practice. *School Leadership and Management*, 22(2), 163–176.

Ireson, J., Hallam, S. and Plewis, I. (2001) Ability grouping in secondary schools: effects on pupils' self-concepts. *British Journal of Educational Psychology*, 71, 315–326.

Jackson, C. (2002) 'Laddishness' as a self-worth protection strategy. *Gender and Education*, 37–51.

Jackson, C. (2003) Motives for 'laddishness' at school: fear of failure and fear of the 'feminine'. *British Educational Research Journal*, 29, 583–598.

Jackson, C. (2004) 'Wild' girls? An exploration of 'ladette' cultures in secondary schools. Paper presented at the British Educational Research Association Conference, Manchester, September.

Jama, D. and Dugdale, G. (2010) *Literacy: State of the Nation*. London: National Literacy Trust.

Jeffrey, P. (1984) *Rogers' Personal Adjustment Inventory*. Windsor: NFER-Nelson.

Jenkins, A., Levacic, R. and Vignoles, A. (2006) *Estimating the Relationship Between School Resources and Pupil Attainment at GCSE*. DfES Research Report 727. London: DfES.

Jenks, K., de Moor, M.J. and van Lieshout, E. (2009) Arithmetic difficulties in children with cerebral palsy are related to executive function and working memory. *Journal of Child Psychology and Psychiatry and Allied Disciplines*, 50(7), 824–833.

Jensen, A. (1973) *Educability and Group Differences*. London: Methuen Barnett.

Jimerson, S.R., Graydon, K., Farrell, P., Kikas, E., Hatzichristou, S., Boce, E. and Bashi, G. (2004) The international school psychology survey: development and data. *School Psychology International*, 25, 259–286.

Johnson, C.J., Beitchman, J.H. and Brownlie, E.B. (2010) Twenty year follow-up of children with and without speech-language impairments: family, educational, occupational and quality of life outcomes. *American Journal of Speech-Language Pathology*, 19, 51–65.

Johnson, J.S. and Newport, E.L. (1989) Critical period effects in second language learning: the influence of maturational state on the acquisition of English as a second language. *Cognitive Psychology*, 21, 60–99.

Johnson, M. and Kress, R. (1964) Individual reading inventories. In *Proceedings of the 21st Annual Reading Institute*. Newark: International Reading Association.

Johnson, S., Cooper, C., Cartwright, S., Donald, I., Taylor, P. and Millet, C. (2005) The experience of work-related stress across occupations. *Journal of Managerial Psychology*, 20, 178–187.

Johnson-Laird, P.N. (1983) *Mental Models*. Cambridge: Harvard University Press.

Johnston, C., Fine, S., Weiss, M., Weiss, J., Weiss, G. and Freeman, W.S. (2000) Effects of stimulant medication treatment on mothers' and children's attributions for the behavior of children with attention deficit hyperactivity disorder. *Journal of Abnormal Child Psychology*, 28(4), 371–382.

Johnston, J., Durieux-Smith, A. and Bloom, K. (2005) Teaching gestural signs to infants to advance child development: a review of the evidence. *First Language*, 25, 235–251.

Johnston, R.S., Rugg, M.D. and Scott, T. (1987) The influence of phonology on good and poor readers when reading for meaning. *Journal of Memory and Language*, 26, 57–68.

Johnston, R.S., Watson, J.E. and Logan, S. (2009) Enhancing word reading, spelling, and reading comprehension skills with synthetic phonic teaching: studies in Scotland and England. In C. Wood and V. Connelly (eds) *Contemporary Perspectives on Reading and Spelling*. London: Routledge.

Joliffe, D. and Farrington, D.P. (2010, in press) Is low empathy related to bullying after controlling for individual and social background variables? *Journal of Adolescence*. Online, available at: www.sciencedirect.com/science/journal/01401971.

Jones, P. (1992) The timing of the school day. *Educational Psychology in Practice*, 8(2), 82–85.

Jones, S. and Myhill, D. (2004) Seeing things differently: teachers' constructions of underachievement. *Gender and Education*, 16(4), December.

Jordan, R. (1999) *Autistic Spectrum Disorders: an Introductory Handbook for Practitioners.* London: David Fulton.

Joy, L., Kimball, M. and Zabrack, M. (1986) Television and children's aggressive behaviour. In T. Williams (ed.) *The Impact of Television: a Natural Experiment in Three Settings.* New York: Academic Press.

Judd, J. (1998) Earlier start to lessons leaves British children behind. *Independent*, 28 January, p. 13.

Jung, C. (1964) *Man and His Symbols.* New York: Doubleday.

Justice, J.M., Kaderavek, J., Bowles, R. and Grimm, K. (2005) Language impairment, parent–child shared reading and phonological awareness. *Topics in Early Childhood Special Education*, 25(3), 143–156.

Justice, L.M. and Ezell, H.K. (2000) Enhancing children's print and word awareness through home-based parent intervention. *American Journal of Speech-Language Pathology*, 9(3), 257–269.

Kagan, J., Rosman, B., Day, D., Albert, J. and Phillips, W. (1964) Information processing and the child significance of analytic and reflective attitudes. *Psychological Monographs*, 78(1).

Kameenui, E., Simmons, D., Chard, D. and Dickson, S. (1997) Direct instruction in reading. In S.A. Stahl and D.A. Hayes (eds) *Instructional Models in Reading.* Hillsdale: Erlbaum.

Kammi, C. (1994) *Young Children Continue to Reinvent Arithmetic: 3rd Grade.* New York: Teacher's College Press.

Kammi, C. (2004) *Young Children Continue to Reinvent Arithmetic: 2nd Grade* (2nd edition). New York: Teacher's College Press.

Kamphaus, R.W., Thorpe, J.S., Winsor, A.P., Kroncke, A.P., Dowdy, E.T. and VanDeventer, M.C. (2007) Development and predictive validity of a teacher screener for child behavioral and emotional problems at school. *Educational and Psychological Measurement*, 67(2), 342–356.

Katz, R.T. (2009) Are children with cerebral palsy and developmental disability living longer? *Journal of Developmental and Physical Disabilities*, 21(5), 409–424.

Kaufmann, A.S. and Kaufmann, D.P. (2004) *The Essentials of the WISC IV Assessment.* New Jersey: Wiley.

Kay, D.A. and Anglin, J.M. (1982) Over extension and underextension in the child's expressive and receptive speech. *Journal of Child Language*, 9, 83–98.

Kearney, C. (2002) Identifying the function of school refusal behaviour: a revision of the School Refusal Assessment Scale. *Journal of Psychopathology and Behavioural Assessment*, 24, 235–245.

Kearney, C. (2008) School absenteeism and school refusal behaviour in youth: a contemporary review. *Clinical Psychology Review*, 28, 451–471.

Kellett, M. (2010) Children's experiences of education. In K. Littleton, C. Wood and J. Kleine-Staarman (eds) *The International Handbook of Psychology in Education.* Bingley: Emerald.

Kelley, H. (1967) Attribution theory in social psychology. In D. Levine (ed.) *Nebraska Symposium on Motivation*, vol. 15. Lincoln: University of Nebraska Press.

Kelly, A. (1988) Gender differences in teacher–pupil interactions: a meta-analytic review. *Research in Education*, 39, 1–23.

Kelly, E. (1994) Racism and sexism in the playground. In P. Blatchford and S. Sharp (eds) *Break-Time and the School.* London: Routledge.

Kelly, A., Carey, S., Carthy, S. and Coyle, C. (2007) Challenging behaviour: principals' experience of stress and perception of the effects of challenging behaviour on staff in special schools in Ireland. *European Journal of Special Needs Education*, 22, 161–181.

Kelly, G.A. (1955) *The Psychology of Personal Constructs.* New York: Norton.

Kelly, R. (2005) *Education and Social Progress.* Keynote address, Institute for Public Policy Research, July.

Keogh, E., Bond, F.W. and Flaxman, P.E. (2006) Improving academic performance and mental health through a stress management intervention: outcomes and mediators of change. *Behaviour Research and Therapy*, 44, 339–357.

Keown, L. and Woodward, L.J. (2002) Early parenting and family relationships of preschool children with pervasive hyperactivity. *Journal of Abnormal Child Psychology*, 30, 541–553.

Kern, M.L. and Friedman, H.S. (2008) Do conscientious individuals live longer? A quantitative review. *Health Psychology*, 27, 505–512.

Keslair, F. and McNally, S. (2009) *Special Educational Needs in England. Final Report for the National Equality Panel.* Online, available at: www.equalities.gov.uk/.../Special%20Educational%20Needs%20in%20England.pdf (accessed 21 March 2010).

Kim, I.-H., Anderson, R., Nguyen-Jahiel, K. and Archodidou, A. (2007) Discourse patterns during children's online discussions. *Journal of the Learning Sciences*, 16, 333–370.

Kimber, M. (2003) *Does Size Matter? Distributed Leadership in Small Secondary Schools. Summary Practitioner Report.* Nottingham: National College for School Leadership.

Kintsch, W. and Vipond, D. (1979) Reading comprehension and readability in educational practice and psychological theory. In L. Nilsson (ed.) *Perspectives in Memory Research*. Hillsdale: Lawrence Erlbaum.

Kirkcaldy, B., Furnham, A. and Siefen, G. (2009) Intelligence and birth order among children and adolescents in psychiatric care. *School Psychology International*, 30(1), 43–55.

Kivilu, J. and Rogers, W. (1998) A multi-level analysis of cultural experience and gender influences on causal attributions to perceived performance in mathematics. *British Journal of Educational Psychology*, 68, 25–37.

Klare, G. (1975) *The Measurement of Readability*. Ames: Iowa State University Press.

Klatt, K.P. and Morris, E.K. (2001) The Premack Principle, response deprivation, and establishing operations. *The Behavior Analyst*, 24, 173–180.

Klein, R. (1996) A steering hand away from trouble. *Times Educational Supplement*, 12 January, p. 5.

Klein, S.B. (1996) *Learning: Principles and Applications*. New York: McGraw Hill.

Kleine Staarman, J. (2008) *Collaboration in CSCL: Social Interaction in Primary School Computer-Supported Collaborative Learning Environments*. Doctoral Thesis submitted to Radboud University Nijmegen, the Netherlands, Institute of Behavioural Sciences.

Kleinman, R., Murphy, J., Little, M., Pagano, M., Wehler, C., Regal, K. and Jellinek, M. (1998) Hunger in children in the United States: potential behavioural and emotional correlates. *Paediatrics*, 101, e3.

Knowles, W. and Masidlover, M. (1982) *Derbyshire Language Scheme*. Private publication, Ripley, Derbyshire.

Kornell, N. and Bjork, R.A. (2007a) Learning concepts and categories: is space the 'enemy of induction'? *Psychological Science*, 19, 585–592.

Kornell, N. and Bjork, R.A. (2007b) The promise and peril of self-regulated study. *Psychonomic Bulletin and Review*, 14, 219–224.

Kristensen, P. and Bjerkedal, T. (2007) Explaining the relation between birth order and intelligence. *Science 22*, 316(5382), 1717–1723.

Kuhn, D. (2006) Do cognitive changes accompany developments in the adolescent brain? *Perspectives on Psychological Science*, 1, 59–67.

Kulik, J., Kulik, C. and Bangert-Drowns, R. (1990) Effectiveness of mastery learning programs: a meta-analysis. *Review of Educational Research*, 60, 265–299.

Kumar, S., Young, G. and James, G.D.H. (2009) Communication outcomes of children with permanent hearing loss developing speaking and signing concurrently: a review. *International Journal of Speech-Language Pathology*, 11(2), 135–146.

Kumpulainen, K. and Wray, D. (eds) (2002) *Classroom Interaction and Social Learning: From Theory to Practice*. London: Routledge-Falmer.

Kutash, K., Duchnowski, A. and Lynn, N. (2009) The use of evidence-based instructional strategies in special education settings in secondary schools: development, implementation and outcomes. *Teaching and Teacher Education*, 25(6), 917–923.

Kutnick, P. (2005) Relational training for group working in classrooms: experimental and action research perspectives. Paper presented as part of the Educational Dialogue Research Unit Seminar Series, The Open University, Milton Keynes, June.

Kutnick, P., Blatchford, P. and Baines, E. (2002) Pupil groupings in primary school classrooms: sites for learning and social pedagogy? *British Educational Research Journal*, 28(2), 187–206.

Kutnick, P., Blatchford, P., Clark, H., MacIntyre, H. and Baines, E. (2005) Teachers' understandings of the relationship between within-class (pupil) grouping and learning in secondary schools. *Educational Research*, 47(1), 1–24.

Kutnick, P., Otab, C. and Berdondinil, L. (2008) Improving the effects of group working in classrooms with young school-aged children: facilitating attainment, interaction and classroom activity. *Learning and Instruction*, 8(1), 83–95.

Labov, W. (1979) The logic of non-standard English. In V. Lee (ed.) *Language Development*. London: Croom Helm/Open University.

Lacey, P., Layton, L., Miller, C., Goldbart, J. and Lawson, H. (2007) What is literacy for students with severe learning difficulties? Exploring conventional and inclusive literacy. *Journal of Research in Special Educational Needs*, 7(3), 149–160.

Lambirth, A. (2006) Challenging the laws of talk: ground rules, social reproduction and the curriculum. *The Curriculum Journal*, 17(1), 59–71.

Landauer, T.K. and Bjork, R.A. (1978) Optimum rehearsal patterns and name learning. In M.M. Gruneberg, P.E. Morris and R.N. Sykes (eds) *Practical Aspects of Memory*. London: Academic Press.

Lange, G. and Adler, F. (1997) Motivation and achievement in elementary children. Paper presented at the Biennial Meeting of the Society for Research in Child Development, 62nd, Washington, DC. ERIC: ED413059.

Langley, K., Fowler, T., Ford, T., Thapar, A.K, van den Bree, M., Harold, G. and Owen, M.J. (2010) Adolescent clinical outcomes for young people with attention-deficit hyperactivity disorder. *The British Journal of Psychiatry*, 196, 235–240.

Larkina, M. and Güler, O.E. (2008) Maternal provision of structure in a deliberate memory task in relation to their pre-school children's recall. *Journal of Experimental Child Psychology*, 100, 235–251.

Larson, M.S. (2003) Gender, race, and aggression in television commercials that feature children. *Sex Roles*, 48, 67–75.

Latane, B. and Darley, J. (1970) *The Unresponsive Bystander: Why Doesn't He Help?* New York: Appleton Century Crofts.

Law, J., Boyle, J., Harris, F., Harkness, A. and Nye, C. (2000) Prevalence and natural history of primary speech and language delay: findings from a systematic review of the literature. *International Journal of Language and Communication Disorders*, 35, 165–188.

Lawrence, D. (1971) The effects of counselling on retarded readers. *Educational Research*, 13(2), 119–124.

Leach, D. and Tan, R. (1996) The effects of sending positive and negative letters to parents on the classroom behaviour of secondary school students. *Educational Psychology*, 16(2), 141–154.

Leeson, L. (2009) *SIGNALL: a European Partnership Approach to Deaf Studies via New Technologies*. Online, available at: www.tara.tcd.ie/jspui/handle/2262/26999 (accessed 21 March 2010).

Lefrancois, G. (1994) *Psychology for Teaching*. Belmont: Wadsworth.

Lefstein, A. (2010) More helpful as problem than solution: some implications of situating dialogue in classrooms. In K. Littleton and C. Howe (eds) *Educational Dialogues: Understanding and Promoting Productive Interaction*. London: Routledge.

Lenhart, A. (2007) *Cyberbullying and Online Teens: Pew Internet and American Life Project*. Online, available at: www.pewinternet.org/Reports/2007/Cyberbullying.aspx (accessed 21 November 2009).

Lenneberg, E.H. (1967) *Biological Foundations of Language*. New York: Wiley.

Lepper, M. and Greene, D. (1978) *The Hidden Costs of Reward*. Hillsdale: Lawrence Erlbaum.

Lepper, M., Greene, D. and Nisbett, R. (1973) Understanding children's intrinsic interest with extrinsic reward: a test of the overjustification hypothesis. *Journal of Personality and Social Psychology*, 28, 129–137.

Levacic, R. and Marsh, A.J. (2007) Secondary modern schools: are their pupils disadvantaged? *British Educational Research Journal*, 33(2), 155–178.

Levitt, E. (1957) The results of psychotherapy with children: an evaluation. *Journal of Consulting Psychology*, 21, 181–196.

Levy, F., Hay, D., McLaughlin, M., Wood, C. and Waldman, I. (1996) Twin-sibling differences in parental reports of ADHD, speech, reading and behaviour problems. *Journal of Child Psychology and Psychiatry*, 37(5), 569–578.

Lewis, A. (1972) The self-concepts of adolescent educational subnormal boys. *Educational Research*, 15, 16–20.

Lewis, A. and Lindsay, G. (eds) (2000) *Researching Children's Perspectives*. Buckingham: Open University Press.

Lewis, M. and Sullivan, M.W. (2005) The development of self-conscious emotions. In A.J. Elliot and C.S. Dweck (eds) *Handbook of Competence and Motivation*. New York: Guildford Press.

Lewis, R., Romi, S., Qui, X. and Katz, Y. (2008) Students' reaction to classroom discipline in Australia, Israel and China. *Teaching and Teacher Education*, 24, 715–724.

Light, P. and Littleton, K. (1999) *Social Processes in Children's Learning*. Cambridge: Cambridge University Press.

Lightfoot, C., Cole, M. and Cole, S. (2009) *The Development of Children* (6th edition). New York: Worth.

Lindsay, G. (1981) *Infant Rating Scale*. Sevenoaks: Hodder and Stoughton.

Lindsay, G. (2007) Educational psychology and the effectiveness of inclusive education/mainstreaming. *British Journal of Educational Psychology*, 77(1), 1–24.

Lipman, M., Sharp, A.M. and Oscanyan, F.S. (1980) *Philosophy in the Classroom*. Philadelphia: Temple University Press.

Littleton, K. (1999) Productivity through interaction: An overview. In K. Littleton and P. Light (eds) *Learning with Computers: Analyzing Productive Interaction*. London: Routledge.

Littleton, K. and Howe, C. (2010) *Educational Dialogues: Understanding and Promoting Productive Interaction*. London: Routledge.

Littleton, K. and Miell, D. (2004) Children's interactions: siblings and peers. In S. Ding and K. Littleton (eds) *Children's Personal and Social Development*. London: Blackwell.

Littleton, K., Wood, C. and Chera, P. (2006) Interactions with talking books: phonological proficiency affects boys' use of talking books. *Journal of Computer Assisted Learning*, 22, 382–390.

Livingstone, M.S., Rosen, G.D., Drislane, F.W. and Galaburda, A.M. (1991) Physiological and anatomical evidence for a magnocellular deficit in developmental dyslexia. *Proceedings of the National Academy of Science*, 88, 7943–7947.

Lloyd, S. (1998) *The Phonics Handbook: Jolly Phonics* (3rd edition). Chigwell: Jolly Learning.

Locke, A., Ginsborg, J. and Peers, I. (2002) Development and disadvantage: implications for the early years and beyond. *International Journal of Language and Communication Disorders*, 37, 3–15.

Lohman, D.L., Hagen, E.P. and Thorndike, R.L. (2009) *Cognitive Abilities Test – CAT*. London: GL Assessment.

Long, M. (1984) *An Investigation of Learning Ability in a Primary School Population*. Unpublished MEd thesis. University of Exeter.

Long, M. (1988) Goodbye behaviour units, hello support services. *Educational Psychology in Practice*, April, 17–23.

Long, M. (2000) *The Psychology of Education*. Oxford: Routledge-Falmer.

Lovaas, O. (1996) The UCLA young autism model of service delivery. In C. Maurice (ed.) *Behavioural Intervention for Young Children with Autism*. Austin: Pro-Ed.

Lovaas, O., Koegel, R., Simmons, J. and Long, J. (1973) Some generalisation and follow-up measures on autistic children in behaviour therapy. *Journal of Applied Behavior Analysis*, 6, 131–166.

Lovegrove, W.J. (1991) Spatial frequency processing in dyslexic and normal readers. In J.F. Stein (ed.) *Vision and Visual Dysfunction: Vision and Visual Dyslexia*, Volume 13. Boca Raton: CRC Press.

Mac an Ghaill, M. (1994) *The Making of Men: Masculinities, Sexualities and Schooling*. Buckingham: Open University Press.

Macbeath, J. and Galton, M. (2004) *A Life in Secondary Teaching: Finding Time for Learning: a Report Commissioned by the National Union of Teachers Concerning the Workloads in Secondary Schools*. Cambridge: Cambridge University Press.

McCann, D., Barrett, A., Cooper, A., Crumpler, D., Dalen, L., Grimshaw, K., Kitchin, E., Lok, K., Porteous, L., Prince, E., Sonuga-Barke, E., Warner, J.O. and Stevenson, J. (2007) Food additives and hyperactive behaviour in 3-year-old and 8/9-year-old children in the community: a randomised, double-blinded, placebo-controlled trial. *Lancet*, 3(9598), 1560–1567.

McCartney, E., Ellis, S. and Boyle, J. (2009) The mainstream primary classroom as a language-learning environment for children with severe and persistent language impairment; implications of recent language intervention research. *Journal of Research in Special Educational Needs*, 9(2), 80–90.

McDougall, S., Hulme, C., Ellis, A.W. and Monk, A. (1994) Learning to read: the role of short-term memory and phonological skills. *Journal of Experimental Child Psychology*, 58, 112–23.

McGarrigle, J. and Donaldson, M. (1974) Conservation accidents. *Cognition*, 3, 341–350.

McGee, R., Williams, S., Share, D., Anderson, J. and Silva, P. (1986) The relationship between specific reading retardation, general reading backwardness and behavioural problems in a large sample of Dunedin boys: a longitudinal study from five to eleven years. *Journal of Child Psychology and Psychiatry*, 27(5), 597–610.

McGuinness, C. and McGuinness, G. (1998) *Reading Reflex*. London: Penguin.

McLeod, S. and McKinnon, D.H. (2007) Prevalence of communication disorders compared with other learning needs in 14,500 primary and secondary school students. *International Journal of Language and Communication Disorders*, 41(S1), 37–59.

McNamara, E. (1979) Pupil self-management in the secondary school: the goal of behavioural intervention. *AEP Journal*, 3, 1.

McSporran, E. (1997) Towards better listening and learning in the classroom. *Educational Review*, 49, 13–20.

Maier, N. (1931) Reasoning in humans. 2. The solution of a problem and its appearance in consciousness. *Journal of Comparative Psychology*, 12, 181–194.

Maines, B. and Robinson, G. (1991) Don't beat the bullies! *Educational Psychology in Practice*, 7(3), 168–72.

Male, D. (1996) Who goes to MLD schools? *British Journal of Special Education*, 23(1), 35–41.

Mandler, J. (1987) On the psychological reality of story structure. *Discourse Processes*, 10, 1–29.

Markman, E. (1987) How children constrain the possible meanings of words. In U. Neisser (ed.) *Concepts and Conceptual Development: Ecological and Intellectual Factors in Categorisations*. New York: Cambridge University Press.

Marland, M. (1993) *The Craft of the Classroom*. London: Heinemann Educational.

Marra, M. (1982) How are you doing now? A followup study of 48 ex-pupils of an ESN(M) day special school. *Remedial Education*, 17(3), 115–118.

Marsh, H.W. (1984) Self-concept: the application of a frame of reference model to explain paradoxical results. *Australian Journal of Education*, 28, 165–181.

Marsh, H.W. (1989) Age and sex effects in multiple dimensions of self-concept: preadolescence to early-adulthood. *Journal of Educational Psychology*, 81, 417–430.

Marsh, H.W. (2007) *Self-Concept Theory, Measurement and Research into Practice: the Role of Self-Concept in Educational Psychology*. Leicester: British Psychological Society.

Marsh, H.W. and Yeung, A.S. (1997) The causal effects of academic self-concept on academic achievement: structural equation models of longitudinal data. *Journal of Educational Psychology*, 89, 41–54.

Marsh, H.W., Byrne, B.M. and Shavelson, R. (1988) A multifaceted academic self-concept: its hierarchical structure and its relation to academic achievement. *Journal of Educational Psychology*, 80, 366–380.

Marsh, H.W., Chessor, D., Craven, R.G. and Roche, L. (1995) The effects of gifted-and-talented programmes on academic self-concept: the big fish strikes again. *American Educational Research Journal*, 32, 285–319.

Martino, W. and Berrill, D. (2003) Boys, schooling and masculinities: interrogating the 'right' ways to educate boys. *Educational Review*, 55, 99–117.

Martino, W. and Pallotta-Chiarolli, M. (2003) *So What's a Boy? Addressing Issues of Masculinity and Schooling*. Buckingham: Open University Press.

Marx, A., Fuhrer, U. and Hartig, T. (2000) Effects of classroom seating arrangements on children's question asking. *Learning Environments Research*, 2, 249–263.

Maslow, A. (1954) *Motivation and Personality*. New York: Harper and Row.

Mathews, V.P., Kronenberger, W.G., Wang, Y., Lurito, J.T., Lowe, M.J. and Dunn, D. (2005) Media violence exposure and frontal lobe activation measured by functional magnetic resonance imaging in aggressive and nonaggressive adolescents. *Journal of Computer Assisted Tomography*, 29, 287–292.

Maxwell, W. (1990) The nature of friendship in the primary school. In C. Rogers and P. Kutnick (eds) *The Social Psychology of the Primary School*. London: Routledge.

Maxwell, W. (1994) Special educational needs and social disadvantage in Aberdeen city school catchment zones. *Educational Research*, 36(1), 25–37.

Mayer, R. (2003) *Learning and Instruction*. New Jersey: Pearson Education.

Mayo, L.H., Florentine, M. and Buus, S. (1997) Age of second-language acquisition and perception of speech in noise. *Journal of Speech, Language and Hearing Research*, 40, 686–693.

Mead, G. (1934) *Mind, Self and Society*. Chicago: University of Chicago Press.

Meadows, S., Herrick, D. and Feiler, A. (2007) Improvement in national test reading scores at Key Stage 1: grade inflation or better achievement? *British Educational Research Journal*, 33(1), 47–59.

Measor, L. and Woods, P. (1988) Initial fronts. In M. Woodhead and A. McGrath (eds) *Family, School and Society*. London: Hodder & Stoughton.

Meichenbaum, D. (1977) *Cognitive Behaviour Modification: an Integrative Approach*. New York: Plenum.

Melhuish, E., Belsky, J., Leyland, A.H. and Barnes, J. (2008) The National Evaluation of Sure Start Research Team. Effects of fully-established Sure Start Local Programmes on 3-year-old children and their families living in England: a quasi-experimental observational study. *Lancet*, 372, 1641–1647.

Melhuish, E., Romaniuk, H., Sammons, P., Sylva, K., Siraj-Blatchford, I. and Taggart, B. (2006) Effective Pre-school and Primary Education 3–11 (EPPE 3–11) project. The effectiveness of primary schools in England in Key Stage 2 for 2002, 2003 and 2004. *DfES Research Brief X06–06*. Nottingham: DfES.

Meltzer, H., Gatward, R., Goodman, R. and Ford, T. (2000) *Mental Health of Children and Adolescents in Great Britain*. London: TSO.

Meltzer, L., Levine, M., Karniski, W., Palfrey, J. and Clarke, S. (1984) An analysis of the learning style of adolescent delinquents. *Journal of Learning Disabilities*, 17, 600–608.

Mercer, N. (1995) *The Guided Construction of Knowledge: Talk Amongst Teachers and Learners*. Clevedon: Multilingual Matters.

Mercer, N. (2000) *Words and Minds: How We Use Language to Think Together*. London: Routledge.

Mercer, N. (2008) The seeds of time: why classroom dialogue needs a temporal analysis. *Journal of the Learning Sciences*, 17(1), 33–59.

Mercer, N. and Hodgkinson, S. (2008) *Exploring Talk in School*. London: Sage.

Mercer, N. and Littleton, K. (2007) *Dialogue and the Development of Children's Thinking: a Socio-Cultural Approach*. London: Routledge.

Mercer, N., Dawes, R., Wegerif, R. and Sams, C. (2004) Reasoning as a scientist: ways of helping children to use language to learn science. *British Educational Research Journal*, 30(3), 367–385.

Merrell, K., Gueldner, B., Ross, S. and Isava, D. (2008) How effective are school bullying intervention programs? A meta-analysis of intervention research. *School Psychology Quarterly*, 23, 26–42.

Merrett, F. and Wheldall, K. (1986) *Observing Pupils and Teachers In Classrooms (OPTIC): a Behavioural Observation Schedule for Use in Schools*. London: Routledge.

Metsala, J.L. (1997) Spoken word recognition in reading disabled children. *Journal of Educational Psychology*, 89, 159–169.

Meyer, D.K. and Turner, J.C. (2006) Re-conceptualizing emotion and motivation to learn in classroom contexts. *Educational Psychology Review*, 18, 377–390.

Meyer, L., Stahl, A., Linn, R. and Wardrop, J. (1994) Effects of reading storybooks aloud to children. *Journal of Educational Research*, 88(2), 69–85.

Michaels, S. and O'Connor, M.C. (2002) *Accountable Talk: Classroom Conversation That Works*, CD-ROM: University of Pittsburgh.

Miell, D. and Littleton, K. (2004) *Collaborative Creativity: Contemporary Perspectives*. London: Free Association Books.

Miles, S.B. and Stipek, D. (2006) Contemporaneous and longitudinal associations between social behavior and literacy achievement in a sample of low-income elementary school children. *Child Development*, 77(1), 103–117.

Milgram, S. (1974) *Obedience to Authority*. New York: Harper & Row.

Miller, A. (1996) *Pupil Behaviour and Teacher Culture*. London: Cassell.

Miller, A. (1997) *Business and Community Mentoring in Schools*. Research Report no. 43. London: Department for Education and Employment.

Miller, D.J. and Moran, T.R. (2007) Theory and practice in self-esteem enhancement: circle-time and efficacy-based approaches: a controlled evaluation. *Teacher and Teaching: Theory and Practice*, 13(6), 601–615.

Miller, G.A. (1956) The magic number seven, plus or minus two: some limits on our capacity for processing information. *Psychological Review*, 63, 81–97.

Miller, S.P., Harris, C.A., Strawser, S., Jones, W.P. and Mercer, C.D. (1998) Teaching multiplication to second graders in inclusive settings. *Focus on Learning Problems in Mathematics*, 20, 50–70.

Mischel, W. (1986) *An Introduction to Personality*. New York: Holt, Rinehart and Winston.

Mittler, P. (2004) *Working Towards Inclusive Education: Social Contexts*. London: David Fulton Publishers.

Molenda, M. (2008) The programmed instruction era: when effectiveness mattered. *TechTrends*, 52(2), 52–58.

Monks, C.P., Smith, P.K., Naylor, P., Barter, C., Ireland, J.L. and Coyne, I. (2009) Bullying in different contexts: commonalities, differences and the role of theory. *Aggression and Violent Behavior*, 14, 146–156.

Montessori, M. (1936) *The Secret of Childhood*. Calcutta: Orient Longmans.

Mortimore, P. and Whitty, G. (1997) *Can School Improvement Overcome the Effects of Disadvantage?* London: Institute of Education.

Moseley, D. (1989) How lack of confidence in spelling affects children's written expression. *Educational Psychology in Practice*, April, 42–46.

Mraz, M. and Rasinski, T.V. (2007) Summer reading loss. *Reading Teacher*, 60(8), 784–789.

Mueller, C. and Dweck, C. (1998) Praise for intelligence can undermine children's motivation and performance. *Journal of Personality and Social Psychology*, 75, 33–52.

Muijs, D. and Reynolds, D. (2003) The effectiveness of the use of learning support assistants in improving the mathematics achievement of low achieving pupils in primary school. *Educational Research*, 45(3), 219–230.

Munn, P., Sharp, S., Lloyd, L., Macleod, G., McCluskey, G., Brown, J. and Hamilton, L. (2009) *The Behaviour in Scottish Schools 2009*. Online, available at: www.scotland.gov.uk/Publications/2009/11/20101438/5 (accessed 22 February 2010).

Murphy, P. (2000) Understanding the process of negotiation in social interaction. In R. Joiner, K. Littleton, D. Faulkner and D. Miell (eds) *Rethinking Collaborative Learning*. London: Free Association Press.

Murphy, P. and Whitelegg, E. (2006) *Girls in the Physics Classroom: a Review of the Research on the Participation of Girls in Physics*. London: Institute of Physics.

Murray, H. (1938) *Explorations in Personality: a Clinical and Experimental Study of Fifty Men of College Age.* New York: Oxford University Press.

Myhill, D. and Jones, S. (2006) 'She doesn't shout at no girls': pupils' perceptions of gender inequality in the classroom. *Cambridge Journal of Education*, 36(1), 99–113.

NACCCE (1999) *All Our Futures: Creativity, Culture and Education.* Sudbury: DfEE.

NAGC (1989) *Help with Bright Children.* Milton Keynes: National Association for Gifted Children.

Naglieri, J., LeBuffe, P. and Pfeiffer, S. (1992) *Devereux Behaviour Rating Scale – School Form.* Sidcup: the Psychological Corporation.

Naigles, L. and Mayeux, L. (2001) Television as incidental language teacher. In D.G. Singer and J.L. Singer (eds) *Handbook of Children and the Media.* Thousand Oaks: Sage.

Naigles, L., Singer, D., Sinmger, J., Jean-Louis, B., Sells, D. and Rosen, C. (1995) Watching 'Barney' affects preschoolers' use of mental state verbs. Paper presented at the annual meeting of the American Psychological Association, New York.

NASS (National Association of Independent Schools and Non-Maintained Special Schools) (2007) *Making Sense of Mental Health: the Emotional Wellbeing of Children and Young People with Complex Needs in Schools.* Research Report. Northampton: the University of Northampton. Online, available at: www.nasschools.org.uk/pages/documents/makingsenseofmentalhealth.doc. (accessed 17 December 2008).

Nathan, L., Stackhouse, J., Goulandris, N. and Snowling, M.J. (2004) Educational consequences of developmental speech disorder. *British Journal of Educational Psychology*, 74, 173–186.

National Assembly for Wales (2002) *Special Educational Needs Code of Practice for Wales.* Cardiff: National Assembly for Wales.

National Collaborating Centre for Mental Health (NCCMH) (2005) *National Institute for Health and Clinical Excellence: Depression in Children and Young People, Identification and Management in Primary, Community and Secondary Care.* National Clinical Practice Guideline Number 28. London: National Collaborating Centre for Mental Health.

National Collaborating Centre for Mental Health (NCCMH) (2008) *Attention Deficit Hyperactivity Disorder: Diagnosis and management of ADHD in Children, Young People and Adults.* National Clinical Practice Guideline Number 72. London: National Collaborating Centre for Mental Health.

National Evaluation of Sure Start (NESS) (2008) *The Impact of Sure Start Local Programmes on Three Year Olds and their Families.* London: Institute for the Study of Children, Families and Social Issues, Birkbeck, University of London, NESS/2008/FR/027.

National Literacy Trust (2009) *Manifesto for Literacy.* London: NLT.

National Union of Teachers (2008) *Teacher Stress in Context.* Online, available at: www.teachers.org.uk/node/8661 (accessed 21 April 2010).

Neale, M. (1989) *Neale Analysis of Reading Ability.* Windsor: NFER-Nelson.

Neale, M.D. (1997) *Neale Analysis of Reading Ability – Revised (NARA II).* Windsor: NFER-Nelson.

Neill, S. and Caswell, C. (1993) *Body Language for Competent Teachers.* London: Routledge.

Nelson, K. (1988) Constraints on word learning. *Cognitive Development*, 3, 221–246.

Nelson, P.B. and Soli, S. (2000) Acoustical barriers to learning: children at risk in every classroom. *Language, Speech, and Hearing Services in Schools*, 31(4), 356–361.

Newton, P.E. (2007) Clarifying the purposes of educational assessment. *Assessment in Education*, 14(2), 149–170.

NFER (National Foundation for Educational Research) (2004) *Excellence in Cities.* Slough: NFER.

NICE (2008) *Attention Deficit Hyperactivity Disorder: the NICE Guideline on Diagnosis and Management of ADHD in Children, Young People and Adults.* National Institute for Health & Clinical Excellence. National Clinical Practice Guideline Number 72. The British Psychological Society and The Royal College of Psychiatrists. Online, available at: www.nice.org.uk/CG72.

Nicholson, T. and Hill, D. (1985) Good readers don't guess: taking another look at the issue of whether children read words better in context or in isolation. *Reading Psychology*, 6, 181–198.

Nicolson, R.I. and Fawcett, A.J. (1990) Automaticity: a new framework for dyslexia research? *Cognition*, 30, 159–182.

Nicolson, R.I. and Fawcett, A.J. (1994) Reaction times and dyslexia. *Quarterly Journal of Experimental Psychology*, 47A, 29–48.

Nicolson, R. and Fawcett, A. (2004) *Dyslexia Early Screening Test (DEST).* Oxford: Pearson Education.

Nicolson, R.I., Fawcett, A.J., Berry, E.L., Jenkins, H., Dean, P. and Brooks, D. (1999) Association of abnormal cerebellar activation with motor learning difficulties in dyslexic adults. *The Lancet*, 353, 1662–1667.

Nikah, R. (2005) *Alarm as Prescriptions of Ritalin to Children Reach a Record High*. The International Child and Youth Care Network. Online, available at: www.cyc-net.org/otherjournals/oj-september2005.html (accessed 12 February 2009).

Nind, M. and Kellett, M. (2002) Responding to individuals with severe learning difficulties and stereotyped behaviour: challenges for an inclusive era. *Journal of Special Needs Education*, 17(3), 265–282.

Nind, M. and Weare, K. (2009) Evidence and outcomes of school based programmes for promoting mental health in children and adolescents. In *European Conference of Educational Research, Vienna, Austria 28–30 September 2009*. Southampton, UK, 10 pp.

Nind, M., Wearmouth, J. with Collins, J., Hall, K., Rix, J. and Sheehy, K. (2004) A systematic review of pedagogical approaches that can effectively include children with special educational needs in mainstream classrooms with a particular focus on peer group interactive approaches. In *Research Evidence in Education Library*. London: EPPI-Centre, Social Science Research Unit, Institute of Education, University of London.

Norman, K. (ed.) (1992) *Thinking Voices: the Work of the National Oracy Project*. London: Hodder and Stoughton.

Nuffield Science Teaching Project (1967) Harmondsworth: Penguin.

Oakhill, J.V. (1984) Inferential and memory skills in children's comprehension of stories. *British Journal of Educational Psychology*, 54, 31–39.

Oakhill, J.V. (1993) Children's difficulties in reading comprehension. *Educational Psychology Review*, 5, 223–237.

O'Connor, E. and McCartney, K. (2007) Examining teacher–child relationships and achievement as part of an ecological model of development. *American Educational Research Journal*, 44, 340–369.

O'Connor, T. and Rutter, M. (2000) Attachment disorder behavior following early severe deprivation: extension and longitudinal follow-up. *Journal of the American Academy of Child and Adolescent Psychiatry*, 31, 518–524.

OECD (2006) *PISA 2006: Science Competencies for Tomorrow's World*. OECD briefing note for the United Kingdom.

OECD (2009) *Education at a Glance*. Paris: OECD Publishing.

Office of the Qualifications and Examinations Regulator (Ofqual) (2009) *National Curriculum Assessment: Regulatory Framework*. Coventry: Ofqual.

Ogilvy, C. (1994) Social skills training with children and adolescents: a review of the evidence on effectiveness. *Educational Psychology*, 14(1), 73–86.

O'Leary, D., Kaufman, K., Kass, R. and Drabman, R. (1970) The effects of loud and soft reprimands on the behaviour of disruptive students. *Exceptional Children*, 37, 145–155.

Olson, C.K., Kutner, L.A., Baer, L., Beresin, E.V., Warner, D.E. and Nicholi, A.M. (2009) M-rated video games and aggressive or problem behavior among young adolescents. *Applied Developmental Science*, 13(4), 1–11.

Olweus, D. (1993) *Bullying at School*. Oxford: Blackwell.

Oppenheim, C. (1993) *Poverty: the Facts*. London: Child Poverty Action Group.

Osborn, M., McNess, E. and Pollard, A. (2006) Identity and transfer: a new focus for home–school knowledge exchange. *Educational Review*, 58(4), 415–433.

Owen-Yeates, A. (2005) Stress in Year 11 students. *Pastoral Care*, 23(4), 42–51.

Pagani, L., Boulerice, B., Tremblay, R. and Votaro, F. (1997) Behavioural development in children of divorce and remarriage. *Journal of Child Psychology and Psychiatry*, 38, 769–781.

Paige-Smith, A. (2005) *Managing Behaviour in Schools* (E804). Milton Keynes: Open University.

Paivio, A. (1969) Mental imagery in associative learning and memory. *Psychological Review*, 76, 241–263.

Palfrey, J., Boyd, D. and Sacco, D. (2008) *Enhancing Child Safety and Online Technologies* Final Report of the Internet Safety Technical Task Force to the Multi-State Working Group on Social Networking of State Attorneys General of the United States. Durham: Carolina Academic Press.

Palincsar, A.S., Magnusson, K.M.C., Collins, K.M. and Cutter, J. (2001) Making science accessible to all: results of a design experiment in inclusive classrooms. *Learning Disability Quarterly*, 24, 15–32.

Panerai, S., Ferrante, L. and Caputo, V. (1997) The TEACCH strategy in mentally retarded children with autism: a multidimensional assessment. Pilot study. Treatment and Education of Autistic and Communication Handicapped children. *Journal of Autism and Developmental Disorders*, 27(3), 345–347.

Panerai, S., Zingale, M., Trubia, G., Finocchiaro, M., Zuccarello, R., Ferri, R. and Elia, M. (2009) Special education versus inclusive education: the role of the TEACCH Program. *Journal of Autism and Developmental Disorders*, 39(6), 874–882.

Parsons, C. and Howlett, K. (1996) Permanent exclusions from school: a case where society is failing its children. *Support for Learning*, 11(3), 109–112.

Pashler, H., Rohrer, D., Cepeda, N.J. and Carpenter, S.K. (2007) Enhancing learning and retarding forgetting: choices and consequences. *Psychonomic Bulletin and Review*, 14, 187–193.

Passenger, T. (1997) *The Contribution of Phonological Awareness and Phonological Memory to Early Literacy*. Unpublished PhD, University of Bristol.

Patterson, G. (1982) *Coercive Family Process*. Eugene: Castalia.

Patterson, G. (1986) Performance models for antisocial boys. *American Psychologist*, 41(4), 432–444.

Patterson, G., Littman, R. and Bricker, W. (1967) Assertive behaviour in children: a step toward a theory of aggression. *Monographs of the Society for Research in Child Development*, 32, 1–43.

Pavlov, I. (1927) *Conditioned Reflexes*. Oxford: Milford.

Peer, L. (2002) What is dyslexia? In M. Johnson and L. Peer (eds) *The Dyslexia Handbook 2002*. London: British Dyslexia Association.

Peers, I. and Johnston, M. (1994) Influence of learning context on the relationship between A-level attainment and final degree performance: a meta-analytic review. *British Journal of Educational Psychology*, 64, 1–18.

Peeters, T. and Gillberg, C. (1999) *Autism: Medical and Educational Aspects*. London: Whurr.

Pelham, W.E. and Fabiano, G.A. (2008) Evidence-based psychosocial treatment for ADHD: an update. *Journal of Clinical Child and Adolescent Psychology*, 37, 184–214.

Pell, T., Galton, M., Steward, S., Page, C. and Hargreaves, L. (2007) Group work at Key Stage 3: solving an attitudinal crisis among young adolescents? *Research Papers in Education*, 22(3) 309–332.

Pennington, B., Johnson, C. and Welsh, M. (1987) Unexpected reading precocity in a normal preschooler: implications for hyperlexia. *Brain and Language*, 30(1), 165–180.

Perret-Clermont, A.-N. (1980) *Social Interaction and Cognitive Development in Children* (European Monographs in Social Psychology). London: Academic Press Inc.

Peterson, E.R., Deary, I.J. and Austin, E.J. (2005) Are intelligence and personality related to verbal–imagery and wholistic–analytic cognitive styles? *Journal of Personality and Individual Differences*, 39, 201–213.

Petitto, L.A., Katerlos, M., Levy, B.G., Gauna, K., Tetreault, K. and Ferraro, V. (2001) Bilingual signed and spoken language acquisition from birth: implications for the mechanisms underlying early bilingual language acquisition. *Journal of Child Language*, 28, 453–496.

Petrides, K.V., Chamorro-Premuzic, T., Frederickson, N. and Furnham, A. (2005) Explaining individual differences in scholastic behaviour and achievement. *British Journal of Educational Psychology*, 75(2), 239–255.

Pettit, G.S., Yu, T., Dodge, K.A. and Bates, J.E. (2009) A developmental process analysis of cross-generational continuity in educational attainment. *Merrill-Palmer Quarterly*, 55(3), 250–283.

Phelan, S. and Young, A.M. (2003) Understanding creativity in the workplace: an examination of individual styles and training in relation to creative confidence and creative self-leadership. *Journal of Creative Behavior*, 37(4), 266–281.

Phillips, N. and Lindsay, G. (2006) Motivation in gifted students. *High Ability Studies*, 17(1), 57–73.

Piaget, J. (1932) *The Moral Judgement of the Child*. London: Routledge/Kegan Paul.

Piaget, J. (1951) *Play, Dreams and Imitation in Childhood*. London: Routledge and Kegan Paul.

Piaget, J. (1959) *The Language and Thought of the Child* (3rd edition). London: Routledge.

Piaget, J. (1966) *The Origins of Intelligence in Children*. New York: International Universities Press.

Piaget, J. (1967) *Six Psychological Studies*. New York: Vintage Books.

Piaget, J. (1972) *The Principles of Genetic Epistemology*. New York: Basic Books.

Pianta, R.C. and Walsh, D.J. (1996) *High-Risk Children in Schools: Constructing Sustaining Relationships*. New York: Routledge.

Piliavin, J., Dovidio, J., Gaertner, S. and Clark, R. (1981) *Emergency Intervention*. New York: Academic Press.

Pinker, S. (1994) *The Language Instinct*. New York: W. Morrow.

Pinker, S. (2002) *The Blank Slate: the Modern Denial of Human Nature*. New York: Penguin.

Plester, B., Wood, C. and Joshi, P. (2009) Exploring the relationship between children's knowledge of text message abbreviations and school literacy outcomes. *British Journal of Developmental Psychology*, 27, 145–161.

Plewis, I. and Veltman, M. (1996) Where does all the time go? In M. Hughes (ed.) *Teaching and Learning in Changing Times*. Oxford: Blackwell.

Plomin, R. (1995) Genetics and children's experiences in the family. *Journal of Child Psychology and Psychiatry*, 36, 33–68.

Plucker, J.A. (1999) Is the proof in the pudding? Reanalyses of Torrance's (1958 to present) longitudinal data. *Creativity Research Journal*, 12, 103–114.

Pollard, A. (1987) Goodies, jokers and gangs. In A. Pollard (ed.) *Children and their Primary Schools*. Lewes: Falmer.

Pollard, A., Triggs, P., Broadfoot, P., McNess, E. and Osborn, M. (2000) *What Pupils Say: Changing Policy and Practice in Primary Education*. London: Continuum International Publishing Group.

Pontefract, C. and Hardman, F. (2005) Classroom discourse in Kenyan primary schools. *Comparative Education*, 2, 87–106.

Portwood, M. (2005) Dyspraxia. In A. Lewis and B. Norwich (eds) *Special Teaching for Special Children? Pedagogies for Inclusion*. Maidenhead: Open University Press/McGraw Hill, pp. 150–165.

Prabhu, V., Sutton, C. and Sauser, W. (2008) Creativity and certain personality traits: understanding the mediating effect of intrinsic motivation. *Creative Research Journal*, 20(1), 53–66.

President's Commission on Excellence in Special Education (2002) *A New Era: Revitalizing Special Education for Children and their Families*. Online, available at: www.ed.gov/inits/commissionsboards (accessed 22 February 2010).

PricewaterhouseCoopers (2001) *An Empirical Assessment of the Relationship Between Schools' Capital Investment and Pupil Performance*. Research Report 242. London: DFEE.

Probst and Leppert (2008) Outcomes of a teacher training program for Autism Spectrum Disorders. *Journal of Autism and Developmental Disorders*, 38(9), 1791–1796.

Prosser, B. (2006) *ADHD: Who's Failing Who?* Sydney: Finch.

QCA (1998) *The Grammar Papers: Perspectives on the Teaching of Grammar in the National Curriculum*. Middlesex: QCA Publications.

QCA (2004) *Geography in Secondary Schools 2003–4*. London: QCA.

QCA (2009a) *Assessing Pupils' Progress Handbook*. Nottingham: DCSF Publications.

QCA (2009b) *Planning, Teaching and Assessing the Curriculum for Pupils with Learning Difficulties*. Online, available at: www.qcda.gov.uk/curriculum/3605.aspx (accessed 21 March 2010).

Quality and Curriculum Development Agency (QCDA) (2009) *Getting to Grips with Assessing Pupils' Progress (APP)*. Coventry: QCDA.

Quinn, P.C. and Eimas, P.D. (1996) Perceptual organization and categorization in young infants. In C. Rovee-Collier and L.P. Lipsitt (eds) *Advances in Infancy Research – Vol. 10*. Norwood: Ablex.

Quinn, P.C., Slater, A.M., Brown, E. and Hayes, R.A. (2001) Developmental change in form categorization in early infancy. *British Journal of Developmental Psychology*, 19, 207–218.

Rae, C., Harasty, J.A., Dzendrowskyj, T.E., Talcott, J.B., Simpson, J.M., Blamire, A.M. *et al.* (2002) Cerebellar morphology in developmental dyslexia. *Neuropsychologia*, 40, 1285–1292.

Raffo, C., Dyson, A., Gunter, H., Hall, D., Jones, L. and Kalambouka, A. (2007) *Education and Poverty: a Critical Review of Theory, Policy and Practice*. York: Joseph Rowntree Foundation.

Raizada, R., Richards, T., Meltzoff, A. and Kuhl, P. (2008) Socioeconomic status predicts hemispheric specialisation of the left inferior frontal gyrus in young children. *NeuroImage*, 40(3), 1392–1401.

Ramjhun, A.F. (2001) *Rhetoric and Reality of Inclusion: an Examination of Policy and Practice in Southampton Local Education Authority*. EdD research thesis, Milton Keynes, Open University.

Randall, P. (1997) *A Community Approach to Bullying*. Stoke-on-Trent: Trentham Books.

Rasmussen, I. (2005) *Project Work and ICT: Studying Learning as Participation Trajectories*. Doctoral thesis, Faculty of Education, University of Oslo, Norway.

Rathus, S. (1988) *Understanding Child Development*. New York: Holt, Rinehart and Winston.

Raven, J.C. (2008) *Raven's Progressive Matrices and Vocabulary Scales*. London: Pearson.

Reay, D. (2007) 'Spice girls', 'Nice girls', 'Girlies' and 'Tomboys': gender discourses, girls' cultures and femininity in the primary school classroom. In N. Cook (ed.) *Gender Relations in Global Perspective: Essential Readings*. Toronto: Canadian Scholars Press.

Reddy, L.A. and Newman, E. (2009) School-Based programs for children with emotional disturbance: obstacles to program design and implementation and guidelines for school practitioners. *Journal of Applied School Psychology*, 25(2), 169–186.

Rees, R. (2001) Principles of psycholinguistic intervention. In J. Stackhouse and B. Wells (eds) *Children's Speech and Literacy Difficulties: 2 Identification and Intervention*. London: Whurr.

Reeve, J., Deci, E.L. and Ryan, R.M. (2004) Self-determination theory: a dialectical framework for understanding sociocultural influences on student motivation. In D.M. McInerney and S. Van Etten (eds) *Big Theories Revisited*. Greenwich: Information Age Publishing.

Reid, K. (2009) Improving attendance and behaviour in Wales: the action plan. *Educational Studies*, 1–15.

Remington, B., Hastings, R.P., Kovshoff, H., degli Espinosa, F., Jahr, E., Brown, T., Alsford, P., Lemaic, M. and Ward, N. (2007) Early intensive behavioral intervention: outcomes for children with autism and their parents after two years. *American Journal of Mental Retardation*, 112(6), 418–438.

Repovs, G. and Baddeley, A.D. (2006) *Multi-component model of working memory: explorations in experimental cognitive psychology. Neuroscience* Special Issue, 139, 5–21.

Resnick, L.B. (1999) Making America smarter. *Education Week Century Series*, 18, 38–40.

Reyna, C. (2008) Ian is intelligent but Leshaun is lazy: antecedents and consequences of attributional stereotypes in the classroom. *European Journal of Psychology of Education*, XIII(4), 439–458.

Reynolds, D. (1987) The effective school: do educational psychologists help or hinder? *Educational Psychology in Practice*, 3(2), 22–28.

Reynolds, D. and Sullivan, M. (1981) The effects of school: a radical faith re-stated. In B. Gillham (ed.) *Problem Behaviour in the Secondary School*. London: Croom Helm.

Reynolds, S., MacKay, T. and Kearney, M. (2009) Nurture Groups: a Large-Scale, Controlled Study of Effects on Development and Academic Attainment. *British Journal of Special Education*, 36(4), 204–212.

Rhode, T.E. and Thompson, L.A. (2007) Predicting academic achievement with cognitive ability. *Intelligence*, 35, 83–92.

Rhodes, J. (1993) The use of solution-focused brief therapy in schools. *Educational Psychology in Practice*, 9(1), 27–34.

Rhodes, J. and Ajmal, Y. (1995) *Solution Focused Thinking in Schools*. London: BT Press.

Richardson, C. (2009) *Assessing Gifted and Talented Children*. London: QCA.

Riding, R. and Anstey, L. (1982) Verbal-imagery learning style and reading attainment in eight-year-old children. *Journal of Research in Reading*, 5, 57–66.

Riding, R. and Cheema, I. (1991) Cognitive styles: an overview and integration. *Educational Psychology*, 11(3 and 4), 193–215.

Riding, R. and Douglas, G. (1993) The effect of cognitive style and mode of presentation on learning performance. *British Journal of Educational Psychology*, 63, 297–307.

Riding, R. and Mathias, D. (1991) Cognitive styles and preferred learning mode, reading attainment and cognitive ability in 11-year-old children. *Educational Psychology*, 11, 383–393.

Riding, R. and Pearson, F. (1994) The relationship between cognitive style and intelligence. *Educational Psychology*, 14(4), 413–425.

Riding, R. and Rayner, S. (1998) *Cognitive Styles and Learning Strategies*. London: David Fulton.

Riding, R., Grimley, M., Dahraei, H. and Banner, G. (2003) Cognitive style, working memory and learning behaviour and attainment in school subjects. *British Journal of Educational Psychology*, 73, 149–169.

Riding, R.J. (1991) *Cognitive Styles Analysis*. Birmingham: Learning and Training Technology.

Riding, R.J., Dahraei, H., Grimley, M. and Banner, G. (2001) *Working Memory, Cognitive Style and Academic Attainment*. In R. Nata (ed.) *Progress in Education*, Vol. 5. New York: Nova Science Publishers Inc.

Rigby, K. (2002) *New Perspectives on Bullying*. London: Jessica Kingsley.

Ring, E. and Travers, J. (2005) Barriers to inclusion: a case study of a pupil with severe learning difficulties in Ireland. *European Journal of Special Needs Education*, 20(1), 41–56.

Rivlin, L. and Rothenberg, M. (1976) The use of space in open classrooms. In H. Proshanski, W. Ittelson and L. Rivlin. (eds) *Environmental Psychology: People and their Physical Settings*. New York: Holt, Rhinehart and Winston.

Rix, J. (2004) Building on similarity: a whole class use for simplified language materials. *Westminster Studies in Education*, 27(1), 57–68.

Robbins, C. and Ehri, L.C. (1994) Listening to stories helps kindergartners learn new vocabulary words. *Journal of Educational Psychology*, 86, 54–64.

Roberts, C., Mazzucchelli, T., Taylor, K. and Reid, R. (2003) Early intervention for behaviour problems in young children with developmental disabilities. *International Journal of Disability, Development and Education*, 50(3), 275–292.

Roberts, D.F., Foehr, U.G., Rideout, V.G. and Brodie, M. (1999) *Kids and Media @ the New Millennium*. Menlo Park: Kaiser Family Foundation.

Robinson, P. (1997) *Literacy, Numeracy and Economic Performance*. London: Centre for Economic Performance.

Robinson, G. and Maines, B. (1994) Assertive discipline: jumping on a dated wagon. *Educational Psychology in Practice*, 9(4), 195–200.

Robinson, R., Smith, S., Miller, D. and Brownell, M. (1999) Cognitive behaviour modification of hyperactivity–impulsivity and aggression: a meta-analysis of school-based studies. *Journal of Educational Psychology*, 91, 195–203.

Rodgers, J.L., Cleveland, H.H., van den Ord, E.J.C.G. and Rowe, D.C. (2000) Do large families make low-IQ children, or do low-IQ parents make large families? *American Psychologist*, 55, 599–612.

Rodkin, P.C. and Hodges, E.V.E. (2003) Bullies and victims in the peer ecology: four questions for psychologists and school professionals. *School Psychology Review*, 32(3), 384–400.

Rogers, B. (1994) Teaching positive behaviour to behaviourally disordered students in primary schools. *Support for Learning*, 9(4), 166–170.

Rogers, B. (2000) *Behaviour Management: a Whole-School Approach*. London: Paul Chapman.

Rogers, B. (2004) *Behaviour Recovery*. London: Sage Publications.

Rogers, C. (1951) *Client-Centred Therapy*. Boston: Houghton Mifflin.

Rogoff, B. (1990) *Apprenticeship in Thinking: Cognitive Development in Social Context*. Oxford: Oxford University Press.

Rogoff, B. (2003) *The Cultural Nature of Human Development*. Oxford: Oxford University Press.

Rose, R., Howley, M., Fergusson, A. and Jament, J. (2009) Mental health and special educational needs: exploring a complex relationship. *British Journal of Special Education*, 36(1), 3–8.

Rosenberg, M., Schooler, C., Schoenbach, C. and Rosenberg, F. (1995) Global self-esteem and specific self-esteem: different concepts, different outcomes. *American Sociological Review*, 60, 141–156.

Rosenshine, B. (1970) Enthusiastic teaching: a research review. *School Review*, 78, 499–514.

Rosenthal, R. (1985) From unconscious experimenter bias to teacher expectancy effects. In J. Dusek (ed.) *Teacher Expectancies*. London: Lawrence Erlbaum.

Rosenthal, R. and Jacobson, L. (1968) *Pygmalion in the Classroom*. New York: Holt, Rinehart and Winston.

Ross, A. and Hutchings, M. (2003) *Attracting, Developing and Retaining Effective Teachers in the United Kingdom*. Paris: OECD Publishing.

Rotter, J. (1966) Generalised expectancies for internal vs external control of reinforcement. *Psychological Monographs*, 80, 1.

Royal-Dawson, L. and Baird, J.A. (2009) The impact of teaching experience upon marking reliability in KS3 English. *Educational Measures: Issues and Practice*, 28(2), 2–8.

Rubie-Davies, C.M. (2006) Teacher expectations and student self-perceptions: exploring relationships. *Psychology in the Schools*, 43(5), 537–552.

Rubie-Davies, C.M. (2007) Classroom interactions: exploring the practices of high- and low-expectation teachers. *British Journal of Educational Psychology*, 77(2), 289–306.

Rudduck, J., Chaplain, R. and Wallace, G. (1996) *School Improvement: What Can Students Tell Us?* London: David Fulton.

Rumelhart, D. and McClelland, J. (1986) On learning the past tenses of English verbs. In J. McClelland, D. Rumelhart and the PDP Research Group (eds) *Parallel Distributed Processing II*. Cambridge: MIT Press.

Runco, M.A. (2006) Divergent thinking: an introduction to the special issue. *Creativity Research Journal*, 18(3), 249–250.

Rusby, J.C., Forrester, K.K., Biglan, A. and Metzler, C.W. (2005) Relationships between peer harassment and adolescent problem behaviors. *Journal of Early Adolescence*, 25(4), 453–477.

Rutter, M. (1967) A children's behaviour questionnaire for completion by teachers: preliminary findings. *Journal of Child Psychology and Child Psychiatry*, 8, 1–11.

Rutter, M. (1989) Isle of Wight revisited: twenty-five years of child psychiatric epidemiology. *Journal of the American Academy of Child and Adolescent Psychiatry*, 28(5), 633–653.

Rutter, M. and Madge, N. (1976) *Cycles of Disadvantage*. London: Heinemann.

Rutter, M. and Smith, D. (1995) *Psychosocial Disorders in Young People*. London: Wiley.

Rutter, M. and Yule, W. (1975) The concept of specific reading retardation. *Journal of Child Psychology and Psychiatry*, 16, 181–197.

Rutter, M., Maughan, B., Mortimore, P. and Ouston, J. (1979) *Fifteen Thousand Hours: Secondary Schools and Their Effects*. Wells: Open Books.

Ryan, C. (2009) Change primary tests – but don't scrap them. *Independent*, 12 February. Online, available at: http://conorfryan.blogspot.com.

Ryan, J. and Peterson, R. (2004) Physical restraint in school. *Behavioral Disorders*, 29(2), 154–168.

Ryan, R.M. and Deci, E.L. (2000) Intrinsic and extrinsic motivations: classic definitions and new directions. *Contemporary Educational Psychology*, 25, 54–67.

Rye, J. (1982) *Cloze Procedures and the Teaching of Reading*. London: Heinemann.

Sachs, J., Bard, B. and Johnson, M. (1981) Language with restricted input: case studies of two hearing children of deaf parents. *Applied Psycholinguistics*, 2, 33–54.

St James-Roberts, I. (1994) Assessing emotional and behavioural problems in reception class school-children: factor structure, convergence and prevalence using the PBCL. *British Journal of Educational Psychology*, 64, 105–118.

Salmon, P. (1988) *Psychology for Teachers: an Alternative Approach*. London: Century Hutchison.

Sammons, P., Sylva, K., Melhuish, E., Siraj-Blatchford, I., Taggart, B., Grabbe, Y. and Barreau, S. (2007) *Summary Report: Influences on Children's Attainment and Progress in Key Stage 2: Cognitive Outcomes in Year 5*. Research Report No. RR828. Nottingham: DfES Publications.

Sammons, P., Taggart, B., Sylva, K., Melhuish, E., Siraj-Blatchford, I., Barreau, S. and Manni, L. (2006) Variations in teacher and pupil behaviours in Year 5 classes. *DfES Research Brief 817*. Nottingham: DfES.

Scarr, S. and Weinberg, R. (1976) IQ test performance of black children adopted by white families. *American Psychologist*, 31, 726–739.

Schaffer, R. (2003) *Introducing Child Psychology*. Oxford: Blackwell.

Schagen, I. and Schagen, S. (2003) Analysis of national value-added datasets to assess the impact of selection on pupil performance. *British Educational Research Journal*, 29(4), 561.

Schank, R. and Abelson, R. (1977) *Scripts, Plans, Goals and Understanding*. Hillsdale: Erlbaum.

Schlapp, U., Wilson, V. and Davidson, J. (2001) *An Extra Pair of Hands? Evaluation of the Classroom Assistants Initiative. Interim Report*. Edinburgh: Scottish Council for Research in Education.

Schlesinger, I. (1988) The origin of relational categories. In Y. Levy, I. Schlesinger and M. Braine (eds) *Categories and Processes in Language Acquisition*. Hillsdale: Lawrence Erlbaum.

Schon, D. (1983) *The Reflective Practitioner*. London: Temple Smith.

Schonell, F. (1955) *Schonell Graded Word Reading Test*. Edinburgh: Oliver and Boyd.

Schopler, E., Bourgondien, M., Wellman, G. and Love, S. (2010) *Childhood Autism Rating Scales 2*. London: Pearson.

Schopler, E., Mesibov, G., Devellis, R. and Chort, A. (1981) Treatment outcomes for autistic children and their families. In P. Mittler (ed.) *Frontiers of Knowledge in Mental Retardation: Social, Educational and Behavioral Aspects*. Baltimore: University Park Press.

Schunk, D.H. (1984) Sequential attributional feedback and children's achievement behaviors. *Journal of Educational Psychology*, 76, 1159–1169.

Schunk, D.H. and Pajares, F. (2005) Competence perceptions and academic functioning. In A.J. Elliot and C.S. Dweck (eds) *Handbook of Competence and Motivation*. New York: The Guildford Press.

Schunk, D.H. and Rice, J.M. (1986) Extended attributional feedback: sequence effects during remedial reading instruction. *Journal of Early Adolescence*, 6, 55–66.

Schwarz, K., Yeung, S., Symons, N. and Bradbury, J. (2002) Survey of school children with visual impairment in Bradford. *Eye*, 16(5), 530–534.

Schweinhart, L. and Weikart, D. (1993) *Significant Benefits: the High/Scope Perry Preschool Study Through Age 27*. Ypsilanti: High/Scope Press.

Scott, P., Ametller, J., Mortimer, E. and Emberton, J. (2010) Teaching and learning disciplinary knowledge: developing the dialogic space for an answer when there isn't even a question. In K. Littleton and C. Howe (eds) *Educational Dialogues: Understanding and Promoting Productive Interaction*. London: Routledge.

Scott, P., Mortimer, E. and Aguiar, O. (2006) The tension between authoritative and dialogic discourse: a fundamental characteristic of meaning making interactions in high school science lessons. *Science Education*, 90, 605–631.

Scott, S. (2010) National dissemination of effective parenting programmes to improve child outcomes. *The British Journal of Psychiatry*, 196, 1–3.

Scott, V. (1990) Explicit and implicit grammar teaching strategies: new empirical data. *The French Review*, 63, 779–789.

Scottish Council for Research in Education (1956) *Hearing Defects of School Children*. London: University of London Press.

Seidenberg, M.S. and McClelland, J.L. (1989) A distributed, developmental model of word recognition. *Psychological Review*, 96, 523–568.

Sejnowski, T. and Rosenberg, C. (1987) Parallel networks that learn to pronounce English text. *Complex Systems*, 1, 145–168.

Select Committee on Education and Skills (2006) Online, available at: www.publications.parliament.uk/pa/cm200506/cmselect/cmeduski/478/47807.htm (accessed 22 February 2010).

Seligman, M. (1975) *Helplessness: On Depression, Development and Death*. San Francisco: W.H. Freeman.

Selye, H. (1956) *The Stress of Life*. New York: McGraw-Hill.

Shah, S. and Priestley, M. (2009) Home and away: the impact of educational policies on disabled children's experiences of family and friendship. *Research Papers in Education*, 1–21.

Shapiro, L.R. and Solity, J. (2008) Delivering phonological and phonics training within whole-class teaching. *British Journal of Educational Psychology*, 78(4), 597–620.

Share, D. and Stanovich, K. (1995) Cognitive processes in early reading development. *Issues in Education*, 1(1), 1–57.

Sharp, C. and Hutchinson, D. (1997) How do season of birth and length of schooling affect children's attainments at Key Stage 1? A question revisited. Paper presented at Annual Conference of the British Research Association. 10–14 September, University of York.

Sharpe, S. (1976) *Just Like a Girl: How Girls Learn to be Women*. London: Penguin.

Sharpe, S. (1998) *Restorative Justice: a Vision for Healing and Change*. Edmonton: The Edmonton Victim Offender Mediation.

Shayer, M. (1996) *The Long-term Effects of Cognitive Acceleration on Pupils' School Achievements*. London: Centre for the Advancement of Thinking, King's College.

Shayer, M. (2008) Intelligence for education: as *described* by Piaget and *measured* by psychometrics. *British Journal of Educational Psychology*, 78, 1–29.

Sheehy, K. and Duffy, H. (2009) Attitudes to Makaton in the ages of inclusion and integration. *International Journal of Special Education*, 24, 91–102.

Sheehy, K. and Johnston-Wilder, S. (2005) *Robotics and Inclusive Education*. RoboFesta-UK 5th Annual Educational Robotics. The Open University. November.

Sheehy, K. and Littleton, T. (2010) The business of child protection in educational virtual worlds. In K. Sheehy, R. Ferguson and G. Clough (2010) *Virtual Worlds: Controversies at the Frontier of Education*. New York: Nova Science Publishers.

Sheehy, K. and Nind, M. (2005) Emotional well-being for all: mental health and people with profound and multiple disabilities. *British Journal of Learning Disabilities*, 33, 34–38.

Sheehy, K. and Rix, J.R.M., with Collins, K., Hall, K., Nind, M. and Wearmouth, J. (2009) *A Systematic Review of Whole Class, Subject Based, Pedagogies with Reported Outcomes for the Academic and Social Inclusion of Pupils with Special Educational Needs in Mainstream Classrooms*. In Research Evidence in Education Library. London: EPPI-Centre, Social Science Research Unit, Institute of Education.

Shepherd, J. (2009) Not in my school yard. *Guardian*, 19 May.

Short, G. (1999) Children's grasp of controversial issues. In M. Woodhead, D. Faulkner and K. Littleton (eds) *Making Sense of Social Development*. London: Routledge.

Shute, R., Foot, H. and Morgan, M. (1992) The sensitivity of children and adults as tutors. *Educational Studies*, 18(1), 21–36.

Siegler, R.S. and Alibali, M.W. (2005) *Children's Thinking* (4th edition). New Jersey: Pearson/Prentice Hall.

Sigafoos, J., Didden, R., Schlosser, R., Green, V.A., Reilly, M.F. and Lancioni, G.E. (2008) A review of intervention studies on teaching AAC to individuals who are deaf and blind. *Journal of Developmental and Physical Disabilities*, 20(1), 71–99.

Silverman, D. (2005) *Doing Qualitative Research* (2nd edition). London: Sage.

Silverman, W.K., Pina, A.A. and Viswesvaran, C. (2008) Evidence-based psychosocial treatments for phobic and anxiety disorders in children and adolescents. *Journal of Clinical Child and Adolescent Psychology*, 37, 105–130.

Simmons, K., Wearmouth, J., Swan, D., Tremer, S., Richmond, R., Beckett, M., Booth, T., Ralston, J., Fraser, I., Flynn, A. and Moran, S. (2006) *The Legal Framework*. Milton Keynes: The Open University.

Simonoff, E., Bolton, P. and Rutter, M. (1996) Mental retardation: genetic findings, clinical implications and research agenda. *Journal of Child Psychology and Psychiatry*, 37(3), 259–280.

Simonoff, E., Pickles, A., Chadwick, O., Gringras, P., Wood, N., Higgins, S., Maney, J.-A., Karia, N., Iqbal, H. and Moore, A. (2006) The Croydon Assessment of Learning Study: prevalence and educational identification of mild mental retardation. *Journal of Child Psychology and Psychiatry and Allied Disciplines*, 47(8), 828–839.

Simons, J., Dewitte, S. and Lens, W. (2004) The role of different types of instrumentality in motivation, study strategies and performance: know why you learn, so you'll know what you learn! *British Journal of Educational Psychology*, 74, 343–360.

Sinclair, J. and Coulthard, M. (1975) *Towards an Analysis of Discourse: the English Used by Teachers and Pupils*. Oxford: Oxford University Press.

Siraj-Blatchford, I. (2009) Conceptualising progression in the pedagogy of play and sustained shared thinking in early childhood education: a Vygotskian perspective. *Educational and Child Psychology*, 26(2), 77–89.

Siraj-Blatchford, I. and Siraj-Blatchford, J. (2009) *Improving Development Outcomes for Children Through Effective Practice in Integrating Early Years' Services*. London: C4EO.

Siraj-Blatchford, I., Taggart, B., Sylva, K., Sammons, P. and Melhuish, E. (2008) Towards the transformation of practice in early childhood education: the effective provision of pre-school education (EPPE) project. *Cambridge Journal of Education*, 38(1), 23–36.

Skidmore, D. (2004) *Inclusion: the Dynamic of Social Development*. Buckingham: Open University Press.

Skidmore, D. (2006) Pedagogy and dialogue. *Cambridge Journal of Education*, 36(4), 503–514.

Skinner, B. (1938) *The Behavior of Organisms*. New York: Appleton Century Crofts.

Skinner, B. (1954) The science of learning and the art of teaching. *Harvard Educational Review*, 24, 86–97.

Skinner, B. (1957) *Verbal Behavior*. New York: Appleton Century Crofts.

Skinner, N. (1985) University grades and time of day instruction. *Bulletin of the Psychonomic Society*, 23, 67.

Skritc, T.M. (1991) The special education paradox: equity as the way to excellence. *Harvard Educational Review*, 61(2), 148–206.

Slavin, R.E. (1980) Co-operative learning. *Review of Educational Research*, 50(2), 315–342.

Slobin, D. (1966) Grammatical transformations and sentence comprehension in childhood and adulthood. *Journal of Verbal Learning and Verbal Behaviour*, 5, 219–227.

Smallridge, P. and Williamson, A. (2008) *Independent Review of Restraint in Juvenile Secure Settings*. London: HMSO.

Smith, C. and Ellsworth, P. (1987) Patterns of appraisal and emotion related to taking an exam. *Journal of Personality and Social Psychology*, 52, 475–488.

Smith, F. (1973) *Psycholinguistics and Reading*. New York: Holt, Rinehart and Winston.

Smith, F., Hardman, F., Wall, K. and Mroz, M. (2004) Interactive whole class teaching in the National Literacy and Numeracy strategies. *British Educational Research Journal*, 30(3), 395–411.

Smith, F., Hardman, F. and Higgins, S. (2006) The impact of interactive whiteboards on teacher–pupil interaction in the National Literacy and Numeracy strategies. *British Educational Research Journal*, 32(3), 443–457.

Smith, G. (1975) *Educational Priority*, vol. 4. London: HMSO.

Smith, P. and Hagues, N. (2009) *Non-Verbal Reasoning Test Series*. London: GL-Assessment.

Smith, P., Fernandes, C. and Strand, C. (2001) *Cognitive Abilities Test 3*. Windsor: NFER-Nelson.

Smith, P., Smith, C., Osborn, R. and Samara, M. (2008) A content analysis of school anti-bullying policies: progress and limitations *Educational Psychology in Practice*, 24(1), 1–12.

Smith, P.K. and Watson, D. (2004) *Evaluation of the CHIPS (ChildLine in Partnership with Schools) Programme*. Research report RR570, DfES publications.

Smith, P.K., Bowers, L., Binney, V. and Cowie, H. (1999) Relationships of children involved in bully/victim problems at school. In M. Woodhead, D. Faulkner and K. Littleton (eds) *Cultural Worlds of Early Childhood*. London: Routledge.

Smith, S.M., Ward, T.B. and Finke, R.A. (eds) (1995) *The Creative Cognition Approach*. Cambridge: MIT Press.

Snow, R. (1969) Unfinished Pygmalion. *Contemporary Psychology*, 14, 197–199.

Snowling, M.J. (2000) *Dyslexia* (2nd edition). Oxford: Blackwell.

Snowling, M.J., Stothard, S.E., Clarke, P., Bowyer-Crane, C., Harrington, A., Truelove, E. and Hulme, C. (2008) *York Assessment of Reading for Comprehension*. London: GL Assessment.

Snowling, M.J., van Wagtendonk, B. and Stafford, C. (1988) Object-naming deficits in developmental dyslexia. *Journal of Research in Reading*, 11, 67–85.

Solity, J., Deavers, R., Kerfoot, S., Crane, G. and Cannon, K. (1999) Raising literacy attainments in the early years: the impact of instructional psychology. *Educational Psychology*, 19(4), 373–397.

Solity, J.E. and Vousden, J.I. (2009) Real Books vs. Reading Schemes: a new perspective from instructional psychology. *Educational Psychology*, 29, 469–511.

Solomon, D., Battistich, V., Watson, M., Schaps, E. and Lewis, C. (2000). A six-district study of educational change: direct and mediated effects of the Child Development Project. *Social Psychology of Education*, 4, 3–51.

Sommers, C. (2000) *The War Against Boys: How Misguided Feminism is Harming Our Young Men*. New York: Simon and Schuster.

Sonstroem, A. (1966) *Manipulating, Labeling and Screening in the Learning of Conservation*. Unpublished PhD thesis, Harvard University.

Spaulding, C. (1992) *Motivation in the Classroom*. New York: McGraw-Hill.

Spearman, C. (1904) General intelligence, objectively determined and measured. *American Journal of Psychology*, 15, 210–293.

Special Educational Needs and Disability Act (SENDA) (2001) Online, available at: www.opsi.gov.uk/acts/acts2001/ukpga_20010010_en_1 (accessed 22 February 2010).

Spence, S. (1995) *Social Skills Training: Enhancing Social Competence with Children and Adolescents*. Windsor: NFER-Nelson.

Spielhofer, T., Benton, T. and Schagen, S. (2004) A study of the effects of school size and single-sex education in English schools. *Research Papers in Education*, 19(2), 133–159.

Spinath, B., Spinath, F.M., Harlaar, N. and Plomin, R. (2006) Predicting school achievement from intelligence, self-perceived ability and intrinsic value. *Intelligence*, 34, 363–374.

Sprafkin, J.N. and Rubinstein, A. (1979) A field correlational study of children's television viewing habits and prosocial behavior. *Journal of Broadcasting*, 23, 265–276.

Squire, L.R. (1992) Declarative and non declarative memory: multiple brain systems supporting learning and memory. *Journal of Cognitive Neuroscience*, 4, 232–243.

Stahl, S.A. (1998) Teaching children with reading problems to decode: phonics and 'not-phonics' instruction. *Reading and Writing Quarterly*, 14, 165–188.

Stainthorp, R. and Hughes, D. (2004) What happens to precocious readers' performance by the age eleven? *Journal of Research in Reading*, 27, 357–372.

Stannard, J. (2009) *Keynote Address to London Regional GandT Conference*, 11 June. Online, available at: www.cfbt.com/.../G%20and %20T%20Briefing%20Paper%20August%202009.doc (accessed 2 March 2010).

Stanovich, K. (1986) Matthew effects in reading: some consequences of individual differences in the acquisition of literacy. *Reading Research Quarterly*, 21, 360–407.

Stanovich, K. (1991) Discrepancy definitions of reading disability. *Reading Research Quarterly*, 26(1), 29.

Stanovich, K. (1994) Annotation: does dyslexia exist? *Journal of Child Psychology and Psychiatry*, 35(4), 579–595.

Stanovich, K.E. and Siegel, L.S. (1994) Phenotypic performance profile of children with reading disabilities: a regression-based test of the phonological-core variable-difference model. *Journal of Educational Psychology*, 86, 24–53.

Steer, A. (2009) *Learning Behaviour: Lessons Learned, a Review of Behaviour Standards and Practices in our Schools*. Nottingham: DCSF.

Stein, J.F. (1994) Developmental dyslexia, neural timing and hemispheric lateralization. *International Journal of Psychophysiology*, 18(3), 241–249.

Steinberg, D. (1986) Psychiatric aspects of problem behaviour: a consultative approach. In D. Tattum (ed.) *Management of Disruptive Pupil Behaviour in Schools*. London: Wiley.

Sternberg, R.J. (1988) Explaining away intelligence: a reply to Howe. *British Journal of Psychology*, 79, 527–533.

Sternberg, R.J. (2003) Creative thinking in the classroom. *Scandinavian Journal of Educational Research*, 47, 325–338.

Sternberg, R.J. (2006) The nature of creativity. *Creativity Research Journal*, 18(1), 87–98.

Sternberg, R.J., Grigorenko, E.L. and Bundy, D.A. (2001) The predictive value of IQ. *Merrill-Palmer Quarterly*, 47, 1–41.

Sternberg, R.J., Grigorenko, E. and Kidd, K.K. (2005) Intelligence, race, and genetics. *American Psychologist*, 60(1), 46–59.

Sterzer, P., Stadler, C., Krebs, A., Kleinschmidt, A. and Poustka, F. (2003) Reduced anterior cingulate activity in adolescents with antisocial conduct disorder confronted with affective pictures. *NeuroImage*, 19(Supp. 1), 23.

Stevenson, J. (2009) Food additives and children's behaviour: evidence-based policy at the margins of certainty. *Journal of Children's Services*, 4(2), 4–13.

Stiggins, R. (2007) Assessment through student eyes. *Educational Leadership*, 64(8), 22–26.

Stott, D. (1971) *Manual of the Bristol Social-Adjustment Guides*. London: University of London Press.

Stott, D.H. (1987) *The Social Adjustment of Children: Manual to the Bristol Social Adjustment Guides*. London: Hodder and Stoughton.

Strand, S. and Lindsay, G. (2009) Evidence of ethnic disproportionality in special education in an English population. *Journal of Special Education*, 43(3), 174–190.

Strand, S., Deary, I.J. and Smith, P. (2006) Sex differences in Cognitive Abilities Test scores: a UK national picture. *British Journal of Educational Psychology*, 76, 463–480.

Stroop, J. (1935) Studies of interference in serial verbal reactions. *Journal of Experimental Psychology*, 18, 643–662.

Stuart, M., Masterson, J. and Dixon, M. (2000) Spongelike acquisition of sight vocabulary in beginning readers? *Journal of Research in Reading*, 23, 12–27.

Stuckless, E. and Birch, J. (1966) The influence of early manual communication on the linguistic development of deaf children. *American Annals of the Deaf*, 111, 499–504.

Stuebing, K.K., Barth, A.E., Holfese, P.J., Weiss, B. and Fletcher, J.M. (2009) IQ is not strongly related to response to reading instruction: a meta-analytic interpretation. *Exceptional Children*, 76, 31–51.

Sue, D., Sue, D. and Sue, S. (1990) *Understanding Abnormal Behaviour* (3rd edition). Boston: Houghton Mifflin.

Sutherland, S. (2008) *An Independent Inquiry into the Delivery of National Curriculum Tests in 2008: a Report to Ofqual and the Secretary of State for Children, Schools and Families (The Sutherland Report)*. London: TSO.

Sutton, L., Smith, N., Dearden, C. and Middleton, S. (2007) *A Child's Eye View of Social Difference*. York: Joseph Rowntree Foundation.

Swann, J. (1992) *Girls, Boys and Language*. London: Blackwell.

Swinson, J. and Harrop, A. (2009) Teacher talk to boys and girls and its relationship to their behaviour. *Educational Studies*, 35, 5.

Swinson, J. and Melling, R. (1995) Assertive Discipline: four wheels on this wagon – a reply to Robinson and Maines. *Educational Psychology in Practice*, 11(3), 3–8.

Sylva, K., Melhuish, E.C., Sammons, P., Siraj-Blatchford, I. and Taggart, B. (2004) *The Effective Provision of Pre-School Education (EPPE) Project: Technical Paper 12 – The Final Report: Effective Pre-School Education*. London: DfES/Institute of Education, University of London.

Sylva, K., Melhuish, E., Sammons, P., Siraj-Blatchford, I. and Taggart, B. (2008a) *Final Report from the Primary Phase: Pre-school, School and Family Influences on Children's Development During Key Stage 2 (7–11)*. Nottingham: DCSF.

Sylva, K., Melhuish, E., Sammons, P., Siraj-Blatchford, I., Taggart, B., Jelicic, H., Barreau, S., Grabbe, Y., Smees, R. and Welcomme, W. (2008b) *Pre-School, School and Family Influences on Children's Development During Key Stage 2 (age 7–11): Final Report*. Research Brief DCSF: RB061. Nottingham: DfES Publications.

Tajfel, H. (1981) *Human Group and Social Categories*. Cambridge: Cambridge University Press.

Tardif, T. (1996) Nouns are not always learned before verbs: evidence from Mandarin speakers' early vocabularies. *Developmental Psychology*, 32(3), 492–504.

Tannock, R. (1998) Attention deficit hyperactivity disorder: advances in cognitive, neurobiological, and genetic research. *Journal of Child Psychology and Psychiatry*, 39(1), 65–99.

Tattum, D. (1982) *Disruptive Pupils in Schools and Units*. Chichester: Wiley.

Terman, L. (1925) *Genetic Studies of Genius: Volumes 1–5*. Stanford: Stanford University Press.

Thakkar, R.R., Garrison, M.M. and Christakis, D.A. (2009) A systematic review for the effects of television viewing by infants and preschoolers. *Pediatrics*, 118(5), 2025–2031.

Tharp, R. and Gallimore, R. (1998) A theory of teaching as assisted performance. In D. Faulkner, K. Littleton and M. Woodhead (eds) *Learning Relationships in the Classroom*. London: Routledge.

Theodore, L.A., Bray, M.A., Kehle, T.J. and Dioguardi, R.J. (2003) Contemporary review of group-oriented contingencies for disruptive behavior. *Journal of Applied School Psychology*, 20(1), 79–101.

Thomas, A. and Chess, S. (1977) *Temperament and Development*. New York: Brunner/Mazel.

Thorndike, R.L., Hagen, E. and France, N. (1986) *Cognitive Abilities Test* (2nd edition). Windsor: NfER Nelson.

Thrupp, M. (1998) The art of the possible: organising and managing high and low socio-economic schools. *Journal of Educational Policy*, 13, 197–219.

Tidman, L., Saravanan, K. and Gibbs, J. (2003) Epilepsy in mainstream and special educational primary school settings. *Siezure*, 12(1), 77–51.

Titus, J.B. and Thio, L.L. (2009) The effects of antiepileptic drugs on classroom performance. *Psychology in the Schools*, 46(9), 885–891.

Tomasello, M. (2003) *Constructing a Language: a Usage-Based Theory of Language Acquisition*. Cambridge: Harvard University Press.

Tomlinson-Keasey, C., Eisert, D., Kahle, L., Hardy-Brown, K. and Keasey, C.B. (1979) The structure of concrete operational thought. *Child Development*, 50, 1153–1163.

Topping, K. (1983) *Educational Systems for Disruptive Adolescents*. London: Croom Helm.

Topping, K. and Ferguson, N. (2005) Effective literacy teaching behaviours. *Journal of Research in Reading*, 28(2), 125–143.

Topping, K. and Trickey, S. (2007) Collaborative philosophical enquiry for school children: cognitive effects at 10–12 years. *British Journal of Educational Psychology*, 77, 271–288.

Topping, K. and Whiteley, M. (1990) Participant evaluation of parent-tutored and peer-tutored projects in reading. *Educational Research*, 32(1), 14–27.

Torgerson, C. and Zhu, D. (2003) A systematic review and meta-analysis of the effectiveness of ICT on literacy learning in English, 5–16. In *Research Evidence in Education Library*. London: EPPI-Centre, Social Science Research Unit, Institute of Education.

Torgerson, C., Brooks, G. and Hall, J. (2006) *A Systematic Review of the Research Literature and Use of Phonics in the Teaching of Reading and Spelling*. DfES, research reports RR711. Online, available at: www.dfes.gov.uk/research/data/uploadfiles/RR711_.pdf (accessed 2 March 2010).

Torgesen, J., Wagner, R. and Rashotte, C. (1994) Longitudinal studies of phonological processing and reading. *Journal of Learning Disabilities*, 27, 276–286.

Torrance, E.P. (1963) *Education and the Creative Potential*. Minneapolis: University of Minnesota Press.

Torrance, E.P. (1988) The nature of creativity as manifest in its testing. In R. Sternberg (ed.) *The Nature of Creativity*. New York: Cambridge University Press.

Touretzky, D. (ed.) (1991) *Connectionist Approaches to Language Learning*. Dordrecht: Kluwer.

Tracey, D.K., Marsh, H.W. and Craven, R.G. (2003) Self-concepts of preadolescent students with mild intellectual disabilities: issues of measurement and educational placement. In H.W. Marsh, R.G. Craven and D.M. McInerney (eds) *International Advances in Self Research, Vol. 1*. Greenwich: Information Age.

Tudge, J. (1989) When collaboration leads to regression: some negative consequences of socio-cognitive conflict. *European Journal of Social Psychology*, 19, 123–138.

Tulving, E. (1983) *Elements of Episodic Memory*. Oxford: Oxford University Press.

Turner, J., Thorpe, P. and Meyer, D. (1998) Students' reports of motivation and negative affect: a theoretical and empirical analysis. *Journal of Educational Psychology*, 90, 758–771.

Turner, M. and Smith, P. (2009) *Dyslexia Screener*. London: GL-Assessment.

Ulicsak, M. and Cramer, S. (2010) *Gaming in Families: Final Report*. Bristol: Futurelab.

Underwood, J. and Underwood, G. (1999) Task effects in co-operative and collaborative learning with computers. In K. Littleton and P. Light (eds) *Learning with Computers: Analysing Productive Interaction*. London: Routledge.

Unis, A., Cook, E., Vincent, J., Gjerde, D., Perry, B., Mason, C. and Mitchell, J. (1997) Platelet serotonin measures in adolescents with conduct disorder. *Biological Psychiatry*, 42(7), 553–559.

United Nations Educational, Scientific and Cultural Organization (UNESCO) (1999) *Salamanca Five Years On: a Review of UNESCO Activities in the Light of the Salamanca Statement and Framework for Action*. Paris: UNESCO. Online, available at: http://unesdoc.unesco.org/images/0011/001181/118118eo.pdf (accessed 2 September 2009).

United Nations Educational, Scientific and Cultural Organization (UNESCO) (2000) *The Right to Education: Towards Education for All Throughout Life*. Paris: World Education Report.

United Nations Educational, Scientific and Cultural Organization (UNESCO) (2004) *FRESH Tools for Effective School Health* (1st edition). Online available at: www.unesco.org/education/fresh (accessed 12 January 2010).

University of Warwick and Department for Education and Skills (2003) Gifted and talented youth: the national academy. *Gifted Education International*, 17(2), 130–133.

Van Boxtel, C., Van der Linden, J. and Kanselaar, G. (2000) Collaborative learning tasks and the elaboration of conceptual knowledge. *Learning and Instruction*, 10(4), 311–330.

van de Grift, W. and Houtveen, T. (2007) Weaknesses in underperforming schools. *Journal of Education for Students Placed at Risk*, 12(4), 383–403.

Van Oers, B. and Hännikäinen, M. (2001) Some thoughts on togetherness: an introduction. *International Journal of Early Years Education* 9(2), 101–108.

Van Petten, C., Coulson, S., Rubin, S., Plante, E. and Parks, M. (1999) Time course of word identification and semantic integration in spoken language. *Journal of Experimental Psychology: Learning, Memory and Cognition*, 25, 394–417.

Varham, S. (2005) Seeing things differently: restorative justice and school discipline. *Education and the Law*, 17(3), 87–104.

Vass, E. (2003) *Understanding Collaborative Creativity: an Observational Study of the Effects of the Social and Educational Context on the Processes of Young Children's Joint Creative Writing*. Doctoral Thesis, Milton Keynes: The Open University.

Vernon, P. (1977) *Graded Word Spelling Test*. Sevenoaks: Hodder and Stoughton.

Volkmar, F.R., Lord, C., Bailey, A., Schultz, R.T. and Klin, A. (2004) Autism and pervasive developmental disorders. *Journal of Child Psychology and Psychiatry*, 45(1), 135–170.

Vousden, J.I. (2008) Units of English spelling-to-sound mapping: a rational approach to reading instruction. *Applied Cognitive Psychology*, 22, 247–272.

Vygotsky, L. (1962) *Thought and Language*. Cambridge: MIT Press.

Vygotsky, L. (1978) *Mind in Society*. Cambridge: Harvard University Press.

Wagner, P. (1995) *School Consultation: Frameworks for the Practising Educational Psychologist*. London: Kensington and Chelsea Education Psychology Service.

Wainscot, J., Naylor, J., Sutcliffe, P., Tantam, D. and Williams, J. (2008) Relationships with peers and use of the school environment of mainstream secondary school pupils with Asperger syndrome (high-functioning autism): a case control study. *International Journal of Psychology and Psychological Therapy*, 8, 25–38.

Walberg, H.J. (1984) Quantification reconsidered. In E. Gordon (ed.) *Review of Research in Education*. Washington, DC: American Educational Research Association.

Walker, B. (1998) Meetings without communication: a study of parents' evenings in secondary schools. *British Educational Research Journal*, 24, 163–179.

Wallace, A. (1986) Giftedness and the construction of a creative life. In F. Horowitz and M. O'Brien (eds) *The Gifted and the Talented: Developmental Perspectives*. Washington, DC: American Psychological Association.

Wallas, G. (1926) *The Art of Thought*. London: Cape.

Wang, A. and Thomas, M. (1995) Effect of keywords on long-term retention: help or hindrance? *Journal of Educational Psychology*, 87, 468–475.

Wang, M., Haertel, G. and Walberg, H. (1990) What influences learning? A content analysis of review literature. *Journal of Educational Research*, 84, 30–43.

Wang, M.C. and Finn, J.D. (2000) Small classes in practice: the next steps. In M.C. Wang and J.D. Finn. (eds) *How Small Classes Help Teachers Do Their Best*. Philadelphia: Temple University Center for Research in Human Development.

Ware, J. (2004) Ascertaining the views of people with profound and multiple learning disabilities. *British Journal of Learning Disabilities*, 32, 175–179.

Warnock Committee (1978) *Special Educational Needs: The Warnock Report*. London: DES.

Warrington, M. and Younger, M. (1999) Perspectives on the gender gap in English secondary schools', *Research Papers in Education*, 14, 51–77.

Wasik, B. and Slavin, R. (1993) Preventing early reading failure with one-to-one tutoring: a review of five programmes. *Reading Research Quarterly*, 28(2), 179–200.

Waters, M. (1996) Success in the primary classroom: we are all in it together. *Support for Learning*, 11, 68–73.

Watkins, C. and Wagner, P. (2000) *Improving School Behaviour*. London: Paul Chapman Publishing.

Watson, A. (2006) Some difficulties in informal assessments in maths. *Assessment in Education: Principles, Policy and Practice*, 13(3), 289–303.

Watson, J. (1925) *Behaviorism*. New York: Norton.

Watson, J.B. (1930) *Behaviorism* (revised edition). Chicago: University of Chicago Press.

WCA (World Class Arena) (2004) *Should My Students do World Class Tests?* Online, available at: www.worldclassarena.org (accessed 2 March 2005).

Webb, N.M. (1989) Peer interaction and learning in small groups. *International Journal of Educational Research*, 13(1), 21–39.

Weber, R., Ritterfeld, U. and Mathiak, K. (2006) Does playing violent video games induce aggression? Empirical evidence of a functional magnetic resonance imaging study. *Media Psychology*, 8, 39–60.

Webster, A. (1985) Deafness and reading. 1. Children with conductive hearing losses. *Remedial Education*, 20(2), 68–71.

Webster, A. and McConnell, C. (1987) *Special Needs in Ordinary Schools: Children with Speech and Language Difficulties.* London: Cassell.

Webster, A. and Wood, D. (1989) *Children with Hearing Difficulties.* London: Cassell.

Wechsler, D. (2003) *Wechsler Intelligence Scale for Children – Fourth Edition: Technical and Interpretive Manual.* San Antonio: Psychological Corporation.

Wechsler, D. (2004) *Wechsler Intelligence Scale for Children – Fourth UK Edition.* London: Harcourt Assessment.

Wechsler, D. (2005) *Wechsler Individual Achievement Test – Second UK Edition.* London: Harcourt Assessment.

Wegerif, R. and Dawes, L. (2004) *Thinking and Learning with ICT: Raising Achievement in Primary Classrooms.* London: Routledge.

Wegerif, R. and Scrimshaw, P. (eds) (1997) *Computers and Talk in the Primary Classroom.* Clevedon: Multilingual Matters.

Wegerif, R., Mercer, N. and Dawes, L. (1999) From social interaction to individual reasoning: an empirical investigation of a possible socio-cultural model of cognitive development. *Learning and Instruction*, 9, 493–516.

Weiner, B. (1985) An attributional theory of motivation and emotion. *Psychological Review*, 92, 548–573.

Weiner, B. (1992) *Human Motivation: Metaphors, Theories and Research.* Newbury Park: Sage.

Weiner, B. (1994) Integrating social and personal theories of achievement striving. *Review of Educational Research*, 64, 557–573.

Weinstein, R.S. (2002) *Reaching Higher: the Power of Expectations in Schooling.* Cambridge: Harvard University Press.

Weisberg, D.S., Keil, F.C., Goodstein, J., Rawson, E. and Gray, J.R. (2008) The seductive allure of neuroscience explanations. *Journal of Cognitive Neuroscience*, 20, 470–477.

Wells, G. (1986) *The Meaning Makers.* London: Hodder and Stoughton.

Wells, G. (1999) *Dialogic Enquiry: Toward a Sociocultural Practice and Theory of Education.* Cambridge: Cambridge University Press.

Wendt, H. (1955) Motivation, effort and performance. In D. McClelland (ed.) *Studies in Motivation.* New York: Appleton Century Crofts.

Wertsch, J.V. (1991) A sociocultural approach to socially shared cognition. In L.B. Resnick, J.M. Levine and S.D. Teasley (eds) *Perspectives on Socially Shared Cognition.* Washington, DC: American Psychological Association.

West, P., Sweeting, H. and Leyland, A. (2004) School effects on pupils' health behaviours: evidence in support of the health promoting school. *Research Papers in Education*, 19(3), 261–291.

Wheldall, K. (1991) Managing troublesome classroom behaviour in regular schools: a positive perspective. *International Journal of Disability, Development and Education*, 38, 99–116.

Wheldall, K., Merrett, F. and Borg, M. (1985) The Behavioural Approach to Teaching Package (BATPAK): an experimental evaluation. *British Journal of Experimental Psychology*, 55, 65–75.

Wheldall, K., Merrett, F. and Russell, A. (1983) *The Behavioural Approach to Teaching Package.* Birmingham: Centre for Child Study, University of Birmingham.

Whitehead, M.R. (1997) *Language and Literacy in the Early Years* (2nd edition). London: Paul Chapman.

Whitehead, M.R. (2009) *Supporting Language and Literacy Development in the Early Years* (2nd edition). Maidenhead: Open University Press.

Whitehurst, G., Arnold, D., Epstein, J., Angell, A., Smith, M. and Fischel, J. (1994) A picture book reading intervention in daycare and home for children from low-income families. *Developmental Psychology*, 30, 679–689.

Whitney, I. and Smith, P. (1993) A survey of the nature and extent of bully/victim problems in junior/middle and secondary schools. *Educational Research*, 35, 3–25.

Whitty, G. (2006) Education(al) research and education policy making: is conflict inevitable? *British Educational Research Journal*, 32(2), 159–176.

Whorf, B. (1956) *Language, Thought and Reality: Selected Writings of Benjamin Lee Whorf.* New York: Wiley.

Wiborg, S. and Green, A. (2006) Comprehensive schooling and educational inequality: an international perspective. In M. Benn and C. Chitty (eds) *A Tribute to Caroline Benn: Education and Democracy.* London: Continuum.

Wiederholt, J.L. and Blalock, G. (2000) *Gray Silent Reading Test (GSRT).* London: Pearson Publishing.

Wiederholt, J.L. and Bryant, B.L. (2001) *Gray Oral Reading Test (GORT-4).* London: Pearson Publishing.

Wigfield, A. (1994) Expectancy-value theory of achievement motivation: a developmental perspective. *Educational Psychology Review*, 6, 49–78.

Wigfield, A. and Eccles, J.S. (2002) The development of competence beliefs, expectancies for success, and achievement values from childhood through adolescence. In A. Wigfield and J.S. Eccles (eds) *Development of Achievement Motivation*. San Diego: Academic Press.

Wikeley, F., Bullock, K., Muschamp, Y. and Ridge, T. (2007) *Educational Relationships Outside School: Why Access is Important*. York: Joseph Rowntree Foundation.

Wilgosh, L. and Paitich, D. (1982) Delinquency and learning disabilities: more evidence. *Journal of Learning Disabilities*, 15(5), 278–279.

Wiliam, D. (2002) Assessing the best method of learning. *The Scotsman*, 5 February.

Wilkin, A., White, R. and Kinder, K. (2003) *Towards Extended Schools: a Literature Review* (Research Report RR432). Slough: National Foundation of Educational Research.

Wilkinson, G.S. and Robertson, G.J. (2006) *WRAT 4 – Wide Range Achievement Test 4*. Oxford: Hogrefe.

Wilkinson, I. and Fung, I. (2002) Small group composition and peer effects. *International Journal of Educational Research*, 37, 425–447.

Williams, S. and McGee, R. (1994) Reading attainment and juvenile delinquency. *Journal of Child Psychology and Psychiatry*, 35, 441–461.

Wilson, G. (2000) The effects of season of birth, sex and cognitive abilities on the assessment of special educational needs. *Educational Psychology*, 20(2), 153–166.

Wilson, J. and Hernstein, R. (1985) *Crime and Human Nature*. New York: Simon and Schuster.

Wing, L. (1997) Asperger's syndrome: management requires diagnosis. *Journal of Forensic Psychiatry and Psychology*, 8(2), 253–257.

Wishart, J. (2004) Internet safety in emerging educational contexts. *Computers and Education*, 43,193–204.

Wishart, J.G. (2005) Learning in children with Down's syndrome. In A. Lewis and B. Norwich (eds) *Special Teaching for Special Children? Pedagogies for Inclusion*. Maidenhead: Open University Press/McGraw Hill, pp. 81–95.

Withers, R. and Eke, R. (1995) Reclaiming 'match' from the critics of primary education. *Educational Review*, 47, 59–73.

Witkin, H.A., Moore, C.A., Goodenough, D.R. and Cox, P.W. (1977) Field dependent and field independent cognitive styles and their educational implications. *Review of Educational Research*, 47, 1–64.

Wolak, J., Finkelhor, D. and Mitchell, K. (2008) Is talking online to unknown people always risky? Distinguishing online interaction types in a national sample of youth Internet users. *CyberPsychology and Behavior*, 11(3), 340–343.

Wolf, M. and Bowers, P. (1999) The 'Double-Deficit Hypothesis' for the developmental dyslexias. *Journal of Educational Psychology*, 91(3), 1–24.

Wolfe, R. and Johnson, S. (1995) Personality as a predictor of college performance. *Educational and Psychological Measurement*, 55(2), 177–185.

Wollin, D. and Montagne, M. (1981) College classroom environment. *Environment and Behaviour*, 13, 707–716.

Wood, C. (2002) Parent–child pre-school activities can affect the development of literacy skills. *Journal of Research in Reading*, 25, 241–258.

Wood, C. and Terrell, C. (1998) Poor readers' ability to detect speech rhythm and perceive rapid speech. *British Journal of Developmental Psychology*, 16, 397–413.

Wood, C., Wade-Woolley, L. and Holliman, A.J. (2009) Phonological awareness: beyond phonemes. In C. Wood and V. Connelly (eds) *Contemporary Perspectives on Reading and Spelling*. London: Routledge.

Wood, D. (1992) Teaching talk. In K. Norman (ed.) *Thinking Voices: the Work of the National Oracy Project*. London: Hodder and Stoughton.

Wood, D. and Middleton, D. (1975) A study of assisted problem solving. *British Journal of Psychology*, 66, 181–191.

Wood, D., Bruner, J. and Ross, G. (1976) The role of tutoring in problem solving. *Journal of Child Psychology and Psychiatry*, 17, 89–100.

Wood, S. and Shears, B. (1986) *Teaching Children with Severe Learning Difficulties: a Radical Reappraisal*. London: Croom Helm.

Woodhead, M., Rhodes, S. and Oates, J. (2005). Disturbed and disturbing development. In S. Ding and K. Littleton (eds) *Children's Personal and Social Development*. Oxford/Milton Keynes: Blackwell/Open University, pp. 53–92.

Woods, K. (2007) Access to General Certificate of Secondary Education (GCSE) examinations for students with special educational needs: what is 'best practice'? *British Journal of Special Education*, 34(2), 89–95.

Woods, P. (1990) *The Happiest Days? How Pupils Cope with School*. Basingstoke: Falmer Press.

Woolford, H. and McDougall, H. (1998) *The Teacher as a Role Model: the Effects of Teacher Gender on Boys' vs Girls Reading Attainment*. Swansea: University of Wales.

Woolner, P., Hall, E., Higgins, S., McCaughey, C. and Wall, K. (2007) A sound foundation? What we know about the impact of environments on learning and the implications for Building Schools for the Future. *Oxford Review of Education*, 33(1), 47–70.

Word, E., Johnson, J., Bain, H., Fulton, B., Zaharias, J., Achilles, C., Lintz, M., Folger, J. and Breda, C. (1994) *The State of Tennessee's Student/Teacher Achievement (STAR) Project: Technical Report 1985–1990*. Tennessee: Tennessee State Department of Education.

Worth, K., Gibson Chambers, J. and Nassau, D.H. (2008) Exposure of US adolescents to extremely violent movies. *Pediatrics*, 122, 306–312.

Wragg, E. (1984) *Classroom Teaching Skills*. London: Croom Helm.

Wright, A. (1992) Evaluation of the first British reading recovery programme. *British Educational Research Journal*, 18(4), 351–368.

Yerkes, R. and Dodson, J. (1908) The relation of strength of stimulus to rapidity of habit-formation. *Journal of Comparative Neurology and Psychology*, 18, 459–482.

Young, S. (1998) The support group approach to bullying in schools. *Educational Psychology in Practice*, 14, 32–39.

Younger, M. and Warrington, M. (1996) Differential achievement of girls and boys at GCSE: some observations from the perspective of one school. *British Journal of Sociology of Education*, 17, 299–313.

Younger, M. and Warrington, M., with Gray, J., Rudduck, J., McLellan, R., Kershner, R., Bearne, E. and Bricheno, P. (2005) *Raising Boys' Achievement: Final Report*. London: DfES.

Youngman, M. (1979) Assessing behavioural adjustment to school. *British Journal of Educational Psychology*, 49, 258–264.

Youngman, M. and Szaday, C. (1985) Further validation of the Behaviour in School Inventory. *British Journal of Educational Psychology*, 55, 91–93.

Youniss, J. (1999) Children's friendship and peer culture. In M. Woodhead, D. Faulkner and K. Littleton (eds) *Making Sense of Social Development*. London: Routledge.

Zajonc, R.B. (2001) The family dynamics of intellectual development. *American Psychologist*, 56(6/7), 490–496.

Zembylas, M. (2003) Interrogating teacher identity: emotion, resistance and self-formation. *Educational Theory*, 53, 107–127.

Zevenbergen, A.A., Whitehurst, G.J. and Zevenbergen, J.A. (2003) Effects of a shared-reading intervention on the inclusion of evaluative devices in narratives of children from low-income families. *Applied Developmental Psychology*, 24, 1–15.

Zillmann, D. (1988) Cognition–excitation interdependencies in aggressive behaviour. *Aggressive Behaviour*, 14, 51–64.

Zimbardo, P. (1970) The human choice: individuation, reason and order versus deindividuation, impulse and chaos. In W. Arnold and D. Levine (eds) *Nebraska Symposium on Motivation*, vol. 16. Lincoln: University of Nebraska Press.

Zimmerman, B., Bandura, A. and Martinez-Pons, M. (1992) Self motivation for academic attainment: the role of self-efficacy beliefs and personal goal setting. *American Educational Research Journal*, 29, 663–676.

Index

Note: Page numbers in **bold** denote figures or illustrations, those in *italic* denote tables.